AF166229

Communications in Computer and Information Science   2198

Rationale

The CCIS series is devoted to the publication of proceedings of computer science conferences. Its aim is to efficiently disseminate original research results in informatics in printed and electronic form. While the focus is on publication of peer-reviewed full papers presenting mature work, inclusion of reviewed short papers reporting on work in progress is welcome, too. Besides globally relevant meetings with internationally representative program committees guaranteeing a strict peer-reviewing and paper selection process, conferences run by societies or of high regional or national relevance are also considered for publication.

Topics

The topical scope of CCIS spans the entire spectrum of informatics ranging from foundational topics in the theory of computing to information and communications science and technology and a broad variety of interdisciplinary application fields.

Information for Volume Editors and Authors

Publication in CCIS is free of charge. No royalties are paid, however, we offer registered conference participants temporary free access to the online version of the conference proceedings on SpringerLink (http://link.springer.com) by means of an http referrer from the conference website and/or a number of complimentary printed copies, as specified in the official acceptance email of the event.

CCIS proceedings can be published in time for distribution at conferences or as postproceedings, and delivered in the form of printed books and/or electronically as USBs and/or e-content licenses for accessing proceedings at SpringerLink. Furthermore, CCIS proceedings are included in the CCIS electronic book series hosted in the SpringerLink digital library at http://link.springer.com/bookseries/7899. Conferences publishing in CCIS are allowed to use Online Conference Service (OCS) for managing the whole proceedings lifecycle (from submission and reviewing to preparing for publication) free of charge.

Publication process

The language of publication is exclusively English. Authors publishing in CCIS have to sign the Springer CCIS copyright transfer form, however, they are free to use their material published in CCIS for substantially changed, more elaborate subsequent publications elsewhere. For the preparation of the camera-ready papers/files, authors have to strictly adhere to the Springer CCIS Authors' Instructions and are strongly encouraged to use the CCIS LaTeX style files or templates.

Abstracting/Indexing

CCIS is abstracted/indexed in DBLP, Google Scholar, EI-Compendex, Mathematical Reviews, SCImago, Scopus. CCIS volumes are also submitted for the inclusion in ISI Proceedings.

How to start

To start the evaluation of your proposal for inclusion in the CCIS series, please send an e-mail to ccis@springer.com.

A. Mirzazadeh · Zohreh Molamohamadi ·
Babek Erdebilli · Erfan Babaee Tirkolaee ·
Gerhard-Wilhelm Weber

Editors

Science, Engineering Management and Information Technology

Second International Conference, SEMIT 2023
Ankara, Turkey, September 14–15, 2023
Proceedings, Part-I

 Springer

Editors
A. Mirzazadeh 🆔
Kharazmi University
Tehran, Iran

Babek Erdebilli 🆔
Ankara Yildirim Beyazit University
Ankara, Türkiye

Gerhard-Wilhelm Weber 🆔
Poznań University of Technology
Poznań, Poland

Zohreh Molamohamadi 🆔
Kharazmi University
Tehran, Iran

Erfan Babaee Tirkolaee 🆔
Istinye University
Istanbul, Türkiye

ISSN 1865-0929   ISSN 1865-0937 (electronic)
Communications in Computer and Information Science
ISBN 978-3-031-72283-7   ISBN 978-3-031-72284-4 (eBook)
https://doi.org/10.1007/978-3-031-72284-4

Preface

The International Conference on Science, Engineering Management and Information Technology (SEMIT 2023) was held virtually in Ankara, Turkey on September 14–15, 2023 at Yildirim Beyazit University. It provided an energetic knowledge-transferring atmosphere for participants (as several feedbacks revealed).

SEMIT 2023 attracted the attention of students and professionals internationally. The covered subjects included, but were not limited to, "IT- and EM-based case studies of manufacturing/service industries (including automotive, food, tourism, petroleum, healthcare, insurance and banking, energy, etc.)", "E-government, E-commerce, E-learning", "Marketing and E-marketing for resources management", "Data science, big data, data mining, and knowledge management in EM", "Decision making and support systems in an uncertain environment and risk management", "Industry 4.0, supply chain 4.0, and logistics 4.0", "Supply chain management (green SCM, sustainable SCM, agile SCM, JIT SCM, global SCM, etc.)", "Optimization and decision making: methods and algorithms", "Applied soft computing in engineering management", "Metaheuristic algorithms and applications", "Blockchain in engineering management", "Artificial intelligence and expert systems", "Digital city", "Internet of things (IoT)", and "Other fields of study related to EM and IT".

SEMIT 2023 was honored to be enriched by outstanding keynote speakers from France, Poland, Mexico, Vietnam, and Turkey. In this event, fifteen universities from USA, UK, Czech Republic, Tunisia, Malaysia, Algeria, Pakistan, and Turkey were present as scientific sponsors.

The conference included participation of 54 countries. The geographical diversity of international scientific committee members was from 20 countries.

The conference team received 409 English and Turkish papers, which were reviewed by at least three international reviewers (single-blind reviews). Considering the reviewers' comments in the first round of review, the papers were reviewed once more with stricter criteria to select the most appropriate ones for these two Springer CCIS proceedings volumes. Finally, the two-round review process resulted in the selection of 46 papers (around 11%) for Springer.

The review criteria in this step were: content; originality; relevance; contribution to the professional literature; significance and potential impact of the paper; language accuracy; study validity; accuracy of methodology and analysis; paper organization, required relevant data, citations, and references; adequate reference to background information; consistency of references, symbols, and units throughout the paper; quality and clarity of tables and figures.

The papers in SEMIT 2023 were presented in 20 panel sessions: "Artificial intelligence and expert systems", "Advanced intelligent systems and sustainable development", "IT- and EM-based case studies", "Data science, big data, data mining, and knowledge management in EM", "Safety and reliability engineering, system engineering and system safety, safety in industry 4.0", "Applied soft computing in engineering management", "Optimization, decision making, and support systems", "Neural networks: analysis, modelling and numerical computations, and data science", "Advancing innovation and collaboration in science, engineering, and information technology", "Uncertain decision making", "Industry 4.0, supply chain 4.0, and logistics 4.0", "Marketing and e-marketing for resources management", "Humanities and social sciences", "Advances in engineering: machine learning techniques", "Artificial intelligence innovations", "Inventory control, production planning, and scheduling", "Multi-criteria decision-making", "Smart marketing", "Quality, productivity, and project management", and "Other fields of study related to EM and IT".

SEMIT 2023 included four applied workshops by outstanding lecturers with large of audiences. The workshop subjects were very well received by the participants and were entitled: "Product as a service (paas) with value retention processes: research implications for engineering management of introducing circular business models"; "Latest digital transformation & digital technology trends in the global business world"; "Supervised machine learning using the Scikit-learn Library"; and "Dissemination of digital youth life health platform (DYL-HP)".

December 2023

A. Mirzazadeh
Zohreh Molamohamadi
Babek Erdebilli
Erfan Babaee Tirkolaee
Gerhard-Wilhelm Weber

The original version of the book has been revised. The 4th editor name has been corrected. A correction to this book can be found at https://doi.org/10.1007/978-3-031-72284-4_28

Organization

Conference Chairs

Abolfazl Mirzazadeh	Kharazmi University, Iran
Mete Gundogan	Yildirim Beyazit University, Turkey

Patrons

Ali Cengiz Köseoğlu	Ankara Yildirim Beyazit University
Hasan Okuyucu	Ankara Yildirim Beyazit University
Babek Erdebilli	Ankara Yildirim Beyazit University

Conference Coordinators

Leila Chehreghani	Ulster University Birmingham, UK
Zohreh Molamohamadi (Scientific Coordinator)	Kharazmi University, Iran
Roya Soltani (Development Manager)	Khatam University, Iran

Program Committee Chairs

Erfan Babaee Tirkolaee	Istinye University, Turkey
Babek Erdebilli	Yildirim Beyazit University, Turkey
Zohreh Molamohamadi	Kharazmi University, Iran
A. Mirzazadeh	Kharazmi University, Iran
Gerhard-Wilhelm Weber	Poznań University of Technology, Poland

Editorial Committee Members

Arpan Kumar Kar	Indian Institute of Technology Delhi, India
Elif Kılıç Delice	Ataturk University, Turkey
Eloisa Macedo	University of Aveiro, Portugal
Mustapha Oudani	International University of Rabat, Morocco

Tatiana Tchemisova   University of Aveiro, Portugal
Dinh Tran Ngoc Huy   International University of Japan, Japan

Steering Committee Members

Sırma Zeynep Alparslan Gök   Suleyman Demirel University, Turkey
Babek Erdebilli   Yildirim Beyazit University, Turkey
Kok Lay Teo   Sunway University, Malaysia/Curtain University,
                                           Australia
A. Mirzazadeh   Kharazmi University, Iran
Janny M.Y. Leung   University of Macau, China
Ruben Ruiz Garcia   Polytechnic University of Valencia, Spain
Yavuz Selim Ozdemir   Ankara Science University, Turkey
Chefi Triki   University of Kent, UK
Gerhard-Wilhelm Weber   Poznań University of Technology, Poland
Abdullah Yildizbasi   Yildirim Beyazit University, Turkey
Ibrahim Yilmaz   Yildirim Beyazit University, Turkey

Scientific Committee Members

Maher Agi   Rennes School of Business, France
Nasr Hamood Mohamed Al-Hindi   Sultan Qaboos University, Oman
Sadia Samar Ali   King Abdulaziz University, Saudi Arabia
Bernardo Almada-Lobo   University of Porto, Portugal
Yavuz Can   Halic University, Turkey
Aybike Özyüksel Çiftçioğlu   Manisa Celal Bayar University, Turkey
Sadeq Damrah   Australian University of Kuwait, Kuwait
Alexandre Dolgui   IMT Atlantique, France
Leopoldo Eduardo   Tecnológico de Monterrey, Mexico
  Cárdenas-Barrón
Ergun Eraslan   Ankara Yildirim Beyazit University, Turkey
Vijai Kumar Gahwalat   National Institute of Food Technology
                                           Entrepreneurship and Management, India
Paulina Golinska   Poznań University of Technology, Poland
Hakan Gultekin   Sultan Qaboos University, Oman
Mete Gundogan   Yildirim Beyazit University, Turkey
Marwa Hasni   University of Sfax, Tunisia
M. Irfan Uddin   Kohat University of Science and Technology,
                                           Pakistan

Josef Jablonsky — Prague University of Economics and Business, Czech Republic

Josef Jablonsky	Prague University of Economics and Business, Czech Republic
Dariusz Jacek Jakóbczak	Koszalin University of Technology, Poland
Peren Jerfi Janatalay	Halic University, Turkey
Mehmet Kabak	Gazi University, Turkey
Burçin Kaplan	Istanbul Aydin University, Turkey
Michael G. Kay	North Carolina State University, USA
Mohammed Khalil	Halic University, Turkey
Baris Bulent Kirlar	Suleyman Demirel University, Turkey
Safa Bhar Layeb	University of Tunis El Manar, Tunisia
Taicir Moalla Loukil	University of Sfax, Tunisia
M. M. Nadakatti	KLS Gogte Institute of Technology, India
Eren Ozceylan	Gaziantep University, Turkey
Stefan Pickl	Bundeswehr University Munich, Germany
Sujan Piya	University of Sharjah, United Arab Emirates
Sankar Kumar Roy	Vidyasagar University, India
Sita Ram Sharma	Chitkara University, India
Kathryn Stecke	University of Texas at Dallas, Naveen Jindal School of Management, USA
Jie Sun	National University of Singapore, Singapore
Kamran Yeganegi	Islamic Azad University, Zanjan Branch, Iran
Abdullah Yildizbasi	Yildirim Beyazit University, Turkey

Keynote Speakers

Sırma Zeynep Alparslan Gök	Süleyman Demirel University, Turkey
Alexandre Dolgui	IMT Atlantique, France
Mostafa Hajiaghaei-Keshteli	Tecnológico de Monterrey, Mexico
Anand Nayyar	Duy Tan University, Vietnam
Gerhard-Wilhelm Weber	Poznań University of Technology, Poland

Workshop Organizers

Safa Bhar Layeb	National Engineering School of Tunis, University of Tunis El Manar, Tunisia
Rezzy Eko Caraka	National Research and Innovation Agency (BRIN), Indonesia/Ulsan National Institute of Science and Technology (UNIST), South Korea/Pukyong National University (PKNU), South Korea

Marwa Hasni	National Engineering School of Tunis, University of Tunis El Manar, Tunisia
Paulina Golinska-Dawson	Poznań University of Technology, Poland
Meenakshi Kaushik	Trinity Institute of Innovations in Professional Studies, Guru Gobind Singh Indraprastha University, India
Servet Soygüder	Ankara Yıldırım Beyazıt University, Turkey

Reviewers

Houda Ait Aabdelmalk	ENSAM-Rabat, Mohammed V University, Morocco
Khawar Abbas	Xian Jiaotong University, China
Mohammad Abdel-Aal	King Fahd University of Petroleum & Minerals, Saudi Arabia
Mohamed Nezar Abourraja	Siemens Gamesa, Denmark
Chales Adusei	Garden City University College, Ghana
Oludele Afolabi	Modibbo Adama University Yola, Nigeria
Adeyinka Ajayi	Redeemer's University, Nigeria
Ghada Alhudhud	King Saud University, Saudi Arabia
Sadia Samar Ali	King Abdulaziz University, Saudi Arabia
Richard Allmendinger	University of Manchester, UK
Luma Al Kindi	University of Technology, Iraq
Zeynep Alparslan	Suleyman Demirel University, Turkey
Minwir AlShammari	University of Bahrain, Bahrain
Elizabeth Altman	USA
Yağmur Arıöz	Yıldırım Beyazıt University, Turkey
Melisa Antonio	Middle East College, Oman
Mamoon Atout	Society of Engineers, UAE
Nadia Serhan Aydin	Istinye University, Turkey
Erfan Babaee Tirkolaee	Istinye University, Turkey
Eric Bang	Broad Institute of MIT and Harvard, USA
Igor Barahona	Universidad Nacional Autónoma de México, Mexico
Abderaouf Benghalia	Algiers I University, Algeria
Shazia Bilal	COMSATS Institute of Information Technology, Pakistan
Marilisa Botte	University of Naples, Italy
Yavuz Can	Friedrich-Alexander-University, Germany
Ibrahim Chaloob	Al-Esraa University College, Iraq
Wirapong Chansanam	Khon Kaen University, Thailand

Leyla Chehreghani	RefConf Institution, UK
Aybike Özyüksel Çiftçioğlu	Manisa Celal Bayar University, Turkey
Soumen Kumar Das	Vidyasagar University, India
Mouna Derbel	University of Sfax, Tunisia
Erkan Dogan	Manisa Celal Bayar University, Turkey
Esra Sipahi Dongul	Aksaray University, Turkey
Skalli Dounia	Hassan 1st University, Morocco
Tugrul Erdem	Manisa Celal Bayar University, Turkey
Islam Gamal	Helwan University, Egypt
Suresh Garg	DTU University, India
Michel Gendreau	École Polytechnique de Montréal, Canada
Alireza Goli	University of Isfahan, Iran
Parul Gupta	Global Institute of Technology & Management (GITM), India
Achraf Haibi	Moulay Ismail University, Morocco
Doha Haloui	Moulay Ismail University, Morocco
Mohamed Houasni	Khemis Miliana University, Algeria
Tarak Housein	Benghazi University, Libya
Change-Ling Hsu	Ming Chuan University, Taiwan
Dinh Tran Ngoc Huy	International University of Japan, Japan
Dina M. Ibrahim	Qassim University, Saudi Arabia
Kanthavelkumaran Natesan	Anna University, India
Yasaman Karimian	Sabancı University, Turkey
Bilal Karroumi	Abdelmalek Essaadi University, Morocco
Mohd Khairol Anuar b. Mohd Ariffin	Universiti Putra Malaysia, Malaysia
Rakesh Kumar	University of Science and Technology, Namibia
Flevy Lasrado	American University in the Emirates, UAE
Ramesh Lekurwale	Somaiya College of Engineering, India
Zulkiflle b. Leman	Universiti Putra Malaysia, Malaysia
Jorge Hernandez Lopez	University of Ibague, Colombia
Eloisa Macedo	University of Aveiro, Portugal
Gour Mahata	Sidho Kanho Birsha University, India
Fouad Maliki	Abou Bakr Belkaid University of Tlemcen, Algeria
Sachin Kumar Mangla	University of Plymouth, UK
El Hassania Messaoud	Private University of Fez, Morocco
Froilan Mobo	Philippine Merchant Marine Academy, Philippines
Emine Nur Nacar	Yıldırım Beyazıt University, Turkey
Mahantesh Nadakatti	Gogte Institute of Technology, India
Mehdi Najib	International University of Rabat, Morocco

Scientific Sponsors

International University of Rabat, Morocco

The University of Texas at Dallas, USA

Prague University of Economics and Business, Czech Republic

Kent Business School, UK

University of Sfax, Tunisia Faculty of Economics and Management

University of Sfax, Tunisia

Sunway University, Malaysia

Ankara Science University, Turkey

Manisa Celal Bayar University, Turkey

Manufacturing Engineering Laboratory of Tlemcen, Algeria

Abou Bekr Belkaid Tlemcen University, Algeria

Suleyman Demirel University, Turkey

Halic University, Turkey

Kohat University of Science & Technology, Pakistan

The Laboratory of Operations Research, decision and Control,
Tunis University, Tunisia

Contents – Part I

Smart Production, Transportation and Supply Chain Systems

Information Technology and Data Science in Industry

Contents – Part II

Digitalization and Artificial Intelligence in Manufacturing/Service Industries

Soft Computing and Artificial Intelligence in Engineering Management and Marketing

Decision Analysis and Expert Systems

Constructing the Criteria in Determining the Product Groups for Agriculture 4.0 Applications

Melike Erdoğan[1]([✉]) [iD], Zekeriya Konurhan[2] [iD], Melih Yücesan[3] [iD], and Muhammet Gül[4] [iD]

[1] Computer Engineering Department, Duzce University, Duzce, Turkey
`melikeerdogan@duzce.edu.tr`
[2] Department of Geography, Munzur University, Tunceli, Turkey
`{zkonurhan,melihyucesan}@munzur.edu.tr`
[3] Department of Emergency Aid and Disaster Management, Munzur University, 62000 Tunceli, Turkey
[4] Department of Transportation and Logistics, Istanbul University, Istanbul, Turkey
`muhammetgul@istanbul.edu.tr`

Abstract. With Agriculture 4.0, the use of techniques such as sensors, robots, artificial intelligence, and machine learning in agriculture has started. It is aimed to increase productivity in agriculture by reducing food loss and waste through Agriculture 4.0. It is a critical decision to determine which products should be handled first for Turkey to benefit from the advantages of Agriculture 4.0 as soon as possible compared to developed countries in the field of agriculture. At this point, the problem of which factors should be addressed in the determination of product & product groups arises. To handle this, in this study, a multi-criteria analysis has been applied to prioritize the factors that should be considered in the determination of the critical fruit and vegetable group for export, which should be considered as a priority within the scope of Agriculture 4.0. In this context, a multi-criteria analysis has been carried out by adopting the Bayesian Best Worst Method BWM (B-BWM), which is an improved version of a pairwise comparison-based BWM method and applied to group decisions. As a result of the analysis, the most important and least important criteria to be used in determining which products or product groups are more suitable for Agriculture 4.0 applications in Turkey and which should be invested in priority have been determined.

Keywords: Agriculture 4.0 · Bayesian Best Worst Method · Evaluation Criteria · MCDM

1 Introduction

Agriculture 4.0, which cannot be separated from the concept of sustainable agriculture, is based on the application of the technological advances of Industry 4.0 in the field of agriculture [1]. It includes the use of techniques such as sensors, robots, artificial

A. Mirzazadeh et al. (Eds.): SEMIT 2023, CCIS 2198, pp. 3–17, 2024.
https://doi.org/10.1007/978-3-031-72284-4_1

intelligence, and machine learning in agriculture [2–4]. It is thought that Agriculture 4.0 will provide great improvements in terms of increasing the efficiency of agriculture and food systems, improving the quantity, quality and accessibility of agricultural products, adapting to climate change, reducing food loss and waste, and optimizing its use. However, both the technological developments and the geographical, economic, environmental, supply chain and social criteria that Agriculture 4.0 is related to reveal the problem of which product or product group will be most suitable for the entrepreneurs who are considering investing in this field. Appropriate application areas are mentioned rather than suitable products for Agriculture 4.0 in academic literature and practical applications [5]. The whole thematic concept of Agriculture 4.0 is discussed under four main classes: monitoring, forecasting, logistics and control [3]. Many subclasses related to these subclasses are also mentioned, such as crop and soil data collection, yield forecasting, market demand, irrigation, harvesting, storage problems, and supply chain management [5, 6]. However, for countries with rich agricultural diversity such as Turkey, it is unthinkable to determine the agricultural practices to be made based on these technologies alone. In this case, besides the technological convenience dimension, the effect of other location-centered criteria should also be considered. In this direction, besides the relatively essential agricultural products such as cotton, corn, potato, and sunflower in Turkey, it is necessary to analyze the suitability of the fruit and vegetable group, which is important for exports, in the context of Agriculture 4.0. Unlike these groups, some special and rare species are also valuable in terms of the inclusiveness of the selection model to be considered within the scope of the evaluation.

It is undoubtedly a multi-criteria decision-making (MCDM) problem to determine which investment opportunity suitable for Agriculture 4.0 should start for the a forementioned agricultural products [7]. Multi-criteria decision analysis, which has been extensively studied in the literature and many methods have been developed, focuses on the selection, ranking, or sorting of alternatives under many different types and conflicting criteria [8]. In addition to pairwise comparison-based methods such as analytical hierarchy process (AHP), analytical network process (ANP), best-worst method (BWM), compromise, outranking and preference-based methods (TOPSIS, VIKOR, ELECTRE, PROMETHEE, etc.) also find their place in the field of application [9–14].

In this study, an MCDM model developed under a series of criteria is presented in order to determine which product or product groups are more suitable for Agriculture 4.0 applications in Turkey and which of them should be invested in priority. For this model, B-BWM [15], which is an improved version of the BWM suggested for group decision-making, is preferred. To this aim, initially, the focus is on determining the importance weights for a hierarchy consisting of nine criteria. The results obtained here will provide preliminary input for the problem of determination and selection of suitable product groups for Agriculture 4.0. In this context, this model will contribute to determining which product/product group is more suitable for Agriculture 4.0 applications. As the authors know, it can be claimed that this study is the first to prioritize the factors for determining product groups in terms of Agriculture 4.0 applications primarily.

With this study, the literature contains the initial determination of the criteria for which items or product groupings should be applied to Agriculture 4.0. A baseline study has been provided in this context for researchers who want to work in this area.

Furthermore, it may be argued that, as the initial investigation in this area, it validates the efficacy of MCDM techniques. As a result, it may be said that this study highlights a recent and significant gap in the literature. Taking into account all of these conclusions, it can be said that this work is the first to rank product groupings according to Agriculture 4.0 applications.

In the context of this motivation, the following research questions are valid for the study.

- RQ#1: What are the criteria that have an impact on the problem of what are the most suitable products/product groups for Agriculture 4.0 applications?
- RQ#2: What are the importance weights of these criteria?

To answer these RQs, the model has the following research objectives (ROs):

- RO#1: To determine the criteria by examining the literature.
- RO#2: To obtain the importance weight of each determined criterion with BBWM.

The organization of the next parts of the study is as follows. Section 2 provides a literature review. Section 3 is about the research method and data. The Sect. 4 is about the application and the numerical results obtained. Section 5 presents results and discussion, and Sect. 6 contains conclusions and recommendations for future work.

2 Literature Review

In this section, the studies that could form the background for the suggested paper have been examined. For this aim, the keywords "Agriculture 4.0", "multi-criteria decision making", and "bayesian", etc. have been adopted. In this review process, it has been investigated which concepts are given more attention in Agriculture 4.0, which methods are used more frequently, and which approaches are used more in modeling uncertainty. During this research, all studies have been examined without distinction of year or country. However, the studies whose full text could not be reached, have not been written in English and have not been sufficiently relevant to the subject have been extracted. Thus, the core studies that have been used while handling the paper have been revealed and examined. The studies reviewed are listed in Table 1:

When the literature research results are examined in detail, it can be said that the subject of interest is a very hot topic and there are research gaps in this field. Another conclusion drawn from the literature research is that multi-criteria decision-making approaches have been initiated to be used for decision-making problems in Agriculture 4.0, but the handling of uncertainty is often ignored. Although there are studies that use fuzzy logic to handle uncertainty, no study that adopts the Bayesian Approach has been found. Although there are a few studies conducted for Turkey, no studies have been found on determining the products & product groups that should be considered as a priority for investing in Agriculture 4.0 applications for both our country and the world. The criteria for which products or product groups should be primarily applied to Agriculture 4.0 have been determined for the first time in the literature, and in this context, baseline research has been presented for researchers who will work in this field. In addition, since it is the first study in this field, it can be claimed that it is a study that proves the effectiveness

Table 1. Literature Search Results

Author(s)	Year	Aim of study	Adopted Approach(es)	Country
Haloui et al. [16]	2023	To contribute to the development of more sustainable and smart agricultural production models by developing different strategies in the agriculture 4.0 concept	Multi-objective linear programming, MARCOS	-
Singh et al. [17]	2023	To analyse and predict vibration exposure of five male tractor drivers working in a real agricultural field	Spectral analysis	India
Talukdar et al. [18]	2022	To build a robust agricultural suitability model for India	Fuzzy Logic, AHP	India
Büyük et al. [19]	2020	To present a digital maturity assessment model for companies in terms of Smart Agriculture	BWM, SAW	-
Yücenur et al. [20]	2022	To demonstrate sustainable production and productivity increase in the agricultural sector by automating data management with smart networks	SWARA, EDAS	Turkey
Erdoğan [7]	2022	To measure farmers' view of Agriculture 4.0 technologies and to present a prioritization study based on the perception of use among these technologies	SWARA, MAIRCA, Interval-valued spherical fuzzy set	Turkey
Scuderi et al. [21]	2020	To explore Italian agribusinesses' perceptions of the opportunities and limits of smart agrifood adoption	NAIADE	Italy

(*continued*)

Table 1. (*continued*)

Author(s)	Year	Aim of study	Adopted Approach(es)	Country
Ilieva and Yankova [22]	2022	To analyze the applications of IoT in agriculture and compare the most widely used IoT platforms	MABAC, Intuitionistic fuzzy sets	-
Scuderi et al. [23]	2022	To contribute to the knowledge that will increase the tendency of agricultural operators to use digital solutions of Agriculture 4.0	NAIADE, SWOT	Italy
Zhai et al. [2]	2020	To investigate the upcoming challenges of using agricultural decision support systems in Agriculture 4.0	Review paper	-
Lezoche et al. [24]	2020	To examine studies on new technologies and new existing methods of supply chains to understand the future paths of the Agri-Food	Review paper	-
Reina-Usuga et al. [25]	2022	To present the role of knowledge transfer in the framework of digital transformation in the Andalusian olive landscape	AHP	Spain
Ivale and de Alencar Nääs [26]	2022	To explore the impact of Precision Agriculture on food production in Brazil	AHP	Brazil
Baierle et al. [27]	2022	To analyze the current application status of digital technologies in different industrial sectors and which digital technologies should be used to improve the performance of the agribusiness system	MOORA, Fuzzy Delphi	Brazil

of the use of MCDM methods. Therefore, it can be claimed that this research points to a current and notable gap in the literature. In light of all these inferences, it can be stated that this paper is the first study to prioritize product groups in terms of Agriculture 4.0 applications. In the following sections, the details of the adopted methodology and real-life application are introduced. Then results and discussion section is presented and finally, last section includes the conclusion and future directions.

3 Proposed Methodology

The Best Worst Method (BWM) method was proposed by Rezaei [14]. It has been used extensively in the literature, especially in recent years, because it requires less evaluation than other weighting methods, such as AHP.

The preference for a lean method in multi-criteria decision-making processes is that the criteria or alternatives in the decision-making process can be evaluated in a precise and explicit way. Lean methods such as B-BWM allow prioritization of specific criteria by providing clear weights and evaluations. Furthermore, a lean method was chosen for precision and clarity in the decision-making process. In conclusion, a lean method was chosen because it is in line with the specific needs and expectations to achieve clear and precise results, to make the process more understandable and to make the implementation process more effective [15, 41–43].

BWM allows consistency calculation since it uses two vectors. This method determines the best (most desirable, best) and worst (least desirable, least important) criteria. Then the best and worst criteria are compared with other criteria. A scale of 1–9 is used for comparison. The value of 1 given in the comparison indicates that the two criteria are equally important, and the value of 9 indicates a significant difference between the two criteria [14, 28]. Although BWM allows easy applicability and high consistency evaluation, it does not allow solutions to group decision-making problems. Therefore, BWM is extended as B-BWM by Mohammadi and Rezaei [15]. In B-BWM, data is prepared similarly to the BWM method proposed by Rezaei [14]. Unlike BWM, Monte Carlo [29] and JAGs [30] are used in the solution. B-BWM method collects the evaluations of decision-makers in a probabilistic environment. In addition, it obtains the results by calculating all probability probabilities of the evaluations of the decision makers by preventing information loss. For details, please refer to Mohammadi and Rezaei [15]. Examples of the use of the B-BWM method include studies such as bridge infrastructure resilience assessment, analysis and prioritization of Quality 4.0 dimensions, assessing blockchain technology and determining the best insulation material [31–34].

The procedural steps of B-BWM are detailed below.

Step 1: The evaluation criteria used in the determination of which products or product categories are appropriate for Agriculture 4.0 applications in Turkey and which should be prioritized for investment primarily are identified. The names of each criterion are as in Table 2 and the detailed definitions are also provided in Sect. 4.

Step 2: The expert team decided on the best and worst criteria with the aid of a designed questionnaire. In this questionnaire, we ask the participating expert group: "*Which is the most important and least important criterion in determining which products or product categories are appropriate for Agriculture 4.0 applications in Turkey and which should be prioritized for investment primarily?".*

Step 3: In this step, the best criterion (c_B^k) has been determined, the expert (stated as k) is asked to compare (c_B^k) with the rest of the criteria (a_{Bj}^k) using a 9-point scale. In this scale, 1 means the criterion considered is equally important compared to the other criterion, and 9 means that the criterion is more important. The result of this step is to obtain the so-called best-to-others vector (A_B^k). It is as follows:

$$A_B^k = \left(a_{B1}^k, a_{B2}^k, \ldots, a_{Bn}^k\right), k = 1, 2, \ldots, K \qquad (1)$$

Step 4: In this step, the worst criterion (c_W^k) has been determined. The expert (stated as k) is asked to compare the rest of the criteria (a_{jW}^k) with (c_W^k) using a 9-point scale. In this scale, 1 means the criterion considered is equally important compared to the other criterion, and 9 means that the criterion is more important. The result of this step is to obtain the so-called others-to-worst vector (A_W^k). It is as follows:

$$A_W^k = \left(a_{1W}^k, a_{2W}^k, \ldots, a_{nW}^k\right)^T \qquad (2)$$

Step 5: The weights of the criteria by each expert and the aggregated criteria weights of all experts are calculated using the transformations of the probability distributions in the B-BWM algorithm [15]. Some transformations of multinomial, Dirichlet, Gamma distributions, and a Markov-chain Monte Carlo sampling are used in the algorithm. The mathematical models regarding B-BWM in this step are solved by MATLAB.

4 Real Case Analysis

In this paper, an MCDM approach is suggested to determine which products or product categories are appropriate for Agriculture 4.0 applications more in Turkey and which should be prioritized for investment primarily. The paper framework consists of 5 steps.

Step 1: In the first stage of the study, the authors determined the parameters that would affect the parameters within the scope of Agriculture 4.0. In this context, first, literature research was conducted and then A1-A8 criteria were determined.

Step 2: Experts to evaluate these criteria have been determined. Since experts were determined in different disciplines, 4 experts were determined to evaluate the Criteria. Three associate professor and one professor is included in the expert team.

Step 3: The evaluations of each expert were collected in surveys suitable for the use of the BWM method. These surveys were created in the Word program and contain information about what decision makers will do at what stages. The survey consists of 2 parts. The first part of the survey includes a best-to-others evaluation. In this evaluation, the most important criterion is selected first. Then the other criteria are compared pairwise according to the best criterion. Similarly, in the second part, the least important criterion is selected, and the least important criterion and other criteria are compared pairwise.

Step 4: The created evaluations were checked for input-based consistency [44]. Inconsistent evaluations were sent back to the decision maker. Thus, it was possible to obtain more effective weights.

Step 5: Since the expert team consists of professors from different disciplines, there is no consensus in their decisions. The evaluations were entered into the MATLAB program with the procedure created by Mohammadi and Rezaei [15] and the final weights and credal rankings were obtained.

The relevant literature has been searched in detail and evaluation criteria that could be used in the prioritization process have been determined. Afterward, MCDM analysis has been used to prioritize the evaluation criteria. Besides, the modeling of uncertainty has not been ignored and the MCDM approach has been applied in the Bayesian environment. The criteria set out as a result of a detailed and systematic literature search are shown in Table 2.

Table 2. Evaluation Criteria

A1: Social Factors
A2: Economic conditions
A3: Topography conditions
A4: Climate conditions
A5: Supply chain
A6: Technology
A7: Environmental conditions
A8: Agricultural management

Detailed explanations of the criteria are as follows:

Social Factors (A1): The social participation of farmers and the public in the use of technology is important in Agriculture 4.0. In addition, farmers need to be trained in technology from a social perspective, which is an important issue in agricultural methodology. In this study, economic conditions that affect both input and output in the agricultural sector and social conditions that are important in social life are evaluated as criteria.

Economic Conditions (A2): Economic conditions include various criteria such as value-added, the return rate of agricultural investments, import amounts, and profit share. One of the objectives of Agriculture 4.0 is to increase agricultural productivity with smart methods and to ensure the development of a sustainable economic return [35].

Topography Conditions (A3): In agriculture, topography conditions are effective on many issues, such as slope, elevation, aspect, soil type, climate, transport, irrigation, and land use. It is very important to consider topography conditions for agricultural production [36]. Geographical Information Systems (GIS), one of the agriculture 4.0 technologies, can help to identify suitable agricultural areas by evaluating various criteria. Therefore, topography conditions are a subject considered in agricultural studies, and it was also considered a criterion in this study.

Climate conditions (A4): For a product to grow in agriculture, it is very important to have suitable climatic conditions for the product. Even if suitable climatic conditions do not occur, the conditions required by the product can be provided to a certain extent with applications such as irrigation systems and greenhouses. However, climate change has shown that its effect negatively affects agriculture, especially in recent years. This makes the use of technology in agriculture a necessity. As a matter of fact, agriculture 4.0 facilitates the work of producers and increases productivity by showing how much and what kind of fertilizers should be given to which areas, weather conditions, minerals and irrigation needed by plants, soil condition, pest control, estimated harvest time in a detailed and real-time manner [35, 37]. Therefore, using technology in agriculture is important in providing suitable climatic conditions for the product to be grown.

Supply chain (A5): A supply chain is a system that involves the movement of products or services from the producer to the customer and the organizations, people, technology, and resources involved in this process. The supply chain basically includes various processes of production, storage, processing, and distribution [38]. With Agriculture 4.0, the integration of agriculture and the internet, and new supply models such as online-to-offline, social commerce, and customer-to-customer have also developed in the supply chain [6]. Therefore, the supply chain in the agricultural sector is a fundamental factor in the process from production to consumption and is considered a criterion in this study.

Technology (A6): Technology is one of the most prominent features of Agriculture 4.0. The integration of agricultural production with the internet has been achieved with Agriculture 4.0 and has realized the applicability of issues that require technology, such as precision agriculture, livestock monitoring, smart greenhouse, fisheries management, and weather monitoring. The technology used in agriculture also allows for increased productivity [6]. The technology used as a criterion in this study on Agriculture 4.0 is very important.

Environmental Conditions (A7): Environmental conditions in agriculture are especially important due to environmental pollution. Practices such as excessive irrigation, excessive and incorrect spraying, and fertilization are very important in environmental pollution [35, 39]. As mentioned, with Agriculture 4.0, irrigation, spraying, and fertilization are applied reasonably, and environmental pollution can be prevented.

Agricultural Management (A8): Agricultural management of agricultural activities by state and relevant stakeholders is essential. In agricultural management, issues with a comprehensive framework, such as product-based restrictions or incentives of the state in agricultural management, its involvement in agricultural production in specific periods, management of farmers and providing various pieces of training, and product determination of relevant stakeholders according to the conjuncture are included in agricultural management [40]. An appropriate agricultural management system is necessary for increasing agricultural productivity and using Agriculture 4.0.

After the evaluation criteria have been determined, the prioritization phase has been initiated. For this aim, B-BWM approach is adopted, and the results are explained in the following section Fig. 1 shows the flowchart for the proposed study.

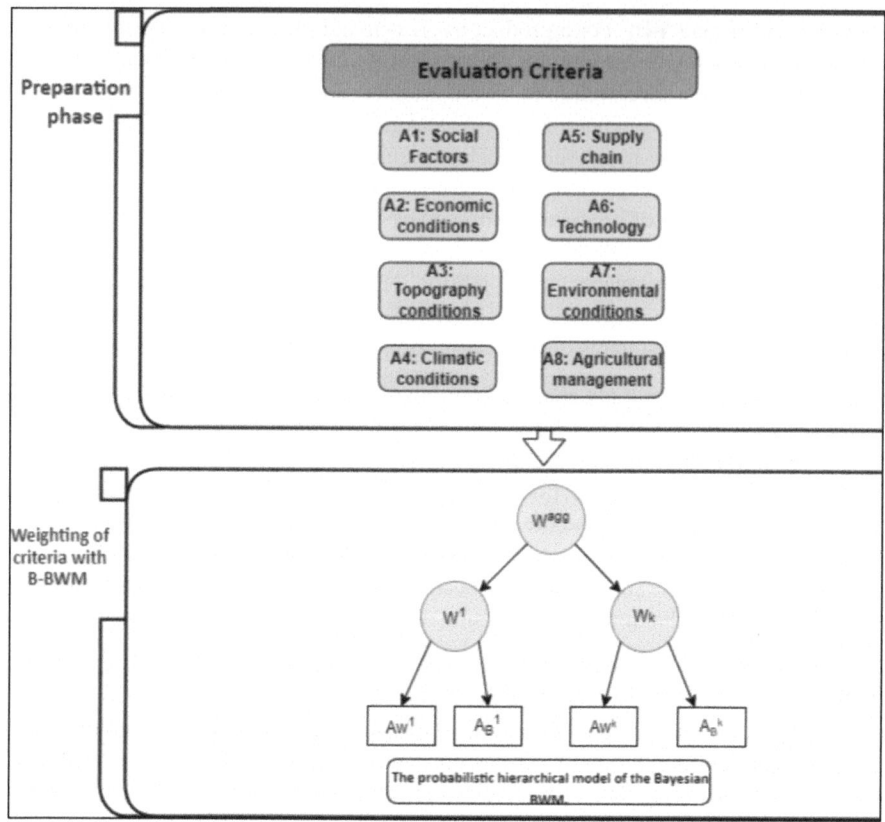

Fig. 1. The weighting of criteria with B-BWM.

5   Results and Discussion

In this study, which tried to determine the criteria that should be considered as a priority for Agriculture 4.0 applications, the criteria weights in Table 3 have been obtained as a result of the B-BWM applied.

The most important criterion for Agriculture 4.0 has been determined as A2 (Economic Conditions) with 0.1847. Due to the rise in food prices and disruptions in food supply after COVID-19, agriculture 4.0 applications must be economically feasible. In addition, the high initial investment costs required for Agriculture 4.0 necessitated the sustainability of the investments made from an economic perspective. The second most important criterion has been identified as A6 (Technology), with 0.1842. It is one of the leading elements in the criteria required for the problem of determining which products or product groups are suitable for agriculture 4.0. In the selection of the product or product group, the technology requirement in the life cycle, technological efficiency and applicability factors shape the content of the technology criterion. As a result of evaluating these factors, it will be revealed which product or product group is preferable. Of course, this is only one part of the problem. The main thing is to determine the

Table 3. Criterion weights.

Criterion	Weight
A1	0.0605
A2	0.1847
A3	0.1015
A4	0.1372
A5	0.1092
A6	0.1842
A7	0.0925
A8	0.1301

suitable lands after selecting the type to be invested in. Therefore, the question sought to be answered in this study is expected to shed light on more than one study topic for future studies. On a different track, the suitability of the technological infrastructure in the relevant region is vital for implementing Agriculture 4.0 applications. The features of this infrastructure should be customized according to the product groups to be produced.

Figure 2 presents the credal ranking graph showing at which level the criteria are superior to each other. The value on the arrow from one criterion to the other varies between 0.5 and 1, and 1 indicates that the relevant criterion is definitely superior. In this graph, A2 is almost 100% superior to A1, A7, A5 and A3. Besides, A2 and A6 are very close to each other. Values in other arrows are interpreted similarly.

The situation is similar for criteria A4 (0.1372) and A8 (0.1301), which are in the third and fourth places in the importance ranking. It would not be right to talk about the obvious superiority of these two criteria over each other. Because the value on the arrow between the two nodes is 0.57. However, the superiority of both criteria over other criteria can be clearly seen. Here, the A4 climate conditions criterion is important in determining the product or product group for Agriculture 4.0. Because not every product can be grown in every climate condition. The fact that climatic conditions come after technology and economy criteria is actually because the technological competence that Agriculture 4.0 will bring is related to the product's ability to intervene in ensuring climatic conditions. Advanced technologies such as robots, temperature and humidity sensors, aerial images and GPS technology will be used in the agriculture of the future. These advanced devices and precision farming and robotic systems will enable farms to be more profitable, efficient, safe and environmentally friendly.

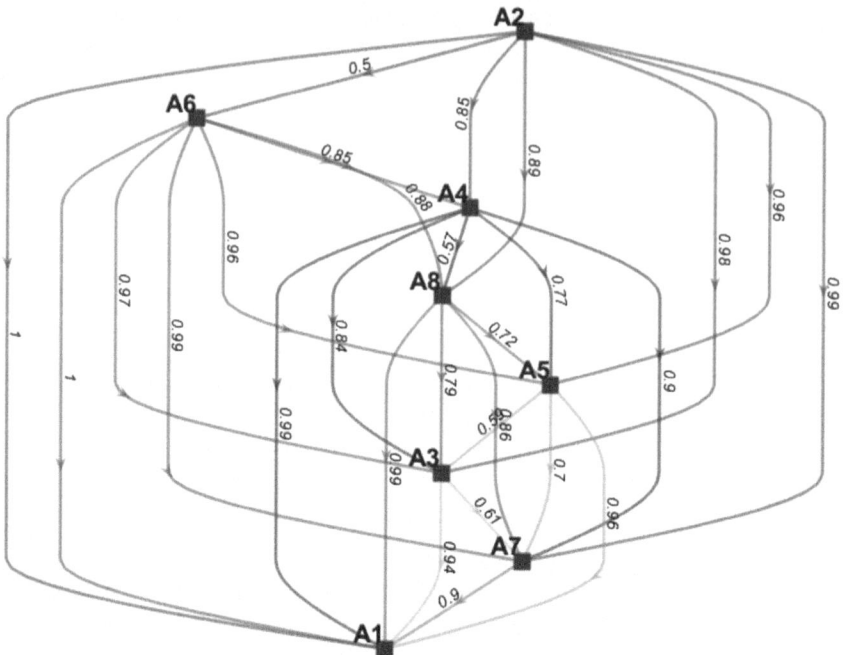

Fig. 2. Credal Ranking Chart.

6   Conclusion and Future Directions

With Agriculture 4.0, it is aimed to increase productivity in agricultural activities by using techniques such as sensors, robots, artificial intelligence, and machine learning. Determining which product or product group should be prioritized in the investments to be made for Agriculture 4.0 can also be mentioned as one of the priority issues in order to increase the benefit to be obtained from the Agriculture 4.0 applications. In this context, it is necessary to analyze the suitability of the fruit and vegetable group, which is important for export, in the context of Agriculture 4.0, as well as agricultural products such as cotton, corn, potatoes, and sunflowers, which are relatively essential in Turkey. For this purpose, a multi-criteria analysis (B-BWM) has been carried out, suggesting which factors should be considered as a priority in determining the product or product groups that will be considered as a priority for Agriculture 4.0 applications in Turkey. As a result of the Bayesian-based multi-criteria analysis, it has been determined that the most important criterion is the Economic Conditions and the least important criterion is the social criterion. In line with these findings, managers should primarily consider economic conditions when planning their investments in agricultural activities. However, some practical guidelines are suggested to put these findings into a broader context and increase their applicability. When determining the most suitable products or product groups for Agriculture 4.0, it is important to consider factors such as environmental sustainability, technological infrastructure, market demand and existing farm capacity, in addition to economic conditions.

To our knowledge, there is no other study aimed at determining which products are suitable for Agriculture 4.0. Although the use of computer systems, IoT and robots is encouraged in the agricultural sector, the issue of feasibility of production attracts attention. The selection of products or product groups is the key factor for success in transferring relevant investments to this sector. The purpose of this study is to emphasize the importance of this issue and to ensure the weighting of the criteria for the relevant field.

This study has some limitations as well as its contribution and originality for Agriculture 4.0. First, it has been built on the opinions of a decision-maker group, including experts from Turkey, for the study, which shows the relative importance levels of the criteria determined by B-BWM and followed in predicting which product or product group will be more suitable for Agriculture 4.0. In this context, more global results can be obtained by selecting this expert group from different countries for further studies. A second limitation is that this model solves some of the problems of determining the suitable product for Agriculture 4.0. At this point, studies are planned on the second part, which includes the selection problem. Third, methodologically chosen B-BWM is revised with a new model that will consider the changes in expert evaluations in the evaluation of criterion weights depending on the potential states that will occur in the future. This can be possible by adding the philosophy of stratification to B-BWM. It is planned to work on this aspect in future studies. Besides, a sub-criteria hierarchy can be established to investigate the effect of the factors in detail, or the prioritization analysis can be added to paper as the further research.

References

1. Walter, A., Finger, R., Huber, R., Buchmann, N.: Smart farming is key to developing sustainable agriculture. Proc. National Acad. Sci. U.S.A. **114**(24), 6148–6150 (2017)
2. Zhai, Z., Martínez, J.F., Beltran, V., Martínez, N.L.: Decision support systems for agriculture 4.0: survey and challenges. Comput. Electron. Agric. **70**, 105256 (2020)
3. Araújo, S.O., Peres, R.S., Barata, J., Lidon, F., Ramalho, J.C.: Characterising the agriculture 4.0 landscape—emerging trends, challenges and opportunities. Agronomy **11**, 667 (2021)
4. Abbasi, R., Martinez, P., Ahmad, R.: The digitization of agricultural industry – a systematic literature review on agriculture 4.0. Smart Agric. Technol. **2**, 100042 (2022)
5. Javaid, M., Haleem, A., Singh, R.P., Suman, R.: Enhancing smart farming through the applications of agriculture 4.0 technologies. Int. J. Intell. Networks **3**, 150–164 (2022)
6. Liu, Y., Ma, X., Shu, L., Hancke, G.P., Abu-Mahfouz, A.M.: From industry 4.0 to agriculture 4.0: current status, enabling technologies, and research challenges. IEEE Trans. Ind. Informatics **17**(6), 4322–4334 (2021)
7. Erdoğan, M.: Assessing farmers' perception to Agriculture 4.0 technologies: a new interval-valued spherical fuzzy sets based approach. Int. J. Intell. Syst. **37**(2), 1751–1801 (2022)
8. Ishizaka, A., Nemery, P.: Multi-Criteria Decision Analysis Methods and Software: General Introduction, pp. 1–9 (2013)
9. Saaty, T.L.: Decision making — the analytic hierarchy and network processes (AHP/ANP). J. Syst. Sci. Syst. Eng. **13**(1), 1–35 (2004)
10. Hwang, C.-L., Yoon, K.: Multiple Attributes Decision Making Methods and Applications. Springer, Berlin (1981)
11. Opricovic, S., Tzeng, G.H.: Extended VIKOR method in comparison with outranking methods. Eur. J. Oper. Res. **178**(2), 514–529 (2007)

12. Roy, B.: The outranking approach and the foundations of electre methods. Theory Decis. **31**(1), 49–73 (1991)
13. Brans, J.-P., Mareschal, B.: Promethee Methods. In: Multiple Criteria Decision Analysis: State of the Art Surveys. ISORMS, vol. 78, pp. 163–186. Springer, New York (2005). https://doi.org/10.1007/0-387-23081-5_5
14. Rezaei, J.: Best-worst multi-criteria decision-making method. Omega **53**, 49–57 (2015)
15. Mohammadi, M., Rezaei, J.: Bayesian best-worst method: a probabilistic group decision making model. Omega **96**, 102075 (2020)
16. Doha, H., Kenza, O., Mustapha, O., Khalid El, Y.: A combined multi-objective and multi criteria decision making approach for wireless sensors location in agriculture 4.0. In: Science, Engineering Management and Information Technology (2023)
17. Singh, A., Nawayseh, N., Singh, H., Kumar Dhabi, Y., Samuel, S.: Internet of agriculture: Analyzing and predicting tractor ride comfort through supervised machine learning. Eng. Appl. Artif. Intell. **125**, 106720 (2023). https://doi.org/10.1016/j.engappai.2023.106720
18. Talukdar, S., et al.: Coupling geographic information system integrated fuzzy logic-analytical hierarchy process with global and machine learning based sensitivity analysis for agricultural suitability mapping. Agric. Syst. **196**, 103343 (2022). https://doi.org/10.1016/j.agsy.2021.103343
19. Büyük, A.M., Ateş, G., Burghli, S., Yılmaz, D., Temur, G.T., Sivri, Ç.: Digital maturity assessment model for smart agriculture. In: Durakbasa, N.M., Gençyılmaz, M.G. (eds.) Digital Conversion on the Way to Industry 4.0: Selected Papers from ISPR2020, September 24-26, 2020 Online – Turkey, pp. 289–301. Springer International Publishing, Cham (2021). https://doi.org/10.1007/978-3-030-62784-3_24
20. Yücenur, G.N., Azakli, A.S., Bahadir, K., Tel, M.E., Arabaci, S.N.: Prioritisation of Industry 4.0 implementations in agricultural sector with SWARA/EDAS. Int. J. Sustain. Agric. Manag. Informatics **8**(3), 326–344 (2022)
21. Scuderi, A., La Via, G., Timpanaro, G., Sturiale, L.: Current and future opportunities of digital transformation in the agrifood sector. CEUR Workshop Proc. **2761**, 317–326 (2020)
22. Ilieva, G., Yankova, T.: IoT system selection as a fuzzy multi-criteria problem. Sensors **22**, 4110 (2022)
23. Scuderi, A., La Via, G., Timpanaro, G., Sturiale, L.: The digital applications of 'agriculture 4.': strategic opportunity for the development of the Italian citrus chain. Agriculture **12**, 400 (2022)
24. Lezoche, M., Panetto, H., Kacprzyk, J., Hernandez, J.E., Alemany Díaz, M.M.E.: Agri-food 4.0: a survey of the Supply Chains and Technologies for the Future Agriculture. Comput. Ind. **117**, 103187 (2020)
25. Reina-Usuga, L., Parra-López, C., Carmona-Torres, C.: Knowledge transfer on digital transformation: an analysis of the olive landscape in Andalusia. Spain. Land **11**(1), 63 (2022)
26. Ivale, A.H., de Alencar Nääs, I.: Precision agriculture impact on food production in Brazil. In: Kim, D.Y., von Cieminski, G., Romero, D. (eds.) Advances in Production Management Systems. Smart Manufacturing and Logistics Systems: Turning Ideas into Action: IFIP WG 5.7 International Conference, APMS 2022, Gyeongju, South Korea, September 25–29, 2022, Proceedings, Part II, pp. 43–49. Springer Nature Switzerland, Cham (2022). https://doi.org/10.1007/978-3-031-16411-8_6
27. Baierle, I.C., et al.: Competitiveness of food industry in the era of digital transformation towards agriculture 4.0. Sustain **14**, 11779 (2022)
28. Rezaei, J.: Best-worst multi-criteria decision-making method: some properties and a linear model. Omega **64**, 126–130 (2016)
29. Markov Chain Monte Carlo in Practice. Markov Chain Monte Carlo Pract. (1995)
30. Just Another Gibbs Sampler (JAGS): Flexible Software for MCMC Implementation. https://www.jstor.org/stable/26447820?seq=10. Accessed 28 Apr 2023

31. Ayyildiz, E., Erdoğan, M. : Identifying and prioritizing the factors to determine best insulation material using Bayesian best worst method. Proc. Inst. Mech. Eng. Part E J. Process Mech. Eng. (2022)

32. Munim, Z.H., Balasubramaniyan, S., Kouhizadeh, M., Hossain, N.U.I.: Assessing blockchain technology adoption in the Norwegian oil and gas industry using Bayesian Best Worst Method. J. Ind. Inform. Integr. **28**, 100346 (2022). https://doi.org/10.1016/j.jii.2022.100346

33. Jamkhaneh, H.B., Jalali, R., Shahin, R., Lima, R.M., Rasouli, E., Jamali, G.: Analysis and Prioritization of Quality 4.0 dimensions and companies' readiness to adapt to industry 4.0 evolutions through Bayesian Best – Worst method. In: International Conference on Quality Engineering and Management, pp. 1–17 (2022)

34. Khan, M.S.A., Etonyeaku, L.C., Kabir, G., Billah, M., Dutta, S.: Bridge infrastructure resilience assessment against seismic hazard using Bayesian best worst method. Can. J. Civ. Eng. **49**(11), 1669–1685 (2022). https://doi.org/10.1139/cjce-2021-0503

35. Rapela, M.A.: Post-malthusian dilemmas in agriculture 4.0. In: Rapela, M.A. (ed.) Fostering innovation for agriculture 4.0: A comprehensive plant germplasm system, pp. 1–16. Springer International Publishing, Cham (2019). https://doi.org/10.1007/978-3-030-32493-3_1

36. Bulut, İ.: Genel Tarım Bilgileri ve Tarımın Coğrafi Esasları – COĞRAFYA KİTAPLARI – Yayinlar – Türk Coğrafya Kurumu. Gündüz Eğitim Yayıncılık (2010)

37. Kılavuz, E., Erdem, İ: Dünyada Tarım 4.0 Uygulamaları ve Türk Tarımının Dönüşümü. Soc. Sci. **14**(4), 133–157 (2019)

38. Borodin, V., Bourtembourg, J., Hnaien, F., Labadie, N.: Handling uncertainty in agricultural supply chain management: a state of the art. Eur. J. Oper. Res. **254**(2), 348–359 (2016)

39. Sørensen, C.G., et al.: Conceptual model of a future farm management information system. Comput. Electron. Agric. **72**(1), 37–47 (2010)

40. Özdemir, H.Ö., Kan, M.: Tarım işletmelerinin yönetiminde kullanilan tarimsal bilgi kaynaklari: kirşehir ili örneği. Türk Tarım ve Doğa Bilimleri Dergisi **7**(2), 500–509 (2020). https://doi.org/10.30910/turkjans.725990

41. Guo, S., Zhao, H.: Fuzzy best-worst multi-criteria decision-making method and its applications. Knowl.-Based Syst. **121**, 23–31 (2017). https://doi.org/10.1016/j.knosys.2017.01.010

42. Kurniawan, V.R.B., Puspitasari, F.H.: A fuzzy bwm method for evaluating supplier selection factors in a SME paper manufacturer. IOP Conf. Ser.: Mater. Sci. Eng. **1071**(1), 012004 (2021). https://doi.org/10.1088/1757-899X/1071/1/012004

43. Yalcin Kavus, B., Ayyildiz, E., Gulum Tas, P., Taskin, Alev, et al.: A hybrid Bayesian BWM and Pythagorean fuzzy WASPAS-based decision-making framework for parcel locker location selection problem. Environ. Sci. Pollut. Res. **30**(39), 90006–90023 (2022). https://doi.org/10.1007/s11356-022-23965-y

44. Liang, F., Brunelli, M., Rezaei, J.: Consistency issues in the best worst method: Measurements and thresholds. Omega **96**, 102175 (2020)

Academic Misconduct After the Rapid Transition to Remote Learning

Sari Andayani[1], Endah Susilowati[1], Diah Hari Suryaningrum[1](✉)📧, Andi Indrawati[2],
Evinda Dwi Nur Aini[3], Wandah Nur Aliyyah[3], Singgih Alfiyahya[3],
Naufan Rahmanda Tasri[3], and Mochammad Idris[3]

[1] Universitas Pembangunan Nasional Veteran Jawa Timur, Jl. Raya Rungkut Madya No.1,
Surabaya, Jawa Timur 60294, Indonesia
`diah.suryaningrum.ak@upnjatim.ac.id`
[2] Universitas 17 Agustus 1945 Samarinda, Jl. Ir. H. Juanda, No.80 Air Hitam, Kec. Samarinda
Ulu, Kota Samarinda, Kalimantan Timur 75123, Indonesia
[3] Universitas Pembangunan Nasional Veteran Jawa Timur, Jl. Raya Rungkut Madya No.1,
Surabaya, Jawa Timur 60294, Indonesia

Abstract. The rapid transition to remote learning during and after the COVID-19 pandemic may impact academic misconduct rates due to changes in learning and evaluation systems. Further understanding of the impact of the rapid transition to distance learning. We attempted to further this study from a gender and XYZ generation perspective, which will be essential to identifying specific problems and challenges and developing practical solutions. Therefore, this study examines the factors that influence academic misconduct from the perspective of gender and the XYZ generation after the rapid change. We analyzed technology accessibility, the demands of family responsibilities, social and technical support, stress and mental well-being, and preferences for learning and communication styles. Our study is an exploratory study using a descriptive-quantitative approach. In December 2022, we conducted an online survey by distributing questionnaires to accounting students and lecturers at three universities on the Indonesian island of Java. The three universities represent West Java, Central Java, and East Java. A total of 155 questionnaires were analyzed. We found that technology accessibility, communication styles, and social and technical support affect academic misconduct. Our findings are essential, as they provide insight and knowledge into the culture of academic integrity in the face of rapidly changing learning technologies. We suggest conducting in-depth interviews with several respondents—students and lecturers—to help understand more deeply the factors that influence deciding to commit academic misconduct.

Keywords: academic misconduct · Indonesia · remote learning

1 Introduction

The 2019 COVID-19 outbreak forced higher education institutions to abruptly switch from face-to-face sessions on campus to online distance learning [1, 2]. There was a rapid transition to remote learning. Universities worldwide were forced to rapidly transition

A. Mirzazadeh et al. (Eds.): SEMIT 2023, CCIS 2198, pp. 18–36, 2024.
https://doi.org/10.1007/978-3-031-72284-4_2

from face-to-face learning on campus to online distance learning in response to the threat of spreading the virus. This transition occurred quickly, often within a few weeks or even days. Colleges were faced with evaluating their technology infrastructure, including online learning platforms and online resources. Faculty and teaching staff suddenly had to learn how to teach effectively via virtual platforms, and students had to adjust to self-paced, technology-based learning.

Additionally, this transition brings social and psychological challenges. Loss of social interaction on campus, feelings of isolation, and drastic changes in study routines can impact a student's well-being. Despite the rapid transition, this distance learning experience has sparked innovation and increased the use of technology in higher education. Educational institutions continuously strive to ensure effective and inclusive learning in any scenario. The COVID-19 pandemic has shifted the educational paradigm, prompting more colleges to incorporate elements of online learning into their existing models.

The most common approach is synchronous meetings and embedding the existing course in a learning management system (LMS) [3, 4]. This remote change followed similar face-to-face learning procedures, exercises, and results. Online learning has experienced a surge in popularity in recent years, becoming more than just a temporary trend. Despite its benefits in providing broader educational access, flexibility, and ease of access to learning resources, online learning also brings serious challenges. One of the critical challenges that has emerged with the rapid transition to distance learning is the increase in academic cheating.

Academic cheating, which includes everything from cheating on online exams to plagiarism in online assignments, is a problem that has existed for years in educational settings [5]. However, in the increasingly dominant world of online learning, this action seems to be becoming more widespread and easier to do. The emergence of diverse online platforms and easy access to online information resources has allowed dishonest students to exploit this loophole. It is important to recognize that most students and course participants in online learning environments are individuals of honesty and integrity. They try to study diligently and continue their education in the right way. However, we cannot ignore the fact that integrity challenges such as academic cheating remain a serious threat to the quality of education.

In this article, we will explore the phenomenon of academic cheating in the context of online learning, analyze the factors that drive it, and explore strategies that educational institutions, educators, and students can use to address this problem. We discuss the importance of a holistic approach to promoting academic ethics and integrity in this digital era. Ultimately, our goal is to understand the challenges and potential solutions related to academic cheating in online learning so that we can ensure that education in this digital era remains relevant, high quality, and fair for all.

The rapid transition to distance learning during the COVID-19 pandemic has had some impacts on academic misconduct rates [5, 6]. Changes in learning and evaluation systems cause shifts in academic dynamics, which can trigger several challenges, such as more likely academic misconduct. Changing how students were evaluated, such as changing the format of exams or making fewer assignments. The asynchronous format allows students to move through course content more flexibly and at their own pace.

In an online learning environment, some students may face the temptation to engage in cheating, such as cheating, copying, or colluding with friends in online evaluation situations. Limited direct supervision may make such actions easier. During this transition, educational institutions must increase awareness of academic ethics and develop evaluation strategies appropriate to distance learning. Meanwhile, students need to maintain academic honesty in this challenging situation. Therefore, this present study aims to examine further the factors that influence academic misconduct from the perspective of gender and the XYZ generation after the rapid change.

2 Literature Review

2.1 Academic Misconduct

Academic misconduct is also known as academic cheating or dishonesty. It refers to actions or behavior that violate academic integrity and ethics in an educational context. It covers a wide range of offenses. Examples of academic misconduct include plagiarism, cheating, and collusion [7, 8].

Plagiarism is the act of taking another person's work, such as text, ideas, or works of art, without appropriate acknowledgment or permission. The relationship between plagiarism, gender, and generation XYZ can vary. Gender factors may influence the prevalence of plagiarism, with research showing that some women tend to be more wary of the concept of academic honesty. The XYZ generation, consisting of individuals born between the mid-1990s to the mid-2000s, is often more familiar with technology and has greater access to online resources, which may influence the level of understanding of plagiarism [5]. However, the approach to plagiarism depends on an individual's education, culture, and values [9, 10]. Therefore, it is important not to generalize but to promote awareness and education about academic ethics across all gender groups and generations.

Behaviors such as cheating on exams and copying friends' answers are plagiarism in an educational context. Use of unauthorized materials in exams means any written or printed material that is generally or specifically prohibited from being brought into the examination room, including but not limited to notes, books, and handkerchiefs in which information is written or written on any part of the body. Its relationship with gender and generation XYZ can be seen from a social and technological perspective. First, gender factors may play a role in this behavior. Some research suggests that in some cultures, men and women can have different approaches to risk, ethics, and academic honesty [5, 11]. Sometimes, social pressure or the need for achievement can influence students of different genders to engage in acts of plagiarism [12, 13]. Second, generation XYZ grew up in the era of digital technology. They have greater access to online resources and tools that allow easy copy-pasting [6, 14]. This can make them more likely to try copying a friend's answer or looking up an answer instantly without understanding the material.

Collusion, cooperation, or tacit agreements to deceive others to achieve mutual benefit are behaviors found in various social contexts, including in education and work environments. Its relationship with gender and the XYZ generation can be seen from a social and cultural perspective. This collusive behavior is not exclusively related to one gender or generation. However, sometimes, gender may influence how individuals' approach or rationalize such actions. For example, research suggests that some men may be more likely to engage in risky behavior to gain mutual benefit [15]. The XYZ generations, growing up in the age of technology, may have greater access to communication tools such as text messaging, social media, or information-sharing platforms [5, 16]. This can facilitate collusion or tacit cooperation but can also be a tool for detecting such behavior through security and surveillance technologies. It is important to remember that acts of collusion are serious ethical violations in educational and business contexts.

Several researchers have examined factors that can influence academic cheating, namely technological accessibility [17–19], the demands of family responsibilities [20, 21], social support and technical support [22–24], stress and mental well-being [25–27], and preferences for learning and communication styles [19, 28, 29].

2.2 The Relationship Between Technology Accessibility and Academic Misconduct

Refers to the extent to which technology, such as computers or the internet, is available and accessible to individuals [17–19]. Technology accessibility significantly impacts daily life, including aspects of the economy, education, work, health, and social interactions. The accessibility of technology creates inequalities in society [17, 18]. Individuals with limited access may have difficulty keeping up with digital developments and accessing services that rely heavily on technology. This can impact education, with students who do not have internet access and devices may struggle with distance learning. In the world of work, technology accessibility can impact job opportunities and productivity.

Koswara [30] found that technological developments information and communication makes things easier individuals to commit acts of plagiarism because internet information makes it easier transfer (copy-paste), storage, and editing. In addition, Roberts, et al. [31] studied 422 students for one year. Their results showed that at least the student has been involved in one type academic violations, namely actions plagiarism via the Internet, e-mail, and tools other digital communications. Easy access to technology can trigger misuse of technology if someone has the knowledge and skills, understands the sophistication of information technology, and uses information technology for a long time [19, 32].

2.3 The Relationship Between the Demands of Family Responsibilities to Academic Misconduct

Refers to the responsibilities an individual must fulfill towards his family, which can influence a person's ability to participate in education [20, 21]. Its relationship to gender and generation XYZ illustrates how this view has changed over time. In the millennial generation, there was a significant change in views regarding the demands of family responsibilities. In some societies, this generation tends to be more open to more equal family roles between men and women. They may be more open to the concept of an equally shared family, where child care, household chores, and financial responsibilities do not fall solely on one gender [33].

However, gender differences still influence the view of the demands of family responsibilities in many places. Women often still face traditional expectations of caring for children and the household. This creates tension between social expectations and individual aspirations [34]. It is essential to continue to push for gender equality and enable the XYZ generation to develop family dynamics that are more inclusive and in line with modern values, where family responsibilities are not solely shouldered by one gender but are shared equally based on abilities and desires.

In term of academic misconduct, sometimes students wait until the last minute to complete assignments and study for tests because they haven't figured out how to manage numerous significant course projects or exams at once, or how to prioritize and organize their workload. In addition to their academic education, some students have heavy commitments to extracurricular activities, outside jobs, or family duties. In an effort to improve their GPA, a student may, whether knowingly or unknowingly, turn to dishonest methods in such situations [35].

2.4 The Relationship Between Social and Technical Support to Academic Misconduct

Social support can help overcome stress and difficulties, while technical support helps resolve technical issues may influence academic misconduct [22–24]. Social support is emotional, social, or psychological assistance individuals or groups provide to someone in a difficult or stressful situation. This could be support from friends, family, coworkers, or the community. Social support can include listening, giving advice, or simply providing a feeling of comfort and understanding. This support is essential for a person's mental and emotional well-being, helping to reduce stress and improve quality of life [36].

On the other hand, technical support refers to assistance or resources provided in the form of technical knowledge or skills. It is often related to solutions to practical problems or improvements in certain technical aspects, such as technical support in particular computers, software, or equipment. Technical support aims to help individuals or organizations overcome technical problems that may arise and ensure that various systems or devices operate correctly [37]. Social and technical support play an important role in everyday life, each supporting a person's emotional and technical aspects.

According to Parnther [23, 38], student behaviors are influenced by contextual elements including the peer groups, organization, and atmosphere of the institution. Value judgment issues, like academic misbehavior, call for a global perspective. Individualism vs collectivism, power distance (the degree of social hierarchy), uncertainty avoidance, masculinity versus femininity (task orientation versus person-orientation, long-term orientation, and indulgence versus self-restraint) are among Hofstede's six cultural dimensions. Therefore, the social environment in every culture might have an impact on academic misconduct. Meanwhile, Sarirah, et al. [22], found that there was a relationship between self-regulated learning and peer social support and academic achievement, but peer social support was not related to academic achievement. Social support from classmates, family, or mentors can improve students' understanding of subject matter and increase learning motivation. Students who feel supported may be more likely to put effort into their studies, reducing the need to engage in academic cheating [24].

2.5 The Relationship Between Stress and Mental Well-Being to Academic Misconduct

Stress is a person's emotional or psychological pressure in certain situations. Stress can arise from work stress, personal problems, life changes, or other situations that require adaptation and overcoming challenges [27]. Mental well-being refers to a person's overall emotional and psychological condition. Mental well-being, on the other hand, refers to a person's overall emotional and psychological condition [26]. It covers various aspects such as happiness, life satisfaction, inner calm, emotional balance, and coping with stress. Excessive or chronic stress can have a negative impact on mental well-being. This can cause problems such as anxiety, depression, or sleep disorders. Therefore, it is crucial to manage stress well to maintain optimal mental well-being. Efforts to improve mental well-being include effective stress management, social support, maintaining physical health, and seeking help when needed. Understanding the relationship between stress and mental well-being is important to ensure that individuals can better cope with life's stresses and maintain emotional balance [26].

Perceptions of the incidence of misconduct and a rise in it during the home quarantine period were linked to stress levels. When compared to their male counterparts, female professors believed that student wrongdoing increased and occurred more frequently during the quarantine. The findings indicate a gender issue that is probably caused by an imbalance in household chores, which raises stress levels and the feeling of wrongdoing [25].

2.6 The Relationship Between Preferences for Learning and Communication Style to Academic Misconduct

According to Edwards [28], preferences for learning and communication styles refer to how an individual learns and communicates most effectively. Each person has unique preferences in this regard, and understanding these preferences can improve learning and communication effectiveness. Learning styles include various methods, such as visual, auditory, kinesthetics learning, or a combination of the three. Some individuals may prefer to understand information through pictures or graphs (visual style), while others prefer to listen to explanations (auditory style), and still, others are more effective when they can experience concepts through physical action or interaction [29].

Meanwhile, communication preferences include the way individuals communicate with other people. Some may prefer oral or face-to-face conversations, while others prefer written communication via text messages or emails. Understanding these preferences helps personalized teaching and delivers messages more effectively. It also promotes collaboration and more effective communication in various aspects of life, whether in the context of education, work, or personal relationships [39].

Students have different learning styles, such as visual, auditory, or kinesthetic [40]. If teaching methods do not suit a person's learning style, students may need help understanding the material well. In this situation, it is possible that students look for instant means, such as cheating, to overcome comprehension difficulties. Additionally, communication styles that often involve technology, such as text messaging or online chat, can make it easier to exchange information related to cheating. Students may find it easier to communicate or collaborate unethically using digital platforms [39].

2.7 The Relationship Between Gender and XYZ Generation to Academic Misconduct

Men and women have diverse objectives when it comes to ethical action because of the differences in how human sociality is formed between them. While men's morality is based on the concepts of fairness or equal rights, women demonstrate concern [41]. According to Susilowati et al. [5], regarding academic fraud, women were more cautious than men. But based on historical experience, women tend to copy and paste more than men do.

It was discovered that the practice of copying and pasting was becoming more common among the XYZ generation [42]. The digital era 5.0, which facilitates quick and easy access to digital information, maybe the source. Furthermore, the younger generation has more advanced digital skills than the older generation. When instances of academic misconduct arise between instructors or staff and students, it can send a bad message to students and the community at large about the value of integrity and ethical behavior [5].

3 Research Method

3.1 Research Model

Figure 1 depicts the research model that describes the relationship of factors such as technology accessibility, family responsibility, social and technical support, stress and mental well-being, preferences for learning, communication style, gender, and XYZ generation with academic misconduct. From the figure, there are 8 statements of hypotheses:

H1: Technology accessibility positively affects academic misconduct.
H2: Family responsibility positively affects academic misconduct.
H3: Social and technical support positively affects academic misconduct.
H4: Stress and mental well-being positively affect academic misconduct.
H5: Preferences for learning positively affect academic misconduct.
H6: Communication style positively affects academic misconduct.
H7: Gender affects academic misconduct.
H8: XYZ generation affects academic misconduct.

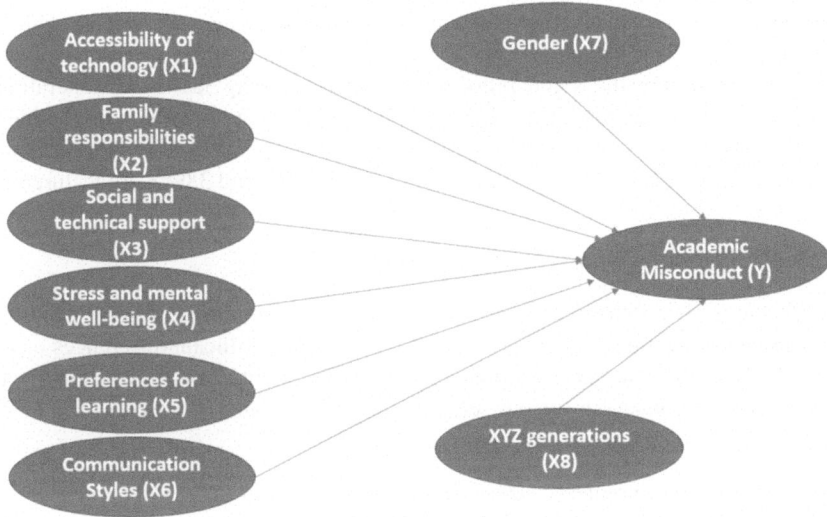

Fig. 1. Research Model

3.2 Sample and Procedures

The sample in this study was students and lecturers from three universities in Indonesia. Questionnaires were made using Google Forms and distributed to respondents through emails. Respondents are notified that their participation is voluntary, and their responses will remain anonymous. They are also told that there is no entirely right or wrong answer, so they only need to respond based on their thoughts and beliefs regarding each question or statement. A total of 155 questionnaires were filled out, and the data could be processed. The information about the respondents is shown in Table 1.

Table 1. Respondents Information (Source: Data processed (2022)).

No	Description		Frequency	Percentage
1	Gender	Male	47	30%
		Female	108	70%
2	Generations	X	43	28%
		Y	38	24%
		Z	74	48%
3	Education	Student	96	62%
		Master	31	20%
		Doctor	28	18%
4	Occupation	Student	96	62%
		Lecturer	69	38%

Based on Table 1, there are more female respondents than male respondents (females make about 70% of the sample). With 74% of the total, the Z generation is the largest generation, followed by the X generation (43%). The remaining 38% are Y generations. Students make up more than 50% of the educated population, with doctors coming in last at 18%. A bachelor's degree is not held by any of the responders. Given the academic nature of the survey, 62% of the respondents were students, and 38% were lecturers.

3.3   Model Evaluation and Hypothesis Testing

Model evaluation helps ensure that the model used fits the data, while hypothesis testing helps understand whether findings in the data result from significant differences or just chance (Table 2). Both are key components in the scientific method for examining and understanding phenomena in various scientific disciplines using SmartPLS [43].

Table 2. Model Evaluation and Hypothesis Testing (Source: Smart-PLS 3.0 application [43]).

Model Evaluation	Criteria
Outer model	
Convergent	Loading factor > 0.70
Average Variance Extracted (AVE)	AVE > 0.5
Discriminant validity	Cross loading > 0.70
Composite reliability	Value > 0.70
Inner model	
R-square	R^2 0.75 (strong); 0.5 (moderate); and 0.25 (weak)
Hypothesis test	p-value < 0.05; 0.01
Effect size	Score 0.35 (strong); 0.15 (moderate); and 0.02 (weak)

4   Results and Discussion

4.1   Results

Outer Model. The outer model relates to the measurement of variables or indicators used in the analysis, namely the measurement of latent variables (constructs that cannot be measured directly) through variables that can be measured (indicators). The results of the outer model analysis can provide insight into the extent to which these indicators correspond to the construct under study.

Convergent Validity: Loading factor > 0.70 (some questionnaires are deleted because of the loading factor < 0.70). Table 3 shows the reliability of the five constructs as measured by composite reliability and Average Variance Extracted (AVE). Composite Reliability for all variables has met the acceptable level of 0.70. Average Variance

Table 3. Reliability and Validity test.

	Composite Reliability	Average Variance Extracted (AVE)
Academic misconduct	0.848	0.736
Accessibility of technology	0.889	0.729
Communication styles	0.938	0.716
Family responsibilities	0.801	0.505
Gender	1.000	1.000
Generations	1.000	1.000
Preferences for learning	0.747	0.501
Social and technical support	0.879	0.711
Stress and mental well-being	0.876	0.504

Source: Smart-PLS results (2022)

Extracted (AVE) ranged between 50.4% and 73.6%, above the recommended level of 0.5. It can be concluded that the convergent validity of the construct is adequate [44].

Figure 2 shows the relationship between independent variables (X1 to X8) and the dependent Variable (Y) with their t-value. The figure shows t-value of each variable as follows:

√ Accessibility to technology (5.342)
√ Family responsibilities (1.596)
√ Social and technical support (2.008)
√ Stress and mental well-being (0.180)
√ Preferences for learning (0.350)
√ Communication styles (2.646)
√ Gender (1.389)
√ XYZ generation (0.367)

Table 4. R Square Results (Source: Smart-PLS results (2022)).

	R Square	R Square Adjusted
Academic misconduct	0,467	0,437

Model testing. R squared in PLS assesses the model's ability to explain and predict the dependent variable (response variable) based on the independent variables (predictor or indicator variables). In general, the higher the R squared value, the better the model can explain variations in the data. Table 4 shows R2 and adjusted R2 of 0.467 (46.7%) and 0.437 (43.7%), respectively. This value indicates a moderate relation between dependent and independent variables.

The relationship test in Table 5 using p-values < 0.05 indicates that from 8 independent variables, only 3 (three) variables affected academic misconduct:

√ Accessibility of technology (0.000)
√ Communication styles (0.008)
√ Social and technical support (0.045)
√ Variables did not influence academic misconduct:
√ Gender (0.165)
√ XYZ Generations (0.714)
√ Family responsibilities (0.111)
√ Preferences for learning (0.727)
√ Stress and mental well-being (0.857)

4.2 Discussion

The Effect of Technology Accessibility on Academic Misconduct. Access to technology can influence academic misconduct in several ways, especially in the context of online education and the use of technology in exams or assignments [19, 45]. Technology accessibility refers to the extent to which individuals or groups have access to digital devices, the internet, or software necessary for learning. When this access is uneven, it can encourage academic misconduct. Inequalities in technology access can create incentives for violations such as cheating, copying, or colluding. Students with limited access may feel forced to look for instant solutions to evaluation challenges, especially when they face pressure to get good results. Supervision becomes more complex with online learning, and students may feel free to cheat. Educational institutions must address technology accessibility issues and appropriately support students with limited access.

Use of unauthorized applications and software. Students who use unauthorized applications or software during exams or assignments may utilize technology to attempt to cheat or circumvent academic rules. In online courses, there is the potential for students to let someone else take their exams or do their assignments. This may occur if identity and presence cannot be verified directly. Additionally, the ease of collaborating without supervision can increase academic misconduct. In an online setting, students can easily collaborate without direct supervision. This can lead to collusion or sharing of answers without permission. Easy access to the internet allows students to quickly copy and paste text from online sources into their assignments without providing proper attribution. This leads to cases of plagiarism, a common form of academic misconduct. Lastly, students who are unwilling or unable to do their assignments can take advantage of this access to purchase other people's work, which is a form of misconduct. Technology such as smartphones and smartwatches can be used to keep notes or access information during an exam. This makes cheating more accessible and more challenging to detect.

However, it is essential to realize that technology can also prevent academic misconduct, such as using anti-plagiarism software to detect plagiarism, online exam proctoring platforms, and strict computer security during online exams. However, using this technology must be balanced with efforts to teach academic integrity and ethics to students. Additionally, it is vital to raise awareness about academic ethics and the consequences

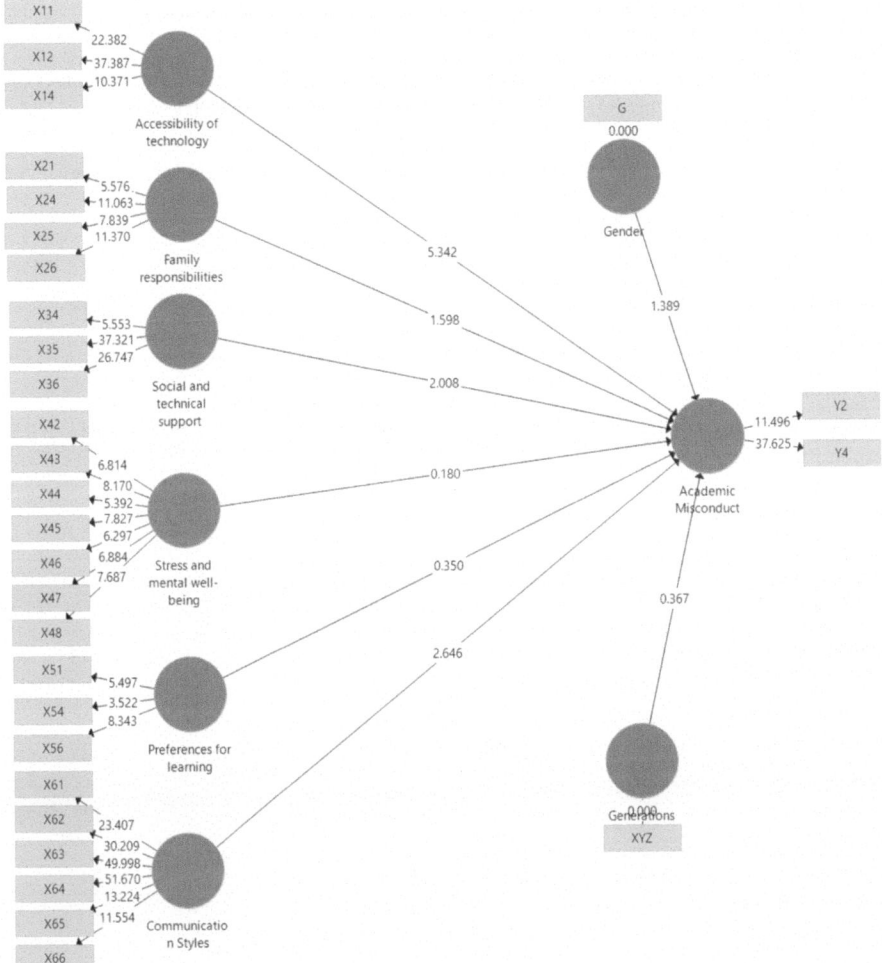

Fig. 2. Research model and the t-value

of academic misconduct, regardless of the level of technology access. Thus, students will be more likely to follow the principles of academic honesty in an online learning environment.

The Effect of Communication Styles on Academic Misconduct. Communication style can influence academic misconduct in several ways [23, 38]. This relates not only to individual communication styles but also how communication occurs between individuals, especially in education and academic environments. Unauthorized collaboration of communication styles encouraging collaboration without permission or sharing answers may facilitate academic misconduct. Students who communicate this way can help each other share answers during exams or work on assignments without the instructor's knowledge. Communication styles among friends or classmates can sometimes create social

Table 5. P-Value Test (Source: Smart-PLS results (2022)).

	Original Sample (O)	Sample Mean (M)	Standard Deviation (STDEV)	T Statistics (IO/STDEVI)	P Values
Accessibility of technology -> Academic misconduct	0.497	0.499	0.093	5.342	0.000
Communication styles -> Academic misconduct	0.320	0.313	0.121	2.646	0.008
Family responsibilities -> Academic misconduct	0.167	0.180	0.104	1.598	0.111
Gender -> Academic misconduct	−0.088	−0.080	0.063	1.389	0.165
Generations -> Academic misconduct	−0.027	−0.026	0.073	0.367	0.714
Preferences for learning -> Academic misconduct	−0.028	−0.010	0.079	0.350	0.727
Social and technical support -> Academic misconduct	−0230	−0.224	0.115	2.008	0.045
Stress and mental well-being -> Academic misconduct	−0.017	−0.016	0.096	0.180	0.857

pressure to commit academic misconduct. Individuals may feel compelled to participate in misconduct if the culture surrounding a peer group values academic achievement more highly than integrity. Modern technology allows easy and fast communication via text messages, chat, or social media. In educational contexts, it can be used to exchange information or answers during online exams or assignments, facilitating cheating.

Therefore, an open and inclusive communication style can encourage students to more easily seek help and discuss academic problems with lecturers or fellow students. This can reduce the stress that might trigger cheating behavior, because students feel more comfortable seeking solutions through effective communication. Lecturers need to play an active role in ensuring that online communications are carried out clearly and comply with academic ethics. Communication style also plays a role in monitoring and reporting academic misconduct. When students feel safe to report cheating, academic misconduct becomes more accessible to detect and address. The stigma or threats associated with reporting academic misconduct can hinder effective communication. Effective education and communication about the values of academic integrity can help minimize academic misconduct.

Overall, it is essential to recognize the role of communication styles in creating an honest and fair academic environment. Lecturers and educational institutions must promote effective communication, awareness of academic ethics, and reporting of academic violations to maintain educational integrity. It is crucial to create an environment where honest and open communication is encouraged, academic misconduct is dealt with firmly, and academic ethics, especially ethics in learning, is emphasized. This can help reduce the negative impact of communication styles that support academic misconduct.

The Effect of Social and Technical Support on Academic Misconduct. Social and technical support are two important factors that can influence individual behavior in the context of academic misconduct. Social support includes emotional, psychological, and social assistance provided by friends, family, or colleagues in an educational setting [46]. Technical support, on the other hand, refers to technical assistance or resources that can help individuals with academic matters, such as access to online resources, software, or technical tutoring.

Social and technical support can influence individuals to commit academic misconduct through several different mechanisms and situations. Social support from family, friends, or classmates to achieve particular academic successes can make individuals feel compelled to seek dishonest ways to meet these expectations. This pressure can encourage academic misconduct in an effort to achieve desired results [4, 22]. Social support from friends or classmates can facilitate collusion or sharing answers during exams or assignments. When individuals feel supported by others in cheating, they may be more likely to commit it.

On the other hand, technical support can provide easier access to resources or tools that can be used for academic misconduct. For example, technical assistance in the form of software that allows plagiarism or access to unauthorized question banks can make cheating easier to commit. When individuals see others in their environment committing academic misconduct and receive social support from their peers, norms around the behavior can be created. Social norms that support cheating may make it seem like a more acceptable option.

Creating an educational environment that encourages positive support, a robust academic ethic and open communication about cheating is vital. Involving all relevant parties in the promotion of academic integrity is an essential step in reducing the impact of social and technical support on academic misconduct.

On the contrary, strong social support can help prevent academic misconduct. Friends, family, or peers who provide emotional support and guidance can help students overcome academic pressure and stress. They can also help promote academic responsibility and ethics. Technical support, such as easy access to online resources and technical assistance, can influence student behavior. If students find it difficult to access necessary resources or face significant technical obstacles, they may be inclined to look for shortcuts, such as copying or cheating. Identifying needed support and providing appropriate technical and social support can help prevent academic misconduct. Effective educational interventions can also strengthen academic ethical awareness.

Overall, a balanced approach between social and technical support, along with strong academic ethics education, can help create an educational environment that promotes academic integrity and reduces academic misconduct. Lecturers, academic staff, and educational institutions must play an essential role in providing resources and supporting students to achieve academic success without resorting to unethical means.

Gender and XYZ Generation Perspectives. This research focuses on the influence of gender and XYZ generation on academic misconduct. However, these two factors do not influence academic misconduct. Some research shows differences in misconduct rates between male and female students, with some showing that males are more prone to certain types of misconduct [5, 41, 47]. This research does not support this opinion. The same thing happens to the influence of the XYZ generation on academic misconduct. Some research argues that the XYZ generation may have different educational, honesty, and ethical values [1, 5, 48]. This may influence how individuals feel it is crucial to avoid academic misconduct. The results of this research do not support this opinion.

This is possibly caused by a sudden change in the learning process, which is still being studied equally by all parties involved so that gender and generation XYZ have not or do not influence academic misconduct. These results might be related to the method of gathering information using questionnaires since filling out the questionnaire via Google Forms could possibly be done by someone else, so the results may not be relevant to the respondent's opinion.

5 Conclusion

This study found that accessibility to technology, communication styles, and social and technical support affect individuals' willingness to commit academic misconduct. On the contrary, gender, XYZ generations, family responsibilities, preferences for learning, and stress and mental well-being did not influence academic misconduct. Based on the results, it is important for education to be aware of the use of technology, which must be balanced with efforts to teach academic integrity and ethics to students. Besides, creating an environment that encourages positive support where honest and open communication is encouraged, academic misconduct is dealt with firmly, and academic ethics is emphasized.

However, we cannot find a relationship between gender and XYZ generation with academic misconduct. Certain research methods may have limitations. For example, we only use quantitative data in our study, while the qualitative aspects of the academic misconduct phenomenon may need to be fully represented. Therefore, it is essential to investigate factors affecting academic misconduct using qualitative research for future research. This method might be a way to minimize the disadvantages of using questionnaires. Conducting in-depth interviews with several respondents of students and lecturers that represent the gender and XYZ generation will help understand the factors that influence the decision to commit academic misconduct more deeply. Future research may also combine quantitative and qualitative research methods to gain a deeper understanding of academic misconduct. Interviews and case studies can provide richer insights than relying solely on statistical data.

Even though we have tried to maintain the validity and reliability of the data and research results, it cannot be denied that there are still several research limitations. First, it is related to the generalization of research results. Research results may only reflect certain situations or populations. In this case, the data may not easily apply to other contexts or populations. For example, the findings may only apply to students at a particular college level or geographic area. Second, some variables not included in the study may influence the relationships between the factors investigated. It is possible that variables that are not measured or considered could impact academic misconduct. So, future research may be beneficial to involve factors that may impact academic cheating in various contexts, such as across educational institutions, levels of education, or levels of learning. This can provide a more thorough understanding of the factors influencing academic misconduct. Second, conduct research that involves monitoring over longer periods to understand the changing trends and dynamics of academic misconduct. This can help identify factors that may develop over time. Third, consider control variables by considering additional variables that might influence academic misconduct. For example, it involves variables such as the course's difficulty level or the type of evaluation used.

References

1. Susilowati, E., et al.: Bibliometric analysis of ethics and online learning using VOSviewer software. Proc. IMCEIS **2022**(October), 1–15 (2022)
2. Huang, C.L., Wu, C., Yang, S.C.: How students view online knowledge: epistemic beliefs, self-regulated learning and academic misconduct. Comput. Educ. **200**, 104796 (2023). https://doi.org/10.1016/j.compedu.2023.104796
3. Alturki, U., Aldraiweesh, A.: Application of learning management system (Lms) during the covid-19 pandemic: a sustainable acceptance model of the expansion technology approach. Sustain. **13**(19), 1–16 (2021). https://doi.org/10.3390/su131910991
4. Raza, S.A., Qazi, W., Khan, K.A., Salam, J.: Social isolation and acceptance of the learning management system (LMS) in the time of COVID-19 pandemic: an expansion of the UTAUT model. J. Educ. Comput. Res. **59**(2), 183–208 (2021). https://doi.org/10.1177/0735633120960421
5. Susilowati, E., Suryaningrum, D.H., Andayani, S.: Gender and Xyz generations perspective on academic misconduct: evidence from Indonesia. J. Namibian Stud.: History Polit. Cult. **33**, 1416–1438 (2023). https://doi.org/10.59670/jns.v33i.2907
6. Stoesz, B.M., Quesnel, M., De Jaeger, A.E.: Student perceptions of academic misconduct amongst their peers during the rapid transition to remote instruction. Int. J. Educ. Integr. **19**(1), 14 (2023). https://doi.org/10.1007/s40979-023-00136-1
7. Parkinson, A.L., Hatje, E., Kynn, M., Kuballa, A.V., Donkin, R., Reinke, N.B.: Collusion is still a tricky topic: student perspectives of academic integrity using assessment-specific examples in a science subject. Assess. Eval. High. Educ. **47**(8), 1416–1428 (2022). https://doi.org/10.1080/02602938.2022.2040947
8. Siddhpura, A., Siddhpura, M.: Plagiarism, contract cheating and other academic misconducts in online engineering education: analysis, detection and prevention strategies. In: 2020 IEEE International Conference on Teaching, Assessment, and Learning for Engineering (TALE), pp. 112–119 (2020). https://doi.org/10.1109/TALE48869.2020.9368311

9. Heckler, N.C., Forde, D.R.: The role of cultural values in plagiarism in higher education. J. Acad. Ethics **13**(1), 61–75 (2015). https://doi.org/10.1007/s10805-014-9221-3
10. Mahmud, S., Bretag, T., Foltýnek, T.: Students' perceptions of plagiarism policy in higher education: a comparison of the United Kingdom, Czechia, Poland and Romania. J. Acad. Ethics **17**(3), 271–289 (2019). https://doi.org/10.1007/s10805-018-9319-0
11. Zhang, Y., Yin, H., Zheng, L.: Investigating academic dishonesty among Chinese undergraduate students: does gender matter? Assess. Eval. High. Educ. **43**(5), 812–826 (2018). https://doi.org/10.1080/02602938.2017.1411467
12. de Lima, J.Á., Sousa, Á., Medeiros, A., Misturada, B., Novo, C.: Understanding undergraduate plagiarism in the context of students' academic experience. J. Acad. Ethics **20**(2), 147–168 (2022). https://doi.org/10.1007/s10805-021-09396-3
13. Hosny, M., Fatima, S.: Attitude of students towards cheating and plagiarism: university case study. J. Appl. Sci. **14**(8), 748–757 (2014). https://doi.org/10.3923/jas.2014.748.757
14. Riaz, S., Mushtaq, A.: Qualitative assessment of tangible-intangible outcomes and challenges of massive open online courses. In: 2023 Advances in Science and Engineering Technology International Conferences (ASET), pp. 1–6 (2023). https://doi.org/10.1109/ASET56582.2023.10180609
15. Simon, C.A., Carr, J.R., Mccullough, S.M., Morgan, S.J., Oleson, T., Ressel, M.: Gender, student perceptions, institutional commitments and academic dishonesty: who reports in academic dishonesty cases? Assess. Eval. High. Educ. **29**(1), 75–90 (2004). https://doi.org/10.1080/0260293032000158171
16. Dhanapal, S., Vashu, D., Subramaniam, T.: Perceptions on the challenges of online purchasing: a study from 'baby boomers', generation 'X' and generation 'Y' point of views. Contaduría y Adm. **60**, 107–132 (2015). https://doi.org/10.1016/j.cya.2015.08.003
17. Mulyadi, C.F.P., Diana, N., Mawardi, M.C.: Pengaruh Motivasi Belajar, Penyalahgunaan Teknologi Informasi dan Integritas Mahasiswa terhadap Perilaku Kecurangan Akademik Mahasiswa Akuntansi sebagai Calon Akuntan (Studi Kasus Pada Mahasiswa Akuntansi Universitas Islam Malang) - The Influence of Learn. E-JRA e-Jurnal Ilm. Ris. Akunt. **10**(6), 16–23 (2021). https://jim.unisma.ac.id/index.php/jra/article/view/12705
18. Nurjanah, Y., Anggraeni, E.P., Van Melle, J.: Pengaruh Dimensi Fraud Diamond dan Penyalahgunaan Teknologi Informasi Terhadap Perilaku Kecurangan Akademik Mahasiswa Akuntansi saat Perkuliahan Online (The influence of fraud diamond dimensions and misuse of information technology on the academic fraud B). JAS-PT (Jurnal Anal Sist. Pendidik. Tinggi Indones. **5**(2), 103 (2021). https://doi.org/10.36339/jaspt.v5i2.462
19. Sososutiksno, C.: Faktor yang Berpengaruh terhadap Perilaku Kecurangan Akademik di Masa Pandemi Covid-19 (Factors that Influence Academic Cheating Behavior during the Covid-19 Pandemic). JMBI UNSRAT (Jurnal Ilm. Manaj. Bisnis dan Inov. Univ. Sam Ratulangi) **10**(1), 137–150 (2023). https://doi.org/10.35794/jmbi.v10i1.45681
20. Yaqin, A., Suadi, S.: Kecurangan Akademik dalam Moda Pembelajaran Digital di Perguruan Tinggi (Academic cheating in digital learning modes in higher education). Hikmah **19**(2), 96–107 (2022). https://e-jurnal.staisumatera-medan.ac.id/index.php/hikmah/article/view/164
21. Karima, R., Octavia, L.G.V., Fahmi, K.: Lunturnya Moralitas Pelajar Indonesia? (Is the morality of indonesian students fading?). Literaksi J. Manaj. Pendidik **1**(2), 17–20 (2023). https://literaksi.org/index.php/jmp/article/view/11
22. Sarirah, T., Rachmayani, D., Supriyono, Y.: Peran Academic Dishonesty Dalam Menjelaskan Hubungan Antara Self-Regulated Learning dan Dukungan Sosial Teman Sebaya dengan Prestasi Akademik (The role of academic dishonesty in explaining the relationship between self-regulated learning and peer social S). Mediapsi **03**(01), 1–8 (2017). https://doi.org/10.21776/ub.mps.2017.003.01.1

23. Parnther, C.: International students and academic misconduct: considering culture, community, and context. J. Coll. Character **23**(1), 60–75 (2022). https://doi.org/10.1080/2194587X.2021.2017978

24. Tarista, M.: Pengaruh Faktor Triangle Fraud dan Faktor Sosial terhadap Kecurangan Akademik yang Dilakukan oleh Mahasiswa Akuntansi (The influence of triangle fraud factors and social factors on academic fraud committed by accounting students). Dsp. Univ. Islam Indones. (August) (2023). https://dspace.uii.ac.id/handle/123456789/45485

25. Parlangeli, O., Palmitesta, P., Bracci, M., Marchigiani, E., Di Pomponio, I., Guidi, S.: University teachers during the first lockdown due to SARS-CoV-2 in Italy: stress, issues and perceptions of misconduct. Sci. Eng. Ethics (2022). https://doi.org/10.1007/s11948-022-00362-9

26. Griffin, M.A., Clarke, S.: Stress and well-being at work. In: Zedeck, S. (ed.) APA handbook of industrial and organizational psychology, Vol 3: Maintaining, expanding, and contracting the organization., pp. 359–397. American Psychological Association, Washington (2011). https://doi.org/10.1037/12171-010

27. Lazarus, R.S.: Theory-based stress measurement. Psychol. Inq. **1**(1), 3–13 (1990). https://doi.org/10.1207/s15327965pli0101_1

28. Edwards, P.M.: A Comparative Analysis of Adult Learning Styles and Interpersonal Communication Techniques. Master of Education Field Project, Western Washington University (1994). https://eric.ed.gov/?id=ED374209

29. Tlili, A., Essalmi, F., Jemni, M., Kinshuk, Chen, N.-S.: Role of personality in computer based learning. Comput. Human Behav. **64**, 805–813 (2016). https://doi.org/10.1016/j.chb.2016.07.043

30. Koswara, A.N.M.: Pengaruh Kemudahan Akses Informasi Internet melalui Konteks Sosial Pelajar terhadap Kecenderungan Tindakan Plagiarisme dalam Penulisan Karya Tulis di Kalangan Pelajar. Masyarakat Telematika Dan Informasi: Jurnal Penelitian Teknologi Informasi dan Komunikasi **9**(1), 51 (2018). https://doi.org/10.17933/mti.v9i1.115

31. Roberts, P., Anderson, J., Yanish, P.: Academic misconduct: where do we start?. In: the Annual Conference of the Northern Rocky Mountain Educational Research Association, pp. 1–26. Jackson, WY (1997). https://eric.ed.gov/?id=ED415781

32. Mulyadi, C.F.P., Diana, N., Mawardi, M.C.: Pengaruh Motivasi Belajar, Penyalahgunaan Teknologi Informasi dan Integritas Mahasiswa terhadap Perilaku Kecurangan Akademik Mahasiswa Akuntansi sebagai Calon Akuntan (Influence of Learning Motivation, Misuse of Technology Information and Student Integrit), E-JRA e-Jurnal Ilm. Ris. Akunt. **10**(6), 16–23 (2021), https://jim.unisma.ac.id/index.php/jra/article/view/12705

33. Donnelly, K., Twenge, J.M., Clark, M.A., Shaikh, S.K., Beiler-May, A., Carter, N.T.: Attitudes toward women's work and family roles in the United States, 1976–2013. Psychol. Women Q. **40**(1), 41–54 (2016). https://doi.org/10.1177/0361684315590774

34. Cerrato, J.. Cifre, E: Gender inequality in household chores and work-family conflict. Front. Psychol. **9**(August), 1330 (2018). https://doi.org/10.3389/fpsyg.2018.01330

35. GSI_Teaching: Factors that Can Contribute to Academic Misconduct," Berkeley Graduate Division (2015). https://gsi.berkeley.edu/gsi-guide-contents/academic-misconduct-intro/factors/. Accessed 13 Oct 2023

36. Drageset, J.: Social support. In: Haugan, G., Eriksson, M. (eds.) Health Promotion in Health Care – Vital Theories and Research, pp. 137–144. Springer International Publishing, Cham (2021). https://doi.org/10.1007/978-3-030-63135-2_11

37. Das, A.: Knowledge and productivity in technical support work. Manage. Sci. **49**(4), 416–431 (2003). https://doi.org/10.1287/mnsc.49.4.416.14419

38. Parnther, C.: Academic misconduct in higher education: a comprehensive review. J. High. Educ. Policy Leadersh. Stud. **1**(1), 25–45 (2020). https://doi.org/10.29252/johepal.1.1.25

39. Giri, V.N.: Culture and communication style. Rev. Commun. **6**(1–2), 124–130 (2006). https://doi.org/10.1080/15358590600763391

40. Yulmiastri, Y., Atmowardoyo, H., Salija, K.: The Learning Styles of Students and Their Problems in Speaking English at the Second Grade of MAN Pangkep. e-print UNM, p. 12752 (2019). http://eprints.unm.ac.id/12752/1/ARTICLE%20YUYU.pdf

41. Rapoho, B.D.: Etika Kepedulian dan Etika Keadilan Bias Gender Dalam Moralitas (Ethics of Caring and Ethics of Justice Gender Bias in Morality) (2019). https://www.researchgate.net/publication/335753948_Etika_Kepedulian_dan_Etika_Keadilan_Bias_Gender_Dalam_Moralitas

42. Rahardyan, T.M., Bakri, M.R., Utami, An.: Generation gap in fraud prevention: Study on generation Z, generation X, millennials, and boomers. Int. J. Res. Busi, Soc. Sci. (2147-4478) **12**(3), 361–375 (2023). https://doi.org/10.20525/ijrbs.v12i3.2566

43. Ringle, C.M., Wende, S., Becker, J.-M.: Smart PLS 3.0. Boenningstedt: SmartPLS GmbH (2015). http://www.smartpls.com

44. Cheung, G.W., Cooper-Thomas, H.D., Lau, R.S., Wang, L.C.: Reporting reliability, convergent and discriminant validity with structural equation modeling: a review and best-practice recommendations. Asia Pacific J. Manag. (2023). https://doi.org/10.1007/s10490-023-09871-y

45. Djokovic, R., Janinovic, J., Pekovic, S., Vuckovic, D., Blecic, M.: Relying on technology for countering academic dishonesty: the impact of online tutorial on students' perception of academic misconduct. Sustainability **14**(3), 1756 (2022). https://doi.org/10.3390/su14031756

46. Peled, Y., Eshet, Y., Barczyk, C., Grinautski, K.: Predictors of academic dishonesty among undergraduate students in online and face-to-face courses. Comput. Educ. **131**, 49–59 (2019). https://doi.org/10.1016/j.compedu.2018.05.012

47. Pelch, M.: Gendered differences in academic emotions and their implications for student success in STEM. Int. J. STEM Educ. **5**(1), 33 (2018). https://doi.org/10.1186/s40594-018-0130-7

48. Pizzolato, D., Dierickx, K.: The mentor's role in fostering research integrity standards among new generations of researchers: a review of empirical studies. Sci. Eng. Ethics **29**(3), 19 (2023). https://doi.org/10.1007/s11948-023-00439-z

Verification and Validation of Knowledge Engineering Systems: A Life Cycle Framework

Ghazi Alkhatib(✉) ⬤

The Hashemite University, Zarqa, Jordan
g.alkhatib@hu.edu.jo

Abstract. The aim of this paper is to develop a life cycle framework for knowledge engineering systems' development, use, and maintenance. The framework integrates verification and validation (V&V) paradigms of software engineering into the different Knowledge Engineering Systems (KES). A simple generic life cycle model is used, consisting of knowledge input, construction, and use. The paper proposes three strategies for incorporating V&V into building and maintaining reliable systems. During development and during operation, conduct periodic and perpetual V&V. The framework provides a comprehensive treatment of V&V to support the operation of KES throughout its expected life cycle span. Future research will provide a detailed, individualized framework for incorporating V&V into generative AI systems.

Keywords: knowledge engineering systems · verification · validation · machine learning · artificial intelligennce · generative artificial intelligence · expert systems · decision support systems

1 Introduction

According to Gartner, the top ten strategic technology trends 2024 included: 1. AI Trust, Risk and Security Management (AI TRiSM), 5. AI-Augmented Development, 7. Intelligent Applications, and 8. Democratized Generative AI [1]. This highlights and supports the importance of the theme of this paper.

The report puts AI TRiSM and democratized Generative AI among the factors that "Protect your investment to secure the benefits from the past and future strategic technology decision to make them last." It present a case in action for AI TRiSM of Fidelity Investment who used many AI models and improved the time to find and resolve issues by 80%, cutting the time from weeks to hours. AI TRiSM has three technology components: content anomaly detection, data protection, and application security. The three components are connected to AI Systems. Gartner predict that applying TRiSM controls to AI applications will increase accuracy of the decision making process by removing 80% of faulty and illegitimate information. AI augmented development involves using AI technologies, such as generative AI and machine learning to assist software engineers in creating, testing and development applications. Gartner predicts that by 2026, 30% of new intelligent application will deploy AI to generate effective user interfaces.

A. Mirzazadeh et al. (Eds.): SEMIT 2023, CCIS 2198, pp. 37–55, 2024.
https://doi.org/10.1007/978-3-031-72284-4_3

Generative AI (GAI) will lead to the development of new content of different data types, such as images, speech, text for widespread use by user and organizations. GIA as the most disruptive trend in coming decade, users will access knowledge and technical skills through open source technologies. This will dictate the need for new regulations and self-governance, as well as increasing workforce productivity. All these factors emphasize the need for developing a framework that will ensure the development of verified and validated AI systems, wither for the public use or for organization use.

1.1 Data Hierarchy

The hierarchical structure of data from the bottom of the organization to the top is as follows: data, information, knowledge, and intelligence. Knowledge Engineering Systems follow the flowing pattern:

At the bottom is the transaction processing system (TPS) for routine decisions, which is considered the backbone of all other systems.

– Decision Support Systems for semi-structured decisions. For example, the basis of the Analytical Hierarchical Process (AHP) using Expert Choice Shell,
– Expert Systems for automatic decision-making using a knowledge base having a reasoning logic constructed on intricate rules of IF\THEN\ELSE or case-based reasoning using expert system shells such as ES-Builder and Java Expert System Shell (JESS),
– Intelligent systems (artificial intelligence and machine learning) with human mind emulation, of which the most standout software is ChatGPT.

1.2 Software Development Life Cycle (SDLC)

Many SDLC models are proposed in software engineering books [2], as well as systems analysis and design books [3]. Each of these KES has its own detailed SDLC model. These discussions are beyond the scope of this paper.

For the purpose of developing the V&V framework, the paper will adopt a simplified generic model of how to implement the three types of KES development and use. Such SDLC consists of three major phases: front-end, construction, and use.

1.3 Verification and Validation (V&V)

In software engineering, verification and validation are not the same thing. Verification shows conformance with specifications; validation shows that the program meets the customer's needs. In uncertain cases where the development methodologies cannot be verified from prior experiences, a prototype is normally constructed and tested using the most suggested methodology, or model [2, 3]. In another reference, the author stated that the verification and validation (V&V) technique is a critical component of the knowledge engineering process. The author defines verification as building the system right, and validation as building the right system. Then the paper exposed five studies on KES projects and concluded that without similar studies, knowledge engineering will remain very much an art [4]. This paper is a current effort to support the importance of V&V in KES.

Figure 1 below displays how the components and V&V factors are linked together with the hierarchy of KES.

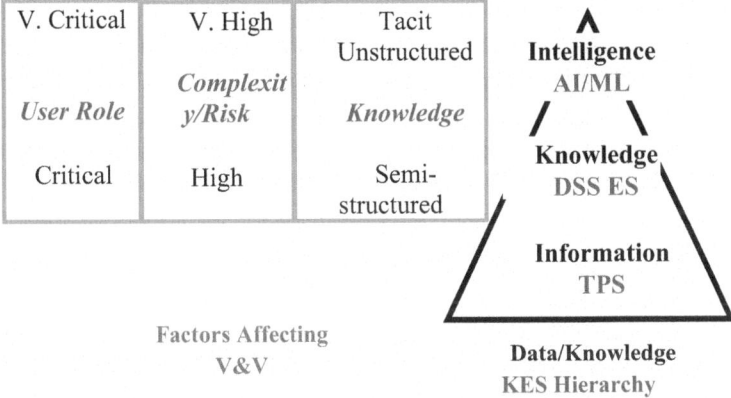

V. Critical	V. High	Tacit Unstructured
User Role	*Complexit y/Risk*	*Knowledge*
Critical	High	Semi-structured

Factors Affecting
V&V

Intelligence
AI/ML

Knowledge
DSS ES

Information
TPS

Data/Knowledge
KES Hierarchy

Fig. 1. Relationships among factors affecting V&V and KES and Data/Knowledge Hierarchies

2   Review of Literature

The verification and validation of KESs are crucial to ensuring their reliability, safety, and effectiveness. KESs can be complex and often involve machine learning algorithms, neural networks, and data- and knowledge-driven decision-making processes involving structured and unstructured data and knowledge. Here's how verification and validation are applied to KES, as stated in [5]. In addition, the paper provides supporting references as appropriate.

2.1   Verification Activities

Requirements Verification. Ensure that the requirements for KES are well-defined, unambiguous, and reflect the desired behavior and performance. Involve domain experts and stakeholders in validating that the requirements align with real-world needs.

Data Verification. Data is a fundamental component of many AI systems. Validate the quality, completeness, and consistency of the training data. One major aspect of an AI/ML system is to ensure that the data used for training is representative of the problem domain.

Model/frameworks/shells Verification. Validate the models used in the KES development. Check for overfitting and underfitting, and ensure that the models generalize well to new data. Overfitting is when the model performs well in the training set but fails to generalize the learning to the testing set. Underfitting becomes obvious when the model is too simple and cannot create a relationship between the input and the output [6]. Gartner also published steps to improve test data management guidelines [7].

Testing and Verification During Development. Conduct various types of testing, such as unit testing, integration testing, and system testing, by creating test cases and datasets to evaluate the KES's performance and identify potential issues [8, 9].

Perpetual and Periodic Verification. User communities of practice must continuously provide feedback individually of collectively during sponsored meetings to ensure the KES meet user expectations [10].

Validation Before Release of the KES. Three approaches may be recommended from practice: use employee to test the system, use beta sites, and/or use usability testing lab with selected representative samples from the target user population.

User Acceptance Testing. During testing Involve users or stakeholders in testing the KES to ensure it meets their expectations and needs [11].

Human-in-the-Loop Verification and Validation. Use human experts to validate the KES's outputs and provide feedback. Implement mechanisms for humans to intervene in or override KES decisions when necessary. This involves bridging the gap between technical developers and decision-makers. What is called the "IT-user divide" includes handling the following issues: technical jargon for lack of user understanding of IT terminologies, which could be handled with user training, and lack of user involvement, which could be handled by following suggested best practices like agile methodologies [12]. Verification of decision-making during development and validation during use ensure that the KES's decisions align with its intended purpose. Develop mechanisms for the explanation and interpretability of KES decisions. KES must provide justifications for decisions after the decision is made.

Continuous Monitoring and Verification and Validation. KES should be continuously monitored for verification and validation, as they may drift over time due to changing data sources and distributions, outdated data, and knowledge and skill decay over time.

Documentation and Record-Keeping. Maintain detailed records of verification and validation activities for auditing and compliance purposes. This could be part of the Quality Assurance Department using quality audits [13].

In summary, the verification and validation process should be ongoing, iterative, and adaptable, as KES may evolve and adapt to new data, knowledge, and scenarios. The level of rigor and the specific methods used will vary depending on the complexity and criticality of the KES, as well as the industry and application domain. Additionally, it's important to keep up with best practices and emerging standards for KES verification and validation.

List of Selected Standards related to V&V Activities. The following is a list of selected major standards that could assist in KES verification and validation in specific areas [5], with supporting references:

– ISO/IEC Standard 25000 – Software Quality Requirements and Evaluation (SQuaRE): This standard provides guidance on software quality requirements and evaluation, which can be applied to AI systems. It covers various aspects of software quality, including functionality, performance, security, and usability [14]. NIST Special Publication 800–183 – Automation Support for Security Control Assessments: This publication by the National Institute of Standards and Technology (NIST) discusses the use of automation to support security control assessments, which is highly relevant in the context of AI system verification and validation [15].

– EU Guidelines for Trustworthy AI: The European Commission has published guidelines for trustworthy AI, which include specific recommendations for assessing and validating AI systems in terms of ethics, transparency, and accountability [16].
– IEEE Standard 7000 – Model for IoT and AI Ethics: This standard from the Institute of Electrical and Electronics Engineers (IEEE) provides a framework for considering ethical issues in AI and IoT systems, including verification and validation practices [17].

Researchers list the following as knowledge-aware applications: natural language understanding, question answering, dialogue systems, and recommender systems. These applications are all related to the AI/ML systems category [18]. But the same ideas can be used to help represent knowledge in shells that are used to build DSS, connecting implicit and explicit knowledge. For example, the effect of the government's political stability on investment analysis, and in ES (decision rules structure and sequencing) The preceding paper also addresses issues related to knowledge acquisition to arrive at a suitable representation of the knowledge graph by removing ambiguities and improving the alignment of entities.

3   Research Methodology

The research methodology uses the integration approach of linking several technologies to build the framework. In particular linking software engineering V&V and KES. It encompassed the following steps of building the framework, as shown in Fig. 2. The first step presents an introduction to the importance of verification and validation (V&V) of information systems and KES, followed by a review of related literature to the theme of the paper. The second step consists of a literature survey of major issues related to V&V of KES, leading to a body of knowledge that will facilitate the construction of the framework. The literature survey includes an analysis of links between the three KES identified in the paper: expert systems (ES), decision support systems (DSS), and artificial intelligence/machine learning systems (AI/ML)/Generative AI. As the discussion ensues, similarities and differences among the three types of systems will be highlighted, as shown in the Fig. 1 above. This analysis would assist in developing a generalized macro framework, delineating a simplified life cycle model that applies to all three systems. This simplified model will then be used to present V&V strategies that apply throughout the life cycle stages.

3.1   Framework Foundation

This section provides a comprehensive review of the existing literature on the relationship between Knowledge Engineering Systems (KES) and the verification and validation processes, drawing on both past and current research. The focus is on how software engineering principles are used in this context. The evaluation establishes the fundamental basis of a knowledge framework that will be used in the construction of the formwork.

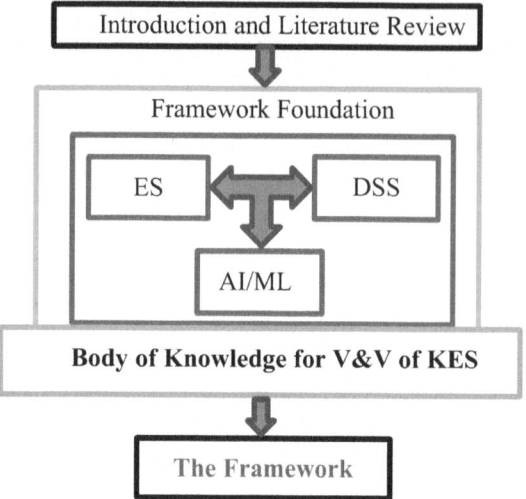

Fig. 2. Steps in Research Methodology.

In their study, Gupta conducted a comprehensive analysis of the verification and validation processes pertaining to knowledge-based systems [18]. Regarding basic challenges in verification and validation (V&V), the author has recognized the following: KES should consider the development of their own verification and validation (V&V) procedures, since knowledge engineering systems (KES) are designed to address heuristic issues that include several levels of reasoning and uncertainty. Consequently, these systems exhibit increased complexity and intricacy. In order to establish dependable systems, it is essential for KES to start their development process by incorporating well investigated theories in knowledge engineering. Therefore, it is essential to ensure that knowledge engineering is generated, managed, and assessed with the same level of precision and rigor as any other discipline within the area of engineering. This work aims to examine the prevailing concerns in the existing body of research pertaining to the V&V of Knowledge Engineering Systems (KES). The knowledge-aware applications identified by another research includes Natural Language Understanding, question answering, conversation systems, and recommender systems. These applications are all under the area of AI/ML systems. The aforementioned study additionally examines concerns pertaining to the acquisition of information in order to get an appropriate depiction of the knowledge graph via the elimination of ambiguities and enhancement of entity alignment [19].

In subsequent years, the development approaches of Knowledge Engineering Systems (KES) saw advancements via the incorporation of shells, as shown by the ones discussed in reference [20] for the construction of Expert Systems (ES), and the use of Analytical Hierarchical Process inside Expert Choice for Decision Support Systems (DSS) as mentioned in reference [21]. Previous studies have shown a connection between ES and artificial intelligence (AI) [22, 23]. Currently, there are two distinct attributes of ES that provide potential advantages: one that should be avoided and another that should be used as a model. The first statement pertains to the observation that ES produces choices and initiates actions, whilst the latter is advantageous due to the inclusion of an explanation model inside the ES framework. This model elucidates the sequence of decision rules or frames used in reaching the decision. According to Gupta's findings, the primary existing deficiencies include the absence of automated mechanisms for information collection, verification of knowledge bases, system testing, and refining and maintenance of knowledge [18]. The author expresses optimism that this framework has the potential to effectively emphasize the crucial components in Knowledge Engineering Systems (KES) and subsequently facilitate the creation of corresponding tools.

Numerous scholarly articles have highlighted the significance of knowledge graphs in the context of generative artificial intelligence [24]. The researchers reached the conclusion that knowledge graphs are beneficial for effectively summarizing the document(s). Moreover, the research findings indicate that the suggested model effectively mitigates issues related to capacity limitations in language models, such as BART and ChatGPT [25]. The aforementioned results were derived using a model that was devised by the authors with the aim of effectively condensing textual content. The authors emphasized the significance of generating knowledge graphs for LLMs in their study. They accomplished this by creating a taxonomy of generative knowledge graph creation techniques, examining their theoretical foundations, and conducting empirical research. Authors of a study have devised a generative model that specifically tackles the problem of numerous relation semantics in knowledge graph embedding [26]. The used methodology included the utilization of a generative Bayesian non-parametric infinite mixture embedding technique. The research discovered that the model had the capability to autonomously discern the implicit connotations of a relationship and modify its various components in order to integrate them into the generative knowledge graph. In the realm of generative AI systems, the significance of knowledge graphs cannot be overstated since they play a crucial role in accurately capturing knowledge.

In the realm of knowledge input verification, previous studies have presented a methodology for assessing user reviews within the context of open source platforms [27]. This aspect has significant importance across all knowledge exchange systems (KES). The parties involved in the evaluation of decision support systems (DSS) and expert systems (ES) may consist of decision makers, IT professionals engaged in the development of all three knowledge-based expert systems (KES), and feedback from decision makers. However, it is particularly important to gather feedback from user communities accessing Large Language Models (LLM), such as ChatGPT.

The use of artificial intelligence (AI) in the realm of business strategy has been duly recognized by the writers, as it serves the purpose of mitigating risk and fostering enhanced cooperation within businesses [28]. The significance of this matter lies in the fact that generative artificial intelligence (AI) is specifically aimed at corporations in order to promote its widespread use. According to IBM, there is a prevailing skepticism surrounding the utilization of generative artificial intelligence (AI) in enterprises. IBM's research indicates that 64% of CEOs are experiencing substantial pressure from various stakeholders, including investors, creditors, and lenders, to expedite the implementation of generative AI [29]. The source provided by IBM offers further insights into the adoption and implications of generative AI in the enterprise context [29].

3.2 Body of Knowledge for V&V of KES

The ensuing discussions provide issues related to V&V of KES.

Scope. The scope of the analysis encompasses both a macro perspective and a micro one. The macro perspective encompasses the perspective of a knowledge-based society. A knowledge society is characterized by its capacity to develop, process, disseminate, and provide accessibility to knowledge to all members of its population. The process encompasses the generation, distribution, and application of information and knowledge. Intellectual capital is often recognized as the primary driver of economic prosperity within societies [30]. Government organizations, such as the Jordan Department of Statistics [31], and commercial organization repositories, such as Moody's Analytics [32], house valuable knowledge that may be accessible either at no cost or for a price. This is mostly used in the fields of Expert Science (ES) and Decision Support Systems (DSS). In addition, knowledge is preserved inside publicly accessible repositories, such as social media platforms and open access resources. The latter option is primarily used for the purpose of training generative artificial intelligence and machine learning systems. This practice has elicited demands for the implementation of risk management strategies for artificial intelligence, safeguarding its accessibility, and providing compensation to writers and publishers for its use via legislative measures [15] or legal recourse [33].

The micro perspective refers to the organizational viewpoint. The storage of organizational knowledge and intellectual capital inside an organization is intricately connected to the concepts of organizational memory and learning. The process of converting organizational memory into a knowledge management system is facilitated via the use of information technology. These repositories facilitate the establishment of a culture that promotes ongoing learning and enhancement inside businesses. They also mitigate the negative impact of specialists leaving the company on its performance and effectiveness. Furthermore, they provide less experienced workers with access to the knowledge base, enabling them to use this valuable resource [34]. The culmination of this procedure is the establishment of a knowledge management system that facilitates the discovery, documentation, dissemination, use, and maintenance of information inside an organization. This phenomenon has the potential to result in either degradation or deterioration [35]·

The Phenomenon of Knowledge Deterioration. Over the course of time, it is possible for knowledge to deteriorate inside the cognitive faculties of particular specialists. One instance of such decline may be seen in the context of student retention within the realm of higher education [36]. Over the course of their employment, individuals may see a decline in their skill levels. Numerous firms implement ongoing education requirements for their staff as a means to tackle this problem [37]. Universities and colleges provide opportunities for those seeking to further their learning and acquire novel skills or information via the provision of continuing education courses. Typically, it is customary for workers to be obligated to amass a certain quantity of Continuing Education Unit (CEC) credits in order to fulfill their professional development requirements [38].

Furthermore, the acquisition of knowledge can be compromised due to advancements in products and processes [39], adopting enhancements made to current IT infrastructure [40], and the implementation of patches or upgrades to software systems utilized within organizations. One instance is the implementation of security patch updates for ISO

27001, as discussed in the comprehensive guide on patch management policy available at hightable.io [41]. Another example pertains to the strategic planning of enterprise resource planning (ERP) upgrades, which is explored in detail in the resource provided in [42].

The aforementioned skill maintenance criteria inherently foster a perpetual process of knowledge acquisition and dissemination.

The categorization of knowledge in knowledge management and decision support systems (DSS) is often delineated as outlined in [43]. For future research, nevertheless, it is possible to see parallels with the field of Artificial Intelligence and Machine Learning (AI/ML).

Types of Knowledge. Tacit knowledge is to a kind of information that is often acquired by hands-on experience, displays variation across people, and is acquired without conscious effort. Consequently, the task of delineating and codifying this data presents difficulties, thereby hindering its efficient propagation within the organization. Tacit knowledge may manifest in several areas, including language skills, face recognition capabilities, and proficiency in handling meetings. The verification and validation of this specific sort of knowledge present significant obstacles. The incorporation of diverse knowledge domains, like face recognition and music reflections, inside generative artificial intelligence (AI) systems presents notable complexities.

The concept of implicit knowledge is often examined in scholarly literature, with several sources seeing it as interchangeable with tacit knowledge. Nevertheless, researchers make a clear distinction between the two concepts, saying that tacit knowledge is acquired via an intentional and meticulous procedure. While there are difficulties in the process of codifying tacit information, it is important to note that implicit knowledge does not always face the same obstacle. Nevertheless, the documentation pertaining to implicit knowledge remains inadequate. Operational operations, such as order processing and site selection for new plant establishment, are often witnessed in practice.

Explicit knowledge encompasses information acquired from several sources such as manuals, reports, and recommendations. This kind of knowledge facilitates efficient information dissemination inside enterprises, whether the teams are co-located or operating remotely. Certain academics contend that this specific sort of knowledge is widely acknowledged and thoroughly examined within the current corpus of scholarly works. Examples that demonstrate this concept might include various intellectual resources such as databases, academic publications, and empirical assessments. The preservation of intellectual capital inside an organization is crucial, since it mitigates the impact of specialists leaving and enables effective knowledge transfer to less experienced staff or new recruits.

Knowledge Evolution. The author has developed a sequential model of knowledge development within organizational contexts. The sequence may be described in the following manner: Data refers to factual information that is stored in databases. Information is the result of processing data, which is used to generate repetitive reports and make routine decisions. Knowledge, on the other hand, is created over time through the expertise and experience of skilled individuals. Intelligence involves the intelligent use of knowledge to generate new ideas and improvements in processes, products, and technologies. Ultimately, this can lead to innovation within organizations, which is often necessary for their survival and success, as reflected in the common slogan "innovate or evaporate." Continuous verification and validation (V&V) is necessary in order to ensure the effectiveness and reliability of newly created creative concepts.

Additional forms of knowledge may include heuristics or superficial information that adheres to the notion of a general rule of thumb. One such instance is to the fields of medical diagnostics and psychiatry [44]. Another kind of knowledge is semi-structured knowledge, which pertains to domains like weather patterns or the political stability of a nation. Efforts have been made to develop collaborative and semi-structured resources that facilitate the extraction and dissemination of such knowledge [45].

4   The Framework

4.1   Introduction

Figure 3 demonstrates the dimensions of V&V approaches as used in the development and use of KES. Software development life cycle (SDLC) model could become very detailed depending on the type of KES. This paper adapted and adopted a generic general life cycle because it addresses issues related to three different KES in an attempt to benefit from experiences gained over the years. This approach to software development life cycle assist in concentrating on issues related to all three KES: expert system (ES), decision support system (DSS), and AI/ML systems including Generative AI (GAI). ES and DSS were around for many years with detailed description of SDLS and system's components. However, the latter type of systems are emerging for the last couple of decades as document in the introduction and review of literature. The SDLC for AI/ML and GAI would require more research, and this paper suggests this topic to be part of future research.

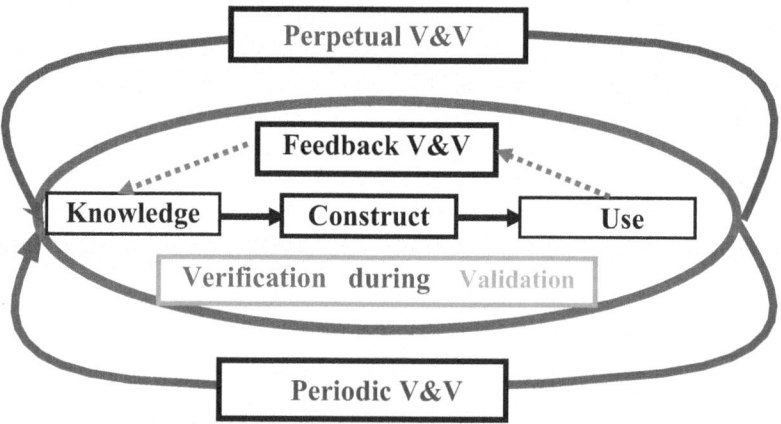

Fig. 3. Dimensions of V&V during software development and use.

4.2   In the Context of the Internal Organization

This could be referred to as the internal perimeter. The backbone of the framework is the internal generic SDLC, shown by the red oval in Fig. 3. The stages start with knowledge acquisition from different sources and different types of knowledge (stored in repositories or solicited from internal, external, published, and social media). These must be verified as to the reliability of the source, age of the knowledge, and relevancy to the KES. The next stage is knowledge representation before starting the construction. This will require different methods for knowledge representation, such as decision rules, multi-attribute utility models using AHP, and AI/ML/GIA models and/or frameworks. During the process of verification, it is important to thoroughly analyze the following aspects: The use of suitable methodologies that encourage ongoing and direct user interaction may enhance the facilitation of model, framework, and language selection, as well as the inclusion of users and IT experts. In addition, effective approaches for narrowing the divide between users and IT experts include reciprocal education and training, fostering confidence in information sources for both sides, and leveraging written or published materials. The move from the verification phase to the validation phase took place inside the organizational context as part of the development process. ES and DSS are domain-specific systems; as such, the move from verification to validation is seamless depending on the SDLC model used, such as prototype, incremental, or other models in software engineering. In the realm of AI/ML/GAI systems, the case is somewhat more cumbersome since users are external to the organization, are in high volume, and have different characteristics and categories. These SDLC models permit continuous verification and validation feedback, as represented in the dotted lines in Fig. 3.

This study aims to provide a verification of the selection of information representation approaches, including knowledge graphs, decision-making rules, and sequences, for Natural Language Processing (NLP) interfaces. The ideal team composition should have people who possess a high level of proficiency in the field of information technology, together with a strong track record of active engagement and use. The process of validating the knowledge sources used in the system requires a more comprehensive evaluation of external sources of information, including semi-structured or unstructured knowledge. The anticipated development in the use and acceptance of LLM and generative AI inside businesses is projected to lead to a higher occurrence of interaction between IT professionals and end-users. The LLM program is seeing a shift towards specialized topics within the realm of business, hence requiring IT professionals to possess a thorough comprehension of these particular fields. Therefore, the matter of reconciling the existing gap between information technology and business becomes apparent. A distinct investigation was undertaken to analyze many knowledge gap evaluations within the framework of integrating knowledge management with software engineering processes [46]. The knowledge gaps pertain to several domains, including process knowledge, product knowledge, technical knowledge, and behavioral knowledge. The study's survey results suggest that it is crucial to take these gaps into account while developing Knowledge Engineering Systems (KES) to optimize the use of knowledge management in the field of software engineering. The research also highlighted the importance of these elements in the advancement of AI knowledge engineering systems (KES). The digital gap, which pertains to the discrepancies between the theoretical comprehension of technology and its actual use, will become more apparent as generative artificial intelligence (AI) systems are integrated into many sectors of the economic world. This research presents compelling data supporting the notion that substantial disparities exist between IT professionals and those responsible for making decisions.

Verification is an essential aspect of the developmental process, wherein it is carried out by implementing suitable testing sequences that span a range of testing approaches, including unit, module, and system testing. Furthermore, a significant quantity of test instances is used in conjunction with statistical testing to guarantee the precision and uniformity of assessments and suggestions. Moreover, the active engagement of users during this period is essential for the eventual effectiveness of the system. Comprehensive and methodical testing protocols enhance the timely identification of errors, thereby reducing the likelihood of further operational interruptions arising from abnormal processing. The analysis showed that fixing a mistake found during operation cost twice as much as fixing a mistake found during the building phase [47]. Another element related to artificial intelligence and machine learning systems concerns the proper distribution of the dataset throughout the training, development, and testing stages. The author presented a division ratio of 80% to 20% between the two entities [48]. This implies that a considerable proportion of the dataset should be used for training the artificial intelligence/machine learning system. The proposed structure should include a system that enables the presentation of the underlying reasons for the recommended output or the justification for a specific choice. The inclusion of this characteristic was taken from the first Knowledge Engineering Systems (KES), in which the ES shell was improved by integrating an explanation module into the ES framework. Furthermore, the use of sensitivity analysis in the context of a Decision Support System (DSS) was noticed during the usage of a software platform such as Expert Choice [49]. Artificial intelligence and machine learning systems, on the other hand, might have more trouble using similar techniques because they use large language models (LLMs) that include complex and varied logic and knowledge structures.

After the first release and the initiation of maintenance efforts, some comments are due. The method of implementation may also include an incremental or iterative approach, depending on the particular development model used. In some circumstances, a prototype may be used. The feedback offered is sourced from the internal user community, which consists of both IT experts and end-users. These individuals actively participated in the implementation process after gaining improved skills and learning fresh perspectives. Furthermore, the addition of a highly skilled individual may result in the emergence of this phenomenon. Feedback may materialize in many ways, ranging from simple modifications to substantial upgrades. Thorough validation throughout the execution phase may not be necessary for simple changes. However, the implementation of substantial alterations or enhancements may require the use of both verification and validation procedures prior to the introduction of the novel product. With few guidelines and procedures in place, IT staff and users may internally handle the V&V process. To enhance the validation process of the revised version, it is recommended to use the established practice of beta testing. This involves selecting users from the community of practice to install the system and provide feedback on any difficulties they experience before the final release of the system.

4.3   In the Context of the External Organizational Environment

It may be referred to as the outer perimeter. The attainment of perpetual verification and validation may be realized via the integration of ongoing input from external users who are not affiliated with the organization. This may include integrating the latest government publications, using commercial sources of data, exploring social media platforms, and utilizing Internet repositories to improve the training and testing of the systems. The aforementioned alterations require the incorporation of both verification and validation procedures. Both types of external V&V can be facilitated by the use of usability laboratories.

Perpetual Verification and Validation. External users should have the ability to propose system improvements, internally review and confirm them, determine their importance, and promptly begin integrating them into the KES. This procedure may be a component of the quality management system aimed at external users. It involves scheduling meetings with specific user categories, such as medical professionals, researchers from other professions, and various sorts of businesses. The main goals are to mitigate the risks associated with the KES, which may escalate with time and alter decision processes and workflows, while also maximizing the benefits of adopting the KES. This paper demonstrates the utilization of ChatGPT 3.5. Users were able to evaluate and adjust their requests using the "Regenerate" option if the provided information was considered unsatisfactory. Appendix A has a screenshot depicting the request mentioned earlier. With the increased utilization of LLM generative artificial intelligence in business, this issue becomes an exemplary case that necessitates perpetual V&V.

Periodic Verification and Validation. The periodic verification and validation methods involve integrating external input into the internal processes. The Quality Assessment Department can conduct these procedures internally or outsource them to a third-party entity. This technique can be applied when the system ages, following the acquisition of new information technology infrastructure and the re-engineering of current systems. The IT department can decide when to conduct verification and validation procedures, such as on a three-year cycle or at other set intervals at major upgrade milestones. The IT department can consistently evaluate the gaps between the current system, including hardware and information systems, and the most recent advancements in any significant new development. Again, with the increased utilization of LLM-generative artificial intelligence in business, this issue becomes an exemplary case that dictates periodic V&V as well.

5   Real-World Cases

This section contains real-world reports on three AI systems and lesson learned from each.

IBM Watson on AI [50]. In 2014, IBM introduced Watson as an AI for health care. It invited clients (but nothing is mentioned about doctors) and journalists (why journalist, are they clients also). IBM promised to become a breakthrough health technology named AI doctor. It turned out to be just as AI assistants that can perform routine tasks.

Lessons learned from this failed project include:

- User doctors were not involvement during the validation or the verification phases. IBM mainly relied on the propaganda hype associated with the new technology, not the real needs of user.
- Process validation and integration were not conducted. IBM acquired companies to bolster the project, but had limited contributions to project.
- Process validation of the natural language processor for genuinely linking the interface to backend databases and retrieve relevant diagnostics to help doctors performing their tasks.
- The system's validation failed to achieve fitness for purpose.
- Failed dataset validation which has 80% of unstructured information on patients. Even liking IBM *Jeopardy!* to its healthcare technology project did not able to handle such dataset.
- The article referenced many external doctors (user experts) trying to help IBM health project achieve its objectives. Those either left the project or criticized the limited success it was accomplishing.

In reference to the framework in Fig. 3 above, IBM was never able to go outside the red circle; it just was repeating the internal life cycle stages and was not able go outside the box and deliver a commercial product.

Other failed cases [51]. The author provided the following lessoned learned after discussing three failed cases: Zillow Real-Estate iBuying, Dutch Government Childcare Welfare Fraud Scandal, and including the one on IBM presented above in a more detailed exposition.

Lesson learned as cited by the author included:

- The biggest lesson is to "Keep humans in the loop", a major factor advocated in this paper's framework at all stages of V&V, both at the internal and external organization stages.
- Algorithms and model must be subjected to a serious effort "to understand them thoroughly, test and validate them, continuously monitor your models, and have the output vetted by human experts using 3rd party data."
- Algorithms and models cannot be accountable for failures. It may lack of major stakeholder of the project form top management, or lower internal users and IT professional who did not conduct the validation as stated in the previous lessons.

Microsoft Chabot—Tay [52]. Microsoft (MS) Tay Chabot was trained using the world from 18–24 year olds on microblogging and chatting sites like Twitter, GroupMe and Kik. Upon initial use, Tay turned racist and sexist within 24 h because the people she spoke to, crowded her with hate and anger.

- Verifying the data used. Was the data used for training the Chabot verified properly to fit user's categories?
- Validation of Tay before release. Since it was developed for an open user community, MS could have invited a representative user samples from the general public, either clustered, stratified or both, to validate system before its release. Users' labs could have been established in mall and/or at the MS cite.

- The SDLC of AI project. An AI project, blending humans and technology together, should not be moved from the internal organization to external organization as a Beta version before properly verified and validated. AI projects could have its own system development life cycle.
- AI software, once it's released, the external environment V&V of periodic and perpetual becomes the crucial activity. The success of such activity depend on how much V&V was conducted in the internal organization. The developing organizations cannot simple depend on the external environment for the improvement of the AI software.
- AI use of big voluminous dataset, and as such, it must be continuous verified and validated at the outset as well as during the use by the external environment. Such dataset must be subject to verification and validation as stipulated in the paper's framework discussions.

6 Conclusions

The verification and validation of IT-based systems, including Transaction Processing Systems (TPS), hold significant importance, even when dealing with ordinary decision-making processes. Undoubtedly, the significance of the knowledge engineering systems (KES) is heightened. The need to develop verified and validated KES that meet customer needs and its continued success throughout the development and use of these systems. This paper developed a life cycle approach framework to achieve such continued success from KES inception to production to use. Although there is a prevailing shift away from the utilization of Expert Systems and Decision Support Systems toward AI systems, empirical studies indicate that these technologies continue to have limited practical implementations. One notable instance is the ES system [53] implemented by American Express in the past, as well as its ongoing endeavor to incorporate generative artificial intelligence (AI) technology. Further information can be found in [54]. The ES system was found to be the sole system that triggers automatic action, which poses challenges in the domain-specific applications, particularly in the field of medical informatics and credit card application approval. The article introduced a paradigm that prioritizes Knowledge Engineering System (KES) verification and validation across the course of the systems' life cycle, leading to ongoing user satisfaction. This is achieved through the mitigation of knowledge erosion and deterioration, as well as the implementation of regular and ongoing verification and validation processes. Certain V&V actions can be derived from either internal sources within the developer company or external sources of knowledge, such as government agencies and social media platforms. The verification process for external sources of knowledge is more challenging compared to that of internal sources.

The proposition put out by researchers entails the creation of an autonomous scientific entity responsible for the verification and validation of generative artificial intelligence [55]. This measure is deemed necessary to mitigate potential risks to scientific progress and public confidence. This paper has the potential to serve as a catalyst in facilitating progress towards that objective. This study also emphasizes an additional concern, as derived from the ES characteristic, which pertains to the necessity for KES to possess the capacity to provide explanations for its suggestions and search outcomes. This assertion is substantiated by a recent discovery that the presence of diverse inconsistencies in findings derived from the use of identical datasets illustrates how the application of different analytical approaches yields differing conclusions [56].

Future research will extensively examine the verification and validation methods of LLM/generative AI systems. SDLC research in software engineering convers several life cycle approaches. Therefore, this justifies the need for further research on developing a new SDLC model specifically for AI generative system.

Appendix A.

Screen shot form the use of ChatGPT 3.5 showing the option to "Regenerated" if the user is not satisfied with the results. An example of perpetual validation.

Validation:

1. **Meets User Needs:** Validation confirms that a system or product meets the user's requirements and expectations. It ensures that what is being built is what the customer actually wants.

2. **Ensures Fitness for Purpose:** Validation ensures that the system or product is fit for its intended purpose and that it will be effective in the real-world context for which it was designed.

3. **Reduces Risk:** By validating a system, you can identify and rectify issues before deployment, reducing the risk of costly errors or failures in the field.

↻ Regenerate

4. **Customer Satisfaction:** Validation helps in ensuring that the final

References

1. Gartner: Gartner Top 10 Strategic Technology Trends 2024. 2024-gartner-top-strategic-technology-trends-ebook.pdf (2023)
2. Sommerville, I.: Software Engineering, 10th edn. Pearson Publishing, London, England (2015)
3. Dennis, A., et al.: Systems Analysis and Design, 8th edn. Wiley, Toronto, Canada (2021)
4. Preece, A.: Building the Right System Right: Evaluating V&V Methods in Knowledge Engineering (2023). http://ksi.cpsc.ucalgary.ca/KAW/KAW98/preece
5. ChatGPT 3.5: (October 2023)
6. Baheti, P.: Overfitting vs. Underfitting: What's the Difference? (2022). https://www.v7labs.com/blog/overfitting-vs-underfitting)
7. Woodward, A.: Gartner: Steps to improving test data management (2023). https://www.computerweekly.com/feature/Gartner-Steps-to-improving-test-data-management
8. Liang, S., Wall, C.: Boost Testing Effectiveness With AI-Infused Tools And Quality Management Practices (2022). A Forrester Report. boost-testing-effectiveness-with-ai-infused-tools-and-quality-management-practices-report.pdf

9. Software Testing Help: 12 Best Automated Unit Testing Tools [LATEST 2024 RANKING] (2024). https://www.softwaretestinghelp.com/best-automated-unit-testing-tools
10. Wenger, E.C., Snyder, W.M.: Communities of Practice: The Organizational Frontier, From the Magazine (January–February 2000). https://hbr.org/2000/01/communities-of-practice-the-organizational-frontier
11. LinkedIn: How do you involve users in your software development process? (2024). https://www.linkedin.com/advice/0/how-do-you-involve-users-your-software
12. Agile Alliance: (2024). https://www.agilealliance.org/agile101
13. Sajith: The Five Essential Functions of Quality Assurance for Effective Business (2023). https://medium.com/@sajiveva1112000/the-five-essential-functions-of-quality-assurance-for-effective-business-operations-d65188147fa5
14. ISO/IEC: ISO/IEC 25000:2005(en) Software Engineering — Software product Quality Requirements and Evaluation (SQuaRE) — Guide to SQuaRE (2023). https://www.iso.org/obp/ui/#iso:std:iso-iec:25000:ed-1:v1:en
15. NIST: NIST Announce the Release of Special Publication 800-183, Network of Things 9 (2016). https://csrc.nist.gov/News/2016/Release-of-Special-Publication-800-183,-Network-of
16. European Commission: Smuha, N. – AI HLEG Coordinator. ETHICS GUIDELINES FOR TRUSTWORTHY AI (2018). https://www.aepd.es/sites/default/files/2019-12/ai-ethics-guidelines.pdf
17. Morandín-Ahuerma, F.: IEEE: a global standard as an ethical AI initiative (2023). https://ieeexplore.ieee.org/document/9536679
18. Gupta, U.: Validation and verification of knowledge-based systems: a survey. J. Appl. Intell. **3**, 343–363 (1993)
19. Ji, S., et al.: A survey on knowledge graphs: representation, acquisition, and applications. IEEE Trans. Neural Netw. Learn. Syst. **33**(2), 494–514 (2022). https://doi.org/10.1109/TNNLS.2021.3070843
20. Siriwardhane, P.: An Introduction to Expert System Shells: A Brief Overview ES Shell Structure and Comparison of Popular Expert System Shells, Published in Nerd For Tech (2022). https://medium.com/nerd-for-tech/an-introduction-to-expert-system-shells-530043914ec0#86b9
21. Ishizaka, A., Labib, A.: Analytic hierarchy process and expert choice: benefits and limitations. OR Insight **22**(4), 201–220 (2009). https://doi.org/10.1057/ori.2009.10
22. Horvitz, E.J., et al.: Decision theory in expert systems and artificial intelligence. Int. J. Approximate Reasoning **2**(3), 247–302 (1988)
23. Jackson, P.: Introduction to expert systems. United States: N. p., Web (1986). https://www.osti.gov/biblio/5675197
24. Kim, B., et al.: Generative model using knowledge graph for document-grounded conversations. Applied Sciences **12**, 3367 (2022). https://doi.org/10.3390/app12073367
25. Ye, H., et al.: Generative Knowledge Graph Construction: A Review, in arXiv:2210.12714v3 [cs.CL]. https://doi.org/10.48550/arXiv.2210.12714
26. Xiao, H. ,et al.: TransG: A Generative Model for Knowledge Graph Embedding. https://arxiv.org/pdf/1509.05488.pdf
27. Simões, G., et al:. Open publication system: evaluating users qualification and reputation. In: Cordeiro, J.M.A., et al. (eds.), CSEDU 2009 – Proceedings of the First International Conference on Computer Supported Education, Lisboa, Portugal, March 23–26, 2009 – Volume 1. 200–205, INSTICC Press (2009)
28. Przegalinska, A., Jemielniak, D.: Strategizing AI in Business and Education: Emerging Technologies and Business Strategy. Cambridge University Press (2023)
29. IBM: Enterprise generative AI: State of the market (2023). https://www.ibm.com/downloads/cas/3YZ1N2PB

30. Tweheyo, R.: Knowledge co-production and sustainable socio-economic development: an engaged scholarly approach. A book chapter in Developing Knowledge Societies for Distinct Country Contexts (2021). https://doi.org/10.4018/978-1-5225-8873-3.ch00In

31. Department of Statistics (2024). https://dosweb.dos.gov.jo

32. Moody's Analytics (2024). https://www.moodysanalytics.com

33. Middleton, C.: Generative AI – authors and artists declare war on AI vendors worldwide (2023). https://diginomica.com/generative-ai-authors-and-artists-declare-war-ai-vendors-worldwide

34. Vrîncianu, M., Anica-Popa, L., Anica-Popa, I.: Organizational memory: an approach from knowledge management and quality management of organizational learning perspectives. Amfiteatru Econ. J. **11**(26), 473–481 (2020)

35. Aris, R., Sensuse, D.: Knowledge management systems development and implementation: a systematic literature review. In: International Conference on Creative Economics, Tourism & Information Management (ICCETIM) (2020)

36. Krygier, D.: Reasons for knowledge decay in higher education and possible solutions. In: Universal Design: Meeting the Teaching and Learning Challenges of 21st Century Higher Education. Cambridge Scholars (2020)

37. AJE Springer Nature. What is Knowledge Management? (2023). https://www.aje.com/arc/what-is-knowledge-management

38. Head Start (ECLKC). Continuing Education Unit (CEU) Credit for Professional Development (2024). https://eclkc.ohs.acf.hhs.gov/professional-development/article/continuing-education-unit-ceu-credit-professional-development

39. Dorin, M.: Product and process innovation: a new perspective on the organizational development. Int. J. Adv. Res. Innov. Ideas Educ. **3**(6), 132–138 (2018). https://www.researchgate.net/publication/330834502_PRODUCT_AND_PROCESS_INNOVATION_A_NEW_PERSPECTIVE_ON_THE_ORGANIZATIONAL_DEVELOPMENT#fullTextFileContent

40. World Wide Technology. Networking Priorities for 2024 (2024). https://www.wwt.com/wwt-research/networking-priorities-for-2024

41. High Table. ISO27001 Patch Management Policy: Ultimate Guide (2024). https://hightable.io/iso-27001-patch-management-policy-ultimate-guide

42. Simon, S.: Everything You Need To Know About ERP Upgrades (2024). https://www.citrincooperman.com/In-Focus-Resource-Center/ERP-upgrade

43. IBM: What is knowledge management? (2024). https://www.ibm.com/topics/knowledge-management

44. Marewski, J.N.: Heuristic decision making in medicine. Dialogues Clin. Neurosci. **14**(1), 77–89 (2012). https://doi.org/10.31887/DCNS.2012.14.1/jmarewski

45. Hovy, E., Navigli, R., Ponzetto, S.P.: Collaboratively built semi-structured content and Artificial Intelligence: the story so far. Artif. Intell. **194**, 2–27 (2013)

46. Georgiev, D.: Exploring knowledge management from a software engineering perspective. Eur. Conf. Knowl. Manag. **24**(2), 1571–1578 (2023). https://doi.org/10.34190/eckm.24.2.1497

47. Boehm, B.W.: Software Engineering Economics, 1st edn. Prentice Hall (1981)

48. Joseph, V.R.: Optimal ratio for data splitting. In Statistical Analysis and Data Mining. Wiley Periodicals LLC (2022). https://doi.org/10.1002/sam.11583

49. Expert Choice: (2024) https://www.expertchoice.com

50. Strickland, E.: IBM Watson, heal thyself: How IBM overpromised and underdelivered on AI health care. IEEE Spectr. **56**(4), 24–31 (2019). https://doi.org/10.1109/MSPEC.2019.8678513

51. Rochford, O.: 3 real-world AI Failures and why we need to keep Humans in the Loop (2022). https://www.linkedin.com/pulse/3-real-world-ai-failures-why-we-need-keep-humans-loop-oliver-rochford

52. Asokan, A.: Three lessons from Microsoft's chatbot debacle (2016). https://www.livemint. com/Opinion/lvBSoyPbnpeAXODk9e3WSJ/Three-lessons-from-Microsofts-chatbot-deb acle.html
53. Holsapple, C.W., Tam, K.Y., Whinston, A.B.: Adapting expert system technology to financial management. Financ. Manage. **17**(3), 12–22 (1988)
54. AI Expert Network. Case Study: The AI Revolution at American Express (2024). https://aie xpert.network/case-study-the-ai-revolution-at-american-express
55. Bockting, C.L., et al.: Living guidelines for generative AI — why scientists must oversee its use. Nature **622**, 693–696 (2023). https://doi.org/10.1038/d41586-023-03266-1
56. Oza, A.: Reproducibility trial: 246 biologists get different results from same data sets. Nature **622**, 677–678 (2023). https://doi.org/10.1038/d41586-023-03177-1

The Critical Factors of Success of Gamification in Digital Banking Services: Using Analytic Hierarchy Process (AHP) Approach

Asif Akhtar[1,2,3](✉) ⬤, Shilpa Chauhan[1,2,3] ⬤, Meenakshi Kaushik[1,2,3],
and Asma Zaheer[1,2,3] ⬤

[1] Department of Business Administration, Aligarh Muslim University, Aligarh, India
asifakh@gmail.com
[2] Trinity Institute of Innovations in Professional Studies, Noida, India
[3] Faculty, Department of Marketing, King Abdulaziz University Jeddah, Jeddah, Saudi Arabia

Abstract. The game elements in serious gamification are well acclaimed and have been experimented with in various contexts, however, the literature seldom noticed any effort to prioritize the gamification elements in the context of digital banking platforms. The current study is written with the purpose to identify, evaluate and prioritize the critical factors of the success of gamification elements in digital banking services, based on the Indian perspective. The study examines critical success factors of gamification elements through a literature review and expert opinion in the banking context. It utilizes analytical hierarchy process (AHP) to arrive at the relative importance of elements using a pair-wise comparison survey instrument. The study evaluates the intensity of criteria, namely assessment, challenge, interactivity, aesthetics, functionality, and control. The survey was conducted, and analysis was done using the AHP approach. The findings identified functionality as the most suitable game element for gamification in digital banking. This study assumes that the criteria for classification of gamification elements are mutually exclusive but in reality, they are overlapping each other particularly in banking context. The study suggests the application of analytical network process (ANP) to mitigate this issue. The study highlights the factors that information technology teams and management of banks must foresee while introducing gamification elements into their digital platform. This study is the first of its kind to acknowledge the significance of elements in the universe of gamification when applied to the banking industry.

Keywords: Game elements · AHP · Digital banking

1 Introduction

Literature is abundant to examine the constructs which enhance digital banking adoption be it internet banking, mobile-banking, or both (Salimon et al., 2017; Alalwan et al., 2016; Dootson et al., 2016). Yet there are certain factors which refrain customers from continuous usage due to concerns like risk, privacy, system quality perception etc.

(Trivedi, 2019; Roy et al. 2017; Liang and Ching, 2014). One of the major concerns pointed by Mishra and Singh (2014) with respect to digital banking is, customers refrain themselves from using such services even if their banks are readily providing those. As a result, banks shall be able to alter customer behaviour to enhances experience with online services (Mbama and Ezepue, 2018). Organizations are turning to gamification as a result of technological advancements to enhance customer interactivity and engagement in areas like education, healthcare, consumption etc. (Kusuma et al., 2018; Koivisto and Hamari, 2014; Nour et al., 2017). Moreover, Clement (2021) reports an exponential growth of gamification market from 4.91 billion dollars (2016) to 11.94 billion dollars (2021).

Briefly gamification is "the use of game design elements in non-game settings" (Deterding et al., 2011) and its elements ranges from game mechanics and dynamics to aesthetics and narratives (Hofacker et al., 2019). However, literature lacks support in determining a framework on key game elements which influences customer engagement with digital banking (Rodrigues et al., 2016). Although several researchers have attempted to correlate gamification elements, yet no published study has been found to order the preference of elements based on the context of digital banking in India. The evaluation of elements used in a gamified banking service involves certain quantitative and qualitative methods which makes it a multi criteria decision making (MCDM) issue. Also, complexity arises while comparing all the elements and prioritizing them in accordance, before building a banking website. To do so, responses were collected from three key stakeholders: bank IT professionals, academicians possessing subject knowledge and customers who have been using digital banking platform on regular basis. This study develops AHP model to evaluate the gamification elements based on digital banking platform.

2   Research Motive:

This study is developed with the following objectives:

- To identify and prioritize the evaluation criteria for selection of gamification elements in context of digital banking using analytical hierarchy process (AHP) approach.
- To support in selection of best alternatives within the context of digital banking.

Although certain game elements are explored widely in literature especially in education and fitness, various criteria and sub criteria have evolved overtime to distinguish gaming elements. However, this categorisation of gaming elements is very much context specific, therefore one game element successful in one context cannot be replicated in the other. The current study aims to identify the gamification elements and develop a research framework to evaluate the best alternative elements amongst the banking channels. Hence, consideration of criteria and their evaluation are based on the gamification elements in banking literature.

3 Conceptual Development and Research Gap

Previous literature has significantly cling to the factors which enhance customer experience with the banking website (Mbama and Ezepue, 2018; Trivedi, 2019; Wasan, 2018), yet there is a viable recognition of the struggle which banks are facing in hands of Fintech service providers, particularly with the engagement and retention (Sivathanu, 2018). More recently, gamification via serious game is transpiring the customer behavior in the desired direction (Dietrich et al., 2018). The term "gamification" arrives from games; however, both differs in terms of objective each seek. While games are characterized by voluntariness, conflict, rules, uncertainty, resolution, and representation (Seaborn and Fels, 2015); gamification seeks a bigger purpose to achieve strategic goals. Gamification is a layer of game added to an existing system (Hamari et al., 2014). In a broader context, gamification literature is united to define it with two perspectives. The first perspective is based on gamification elements and mechanics and defines gamification as "the use of game design elements in non-game context" (Deterding et al., 2011). However, the second perspective defines gamification based on outcome behaviour as "a process of enhancing a service with affordance for gameful experiences and further behavioral outcomes" (Huotari and Hamari, 2012). Hence, gamification is summarized as running game mechanics and elements into a system to enhance customer engagement and alter behavioral outcomes.

Putri et al. (2019) emphasized the adoption of multi criteria forranking of game mechanics while making mobile payments. The same is verified by Curran and Meuter (2005), who proposed the usage of multi criteria while inducing technological advancements in the banking industry. While the impact of these criteria is influenced by the usage of different platforms available for conducting banking transactions (Mishra and Singh, 2014). Also, previous literature, acknowledges that gamification is not the ultimate solution and not all design elements are suitable on all platforms (Hamari et al., 2014; Nasirzadeh and Fathian, 2020). These studies encouraged the idea to compare the importance of game design elements used in banking literature with respect to digital banking platform. The current study is consistent with the classification proposed by Dietrichet al. (2018) in which the authors determine game attributes in context of social marketing programmes. Gamification attributes are broadly classified into reward-based gamification (short term) and meaningful gamification (long term) as proposed by Nicholson's (2015) dichotomy. While reward-based gamification lies within the spectrum of social rewards which are acknowledgments of achievements in the shared community, and economic rewards which are real monetary benefits (Bayuk and Altobello, 2019). Meaningful gamification is "consolidation of customer centred game design elements, and characteristics of non-game settings" (Nicholson, 2012). In the context of this current study, games sought out for the purpose of customer engagement with the banking products are herein referred as "meaningful gamification".

In a similar study, Putri et al. (2019), followed AHP on game mechanics in mobile payments while categorizing the mechanics into Hedonic (enjoyment, passing time); Utilitarian (ease of use, self-presentation, information quality, economic rewards) and Social (social value, social interaction). Nasirzadeh and Fathian (2020) examined the role played by personality traits, demographics, and user type model on selection of gamification elements in e-banking. A banking website shall possess good design and appearance with the certain rules and objectives to be effective by its appearance, design, objectives, rules, and functionality (Rodrigues, 2016). Bayuk and Altobello (2019) explored elements based on social rewards (badges, team challenge and leaderboards) and economic rewards (discounts, coupons, and real money) in financial gaming apps. As scholars started to recognize the potential of gamification, its attributes were introduced to procedural learning within the banking industry.

Table 1 presents the limited studies which have attempted to explore gamification elements in banking to conclude the results holistically based on digital banking context (e-banking, m-banking, and kiosks). Also, no study in banking literature has given clarity to what game elements are effective to particular channels for banking. In order to cover this literature gap, the current study calculates and compare gaming elements based on, Reward-based gamification (Assessments and Challenges) and Meaningful gamification (Interactivity, Aesthetics, Functionality and Control). Next, all the six criteria are used to determine the effectiveness of game elements on digital banking channels.

3.1 Reward Based Gamification

Reward based gamification is not a new phenomenon. They are linked to extrinsic motivation and short-term behavior (Zichermann and Cunningham, 2015). Nicholson's (2012) determines reward-based gamification as BLAP gamification, comprising of Badges, Levels/Leaderboards, Achievements and Points. This study follows Dietrich et al., (2018) to categorize reward-based gamification into assessment and challenges.

Assessment. The criteria 'assessment' of gamification includes certain factors which gives user the opportunity to win or lose in the form of points, badges, levels, progress bars and rewards.Points are the numerical representation of success or achievementwith the tendency to be exchanged with real prizes (Nasirzadeh and Fathian, 2020; Angelina et al., 2019). Pointsdenote the human motivation to gather and achieve. While, assigning tailor made rewards to customers based on achievement are measured by levels (Nasirzadeh and Fathian, 2020) which are indicative of sustained achievements of players overtime (Putri et al., 2019). Nasirzadeh and Fathian (2020) found points and levels to be positively associated with education; ability to use e-banking and weekly hours of using internet, social networks, video games and the like. Badges are virtual achievements in the form of medalsor status indicators with respect to activity (Nasirzadeh and Fathian, 2020; Bayuk and Altobello, 2018). They are even considered as the proactive approach of usage in sharing economy as they provide clear goals and feedback mechanism (Hamari, 2015) while motivation young adults behaviour (Nour et al., 2017). Progress bars on the other hand picturizes completion of any task. A simple profile completion bar on a webpage is a progress bar. Progress bars are also effective while internal assessments and knowledge upgradation among bank staff (Allal-Chérif et al., 2016). Rewards are prizes offered to players in the form of real money, discounts, coupons etc., on successfully achieving the goals (Putri et al., 2019). Rewards are final outcomes of active participation and are one of the successful game elements when applied to internet banking (Angelina et al., 2019). Bayuk and Altobello (2018) determined economic features (ability to earn real money or a high rate of interest) crucial for people having or not having any prior experience with money saving apps.

Challenge. "Comparing oneself with others is an inescapable social phenomenon" (Bayuk and Altobello, 2019). The study subcategorizes challenge into competition, leaderboards and team challenges. Challenge comprises a logical solution to a problem to achieve desired goal while competition arises with the desire to achieve the goal by competing with others (Putri et al., 2019). Xi and Hamari (2019) in an attempt to synthesize the role of gaming features on intrinsic need satisfaction and finds achievement and social related features as crucial for positive results. Another study by Nasirzadeh and Fathian (2020) concluded competition are effective tool to personalize gamified systems in banking. Also, competition influences customer behaviour towards e-banking via motivation (Rodrigues et al., 2017). Further, leaderboards are a depiction of competency, advocacy, and supremacy of one over other. Leader boards leads to recognition among reference group, resulting in motivation to achieve personal saving goals (Bayuk and Altobello, 2019). Nasirzadeh and Fathian (2020) associated leaderboards with extraversion personality traits. Leaderboards also play an effective role in banks internal assessment and training programs. For customers banks may utilize leaderboards for customers with most profitable investment returns (Rodrigues et al., 2017). Team challenges are framed in groups and tend people to collaborate for an activity. Bayuk and Altobello (2019) examines team challenge as a social reward and concludes that application of game elements in financial apps depends on the individual experience and expertise as people with longer experience favoured social rewards above economic rewards which were preferred by people with short experience.

3.2 Meaningful Gamification

While reward-based gamification focuses on scoring elements, meaningful gamification elements are enabled to induce a feeling of play in a user (Nicholson, 2012). Meaningful gamification prioritizes individual needs and goals over organizational goals yet are effective in long term customer engagement rather than reward-based gamification for altering short term customer behaviour (Nicholson, 2015). Following Dietrich (2018), this study categorizes meaningful gamification into: interactivity, aesthetics, functionality, and control as follows:

Interactivity. "Components of the game which engage the player to the point, whereby they are engrossed within the game experience" (Dietrich, 2018). The criterion of interactivity includes elements of digital feedback, easy navigation, product ranking and customer support. Digital Feedback is the acknowledgement given to user. In its simpler form it includes notifications and congratulations given to players for achieving goals (Putri et al., 2019). Cechella (2021) studied the impact of digital feedback system in Brazilian banks and concluded it as an effective measure for internal training. Easy Navigation is the ease with which the webpages of a banking website can be navigated (Rodrigues et al., 2017). A good website design with the features of easy navigation reduces the efforts made towards banking transactions and significantly enhances performance (Rodrigues, 2017). Further website navigation, ease of use, enjoyment features of gamification also influence user adoption of e-banking (Rahi and Ghani, 2018). Product ranking features indulges customers to rank bank's products with the ability to share them on social media enhances awareness of banking products with referral groups (Rodrigues, 2017). Rodrigues et al. (2016) determines customer support as sub-component of the process dimension of game elements while designing software in e-banking.

Aesthetics. The element of aesthetics includes the visual and graphic components as observed by users. Aesthetics are related to confidence, creativity, community, cognizance, commendation, compliance and describe the feeling of users (Kusuma et al., 2018). The current study extends aesthetics based on banking literature to subcategorize into: avatar, graphics, and animation. Avatar are thumbnail images as a customer icon in a personal profile with the purpose to initiate a bond between user and their symbolic representation (Nasirzadeh and Fathian, 2020; Cechella et al., 2021). Avatars are "digital doppelgängers" to encourage customer interaction (Allal-Chérif (2016). The study by Nasirzadeh and Fathian (2020) concludes women and extroverts' preference for avatars in e-banking usage. Help-avatars, graphic information, search tools, animated content are the vital elements to provide product related information and enhance decision making with the banking products (Rodrigues et al., 2017).

Functionality. Functionality is an intended purpose behind adding gaming features into a webpage (Dietrich et al., 2018). The criterion of functionality includes information, ease of use and efficiency for a banking channel to deliver. While Sam and Tahir (2009) documented information as the primary requirement for a webpage which includes instructions, explanation of banking guidelines, product warnings (e.g. market instruments) and detailed information (Rodrigues et al., 2016). Rahi and Ghani (2018) define gamification as information, game characteristics and processes to enhance customer engagement with internet banking website. Also, banks with complex products shall significantly add informing elements to their web channels (Nasirzadeh and Fathian, 2020). Hamari and Koivisto (2015) conceptualized ease of use a utilitarian element of gamification. Ease of use is also the most valuable factor to form positive association with the website usage (Aydin, 2015). Gamification and socialness improve the ease of use with technology which influences intention to adopt the banking technology in future (Rodrigues et al., 2016b). Golian and Ghasemi (2018) measured the effect of efficiency element in Iranian bank and found it to positively influence customer behaviour.

Control. Dietrich et al. (2018) determines control from the aspect of gamification as the elements under check which allows choice, action, or customization. The study subcategorizes control into choice and customization. A bank website design must bestow user with financial freedom of choice (Bayuk and Altobello, 2019). Customization is the form of products suggestions based on demographics and personality traits of the customer. Online personalization is effective in banking when the content relevant messages match the goals of the user (Sunikka et al., 2011). This may include the elements of money saving goal based on the future "dreams" of an individual (Bayuk and Altobello, 2019).

Table1. Most investigated gaming elements in digital banking.

S. no.	Criteria	Constituents	Reference
1	Assessment	Points, Levels, Badges, Progress Bars, Rewards	Nasirzadeh and Fathian (2020); Angelina et al. (2019); Baptista and Oliveira (2017); Bayuk and Altobello (2019); Allal-Chérif et al. (2016); Rodrigues et al. (2017)
2	Challenge	Competition, Leaderboards, Team Challenges	Nasirzadeh and Fathian (2020); Bayuk and Altobello (2019); Rodrigues et al. (2017); Cechella et al. (2021)
3	Interactivity	Digital Feedback, Easy Navigation, Product Ranking, Customer Support	Cechella et al. (2021); Rodrigues et al. (2017); Rahi and Ghani (2018); Rahi and Ghani (2018) a; Rodrigues et al. (2016)
4	Aesthetics	Avatar, Graphics, Animation	Nasirzadeh and Fathian (2020); Rodrigues et al. (2017); Allal-Chérif et al. (2016), Cechella et al. (2021); Rahi and Ghani (2018)
5	Functionality	Information, Ease of use, Efficiency	Nasirzadeh and Fathian (2020); Rodrigues et al. (2016) a; Rodrigues et al. (2017); Rahi and Ghani (2018) a; Golian and Ghasemi (2018)
6	Control	Choice, Customization	Nasirzadeh and Fathian (2020); Rahi and Ghani (2018)

4   Research Methodology

Gamification elements are wide, overlapping, loosely defined and context specific which increases the complexity of picking right elements while decision making. This makes it a multi criteria decision making problem.

Therefore, the criteria have been identified through extensive literature review through a team of experts. The decision group was formed comprising of two academicians and one professional from banking industry. All the three experts have experience of more than 8 years in their respective fields and are competent in decision making. For selection of right mix of elements for digital banking channels, a three phased methodology has been adopted as supported by Garg (2016). Phase-I started with decomposition of problem into goal, criteria, sub-criteria, and the alternatives (Perc͵in, 2006). Next in Phase-II, pair wise comparison based on numerical values of 1-3-5-7-9 scale as proposed by Saaty (1988) was obtained from decision makers input (Mishra and Singh, 2014). In Phase-III, results were analysed on the basis of relative weights obtained from hierarchical structure using eigenvector derivation procedure. This approach of research is Analytical Hierarchy Process (AHP) Approach.

4.1 Analytical Hierarchy Process (AHP) approach

AHP as introduced by Saaty (1980) is a multi-criteria decision making (MCDM) approach with the ability to incorporate both quantitative and qualitative factors and to aligns factors from general criteria to more specific sub-criteria (Perçin, 2006).This approach follows the step-by-step process of structuring a complex decision problem; identifying the goal, criteria, and sub-criteria; measuring pair wise interaction among them; and finally analysing those arrived weights to depict preferences (Phuong Ta and Yin Har, 2000).

While other Multi Criteria Decision Making (MCDM) methods could have been selected for application to our problem, these methods do not have ready provisions for testing of key parameters using sensitivity analysis, or checking for inconsistency to enable correction of results should the selected participants in the study generate inconsistent ranking of alternatives. One of the other main benefits of the AHP is that it gives coherence to and allows the ranking of expert's knowledge about competing alternatives with multiple attributes. The AHP procedure involves six essential phases (Lee et al., 2008).

1. Definition of the unstructured problem
2. Developments of the AHP hierarchy
3. Pair-wise comparison
4. Estimation of relative weights
5. Check for consistency
6. Establishment of overall rating

These steps are briefly explained as follows:

Step 1: Define the unstructured problem
This is the first phase of AHP procedure where the unstructured problem is determined. It starts with clearly laying out the objectives and outcomes.
Step 2: Developing the AHP hierarchy
Thereafter the decision problem is decomposed to arrive at most important elements (Boroushaki and Malczewski, 2008). In this step the complex problem is decomposed into a hierarchical structure with decision elements (Fig. 1).

Step 3: Pair-wise comparison

For each element of the hierarchy structure, pair wise comparison of all the associated elements is carried out in pair-wise comparison matrices as follows:

$$A = \begin{bmatrix} 1 & \frac{w_1}{w_2} & \cdots & \frac{w_1}{w_n} \\ \frac{w_2}{w_1} & 1 & \cdots & \frac{w_2}{w_n} \\ \frac{w_n}{w_1} & \frac{w_n}{w_2} & \cdots 1 \end{bmatrix} \tag{1}$$

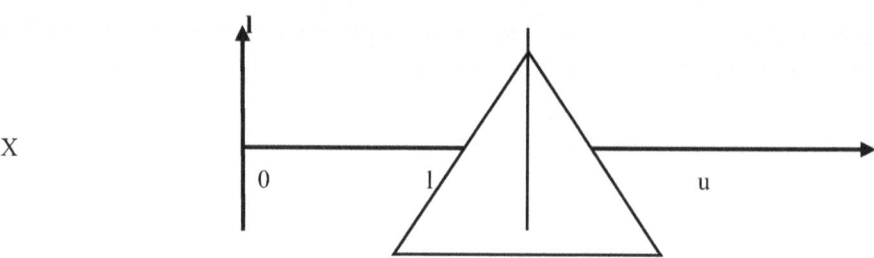

Fig. 1. Triangular membership function.

where: A = comparison pair − wise matrix

$$w_1 = weight\ of\ element\ 1,$$

$$w_2 = weight\ of\ element\ 2,$$

$$w_n = weight\ of\ element\ n,$$

In order to determine the relative preference for two elements of the hierarchy in matrix A, an underlying semantic scale is employed with values ranging from 1 to 9 to rate relative importance (Table 2).

Table 2. Scale for pair-wise comparison (Saaty, 1980).

Preference expressed in linguistic variables	Preference expressed in numeric variables	Reciprocal (decimal)
Extreme importance	9	1/9 (0.111)
Very strong to extremely	8	1/8 (0.125)
Very strong importance	7	1/7 (0.143)
Strongly to very strong	6	1/6 (0.167)
Strong Importance	5	1/5 (0.200)
Moderately to strong	4	1/4 (0.250)
Moderate Importance	3	1/3 (0.333)
Equally to Moderately	2	1/2 (0.500)
Equal Importance	1	1 (1.000)

Step 4: Estimate the relative weights
    Some methods like eigenvalue method are used to calculate the relative weights of elements in each pairwise comparison matrix. The relative weight (W) of matrix A is calculated from following equation:

$$A \times W = \lambda_{max} \times W \qquad (2)$$

where λ_{max}=the biggest eigenvalue of matrix A, I = unit matrix
Step 5: Check the consistency

In this step the consistency property of matrices is checked to ensure that the judgments of decision makers are consistent. For this end some pre-parameter is needed. Consistency Index (CI) is calculated as:

$$CI = \frac{\lambda_{max} - n}{n - 1} \tag{3}$$

The consistency index of a randomly generated reciprocal matrix shall be called to the random index (RI), with reciprocals forced. An averageRIfor the matrices of order 1-15 was generated by using a sample size of 100 (Nobre et al., 1999). The table of random indexes of the matrices of order 1-15 can be seen in Saaty (1980). The last ratio that has to be calculated is CR (Consistency Ratio). Generally, if CRis less than 0.1, the judgements are consistent, so the derived weights can be used. The formulation of CR is:

$$CR = \frac{CI}{RI} \tag{4}$$

Step 6: Obtain the overall rating

In last step the relative weights of decision elements are aggregated to obtain an overall rating for the alternatives as follows:

$$w_i^s = \sum_{j=1}^{m} w_{ij}^s w_j, \quad i = 1, 2, \ldots, n \tag{5}$$

$w_i^s = totalweightofalternativei,$
$w_{ij}^s = weightofalternativeiassociatedtoattributej,$
$w_j = weightofattributej,$
$m = numberofattributes,$
$n = numberofalternatives.$

5 Results and Discussion

The selection criteria should understand gamification and its elements and which elements are pertinent for inclusion in banking channels. Keeping this in mind, a three-member decision group was formed of academician's which are subject experts and bank official with experience in IT department who is also a researcher in this field. The identification of criteria and sub-criteria involved brainstorming gamification literature in banking by the decision group. For the construct of the proposed model, the following 6 drivers which comprise the various dimensions of gamification in digital banking viz. reward-based gamification and meaningful gamification are considered as given in Table 3 below:

A second decision group including the members from previous group was formed. The second group consisted of 5 members from banks working in IT department, 5 members from academics having prior knowledge of the subject and 7 members from customers conducting banking transactions through digital banking on regular basis.

Table 3. Gamification elements in digital banking.

S. No.	Criteria
1	Assessment
2	Challenge
3	Interactivity
4	Aesthetics
5	Functionality
6	Control

Following this approach respondents were given paired comparison to express their preference between criteria. With the use of questionnaire, each respondent was asked to highlight their preference as equally important, moderately important, strongly important, very strongly important, and extremely important. Having identified the various drivers which affect gamification in digital banking, the next step in the AHP method is formulation of Criteria Comparison Matrix (Table 4).

Table 4. Criteria Comparison Matrix.

Criteria		Reward based gamification		Meaningful gamification			
		Assessment	Challenge	Interactivity	Aesthetics	Functionality	Control
Reward based gamification	Assessment	1.000	5.852	0.288	0.524	0.171	0.330
	Challenge	0.171	1.000	0.226	0.384	0.236	0.252
Meaningful gamification	Interactivity	3.469	4.432	1.000	2.235	0.576	0.681
	Aesthetics	1.907	2.607	0.447	1.000	0.396	0.582
	Functionality	5.857	4.239	1.737	2.523	1.000	2.390
	Control	3.034	3.967	1.469	1.717	0.418	1.000
Sum		15.439	22.097	5.167	8.383	2.797	5.235

The next step is normalization of Criteria Comparison Matrix.

Normalization of Comparison Matrix: Normalization of matrix is made by dividing each criterion with sum of the respective column (Table 5).

After arriving at Normalized matrix, a Criteria Weight matrix is to be calculated.

Criteria weight{W}: It can be found out by taking average of each row which is shown as follows:

$$\{W\} = \begin{vmatrix} 0.095 \\ 0.046 \\ 0.204 \\ 0.117 \\ 0.337 \\ 0.201 \end{vmatrix} \tag{6}$$

Table 5. Normalized Criteria Matrix.

Criteria		Assessment	Challenge	Interactivity	Aesthetics	Functionality	Control
Reward based gamification	Assessment	0.065	0.265	0.056	0.063	0.061	0.063
	Challenge	0.011	0.045	0.044	0.046	0.084	0.048
Meaningful gamification	Interactivity	0.225	0.201	0.194	0.267	0.206	0.130
	Aesthetics	0.124	0.118	0.087	0.119	0.142	0.111
	Functionality	0.379	0.192	0.336	0.301	0.358	0.457
	Control	0.197	0.180	0.284	0.205	0.150	0.191

Now the consistency of the criteria matrix is to be checked. The check for consistency ascertains that the ranking that emerges is practically feasible.

The priorities of the different drivers considered for the study are assigned on the basis of their calculated weights. This helps to rank (Table 6) all the drivers of gamification starting from most effective to least effective.

Table 6. Ranking of factors.

Criteria	Criteria Weight (W)	Rank
Assessment	0.095	5
Challenge	0.046	6
Interactivity	0.204	2
Aesthetics	0.117	4
Functionality	0.337	1
Control	0.201	3

Using the ranking based on the calculated criteria weights, a hierarchical model is developed (Fig. 2).

The above figure signifies the importance of each element of gamification in the context of digital banking.

6 Findings

Among the drivers of gamification elements considered for the study, it emerges from the developed AHP model that the role of functionality with the system is primarily important for increasing the customer engagement with digital platform in India. It is considered that the platform that emerges after the application of gamification on digital platform must be efficient, easy to use and loaded with sufficient information. So, management and information technology team of banks shall develop a system to foster functionality of the platform. Functional quality is a crucial component of the bank website as it commands control on the accounting transactions (Khan et al. 2016). Several

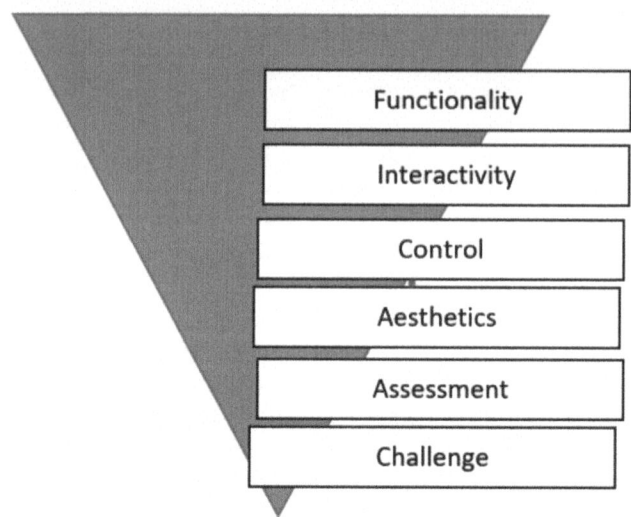

Fig. 2. AHP Model.

other research which places significant impact of utilitarian aspect of website includes (Mbama and Ezepue, 2018; Tirado et al., 2016; Amin, 2016).Another crucial element while implementing gamification elements is interactivity. In our study interactivity is explained by ease in navigation between sites, availability of ranking of products based on individual requirement, provision of feedback so that customer can co-create their experience and, efficient customer support in case of service failure. A baking website which empowers customers to make comparison of their banks products with the other competitor products (for e.g. FDR rates, loans products and their interest rates, etc.) is a preferred characteristic. Also, customer prefer fair treatment in case of any service recovery. A bank website shall be able to track the status of any service failure. Further, it is seen that control plays an equally important role. Control is determined by the ability of banking platform to be able to personalize based on the customer requirements. Herein for this study it also signifies the availability of choices with customer with respect to products. Customers prefer banking websites which are able to recommend products according to their needs and future expectations. So, a bank website shall contain features like investments and saving options according to the monthly income and expenses of the customer. Credit options available to the customer according to their account transactions. Aesthetics in the form of avatars, graphics and animation on the website play another significant role while developing a website. The use of artificial intelligence and chatbot technology to update customer with Frequently Asked Questions (FAQ's) and availability of information to enhance navigation is another preferred characteristic of gamification. Reward based gamification which comes in the form of challenges and assessment comes in the lower end of the continuum as they might appeal to the younger generation and might be relative of personality characteristics of customers.

7 Conclusion

The present study demonstrates that Analytic Hierarchy Process (AHP) can be applied to help decision makers to design the website which includes gamification elements in banking context. It is unique in the sense that the application of AHP as a tool to determine the elements of gamification has not previously undertaken. Here, AHP is applied to assign weights to the various elements of gamification. The study is relevant for management of banks to competitively align elements of gamification while designing their website. The rank ordering various elements of gamification using the AHP tool will help banks emphasising the importance of each element.

The successful application of AHP to aid decisions regarding gamification inclusion parameters paves the way for further application in this domain. Future research may be conducted in other countries by considering variables suitable in the respective contexts. Also, the present study may be expanded by the identification of more variables for hierarchical modelling.

References

Aydin, G.: Adoption of Gamified Systems: a study on a social media gamification website. Int. J. Online Market. **5**(3), 18–37 (2015)

Boroushaki, S., Malczewski, J.: Implementing an extension of the analytical hierarchy process using ordered weighted averaging operators with fuzzy quantifiers in ArcGIS. Comput. Geosci. **34**(4), 399–410 (2008)

Cechella, F., Abbad, G., Wagner, R.: Leveraging learning with gamification: an experimental case study with bank managers. Comput. Hum. Behav. Reports **2**, 100044 (2021)

Clement, J.: Value of gamification market worldwide in 2016 and 2021 (2021). https://www.sta tista.com/statistics/608824/gamification-market-value-worldwide/. Accessed on 12 May 2021

Curran, J.M., Meuter, M.L.: Self-service technology adoption. J. Serv. Market. **19**(2), 103–113 (2005)

Garg, C.P.: A robust hybrid decision model for evaluation and selecting of the strategic alliance partner in the airline industry. J. Air Transp. Manag. **52**(2016), 55–66 (2016)

Hamari, J.: Do badges increase user activity? A field experiment on effects of gamification. Comput. Hum. Behav. **71**(2017), 469–478 (2015)

Hamari, J., Koivisto, J.: Why do people use gamification services? Int. J. Inform. Manag. **35**(2015), 419–431 (2015)

Hamari, J., Koivisto, J., Sarsa, H.: Does gamification work? -a literature review of empirical studies on gamification. In: 2014 47th Hawaii International Conference on System Sciences (HICSS), pp. 3025–3034. IEEE (2014)

Hofacker, H.F., de Ruyter, K., Lurie, N.H., Manchanda, P., Donaldson, J.: Gamification and mobile market effectiveness. J. Interact. Market. **34**(2016), 25–36 (2016)

Koivisto, J., Hamari, J.: Demographic differences in perceived benefits from gamification. Comput. Human Behav. **35**(2014), 179–188 (2014)

Kusuma, G.P., Wigati, E.K., Utomo, Y., Suryapranata, L.K.P.: Analysis of gamification models in education using MDA framework. Procedia Comput. Sci. **135**(2018), 385–392 (2018)

Lee, A.H., Chen, W.C., Chang, C.J.: A fuzzy AHP and BSC approach for evaluating performance of IT department in the manufacturing industry in Taiwan. Expert Syst. Appl. **34**(1), 96–107 (2008)

Mishra, V., Singh, V.: Selection of appropriate electronic banking channel alternative: critical analysis using analytical hierarchy process. Int. J. Bank Market. **33**(3), 223–242 (2015)

MohdSam, M., NorHayati, T.: Website quality and consumer online purchase intention of air ticket. Int. J. Basic Appl. Sci. **9**(10), 2009 (2009)

Nicholson, S.: A User-centered theoretical framework for meaningful gamification. Paper Presented at Games+Learning+Society 8.0, Madison, WI (2012). https://scottnicholson.com/pubs/meaningfulframework.pdf

Nobre, F.F., Trotta, L.T.F., Gomes, L.F.A.M.: Multi-criteria decision making-an approach to setting priorities in health care. Stat. Med. **18**(23), 3345–3354 (1999)

Nour, M.M., Rouf, A.S., Allman-Farinelli, M.: Exploring young adult perspectives on the use of gamification and social media in a smartphone platform for improving vegetable intake. Appetite **120**(2018), 547–556 (2018)

Putri, M.F., Hidayanto, A.N., Negara, E.S., Abidin, Z., Utari, P., Budi, N.F.A.: Ranking of game mechanics for gamification in mobile payment using AHP-TOPSIS: uses and Gratification Perspective. In: 2019 3rd International Conference on Informatics and Computational Sciences (ICICoS) (2019). https://doi.org/10.1109/ICICoS48119.2019.8982458.

Saaty, T.L.: The Analytical Hierarchy Process. McGraw-Hill, New York (1980)

Sunikka, A., Bragge, J., Kallio, H.: The effectiveness of personalized marketing in online banking: a comparison between search and experience offerings. J. Financ. Serv. Mark. **16**(3–4), 183–194 (2011)

Ta, H.P., Har, K.Y.: A study of bank selection decisions in Singapore using the Analytical Hierarchy Process. Int. J. Bank Market. **18**(4), 170–180 (2000)

Xi, N., Hamari, J.: Does Gamification satisfy needs? A study on the relationship between gamification features and intrinsic need satisfaction. Int. J. Inform. Manag. **46**(2019), 210–221 (2019)

Zhang, K.: What does smart banking look like in 2021? (2021). https://www.sld.com/blog/brand-strategy/smart-banking-2021/. Accessed on 25 May 2021

E-Shopping Sites Preference Analysis
with Multi-criteria Decision-Making Methods

Vuslat Erat[1]([✉]) and Babek Erdebilli[2]

[1] TOBB University of Economics and Technology, Söğütözü 43, 06510 Çankaya, Ankara,
Turkey
verat@etu.edu.tr

[2] Department of Industrial Engineering, Ankara Yildirim Beyazit University, 06010 Ankara,
Turkey

Abstract. In light of advancing technology, the prevalence of internet usage has
significantly increased. Presently, individuals inclined to optimize their time grav-
itate towards e-commerce platforms. This research focuses on evaluating the five
most popular e-shopping sites in Turkey, namely Trendyol, Hepsiburada, Amazon,
Getir, and Morhipo. Seven criteria were employed for the assessment: site design,
product variety, reliability, detailed filtering, service quality, ease of site use, and
price. The study utilized the Multi- Criteria Decision Making (MCDM) methods,
specifically MOOSRA, MOORA, and TOPSIS, and compared their outcomes.
The Pairwise Comparison method was employed to determine criterion weights.
The findings revealed that price emerged as the most pivotal criterion, whereas
site design held the least significance. Application of MOOSRA, MOORA, and
TOPSIS consistently ranked Trendyol as the top-performing e-shopping site.

Keywords: Multiple Criteria Decision Making (MCDM) · MOOSRA ·
MOORA · TOPSIS · e-shopping · Pairwise Comparison

1 Introduction

Multi-Criteria Decision-Making (MCDM) methodologies play a pivotal role across
diverse domains such as business, engineering, and environmental management. They
provide systematic frameworks for evaluating and selecting optimal alternatives from a
set of options, particularly when faced with multiple conflicting criteria or objectives.

The growing complexity of decision-making processes in today's dynamic and competitive environments has spurred increased interest in the application of MCDM methods in recent years. By encompassing both quantitative and qualitative factors, these
methods offer decision-makers a comprehensive approach to analyze and prioritize
alternatives based on their preferences and constraints.

© The Author(s), under exclusive license to Springer Nature Switzerland AG 2024
A. Mirzazadeh et al. (Eds.): SEMIT 2023, CCIS 2198, pp. 71–97, 2024.
https://doi.org/10.1007/978-3-031-72284-4_5

The surge in online shopping, fueled by the rapid development of the internet, has eclipsed traditional retail practices. In 2022, the global e-commerce sector achieved a staggering $5.9 trillion in sales, exhibiting a notable growth rate of 9.26% in e-commerce purchases. Key players in this market are prominent in various countries, with China leading in online sales volume, closely followed by the USA. Additionally, countries like Japan, Germany, the UK, South Korea, India, France, Indonesia, and Brazil boast significant e-commerce markets, each featuring leading platforms tailored to diverse consumer needs (Herpin, Top 10 Countries with the Largest E-commerce Industry, 2023).

Turkey's online shopping sector has witnessed steady growth, driven by factors such as increased internet penetration, heightened credit card usage, and a youth demographic prioritizing consumption over savings. The COVID-19 pandemic has further accelerated this trend, aligning with the global surge in e-commerce. Popular categories for online shopping in Turkey include household goods, electronics, fashion, apparel, and food/groceries. This trend mirrors the diverse offerings provided by e-commerce platforms in other countries, reflecting changing consumer behaviors and preferences (E-Commerce in Turkey: Outlook & Retail Trends in 2023, 2023).

The combination of online shopping with Multi-Criteria Decision-Making (MCDM) methods offers a potent framework for enhancing the customer shopping experience and optimizing business operations in e-commerce platforms. By integrating MCDM techniques, businesses can provide personalized recommendations, enhance product assortment, and streamline decision-making for both customers and retailers.

In addressing the evolving demands of consumers seeking time-efficient and product-comparison features, e-shopping site owners play a crucial role in fostering long-term customer loyalty. Various criteria influence customers' choice of e-shopping platforms, with seven selected for this study: site design, product variety, reliability, detailed filtering, service quality, ease of site use, and price. The study focuses on five popular e-shopping sites in Turkey: Trendyol, Hepsiburada, Amazon, Getir, and Morhipo.

The subsequent sections of this study, following the introduction, encompass the methods utilized and a literature review pertaining to online shopping. The third section details the criterion weighting method and the procedural steps of the employed multi-criteria decision-making methods. The fourth section presents the applications of these methods, while the discussion and conclusion section compares the results obtained.

2 Literature Review

This segment encompasses a review of literature on online shopping, exploring the MOOSRA, MOORA, and TOPSIS methodologies.

In 2020, Guru, Nenavani, Patel, and Bhatt employed the AHP method to rank India's leading B2C e-commerce brands. The chosen criteria for assessment included three shopper-perceived risks: performance risk, financial risk, and time loss risk.

Azhar, Mulyani, Hutahaean, and Mayhaky, in 2022, utilized the MOOSRA method for a decision analysis on the best e-commerce company. The study involved eight identified alternatives, with evaluation based on four criteria: ease of use, ease of access, reliability, and price.

Durmus and Tayyar (2017) employed both AHP and TOPSIS methodologies to select Turkey's top three online shopping sites. The assessment incorporated four criteria: reliability/confidentiality, ease of payment, product information and diversity, and website performance.

In 2018, Mardhia and Normawati determined the three most popular shopping sites in Indonesia, utilizing five criteria: price, seller location, seller reputation, number of products sold, and transportation support.

Şahin and Sara (2019) conducted a comparative analysis of online shopping sites using the VIKOR method. The study encompassed five alternatives and eleven criteria, including accessibility, home page design, site design, text appearance on the website, search box, detailed filtering, reliability, product variety, navigation structure, updateability, and ease of communication with the website.

Writer/ Writers	Criteria 1 Reliability	Criteria 2 Ease of payment	Criteria 3 Product variety	Criteria 4 Website performance	Criteria 5 Price	Criteria 6 Seller location	Criteria 7 Seller reputation	Criteria 8 Number of products sold	Criteria 9 Transportation support	Criteria 10 Accessibility	Criteria 11 Home page design
Durmuş, Tayyar (2017)	✓	✓	✓	✓							
Mardhia ,Normawati (2018)					✓	✓	✓	✓	✓		
Şahin, Sara (2019)										✓	✓
Guru, Nenavani,Patel, Bhatt (2020)					✓						
Azhar, Mulyani,Hutahaean, Mayhaky (2022)	✓									✓	
Criteria used in This Study	✓		✓		✓						

Writer/Writers	Criteria 12 Site design	Criteria 13 Text appearance on the website	Criteria 14 Search box	Criteria 15 Detailed filtering	Criteria 16 Navigation structure	Criteria 17 Updateability	Criteria 18 Easy communication with the website	Criteria 19 Ease of site use	Criteria 20 Performance risk	Criteria 21 Financial risk	Criteria 22 Time loss risk	Criteria 23 Service quality
Durmuş, Tayyar (2017)												
Mardhia, Normawati (2018)												
Şahin, Sara (2019)	✓	✓	✓	✓	✓	✓	✓					
Guru, Nenavani, Patel, Bhatt (2020)									✓	✓	✓	
Azhar, Mulyani, Hutahaean, Mayhaky (2022)								✓				
Criteria used in This Study	✓			✓				✓				✓

2.1 Online Shopping Literature

Writer/Writers	Title	Subject of the Study	Method Used	Journal Name
Zhifeng Li, Liyi Zhang (2013)	The Research of Online Shopping Evaluation Based on Grey Linguistic Multiple Criteria Decision Making System	Online shopping review	Grey linguistic	2013 İeee İnternational Conference On İndustrial Engineering And Engineering Management
Mert Durmuş, Nezih Tayyar (2017)	Usage of Different Criterion Weighting Methods with AHP and TOPSIS and Comparison with Decision Makers' Opinions	Comparison of Turkey's three most well-known online shopping sites	AHP TOPSIS SWARA MAX100	Eskisehir Osmangazi Universitesi İibf Dergisi-Eskisehir Osmangazi University Journal Of Economics And Administrative Sciences
Murein Miksa Mardhia, Dwi Normawati (2018)	Marketplace Seller Recommender with User- Based Multi Criteria Decision Making	Comparison of the most popular online stores in Indonesia	Fuzzy Simple Additive Weighting	2018 12Th İnternational Conference On Telecommunication Systems, Services, And Applications (TSSA)
Gaurav Kumar (2018)	A Multi-Criteria Decision Making Approach for Recommending a Product using Sentiment Analysis	Product evaluation by analyzing customer comments on online platforms	AHP TOPSIS	2018 12Th İnternational Conference On Research Challenges İn İnformation Science (RCIS)
Yıldız Şahin, Deniz Merve Sara (2019)	E-Shopping Sites Preference Analysis with Multi-Criteria Decision-Making Methods	Comparison of the preferability of online websites in the shopping industry	VIKOR	Bilişim Teknolojileri Dergisi

(continued)

(*continued*)

Writer/Writers	Title	Subject of the Study	Method Used	Journal Name
Sunita Guru, Jitendra Nenavani, Vipul Patel, Nityesh Bhatt (2020)	Ranking of perceived risks in online shopping	Ranking India's top B2C eCommerce brands	AHP	Decision
Liu Fan, Ronald R. Yager, Radko Mesiar, LeSheng Jin (2020)	Two-level multi-criteria comprehensive evaluation for preference vectors in online shopping platform evaluation	Evaluation of online shopping platforms	Weighted averaging aggregation	Journal Of Intelligent & Fuzzy Systems
Ganeshsree Selvachandran, Shio Gai Quek, Le Hoang Son, Pham Huy Thong, Bay Vo, Tahani A. Abdusalam Hawari, Abdul Razak Salleh (2021)	Relations and compositions between interval-valued complex fuzzy sets and applications for analysis of customers' online shopping preferences and behavior	Application of the proposed Multi-Criteria Decision Method to customers' online shopping preferences and behaviors	CFS model	Applied Soft Computing
Ade Febransyah, Joklan I C Goni (2022)	Measuring the supply chain competitiveness of e-commerce industry in Indonesia	Measuring the supply chain competitiveness of the e-commerce industry in Indonesia	AHP	Competitiveness Review
Ramona Ramli, Asmidar Abu Bakar, Fiza Abdul Rahim (2022)	What Influences Customer's Trust on Online Social Network Sites (SNSs) Sellers?	Evaluation of dimensions and criteria affecting customer trust	AHP	International Journal Of Advanced Computer Science And Applications

(*continued*)

(continued)

Writer/Writers	Title	Subject of the Study	Method Used	Journal Name
Cheng Zhang, Sheng Ang, Feng Yang (2023)	**A new hybrid entropy-based decision support method and its application to online shopping selection**	Online furniture selection	**Hybrid entropy-based decision (HEBM)**	Computers & Industrial Engineering
Saurabh Pratap, Sunil Kumar Jauhar, Yash Daultani, Sanjoy Paul (2023)	Benchmarking sustainable E-commerce enterprises based on evolving customer expectations amidst COVID-19 pandemic	Performance evaluation for e-commerce businesses based on evolving customer expectations due to COVID-19	Fuzzy VIKOR	Business Strategy And The Environment

2.2   MOOSRA, MOORA and TOPSIS Literature

Writer/Writers	Title	Subject of the Study	Method Used	Journal Name
Manik Chandra Das, Bijan Sarkar, Siddhartha Ray (2015)	A performance evaluation framework for technical institutions in one of the states of India	Performance evaluation of the engineering faculty	Fuzzy AHP MOOSRA	Benchmarking-An International Journal
Asis Sarkar, Subhas Chandra Panja, Dibyendu Das, Bijan Sarkar (2015)	Developing an efficient decision support system for non-traditional machine selection: an application of MOORA and MOOSRA	Finding an effective decision support method for non-traditional machine selection	MOORA MOOSRA	Production And Manufacturing Research-An Open Access Journal
Shivam Sharma, Anoop Pandey (2017)	Comparison of results of benchmarking performed through various techniques in an engineering college of Delhi NCR	Performance comparison of 6 academic departments	MAUT MOOSRA SDV MOORA	–2017 3Rd Ieee International Conference On Computational Intelligence &Communication Technology (CICT)
Yahya Dorfeshan, Seyyed Meysam Mousavi, Vahid Mohagheghi, Behnam Vahdani (2018)	Selecting project-critical path by a new interval type-2 fuzzy decision methodology based on MULTIMOORA, MOOSRA and TPOP methods	A case study of an aircraft prototype group	MULTIMOORA MOOSRA TPOP	Computers & Industrial Engineering

(continued)

(continued)

Writer/Writers	Title	Subject of the Study	Method Used	Journal Name
Chiranjib Bhowmik, Amitava Ray (2019)	Comparative Analysis of MCDM Methods for the Evaluation of Optimum Green Energy Sources: A Case Study	Choosing the optimum green energy sources	TOPSIS MOOSRA COPRAS	International Journal Of Decision Support System Technology
Karri Babu Ravi Teja, Navneet Gupta (2019)	Low-k polymer gate dielectric selection for organic thin-film transistors (OTFTs) using material selection methodologies	Selection of low-k polymer gate dielectric for organic thin-film transistors	MOOSRA TOPSIS VIKOR	Journal Of Computational Electronics
J. Anitha, Randip Kumar Das (2020)	Optimization of EDM Process Parameters Using Standard Deviation and Multi-objective Optimization on the Basis of Simple Ratio Analysis (MOOSRA)	Recommending optimized input parametric combination to increase productivity and quality	MOOSRA	Intelligent Manufacturing And Energy Sustainability, Icimes 2019
Soutrik Bose, Nabankur Mandal, Titas Nandi (2020)	Selection and Experimentation of the Best Hybrid Green Composite Using Advanced MCDM Methods for Clean Sustainable Energy Recovery: A Novel Approach	Selection of the best hybrid composite material	ARAS MABAC COPRAS MOOSRA	International Journal Of Mathematical Engineering And Management Sciences
Samayan Narayanamoorthy, Veerappan Annapoorani, Daekook Kang, Dumitru Baleanu, Jeonghwan Jeon, Joseph Varghese Kureethara, Lakshmanaraj Ramya (2020)	A novel assessment of bio-medical waste disposal methods using integrating weighting approach and hesitant fuzzy MOOSRA	Comparison of bio-medical waste disposal methods	Fuzzy MOOSRA	Journal Of Cleaner Production
Elif Kilic Delice, Gulin Feryal Can (2020)	A new approach for ergonomic risk assessment integrating KEMIRA, best-worst and MCDM methods	A new three-stage ergonomic risk assessment approach to determine which worker has the highest level of ergonomic risk	MOORA MOOSRA COPRAS TPOP	Soft Computing
Faranak Feizi, Amir Abbas Karbalaei-Ramezanali, Sasan Farhadi (2021)	**FUCOM-MOORA and FUCOM-MOOSRA: new MCDM-based knowledge-driven procedures for mineral potential mapping in greenfields**	Application of two new hybrid multi-criteria decision-making techniques in mineral potential mapping (MPM)	FUCOM-MOORA FUCOM-MOOSRA	SN Applied Sciences

(continued)

(*continued*)

Writer/Writers	Title	Subject of the Study	Method Used	Journal Name
Zoran Štirbanović, Vojka Gardic, Dragisa Stanujkic, Radmila Markovic, Jovica Sokolovic, Zoran Stevanovic (2021)	Comparative MCDM Analysis for AMD Treatment Method Selection	Selection of acid mine drainage (AMD) treatment methods to purify Robule Lake water contaminated with various metal ions (Fe, Cu, Zn, Mn, Cd, Ni, etc.)	TOPSIS VIKOR MOOSRA WASPAS CoCoSo	Water Resources Management
Fatma Gul Altin, Taner Filiz (2022)	Assessment of the Performance of Logistics Villages Operated by the Turkish State Railways Using MCDM and DEA Methods	Analyzing the logistics performance and efficiency of eight operating logistics villages	EDAS MAUT MOOSRA	Ege Academic Review
Zulfi Azhar, Neni Mulyani, Jeperson Hutahaean, Ade Mayhaky (2022)	Sistem Pendukung Keputusan Pemilihan E-Commerce Terbaik Menggunakan Metode MOOSRA '' MOOSRA Yöntemini Kullanarak En İyi E-Ticaret Seçim Karar Analizi"	Choosing the best e-commerce company	MOOSRA	Jurnal Media İnformatika Budidarma
Nuri Avsarligil, Ercument Dogru, Aysegul Cıger (2023)	The Bank Performance Ranking in the Emerging Markets: A Case of Turkey	Evaluation of the financial performances of Turkey's 13 commercial banks with the highest transaction volume before the pandemic (2019) and during the pandemic period (2020)	ENTROPY ARAS MOORA MOOSRA	Sosyoekonomi
Christos Tzimopoulos, V. Balioti, Chris Evangelides (2013)	Fuzzy Multi-Criteria Decision Making Method for Dam Selection	Dam selection	TOPSIS	Proceedings Of The 13Th İnternational Conference On Environmental Science And Technology
Dhiren Kumar Behera, Asis Sarkar (2013)	A TOPSIS-based multi-criteria approach to faculty recruitment: A Case study	Faculty member selection	Fuzzy TOPSIS	Automatic Control And Mechatronic Engineering II

(*continued*)

(continued)

Ruzanita Mat Rani, Wan Rosmanira Ismail, Siti Fatihah Razali (2014)	Operator Performance Evaluation Using Multi Criteria Decision Making Methods	Operator performance evaluation	TOPSIS AHP Fuzzy AHP ELECTRE PROMETHEE II VIKOR	Proceedings Of The 3Rd İnternational Conference On Mathematical Sciences
Vladimír Rogalewicz, Ivana Jurickova (2014)	Multiple-criteria decision making: application to medical devices	Evaluation of medical devices	TOPSIS WSA	Proceedings İwbbio 2014: İnternational Work-Conference On Bioinformatics And Biomedical Engineering, Vols 1 And 2
Ahamd Radmehr, Shahab Araghinejad (2015)	Flood Vulnerability Analysis by Fuzzy Spatial Multi Criteria Decision Making	Flood Vulnerability Analysis	Fuzzy TOPSIS AHP	Water Resources Management
Javeed Kittur (2015)	Using the PROMETHEE and TOPSIS Multi-Criteria Decision Making Methods to Evaluate Optimal Generation	Evaluation of electricity production types	TOPSIS AHP PROMETHEE	Proceedings Of The 2015 İnternational Conference On Power And Advanced Control Engineering (İcpace)
Qingwei Cao, Jian Wu, Changyong Liang (2015)	An intuitionsitic fuzzy judgement matrix and TOPSIS integrated multi-criteria decision making method for green supplier selection	Green supplier selection	TOPSIS	Journal Of İntelligent & Fuzzy Systems
Gülçin Büyüközkan, Sezin Güleryüz (2016)	Multi Criteria Group Decision Making Approach for Smart Phone Selection Using Intuitionistic Fuzzy TOPSIS	Smart Phone selection	Fuzzy TOPSIS	International Journal Of Computational İntelligence Systems

(continued)

(continued)

Varsha Lokare, Prakash Jadhav (2016)	Using the AHP and TOPSIS methods for Decision Making In Best Course Selection after HSC	Best course selection	TOPSIS AHP	2016 İnternational Conference On Computer Communication And İnformatics (ICCCI)
AmirAli Pourahmadi, Taghi Ebadi, Manouchehr Nikazar (2017)	Industrial Wastes Risk Ranking with TOPSIS, Multi Criteria Decision Making Method	Risk ranking of industrial wastes	TOPSIS	Civil Engineering Journal-Tehran
Serafettin Alpay, Melih Iphar (2018)	Equipment selection based on two different fuzzy multi criteria decision making methods: Fuzzy TOPSIS and fuzzy VIKOR	Selection of equipment for pit mine excavation	Fuzzy TOPSIS Fuzzy VIKOR	Open Geosciences
Mehmet Alper Sofuoğlu (2019)	Development of an ITARA-based hybrid multi-criteria decision-making model for material selection	Material selection	TOPSIS ITARA VIKOR MOORA	Soft Computing
Niharendu Bikash Kar, Anindya Ghosh, Subhasis Das, Debamalya Banerjee (2020)	Fuzzy multi-criteria group decision making approach for grading of mulberry silk cocoons	Silk cocoon grading	Fuzzy TOPSIS	Indian Journal Of Fibre & Textile Research
Shahmir Janjua, Ishtiaq Hassan (2020)	Fuzzy AHP-TOPSIS multi-criteria decision analysis applied to the Indus Reservoir system in Pakistan	Ranking of reservoirs in Pakistan	TOPSIS Fuzzy AHP	Water Supply

(continued)

(continued)

Shafiqur Rehman, Salman A. Khan, Luai M. Alhems (2020)	Application of TOPSIS Approach to Multi-Criteria Selection of Wind Turbines for On-Shore Sites	Wind turbine selection	TOPSIS	Applied Sciences-Basel
Chun-Ho Chen (2021)	A Hybrid Multi-Criteria Decision-Making Approach Based on ANP-Entropy TOPSIS for Building Materials Supplier Selection	Building materials supplier selection	TOPSIS AHP-Entropy Weight	Entropy
Mushfiqur Rahman, Md. Asadujjaman (2021)	Multi-criteria Decision Making for Job Selection	Selection of job sectors for Industrial and Production Engineering (IPE) graduates	TOPSIS	2021 International Conference On Decision Aid Sciences And Application (Dasa)
Pedro Ponce, Citlaly Perez, Aminah Robinson Fayek, Arturo Molina (2022)	Solar Energy Implementation in Manufacturing Industry Using Multi-Criteria Decision-Making Fuzzy TOPSIS and S4 Framework	Evaluation of solar energy companies	Fuzzy TOPSIS	Energies
Bingchao Zhao, Han Wang, Zhihao Huang, Qianqian Sun (2022)	Location mapping for constructing biomass power plant using multi-criteria decision-making method	Biomass power plant location selection	TOPSIS	Sustainable Energy Technologies And Assessments
Zhaoke Huang, Chunhua Yang, Xiaojun Zhou, Weihua Gui (2023)	An improved TOPSIS-based multi-criteria decision-making approach for evaluating the working condition of the aluminum reduction cell	Operating condition evaluation of the aluminum reduction cell	TOPSIS	Engineering Applications Of Artificial Intelligence

(continued)

(*continued*)

Imad Hassan, Ibrahim Alhamrouni, Nurul Hanis Azhan (2023)	A CRITIC-TOPSIS Multi-Criteria Decision-Making Approach for Optimum Site Selection for Solar PV Farm	Assessment of suitable sites and technical potentials for large-scale solar photovoltaic (PV) systems	TOPSIS CRITIC	Energies
Mehmet Ozcalici (2023)	Integrating queue theory and multi-criteria decision-making tools for selecting roll-over car washing machine	Choosing a car wash machine for the petrol station	TOPSIS EDAS CoCoSo TODIM	Operations Research And Decisions

3 Method

In this section, the multi-criteria decision-making methods MOOSRA, MOORA and TOPSIS methods used to compare e-shopping sites in Turkey and the pairwise comparison method used to calculate the criterion weight are included (Fig. 1).

The flow chart of the problem is given above.

3.1 Criteria Weighting Method Used

The data to be used was obtained by survey method in order to weight the criteria and evaluate the alternatives. Necessary questions were asked to 52 e-shopping site users belonging to different age groups, and the answers given were used in the application.

The distribution of the surveyed people in terms of gender and age groups is given in Table 1 and Table 2.

Pairwise comparison method was used to evaluate the impact of the methods on critical weights.

The criteria were determined as site design, product variety, reliability, detailed filtering, service quality, ease of site use and price. In the following sections, they will be shown as site design (SD), product variety (PV), reliability (R), detailed filtering (DF), service quality (SQ), ease of site use (ESU) and price (P).

As a result of the data obtained from the survey, the pairwise comparison matrix in Table 3 was obtained.

According to the results of the pairwise comparison matrix, the weight of the site design criterion was determined as 0.03, product variety as 0.04, reliability as 0.18, detailed filtering as 0.05, service quality as 0.23, ease of site use as 0.10 and price criterion as 0.37 (Table 4).

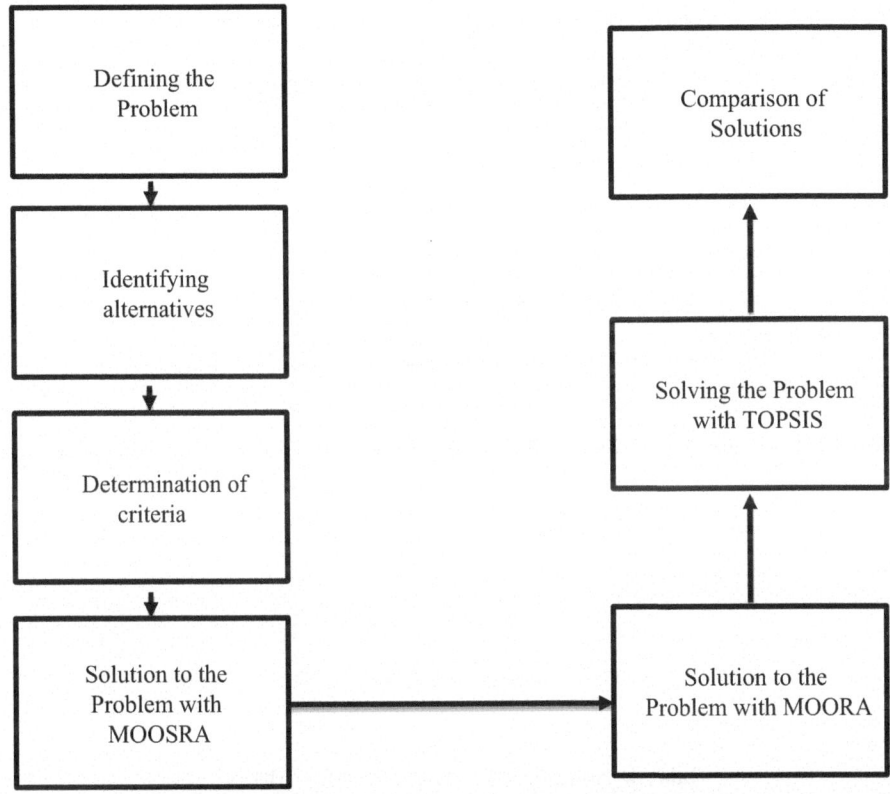

Fig. 1. Flow Chart of the Problem

Table 1. Gender Distribution of Survey Participants by Age Groups

Age Groups	Number	%Distribution	Woman	% Distribution	Man	% Distribution
18–25	14	0,27	7	0,23	7	0,32
26–30	18	0,35	14	0,47	4	0,18
31–40	13	0,25	5	0,17	8	0,36
40+	7	0,13	4	0,13	3	0,14
Total	**52**	**1,00**	**30**	**1,00**	**22**	**1,00**

3.2 Consistency Rate

(λmax) value is 7.455.
    CI value is 0.08.

Since 7 criteria were used in the study, the RI value is determined as 1.32.
Finally, the consistency (CR) of the comparison matrix was found as follows.
0,08/1,32 = 0,0574.

Table 2. Distribution of Survey Participants by Gender

Gender	Number	% Distribution
Woman	30	0,58
Man	22	0,42
Total	52	1,00

Table 3. Pairwise Comparison Matrix.

Criteria	SD	PV	R	DF	SQ	ESU	P
SD	1,00	0,37	0,15	0,26	0,14	0,21	0,12
PV	2,70	1,00	0,18	0,67	0,17	0,40	0,13
R	6,50	5,48	1,00	5,01	0,40	3,50	0,40
DF	3,79	1,50	0,20	1,00	0,16	0,29	0,13
SQ	7,00	6,00	2,50	6,15	1,00	3,00	0,33
ESU	4,86	2,50	0,29	3,50	0,33	1,00	0,22
P	8,5	7,50	2,50	8,00	3,00	4,50	1,00
Total	**34,35**	**24,35**	**6,82**	**24,59**	**5,21**	**12,89**	**2,33**

Table 4. Normalized Pairwise Comparison Matrix.

Criteria	SD	PV	R	DF	SQ	ESU	P
SD	0,03	0,02	0,02	0,01	0,03	0,02	0,05
PV	0,08	0,04	0,03	0,03	0,03	0,03	0,06
R	0,19	0,23	0,15	0,20	0,08	0,27	0,17
DF	0,11	0,06	0,03	0,04	0,03	0,02	0,05
SQ	0,20	0,25	0,37	0,25	0,19	0,23	0,14
ESU	0,14	0,10	0,04	0,14	0,06	0,08	0,10
P	0,25	0,31	0,37	0,33	0,58	0,35	0,43

Since the CR value (0.0574) is less than 0.10, it can be said that the pairwise comparison matrix is consistent.

3.3 MOOSRA Method

The MOOSRA method was developed by Das, Sarkar and Ray in 2012.
The steps of the method are as follows;

Step 1: Creating the decision matrix.

In this step, the decision matrix is created according to the formula (1).

$$R = \left[r_{ij}\right]_{mxn} = \begin{bmatrix} r_{11} & \cdots & r_{1n} \\ \vdots & \ddots & \vdots \\ r_{m1} & \cdots & r_{mn} \end{bmatrix} \tag{1}$$

Step 2: Normalizing the decision matrix.

Normalization of the decision matrix can be found with the formula (2) given below.

$$r_{ij}^* = \frac{r_{ij}}{\sqrt{\sum_{i=1}^{m}\left(r_{ij}\right)^2}} \quad i = 1, 2, \dots \dots, m \text{ and } j = 1, 2, \dots \dots, n \tag{2}$$

Step 3: Finding the total performance score (S_i) of the alternatives.

S_i value (3) is obtained by dividing the sum of the beneficial criteria by the sum of the non-beneficial criteria.

$$S_i = \frac{\sum_{j=1}^{t} w_j x r_{ij}^*}{\sum_{j=t+1}^{n} w_j x r_{ij}^*} \tag{3}$$

Here w_j value is the criterion weight of the jth criterian, t is the total number of useful criteria.

Step 4: The determined S_i values are sorted from largest to smallest. The one with the highest score is chosen as the best alternative.

3.4 MOORA Method

Brauers and Zavadskas introduced the MOORA method to the literature in 2006. There are different solution methods of the MOORA method in the literature, including the ratio system approach, the reference point approach, significance coefficient, full multiplication and the MULTI-MOORA approach.

MOORA-Ratio method and MOORA-Reference point approach were used in this study.

MOORA-Ratio Method. The steps of the method are as follows;

Step 1: Creating the decision matrix.

The decision matrix is obtained with the formula (4) below.

$$D = \left[x_{ij}\right]_{mxn} = \begin{bmatrix} x_{11} & \cdots & x_{1n} \\ \vdots & \ddots & \vdots \\ x_{m1} & \cdots & x_{mn} \end{bmatrix} \tag{4}$$

Step 2: Normalizing the decision matrix.

Normalization of the decision matrix is obtained by the formula (5).

$$x_{ij}^* = \frac{x_{ij}}{\sqrt{\sum_{i=1}^{m}\left(x_{ij}\right)^2}} \quad i = 1, 2, \dots \dots, m \text{ and } j = 1, 2, \dots \dots, n \tag{5}$$

Step 3: Normalized for all purposes i^{th} evaluation of the alternative.

The value $(y_i)^*$ (6) is obtained by subtracting the total of non-beneficial criteria from the total of beneficial criteria.

$$(y_i)^* = \sum_{j=1}^{g} s_j x_{ij}^* - \sum_{j=g+1}^{n} s_j x_{ij}^* \tag{6}$$

$j = 1,\ldots,g$ show the criteria to be maximized, $j = g + 1,\ldots,n$ show the values to be minimized.

$y_i^* = $ is the normalized evaluation of the importance coefficient of the ith alternative according to all criteria.

$s_j = $ represents the importance coefficient of the jth criterion.

Step 4: Alternatives are ranked according to the magnitude of the determined y_i^* values. The alternative with the highest score is chosen as the best alternative.

MOORA-Reference Point. IN the REFERENCE POINT METHODOLOGY, THe MOORA-Ratio method is employed to acquire normalized values. Subsequently, the identification of reference points for each criterion becomes imperative. For beneficial criteria, the reference point (rj) is chosen as the maximum value, while for non-beneficial criteria, it is established as the minimum value. Following this determination, the distances from the alternatives to the specified reference points are computed using the formula (7) as outlined in the work by Özbek (2015)

$$d_{ij}^* = w_j \left| r_j - xij^* \right| \tag{7}$$

$w_j = $ importance coefficient of the jth criterion,

$x_{ij}^* = $ normalized value of the ith alternative in the jth criterion,

$r_j = $ refers to the reference point of the jth criterion.

TchebycheffMin-Max process (8) is applied to the new matrix created.

$$P_i = \min i(\max j dij^*) \tag{8}$$

Accordingly, P_i values are ranked from smallest to largest and the first value is determined as the best alternative.

3.5 TOPSIS Method

The TOPSIS method was first developed by Hwang and Yoon in 1981.

Step 1: Creating the decision matrix.

The decision matrix is obtained with the formula (9).

$$R = [r_{ij}]_{mxn} = \begin{bmatrix} r_{11} & \cdots & r_{1n} \\ \vdots & \ddots & \vdots \\ r_{m1} & \cdots & r_{mn} \end{bmatrix} \tag{9}$$

Step 2: Normalizing the decision matrix.

Formula (10) is used for normalization of the decision matrix.

$$r_{ij}^* = \frac{r_{ij}}{\sqrt{\sum_{i=1}^m (r_{ij})^2}} i = 1, 2, \ldots\ldots, m \text{ and } j = 1, 2, \ldots\ldots, n \qquad (10)$$

Step 3: Weighting of Normalized Decision Matrix.

The value v_{ij} in (11) is obtained by multiplying the importance coefficient of the jth criterion (w_j) with the r_{ij}^* value obtained from the formula (10)

$$v_{ij} = w_j x r_{ij}^* \qquad (11)$$

Step 4: Determining Positive and Negative Ideal Solutions.

Positive ideal and negative ideal solution sets are obtained by using the v_{ij} matrix in Step 3. If the criterion is the criterion that provides benefit, it is the largest values of the columns of the positive ideal solution v_{ij} matrix. The negative ideal solution is determined as the smallest values of the columns of the v_{ij} matrix. If the criterion is a non-beneficial criterion, the positive ideal solution is the smallest values of the columns of the v_{ij} matrix. The negative ideal solution is determined as the largest values of the columns of the v_{ij} matrix.

Positive ideal solution set;

$V^* = (v_1^*, v_2^*, \ldots\ldots v_n^*)$

Negative ideal solution set;

$V^- = (v_1^-, v_2^-, \ldots\ldots v_n^-)$

Step 5: Finding the distances to positive ideal and negative ideal solution values.

The distance to the positive ideal solution set is obtained by the formula in (12), and the distance to the negative ideal solution set is obtained by the formula in (13).

$$S_i^* = \sqrt{\sum_{j=1}^n \left(v_{ij} - v_j^*\right)^2} \qquad (12)$$

$$S_i^- = \sqrt{\sum_{j=1}^n \left(v_{ij} - v_j^-\right)^2} \qquad (13)$$

Step 6: Calculation of Relative Closeness to the Ideal Solution.

The distance to the ideal solution is obtained with the formula (14) below.

$$C_i^* = \frac{S_i^-}{S_i^* + S_i^-} \qquad (14)$$

Step 7: The C_i^* values in Step 6 are listed from largest to smallest and the largest value is selected as the best alternative.

4 Findings and Results

This section includes the application of MOOSRA, MOORA and TOPSIS methods.

In the survey conducted to find the best e-shopping site, 52 people were asked questions in line with the criteria in Table 5.

Table 5. Evaluation Criteria of Alternatives According to Criteria.

1	Very Poor
3	Poor
5	Medium
7	Good
9	Very Good

4.1 MOOSRA Method Application

According to the results obtained from the survey, the decision matrix in Table 6 was created.

Table 6. Decision Matrix.

	Criteria						
	Benefit (max)	Benefit (max)	Benefit (max)	Benefit (max)	Benefit (max)	Benefit (max)	Cost (min)
Criterion Weights	0,03	0,04	0,18	0,05	0,23	0,10	0,37
Alternatives	SD	PV	R	DF	SQ	ESU	P
Trendyol	6,50	7,69	7,04	7,27	7,12	7,50	3,65
Hepsiburada	5,65	6,50	6,46	6,35	6,27	6,04	4,04
Amazon	5,88	6,42	6,46	6,23	6,50	6,23	3,96
Getir	6,31	5,85	6,92	6,00	6,58	7,50	4,58
Morhipo	4,54	4,81	5,73	5,77	5,62	5,46	4,88

According to the MOOSRA method, the ranking of the alternatives is determined as Trendyol- Amazon- Hepsiburada- Getir-Morhipo.

4.2 MOORA Method Application

The MOORA method is the same as the 1st and 2nd steps of the MOOSRA method, and Table 6, Table 7 and Table 8 are the same for this method.

MOORA-Ratio Method Application. Unlike the MOOSRA method, the MOORA-Ratio method involves subtracting the sum of cost criteria from the sum of benefit criteria. Table 6 – Decision Matrix, Table 7 – Normalized Decision Matrix and Table 8 – Weighted Normalized matrix are also valid for the MOORA-ratio method (Table 9).

Table 7. Normalized Decision Matrix.

	Criteria						
	Benefit (max)	Benefit (max)	Benefit (max)	Benefit (max)	Benefit (max)	Benefit (max)	Cost (min)
Criterion Weights	0,03	0,04	0,18	0,05	0,23	0,10	0,37
Alternatives	SD	PV	R	DF	SQ	ESU	P
Trendyol	0,4997	0,5438	0,4815	0,5124	0,4947	0,5084	0,3845
Hepsiburada	0,4344	0,4597	0,4419	0,4476	0,4356	0,4095	0,4256
Amazon	0,4521	0,4540	0,4419	0,4391	0,4516	0,4223	0,4172
Getir	0,4851	0,4137	0,4733	0,4229	0,4572	0,5084	0,4825
Morhipo	0,3491	0,3402	0,3919	0,4067	0,3905	0,3701	0,5141

Table 8. Weighted Normalized Matrix.

	Criteria						
	Benefit (max)	Benefit (max)	Benefit (max)	Benefit (max)	Benefit (max)	Benefit (max)	Cost (min)
Criterion Weights	0,03	0,04	0,18	0,05	0,23	0,10	0,37
Alternatives	SD	PV	R	DF	SQ	ESU	P
Trendyol	0,0150	0,0218	0,0867	0,0256	0,1138	0,0508	0,1423
Hepsiburada	0,0130	0,0184	0,0795	0,0224	0,1002	0,0409	0,1575
Amazon	0,0136	0,0182	0,0795	0,0220	0,1039	0,0422	0,1543
Getir	0,0146	0,0165	0,0852	0,0211	0,1052	0,0508	0,1785
Morhipo	0,0105	0,0136	0,0705	0,0203	0,0898	0,0370	0,1902

Table 9. Performance Scores of Alternatives.

Alternatives	Sum of Benefit Criteria	Sum of Cost Criteria	S_i	Ranking
Trendyol	**0,3137**	**0,1423**	**2,2048**	**1**
Hepsiburada	0,2745	0,1575	1,7431	3
Amazon	0,2793	0,1543	1,8097	2
Getir	0,2934	0,1785	1,6438	4
Morhipo	0,2418	0,1902	1,2712	5

Table 10. Ranking of MOORA-Ratio Method Alternatives.

Alternatives	Sum of Benefit Criteria	Sum of Cost Criteria	y_i^*	Ranking
Trendyol	**0,3137**	**0,1423**	**0,1714**	1
Hepsiburada	0,2745	0,1575	0,1170	3
Amazon	0,2793	0,1543	0,1250	2
Getir	0,2934	0,1785	0,1149	4
Morhipo	0,2418	0,1902	0,0516	5

According to the MOORA-Ratio Method, the ranking of the alternatives is determined as Trendyol- Amazon- Hepsiburada- Getir-Morhipo (Table 10).

MOORA-Reference Point Approach Application. For the MOORA-Reference point approach, Table 6 – Decision Matrix, Table 7 – Normalized Decision Matrix and Table 8 – Weighted Normalized matrix are the same, and an additional reference point must be Found (Table 11, Table 12).

Table 11. Reference Point (rj).

	Criteria						
	Benefit (max)	Benefit (max)	Benefit (max)	Benefit (max)	Benefit (max)	Benefit (max)	Cost (min)
Criterion Weights	0,03	0,04	0,18	0,05	0,23	0,10	0,37
Alternatives	SD	PV	R	DF	SQ	ESU	P
Trendyol	0,0150	0,0218	0,0867	0,0256	0,1138	0,0508	0,1423
Hepsiburada	0,0130	0,0184	0,0795	0,0224	0,1002	0,0409	0,1575
Amazon	0,0136	0,0182	0,0795	0,0220	0,1039	0,0422	0,1543
Getir	0,0146	0,0165	0,0852	0,0211	0,1052	0,0508	0,1785
Morhipo	0,0105	0,0136	0,0705	0,0203	0,0898	0,0370	0,1902
rj	**0,0150**	**0,0218**	**0,0867**	**0,0256**	**0,1138**	**0,0508**	**0,1423**

According to the MOORA-Reference Point Approach, the ranking of the alternatives has been determined as Trendyol- Amazon- Hepsiburada- Getir-Morhipo.

4.3   TOPSIS Method Application

As in the MOOSRA and MOORA methods, in the TOPSIS method, Table 6 – Decision Matrix, Table 7 – Normalized Decision Matrix and Table 8 – Weighted Normalized matrix are found in the same way, so calculations were made using these tables (Table 13, Table 14, Table 15).

Table 12. Reference Point Approach Results.

Alternatives	Pi	Ranking
Trendyol	**0,0000**	1
Hepsiburada	0,0152	3
Amazon	0,0121	2
Getir	0,0362	4
Morhipo	0,0479	5

Table 13. Positive and Negative Ideal Solutions.

	Criteria						
	Benefit (max)	Benefit (max)	Benefit (max)	Benefit (max)	Benefit (max)	Benefit (max)	Cost (min)
Criterion Weights	0,03	0,04	0,18	0,05	0,23	0,10	0,37
Alternatives	SD	PV	R	DF	SQ	ESU	P
Trendyol	0,0150	0,0218	0,0867	0,0256	0,1138	0,0508	0,1423
Hepsiburada	0,0130	0,0184	0,0795	0,0224	0,1002	0,0409	0,1575
Amazon	0,0136	0,0182	0,0795	0,0220	0,1039	0,0422	0,1543
Getir	0,0146	0,0165	0,0852	0,0211	0,1052	0,0508	0,1785
Morhipo	0,0105	0,0136	0,0705	0,0203	0,0898	0,0370	0,1902
V*	0,0150	0,0218	0,0867	0,0256	0,1138	0,0508	0,1423
V−	0,0105	0,0136	0,0705	0,0203	0,0898	0,0370	0,1902

Table 14. Positive and Negative Distance to Ideal Solution Values.

Alternatives	S_i^*	S_i-
Trendyol	0,0000	0,0586
Hepsiburada	0,0243	0,0362
Amazon	0,0199	0,0403
Getir	0,0379	0,0284
Morhipo	0,0586	0,0000

According to the TOPSIS method, the ranking of the alternatives is determined as Trendyol- Amazon- Hepsiburada- Getir-Morhipo.

Table 15. Closeness Coefficient (Ci) Value and Ranking of Alternatives.

Alternatives	S_i*	S_i^-	C_i	Ranking
Trendyol	**0,0000**	**0,0586**	**1,0000**	**1**
Hepsiburada	0,0243	0,0362	0,5983	3
Amazon	0,0199	0,0403	0,6690	2
Getir	0,0379	0,0284	0,4278	4
Morhipo	0,0586	0,0000	0,0000	5

5 Discussion and Conclusion

The study aimed to scrutinize the decision-making processes of five e-shopping sites prevalent in Turkey. To gather data, a survey comprising questions was administered to 52 users of these e-shopping sites, encompassing diverse gender and age demographics. The responses obtained were leveraged in the Pairwise Comparison method to ascertain criterion weighting. Multiple Multi-Criteria Decision-Making methods, namely MOOSRA, MOORA-Ratio Method, MOORA-Reference Point Approach, and TOPSIS, were chosen, and the outcomes were juxtaposed. The MOORA method was applied by adopting both the ratio method and reference point approach from the available solution methods in the literature.

Consequently, across the implemented MOOSRA, MOORA-Ratio Method, MOORA-Reference Point Approach, and TOPSIS methods, the ranking of alternatives was found to be consistent. The preferred order of the five widely-used e-shopping sites in Turkey, based on the determined criteria, was established as Trendyol-Amazon-Hepsiburada-Getir-Morhipo.

The utilization of MOOSRA, MOORA, and TOPSIS methods proves to be suitable for ranking online shopping sites, considering various criteria and objectives pertinent to the e-commerce industry. These methodologies offer systematic approaches, facilitating the evaluation and comparison of alternatives. This, in turn, aids stakeholders in making informed decisions when selecting or ranking online shopping platforms.

This study stands out in the realm of online shopping site comparisons in Turkey due to its distinctive approach and comprehensive methodology. Unlike many existing studies with limited alternatives and criteria, this research provides a more thorough evaluation of online shopping sites. By employing three distinct multi-criteria decision-making methods – MOOSRA, MOORA, and TOPSIS – the study delivers a more robust and detailed analysis of online shopping platforms, enhancing the depth and reliability of its findings.

In future research, the comparison of e-shopping sites could be approached using different multi-criteria decision-making methods and criteria, allowing for comparison with the methods presented in this study. Furthermore, the application of MOOSRA, MOORA, and TOPSIS methods in other decision-making problems could broaden the scope of their utility.

References

Alpay, S., Iphar, M.: Equipment selection based on two different fuzzy multi criteria decision making methods: fuzzy topsis and fuzzy vikor. Open Geosci. **10**(1), 661–677 (2018)

Altin, F.G., Filiz, T.: Assessment of the performance of logistics villages operated by the Turkish state railways using MCDM and DEA methods. EGE Acad. Rev. **22**(2), 169–182 (2022)

Avsarligil, N., Dogru, E., Cıger, A.: The bank performance ranking in the emerging markets: a case of turkey. Sosyoekonomi **31**(55), 69–84 (2023)

Azhar, Z., Mulyani, N., Hutahaean, J., Mayhaky, A.: Sistem pendukung keputusan pemilihan e-commerce terbaik menggunakan metode moosra. Jurnal Media Informatika Budidarma **6**(4), 2346–2351 (2022)

Behera, D.K., Sarkar, A.: A topsıs-based multi-criteria approach to faculty recruitment: a case study. Autom. Control Mechatron. Eng. **II**, 741–744 (2013)

Bhowmik, C., Dhar, S., Ray, A.: Comparative analysis of MCDM methods for the evaluation of optimum green energy sources: a case study. Int. J. Decis. Support Syst. Technol. **11**(4), 1–28 (2019)

Bose, S., Mandal, N., Nandi, T.: Selection and experimentation of the best hybrid green composite using advanced MCDM methods for clean sustainable energy recovery: a novel approach. Int. J. Math. Eng. Manag. Sci. **5**(3), 556–566 (2020)

Büyüközkan G, Güleryüz S. Multi criteria group decision making approach for smart phone selection using ıntuitionistic fuzzy topsıs. International Journal Of Computational İntelligence Systems 9(4), 709–725 (2016)

Cao Q, Wu J, Liang C. An intuitionsitic fuzzy judgement matrix and topsis integrated multi-criteria decision making method for green supplier selection. Journal Of Intelligent & Fuzzy Systems 28(1), 117–126 (2015)

Chen, C.: A hybrid multi-criteria decision-making approach based on anp-entropy topsıs for building materials supplier selection. Entropy **23**(12), 1597 (2021)

Das, M.C., Sarkar, B., Ray, S.: A performance evaluation framework for technical institutions in one of the states of India. Benchmarking **22**(5), 773–790 (2015)

Delice, E.K., Can, G.F.: A new approach for ergonomic risk assessment integrating KEMIRA, best–worst and MCDM methods. Soft. Comput. **24**(19), 15093–15110 (2020). https://doi.org/10.1007/s00500-020-05143-9

Dorfeshan, Y., Mousavi, S.M., Mohagheghi, V., Vahdani, B.: Selecting project-critical path by a new interval type-2 fuzzy decision methodology based on MultıMOORA, MOOSRA and TPOP methods. Comput. Industr. Eng. 120 (2018)

Durmuş, M., Tayyar, N.: Usage of different criterion weighting methods with AHP and Topsis and comparison with decision makers opinions. Eskisehir Osmangazi Universitesi IIBF Dergisi-Eskisehir Osmangazi Univ. J. Econ. Admin. Sci **12**(3), 65–80 (2017)

Fan, L., Yager, R.R., Mesiar, R., Jin, L.: Two-level multi-criteria comprehensive evaluation for preference vectors in online shopping platform evaluation. J. İntell. Fuzzy Syst. **39**(5), 7921–7930 (2020)

Febransyah, A., Goni, J.I.C.: Measuring the supply chain competitiveness of e-commerce industry in Indonesia. Competitiveness Rev. (2022)

Feizi, F., Karbalaei-Ramezanali, A.A., Farhadi, S., FUCOM-MOORA and FUCOM-MOOSRA: new MCDM-based knowledge-driven procedures for mineral potential mapping in Greenfields. Sn Appl. Sci. **3**(3) (2021)

Guru, S., Nenavani, J., Patel, V., Bhatt, N.: Ranking of perceived risks in online shopping. Decision **47**(1), 137–152 (2020)

Hassan, İ., Alhamrouni, İ., Azhan, N.H.: A critic-Topsis multi-criteria decision-making approach for optimum site selection for solar PV farm. Energies **16**(10), 4245 (2023)

Huang, Z., Yang, C., Zhou, X., Gui, W.: An improved Topsis-based multi-criteria decision-making approach for evaluating the working condition of the aluminum reduction cell. Eng. Appl. Artif. Intell. **117**(5), 105599 (2023)

Janjua, S., Hassan, İ: Fuzzy AHP-Topsis multi-criteria decision analysis applied to the Indus reservoir system in Pakistan. Water Supply **20**(5), 1933–1949 (2020)

Kar, N.B., Ghosh, A., Das, S., Banerjee, D.: Fuzzy multi-criteria group decision making approach for grading of mulberry silk cocoons. Indian J. Fibre Textile Res. **45**(2) (2020)

Kittur, J.: Using the promethee and topsis multi-criteria decision-making methods to evaluate optimal generation. In: Proceedings of the 2015 International Conference on Power and Advanced Control Engineering (ICPACE) (2015)

Kumar, G.: A multi-criteria decision-making approach for recommending a product using sentiment analysis. In: 2018 12th International Conference on Research Challenges in Information Science (RCIS) (2018)

Li, Z., Zhang, L.: The research of online shopping evaluation based on grey linguistic multiple criteria decision-making system. In: 2013 IEEE International Conference on Industrial Engineering and Engineering Management (2013)

Lokare, V., Jadhav, P.: Using the AHP and Topsis methods for decision making in best course selection after HSC. In: 2016 International Conference on Computer Communication And Informatics (2016)

Mardhia, M.M., Normawati, D.: Marketplace seller recommender with user- based multi criteria decision making. In: 2018 12th International Conference on Telecommunication Systems, Services, and Applications (Tssa) (2018)

Narayanamoorthy, S., Annapoorani, V., Kang, D., Baleanu, D., Jeon, J., Kureethara, J.V., Ramya, L.: A novel assessment of bio-medical waste disposal methods using integrating weighting approach and hesitant fuzzy moosra. J. Clean. Prod. **275**, 122587 (2020). https://doi.org/10.1016/j.jclepro.2020.122587

Ozcalici, M.: Integrating queue theory and multi-criteria decision-making tools for selecting rollover car washing machine. Oper. Res. Decis. **33**(2), 99–119 (2023)

Özbek, A.. Akademik Dirim Yöneticilerinin MOORA Yöntemiyle Seçilmesi: Kırıkkale Üzerinde Bir Uygulama. Sosyal Bilimler Enstitüsü Dergisi **38**(1), 1–18 (2015)

Ponce, P., Perez, C., Fayek, A.R., Molina, A.: Solar energy implementation in manufacturing industry using multi-criteria decision-making fuzzy topsis and s4 framework. Energies **15**(23), 8838 (2022)

Pourahmadi, A., Ebadi, T., Nikazar, M.: Industrial wastes risk ranking with TOPSIS, multi criteria decision making method. Civ. Eng. J. **3**(6), 372–381 (2017). https://doi.org/10.28991/cej-2017-00000098

Pratap, S., Jauhar, S.K., Daultani, Y., Paul, S.K.: Benchmarking sustainable E-commerce enterprises based on evolving customer expectations amidst COVID-19 pandemic. Bus. Strat. Environ. **32**(1), 736–752 (2023). https://doi.org/10.1002/bse.3172

Radmehr, A., Araghinejad, S.: Flood vulnerability analysis by fuzzy spatial multi criteria decision making. Water Resour. Manage **29**(12), 4427–4445 (2015). https://doi.org/10.1007/s11269-015-1068-x

Rahman, M., Asadujjaman, M.D.: Multi-criteria decision making for job selection. In: 2021 International Conference on Decision Aid Sciences and Application (Dasa), pp. 152–156 (2021)

Ramli, R., Bakar, A.A., Rahim, F.A.: What influences customer's trust on online social network sites (snss) sellers?. Int. J. Adv. Comput. Sci. Appl. **13**(1), 480–489 (2022)

Rani, R.M., Ismail, W.R., Razali, S.F.: Operator performance evaluation using multi criteria decision making methods. In: Proceedings of the 3Rd International Conference on Mathematical Sciences, vol. 1602, no. 1, pp. 559–566 (2014)

Rehman, S., Khan, S.A., Alhems, L.M.: Application of topsis approach to multi-criteria selection of wind turbines for on-shore sites. Appl. Sci. Basel **10**(21), 7595 (2020)

Rogalewicz, V., Jurickova, İ.: Multiple-criteria decision making: application to medical devices. In: Proceedings İwbbio 2014: İnternational Work-Conference on Bioinformatics and Biomedical Engineering, vols. 1 and 2, pp. 1359–1372 (2014)

Sarkar, A., Panja, S.C., Das, D., Sarkar, B.: Developing an efficient decision support system for non-traditional machine selection: an application of MOORA and MOOSRA. Prod. Manuf. Res. **3**(1), 324–342 (2015)

Selvachandran, G., Quek, S.G., Son, L.H., Thong, P.H., Vo, B., Hawari, T.A.A., Salleh, A.R.: Relations and compositions between interval-valued complex fuzzy sets and applications for analysis of customers' online shopping preferences and behavior. Appl. Soft Comput. **114**(2), 108082 (2021)

Sharma, S., Pandey, A.: Comparison of results of benchmarking performed through various techniques in an engineering college of Delhi NCR. In: 2017 3rd IEEE İnternational Conference on Computational Intelligence &Communication Technology (2017)

Štirbanović, Z., Gardić, V., Stanujkić, D., Marković, R., Sokolović, J., Stevanović, Z.: Comparative mcdm analysis for amd treatment method selection. Water Resour. Manage **35**(11), 3737–3753 (2021). https://doi.org/10.1007/s11269-021-02914-3

Şahin, Y., Sara, D.M.: E-shopping sites preference analysis with multi-criteria decision-making methods . Bilişim Teknolojileri Dergisi **12**(4), 265–275 (2019)

Teja, K.B.R., Gupta, N.: Low-k polymer gate dielectric selection for organic thin-film transistors (OTFTs) using material selection methodologies. J. Comput. Electr. 872–881 (2019)

Tzimopoulos, C., Balioti, V., Evangelides, C.: Fuzzy multi-criteria decision making method for dam selection. In: Proceedings of the 13th international conference on environmental science and technology (2013)

Zhao, B., Wang, H., Huang, Z., Sun, Q.: Location mapping for constructing biomass power plant using multi-criteria decision-making method. Sustain. Energy Technol. Assess. **49**(9), 101707 (2022)

Machine Learning, Data Analysis and Computer Vision in Healthcare and Medicine

Advancing Anemia Diagnosis: Harnessing Machine Learning Methods for Accurate Detection

P. Sümeyye Söylemez$^{(\boxtimes)}$ ⓘ and Hilal Arslan ⓘ

Ankara Yıldırım Beyazıt University, Ankara, Turkey
`p.s.soylemez@aybu.edu.tr`

Abstract. Anemia, a condition characterized by insufficient healthy red blood cells to transport oxygen adequately, demands timely detection and treatment to prevent complications. Machine learning methods offer promising avenues for diagnosing anemia, especially in settings with limited medical expertise and resources. This study employed various algorithms, including k-nearest neighbor, support vector machines, decision trees, adaptive boosting, and random forest, to diagnose anemia and its specific types. The dataset encompassed laboratory data from 5,553 anemia patients and 9,747 healthy individuals, with subtypes including iron deficiency-related anemia, hemoglobin insufficiency, B12 deficiency, and folate deficiencies. Using 24 features like B12 levels, blood cell counts, iron levels, and gender, the study aimed to identify the anemia presence and recommend treatment. Notably, the decision tree algorithm emerged highly effective, surpassing other methods with a 96.49% accuracy rate. The study achieved a remarkable 100% accuracy in anemia diagnosis by optimizing hyperparameters through grid search. This outcome holds significant clinical implications, as misdiagnosing anemia can lead to severe complications like hemochromatosis, potentially resulting in organ damage or failure.

Keywords: Anemia · Support Vector Machine · k-Nearest Neighbor · Decision Tree Neural Network

1 Introduction

Anemia, characterized by a deficiency in red blood cells or hemoglobin, remains a significant global public health concern affecting individuals of all ages, particularly in low and middle-income countries. The condition can lead to various adverse health outcomes, including fatigue, impaired cognitive function, and increased mortality rates, emphasizing the critical need for timely and accurate diagnosis. Traditional diagnostic methods, reliant on invasive blood tests, pose challenges in terms of accessibility, cost, and time, especially in resource-limited settings. However, the integration of machine learning techniques into healthcare offers promising avenues for enhancing diagnostic accuracy and efficiency across various medical domains, including anemia diagnosis.

A. Mirzazadeh et al. (Eds.): SEMIT 2023, CCIS 2198, pp. 101–110, 2024.
https://doi.org/10.1007/978-3-031-72284-4_6

This study aims to contribute to the existing body of knowledge by leveraging machine learning algorithms for the automated diagnosis of anemia using non-invasive and easily accessible clinical data. Analyzing a comprehensive dataset comprising demographic information, medical history, and laboratory test results, we seek to develop and evaluate robust predictive models capable of accurately identifying individuals with anemia. The methodology involves feature selection using minimum Redundancy Maximum Relevance (mRMR) to identify the most informative variables for model training. Subsequently, various classification algorithms, including Decision Trees, Random Forest, Support Vector Machines (SVM), and Gradient Boosting Machines (GBM), are applied to classify individuals into anemic and non-anemic groups. The performance of each algorithm is rigorously evaluated using standard metrics such as accuracy.

Additionally, this paper discusses the implications of employing machine learning-based approaches for anemia diagnosis in clinical practice, highlighting the limitations and challenges encountered during the study. Furthermore, potential avenues for future research aimed at refining and improving the proposed methodology are explored. Overall, this research aims to demonstrate the feasibility and effectiveness of using machine learning techniques for enhancing anemia diagnosis, thereby facilitating early intervention, and improving health outcomes for affected individuals.

2 Related Works

Anemia, a condition characterized by a deficiency in red blood cells or hemoglobin, has been a significant focus of medical research due to its widespread prevalence and implications for public health. Recent studies have demonstrated remarkable progress in leveraging machine learning algorithms to enhance the accuracy and efficiency of anemia diagnosis, showcasing the potential of non-invasive approaches, particularly in resource-constrained settings.

One notable avenue of research, as highlighted by Yıldız et al. [1], involves classifying different types of anemia using artificial learning methods. Their study provides a foundational understanding of how machine learning can be applied to categorize anemia types, laying the groundwork for further advancements in diagnosis and treatment strategies.

Building upon this foundation, Zhao et al. [2] developed a sophisticated deep learning framework for predicting hemoglobin concentration and screening for anemia using ultra-wide field (UWF) fundus images. By achieving superior performance metrics such as area under the curve (AUC) and sensitivity, their research underscores the potential of innovative technologies to revolutionize anemia screening and diagnosis, particularly in clinical settings like Peking Union Medical College Hospital (PUMCH).

Moreover, Saputra et al. [3] proposed a novel artificial intelligence approach utilizing extreme learning machines for predicting and analyzing anemia diagnoses. By introducing a new model into the landscape of anemia diagnosis, their study contributes to the ongoing efforts to harness machine learning for improving healthcare outcomes.

Expanding the scope of machine learning applications in anemia diagnosis, several studies have explored diverse methodologies and techniques. Kilicarslan et al. [4] investigated hybrid models combining genetic algorithms and deep learning algorithms for nutritional anemia disease classification, achieving remarkable accuracy rates. They employed SVM-Gaussian, random tree, SVM-Linear, and k-NN methods to diagnose anemia patients and their types, achieving a remarkable accuracy of 96.49% using the random tree method. Meanwhile, Dogan and Turkoglu [5] demonstrated the effectiveness of decision trees in detecting iron-deficiency anemia, showcasing a 100% success rate in matching doctor diagnoses.

Furthermore, Khan et al. [6] focused on predicting childhood anemia in resource-limited settings, emphasizing the feasibility of utilizing machine learning algorithms to analyze socio-economic factors and living conditions. Meena et al. [7] highlighted the significance of various factors such as gender, place of residence, and breastfeeding practices in diagnosing anemia severity, utilizing decision tree algorithms on a large dataset of children.

In the realm of hemoglobin estimation and anemia classification, El-kenawy et al. [8] developed a high-accuracy machine learning model using hybrid classifier algorithms. Additionally, they addressed the association between anemia and COVID-19, demonstrating the potential of using anemia as a marker for disease severity [9].

In summary, the collective efforts of these studies underscore the significant advancements made in the field of anemia diagnosis through the application of machine learning techniques. By addressing various aspects such as classification, prediction, and association with other health conditions, these interdisciplinary endeavors pave the way for more accurate, efficient, and accessible anemia diagnosis and treatment strategies, ultimately improving patient care in the field of hematology.

3   Method

In this section, we present a detailed description of the experimental setup and the tools employed for classification and cross-validation. The experimental results were conducted on a 2.30 GHz Intel Core i7 computer with 16 GB RAM running the Windows 10 Education operating system. The MATLAB software, specifically the Classification Learner tool in MATLAB R2022b, was utilized for performing the classification tasks and conducting cross-validation. This section outlines the specific steps taken to ensure the accuracy and reliability of the experimental procedure, providing a solid foundation for the subsequent analysis and discussion of the results.

3.1   Dataset

The dataset [4] utilized in this study is sourced from clinical records of 15,300 subjects, encompassing a diverse range of demographic backgrounds, medical histories, and laboratory test results. This dataset includes comprehensive measurements of various blood components and characteristics crucial for assessing anemia and related deficiencies. Parameters such as Vitamin B12, Ferritin, Folate, Hemoglobin, White Blood Cells (WBC), and Red Blood Cells (RBC) are among the key variables recorded.

Specifically, the dataset comprises 9,747 individuals without anemia and 5,553 individuals diagnosed with anemia, categorized into distinct types: Iron deficiency anemia (4,182 cases), Hemoglobin deficiency anemia (1,019 cases), B12 deficiency anemia (199 cases), and folate deficiency anemia (153 cases). The distribution of patients across these categories is detailed in Fig. 1.

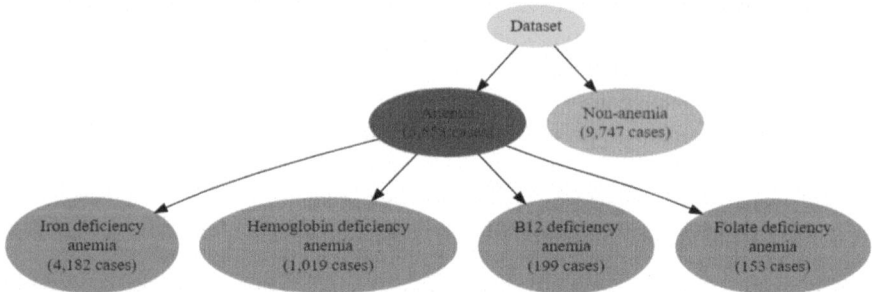

Fig. 1. Anemia Dataset Overview

It is worth noting that this dataset's significance lies in its utility for training and evaluating machine learning models aimed at diagnosing anemia and its specific types using non-invasive clinical data.

3.2   Feature Selection (mRMR)

The visual representation in Fig. 2 offers insight into the feature selection process, demonstrating the application of the Minimum Redundancy Maximum Relevance (mRMR) [10] algorithm. This well-established method in machine learning aims to identify pertinent features within the dataset by maximizing their relevance to the target variable while minimizing redundancy between selected features.

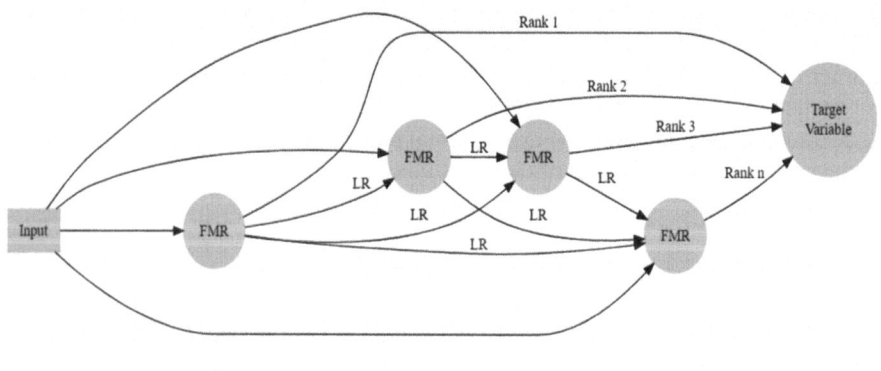

FMR:Feature with Maximum Relevance
LR:Low Redundancy

Fig. 2. Feature Selection with mRMR

In the context of mRMR, relevance refers to the degree of association or importance of a feature with respect to the target variable, often measured by statistical metrics such as mutual information or correlation coefficients. Meanwhile, redundancy quantifies the overlap or similarity between pairs of selected features, ensuring that the chosen features offer distinct and complementary information.

The feature selection process involves computing relevance and redundancy scores for each feature and then selecting a subset that optimally balances relevance and redundancy. Through iterative evaluation and adjustment of feature subsets, mRMR facilitates the identification of the most informative features while mitigating the risk of selecting redundant or irrelevant ones.

3.3 Learning Methods

Various machine learning algorithms were employed for the classification task based on the selected features. These algorithms include Decision Trees, Support Vector Machines (SVM), k-Nearest Neighbors (KNN), and Neural Networks. Each algorithm underwent training using a cross-validation approach to assess its performance accurately.

A *Decision Tree* [11] is a powerful tool in machine learning, dividing data to construct a predictive model. The depth of the tree determines its complexity: fine trees capture intricate details but risk overfitting, medium trees strike a balance, and coarse trees focus on salient patterns. The Gini impurity criterion guides node splitting, while adjusting granularity allows tailoring for complexity versus interpretability. Overall, decision trees remain valuable for their versatility and ease of interpretation in machine learning.

$$Gini\ Index = 1 - \sum_{i=1}^{n} (P_i)^2 \tag{1}$$

In Formula 1, the Gini Index is calculated as 1 minus the sum of the squares of the probabilities of each class, where P_i represents the probability that an element is classified in a specific class. This mathematical formula aids in assessing the impurity of nodes in decision trees.

SVM [12] is a supervised machine learning algorithm used for classification and regression tasks. It works by finding an optimal hyperplane that separates different classes in the input space. The hyperplane is selected in such a way that the margin (distance) between the hyperplane and the nearest data points from each class is maximized. These nearest data points are called support vectors.

In the case of linear SVM, the hyperplane is a straight line in a two-dimensional space or a hyperplane in a higher-dimensional space. Linear SVM uses a linear decision boundary to separate classes.

In contrast, quadratic, cubic, fine Gaussian, medium Gaussian, and coarse Gaussian SVMs use non-linear decision boundaries. These SVM methods use different kernel functions to map the original input space into a higher-dimensional feature space, where a linear hyperplane can separate the data points effectively.

KNN [13] is a machine learning algorithm employed for classification and regression tasks. It is a non-parametric approach that predicts based on the k-closest training samples in the feature space. When comparing different KNN methods, several variations can be observed. Medi-um KNN is a classification method that predicts the mode (most frequent class) among the k nearest neighbors. It is particularly useful for imbalanced datasets or situations where the most common class needs to be determined. Coarse KNN, another classification method, predicts the class that appears the most among the k nearest neighbors, resolving ties randomly if multiple classes have the same frequency. On the other hand, Cosine KNN considers cosine similarity between feature vectors instead of the traditional Euclidean distance. This method is suitable for high-dimensional or sparse data and can be more robust to differences in feature magni-tudes. Weighted KNN, whether for classification or regression, assigns weights to neighbors based on their distances. Closer neighbors have higher weights, indicating a stronger influence on the prediction. Weighted KNN is often employed when certain neighbors are deemed more informative or when varying levels of influence are de-sired. Ultimately, the choice of the KNN method depends on the specific problem at hand, the characteristics of the dataset, and the desired behavior of the algorithm.

Neural Networks [14] are a class of machine learning algorithms inspired by the structure and functioning of the human brain. They are composed of interconnected nodes, called neurons, organized in layers. Each neuron receives inputs, applies a transformation function, and produces an output. The outputs from one layer serve as inputs to the next layer, allowing the network to learn complex patterns and make predictions.

4 Results

Utilizing the mRMR feature selection method, a meticulous process was undertaken to identify a subset of features highly relevant to the target variable while minimizing redundancy. This involved assessing the discriminative power and mutual information among the 24 initial features. Subsequently, subsets containing 16, 20, and all 24 features were carefully chosen based on their significance to the target variable.

These curated feature subsets were then subjected to rigorous evaluation through cross-validation with 3, 5, and 10 folds. This comprehensive approach aimed to analyze the performance of various classification methods across different combinations of feature subsets and cross-validation settings, providing insights into the efficacy of the proposed methodology.

Figure 3 illustrates the classification accuracy achieved by each method across different cross-validation and feature selection settings.

Among the SVM methods, Linear SVM (LSVM) exhibited the highest performance, achieving accuracies ranging from 91.7% to 96%. Quadratic SVM (QSVM) and Cubic SVM (CSVM) also showed competitive results, with accuracies ranging from 81.7% to 83.6% and 90.4% to 95.1%, respectively. Additionally, Fine Gaussian SVM (FGSVM), Medium Gaussian SVM (MGSVM), and Coarse Gaussian SVM (CGSVM) methods achieved accuracies ranging from 71.8% to 83.7%, 91.4% to 94.9%, and 90.1% to 93.4%, respectively.

Regarding Decision Trees, Fine Tree (FT) and Medium Tree (MT) methods exhibited excellent performance, with accuracies ranging from 95.3% to 100% and 95.8% to 100%, respectively. Coarse Tree (CT) method achieved accuracies between 93.8% and 95.2%.

Among KNN methods, Cosine KNN (Cos-KNN) demonstrated the highest accuracy, ranging from 86.8% to 88.2%. Medium KNN (M-KNN) and Weighted KNN (W-KNN) methods also performed well, achieving accuracies between 86.3% and 87.7% and

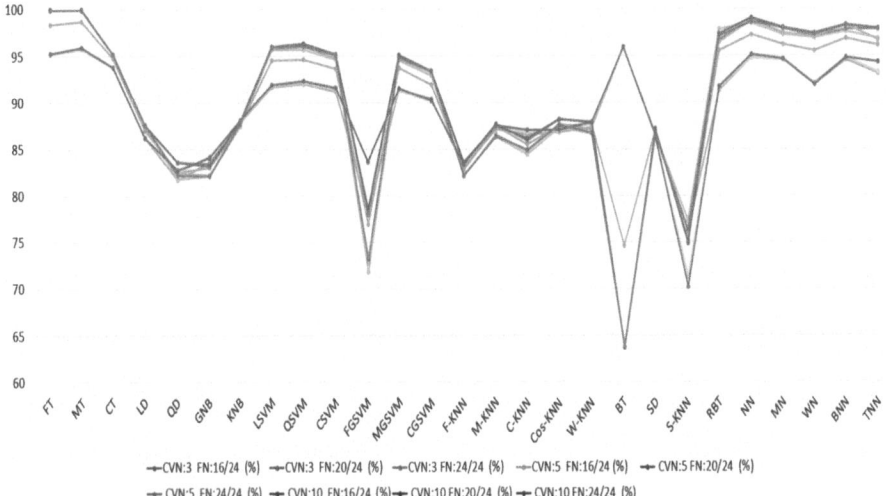

Fig. 3. Classification Algorithm Performance(CVN: Cross Validation Numbers, FN: Feature Numbers)

86.6% and 87.8%, respectively. Fine KNN (F-KNN) and Coarse KNN (C-KNN) methods obtained accuracies ranging from 82.1% to 83.6% and 84.4% to 86.5%, respectively.

Lastly, Neural Network models, including Narrow Neural Network (NN), Medium Neural Network (MN), Wide Neural Network (WN), Bilayered Neural Network (BNN), and Trilayered Neural Network (TNN), were evaluated. NN achieved accuracies between 94.5% and 98.8%, showing promising results. The other Neural Network models also demonstrated competitive performance, with accuracies ranging from 91.9% to 97.9%.

5 Discussion

In contrast to previous efforts [4], which opted for the challenging path of constructing complex hybrid systems but achieved an accuracy of 96.49%, our work takes a different approach. Without relying on supercomputers, we have attained higher accuracy values using simple and previously employed machine learning methods, particularly by leveraging feature selection techniques like mRMR. Our study demonstrates that by utilizing only 20 features selected by mRMR from the original dataset of 24 features, we achieved remarkable accuracy results. For instance, our model employing the Fine Tree algorithm with 10-fold cross-validation achieved a perfect accuracy of 100% (Fine Tree CVN: 10 FN: 20/24), surpassing the accuracy value reported in the previous study. Table 1 showcases accuracy values exceeding 96.49%(Random Tree), and 98.52%(GNN-CNN Model 4)indicating the efficacy of our approach.

The dataset initially comprised a modest 24 features, and while our results are promising, we acknowledge the potential for further enrichment of our analysis. Delving deeper into patient demographics and health parameters could unlock invaluable insights. Factors such as gender, pregnancy status, age demographics, and the presence of nutritional disorders remain pivotal determinants that warrant exploration. Ancillary diagnostic

Table 1. Accuracy Values Exceed the Accuracy Value in Previous Study [4].

Method	Accuracy Range (%)
Random Tree [4]	96.49
GNN-CNN Model 4 [4]	98.52
Fine Tree CVN:10 FN: 20/24	100.0
Fine Tree CVN:5 FN: 20/24	99.9
Fine Tree CVN:3 FN: 20/24	98.4
Medium Tree CVN:10 FN: 20/24	100.0
Medium Tree CVN:5 FN: 20/24	99.9
Medium Tree CVN:3 FN: 20/24	98.7
Narrow NN CVN:10 FN: 20/24	99
Narrow NN CVN:5 FN: 20/24	98.8
Narrow NN CVN:3 FN: 20/24	97.2
Medium NN CVN:10 FN: 20/24	98
Medium NN CVN:5 FN: 20/24	97.9
Medium NN CVN:3 FN: 20/24	96.2

modalities, such as stool tests assessing the microbiome composition, hold untapped potential in elucidating nuanced intricacies of anemia etiology.

The interplay between anemia and gastrointestinal health unveils a realm ripe for exploration. Consider the intriguing nexus between vitamin B12 deficiency anemia and gut microbiota dysbiosis. In cases where malabsorption stemming from compromised gut flora impedes adequate nutrient uptake, conventional dietary interventions may prove futile.

Our study, while showcasing the prowess of machine learning algorithms in anemia diagnosis, underscores the imperative of embracing a holistic approach. By integrating a broader array of information and considering the intricate relationship between anemia and gastrointestinal health, we can enhance diagnostic accuracy and pave the way for more effective treatment strategies.

6 Conclusion

In conclusion, our study presents a comprehensive exploration of machine learning methodologies for the diagnosis of anemia and its specific types using non-invasive clinical data. Leveraging a dataset comprising 15,300 subjects with diverse demographic backgrounds and medical histories, we employed rigorous experimental procedures to evaluate the performance of various classification algorithms. The feature selection process, guided by the mRMR algorithm, ensured the identification of pertinent features while minimizing redundancy. Through meticulous evaluation via cross-validation, we observed notable accuracies across different classification methods. Specifically, Linear

SVM, Decision Trees (Fine and Medium), Cosine KNN, and Neural Networks (Narrow to Trilayered) demonstrated high performance in accurately diagnosing anemia and its types. Our findings indicate that complex hybrid systems, while challenging to construct, may not necessarily outperform simpler machine learning approaches. Notably, without relying on supercomputers, we achieved accuracies surpassing previous studies, highlighting the efficacy of employing well-established machine learning methods on comprehensive clinical datasets.

However, it is essential to acknowledge the limitations of our study. While our approach achieved promising results, the generalizability of our findings may be limited by the specific characteristics of the dataset used. Additionally, the absence of certain demographic and health parameters, such as gender, age demographics, and ancillary diagnostic modalities like microbiome composition assessments, may have impacted the comprehensiveness of our analysis. Future studies should aim to address these limitations by incorporating a broader range of variables and datasets to ensure more robust and generalizable findings.

Moving forward, there are several avenues for future research to explore. One promising direction is to enrich our analysis by incorporating additional patient demographic and health parameters, as mentioned earlier. Exploring the intricate interplay between anemia and gastrointestinal health, particularly in cases of vitamin B12 deficiency anemia, presents another avenue for future research to uncover nuanced etiological insights. By embracing this interdisciplinary perspective, future studies can enhance diagnostic accuracy and pave the way for more effective treatment strategies in clinical practice.

References

1. Yıldız, T.K., Yurtay, N., Öneç, B.: Classifying anemia types using artificial learning methods. Eng. Sci. Technol. Int. J. **24**(1), 50–70 (2021)
2. Zhao, X., et al.: Deep-learning-based hemoglobin concentration prediction and anemia screening using ultra-wide field fundus images. Front. Cell and Develop. Biolo. **10**, 888268 (2022)
3. Saputra, D.C.E., Sunat, K., Ratnaningsih, T.: A new artificial intelligence approach using extreme learning machine as the potentially effective model to predict and analyze the diagnosis of anemia. In: Healthcare, Vol. 11, No. 5, p. 697. MDPI (2023)
4. Kilicarslan, S., Celik, M., Sahin, Ş: Hybrid models based on genetic algorithm and deep learning algorithms for nutritional Anemia disease classification. Biomed. Sig. Proc. Contr. **63**, 102231 (2021)
5. Dogan, S., Turkoglu, I.: Iron-deficiency anemia detection from hematology parameters by using decision trees. Int. J. Sci. Technol. **3**(1), 85–92 (2008)
6. Khan, J.R., et al.: Machine learning algorithms to predict the childhood anemia in Bangladesh. J. Data Sci. **17**(1), 195–218 (2019)
7. Meena, K., et al.: Using classification techniques for statistical analysis of Anemia. Artif. Intell. Medic. **94**, 138–152 (2019)
8. El-kenawy, E.S.M.T.: A machine learning model for hemoglobin estimation and anemia Classification. Int. J. Comp. Sci. Info. Sec. (IJCSIS) **17**(2), 100–108 (2019)
9. El-kenawy, E.-S., Eid, M.M., Ibrahim, A.: Anemia estimation for covid-19 patients using a machine learning model. J. Comp. Sci. Info. Sys. **17**(11), 1451–2535 (2021)
10. Ding, C., Peng, H.: Minimum redundancy feature selection from microarray gene expression data. J. Bioinform. Comput. Biol. **3**(02), 185–205 (2005)

11. Carson, R.T., Richard, T.: Three essays on contingent valuation (welfare economics, non-market goods, water quality). Diss. University of California, Berkeley (1985)
12. Cortes, C., Vapnik, V.: Support-vector networks. Mach. Learn. **20**, 273–297 (1995)
13. Fix, E., Hodges, J.L.: Discriminatory analysis. nonparametric discrimination: consistency properties. Int. Statist. Rev. Revue Internationale de Statistique **57**(3), 238–247 (1989)
14. Crevier, D.: AI: the tumultuous history of the search for artificial intelligence. Basic Books, Inc. (1993)

Monkeypox Detection with K-mer Using Machine Learning Algorithms

Hasret Pınar Tipioğlu[1]([⊠]) and Hilal Arslan[2]

[1] Biology Department, Ankara University, Ankara, Türkiye
hasretpinar@gmail.com

[2] Software Engineering Department, Ankara Yıldırım Beyazıt University, Ankara, Türkiye

Abstract. According to data of World Health Organization, since 2022, Monkeypox cases have been more common around the world, including Europe and America, compared to previous years. Like every disease, correct diagnosis of Monkeypox is very important in terms of treatment and recovery period. In the clinic, Monkeypox and warts are sometimes confused with each other because they have similar symptoms. For this purpose HPV (Human papilloma virus) DNA which causes warts and Monkeypox virus DNA which causes Monkeypox, were selected in our study.

Today, the rapid development of technology allows us to use technology in many areas. The progress in artificial intelligence, especially in the last 20 years, has enabled the use of artificial intelligence in both research and clinics in the field of medicine, as well as in many other fields.

In our study, the full genome sequences of Monkeypox virus and HPV were used to classify these two viruses with supervised machine learning algorithms. As for features, the data obtained by calculating the number of k-mers (4-mer, 5-mer, 6-mer), which is an alignment free approach, and dividing by the full genome length (number of base pairs) for each virus, was used.

According to the classification results, an accuracy of 99% or more was achieved. As a result, these two diseases were successfully distinguished using whole genome virus DNAs.

Keywords: Monkeypox · HPV · Machine Learning · k-mer

1 Introduction

With the rapid development of technology and computer hardware in the last 20 years, groundbreaking developments have occurred in programming that can be used in many areas. Rapid progress has been made, especially in the field of artificial intelligence. Artificial intelligence is involved in many fields with voice assistants, language translations, navigation, social security, medicine, e-commerce and robot applications. Artificial intelligence in medicine; it is used for applications such as diagnosis, treatment protocol, drug development, personalized medicine, patient monitoring and care. Artificial intelligence algorithms can also be used to analyze large amounts of data for disease prevention and diagnosis. In our study, using artificial intelligence algorithms and the full genome sequence of Monkeypox virus and HPV, these two viruses were distinguished from each other on a genome basis. Thus, by using artificial intelligence algorithms in the diagnosis of warts and Monkeypox diseases, whose symptoms are similar to each other in the clinic it has been shown that the diagnosis of these two diseases can be easily distinguished from each other.

The study also explains that artificial intelligence algorithms it has been shown that using the full genome sequence can be used successfully for both virus classification and disease diagnosis with a high percentage of accuracy. For this purpose, it also contributes to future studies.

According to data of the World Health Organization, there has been a spread and increase in Monkeypox cases worldwide for approximately the last 3 years [1]. Monkeypox causes a rash that appears as a bump or pustule on the skin. Monkeypox rash may resemble chickenpox, herpes, warts, or syphilis. Therefore, when diagnosing Monkeypox in the clinic, these skin rashes can sometimes be confused with chickenpox, herpes, warts or syphilis [2]. As with all diseases, accurate and rapid diagnosis of Monkeypox is very important for the treatment process and recovery. Nowadays, machines and computer programs are used for various analysis methods for diagnosis.

DNA detection of viruses is used to diagnose diseases caused by viruses, and thus it is determined that the virus is present in the patient. For DNA detection in viruses, real-time quantitative PCR (qPCR) is used to search for the virus to be detected in patients [3].

The formation of warts is caused by HPV [4]. Both Monkeypox and warts are viruses that carry DNA as their genetic material. Approximately the genome length of Monkeypox is 200 kb and HPV is 8 kb [4, 5].

Recently, artificial intelligence algorithms have been used in genome classification. Machine learning is also a sub-branch of artificial intelligence. Machine learning algorithms; it learns from previously obtained data and builds models to develop predictions on new independent data. Since machine learning can be used in very complex data sets and a high percentage of accuracy is achieved, its use in genome data and many different areas of bioinformatics is becoming increasingly popular day by day [6].

These two viruses were used in the study because their symptoms in the clinic are similar and both viruses are DNA viruses. In addition, the full genome sequences of these two viruses are available as open source. HPV DNA sequences were obtained from NCBI, and Monkeypox virus DNA sequences were obtained from GISAID.

Chen et al. (2021) used 3-mer (trimer), genetic measurements and phylogenetic algorithms to evaluate 640 PV (Papiloma virus) in their study. They found that HPVs found in the same (human) host generally had similar trimer distributions. In the study, they detected HPV types with high accuracy [7].

Asensio-Puig et al. (2022) used machine learning to evaluate HPV16. Genome Wide Association Study (GWAS) was used, identifying 56 lineage-specific Single Nucleotide Polymorphisms (SNPs) using a total of 645 HPV 16 genomes. Different algorithms such as Random Forest (RF), Support Vector Machine (SVM) and K-nearest neighbors (KNN) have been used. Ultimately, the RF model provided identification of HPV 16 with an accuracy of 99.5%. Additionally, Maximum Likelihood Tree (MLT) was also used in the study. However, it has been proven that the RF model is more successful than MLT, both by working faster than MLT and by detecting samples that MLT cannot detect [8].

Tian et al. used deep learning to find the HPV integration site. While 3608 HPV integration sites were used to train the model, 584 revised HPV integration sites were used for testing [9].

In another study, machine learning was used for viral metagenome classification. Random Forest, Feed Forward Neural Networks and Convolutional Neural Networks algorithms were used to classify as virus and non-virus. Hidden Markov Models has been used to identify and classify viral genome sequences in different viral families [10].

Raju et al. (2021) have developed a tool called VirusTaxo with machine learning. The VirusTaxo tool performs taxonomic classification using the genome (DNA or RNA) of viruses. VirusTaxo determines k-mers from the genome sequence to find the order, family, and genus of a virus [11].

Alakus and Baykara (2022) used a deep learning algorithm to classify HPV and Mpox DNAs. A high accuracy rate of 96.08% was achieved in the study. As a result, HPV and Mpox DNAs were effectively classified according to their DNA sequences [12].

Tipioğlu and Arslan (2023) used the full genome sequences of HPV and Monkeypox were binary classified with supervised machine learning algorithms. The results showed that accuracy, F1-Score, precision and recall values are above 99% [13].

2   Data and Methods

Although viruses are not classified as living things, they are classified by taxonomic classification, like other living things, in order to find out the virus types and which family they belong to. And the genetic material of viruses is used for this taxonomic classification.

In traditional virus classification, various phenotypic features of viruses such as molecular composition, structure, proteins, host and pathogenicity are used [14]. However, today, with the development of genome sequencing technologies, classification of viruses is now made according to the genome sequences of viruses rather than their phenotypic features.

In computational methods used for virus taxonomy is based on genome structure similarity and the homologous genes [15]. But these methods require high computational processes and usually expert comment.

To classify viruses according to their genome sequence are used three main approaches. One of them is sequence alignment; these based on similarity search methods and binary distance. The other one is the phylogenetic-based approach. To classif a new virus, the virus genom sequence is realigned with the existing set of reference sequences. Consequently, a new phylogenetic tree is extracted or the virus sequence is placed in the existing phylogenetic tree. The last one is the alignment-free approach, which we used in this study. This approach uses nucleotide correlations and sequence composition [16].

In this study, we used the k-mer methods which is one of the alignment free methods. k-mers are short nucleotide sequences of length k in a genome sequence.

The features which to be used for machine learning algorithms used in the study were created as follows. First of all, 4-mers, 5-mers and 6-mers were created for each virus. And each of these generated k-mers is divided by the genome length (base pair) of each virus. And the obtained numbers were used as features. The purpose of dividing the obtained k-mer numbers by the virus genome length is to eliminate the negative effect that may arise from the different lengths of these two viruses. Thus, calculation errors that may arise from differences in virus genome lengths are minimized.

Dataset is labeled 1 for Mpox and 2 for HPVs.

4-mers: AAAA, AAAT, AAAG, AAAC, ATGC, ... Number of 4-mers $= 4^4 = 256$

5-mers: AAAAA, AAAAT, AAAAG, AAAAC, AATGC,... Number of 5-mers $= 4^5 = 1024$

6-mers: AAAAAA, AAAAAT, AAAAAG, AAAAAC, AAATGC,... Number of 6-mers $4^6 = 4096$

The genome sequences used in the study are complete genome sequences for both viruses. And both of them are in fasta format.

In this study; 623 HPV16 complete genome sequences downloaded from NCBI's open source website were used. 619 humanMonkeypox complete genome sequences downloaded from GISAID's open source website were used.

2.1 Machine Learning Algorithms

Machine learning is inspired by the human learning ability. In machine learning, algorithms have been obtained in which various calculations are made using mathematical equations. As a result, algorithms make calculations using known data and make predictions as a result of these calculations. In our study, supervised learning algorithms were used for classification algorithms.

DT, ANNs, SVM, KNN are some of the machine learning algorithms used for classification [17, 18].

Decision Tree, as the name suggests, creates a tree-like structure with the algorithm. To do this, it compares the feature values with the known real data set, starting from the root node of the tree, and jumps to the next node each time. For each subsequent node, the algorithm compares the attribute value with other child nodes [19].

Artificial Neural Network (ANN): Here, it is inspired by the working principle of the human brain. The neural network in the human brain consists of neurons and the connections between them. Artificial neural networks consist of artificial nerve cells and the connections between them, just like the human brain. Artificial neural networks consist of three basic layers; Input Layer, Intermediate (Hidden) Layers and Output Layer [20].

Information is transmitted to the neural network through the input layer. It is processed in the intermediate layers (information coming to the network is converted into output using the weight values of the network) and the resulting output is sent to the output layer.

KNN algorithm classifies unknown data according to its nearest neighbor. The important thing here is to calculate the k value correctly.The K value is the number of nearest neighbors. It is necessary to calculate the distance between the test and training data [17, 18].

In the KNN algorithm, Euclid (Eq. 1) and Manhattan (Eq. 2) distance measures are used in distance calculation.

$$(x, y) = (\sqrt{\sum_{i=1}^{n} (\mathrm{xi} - \mathrm{yi})^2}) \tag{1}$$

$$(x, y) = \sum_{i=1}^{n} |\mathrm{xi} - \mathrm{yi}| \tag{2}$$

Support Vector Machines (SVM) are good at binary classification based on statistic. SVM is divided into linear and nonlinear. The important thing in this algorithm is to find the best line or decision boundary (hyperplane) that separates the data points of different data classes. The goal is to maximize the margin, which is the distance between the hyperplane and the closest data points of each category, thus classifying the data [17, 18].

In this study, classifier models with different algorithms were used from the MATLAB machine learning toolbox. We used Neural network, KNN algorithm, DT algorithms, and SVM algorithms to classify. All numerical results are obtained using MATLAB R2022b on an Intel processor under Windows 10 operating system.

3   Experimental Result

HPV and Mpox complete genome sequences were classified using Matlab machine learning toolbox algorithms. For this purpose, Fine Tree, Medium Tree, Coarse Tree, Linear SVM, Quadratic SVM, Cubic SVM, Fine Gaussian SVM, Medium Gaussian SVM, Fine KNN, Medium KNN, Coarse KNN, Cosine KNN, Cubic KNN, Weighted KNN, Subspace KNN, Narrow Neural Network, Medium Neural Network, Wide Neural Network, Bilayered Neural Network, Trilayered Neural Network algorithms were used.

Model success is measured via the accuracy metric that was shown in Eq. 3 (TN: TrueNegative, TP: True Positive, FP: False Positive, FN: False Negative). For algorithm validation, 10-fold cross validation was applied. Algorithms for 4-mer, 5-mers and 6-mers were applied separately. Validation accuracy results are given in the Table 1 below.

$$Accuracy = \frac{TN + TP}{TN + FP + FN + TP} \tag{3}$$

Confusion matrix is a measure table used to classification. It can be applied either binary or multiclass classification. A confusion matrix for binary classification is shown in Fig. 1 below.

Confusion matrix represent numbers for predicted and actual values. "TN" means True Negative which shows the number of negative examples classified accurately. "TP" means for True Positive which shows the number of positive examples classified accurately. "FP" means False Positive value, the number of actual negative examples classified as positive. "FN" means False Negative which shows the number of actual positive examples classified as negative [21].

Table 1. Machine learning algorithms for classification HPV and Mpox 4-mer, 5-mer, 6-mer accuracy (mean)

Model Type	4-mer Accuracy	5-mer Accuracy	6-mer Accuracy
Decision Tree	100	100	100
SVM	99,94	99,94	99,90
KNN	100,00	99,98	100
ANN	100,00	98,48	98,58

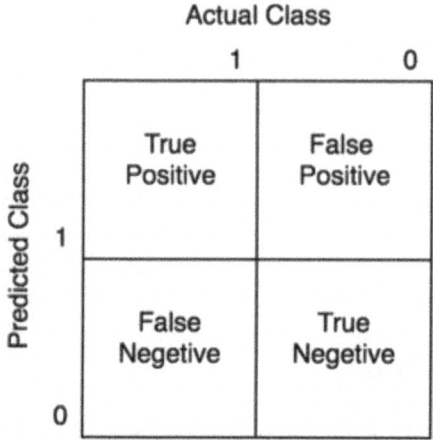

Fig. 1. Confusion matrix for binary classification

ROC AUC curve is a graph showing the classifier's success in distinguishing positive and negative classes. Values can be taken from 0 to 1. A higher ROC AUC indicates better performance. The closer the AUC value of a model is to 1, the higher its discrimination success [22]. The Roc curve is shown below (Fig. 2).

Confusion matrices and Roc curves of some algorithms are shown below (Figs. 3, 4, 5, 6, 7, 8, 9, 10, 11, 12, 13 and 14):

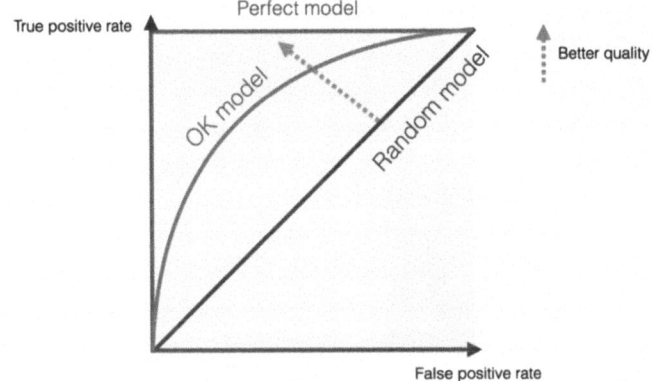

Fig. 2. ROC AUC curve

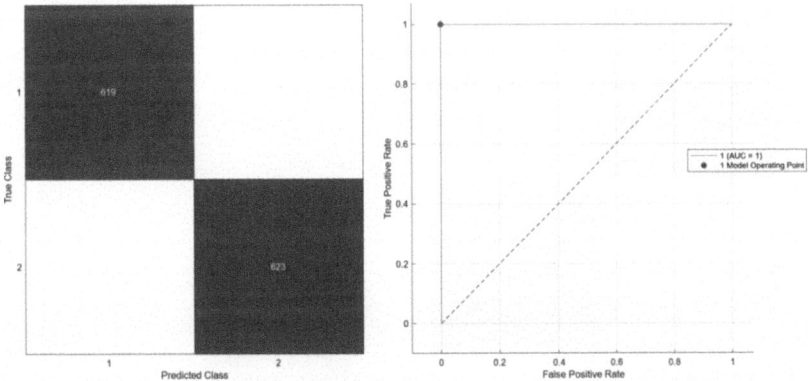

Fig. 3. 4-mer Fine Tree Confusion Matrix and 4-mer Fine Tree ROC Curve

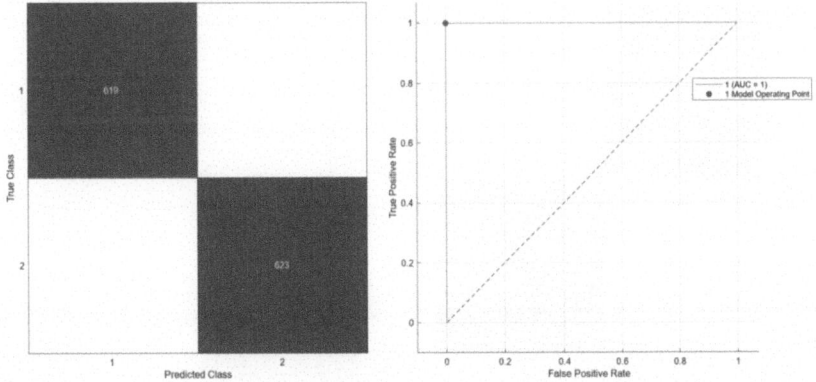

Fig. 4. 4-mer Linear SVM Confusion Matrix and 4-mer Linear SVM Roc Curve

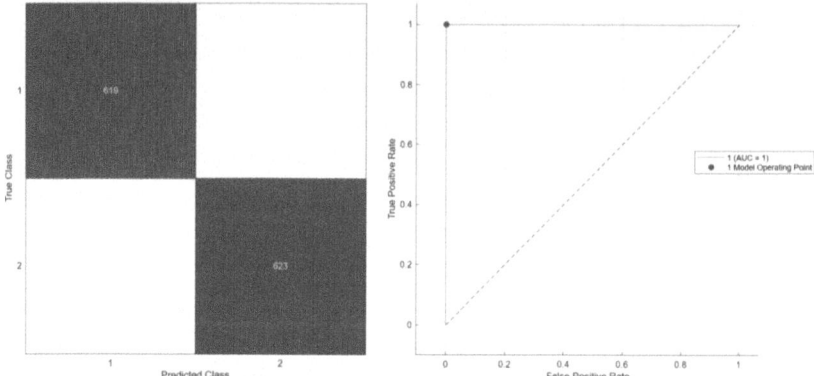

Fig. 5. 4-mer Fine KNN Confusion Matrix and 4-mer Fine KNN Roc Curve

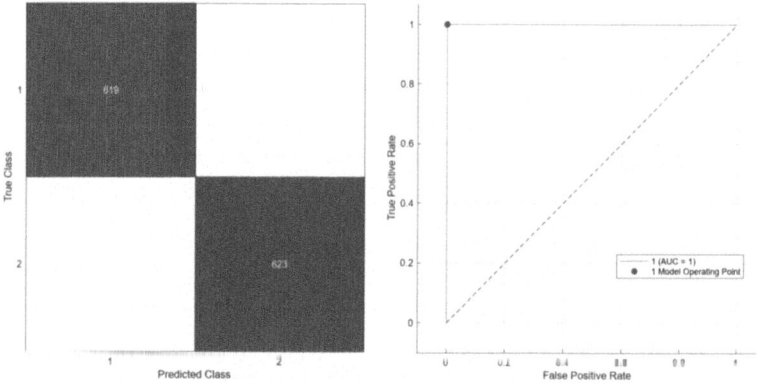

Fig. 6. 4-mer Wide ANN Confusion Matrix and 4-mer Wide ANN Roc Curve

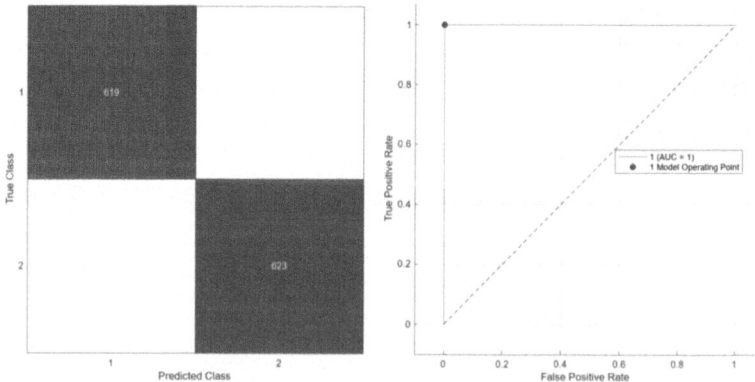

Fig. 7. 5-mer Fine Tree Confusion Matrix and 5-mer Fine Tree Roc Curve

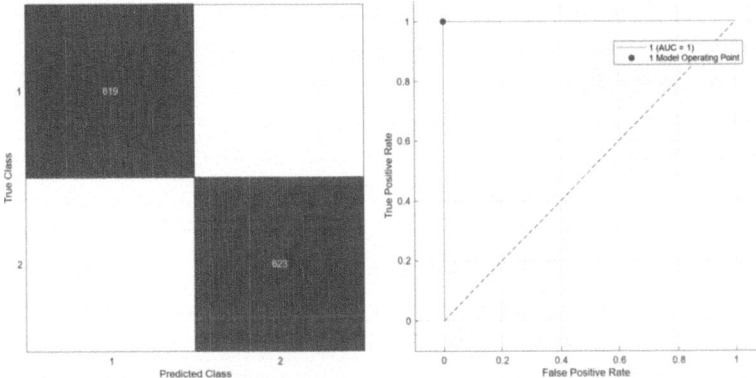

Fig. 8. 5-mer Linear SVM Confusion Matrix and 5-mer Linear SVM Roc Curve

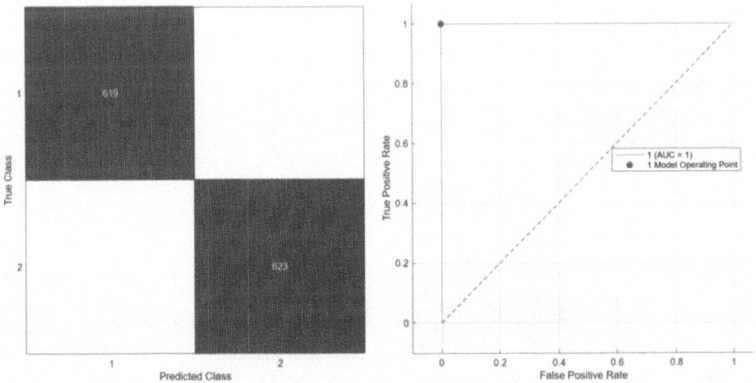

Fig. 9. 5-mer Fine KNN Confusion Matrix and 5-mer Fine KNN Roc Curve

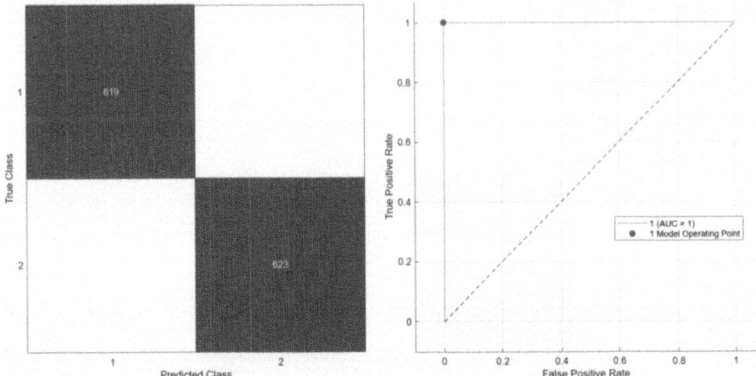

Fig. 10. 5-mer Wide ANN Confusion Matrix and 5-mer Wide ANN Roc Curve

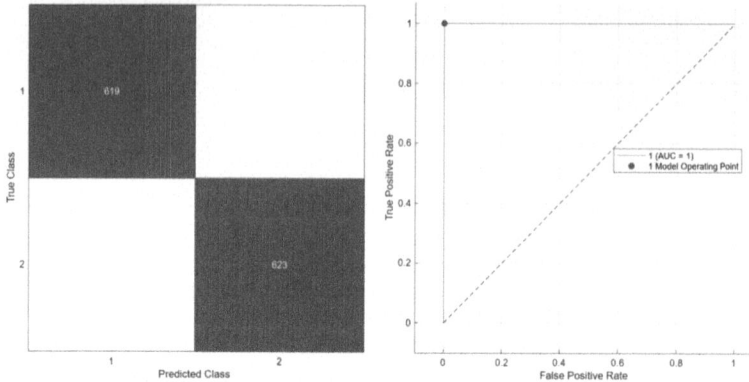

Fig. 11. 6-mer Fine Tree Confusion Matrix and 6-mer Fine Tree Roc Curve

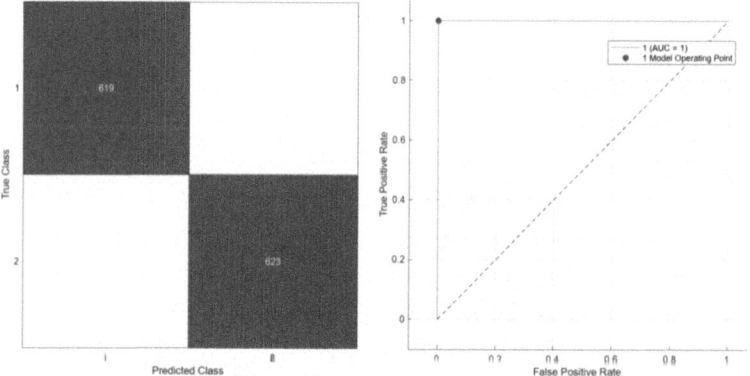

Fig. 12. 6-mer Linear SVM Confusion Matrix and 6-mer Linear SVM Roc Curve

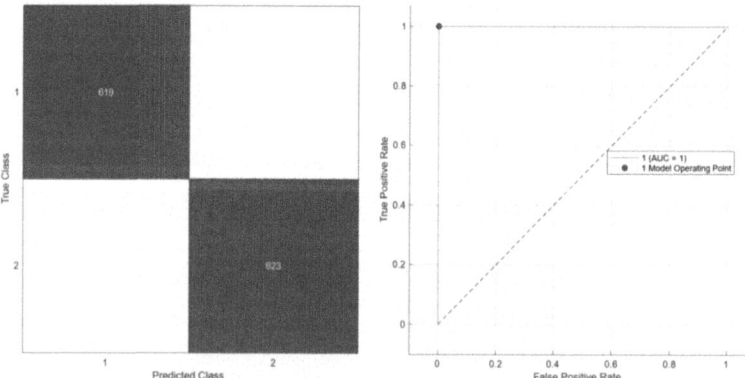

Fig. 13. 6-mer Fine KNN Confusion Matrix and 6-mer Fine KNN Roc Curve

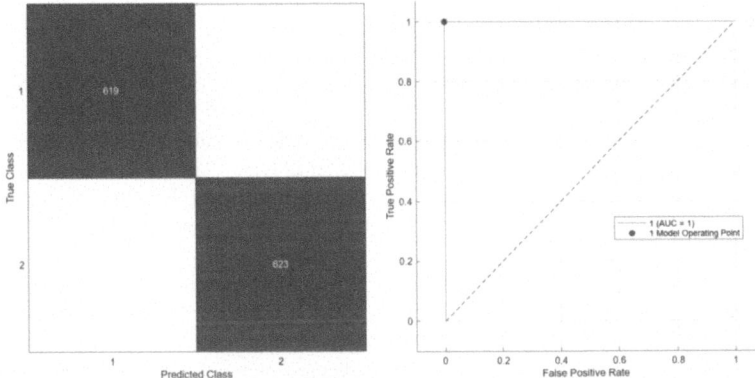

Fig. 14. 6-mer Wide ANN Confusion Matrix and 6-mer Wide ANN Roc Curve

4 Conclusion

The aim of the study is to distinguish between similar diseases with machine learning algorithms. For this purpose, the complete DNA genome sequences of Mpox and HP were used as a data set.

The k-mer method, which is an alignment-free approach, was applied to feature detection. And since virus genome lengths (number of base pairs) are quite different from each other, each k-mer number found is divided by the number of virus's own genome lengths (number of base pairs) when determining the feature. For this purpose, 4-mer, 5-mer and 6-mer were used. The results obtained are shown as accuracy, confusion matrix and Roc curve. 4-mer accuracy results are 99% and above, and 5-mer and 6-mer accuracy results are 98% and above.

In the study, it was shown that the DNA genomes of HPV and Mpox viruses were distinguished from each other by machine learning algorithms. So machine learning algorithms for use in virus classification are a useful bioinformatics method for different future studies.

References

1. World Health Organization Homepage: https://www.who.int/news-room/fact-sheets/detail/monkeypox. Last accessed 20 January 2024
2. Centers for Disease Control and Prevention: Intervention Services for People with or Exposed to Monkeypox. https://www.cdc.gov/poxvirus/monkeypox/health-departments/intervention-services.html. Last accessed 20 January 2024
3. Argüelles, M.E.Á., et al.: Detecting, Quantifying, and Isolating Monkeypox Virus in Suspected Cases, Spain. Emerging Infectious Diseases **29**(7), 1465 (2023)
4. Alp Avcı, G., Bozdayı, G.: İnsan papilloma virüsü. Kafkas J. Med. Sci. **3**(3), 136–144 (2013)
5. Di Gennaro, F., et al.: Human Monkeypox: a comprehensive narrative review and analysis of the public health implications. Microorganisms **10**, 1633 (2022)
6. Ren, J., et al.: Identifying viruses from metagenomic data using deep learning. Quantitative Biology **8**(1), 64–77 (2020)

7. Chen, Z., et al.: K-mer analyses reveal different evolutionary histories of alpha, beta, and gamma papillomaviruses. Int. J. Mol. Sci. **22**(17), 9657 (2021)

8. Asensio-Puig, L., Alemany, L., Pavon, M.A.: A Straightforward HPV16 lineage classification based on machine learning. Frontiers in Artificial Intelligence **5** (2022)

9. Tian, R., et al.: DeepHPV: a deep learning model to predict human papillomavirus integration sites. Briefings in Bioinformatics **22**(4), bbaa242 (2021)

10. Bzhalava, Z.: Machine Learning and Data-Parallel Processing for Viral Metagenomics, (Thesis for Doctoral Degree) Department of Laboratory Medicine Karolinska Institutet 58 (2020)

11. Raju, R.S., Nahid, A.A., Shuvo, P., Islam, R.: VirusTaxo: taxonomic classification of virus genome using multi-class hierarchical classification by k-mer enrichment. bioRxiv, 2021–04 (2021)

12. Alakus, T.B., Baykara, M.: Comparison of Monkeypox and wart DNA sequences with deep learning model. Appl. Sci. **12**(20), 10216 (2022)

13. Tipioğlu, H.P., Arslan, H.: Classification of Monkeypox and HPV with Supervised Machine Learning Algorithms using k-mer. SEMIT 182, 188 (2023)

14. Simmonds, P., et al.: Virus taxonomy in the age of metagenomics. Nature Reviews Microbiology **15**(3), 161–168 (2017)

15. Dougan, T.J., Quake, S.R.: Viral taxonomy derived from evolutionary genome relationships. PLoS ONE **14**(8), e0220440 (2019)

16. Remita, M.A., Halioui, A., Malick Diouara, A.A., Daigle, B., Kiani, G., Diallo, A.B.: A machine learning approach for viral genome classification. BMC Bioinformatics **18**, 1–11 (2017)

17. Akgül, G., Çelik, A.A., Aydin, Z.E., Öztürk, Z.K.: Hipotiroidi Hastalığı Teşhisinde Sınıflandırma Algoritmalarının Kullanımı. Bilişim Teknolojileri Dergisi **13**(3), 255–268 (2020)

18. Özbay Karakuş, M., Er, O.: A comparative study on prediction of survival event of heart failure patients using machine learning algorithms. Neural Comput. Appl. **34**(16), 13895–13908 (2022)

19. Javatpoint Homepage: https://www.javatpoint.com/machine-learning-decision-tree-classification-algorithm. Last accessed 20 January 2024

20. Veribilimiokulu Homepage: https://www.veribilimiokulu.com/yapay-sinir-agiartificial-neural-network-nedir. Last accessed 20 January 2024

21. Kulkarni, A., Chong, D., Batarseh, F.A.: Foundations of data imbalance and solutions for a data democracy. In: Data democracy, pp. 83–106. Academic Press (2020)

22. Evidentlyai Homepage: https://www.evidentlyai.com/classification-metrics/explain-roc-curve. Last accessed 20 January 2024

Cloud Computing Model for Handling Medical Big Data: A Mobile Hospital Pervasive Healthcare Application

Wided Oueslati[1]([✉]), Hela Limam[2], and Sonia Nasri[3]

[1] Ecole Supérieure de Commerce de Tunis Université de La Manouba, Laboratoire BESTMOD, Tunis, Tunisia
Wided.oueslati@esct.uma.tn

[2] Institut Supérieur d'Informatique, Université de Tunis El Manar, Laboratoire BESTMOD, Tunis, Tunisia

[3] Ecole Supérieure de Commerce de Tunis Université de La Manouba, Laboratoire LARODEC, Tunis, Tunisia

Abstract. The handling of big data by cloud computing is becoming a good practice in the management of information systems and can be considered one of the promising and emerging technologies in computing in many domains. Actually, big data is somewhat dependent on the cloud for the flexibility and extensions provided through virtual machines, which aids in making big data accessible. In fact, big data are huge and heterogeneous as they come from different sources and of different types i.e. structured, semi-structured, and unstructured so they require proper storage and high analysis capabilities. Cloud computing seems like a suitable repository to store such data in a decision support system. In fact, data stored in the cloud can be extracted and accessed easily since cloud technology allows access to big data and computer resources from anywhere and at any time that a network connection is available. Big data and cloud computing have opened many research possibilities in different sectors. Among them are those engaged in the field of healthcare. The healthcare sector generates each year a high volume of data to be analyzed to solve organizations' problems, predict epidemics, detect diseases and reduce healthcare costs. The aim of this paper is to shed the light on how cloud computing as an emerging paradigm is improving the healthcare sector, especially in rural zones. To this end, we propose a pervasive healthcare cloud solution to store medical big data collected by medical staff via mobile devices and to deliver that data to the medical cloud center for processing, analysis, and decision-making.

Keywords: cloud computing · Healthcare Pervasive systems · SAAS · Electronic Health Record · Emergency management · Mobile physician · smart connectivity · hospital mobility · Location-based services

1 Introduction

The absence of hospitals in rural regions and the increase in cancer disease make health-care in underdeveloped zone a serious issue. In fact, the limited access to patient health records during the decision-making process and the limited communication between the patient care team can be considered causes of medical diagnostic errors. Cloud computing technology can resolve such problems by providing the healthcare field with all technical requirements. In fact, it allows on-demand access to storage facilities, the support of big data related to radiology images or healthcare records, and the sharing of those medical big data among physicians. The cloud healthcare service can improve significantly clinical outcomes and increases patient satisfaction since data will be available at anytime and anywhere. In our study, the cloud will be useful in the medical domain as a service to store online medical big data collected by mobile hospitals that move in Tunisian rural zone to detect breast cancer disease.

The remainder of this paper is organized as follows: in Sect. 2, we will present the background section in which we define the big data concept, and present cloud computing models (services) and types. In Sect. 3, we will focus on the literature review related the healthcare management on the cloud. In Sect. 4, we will present the benefits of cloud computing in the healthcare domain. In Sect. 5, we will expose our case study concerned with detecting breast cancer disease in rural Tunisian zones. Section 6 proposes our pervasive healthcare system architecture that uses cloud computing technology. In Sect. 7, we will evaluate the performance of the proposed solution. In Sect. 8, we will summarize the work and propose some perspectives to be performed in future works.

2 Background

2.1 Big Data

Please note that the first paragraph of a section or subsection is not indented. The first paragraphs that follows a table, figure, equation etc. does not have an indent, either.

Subsequent paragraphs, however, are indented.

The key dimensions of big data are the "3Vs": volume, velocity, and variety ([1–3]). The volume describes the amount of data generated by companies or individuals. Big Data is usually associated with this feature. Businesses across all industries will need to find ways to manage the ever-increasing volume of data that is created daily.

The velocity describes the frequency at which data is generated, captured, and shared. Due to recent technological evolution, consumers, as well as businesses, are generating more data in much shorter times. At this speed level, companies can only take advantage of this data if they are collected and shared in real-time. It is precisely at this point that many analyses fail. They can only process the data in batches every few hours, at best. However, these data have no longer any value since the cycle of generation of new data has already begun.

The variety is the result of the explosion of data types from sources such as social media and mobile devices that creates an enormous diversity beyond traditional transactional data. The data is no longer in a net structure that is easy to use. New data types include geospatial data, hardware data points, geo-location data, connection data, machine-generated data, mobile data, physical data points, RFID data, flow data, social media data, web data, etc…

2.2 Computing Models

To well understand cloud computing in the healthcare domain, we have to understand the basics of cloud computing in general. For this reason, we present in the following the different models of cloud services. Those latter are available and can be used. In fact, a collaborative service will instead turn to the software as a service model (SAAS), while a specific application development can be implemented using the platform as a service model (PAAS). For the SAAS, the software solution is provided as on-demand service. This service is maintained and updated by a certified health professional that is committed to administering applications, servers and IT services from an asylum on a day-to-day basics.

The choice of the service provider is made according to the functional adequacy of its solution, the security and the confidentiality of the hosted data. Here below we define more each cloud computing model.

- Software As A Service (SAAS): The SAAS is a model where the provider is responsible of the infrastructure, the platform and the applications that are deployed in Cloud. The client can configure applications but cannot control the platform or the infrastructure. Hotmail Messaging Microsoft is a typical example of these client configurable applications.
- Platform As A Service (PAAS): In the PaaS model, the supplier is responsible for the infrastructure and the platform. The client has a quickly available execution environment. He can create, maintain, deploy and configure its applications in the cloud. Google Apps Engine (GAE) represents an example of Platform as a Service.
- Infrastructure As A Service (IAAS): The IAAS is a model where the supplier is responsible of the infrastructure. Users shall benefit from the storage capacities, servers, network capabilities, and other resources are at their disposal. The equipment's maintenance and hosting remain the responsibility of the supplier. The customer can use the available infrastructure to install any operating system and / or other applications.

As we go down the list of models from the SAAS to the IAAS: the subscriber has more control in an IAAS and PAAS than with a SAAS agreement. The cloud provider has less control in an IAAS model than with a SAAS agreement. Cloud computing delivery models are steadily becoming very adopted by organizations that are interested in the healthcare industry. The following schema of Fig. 1 summarizes the cloud computing models:

2.3 Deployment of Cloud Services: Types of Clouds

The National Institute for Standards and Technology has defined four types of Cloud; public cloud, private cloud, community cloud and hybrid cloud [4]. Different cloud types are presented in the following sections ([4, 5]):

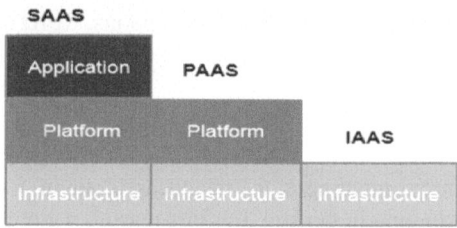

Fig. 1. Cloud computing model.

Public cloud: this type of cloud can be accessed by any subscriber with an internet connection. Services provided by a public cloud are owned and operated by a cloud provider. The user can access cloud services via the public internet without having an idea about where their data are hosted or executed. The information technology resources, and users' databases can be hosted in any provider data center and can move from one data center to another in order to maximize the public cloud provider's capabilities. According to Lui et al. [6], the most known providers to offer this service are Google, Amazon, and Microsoft.

- Private cloud: this type of cloud is established for a specific organization and limits access to just that organization. The cloud infrastructure is managed by the organization or by a third party. Some infrastructure can host multiple virtual private clouds belonging to different users and each user can access to its private cloud via its own network.
- Community cloud: this type of cloud is shared among two or more organizations that have similar cloud requirements. The infrastructure may be owned by the organizations or by a cloud service provider. Sharing resources available in the cloud allows those companies to make attractive savings and ensure more the data security.
- Hybrid cloud: this type of cloud is essentially a combination of at least two clouds, where the clouds included are a mixture of public, private or community.

3   Healthcare Management on the Cloud Overview

Sobhy et al. [7], have proposed a cloud computing system called "medcloud" to store EMRs. This system aims to provide users with essential services for building a cloud healthcare application. They used the Hadoop ecosystem for server implementation.

The most popular cloud platform is Amazon Elastic Compute Cloud [8]. This latter allows users to roll their applications on a virtual computing environment. Google App Engine is a cloud platform that permits users to manage web applications by providing them a web-based administration console and to run web applications writers using java and python language [9].

A solution to automate the process of patient's vital data collection using sensors that are joined to medical equipment is proposed [10]. The aim of this work is to make the information available in the cloud from anywhere to be processed by the medical staff. The scenario is that there are sensors nodes at the patient bedside to collect encode and transmit data through wireless to be stored to an exchange service. This latter receives collected data from sensors and load it into a cloud service. Medical staff can retrieve patients' data from the cloud service. A framework design to treat colorectal cancer images based on Microsoft technologies, image toolkits, and cloud computing concepts is presented [11].

A medical cloud system is also proposed [12]. That system collects patients 'data from legacy medical devices for storage and processing. The benefits of this cloud are providing users with real-time data and reducing possibilities of typing errors by eliminating manual collection work. An emergency medical cloud system for the Greek National Health Service to provide physicians with real-time access to patient data via any computing device from anywhere is proposed [13]. A cloud computing framework for colorectal cancer imaging research and analysis for clinical use is presented [11].

ActiveHealth management is a collaborative care solution using cloud computing architecture [14]. This medical solution allows easy access to electronic medical records, claims, and laboratory data by the medical staff. It permits too to show how patients are acting in response to treatments prescribed by doctors.

A fog-assisted model is presented [1]. It provides healthcare as a cloud service and efficiently manages the data of heart patients, which is coming from different IoT devices. Also, Kumar and Gandhi, [2] proposed an IoT framework that uses logistic regression to develop the prediction model for monitoring heart diseases at the early stage. The system consists of three blocks: data collection, data storage, and data analytics. Wearable sensor devices for the early detection of Alzheimer's disease using a dynamic time-warping algorithm is proposed [3]. Many researchers have focused on cloud computing in big data to improve healthcare services and resolve such problems by developing advanced algorithms to analyze big health data. The use of structured and unstructured data from hospitals along with regional data for building strong prediction models for the estimation of disease outbreaks is suggested [15]. Chen, et al. developed a mobile device-based application for predicting the time waiting for patients [16]. Saba et al. proposed a framework that incorporates a cloud-based decision support system for the detection and classification of malignant cells from breast cytology images [17].

4   Benefits of Cloud Computing in the Healthcare Information Management

Many experts envisage that cloud computing can improve health care services and promote health care research ([18, 19]). In fact, cloud computing can reduce electronic health record expenses (hardware, software, networking, licensing fees) and hence will encourage its adoption. In fact, many companies have invested in the healthcare cloud by extending their contributions to medical records services. This investment promises an explosion in health information online storage and retrieval. The healthcare cloud service allows to handle patient's electronic health records, patient's personal records, and patient's medical images and to keep track of all patient information that can help to speed up treatments and synergy between physicians who can collaborate through this healthcare cloud service and saves overall traveling time for physicians.

Cloud computing is making it possible for doctors to collaborate and to treat their patients better. In fact, the cloud speeds up the research process by storing and sharing big medical data in real-time and by accessing those data from everywhere and at any time. Healthcare analysts can use the cloud to pool and carefully analyze this data then return more meaningful insights to make the able decisions in the future.

In the healthcare field, cloud computing is considered a distant medical practice that uses information and communication technologies. The cloud allows for a patient at risk to have a preventive follow up or post-therapeutic follow up, to request a specialized opinion, and for medical professionals to take a therapeutic decision, to do a diagnostic, to prescribe drugs, to prescribe or to perform services or acts and to monitor the state of the patient.

Cloud computing has many interests for the patient whose follow-up is optimized and for practitioners who can benefit from all the necessary and the available information to perform their work in good conditions.

5   Case Study: The Pink October for of Breast Cancer Screening

The increase of cancer disease makes healthcare in the underdeveloped zones a serious problem [23, 24]. For that reason and on the occasion of the celebration of "Pink October", month of the fight against breast cancer and to encourage preventive health, several health caravans were dedicated to breast cancer screening [25, 26]. This initiative is led by the Tunisian Ministry of Health, the Faculty of Medicine of Tunis in partnership with hospitals in the southwest.

The services of the health caravans which cover the rural Tunisian regions, benefited several women. Indeed, more than 1400 clinical examinations for breast cancer have been carried out in these health caravans. Those free services of early detection of breast cancer as well as education and communication activities aimed at raising awareness of the importance of the early detection and prevention of breast cancer and the adoption of a healthy lifestyle.

A team of 10 doctors (8 general practitioners and 2 gynecologists) and paramedical staff provided around 1,400 free consultations for the benefit of patients in these rural regions.

The scenario is as follows: the rural woman is taken inside the health caravan, see Fig. 2.

The nurse identifies the patient information and does mammography for the woman then she communicates them to the pervasive healthcare cloud service via a mobile device such as Personal Digital Assistant. The generalist doctor will receive that information and depending on the status of the patient, he will send a message to the nurse who is in the mobile hospital to say that this patient has not to treat cancer or to a specialized doctor if the mammography shows that there is a breast cancer disease. In the second case, the specialized doctor sends a message to the nurse and suggests taking the patient to the nearest appropriate specialized hospital in order to be checked by a doctor and do other clinic exams. The nurse in the health caravan has to update the status of the patient in the patient file that is stored in the healthcare cloud system and find the nearest hospital. When the patient is taken to the nearest hospital, other exams like the biopsy will be done. Results of those exams and other data related to patients will be stored in a cloud healthcare system and then can be exploited to support healthcare analysis.

Fig. 2. Tunisian health caravan for breast cancer screening.

6 A Pervasive Healthcare System on the Cloud

After much research and studies, we find that the lack of resources presents a real threat to the patients' lives. Some problems arise: How to access certain medical establishments in a minimum time? Where are the required and available material and human resources for the ongoing emergency? Where is the relevant information about the patient? How to interoperate doctors that are dispersed geographically? How to make the right decision at the right time?

Distant medical services accessible from any point of the planet in seconds are the solution to these problems. That is why, we need a localization service that is able to locate the medical establishments according to the positions of physicians and their expressed preferences, a booking service that is able to book medical resources and medical staff, a patient electronic health record service that is able to provide information about the patient's medical records, medical analyze service that is able to fill in information related to existing analyzes or to edit a new analysis and decision support service that is able to provide decisions, statistics, and reports. These services are referred to as Software as a Service, an essential component of cloud computing, and are implemented as functionalities of the proposed pervasive healthcare system on the cloud.

Our proposed solution introduces a novel approach to healthcare data management in rural zones, leveraging cloud computing technologies. The innovation lies in our user-centric design, which seamlessly integrates a pervasive healthcare system with cloud services to facilitate real-time data collection, analysis, and decision-making.

Before detailing the different SAAS of the proposed pervasive healthcare system on the cloud, we summarize the tasks of the system users in the following Table 1.

A description of the different cloud computing pervasive healthcare services is presented in the following subsections with screenshots of some proposed services.

Table 1. Pervasive healthcare system users 'tasks.

Pervasive healthcare system user	Medical staff tasks
	-Identify the patient information - Do a mammography for the woman - Communicates mammograph to the healthcare cloud service via a mobile device such as PDA - Update the status of the patient in the patient file -Find the nearest hospital for the patient - Book an appointment for the patient
	-Check patient's information - Send a message to the nurse if the patient is healthy according to the mammogram (no breast cancer disease detected) - Send a message to a specialized doctor if there is a possibility that the patient has a breast cancer
	-Check patient's information - Send a message to the nurse to inform the patient that she's affected by breast cancer - ask the nurse to book a medical resource for the patient that has the breast cancer

6.1 Location as a Service

Different questions can be sent to the localization as a service such as: give me the closest hospitals closest to my current position. The answer to this query is a set of points of interest that must be calculated by the localization as a service and displayed on the doctor's mobile device screen via a dedicated network.

Many approaches can be used as SaaS to locate medical establishments, especially those that have been proposed by the KNNs. Hastie and Tibshirani. Are intended form dimension spaces that can be applied to road networks [20].

Khayati and Akaichi. Propose Delaunay TRiangulation (DTR)approach allows the determination of nearest neighbors. It allows finding for a mobile located on the road network the nearest neighbors [21]. The aim is to find the K nearest neighbors (KNNs) by presenting various techniques for KNNs devoted to the Euclidean space and those intended for road networks. In the DTR approach, Delaunay's triangulation is used to represent the networks and effectively evaluate queries such as: "give me the three hospitals closest to my current position". The principle is to divide the network to find the first nearest neighbor in a triangle, by applying a first search algorithm 1NN. Once this 1NN has been found, the algorithm makes it possible to delimit the influence region (IR1) to search by contiguity in the vicinity of the second nearest point. The influence algorithm will extend the influence region (IR1) to a second influence region (IR2) to ensure a valid result. Once the points of interest are marked, they are returned to the medical staff's mobile device such as PDA and will be displayed. Medical establishments can then be selected and booked according to their availability.

When the nurse receives the decision of the specialist indicating that the patient is sick, she will find the nearest hospital for the patient and book an appointment for her to treat breast cancer thanks to the localization as a service of our pervasive healthcare system. The following figure represents the result of this service (Fig. 3).

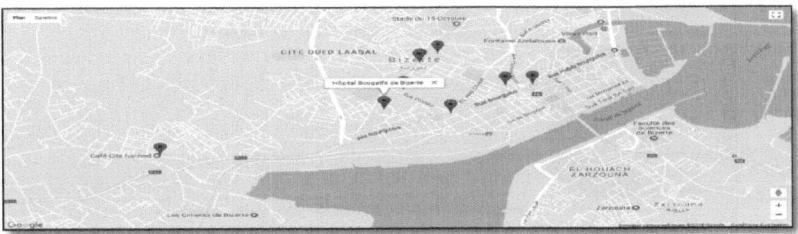

Fig. 3. Geolocation as a service.

6.2   Booking Medical Resource as a Service

The booking as a service allows keeping aside the necessary medical resources such as surgery room and medical equipment, medical staff (for example, specialized nurses and surgical specialists, etc.) related to the selected medical establishment by the localization as a service.

For example, the nurse books an appointment for the patient, she adds her name, phone number, national identifier, the date of reservation and the hospital as shown in the figure.

6.3   Patient Electronic Health Record as a Service

Obviously, the physician needs to find information about his patient in order to analyze and follow closely the evolution of her health state, history of previous treatments, pathologies and other information. The patient electronic health record as a service makes this possible for doctors from anywhere and at any time.

As an example, the generalist doctor will check the patient mammography (stored in the patient electronic health record) then according to that he will change the patient status:

Sick. According to the mammography the doctor decide that the patient is sick and will pass this patient to a specialist doctor.

Not Clear. The doctor can't decide if the patient is sick or not so he will pass the patient information and the mammography to a specialist doctor.

Healthy. According to the mammography the doctor decides that the patient is healthy (Fig. 4).

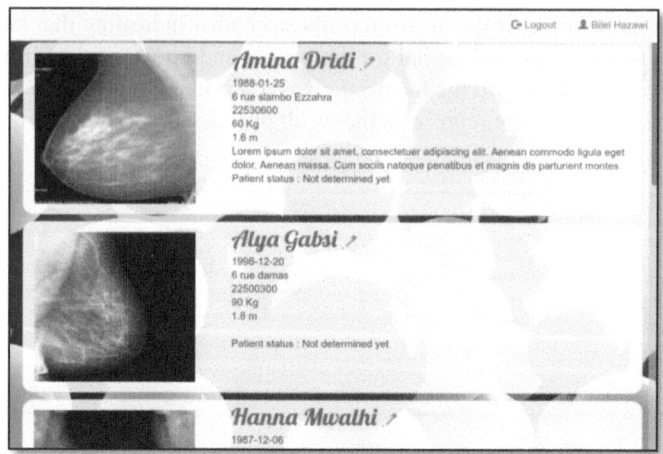

Fig. 4. Electronic health record as a service.

6.4 Medical Analysis as a Service

Doctors have to exchange more information about the patient such as her current or previous health state for analysis and prevention purposes. The stored data will be analyzed by specialized doctors. The analysis reports will be stored in the medical analysis as a service and can serve for scientific research purposes.

The medical analysis as a service allows doctors to interpret online medical images such as mammography and send the report to another specialist to have their diagnostics and point of view.

All sensitive medical data, including patient health records and diagnostic images, are encrypted using encryption algorithms to ensure that data is secure during transmission and storage. To restrict data access only to authorized healthcare professionals, robust access control is established using strong authentication methods, such as multi-factor authentication, to verify the identity of users accessing the system.

To ensure medical data continuous availability, a redundancy measures are proposed for the healthcare services in the event of system failures. In addition, regular backups of medical data are conducted to prevent data loss and facilitate timely recovery.

6.5 Decision Support as a Service

The decision support as a service allows specialists to take decisions online and from everywhere about their patients like transferring them to the nearest hospital or doing other biological analyses or giving them prescriptions, etc. according to the result of diagnostics that are stored in the medical analysis as a service.

If the specialist doctor indicates that the patient is affected by breast cancer so the patient will appear in the system interface in red and in green if she is safe as shown in Fig. 5.

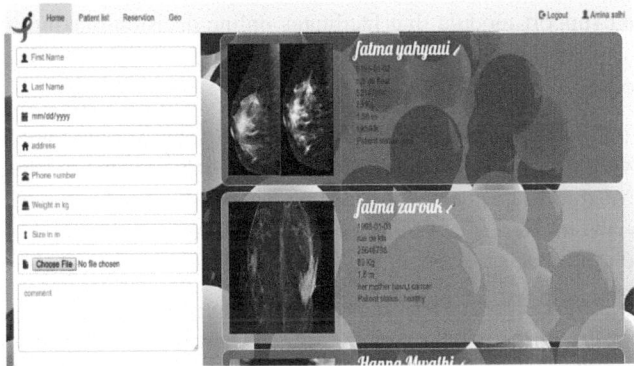

Fig. 5. Medical analysis as a service.

6.6 The Architecture of the Pervasive Healthcare System on the Cloud

We expect that cloud computing technology is the core of healthcare innovation. In fact, it offers new types of services and skillfulness for medical staff and patients. In this regard, we developed a pervasive healthcare solution on the cloud for a mobile hospital to detect the breast cancer disease in rural Tunisian zones. The proposed system supports mobile telemedicine, location-based services, patient monitoring and access to healthcare data. In fact, the architecture is composed of a set of cloud services that communicate directly with users (nurses and doctors) and allows the localization of medical establishments, the booking of medical establishments, the storage of electronic records healthcare (update and retrieval), the doctor diagnosis (analysis) and the doctor decision making.

Our proposed solution leverages a cloud-based pervasive healthcare system, utilizing a multi-tiered architecture for efficient data processing and storage. The components of our architecture are as follows:

- The Mobile Health Caravan that is equipped with mobile devices for data collection, including a mammography and patient information and communicates seamlessly with the cloud-based infrastructure.
- The cloud infrastructure that comprises a scalable and secure cloud environment for data storage, processing, and analysis. It utilizes virtualization technologies to optimize resource allocation.
- The geolocation module that determines the locations of medical establishments and enables healthcare professionals to identify and navigate to the nearest hospitals.
- The booking Service that facilitates the reservation of medical resources and staff based on the identified medical establishments and ensures efficient allocation of resources for patient appointments.
- The Electronic Health Record module that manages and updates patient electronic health records securely in the cloud and provides healthcare professionals with real-time access to patient history and mammography data.
- The medical analysis module that enables the interpretation of medical images, such as mammography and supports the storage of analysis reports for further research.

- The decision support module that facilitates online decision-making by specialists regarding patient diagnoses and treatment plans and it integrates with the medical analysis module to enhance the diagnostic process.

The main purpose of the proposed pervasive healthcare is to provide medical staff and patients with a mobile user interface to determine the nearest hospital, to store, manage, retrieve, query and analyze medical patient health record and medical contents such as biopsy and medical images via a ubiquitous access.

Used cloud models are:

- Software as a Service (SAAS) for healthcare applications, providing on-demand access to software solutions and enables healthcare professionals to interact with applications without
- managing the underlying infrastructure.
- Platform as a Service (PAAS) used for application development, deployment, and maintenance. Besides it streamlines the development process for healthcare specific functionalities.
- Infrastructure as a Service (IAAS) is used for scalable infrastructure resources, including servers and storage. In addition, it offers flexibility and customization of the cloud environment to meet healthcare demands.

The Cloud Deployment model is Hybrid Cloud, since it adopts a hybrid cloud approach for a combination of public and private cloud resources. Besides it ensures a balance between scalability and security in healthcare data management.

Services described in the above sections are running on Google's Android operating system. The communication is performed through web services REST API because it is supported by Android. Medical files and imaging require high capacity of storage and computing. For this reason, they are stored in the cloud especially into a database supported by Android which is the SQLite.

The following figure illustrates our pervasive healthcare system architecture on the cloud (Fig. 6).

The following flowchart illustrates the pervasive healthcare system data flow (Fig. 7).

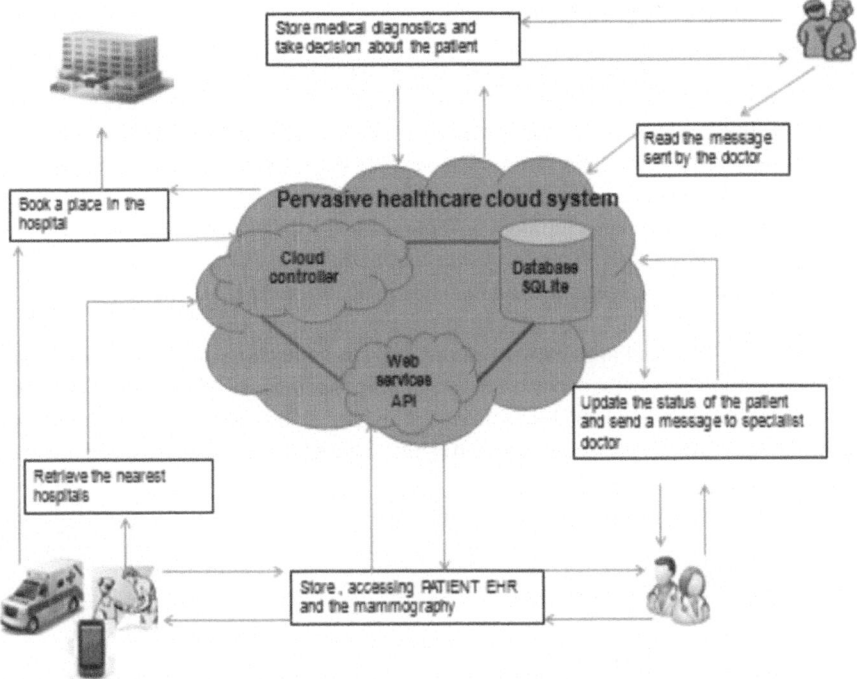

Fig. 6. Pervasive healthcare cloud system architecture.

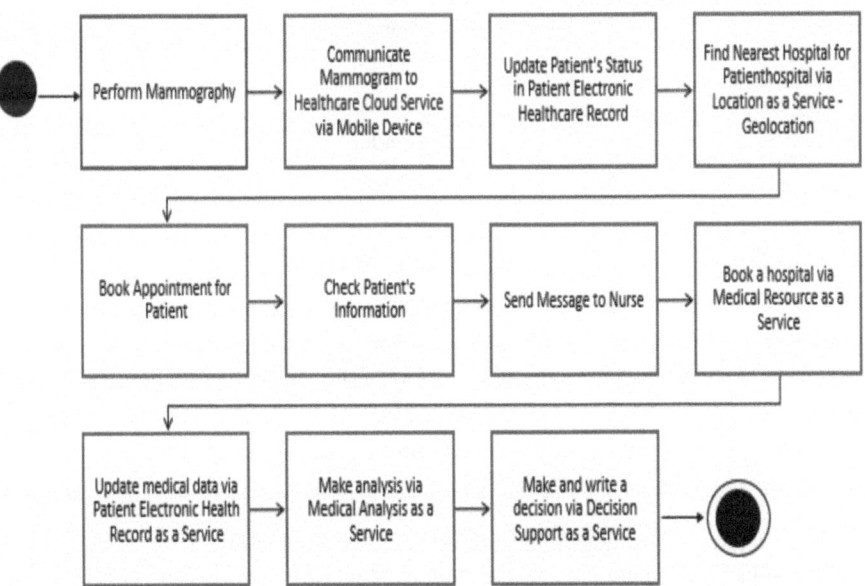

Fig. 7. The pervasive healthcare system based on the cloud data flow flowchart.

7 Performance Evaluation

Our case study is a real-world case study that is the breast cancer screening campaign in Tunisian rural zones known as the "Pink October" initiative. We collaborate with Tunisian healthcare institutions, hospitals, and medical professionals to implement and test the solution in diverse healthcare settings. We extend the testing to multiple sites to capture variations in healthcare practices and infrastructure.

We adopt the iterative development; in fact, we established a continuous improvement cycle based on feedback from real-world testing and we regularly update and refine the solution based on users' feedbacks and emerging healthcare needs.

By incorporating these real-world testing, we aim to provide tangible evidence of the efficacy and practical applicability of our proposed pervasive healthcare solution.

For evaluation purposes, experiments are conducted through an evaluation grid composed of questions related to three metrics which are: Interactivity, consistency, and graphic design. The selected metrics aim to evaluate the ergonomic and functional aspects of the proposed cloud solution.

The grid was addressed to a sample of the target population composed of 10 doctors and 10 patients (Table 2). The performance is tracked and measured according to the proposed metrics.

Table 2. Description of the population sample.

Doctor's profile		Patient's profile	
Characteristics	Number	Characteristics	Number
Age		**Age**	
[30–45]	3	[30 45]	1
45 or above	7	45 or above	9
Gender		**Gender**	
Female	5	Female	10
Male	5	Male	0
Service period		**Service period**	
[1:5]	6	below college	4
5 or above	4	University	6
Experience of using smart devices		**Experience of using smart devices**	
Yes	2	Yes	5
No	8	No	5

The structure and the questions of the grid are detailed in Fig. 8.

We conduct a comparative analysis with existing healthcare systems [22] to showcase the advantages and improvements brought by our proposed solution. We evaluate key metrics such as interactivity, consistency and readability. By incorporating this comparative analysis, we aim to provide a comprehensive evaluation of our proposed cloud

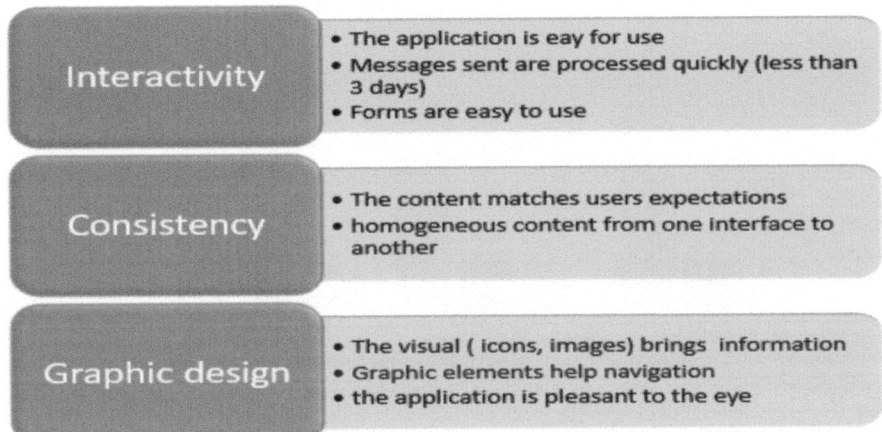

Fig. 8. The structure of the evaluation grid

computing model in relation to existing solutions in the healthcare domain. This addition will contribute to a more thorough understanding of the model's strengths.

The proposed model is scalable since it handles diverse and voluminous nature of medical big data. Besides, it is characterized by the accessibility since it enables seamless access to medical data from any location with an internet connection. Moreover, the proposed model is flexible by the fact that it is flexible in adapting to different types of medical data, including structured, semi-structured, and unstructured data.

We collaborated closely with healthcare professionals, including clinicians and medical practitioners. That allowed us to gather insights and feedback from healthcare professionals throughout the development and testing phases of the proposed solution. In fact, we established a mechanism for continuous feedback from healthcare professionals during the solution's development and implementation phases and we adapted the solution based on the evolving needs and feedback received from interdisciplinary collaborators.

The summary of results is presented in Fig. 9. From the evaluation metrics, we conclude that the results obtained prove the effectiveness of the method and compared to the approach of [22] we used 3 accurate metrics to perform the evaluation instead of 2 general criteria used by authors and we produced better values.

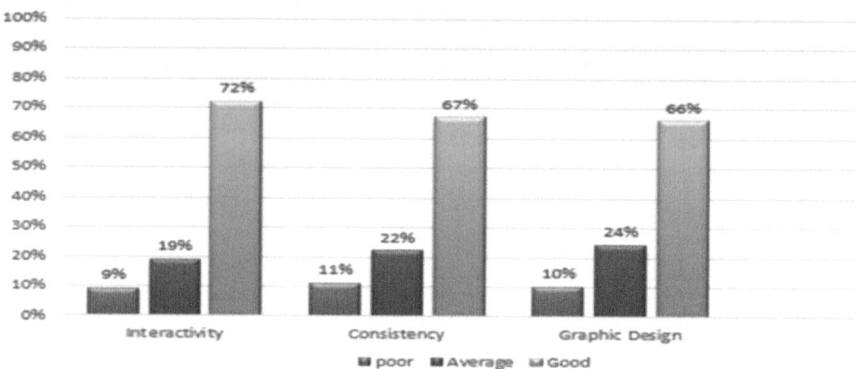

Fig. 9. Cloud computing pervasive healthcare system evaluation according to chosen metric

8   Conclusion and Future Works

In the healthcare field, cloud computing is considered a distant medical practice that uses information and communication technology to enhance the healthcare ecosystem. In this context, we proposed a pervasive healthcare system based on the cloud. The main purpose of the system is to provide seamless communication flow between medical staff in the health caravan and other doctors and to offer more flexibility, more efficiency in IT services and resources. It provides latent opportunities for improving electronic health records espousal and health care services. The main functionality of the proposed solution is to furnish medical teams with an ergonomic user interface to manage healthcare information and analyze them to make decisions that can solve many rural women's lives. The proposed pervasive healthcare system on the cloud will push down the boundaries for modernization and innovation of healthcare applications since it allows rapid remote access to patients' healthcare records, scalability, portability, easy sharing of information, large storage of medical big data, medical diagnosis and medical decision making. Nonetheless, there are still many challenges to promoting cloud computing because of data security and legal issue. Although cloud computing has many advantages, there are still many actual problems that need to be solved. Those concerns will be treated in future works.

References

1. Gill, S.S., Arya, R.C., Wander, G.S., Buyya, R.: Fog-based smart healthcare as a big data and cloud service for heart patients using IoT. In: International Conference on Intelligent Data Communication Technologies and Internet of Things, ICICI 2018, vol. 26, pp. 1376–1383. Coimbatore, India (2019). https://doi.org/10.1007/978-3-030-03146-6_161
2. Kumar, P., Gandhi, U.:A novel three-tier internet of things architecture with machine learning algorithm for early detection of heart diseases. Computers & Electrical Engineering **65**, 222–235 (2018). ISSN 0045-7906, https://doi.org/10.1016/j.compeleceng.2017.09.001
3. Varatharajan, R., Manogaran, G., Priyan, M.K., et al.: Wearable sensor devices for early detection of Alzheimer disease using dynamic time warping algorithm. Cluster Comp. **21**, 681–690 (2018). https://doi.org/10.1007/s10586-017-0977-2

4. Mell, P., Grance, T.: Draft nist working definition of cloud computing. Referenced on June. 3rd (2009)
5. Zeller, M., et al.: Open standards and cloud computing: KDD-2009 panel report in KDD, pp. 11–18. France, Paris (2009)
6. Liu, J., et al.: NIST Cloud Computing Reference Architecture, vol. 500, p. 292. NIST Special Publication (2011)
7. Sobhy. D., El-Sonbaty, Y., Abou Elnasr, M.: MedCloud: Healthcare cloud computing system. In: 2012 International Conference for Internet Technology and Secured Transactions, pp. 161–166 (2012)
8. Mandl, K.D., Szolovits, P., Kohane, I.S.: Public standards and patients' control: how to keep electronic medical records accessible but private. BMJ **322**(7281), 283 (2001)
9. Zeng Shu-Qing, J.B.: The improvement of paas platform. 1st international conference on networking and distributed computing, pp. 156–159 (2010)
10. Carlos, O.F., Becker, L.w.: A cloud computing solution for patient's data collection in healthcare institutions. In: 2010 Second International Conference on eHealth, Telemedicine, and Social Medicine. Netherlands Antilles
11. Avila-Garcia, M.S., Trefethen, A.E., Brady, M., Gleeson, F., Goodman, D.: Lowering the barriers to cancer imaging. In: eScience 2008: IEEE 4th International Conference on eScience. New York, NY: IEEE; 2008 Presented at: The 4th IEEE International Conference on eScience; December 8–12, pp. 63–70. Indiana, USA (2008)
12. Rolim, C.O., et al.: A cloud computing solution for patient's data collection in health care institutions. In: 2010 Feb 10 Presented at: In: Proceedings of the 2nd International Conference on eHealth, Telemedicine, and Social Medicine; February 10–16. New York, NY (2010)
13. Koufi, V., Malamateniou, F., Vassilacopoulos, G.: Ubiquitous access to cloud emergency medical services. In: Proceedings of the 2010 10th IEEE International Conference on Information Technology and Applications in Biomedicine (ITAB). New York, NY: IEEE; 2010 Presented at: The 10th IEEE International Conference on Information Technology and Applications in Biomedicine (ITAB); November 3–5. Corfu, Greece (2010)
14. Campbell, S.: IBM and ActiveHealth management collaborate to transform healthcare in Puerto Rico. EMR Daily News
15. Chen, Y., Crespi, N., Ortiz, A.M., Shu, L.: Reality mining: a prediction algorithm for disease dynamics based on mobile big data. Information Sciences **379**, 82–93 (2017). ISSN 0020-0255, https://doi.org/10.1016/j.ins.2016.07.075
16. Chen, J., Li, K., Tang, Z., Bilal, K., Li, K.: A parallel patient treatment time prediction algorithm and its applications in hospital queuing-recommendation in a big data environment. In: IEEE Access, vol. 4, pp. 1767–1783 (2016). https://doi.org/10.1109/ACCESS.2016.2558199
17. Saba, T., Khan, S.U., Islam, N., et al.: Cloud-based decision support system for the detection and classification of malignant cells in breast cancer using breast cytology images. Microscopy Res. Technics. **82**, 775–785 (2019). https://doi.org/10.1002/jemt.23222
18. Chatman, C.: How cloud computing is changing the face of health care information technology. J. Health Care Compliance **12**(3), 37–70 (2010)
19. Rosenthal, A., Mork, P., Li, M.H., Stanford, J., Koester, D., Reynolds, P.: Cloud computing: a new business paradigm for biomedical information sharing. J. Biomed. Inform. **43**(2), 342–353 (2010)
20. Hastie, T., Tibshirani, R.: Discriminant adaptive nearest neighbor classification. IEEE Trans. Pattern Analy. Mach. Intell. (PAMI) **18**, 607–616 (1996)
21. Khayati, M., Jalel, A.: Incremental approach for Continuous k-Nearest Neighbours queries on road. IJIIDS **2**(2), 203–221 (2008)

22. Hanen, J., Kechaou, Z., Ayed, M.B.: An enhanced healthcare system in mobile cloud computing environment. Vietnam J. Comput. Sci. **3**, 267–277 (2016). https://doi.org/10.1007/s40 595-016-0076-y
23. Oueslati, W., Akaichi, J.: Trajectory data warehouse modeling based on a Trajectory UML profile: Medical example. International Work-Conference on Bioinformatics and Biomedical Engineering (2014)
24. Oueslati, W., Akaichi, J.: A trajectory UML profile for modeling trajectory data: a mobile hospital use case (2011). arXiv preprint arXiv:1102.4429
25. Oueslati, W., Hamdi, H., Akaichi, J.: A mobile hospital trajectory data warehouse modeling and querying to detect the breast cancer disease. In: Proceedings of the International Conference on Intelligent Information Processing, Security and Advanced Communication, p. 93. ACM (2015)
26. Oueslati, W., Akaichi, J.: A framework for the trajectory data warehouse conceptual modeling support: a mobile hospital trajectory case study, Netw. Model. Anal. Health Inf. Bioinform. **4**(1) 11 (2015). https://doi.org/10.1007/s13721-015-0083-4

Harnessing Advanced AI Techniques: An In-Depth Analysis of Machine Learning Models for Improved Diabetes Prediction

Ihtisham Ul Haq[1]([⊠]), Muhammad Anas[2], Hamza Ahmad Khan[3], and Zubair Ahmad Khan[3]

[1] Department of Information and Communication Technologies, University of Calabria, Arcavacata, Italy
Ihtisham.haq@dimes.unical.it

[2] Department of Electrical Engineering, University of Gujrat, Hafiz Hayat Campus Gujrat, Gujrat, Pakistan

[3] Department of Mechatronics Engineering, University of Engineering and Technology Peshawar, Peshawar, Pakistan

Abstract. By 2023, diabetes will have become a major public health problem in Pakistan, affecting an estimated 26.3% of the adult population. The rising death rate is attributable in part to diabetes-related complications, highlighting the critical need for cutting-edge, trustworthy diabetes prediction systems that enable early detection and treatment. Since machine learning (ML) models have the potential to improve the accuracy of diabetes forecasts, this study is focused on exploiting these methods of artificial intelligence (AI) for better predictions. As such, the importance of this research to the field of medical informatics cannot be overstated. A wide range of ML and deep learning models, such as Support Vector Machine (SVM), K-Nearest Neighbors (KNN), Logistic Regression, Naive Bayes, Random Forests, Decision Trees, and a novel ensemble learning approach, were tested and compared. The models were evaluated on a conventional diabetes dataset. Our min-max normalization and other data pre-processing procedures greatly improved model accuracy. At first, the models were only about 70% accurate. However, after the pre-processing phase, we saw a dramatic improvement in performance. In particular, Random Forests reached 96.49 percent accuracy, while both Decision Trees and KNN models hit 96.33 percent. To improve upon the prediction accuracy of the separate models, we used a novel ensemble learning mechanism. This method demonstrates the efficacy of hybrid techniques in AI-driven healthcare solutions by utilizing the strengths of different ML models to create a single optimal model. Our research establishes a new paradigm for the field of illness prediction and has far-reaching consequences for diabetes care and early intervention techniques. We anticipate that our findings will encourage more investigation into the utility of cutting-edge AI techniques for improved disease prediction, ultimately leading to a more secure and manageable future.

Keywords: Diabetes · Ensemble learning · Medical Informatics · Machine learning · Hybrid models

A. Mirzazadeh et al. (Eds.): SEMIT 2023, CCIS 2198, pp. 141–158, 2024.
https://doi.org/10.1007/978-3-031-72284-4_9

1 Introduction

Diabetes mellitus, more commonly referred to as diabetes, is a persistent metabolic illness that is defined by persistent hyperglycemia owing to insulin deficit, insulin resistance, or both. Diabetes is characterized by persistent hyperglycemia due to insulin deficiency, insulin resistance, or both. It is a primary source of illness and mortality around the world, contributing to conditions such as heart disease, kidney failure, blindness, and the amputation of lower limbs. The International Diabetes Federation (IDF) estimates that roughly 26.3% of the adult population in Pakistan is affected by diabetes, highlighting the significant threat to public health posed by this condition [1].

Artificial intelligence (AI) has quickly emerged as a game-changing technology that is transforming a wide range of industries, including the healthcare industry. The ability of artificial intelligence and its subfields, machine learning (ML) and deep learning (DL), to sift through large amounts of data, recognize patterns, and come to conclusions has made it an important tool in the diagnosis, treatment, and management of disease [2]. The application of AI to the task of early disease diagnosis, in particular for persistent conditions such as diabetes, carries with it the potential to revolutionize healthcare delivery and results.

The purpose of this investigation, which is titled "Harnessing Advanced AI Techniques: An In-Depth Analysis of Machine Learning Models for Improved Diabetes Prediction," is to make a contribution to the rapidly expanding field of AI-driven healthcare solutions. We test a wide variety of machine learning models, including Support Vector Machine (SVM), K-Nearest Neighbors (KNN), Logistic Regression, Naive Bayes, Random Forests, Decision Trees, and an innovative method to ensemble learning, to determine how well they can predict diabetes.

Our research extends beyond the use of individual models by investigating methods of ensemble learning. These methods integrate the results of numerous models to provide more accurate predictions. These methods have demonstrated potential in a variety of contexts by capitalizing on the features that distinguish individual models to achieve im-proved prediction accuracy [3]. According to the findings of our investigation, which followed a methodical and stringent evaluation procedure, these ensemble strategies frequently surpass individual models in terms of their accuracy of prediction.

Techniques for data pre-processing, such as normalization, outlier detection, and the management of missing value data, also play an important part in the study that we are conducting. These strategies, despite the fact that they are frequently ignored, have the potential to greatly increase model performance. Following the implementation of these data pre-processing processes, we noticed a discernible rise in the accuracy of our ML models [4].

The contents of the paper are as follows: In the following section, we will evaluate the relevant work, with a focus on earlier research that utilized ML and DL methods for diabetes prediction. The methodology is discussed in further depth in Sect. 3, which includes a comprehensive breakdown of the ML models that were implemented as well as the ensemble learning strategy. In Sect. 4, we will report the findings of our tests, with a particular emphasis on the predictive power of each model and the influence of the pre-processing of the data. The final section of the paper, Sect. 5, provides a summary of our findings, discusses the consequences of those findings, and outlines potential future re-search topics.

2 Literature Review

A great number of studies have focused on the application of AI methods for diabetes prediction, and each of these studies has their own unique contributions and limitations. Here, we discuss several relevant works in this domain:

Artificial neural networks (ANNs) were used in the method that Huang et al. [5] presented as their early diagnostic system for type 2 diabetes. They conducted their study using a dataset consisting of around 400 different patients. In spite of the fact that it made important contributions, the study was constrained by a limited number of participants, which may make it difficult to generalize the findings. In addition, they primarily concentrated on ANNs, completely ignoring the possibilities offered by other ML models.

The Pima Indians Diabetes Dataset (PIDD) was the subject of the research carried out by Yu et al. [6], in which a wide range of machine learning methods were utilized. In this study, decision trees, random forests, and support vector machines were utilized. The Random Forests model achieved the highest level of accuracy, which was 79.95%. Although the work they accomplished is impressive, it did not take into account pre-processing methods, which are methods that have the potential to increase model performance.

Another important contribution was made by Perveen et al. [7] who conducted a comparison study of many ML algorithms for the purpose of diabetes prediction. A number of different algorithms, such as Naive Bayes, Decision Trees, Random Forests, and K-Nearest Neighbors, were utilized. According to the findings of the research, Random Forests is the model that performs the best, with an accuracy of 81.03%. The research, however, did not investigate the application of ensemble learning methods, which are capable of increasing accuracy to an even greater degree.

In a manner analogous to this, Woldaregay et al. [8] concentrated their attention on data-driven modeling strategies for the prediction of diabetes utilizing electronic health records. They found that ensemble models performed better than individual models. However, because the research was limited to data from electronic health records, it is possible that additional potentially significant characteristics for diabetes prediction were overlooked.

In the last study, D'hoore et al. [9] used a logistic regression model to forecast the beginning of diabetes in a Belgian sample. Their work does contribute to a better knowledge of risk variables; nevertheless, the use of a single model that is very straightforward may restrict the predictive usefulness of the research.

A recent study published in 2020 and titled "Predicting Diabetes using an Intelligent System with Probabilistic Neural Network" made significant progress in this area by providing an Intelligent System for the prediction of diabetes that makes use of a Probabilistic Neural Network [10]. The research was restricted by the quality and amount of the data that was used, despite the fact that the accuracy rate that was attained was an astounding 95.4%. In addition, the Probabilistic Neural Network model that was used could not be applicable for all different kinds of datasets, which indicates that there is a want for additional research into the adaptability of the model.

An additional important piece of research published in 2019 "Comparative Study of Machine Learning Algorithms along with Deep Learning for Diabetes Diagnosis" [11] carried out a study that compared several machine learning algorithms for the purpose of diabetes forecasting. The research highlighted the promise of machine learning algorithms in the diagnosis of diabetes; however, the data also revealed that the selection of the algorithm has a significant impact on the accuracy of the prediction. This demonstrates the importance of making a thoughtful choice in the machine learning algorithms to use and fine-tuning those algorithms to achieve optimal performance. In light of these studies, the purpose of our research is to overcome some of the limitations that these studies have by utilizing an ensemble learning strategy, a wider variety of machine learning models, and more robust data pre-processing techniques.

2.1 Prediction of Diabetes Using Machine Learning

Algorithms Machine learning (ML) has demonstrated tremendous potential in the field of medical diagnostics, including prediction of diabetes. In order to accomplish this goal, numerous machines learning techniques, including Logistic Regression, Support Vector Machines, Random Forest, and Decision Trees, have seen widespread application. Random Forest came out on top in terms of accuracy in a notable study [1] that examined different machine learning algorithms using a public diabetes dataset. The researchers concluded that Random Forest performed the best overall. Nevertheless, every one of these models has both positive and negative aspects. For example, decision trees are simple to understand but there is a possibility that they overfit the data, whereas support vector machines are effective in high-dimensional fields but can be computationally demanding.

2.2 Prediction of Diabetes Using Deep Learning Algorithms

Deep learning (DL) algorithms have also been used for diabetes prediction because of their ability to model complex non-linear relationships and automatically build feature representations from raw data. This is one of the reasons why these algorithms have become so popular. For the purpose of diabetes prediction, these models, which include Convolutional Neural Networks (CNNs) and Recurrent Neural Networks (RNNs), have been utilized to assess both organized and unstructured medical data. A deep learning model fared better than typical machine learning models in a study [2], which demonstrates the potential of DL in this area of research. Deep learning models, on the other hand, are frequently referred to as a "black box" because of their limited interpretability and the enormous amounts of data that are necessary for optimal performance.

2.3 Prediction of Diabetes Using a Hybrid Approach

In order to capitalize on the benefits offered by both machine learning and deep learning models, hybrid techniques have been developed. These methods incorporate several different models in order to improve the performance of the prediction. For example, A study in [3] used a combination of neural networks and support vector machines as their method of analysis and discovered that the ensemble model reached a greater level of accuracy than the separate models themselves. This strategy takes advantage of the benefits offered by both models while simultaneously compensating for the shortcomings of each one. However, such approaches can be resource-intensive in terms of processing and need precise adjustment.

In conclusion, the subject of diabetes prediction is incredibly expansive and rapidly developing, with ongoing breakthroughs being made in machine learning, deep learning, and hybrid approaches. The selection of the methodology is frequently determined by the specific requirements of the investigation, which may include the quantity and quality of the data that is readily available, the requirement that the model be interpretable, and the computational resources that are available (Table 1).

Table 1. Comparative Analysis of Machine learning, Deep Learning and Hybrid approaches.

Ref	Dataset Used	Contribution to Scientific Research	Limitations	Accuracy
[1]	Pima Indian Diabetes Dataset	Introduced a novel feature selection approach for SVM	Lack of model interpretability	92%
[2]	National Health and Nutrition Examination Survey	Developed an optimized Random Forest model	Overfitting on high-dimensional data	88%
[3]	Taiwan's National Health Insurance Research Database	Explored ensemble learning methods for prediction	Need for extensive computation resources	94%
[4]	Diabetes-130 US hospitals for years 1999–2008	Introduced the use of logistic regression models for diabetes prediction	Certain models have high false positive rate	89%
[5]	Korean National Health and Nutrition Examination Survey	Investigated K-Nearest Neighbors for diabetes prediction	KNN models can be computationally expensive	85%
[6]	Pima Indian Diabetes Dataset	Applied a deep learning model (CNN) for the first time	Complex model architecture and overfitting	90%
[7]	Taiwan's National Health Insurance Research Database	Explored a new way of preprocessing data for deep learning	Limited to the specific preprocessing method	91%
[8]	UCI ML Diabetes Dataset	Utilized Recurrent Neural Networks (RNNs) for prediction	Dependency on the sequence of data	89%

(*continued*)

Table 1. (*continued*)

Ref	Dataset Used	Contribution to Scientific Research	Limitations	Accuracy
[9]	Diabetes-130 US hospitals for years 1999–2008	Proposed a new loss function for the training of deep learning models	Generalizability of the new loss function	92%
[10]	National Health and Nutrition Examination Survey	Introduced the application of transfer learning in diabetes prediction	Dependency on the pre-trained model	93%
[11]	Pima Indian Diabetes Dataset	Combined ML and DL models in a novel hybrid approach	Complexity in model interpretation	92%
[12]	Taiwan's National Health Insurance Research Database	Integrated statistical and machine learning methods in diabetes prediction	Limitation of statistical methods used	94%
[13]	UCI ML Diabetes Dataset	Incorporated feature engineering in a hybrid ML model	Dependency on expert knowledge for feature engineering	93%
[14]	Diabetes-130 US hospitals for years 1999–2008	Proposed a hybrid ensemble model for prediction	Difficulty in model tuning	91%
[15]	National Health and Nutrition Examination Survey	Utilized transfer learning with a hybrid of ML models	Dependency on the pre-trained model	95%

3 Methodology

Our method for predicting diabetes involves systematically applying different machine learning models and comparing their results across a wide range of parameters. To test and refine these models, we employed the MATLAB programming environment. The procedure we used to put the models into action and assess their performance is detailed in this section.

3.1 Dataset Description

For this research, we used the UCI Machine Learning Repository's PIMA diabetic dataset [1]. This dataset [19] has 768 images, 8 features, and a class property with the values tested positive (1) and tested negative (0). This paper uses two toolboxes, specifically the WEKA (Waikato Environment for Knowledge Analysis) device created by the University of Waikato, New Zealand, which includes apparatuses for data pre-processing, characterization, and relapse [2, 20]. The minimum, maximum, mean, and standard deviation (SD) for each dataset are shown in Table 2.

Table 2. Attributes Description.

Attributes Name	Attributes Description	Min	Max	Mean		St_dev
Pregnancies	Number of times pregnant	0.00	17.00	3.845		3.37
Blood Pressure	Diastolic blood pressure (mm Hg)	0.00	122.00	69.105		19.356
Glucose	2-h plasma glucose concentration in an oral glucose tolerance test	0.00	199.00	120.895		31.973
Skin Thickness	Triceps skin fold thickness (mm)	0.00	99.00	20.536		15.244
MBI	Body mass index (weight in kg/(height in m)^2)	0.00	67.10	31.993		7.884
Insulin	Serum insulin 2 h (mu U/ml)	0.00	846		79.799	115.244
Diabetes Pedigree Function	Diabetes pedigree Function	0.00	2.24	0.472		0.331
Class	Class Variable (1 for positive and 0 for negative)	0.00	1.00	-		-
Age	Age(year)	0.00	81.00	33.241		11.78

3.2 Experimental Result

MATLAB is used to conduct the experiment. Accuracy, error rate, F-measure, PRC (Precision-Recall Curves Area), MCC (Matthew's Correlation Coefficient), and ROC (Receiver Operating Characteristics) areas are compared, graphed, and calculated by MATLAB programming tools, and the result is shown. Classification techniques such as Random Forest, Logistic Regression, K-Nearest Neighbors, Decision Tree, Naive Bayes, Support Vector Machine, LDA, are utilized in these studies.

3.3 Decision Tree

This paper uses the decision tree algorithm because it achieves the highest accuracy percentage in the PIMA dataset and has other advantages such as being easy to read and understand, quick to prepare, and requiring less data cleaning. Artificial intelligence (AI) decision trees are used for both clustering and relapse methods. To be "managed," something must be given a label before being carried out. A decision tree is a model of possible outcomes and resources that is supported by a tree-shaped equipment. Decision trees provide a framework for expressing conditional controls on numerical computations. They feature sub-disciplines that deal with the ever-changing developments that can lead to acceptance of findings [21]. The diabetes analysis decision tree provides a reliable framework for planning and making projections. For instance, the ID3, C4.5, and C5.0 decision trees, as well as the CART, Decision Stump, J48, and Heoffding tree, can be used to categorize data [22].

3.4   Confusion Matrix

A confusion matrix is a table that summarizes the results of a classification model on a set of input data. It presents the count of correct and incorrect predictions for each class [19]. The matrix includes four categories:

True Positive (TP): It is positive for both observed and predicted.
False Negative (FN): It is positive for observed, but negative for predicted.
True Negative (TN): It is positive for predicted, but negative for observed.
False Positive (FP): It is negative for both observed and predicted (Fig. 1).

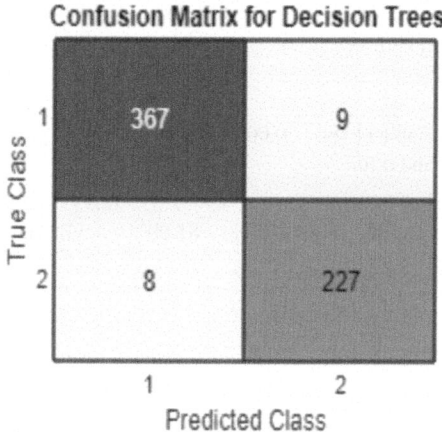

Fig. 1. Confusion Mtrix for Decision tree.

3.5   Logistic Regression

In supervised machine learning, logistic regression is used to estimate the probability of discrete outcomes given a set of input variables. The relationship between several independent factors and a single dependent variable can be better comprehended in this manner [9]. It is a binary algorithm that can only store the numbers 0 and 1. The sigmoid function is the key ingredient in the transition of linear regression into logistic regression. As opposed to predicting a continuous and continuous value (such as a user's total lifetime income), logistic regression predicts a discrete and dichotomous value (such as whether the user will spend or not spend money for the product). This is why some researchers have proposed renaming logistic regression to "logistic classification" [23].

$$y = \beta_o + \beta_1 X_1 + \beta_2 X_2 + \ldots + \beta_n X_o \tag{1}$$

where, y is the dependent variable, and $X_1, X_2, X_3 \ldots$ And X_n are the independent variables (Fig. 2).

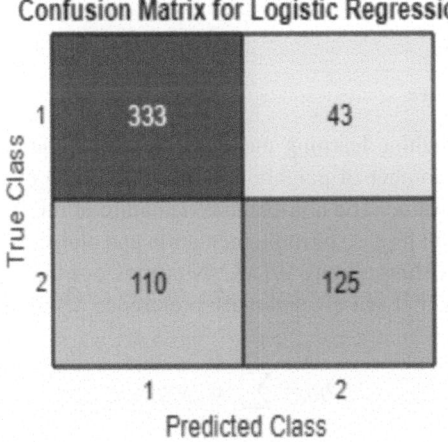

Fig. 2. Confusion Matrix for Logistic Regression.

3.6 Random Forest

Machine learning method random forest is a descendant of the decision tree [24]. Classification models benefit from the use of random forest. Each decision tree algorithm generates a classification for an attribute based on the input data, and then random forest aggregates and predicts the most cast ballot expectation. Each tree's input is essentially a subset of the full dataset. Simply said, random forest is a method that employs numerous decision tree models to get an improved prediction model.

$$MSE = \frac{1}{N} \sum_{i=0}^{N} (f_i - y_i)^2 \tag{2}$$

N is the number of data points f_i is the value returned by the model, and y_i is the actual value (Fig. 3).

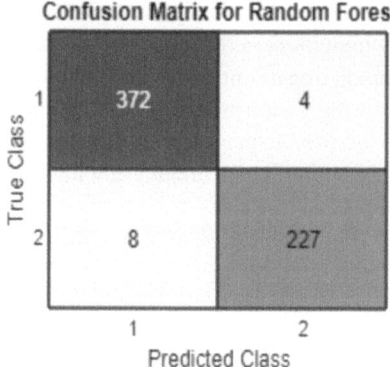

Fig. 3. Confusion Matrix for Random Forest.

3.7 K-Nearest Neighbors

KNN is a supervised machine learning method that focuses on classification [12]. In KNN, K represents the number of neighbors being used. How effectively this method works depends on the K value. The non-parametric nature of this technique makes for a lengthy learning curve, but its ease of implementation and ability to be applied to a huge dataset make up for this shortcoming [9]. KNN carries out three primary operations: distance estimation, neighbor search, and mark preference determination [14] (Fig. 4).

$$D_H = \sum_{i=0}^{k} |x_i - y_i| \tag{3}$$

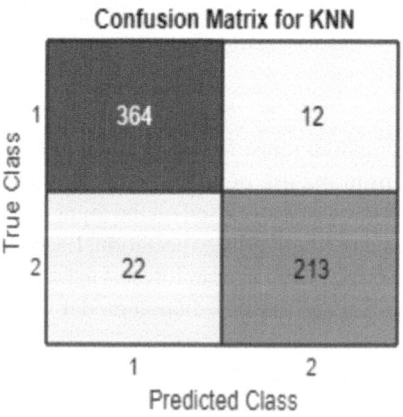

Fig. 4. Confusion Matrix for KNN.

3.8 Naïve Bayes

In the realm of machine learning, the Naive Bayes method falls within the supervised category. The Bayesian theorem, on which Naive Bayes is based, calculates the probability of a hypothesis given its proof. According to this technique, all of the features in a dataset contribute equally and independently to the problematic target class [6]. The naive Bayes approach excels when dealing with massive, high-dimensional datasets [12].

$$P(H|S)\frac{P(S|H)P(H)}{P(S)} \tag{4}$$

P(H): The probability that hypothesis H is correct. P(S): Probability of S data. Previous probability of H.

P(H—S): Probability of hypothesis H given data D.

P(S—H): The probability that the S data is given the hypothesis H (Fig. 5).

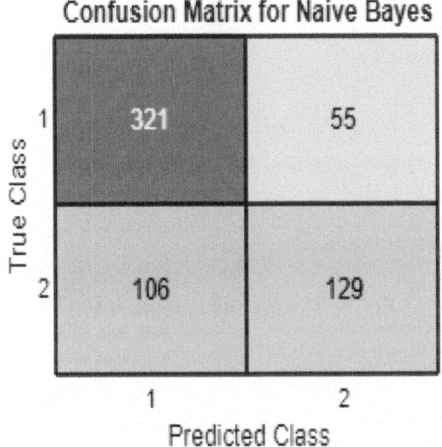

Fig. 5. Confusion Matrix for Naïve Bayes.

3.9 Support Vector Machines

SVM is a sophisticated supervised machine learning technique for classification and regression. SVM uses hyperplanes to divide feature space classes. In a two-class problem, SVM seeks the ideal hyperplane that maximizes the margin, the distance between the hyperplane and the closest support vectors from each class. SVM uses the kernel trick for non-linearly separable data. It converts the input space into a higher-dimensional space where data is linearly separable, allowing an ideal separation hyperplane to be constructed. Linear, polynomial, RBF, and sigmoid kernels are common. SVMs are robust, especially when the number of dimensions exceeds the number of samples. The regularization parameter manages the trade-off between training data error and model complexity, preventing overfitting. SVMs are computationally costly, especially for bigger datasets, and they may require careful parameter tuning and kernel selection to work well.

$$L_p = \frac{1}{2}\vec{W} - \sum_{i=1}^{t} \propto_i y_i\left(\vec{W}.\vec{X}\right) + \sum_{i=1}^{t} \propto_i \qquad (5)$$

where t is the number of prepared models, $\propto_i$, i = 1,..., t, are non-negative numbers, Derivatives of L_p with respect to αi are zero, $\propto_i$ are the Lagrange multipliers, L_p is called Lagrangian and the vector w and the constant b define the hyperplane [27] (Fig. 6).

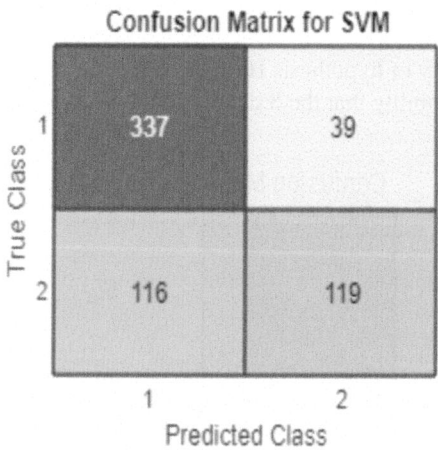

Fig. 6. Confusion Matrix for SVM.

3.10 Linear Discriminant Analysis LDA

In pattern recognition and machine learning, Linear Discriminant Analysis (LDA) is a powerful tool that seeks linear combinations of characteristics to discriminate between two or more classes of objects or events. Its primary goal is to reduce the amount of variation between groups within a given class. Because of its effectiveness in transforming high-dimensional data into a lower-dimensional space, dimensionality reduction is a popular technique for improving classification accuracy. LDA is widely used in fields including facial recognition, medical imaging, and predictive analytics despite the fact that it requires certain assumptions about the distribution of the data (Fig. 7).

3.11 MCC, ROC and PRA Area

The MCC (Matthews Correlation Coefficient) ranges from +1 to −1, with +1 being a perfect score and −1 representing the poorest score; we depict these values and their corresponding graph [28]. Diagnostic values between 0 and 1 are displayed graphically

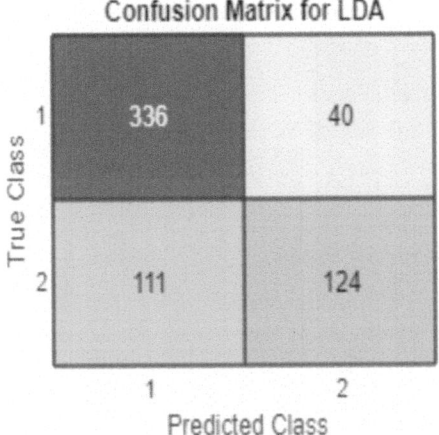

Fig. 7. Confusion Matrix for LDA.

in the ROC (receiver operating characteristics) plot [29]. When there is a moderate to large class imbalance, a PRC (Precision-Recall Curve) should be utilized. PRC values range from 0 to 1 (Table 3).

Table 3. MCC, ROC and PRA area.

MCC, ROC and PRA Curve	MCC	ROC	PRC
Decision Tree	0.515	0.839	0.837
Logistic Regression	0.527	0.848	0.859
Random Forest	0.428	0.832	0.845˙
Naive Bayes	0.458	0.845	0.862
K-NN	0.39	0.697	0.688
SVM	0.489	0.723	0.717

Figure 8 shows the accuracies of multi model machine earning algorithms. Upon Comparison we get to know that random forest and decision tree perform exceptionally well with an accuracy of 98.4% and 97.22% while SVM, Logistic regression and Naïve Bayes perform average with an accuracy of 74%.

3.12 Detailed Accuracy

Generally, we know that the prediction process consists of four main attributes that are called true positive (TP), true negative (TN), false positive (FP), and false negative (FN) [7]. To calculate the precision, recall, MCC, F-score, true positive rate (TPR), true negative rate (TNR), false positive rate (FPR), false negative rate (FNR), and accuracy.

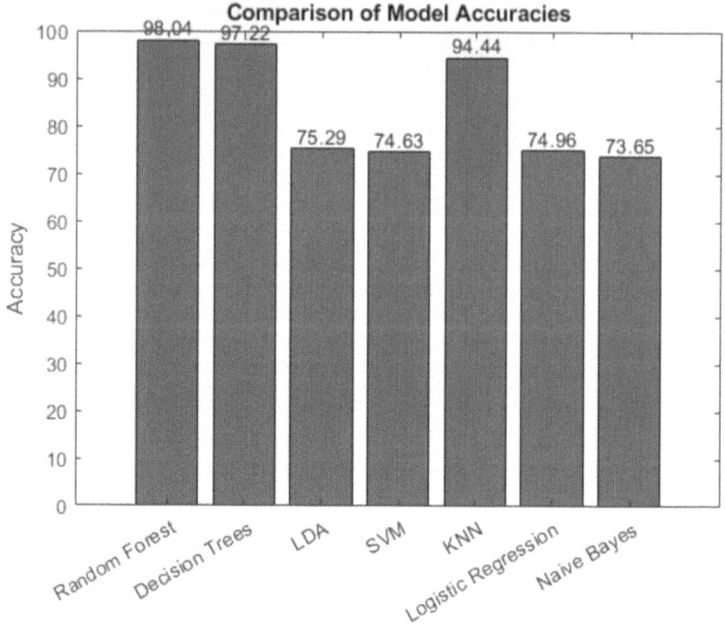

Fig. 8. Comparisons of Model accuracies.

3.13 Precision

A classification model's precision is a metric that assesses its capacity to correctly identify only the pertinent data points [32]. Mathematically, precision can be computed using the formula below:

$$Precision = \frac{TP}{TP + FP} \tag{6}$$

By using Eq. (6) we can calculate the precision value.

3.14 Recall

The recall is a metric that evaluates the ability of a model to identify all the relevant cases within a dataset [32]. Mathematically, recall can be computed using the formula below:

$$Recall = \frac{TP}{TP + FN} \tag{7}$$

By using Eq. (7) we can calculate the Recall value.

3.15 Mathews Correlation Coefficient

The Mathews Correlation Coefficient (MCC) is a more robust statistical measure than others, as it produces a higher score when the model achieves good outcomes across all four classes of the Confusion Matrix (true positive, false negative, true negative, and false positive) relative to the size of the positive and negative components in the dataset [32]. Mathematically the MCC can be calculated by using below formula:

$$MCC = \frac{((TN*TP) - (FN*FP))}{\sqrt{((FP+TP)*(FP+TN)*(FP+TP)*(FP+TN))}} \tag{8}$$

By using Eq. (8) we can calculate the MCC value.

3.16   True Positive Rate

A true positive is an outcome where the model correctly predicts the positive value. Mathematically the True Positive can be calculated by using below formula:

$$TPR = \frac{TP}{FN+TP} \tag{9}$$

By using Eq. (9) we can calculate the TPR value.

3.17   True Negative Rate

In a classification problem, a true negative refers to an outcome where the model correctly predicts the negative class. Mathematically the True negative can be calculated by using below formula:

$$TNR = \frac{TN}{TN+FP} \tag{10}$$

By using Eq. (10) we can calculate the TNR value.

3.18   False Positive Rate

In a classification problem, a false positive is an outcome where the model incorrectly predicts the positive class.
Mathematically the false Positive can be calculated by using below formula:

$$FPR = \frac{FP}{TN+FP} \tag{11}$$

By using Eq. (11) we can calculate the FPR value.

3.19   False Negative Rate

A false negative occurs when the model predicts a negative class. False negatives are a type of error in which the model fails to detect a true positive instance.
Mathematically the false negative can be calculated by using below formula:

$$FNR = \frac{FN}{TP+FN} \tag{12}$$

By using Eq. (12) we can calculate the FNR value.

3.20   Mean Absolute Error

The formula calculates the sum of the absolute differences between each predicted value and its corresponding true value and then divides by the total number of predictions to get the average error. The lower the MAE value, the better the predictive model is performing. Mathematically the MAE can be calculated by using below formula:

$$MAE = \frac{1}{2} \sum_{i=0}^{n} |\hat{y}_i - y_i| \tag{13}$$

By using Eq. (13) we can calculate the MAE value.

3.21   Root Mean Squared Error

RMSE is the standard deviation of errors that occur when predicted on a dataset. This is similar to MSE (Main Squared Error) but the root of the value is considered when determining the accuracy of the model. Mathematically the RMSE can be calculated by using below formula:

$$RMSE = \sqrt{\frac{1}{2} \sum_{i=0}^{n} (Y_i - \hat{Y}_i)^2} \tag{14}$$

By using Eq. (14) we can calculate the RMSE value.

3.22   Relative Absolute Error

Relative absolute error is ex- pressed as a ratio, a minor error is compared to errors produced by a small model. Mathematically the RAE can be calculated by using below formula:

$$RAE = \frac{\left[\sum_{i=1}^{n} (P_i - A_i)^2 \right]^2}{\left[\sum_{i=1}^{n} A_i^2 \right]^2} \tag{15}$$

By using Eq. (15) we can calculate the RAE value.

3.23   Root Relative Absolute Error

RRAE (Relative Ratio Absolute Error) is a metric that can be used to evaluate the performance of a predictive model. It is calculated by dividing the mean absolute error (MAE) of the model by the error of Zero-R classifier, which is a simple classifier that always predicts the most frequent class in the training data.

The formula for RRAE is:

$$RRAE = \sqrt{\frac{\sum_{j=1}^{n} (P_j - T_j)^2}{\sum_{j=1}^{n} (T_j - T_j)^2}} \tag{16}$$

By using Eq. (16) we can calculate the RRAE value.

4 Conclusion

In the midst of an ever-worsening health crisis on a worldwide scale, diabetes stands out as an epidemic that is mostly being ignored. This work, which aims to help in the fight against this silent epidemic, presents a comprehensive comparison of seven different classification algorithms applied to the PIMA diabetes dataset using the processing capacity of MATLAB. Careful tabulation of all experimental results is supported by visual representations to promote a better global comprehension of the data. The ultimate goal of our research is to develop more reliable methods of diagnosing diabetes before symptoms appear. According to the data collected in the experiments, the Random Forest algorithm yields the highest accuracy (98.4%), followed by the Decision Tree model (97.22%). While effective, the accuracy rates achieved by SVM, Naive Bayes, and Logistic Regression are all around 74%. But we go deeper than just accuracy rates when evaluating. We also calculate a variety of metrics, including error rates, precision, recall, and the F-measure, to provide a more nuanced understanding of each algorithm's performance. Our long-term goal is to improve upon this investigation by creating a fully featured web-based application. A medical-specific section, push notifications, and a chat window are all in the works. Our goal is to make our services even more convenient and accessible by making them available as an Android app. Ways to improve system performance and methods for training algorithms to improve predicted accuracy will be investigated in future studies.

References

1. International Diabetes Federation: IDF Diabetes Atlas, 9th edn. International Diabetes Federation, Brussels, Belgium (2023)
2. Amisha, M.P., Pathania, M., Rathaur, V.K.: Overview of artificial intelligence in medicine. J. Family Med. Prim. Care **8**(7), 2328–2331 (2019). https://doi.org/10.4103/jfmpc.jfmpc_440_19
3. Opitz, D., Maclin, R.: Popular ensemble methods: An empirical study. J. Artif. Intell. Res. **11**, 169–198 (1999)
4. Chawla, N.V., Bowyer, K.W., Hall, L.O., Kegelmeyer, W.P.: SMOTE: synthetic minority over-sampling technique. J. Artif. Intell. Res. **16**, 321–357 (2002). https://doi.org/10.1613/jair.953
5. Huang, Y., McCullagh, P., Black, N., Harper, R.: Feature selection and classification model construction on type 2 diabetic patients' data. Artif. Intell. Med. **41**(3), 251–262 (2007)
6. Yu, W., Liu, T., Valdez, R., Gwinn, M., Khoury, M.J.: Application of support vector machine modeling for prediction of common diseases: the case of diabetes and pre-diabetes. BMC Med. Inform. Decis. Mak. **10**(1), 16 (2010)
7. Perveen, S., Shahbaz, M., Guergachi, A., Keshavjee, K.: Performance analysis of data mining classification techniques to predict diabetes. Procedia Comp. Sci. **159**, 292–301 (2019)
8. Woldaregay, A.Z., et al.: Data-driven modeling and prediction of blood glucose dynamics: Machine learning applications in type 1 diabetes. Artif. Intell. Med. **98**, 109–134 (2019)
9. D'hoore, W., Sicotte, C., Tilquin, C.: Risk adjustment in outcome assessment: the Charlson comorbidity index. Methods of Information in Medicine **32**(05), 382–387 (1993)
10. Krishnamoorthi, R., et al.: A novel diabetes healthcare disease prediction framework using machine learning techniques. J. Healthc. Eng. 2022 (2022)

11. Abdollahi, J., Nouri-Moghaddam, B.: Hybrid stacked ensemble combined with genetic algorithms for diabetes prediction. Iran J. Comp. Sci. **5**(3), 205–220 (2022)
12. Obulesu, O., Suresh, K., Ramudu, B.: Diabetes prediction using machine learning techniques. HELIX **10**(2), 136–142 (2020)
13. Das, H., Naik, B., Behera, H.S.: Classification of diabetes mellitus disease (DMD): a data mining (DM) approach. In: Progress in Computing, Analytics and Networking, pp. 539–549. Springer, Singapore (2018)
14. Mahboob Alam, T., et al.: A model for early prediction of diabetes. Informatics in Medicine Unlocked **16**, 100204 (2019)
15. Mukesh, K., Rajan, V., Anshul, A., et al.: Pre-diction of diabetes using Bayesian Network. Int. J. Comp. Sci. Info. Technol. **5**(4), 5174–5178 (2014)
16. Mir, A., Dhage, S.N.: Diabetes disease prediction using machine learning on big data of healthcare. In: 2018 Fourth International Conference on Computing Communication Control and Automation (ICCUBEA), pp. 1–6. IEEE (2018)
17. Naz, H., Ahuja, S.: Deep learning approach for diabetes prediction using PIMA Indian dataset. J. Diab. Metabo. Disord. **19**(1), 391–403 (2020)
18. Iyer, A., Jayalatha, S., Sumbaly, R.: Diagnosis of diabetes using classification mining techniques. Int. J. Data Mining & Knowl. Manage. Process **5**(1), 01–14 (2015)
19. Sisodia, D., Sisodia, D.: Prediction of diabetes using classification algorithms. Procedia Comp. Sci. **132**, 1578–1585 (2018)
20. Cs.aucland.ac.nz (2020). [Online].Available :https://www.cs.auckland.ac.nz/courses/compsc i367s1c/tutorials/IntroductionToWeka.pdf/
21. Jaiswal, S.: Machine Learning Decision Tree Classification Algorithm-Javatpoint (2020). [online] www.javatpoint.com.Available at: https://www.javatpoint.com/machine-learning-decision-tree-classification-algorithm
22. Iyer, A., Jayalatha, S., Sumbaly, R.: Diagnosis of diabetes using classification mining techniques. Int. J. Data Mining & Knowl. Manage. Process **5**(1), 01–14 (2015)
23. Navlani, A.: (Tutorial) Understanding Logistic REGRESSION in PYTHON. DataCampCommunity (2020). [Online].Available:https://www.datacamp.com/community/tutorials/unders tanding-logistic-regression-python/
24. Chen, J., et al.: A parallel random forest algorithm for big data in a spark cloud computing environment. IEEE Transactions on Parallel and Distributed Systems **28**(4), 919–933 (2017). [Online]. Available: https://ieeexplore.ieee.org/abstract/document/7557062/
25. Navlani, A.: KNN Classification using Scikit-learn. DataCamp Community (2020). [Online]. Available: https://www.datacamp.com/community/tutorials/k-nearest-neighbor-cla ssification-scikit-learn
26. Navlani, A.: (Tutorial) Support Vector Machines (SVM) in Scikit-learn. DataCamp Community (2020). [Online]. Available: https://www.datacamp.com/community/tutorials/svm-classi fication-scikit-learn-python/
27. Santhanam, T., Padmavathi, M.: Application of K-Means and Genetic Algorithms for Dimension Reduction by Integrating SVM for Diabetes Diagnosis. Procedia Comp. Sci. **47**, 76–83 (2015)
28. Wu, X., et al.: Top 10 algorithms in data mining. Knowl. Info. Sys. **14**(1), 1–37 (2007)
29. Piatetsky-Shapiro, G.: The Best Metric to Measure Accuracy of Clas- sification Models - KDnuggets. KDnuggets (2020). [Online]. Available: https://www.kdnuggets.com/2016/12/ best-metric-measure-accuracy-classification-models.html/2/
30. Bui, H.: ROC Curve Transforms the Way We Look at a Classification Problem. Medium (2020). [Online]. Available: https://towardsdatascience.com/a-simple-explanation-of-the-roc-curve-and-auc-64db32d75541/
31. Shaukat, Z., Naseem, R., Zubair, M.: A Dataset for Software Requirements Risk Prediction. 978-1-5386-7649 3/18/31.002018IEEE10.1109/CSE.2018.00022, pp. 112–118 (2018)

Image Processing in Toxicology: A Systematic Review

Gayatri Mirajkar[1]([✉]), Lalit Garg[2], Mukil Alaragisamy[3], and Sagar Shinde[4]

[1] Arvind Gavali College of Engineering, Satara, India
gayatrimirajkar@gmail.com
[2] University of Malta, Msida, Malta
[3] Lincoln University College, Kota Bharu, Malaysia
[4] Dr. D. Y. Patil Institute of Technology, Pune, India

Abstract. Cellular imaging has proven to be the key to identifying and applying biomarkers for tracking cell fate and drug activity in vitro. The aim here is to improve the comprehension of the mechanism of action of newly developed drugs. High-throughput imaging investigations, which quantify cellular morphological changes on a large scale, have become an invaluable instrument in the early phases of drug development due to automated microscopy and image processing. In order to document the evolution of cell morphology, photomicrographs have been taken using multi-well assay plates equipped with high-throughput imaging devices. These systems generate a multitude of results that take a lot of effort and subjective interpretation. Designing a step-by-step approach for detecting toxicity in assay images requires the automatic detection and classification of thousands of assay images. This method consists of acquiring images using high-throughput microscopy, processing the images, and analyzing the results. Because of the diversity of nuclei organization patterns associated with drug-induced toxicity, Deep Learning (DL) approaches have only just entered the landscape. These techniques have the significant advantage of screening thousands of images at different time intervals and at different spatial resolutions which would not be possible using manual intervention. We present a systematic review of the different image analysis techniques for toxicity detection in cell assay images. These include background correction, segmentation, and classification techniques. In addition, the review also focuses on the most prominent applications of DL to classify cell assay images as healthy or toxicity-affected. The advantage of DL based techniques is the flexibility of being incorporated in the high-throughput imaging pipeline along with the screening of thousands of assay images.

Keywords: Deep Learning · Image Analysis · convolutional neural networks · Assay images · toxicity affected

1 Introduction

Cellular imaging is essential in identifying and applying biomarkers for tracking cell fate and drug activity in vitro to characterize medications better and understand their mechanism of action. The output of such cellular imaging systems is a digital image

A. Mirzazadeh et al. (Eds.): SEMIT 2023, CCIS 2198, pp. 159–175, 2024.
https://doi.org/10.1007/978-3-031-72284-4_10

of a specific cell type or biological event. Images of cultured cells contain a wealth of information. Cellular imaging uses image-analysis technologies to visualize a cell population, single-cell, or subcellular features [1, 2]. Image-based cell profiling quantifies phenotypic variations between cell groups in a high-throughput manner [1].

The scientific evaluation of the effects of harmful chemical compounds on bacteria or mammalian cell culture is known as in vitro toxicity testing [3]. The application of in vitro testing is the identification of potentially hazardous chemicals. It demonstrates that some toxic properties are absent during the initial phases of developing novel drugs that may be useful [4].

The creation of more biologically relevant cell-based tests for all therapeutic areas that may be employed throughout drug discovery R&D has been made possible by modern cell imaging methods [5]. The ability of cellular imaging technology as a tool for drug discovery has been further enhanced by the ability to automate and multiplex imaging methods to boost throughput [6].

The term "high-throughput imaging" refers to the automated analysis of images and light microscopy of a substantial quantity of samples. In these investigations, cells are frequently grown in multi-well plates, and each well's cells are then treated with a tiny chemical or genetic disruption [4]. This method works especially well for phenotypic screening assays, assessing cell response, cell-based models, or organisms to different perturbagens. Digital image analysis and automated fluorescence microscopy from microtiter plates are used in image-based high-content screening (HCS), a type of high-throughput screening (HTS) [3, 7]. By analyzing images and using automated microscopy, high-throughput imaging tests can quantify cellular morphological changes on a wide scale, making them a useful prediction tool in the early stages of drug development [4, 8].

Prediction of the activity of compounds in apparently unrelated assays has been achieved by using image-based fingerprints of compounds derived from a given image based cellular assay [9, 10]. Predicting a drug toxicity preclinically improves decision-making, lowering development costs and improving patient safety. The model proposed by [11] helps drug safety experts anticipate liver damage using only these variables and the clinical dose. These investigations frequently start with the growth of cells in multi-well plates and end with applying a tiny chemical or genetic disruption to each well of the cells [8].

When used early in drug discovery, the prediction of drug MOAs (Mechanism of Action) using such assays may result in cost savings [8]. In more recent times, high-throughput imaging systems have generated photomicrographs and tracked cell morphology in each well of the multi-well assay plates throughout time [12]. These systems provide numerous findings that must be time-consuming and subjectively interpreted by humans [12].

While manual segmentation limits the number of parameters that can be measured, it is also impossible to analyze the thousands of images generated during experiments by high-throughput systems. Manual data analysis also suffers from the disadvantage of generalized results across all cells in the same plate. Designing a step-by-step approach for detecting toxicity in assay images requires the automatic detection and classification of thousands of assay images. Fully automated toxicity prediction uses raw images as input and does not require segmentation and cropping stages [12]. This systematic review examines the image analysis methods used for toxicity detection in high-throughput microscopy images.

A part of this review also considers applying DL methods for the same purpose. In DL, an algorithm learns effective representations for a given task entirely from the data [13]. A deep neural network (DNN) in essence is just a concatenation of several layers [12]. Each layer can be trained to do something specific, like identifying objects in images or anticipating the chemical to which the cell has been exposed to, by reweighting and transforming data. Data, including unprocessed images or image-based profiles, are introduced into the system through an input layer. Data is reshaped as it passes through the network by each layer. Finally, the output layer exports the fully transformed data [14]. Results from DL techniques imply that automatic classification of cellular images for toxicity detection could increase the throughput [12]. These automatic approaches can quickly screen thousands of images for toxicity, a task that would otherwise be time-consuming and prone to human error. Also, traditional image analysis approaches incorporate segmentation as a critical step. DL architectures perform segmentation in the CNN layer itself.

2 Methods

The research uses a Systematic Literature Review, which identifies, selects, and critically evaluates research to address a well-defined topic [15]. This systematic review follows the Preferred Reporting Items for Systematic Reviews and Meta-Analysis (PRISMA) guidelines. The SLR (Systematic Literature Review) aims to address the research questions by finding all relevant research outcomes from previous studies. The research questions are divided into the following sub-questions:

- Which methods of image analysis are used in toxicity detection in assay images?
- Which are the cell image analysis software's?

We searched various databases such as IEEE Xplore, ScienceDirect, and Google Scholar.

3 Literature Search

A systematic literature search was performed on the ScienceDirect database for original English-language articles published from 1 January 2000 to 14 July 2023. Various combinations of search terms representing "DL toxicology images" and "image analysis toxicology images" were used to retrieve all relevant studies (Fig. 1).

The steps involved in the process of toxicity detection can be depicted as in Fig. 2. The steps involved in this process involve image acquisition along with high-throughput microscopy images followed by image processing techniques and analysis. A summary of the steps can be given as follows [7]:

- Illumination correction
- Segment nuclei

- Segment cell bodies
- Segment other compartments
- Measure features of all compartments (intensity, shape, texture, etc.)
- Classify objects and relate compartments to each other
- Determine the statistical indicators of assay quality

For each test [4, 7], an image analysis pipeline is built using CellProfiler [16], an open-source cell image analysis software. In [4], data cleaning is an important step that handles intensity irregularities occurring inside the staining and imaging process and which impacts the analysis results. Data cleaning or scrubbing aims to produce high-quality, reliable data for analysis and research purposes. The identification of outliers is a significant challenge during the data cleaning stage. The presence of outliers during analysis can result in erroneous conclusions. The data cleaning stage also suffers from other challenges such as extreme data values which result from cell death due to toxic compounds.

During the pre-processing stages, Intensity normalization (background correction and subtraction) across the plate images is carried out to correct for irregular illumination due to optical hardware irregularities and shading. One way of background correction is via morphological techniques. Other techniques include computation of the mean (or median) of the set of pixel values at every location across many fields, followed by smoothing – usually Gaussian or parabola or fitting a plane to the data. The next step is to normalize each pixel value by dividing it by the "mean pixel value" for that particular location. The pre-processing (enhancement) stage also contains the step of feature extraction, i. e., features or measurements for every cell/nuclei. In [4], the cell area is regressed out from all features as several features are impacted by cell area. In [7], 500 to 1000 features are measured per cell. Each cell's and subcellular compartment's sizes and shapes and each stain's intensity and texture inside each cell and subcellular compartment are differentiating features [7, 17].

In [4], the pre-processing steps of feature extraction, segmentation, and illumination correction are performed using the open-source software CellProfiler to automate most of such steps. Because several artefacts might arise during staining and imaging and possibly change study results, the authors [4] stress the importance of data cleaning as a step towards better image-based profiling. Errors at any stage of the pipeline could produce outlier cells (those that deviate from the norm but show no real biological impact) [4].

The pre-processing step ensures obtaining meaningful and stable results. Errors in such images include intensity effects and noisy artefacts in the plate information utilized for normalization. Such effects affect the CellProfiler pipeline. Outlier medications with unexpected side effects on the features are also filtered out during this preliminary processing step [4].

Not every compound induces a significant altercation in the features extracted by CellProfiler. Therefore, it is preferable to examine medications that have a noticeable impact the features only. The techniques for determining outliers are classified as supervised, semi-supervised, and unsupervised methods [4]. Histogram-based outlier score detection is an efficient unsupervised method used for outlier detection.

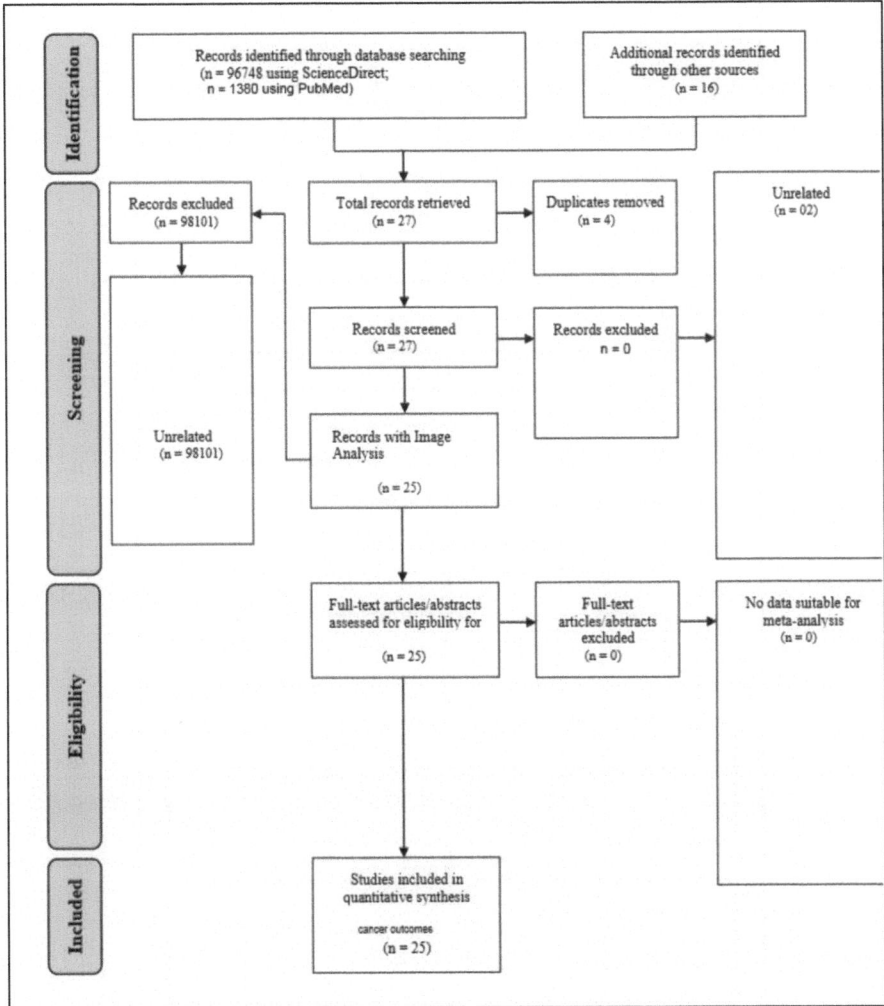

Fig. 1. PRISMA flow diagram for the systematic review of the applications of image processing in toxicology

Furthermore, pre-processing facilitates the regression of cell area relative to all other variables, as a substantial number of them are subsequently influenced by cell area [9]. In the drug development pipeline, image analysis applications are used during the early stages of drug development [4].

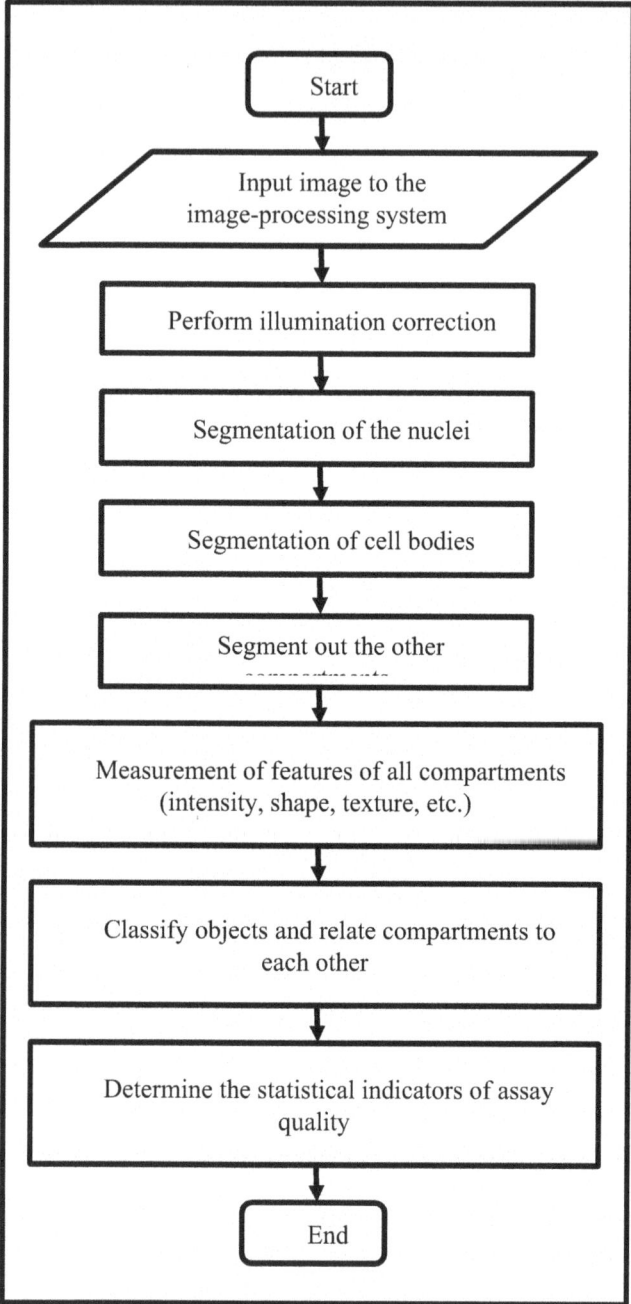

Fig. 2. Steps involved using image processing techniques in toxicity detection in cell assays

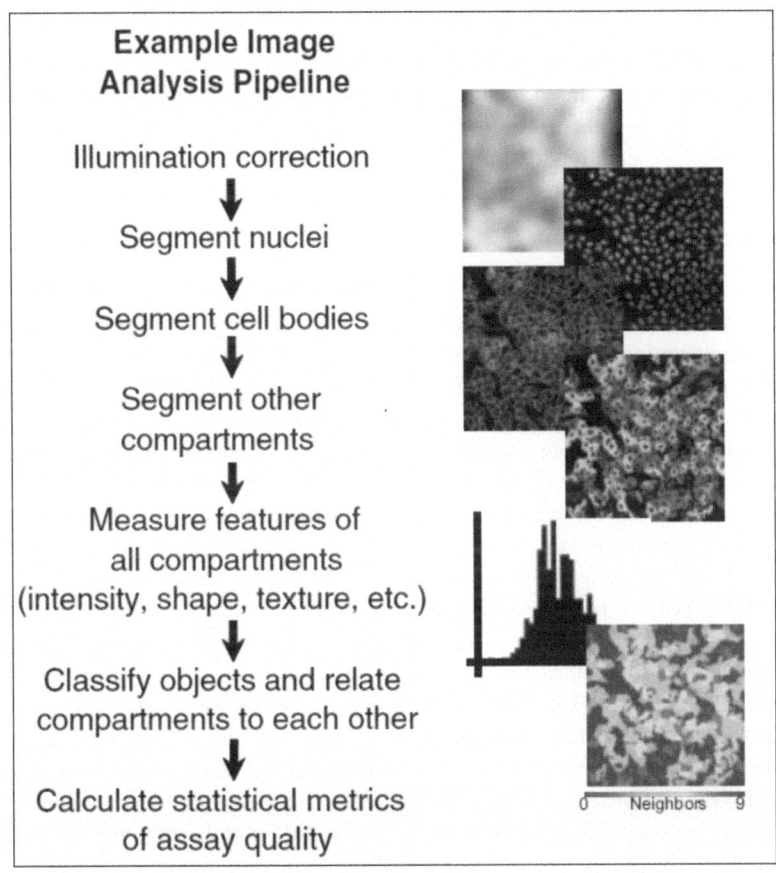

Fig. 3. Diagram illustrating the steps in the pipeline for image analysis [27].

4 Steps Involved in Image Analysis Pipeline

4.1 Pre-processing Steps

CellProfiler [16], an open-source cell image analysis software, is used to construct an image analysis pipeline for each assay [4, 7]. In [4], data cleaning is an important step that handles intensity irregularities occurring in the process of staining and imaging and which impact the analysis results. Intensity normalization (background correction and subtraction) across the plate images is carried out in the pre-processing stages to correct for irregular illumination due to optical hardware irregularities and shading. One way of background correction is via morphological techniques. Other techniques include the computation of the mean (or median) of the set of pixel values at every location across many fields, followed by smoothing – usually parabola to the data or Gaussian or fitting a plane [18]. The next step is to normalize each pixel value by dividing it by the "mean pixel value" for that particular place. The pre-processing (enhancement) stage also contains the feature extraction step, i.e. measurements or features for every cell/nuclei.

All features are regressed [4] as the cell area impacts several characteristics. In [7], 500 to 1000 features are measured per cell. Differentiating features include the size, shape, staining intensity, and staining texture of each cell and subcellular compartments [17]. The enormous number of features that have been retrieved has aided in dimensionality reduction and representation learning.

4.2 Segmentation

The next step, as shown in Fig. 3, is segmentation. Segmentation is identifying, partitioning, and extracting individual cells in the field of view for subsequent analysis [4]. The segmentation process assigns individual pixels to classes such as cell nuclei, individual cells, and other classes such as pixel intensity, texture, and color. Segmentation techniques broadly fall under two categories: region–based and boundary-based— region-based techniques group similar-intensity pixels into common groups. The most common technique to achieve segmentation is thresholding, a simple binary classification of the pixels in the image. However, the technique cannot give satisfactory results when the image contains various intensity levels. Other techniques that are used for segmentation include gradient-based techniques and watershed algorithms. The watershed algorithm is a compelling technique and is used commercially. If, however, seeded watersheds are used, the seed locations must be located manually. This is itself impossible for the hundreds of images produced using screening studies. As a result, automated techniques are employed. Cell-level segmentation is frequently seeded using nuclear-level segmentation on an independently obtained nuclear channel. As shown in Fig. 4, a 2-stage segmentation method employing nuclei as seeds for cell segmentation of seeded watershed is depicted.

Gradient-based techniques are sensitive to noise outliers and can result in false region detection. A window around the cell must be present for segmentation using active contours. Cell boundaries are created by continually deforming the coarse boundary. The Canny Edge Detector is a gradient-based technique that is a multi-stage edge detector and is also applicable to noise-sensitive data. Active-contour-based approaches are also used for cell segmentation in HCA analysis. Graph partitions, clustering, or approaches based on histograms could be used to separate tissues with normal and cancerous phenotypes [18].

Certain applications require tracing, i.e., quantifying numbers, lengths, and relative branching structure sizes in photos at various scales. These might include the microtubules, neurites, and vasculature in HCA applications. Tracking refers to the study of the dynamics of movement inside cells or simply the movement of the cell from one frame to the next. It is accomplished by following the objects from one frame to the next. Particle filtering, a model-based probabilistic approach, is employed to track the movement of cells [19]. The classical segmentation techniques include histogram-based methods like watershed segmentation, edge detection, and thresholding. ML-based methods discover the best segmentation solution by training a classifier with ground truth data and manually selecting labels for image pixels [20].

A brief comparison between model-based and ML-based segmentation techniques is given below:

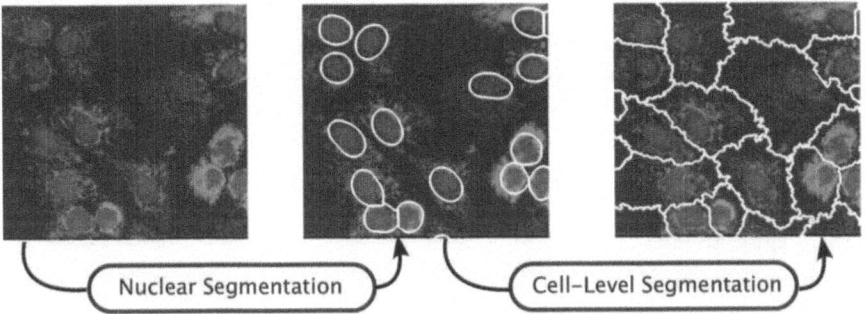

Fig. 4. 2-stage segmentation method employing nuclei as seeds for cell segmentation of seeded watershed

4.3   Feature Extraction

Classification deals with labelling the individual phenotypic and subcellular information segmented out. The labelling is achieved based on the set of features extracted from each of the segmented objects (usually individual cells) and their associated sub-objects (usually subcellular organelles) [21]. The features can be based on texture, color, and intensity or even statistical features such as a cohort's mean and variance. The choice of features depends on the experiment, biological conditions, etc. Among texture-based features, co-occurrence matrices are widely used for texture-based classification. The features extracted can be in hundreds and create a set of quantitative measurements for each cell. This can be considered as the meta-data for each cell. The method usually employed is to derive custom or designed features from the existing library of features [7]. Calculations like ratios of features or the proportion of cells that are higher than a threshold are examples of derived features that use individual cell data [7]. The features extracted include:

- Shape features – roundness, area, and perimeter
- Intensity-based features – statistical features like mean, intensity, and maximum intensity.
- Features of the microenvironment and surroundings, including cell counts and spatial connections in the field of view
- Texture features

CellProfiler [16] can record hundreds of thousands of features, such as the number of cells within each sample that are over a given threshold for each measured feature or the ability to compute a wide array of ratios or features [7]. A disadvantage of increasing the feature set is the increased probability of the existing data and/or producing false positives. The classification step needs to be automated to achieve meaningful and statistically significant phenotypic and morphological classification. Machine learning algorithms are divided into Supervised (training data set) and unsupervised (model-based). Supervised learning methods like KNN ("K – Nearest Neighbours"), SVM ("Support Vector Machines"), and Naive Bayes Classifiers are commonly used in biological operations [21]. Unsupervised learning involves clustering objects based on the maximum variance and maximum correlation to the group of objects [21]. The drawback involved in unsupervised learning is the significant amount of time needed for classification and the generation of unknown classes. One of the possible ways to overcome this difficulty is to use DL methods to achieve classification into cellular and sub-cellular components. Analysis Software available for use in High Content Screening are:

- ImageJ [22]
- CellProfiler [16]
- DetecTiff [23]
- BioImageXD [24]
- ScanR High-Content Screening Solution for Life Science [25]

5   DL Algorithms

The complexity of DNNs (Deep Neural Networks) may be described as factors like the number of layers between input and output or so-called hidden layers [26]. They may alternatively be defined by the model's total number of hidden nodes or the node's total number of inputs and outputs. Convolutional neural networks (CNNs) are the most common models used nowadays and are popular in image-processing applications. CNN consists of three-layer forms with distinct convolutional layers, pooling, and completely related (Fig. 5). Each CNN is separated into two phases: the training phase, the feed-forwards stage, and the back-propagation stage. The most often used CNN architectures are ResNet, GoogleNet, VGGNet, and AlexNet (Table 1).

Table 1. Comparison between model and ML-based segmentation

Sr No	Model-based segmentation	Machine-learning-based segmentation
1	Commonly used	Used primarily for classification
2	Used for fluorescence micros copy images of cultured cells	Used for highly variable cell forms or tissues
3	Manual parameter adjustment for each new experimental setup	Manual labelling of training pixels for each experimental setup and every batch of images

5.1   Extraction of Significant Features

The phenotypes being studied must be thoroughly understood for feature extraction and selection to be effective [27]. This is challenging due to the wide range of nuclei organization patterns associated with drug-induced toxicity [27]. Traditional image analysis relies on feature engineering to find drug compounds that modulate phenotype [20]. In standard practice, the images of drug-treated cell populations are first segmented into single cells [20]. The features are created manually, and their values are measured by some carefully designed automated process [28]. During feature selection, the irrelevant features are manually removed or by a machine learning algorithm [20]. Hence, the phenotypic profile of a drug is a multidimensional measurement of the selected features. Finally, the drug profiles are compared and clustered to determine anomalies.

Feature engineering plays a vital role in the process of HCA ("High Content Analysis") and the overall success of determining anomalies from drug profiles. Unsupervised machine learning approaches in image analysis that provide an alternative to feature engineering are much needed. DL-based image analysis techniques are most suited for feature extraction and subsequent classification of features in HCA. We present three approaches that employ DL techniques for studying and estimating drug toxicity in images. Also, toxicity detection using high-throughput imaging and DL techniques can consist of the steps as shown in Fig. 6.

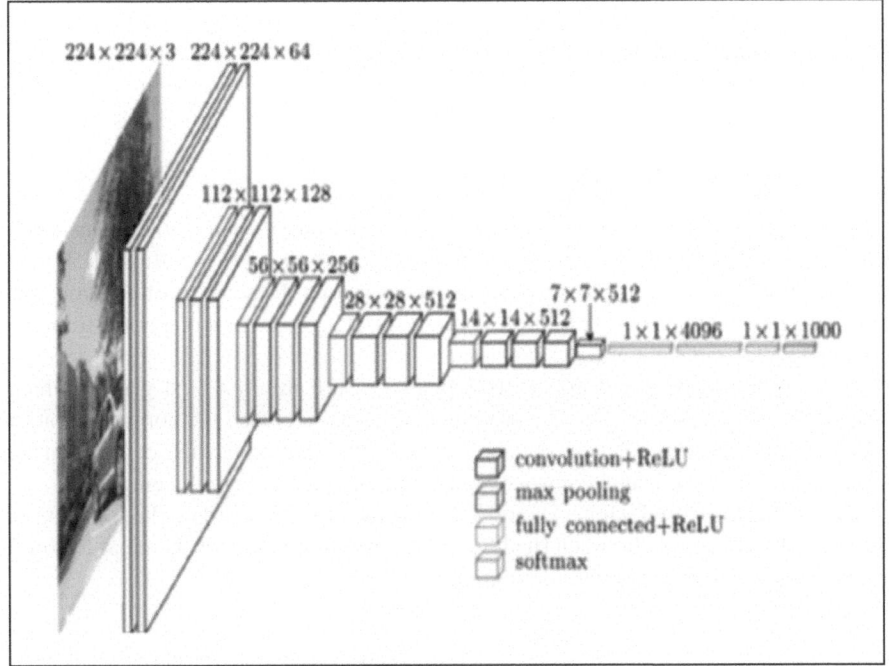

Fig. 5. CNN topology architecture

5.2 Key Features in the Usage of DL [27]

Drug toxicity in fluorescently labelled nuclei images has been studied and estimated using DL [27]. In [27], a deep CNN architecture was implemented to predict cell-based health status obtained from microscopy photos of DAPI-stained nuclei. This allowed for the independent determination of toxicity based on cell density and the identification of pre-lethal toxicity.

Conventional image processing techniques are used to separate the nuclei and cytoplasm based on the DAPI signal. Segmentation is employed to crop images. Independent

CNN models were trained using cropped pictures, each with a mass-centered cell, to provide toxicity predictions [27]. The result of CNN models is a "health status" score as output for every cell, which estimates a binary classification: toxicity or healthy impacted [27]. CNN requires images labelled as per expected O/P (toxicity or healthy impacted) as reference images for training purposes and is thus a supervised learning technique. The "general" toxicity was measured per well based on the proportion of cells the various CNN models deemed healthy [27].

Results:

1. It was observed that the Tox_CNN model, which relies on nuclei cropping, fared better than competing methods when it came to determining the health condition of individual cells [27].
2. When compared to existing toxicity readouts, both Tox_R(CNN) models were more sensitive and had broader specificity, when it came to detecting pre-lethal toxicity from nuclei images [27].
3. The Tox_(R)CNN models offer reliable, sensitive, and affordable in vitro drug-induced toxicity screening techniques [27].

5.3   Key Features in the Usage of DL [30]

In [12], an approach using DL to identify digital assay images automatically has been proposed. A CNN is trained to classify binary and multi-class [12]. A ResNet-50 [13] based CNN has been trained to segment images based on the survival of cell colonies using pre-processed images. To train ResNet-50, a CNN, over a million photos from the ImageNet collection were utilized [12].

A single image of size 1392 × 1036 pixels is split into a 4 × 4 grid in which every tile is of size 348 × 259. The pre-processing step included the normalization of pixel intensities. The conclusion obtained from [12] is that automated cellular image classification can significantly enhance high-throughput toxicology systems.

The application of DL strategies in [12] show the efficiency of DL classification in accurately discriminating between Healthy and Altered monolayers of chemical-exposed hepatic cells in bright field photomicrographs.

Results:

1. According to [12], the CNNs that were designed demonstrate excellent recall, and precision for the majority class across all of the datasets that were utilized in the research studies [12].
2. The model results show a strong link between dosage and the classifier's predicted scores, which suggest that it might be possible to find an image morphological baseline dose (BMD) [12].
3. The results indicate that DL-based automated cellular image segmentation could greatly improve the reliability and validity of cytotoxicity tests for different cell types [12].

5.4   Key Features in the Usage of DL [5]

Another notable application of DL techniques is extracting image-based features from information-rich biological images. The application falls under image-based profiling

[29]. Image-based profiling needs pictures of biological data showing how each case differs.

The processed images extract features that are combined to create profiles [14]. The feature extraction stage has evolved from expert-defined feature extraction to data-driven DL. The collected profiles are examined for biologically significant similarities and differences [14].

Results:

1. By employing DL and single-cell techniques to more effectively extract biological information from photos, drug discovery can be expedited [14].
2. The extensive data inherent in biological images is condensed into a multidimensional profile, which comprises a completion of image-based features that have been extracted [14].
3. Mining these profiles for relevant patterns potentially reveals previously unknown biological activity useful for prediction of drug toxicity [14]. Identifying trends in these profiles may reveal new biological activity valuable for drug toxicity detection [14].

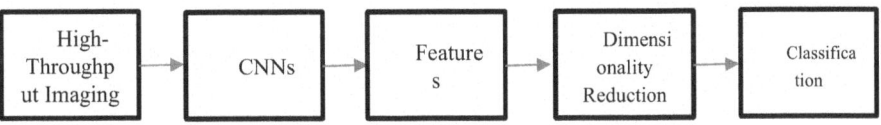

Fig. 6. Steps for toxicity detection using DL technique

6   Limitations and Future Scope

Imaging as a part of in vitro screening is also becoming more widely acknowledged vital in toxicology and pharmacology. Due to imaging, researchers can evaluate integrated features of the biological response to ambient chemical exposures, making it easier to characterize complicated cellular biology dynamics. High-throughput imaging systems generate thousands of results that must be processed for detection and classification to determine the occurrence of cell toxicity. The high-content analysis involves image analysis and automated microscopy. High-content screening systems developed since the one created by Cellomics have undergone many technological advances, thus advancing the need for standards and formats for the images and metadata generated. The lack of a common platform for data exchange and easy interpretation of analysis tools has prevented using multiple image analysis tools for the same dataset of images. Each step in HCA is associated with high degrees of computer-driven automation, thus increasing the computer processing power needed for efficiently performing data analysis and retrieval. The future of HCA systems will involve imaging and the parallel image analysis of living cells in a time-lapse format.

Recent developments in creating more complicated context-based image analysis software tools and machine learning techniques enable the creation of custom image analysis algorithms that can be adapted to more intricate biological models [30]. The findings show that automated DL-based image categorization of changes in cell shape brought on by chemically induced stress may produce exact and repeatable cytotoxicity evaluations across many cell types. Using DNNs, it is now possible to detect subtle, complicated patterns in enormous datasets [30]. DNNs are machine learning techniques that employ a collection of model parameters and operators that, following a training (fitting) process, enable input data to be turned into meaningful outputs. DL techniques can generalize to related data inputs while requiring far less human feature building and parameter adjustment than earlier ML techniques.

The data becomes even more overwhelming as we continue to extract more information from a single cell and as the complexity of some experiments rises. Traditional image analysis may be complex and time-consuming when carried out manually or semi-automatically. There is always a chance for human error and bias due to the challenging and detailed nature of the undertaking. The chance to use machine learning arises when you consider the workflow's repetitive, protracted, and sometimes laborious nature. AI eliminates individual variance, human error, and bias, enhancing data quality and confidence, optimizing processes, and increasing productivity. DL-based image analysis techniques are most suited for feature extraction and subsequent classification of features in HCA.

7 Conclusion

Through automated microscopy and image processing, high-throughput imaging tests have been demonstrated to be an efficient prediction technique in the early phases of drug development, making large-scale measurement of cellular morphological responses possible [4, 8]. In recent years, high-throughput imaging technologies have captured photomicrographs and recorded the cell morphology in each well of multi-well test plates throughout time. These systems provide thousands of findings that require subjective and time-consuming human interpretations. It has been shown in [4] that, data cleaning methods positively impact the quality of extracted features. This affects the mechanisms of actions of different drugs and increases the odds ratio. Removing toxic outliers gives a more real and meaningful odds ratio.

A split-merge watershed technique was created in [8] for fluorescence microscopy cell segmentation. Findings from [8] demonstrated that this approach achieved a satisfactory middle ground between over- and under-segmentation, in addition to exhibiting great accuracy. However, [8] mentions DL architectures out-performing the split-merge watershed method. The advantage of the split-merge watershed method lies in the absence of the training process, making the proposed method suitable for databases with reduced data.

Designing a step-by-step approach for detecting toxicity in assay images requires the automatic detection and classification of thousands of assay images. The steps involved in this process are obtaining high-throughput microscopy images and using them to train CNNs designed to classify cell images as healthy or affected by toxic compounds. Unsupervised machine learning approaches in image analysis provide a much-needed relief to the tedious feature engineering process that requires the manual selection of features. Recently, it has been shown that DL-based image analysis techniques are most suited for feature extraction and subsequent classification of features in HCA. Before the advent of DL, reducing correlation and redundancy in the extracted features using feature selection and transformation techniques was a tedious task [31]. DL techniques replaced this task by learning descriptors directly from data [13].

The DL method has the dual benefit of being able to detect ambiguous areas in images and being resilient to noisy data sets; this is especially helpful for high-throughput toxicity screening, as the effects of a toxin may not be uniform across the cell culture well [12]. Overall, the future for automated classification of cellular data looks quite bright. A major hurdle in the path is the absence of curated datasets that can attract ML experts to propose newer, more accurate, more broadly applicable techniques using DL. The use of transfer-learning strategies can result in obtaining results faster. Such applications can be made available to users as deployment solutions, the results of which can be used to improve applications themselves.

In this review, we have studied the applications of image processing techniques for detecting toxicity in high-throughput microscopy images. We have suggested a step-by-step approach for the analysis of these images. This review also focuses on DL strategies for the same purpose. Though in its early stage, DL strategies have made a remarkable progress in biological image analysis [13]. The success of these approaches lies in their feasibility of being integrated into existing high-throughput toxicology pipeline [12]. DL models have demonstrated robust behavior, sensitivity, and cost-effectiveness for in vitro screening of drug-induced toxicity [27]. Therefore, DL techniques have a promising future in drug-induced toxicity studies and can eliminate the manual screening of large datasets.

Acknowledgements. This research was partially funded by the University of Malta Internal Research Grants Programme's Research Excellence Fund (Grant Reference NICE-Healthcare). Any views or opinions presented herein are those of the authors and do not necessarily represent those of funders, their associates or their sponsors.

References

1. Caicedo, J.C., et al.: Date-analysis strategies for image-based cell profiling. Nat. Methods **14**, 849–863 (2017)
2. Driscoll, M., Zaritsky, A.: Data science in cell imaging. J. Cell Sci. **134**, 1–8 (2021)
3. Flotow, H., Henkel, M.: Assay development for image-based high-content screening. Drug Target Review **3** (2017)
4. Rezvani, A., Bigverdi, M., Rohban, M.H.: Image-based cell profiling enhancement via data cleaning methods. PLOS ONE **17**(5) (2022)
5. Mohs, R., Greig, N.: Data science in cell imaging. J. Cell Sci. **3**, 651–657 (2017)
6. Pegoraro, G., Misteli, T.: High-throughput imaging for the discovery of cellular mechanisms of diseases. Trends Genet. **33**, 604–615 (2017)
7. Logan, D.J., Carpenter, A.E.: Screening Cellular Feature Measurements for Image-Based Assay Development **15**(7), 840–846 (2010)
8. Gamarra, M., Zurek, E., Escalante, H.J., Hurtado, L., San-Juan-Vergara, H.: Split and merge watershed: a two-step method for cell segmentation in fluorescence microscopy images. Biomed. Signal Process. Control, 53 (2019)

9. Simm, J., et al.: Repurposing high-throughput image assays enables biological activity prediction for drug discovery. Cell Chem. Biol. **25**, 616–618 (2018)

10. Aulner, N., Danckaert, A., Ihm, J., Shum, D., Shorte, S.: Next-generation phenotypic screening in early drug discovery for infectious diseases. Trends Parasitol. **37**(7), 559–570 (2019)

11. Semenova, E., et al.: A bayesian neural network for toxicity prediction. Computational Toxicity **16**, 100133 (2020)

12. Tandon, A., et al.: Deep learning image analysis of high-throughput toxicology assay images. SLAS Discovery **27**(1), 29–38 (2022)

13. Moen, E., Bannon, D., Kudo, T., Graf, W., Covert, M., Van Valen, D.: Deep learning for cellular image analysis. Nat. Methods **16**(12), 1233–1246 (2019)

14. Chandrasekaran, S.N., Ceulemans, H., Boyd, J.D., et al.: Image-based profiling for drug discovery: due for a machine-learning upgrade? Nat. Rev. Drug Discov. **20**, 145–159 (2021)

15. Matthews, A., Tan, K., Suharyo, P.B.: A systematic literature review: Image segmentation on brain MRI image to detect brain tumor. 2022 International Conference on Science and Technology (ICOTECH) (2022)

16. Carpenter, A.E., Jones, T.R., Lamprecht, M.R., et al.: Cell Profiler: image analysis software for identifying and quantifying cell phenotypes. Genome Biol. **7**, R100 (2006)

17. Gough, A.H., Johnston, P.A.: Requirements, features, and performance of high content screening platforms. High Content Screening. Methods in Molecular Biology, 356, Humana Press, 41–61 (2007)

18. Sharif, A., Kangas, J., Coelho, L.P., Quinn, S., Murphy, R.F.: Automated image analysis for high content screening and analysis. J. Biomed. Screen. **15**(7), 734–756 (2010)

19. Smal, I., Draegestein, K., Galijart, N., Niessen, W., Meijering, E.: Particle filtering for multiple object tracking in dynamic fluorescence images: application to microtubule growth analysis. IEEE Trans. Med. Imaging **27**, 789–804 (2008)

20. Zeng, D.Z.: Deep learning-based image analysis for high-content screening. M.Sc Thesis. Victoria University of Wellington (2021)

21. Simpson, J.C.: Basics of image analysis in high content screening. European Pharmaceutical Review, 6 (2009)

22. Lind, R.: 5-Open-source software for image processing and analysis: picture this with Image. In: Harland, J.L., Forster, M. (eds.) Open-source software in life science research, pp. 131–149. Woodhead Publishing (2012)

23. Gilbert, D.F., Meinhof, T., Pepperkop, R., Runz, H.: DetecTiff: a novel image analysis routine for high-content screening microscopy. J. Biomed. Screen. **14**(8), 944–955 (2009)

24. Kankaanpää, P., Paavolainen, L., Titta, S., et al.: BioImageXD: an open, general-purpose, and high-throughput image processing platform. Nat. Methods **9**, 683–689 (2012)

25. Olympus Corporation: The Olympus ScanR high-content screening station rapidly acquires quantitative data from cell-based assays. Lab Manager (2019). https://www.labmanager.com/the-olympus-scanr-high-content-screening-station-rapidly-acquires-quantitative-data-from-cell-based-assays-16308

26. Conrad, C., et al.: Automatic identification of subcellular phenotypes on human cell arrays. Genome Res. **14**, 1130–1136 (2004)

27. Jimenez-Carretero, D., et al.: Tox-(R)CNN: Deep learning-based nuclei profiling tool for drug toxicity screening. PLOS Computational Biology **14**(11) (2018)

28. Baatz, M., Arini, N., Schape, A., Binnig, G., Linssen, B.: Object-oriented image analysis for high content screening: detailed quantification of cells and sub cellular structures with the Cellenger software. Cytometry A **69**, 652–658 (2006)

29. Warchal, S.J.: Image informatics approaches to advance cancer drug discovery, PhD Thesis. The University of Edinburgh (2018)

30. Yang, S.J., Lipnick, S.L., et al.: Applying deep neural network analysis to high-content image-based assays. SLAS Discov. **24**, 829–841 (2019)

31. Zheng, H., Wang, R., Yu, Z., Wang, N., Gu, Z., Zhang, B.: Automated plankton image classification combining multiple view features via multiple kernel learning. BMC Bioinform.
18(16), 570 (2017)
32. Jones, T.R., et al.: BMC Bioinformatics **9**, 482 (2008)
33. Rybacka, A., Andersson, P.L.: Considering ionic state in modelling sorption of pharmaceu-
ticals to sewage sludge. Chemosphere **165**, 248–293 (2016)
34. Sino, N.I., Farhan, R.N., Seno, M.E.: Review of deep learning algorithms in computational
biochemistry. J. Phys: Conf. Ser. **1804**, 012135 (2021)
35. Wollman, R., Stuurman, N.: High throughput microscopy: from raw images to discoveries.
J. Cell Sci. **120**, 3715–3722 (2007)

Augmented Reality Immersive World with Hologram Special Effect in Early Childhood Education

Maria Seraphina Astriani[1]([⊠]), Raymond Bahana[1], Arif Priyono Susilo Ahmad[2], Andreas Kurniawan[1], and Lee Huey Yi[3]

[1] Computer Science Department, School of Computing and Creative Arts, Bina Nusantara University, Jakarta 11480, Indonesia
seraphina@binus.ac.id
[2] Creative Advertising Program, Visual Communication Design Department, School of Design, Bina Nusantara University, Jakarta 11480, Indonesia
[3] Water Lily, 75200 Melaka, Malaysia

Abstract. Early childhood education is a critical stage of education because it may establish the foundation for an individual's intelligence. Students of this age group are generally unable to remain seated and study for long periods of time because they get bored easily. They are more likely to be attracted to visual information and enjoy interactive activities. This condition challenges the world of education to keep developing learning methods that are able to help students to learn the materials. The combination of Augmented Reality technology and hologram special effects is a promising solution because it allows students to see an immersive world and allows them to interact with real-life physical objects while learning. Augmented Reality immersive world solution with hologram special effects in early childhood education has successfully been tested and implemented by using two smartphones, one acts as an input-camera and the other acts as an output to display the hologram. This solution is specially designed to make it easier for students to learn the materials without using wearable devices.

Keywords: Augmented Reality · Hologram · Education · Early Childhood · Immersive

1 Introduction

Human personality and intelligence development typically begins in childhood [1]. As a result, early childhood education (from birth up to 8 years) is a critical stage because it can shape the intelligence of an individual. Students of this age group are generally unable to remain seated and study for long periods of time because they tend to get bored. They are more drawn to visual information and enjoy interactive activities [2, 3]. This condition challenges the world of education to keep developing learning methods that can assist students to learn the materials.

A. Mirzazadeh et al. (Eds.): SEMIT 2023, CCIS 2198, pp. 176–186, 2024.
https://doi.org/10.1007/978-3-031-72284-4_11

Researchers generally continue doing the investigation on the discipline of learning methods because they perceive numerous potentials for development that suit current conditions. The rapid advancement of technology is one of the major factors that is influencing the world of education, so the adoption of technology must occur during the learning process. Augmented Reality (AR) is one technology that has the potential to be used in the educational sector because it is able to combine digital content in real-time with objects in the real world (real-life physical objects) so people can experience and feel the immersive world [4, 5].

Educating children at an early childhood has its own challenges because they generally have a shorter attention span compared to adult. Factually, children often struggle to concentrate and get bored easily during study sessions. They generally cannot sit still and pay attention to the teacher's explanation if the learning duration is quite long [2, 3]. They prefer to play, have a high sense of curiosity (especially if there is something new), and get bored more easily. The application of AR in education can help students to learn because it makes learning more interesting and interactive. AR technology makes teaching method presented differently compared to conservative methods since students can play while learning, which keeps them motivated and helps them absorb the information being taught [4, 5].

The concept of a hologram is the illusion of something that does not exist but visible while we see it [6]. This illusion technique has long been discovered and are often used in exhibitions, shows, amusement parks, and so on [7]. Floating hologram is a special effect hologram that uses a transparent screen to project images or videos so that the result looks like it is floating in the air [7]. The use of hologram in education area is still novel. Hologram is predicted to expand significantly in the context of technological applications and research related with effectiveness - utilization [8]. Although hologram technology has been tested and applied in educational settings, the subjects and topics covered were limited [9]. Special effect holograms are not yet widely available in everyday life, so seeing this hologram may astound and cause these moments to be recorded in the memory (brain) [10]. If the benefits of using holograms are applied to the educational sector, it is hoped that the "wow" effect produced by holograms will make students interested and help them remember learning material longer.

The availability of AR and hologram technology has inspired researchers to combine these technologies to provide a solution to solve problems that occur in early childhood education. This solution is expected to enable children to actively interact with objects in real-life and see the projection results in the form of holograms. The study was not discussed the health impacts of devices' radiation and limited to early childhood education, especially preschool teaching materials to teach children to recognize school's stationeries and distinguish whether they belong to the school's stationeries category or not.

2   Method

Based on the research that have been conducted [10], using one device (smartphone) for a portable AR installation solution with hologram special effect is ideal if the target is to provide portable result and does not require many physical devices (Fig. 1). However, in terms of user convenience (especially children), the upward facing position of the smartphone's camera makes it quite difficult to position the object (made from building block toys) within range of the camera that can fully capture the object. The object used as a marker must be placed above the smartphone's camera and fully visible in order for the AR application to detect it. If the object is not completely captured, the software will be unable to process it and produce the expected output. The transparent panel used in this research only uses one panel which is placed in a box with two openings. To ensure that children can see the hologram result, it is recommended to view the hologram from the front side of the box. This installation design dan result is suitable for use by one child. However, this condition is not the right solution if more than one child wants to see the hologram at the same time.

Fig. 1. Result of the previous research [10].

The solution designed for this research takes the consideration of the past research analysis result so that the constraints of earlier research can be avoided. The proposed method involves using two devices separately. One device acts as a camera (input), while the other acts as an output to display the result of the AR application. Using one transparent panel is not an issue if the hologram is only seen by one child. However, to make it easier for the hologram to be seen from other sides and more comfortable if more than one child would like to see the hologram, the transparent panel used can use a pyramid shape so it can be seen from four different sides. Because the output must be reflected on all four sides, the marker's virtual object must be changed from previous research. Previously, it was enough to use one angle of virtual object. If the pyramid shape is used to reflect the hologram, the maker's virtual object needs to be duplicated four times and each of them must be rotated 90°. The number of transparent panels used in this research is one, so each student can focus to learn and use the solution only for them and not bothered with other children to reach child maximum potential. If this research would like to be conducted by other researchers and the number of physical devices available is available and not restricted, it is suggested that a pyramid shape transparent panel can be used so the solution can be enjoyed by four children at once.

AR with hologram special effect in early childhood education solution is able to create an immersive world to combine real-life physical object with virtual object. Two main components are needed to create this solution: physical object and software. It is best to avoid using wearable technology to maintain the simplicity and convenient for children because the main target of the solution intended for children in early childhood education.

Physical devices are all the tools/devices/hardware needed to support the development and usage of the solution. The physical devices needed to create AR with hologram special effects in early childhood education solutions are two smartphones (or one smartphone and one tablet), a tripod/smartphone stand, server (cloud), transparent panel, and various school's stationeries as AR markers. The software used for this solution are remote connectivity software, AR application (web-based), and browser. The AR application used needs to have the ability to design AR (AR maker), capture, process and display AR results on the browser (AR Client).

Researchers use a web-based application because the application can be viewed mostly on all smartphone devices (not limited to smartphone brand, type, or operating system) and only requires browser to access it. In order for the browser to access the smartphone's camera, it is crucial to make sure that both the smartphone and the browser being used still meet minimum requirements. For convenience and performance, researchers recommend that the smartphone and browser used should not be older than 3 years. The AR application used in this solution can be built in-house if there are sufficient resources and time to develop the application. If not, using the existed AR application that have an AR maker can be a right choice [10–12]. Because researchers have done some researches related with AR before, the AR application used in this research was not built from scratch but used a pre-existing AR application.

The two smartphones that been used have two different tasks. One smartphone functions as a camera (input) and the other smartphone functions as a device to display AR results (output) so the output from the smartphone's screen can be reflected on the transparent panel to produce a hologram. To make operation easier, the smartphone that functions as a camera has to have a browser and remote connectivity software installed. The proposed flowchart method used when children use the solution is based on previous research [10], and the results of the enhancement and expansion of the method can be seen in Fig. 2.

The smartphone that functions as a camera (smartphone 1) needs to use the camera installed on the smartphone to be able to capture the object (input). The objects used in this research are school's stationeries that function as AR markers. Smartphone 1 needs to have an internet connection to be able to open the AR application in the browser. When AR application is used, input captured from the smartphone's camera is processed using computer vision technology, and the results will be compared with the object's data that has been stored on the server. If the AR application successfully identifies

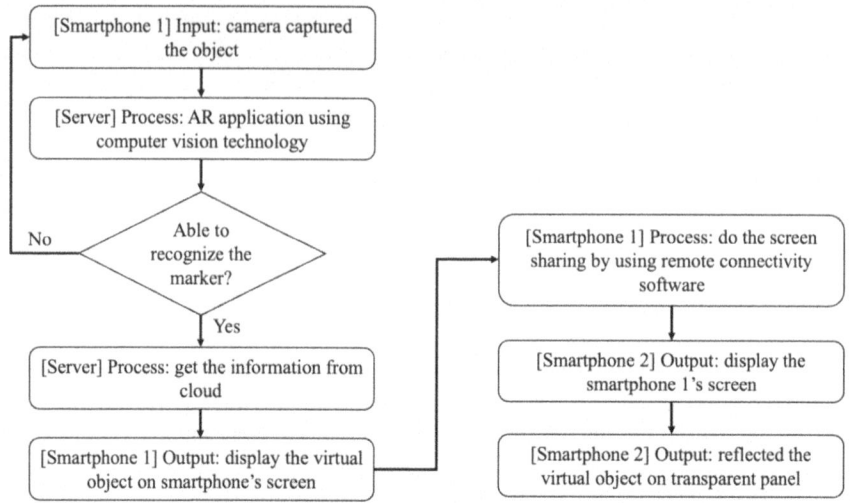

Fig. 2. Flowchart - method.

the marker, then the information related to the marker will be taken from the server to be sent to smartphone 1 and the AR output (virtual object) will be displayed on the smartphone 1 screen. Because remote connectivity software has been installed on both of the smartphones, the output results from smartphone 1 will be forwarded to the other smartphone (smartphone 2). The output produced on smartphone 2 will be exactly the same as seen on smartphone 1. The brightness setting on smartphone 2 needs to be adjusted (bright enough) so the output displayed on the screen can be reflected on the transparent panel to form a holographic display.

3   Result and Discussion

The research is divided into three main stages: preparation, marker creation, and AR-hologram usage. The preparation stage consists of preparing the physical devices and software needed for marker creation and AR application. Marker creation focuses on making AR markers for school's stationeries. AR-hologram usage stage is the solution implementation for users (children) so they can use the solution to learn school's stationeries. The details of the implementation of three stages in this research can be seen in Subsects. 3.1, 3.2, and 3.3. Test results, analysis and research discussion are in Subsect. 3.4.

3.1   Preparation

Architecture and installation design that describe the hardware infrastructure, software needed, and how the solution that will be used by children will look need to be created first to make it easier for researchers to prepare the physical devices and software that will be used. The design of architecture and installation needs to be built to minimize errors or failures that can occur when the solution is developed. Generally, architecture design only displays hardware or software architecture only. However, the architecture and installation design of the AR immersive world solution with hologram special effects in early childhood education is very unique because it combines hardware and software simultaneously in the design (Fig. 3).

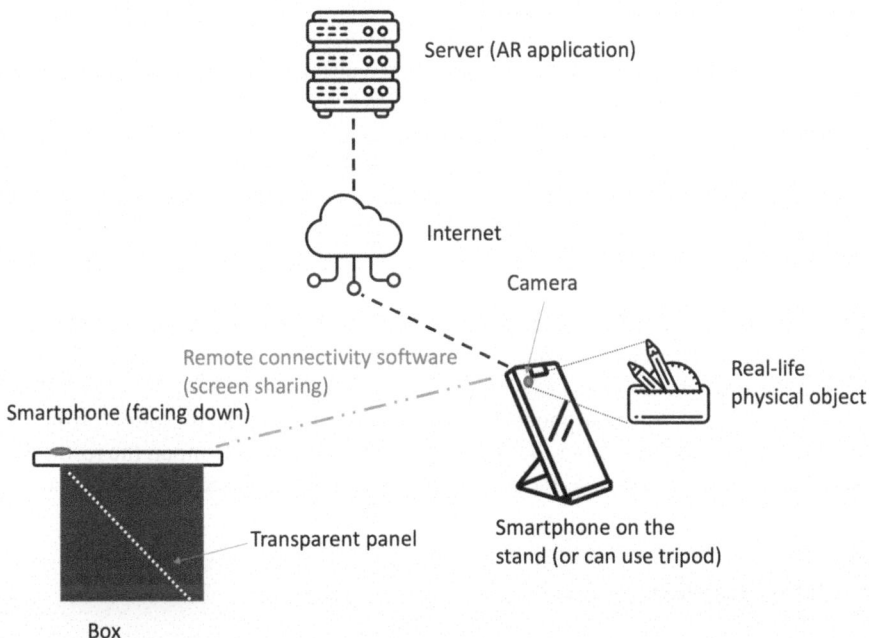

Fig. 3. The design of architecture and installation of the AR immersive world solution with hologram special effects in early childhood education.

Based on the architecture and installation design, it can be concluded that the solution requires two smartphones, tripod/smartphone stand, server (cloud), transparent panel, school's stationeries, AR application, remote connectivity software, and browser. Other components needed are internet and a box with two opening to place the transparent panel.

The AR application used in this research is based on web (web-based application) and can be run in a browser. This AR application has features to be able to design AR display content (AR maker) as well as an AR Client which has features to capture the input from the camera, process the input, and display AR result (virtual object) in the browser. AR applications can be used/accessed using a browser installed on a smartphone 1. Because the AR application is a web-based application, all application files and other data (including marker data and AR display content design results/virtual object) related to this application will be stored on a server in the cloud. Therefore, it is necessary to ensure that smartphone 1 can access the internet smoothly so there will be no issue when the solution is used by children and the results can be seen in real-time.

Because smartphone 1 acts as a camera to capture objects (real-life physical objects), it must be mounted on a tripod or stand so it is sturdy. The objects used in this research are school's stationeries that are generally used by children in early childhood education, such as eraser, pencil, pen, ruler, pencil sharpener, and pencil case. Because the school's stationeries will be needed during the marker creation stage, all of these objects must be prepared first.

Remote connectivity software (ApowerMirror) needs to be installed on smartphone 1 and make sure that the browser has been installed on the smartphone too. To allow the screen sharing between smartphones, smartphone 2 also requires ApowerMirror so that the AR output results that appear on smartphone 1's browser can be seen on smartphone 2's screen.

Smartphone 2 needs to be placed on top of the box with the smartphone's screen facing downwards so the hologram special effect can be reflected by the transparent panel underneath. The box is made from plastic with dimensions of 6 cm length, 7 cm width, 7 cm height, and has 0.1 cm thickness. The box used in this research is very special, because it only has 4 sides and has opening at the top and at the front side. The transparent panel needs to be placed in the box with a 45° angle and facing the front side of the box. The transparent panel used is made of thin acrylic with a thickness of 0.5 cm and has 5.9 cm height and 9.85 cm width.

Internet is needed so smartphone 1 can send the input that been captured from the camera to the cloud server. After the AR application processes the input, the result will be sent back via the internet so the virtual object can be displayed on the browser on smartphone 1.

3.2 Marker Creation

One of the features in AR application is AR maker. This feature has the ability to design AR display content to produce a virtual object. Because the AR application is web-based application and can be opened in a browser, content design creation can be done on a smartphone 1 by using the browser. However, researchers used a computer while using AR Maker to make real-life physical object markers because it is easier to see the results and researcher can comfortably design the AR display content by using a mouse.

Researchers used a browser on the computer to open the AR application and selected the AR maker menu. The appearance of the AR Maker working area uses the concept that been used in the application to create a 3D graphic and the objects placed in this working area can be manipulated (translation, scaling, rotation, flip, coloring, and so on).

The school's stationeries that have been prepared as a markers (eraser, pencil, pen, ruler, pencil sharpener, and pencil case) need to be photographed one by one and it is necessary to ensure that the result of the images are sharp and bright enough. Each of the image then needs to be cropped and be adjusted to the shape of the object (Fig. 4).

If the marker for a pencil case been made, the edited pencil case image can be inserted into the AR Maker working area and placed in the middle, adjusted the size (approximately the length or width of 10 working area grids), and make sure the direction of the marker is facing up (aligned with z axis). The "Pencil Case" text can be added to the working area and the styles (font type, font size, and color) can be edited. To let the

Fig. 4. Pencil case marker that have been cropped and adjusted to fit the object.

children learn how to pronounce "Pencil Case", the audio was added on it. The green checkmark been added to indicate "Pencil Case" is a school's stationery. Because the output produced by smartphone 2 will be reflected on the transparent panel, the entire design needs to be mirrored. The design process for marker creation can be continued until it produced the expected results. If the design process already been done, the working area can be saved and the result (called virtual object) will be stored on the server. If making the design content for the "Pencil Case" has been completed, the process can be continued and work on the remaining markers. An example of the result of the "Pencil Case" design content can be seen in Fig. 5.

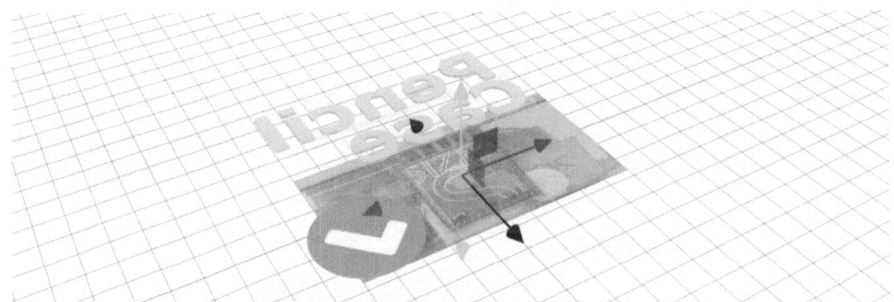

Fig. 5. AR maker – pencil case design content.

3.3 AR-Hologram Usage

The researchers set up the installation according to the design made in Fig. 3. The ApowerMirror application needs to be turned on first and need to be checked to make sure that the smartphone 1 screen result have successfully appeared on smartphone 2.

In order to be able to use the AR immersive world solution with hologram special effects to teaches children in early childhood to recognize school's stationeries and to differentiate whether they are included in the school's stationery category or not, the AR application - AR Client needs to be opened by an adult using a browser on smartphone 1 by entering the web address of the AR application. If there is more than one installation (used by more than one child), all smartphone 1 devices need to be set up.

After setting up the devices, the solution can be directly used by the children. Children can take one of the school's stationary (for example a pencil case) and bring the object closer to the smartphone 1's camera to be captured. As the result, the virtual object for the "Pencil Case" content that has been created on the marker creation will be reflected by transparent panel as a hologram in the box (Fig. 6). Because the audio been added before, the voice that pronounced "Pencil Case" will be played if the pencil case was detected by AR Client.

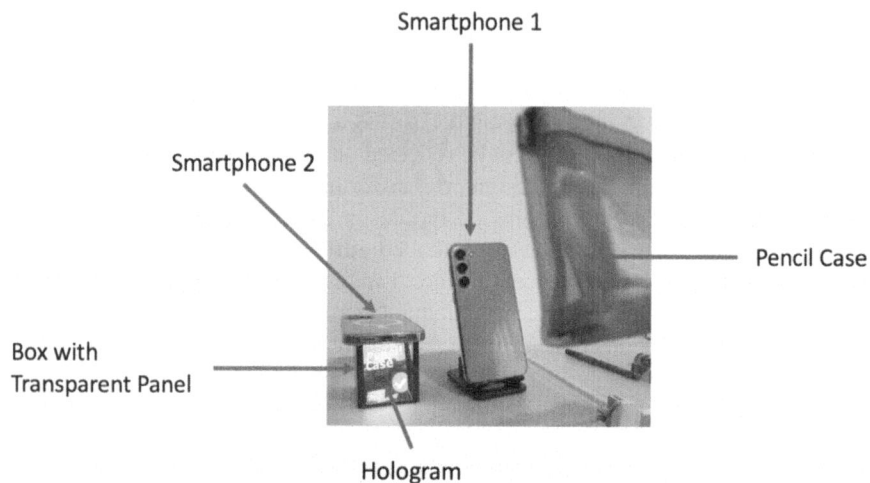

Fig. 6. Solution result

3.4 Test, Analysis, and Discussion

The AR immersive world solution with hologram special effect in early childhood education was tested by a kindergarten child (tester) and used pencil case, pencil sharpener, and other objects that are not included in the school's stationeries. This testing assessed user friendliness, how the tester reacts when using the solution, and the learning outcomes.

Kindergarten child generally still need to be supervised by adults. Because the solution used requires a couple of devices, it is best for the tester to be supervised by an adult to prevent the devices from being tampered to prevent damaged.

The tester entered the room where the installation has been set and the real-life physical objects such as school's stationeries and other objects has been put beside the installation. Tester was given a verbal instruction and demonstrated how to use them. The tester was asked to take a pencil case object, bring the object closer to smartphone 1's camera, and see the hologram result on the box. If the object was categorized as a school's stationery, the tester would saw a virtual object and heard the pronunciation of that object. If the object was not included in school's stationery category, then no virtual object will be shown. This test was conducted by using several real-life physical objects and carried out independently by the tester without the help of adult.

Researchers observed tester, how tester carried out the test and then analyzed the result. The tester was curious and very enthusiastic to try the solution. The tester quickly took the object and placed it near smartphone 1's camera, amazed when saw the hologram result in the box, and wanted to try again to do the same thing but with another object. Tester was able to learn how to pronounce the object by listening to the audio that played if the object categorized as school's stationery.

Separating input and output into two devices was a right decision because the tester can more easily point the object to the camera while seeing the results. Despite the fact that previous researchers' limitations have been conquered, the tester needs to look down a bit to see the results of the hologram in the box because some part of the hologram has been covered by the smartphone 2 placed above it. This condition, however, can be alleviated by positioning the box at the eye level. To engage more user interaction and visibility, the box and the transparent can be made bigger and use a flexible smartphone holder to let the smartphone 1 be adjusted based on user's position. Researchers noticed if the internet connection is not stable, even though the object has been placed in front of the camera, the AR Client still hasn't displayed the virtual object. This problem can possibly be minimized if data compression technology been used to compress the data sent to the server and also compress data from the server to the smartphone. Based on the preliminary research conducted by the researchers, zlib had the highest compression rations but slower compression speed compared to Zstandard. Zlib has the possibility to be used for this solution if the compression speed is not an issue.

Researchers are pleased with the results of the test that have been carried out so researchers can find out the results, impact, and analyze the advantages and disadvantages of this solution. In the future, additional testing could be conducted with diverse groups of young learners to assess the effectiveness of the solution in different contexts and user profiles. There is also an opportunity for collaboration with educators/child development specialist to refine the solution based on pedagogical principles and developmental considerations.

4   Conclusion and Recommendation

AR and hologram technology can be combined to provide a solution to solve problems that occur in early childhood education. AR immersive world solution with hologram special effects in early childhood education successfully been implemented by using two devices as the enhancement from the previous research. One device acts as a camera (input), while the other acts as an output to display the hologram results. This solution enables children to actively interact with objects in real-life, see the hologram, and having a fun time while learning about school's stationeries.

The box is recommended to be placed at the eye level of the user or the box (and also the panel) needs to be made bigger so it can be used more comfortably. Flexible smartphone holder can be used to adjust the position of smartphone 1. Data compression technology, zlib, has a prospect to be used on the solution to compress the data if the internet connection is not stable because the data's file size will be smaller. In the future, additional testing can be conducted with more users and the collaboration with educators/child development specialist needs to be carried out to refine the solution.

Acknowledgement. This work is supported by Research and Technology Transfer Office, Bina Nusantara University as a part of Bina Nusantara University's International Research Grant entitled Teaching and Learning Augmented Reality Installation with Hologram Special Effect with contract number: 029/VRRTT/III/2023 and contract date: 1 March 2023.

References

1. Dunkel, C.S., van der Linden, D., Kawamoto, T.: Maternal supportiveness is predictive of childhood general intelligence. Intelligence **98**, 101754 (2023)
2. Hoon, L.N., Shaharuddin, S.S.: Learning effectiveness of 3D hologram animation on primary school learners. J. Visual Art and Design **11**(2), 93–104 (2019)
3. Gilakjani, A.P.: A study on the impact of using multimedia to improve the quality of English language teaching. J. Lang. Teach. Res. **3**(6) (2012)
4. Kamphuis, C., Barsom, E., Schijven, M., Christoph, N.: Augmented reality in medical education? Perspect. Med. Edu. **3**, 300–311 (2014)
5. Roopa, D., Prabha, R., Senthil, G.A.: Revolutionizing education system with interactive augmented reality for quality education. In: Materials Today on Proceedings **46**, 3860–3863 (2021)
6. Pietroni, E., Ferdani, D., Forlani, M., Pagano, A., Rufa, C.: Bringing the illusion of reality inside museums-A methodological proposal for an advanced museology using holographic showcases. Informatics **6**(1) (2019)
7. Song, S.S., Kim, B.K., Hong, S.D.: Studies on reflection hologram technology applied miniature hologram types. Webology **19**(1), 4716–4723 (2022)
8. Yoo, H., Jang, J., Oh, H., Park, I.: The potentials and trends of holography in education: a scoping review. Comput. Educ. **186**, 104533 (2022)
9. Wójcik, M.: Holograms in libraries–the potential for education, promotion and services. Library Hi Tech. **36**(1), 18–28 (2018)
10. Astriani, M.S., Bahana, R., Ahmad, A.P.S., Yi, L.H.: Portable augmented reality installation with hologram special effect for kids' education to learn everyday objects. In: E3S Web of Conferences, vol. 426, p. 02021 (2023)
11. Astriani, M.S., Bahana, R., Ahmad, A.P.S., Yi, L.H.: Bee AR teacher collaborative learning augmented reality framework. J. Pharmaceut. Negat. Resu. 431–438 (2023)
12. Astriani, M.S., Bahana, R., Ahmad, A.P.S.: Bee AR teacher framework: build augmented reality independently in education. In: Conference on Innovative Technologies in Intelligent Systems and Industrial Applications, pp. 301–309 (2022)

Improving the Visual Ergonomics of Computerised Workplaces Through the Use of Specialised Eye-Rest Software

Tihomir Dovramadjiev$^{(\boxtimes)}$ ⓘ, Darina Dobreva ⓘ, and Ralitsa Zlateva

Department of Industrial Design, Technical University of Varna, Str. Studentska N1, 9010 Varna, Bulgaria
tihomir.dovramadjiev@tu-varna.bg

Abstract. This article focuses on improving the visual ergonomics of computer workstations through the use of specialised eye-rest software, taking into account human factors. Prolonged screen time at computer workstations often leads to visual discomfort and strain, collectively known as Computer Vision Syndrome (CVS). To address this problem, users/workers should be informed of the potential of eye-rest software as a solution. This article highlights how specialised eye-rest software incorporates techniques such as regular eye exercises, break reminders, screen adjustments and blue light filters to reduce visual strain and promote eye comfort. It presents recent research on the effectiveness of eye-rest software in reducing visual discomfort and CVS symptoms, taking into account the individual needs and preferences of users. The article also examines the challenges and opportunities associated with the implementation and adoption of eye-rest software, including user acceptance, software compatibility and organisational support. The potential benefits of ergonomic and eye-rest software in improving productivity and employee well-being by optimising visual ergonomics are detailed. The leading priorities in the article are to provide accessible digital resources to all stakeholders for visual health prevention and to optimal ergonomics in human – computer interaction (HCI) when working with digital workstations.

Keywords: Ergonomics · Human Factors · Workplaces · Computer Vision Syndrome (CVS) · Eye-rest software · Prevention

1 Introduction

In today's computerised workplaces, prolonged screen time has raised concerns about the visual discomfort and strain experienced by users, collectively known as Computer Vision Syndrome (CVS) [1–3]. This phenomenon has prompted researchers and developers to seek innovative solutions to improve the visual ergonomics of computer workstations. One such solution that is gaining traction is specialised eye-rest software that incorporates various techniques to reduce visual strain and promote eye comfort. CVS encompasses a range of symptoms, including eyestrain, dry eyes, blurred vision, headaches, and neck or shoulder pain. Visual discomfort refers to the physical and

A. Mirzazadeh et al. (Eds.): SEMIT 2023, CCIS 2198, pp. 187–198, 2024.
https://doi.org/10.1007/978-3-031-72284-4_12

psychological sensations experienced by users due to prolonged visual tasks, affecting productivity, performance and well-being. To address these challenges, it is essential to consider human factors, which include the psychological, physiological and ergonomic aspects of human behaviour and interaction. Understanding individual visual capabilities, viewing distances, lighting conditions, posture and personal preferences is critical to designing effective solutions. In addition, human-computer interaction (HCI) principles are essential to ensure user-friendly and efficient computer systems [4–6]. Eye-rest software plays a key role in optimising visual ergonomics. By incorporating techniques such as regular eye exercises, break reminders, screen adjustments and blue light filters, this software aims to reduce visual strain and promote eye comfort. The eye-rest software takes into account individual needs and preferences, providing personalised solutions to alleviate visual discomfort and CVS symptoms. Recent research has highlighted the effectiveness of eye-rest software in reducing visual discomfort and improving visual well-being. By providing tailored interventions and reminders, eye-rest software empowers users to adopt healthier visual habits and maintain long-term visual health in computerised work environments. In addition, the implementation and adoption of eye-rest software presents challenges such as user acceptance, software compatibility and organisational support. The importance of eye-rest software lies in its potential to improve employee productivity and well-being. By optimising visual ergonomics, this software can reduce the negative effects of CVS, resulting in increased performance, reduced absenteeism and improved overall wellbeing. In the realm of Human Computer Interaction (HCI), human factors and visual ergonomics play a crucial role in ensuring an optimal user experience and protecting the eyes from the potential risks associated with prolonged computer use. Understanding and addressing human factors and visual ergonomics is essential for the design of user-friendly computer systems and the implementation of specialised software aimed at protecting visual health. Human factors include the psychological, physiological and ergonomic aspects of human behaviour and interaction with technology. When it comes to visual ergonomics, it is essential to consider factors such as individual visual capabilities, viewing distances, lighting conditions, posture and personal preferences. By taking these factors into account, HCI practitioners and software developers can design interfaces and systems that minimise visual strain, enhance usability, and promote overall user well-being. Protecting the eyes with specialised software is in line with the principles of visual ergonomics. Such software, specifically designed to alleviate visual discomfort and reduce the risk of conditions such as CVS, incorporates various features to optimise the visual environment and promote healthy viewing habits. Computer eye safety prevention is an essential aspect of maintaining visual health in our increasingly digital world [7–10]. However, it is unfortunate that awareness and adoption of preventive measures for computer eye protection is not yet widespread among the general population. There is a need to raise awareness and inform society about the importance of taking proactive steps to protect their eyes when using computers. Many people spend long periods of time in front of digital screens, whether for work, education or leisure [11–23]. This prolonged screen time puts an immense strain on the eyes and increases the risk of developing visual discomfort, eye fatigue and long-term eye health problems [24–31]. It is important to recognise that preventive measures can significantly reduce these risks and contribute to better visual well-being [32–39]. An important aspect of specialised eye software is the integration of screen filters and additional tools. These filters and tools allow users to adjust screen brightness, contrast, and colour temperature to reduce eye strain and minimise exposure to harmful blue light emitted by digital screens. By controlling these visual elements, specialised software promotes a more comfortable and eye-friendly viewing experience. Focusing on screen adjustments, specialised software often includes break reminders and adjustable short break durations. These features encourage users to take regular breaks during long computer sessions, reducing eye fatigue and providing opportunities for rest and relaxation. By incorporating break reminders, software developers aim to instil healthy working habits and remind users of the importance of regular eye rest. Some specialised software offers vision therapy features to address common eye problems and improve various visual skills. These features include exercises and activities that target specific visual challenges, such as eye coordination or focusing difficulties. By incorporating vision therapy into the software, users can take proactive measures to correct or prevent visual problems, ultimately contributing to improved visual health. In order to increase the uptake of computer eye strain prevention, the focus needs to be on education and raising awareness of the potential risks of excessive screen time. Society needs to be informed about the symptoms and consequences of CVS, including eye strain, dry eyes, headaches and blurred vision. By understanding the impact of prolonged screen time on visual health, users can be motivated to prioritise eye protection. It is important to emphasise that computer eye protection goes beyond simply wearing glasses or using screen filters. Specialised software, as discussed earlier, offers a comprehensive approach to visual health by incorporating features such as blue light filters, screen adjustments, break reminders and eye exercises. However, many people are unaware of the existence and effectiveness of these solutions. The user interface of specialised vision software also plays an important role in ensuring optimal human-computer interaction. The software strives to provide an eye-pleasing and user-friendly interface that allows users to navigate and use the software effortlessly. A well-designed interface enhances usability, reduces cognitive load and promotes a positive user experience. Given the multifaceted nature of human factors and visual ergonomics, specialised eye software also recognises the importance of multilingual support. Although only partially available in some cases, offering software in multiple languages improves accessibility and ensures that users from different linguistic backgrounds can benefit from the visual health features provided. By incorporating human factors and visual ergonomics into the design and development of specialised eye software, HCI practitioners and software developers aim to create solutions that prioritise visual health, user comfort and productivity. These software tools, with their range of features and user-centred approach, offer a holistic solution to protecting the eyes and promoting healthier visual habits in the context of human-computer interaction. Ultimately, the integration of specialised eye software into computerised work environments is in line with the goal of safeguarding visual health, improving user experience and promoting a more productive and visually comfortable work environment. By combining human factors considerations, visual ergonomics principles, and specialised software features, organisations and users can work to mitigate the risks associated with prolonged computer use and promote long-term visual well-being.

Specialised eye-rest software offers a promising solution for improving visual ergonomics at computer workstations. By taking into account human factors and individual needs, this software aims to reduce visual discomfort, improve visual well-being and promote healthier visual habits. The effective implementation and adoption of eye-rest software has the potential to benefit both individuals (users) and organisations, leading to improved productivity and overall satisfaction in computerised work environments. To gain a better understanding of the software resources available, Table 1 lists some of the leading eye software programmes specialising in visual health prevention and some of their key features. Links to access them are included.

Table 1. Eye-Rest Software.

Eye-Rest Software	License	Main functions/Features	Developer/Link
Eye Pro v3 (ergo)	Free	New in version 3: - Screen filters and add-on tools - In-build work stress relieving mechanism - Eye pleasing and User friendly Interface - Vision Therapy feature to rectify common eye problems and improve various skills - Adjustable short break duration -Trophy and awards section - Multi-language support (partially) -Improved Eye care tips section (eye care tips in picture mode)	Classlesoft https:// classlesoft.in/index.php/eye-pro
EyeRest	Free	- rest eyes every 20 min; - take regular breaks during the day; - have lunch break on time	Microsoft https: //apps.microsoft.com/store/detail/eyerest/9NBLGGH5FLGB ?hl = bg-bg&gl = bg&rtc = 1
Eyes Relax	Free	- Flexible utility - Allows to specify two independent (short and long) work periods, the length of the breaks, break types, notification sounds and other settings	The Mech https: //themech.net/eyesrelax/

(continued)

Table 1. (*continued*)

Eye-Rest Software	License	Main functions/Features	Developer/Link
CareUEyes Pro	Paid	- Blue light filter - Brightness control - Break reminder -Improve productivity	Care-eyes https://care-eyes.com/
Dark Reader for Edge	Free	- Open source eye-care browser extension	Alexander Shutau https://darkreader.org/
Eye Saver	Free	- Blue light filter: Filters out the harmful blue light emitted by the display and makes colors warm and easier on the eyes - No flickering: Eliminates the invisible flickering of the display backlight, a cause of eye strain and headaches - Break reminder: Reminds you to take breaks and provides advice on maintaining good health in front of the computer	Leosoft ltd https://www.eye-saver.net/
Eyeblink	Freemium/Paid	- Measures blink rate by camera - Increases blink rate by blink interaction - Adjusts screen brightness - Reminds PC breaks	Eyeblink https://www.blinkingmatters.com/

Prevention of visual health is a complex care that includes many aspects. In addition to the technical means, it is necessary to comply with the ergonomic requirements for correct work in computerized workplaces. This especially applies to ergonomic human postures in human-computer interaction [40–44]. Figure 1 shows the ergonomic setup of computerized workplaces [Classlesoft Eye Pro v3 (ergo) software].

For customization of specific ergonomic parameters covering the anthropometric data of the person, the ErgoFellow 3.0 (30 days trial/paid version) https://www.fbfsistemas.com/registererg.html software offers extended options. Some important possibilities for ergonomic calculations are shown in Fig. 2 (a) and (b).

To the ergonomic settings, adequate lighting of the environment, the human factor in terms of blinking (not concentrating on the screen for a long time), the very movements of the body and hands that control the mouse and keyboard and others should be determined.

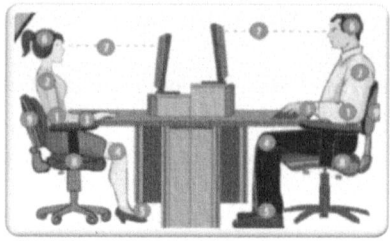

Fig. 1. Ergonomic setup of computerized workplaces [Classlesoft Eye Pro v3 (ergo) software]. 1. Elbows-Above the desk, at 90–110°, relaxed close to body; 2. Shoulders-Relaxed as opposed to hunched; 3. Wrist-inline with forearms; 4. Hips, knees, ankles-at 90°, whilst seated; 5. Feet-Flat on ground or footrest; 6. Head-upright with ears aligned with shoulders; 7. Eyes-Top of monitor casing shall be 2–3 inchs above eye level; 8. Seat Lengths-should be long enough to provide support beneath thighs; 9. Backrest-Angled at 90–110°, with adequate support.

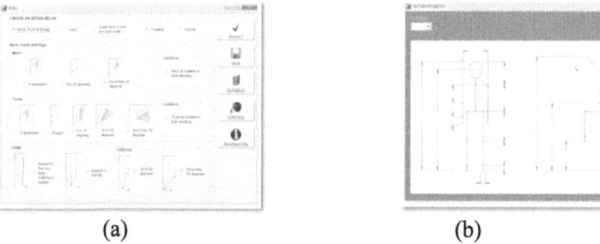

(a)   (b)

Fig. 2. Ergonomic software ErgoFellow 3.0 (a) REBA [https://www.fbfsistemas.com/images/reb aeng.jpg] and (b) Anthropometry [https://www.fbfsistemas.com/images/anthropometryeng.jpg].

2   Methods and Implementations

Assuming that the ergonomic setups are approved and the protocol for the proper operation of computerized workplaces is properly followed, visual health prevention includes the application of specialized eye software that must possess certain qualities and functions and other significant priorities as shown in Fig. 3. First of all, there must be access to resource (download) of the software by the users (the license is relevant, respectively). Second, users should be encouraged to use specialized software with a friendly interface that has the necessary good design. Third, the software must have all the necessary functions ensuring prevention and protection of visual health.

By using specialised eye health software, users can proactively prevent eye health problems associated with computer use. Through incorporating such software users can protect their eyes and maintain better long-term eye health. The prevention of eye health problems can be effectively addressed through the use of specialised software designed to promote visual well-being:

- Blue light filters: Blue light has been linked to eye strain, fatigue and sleep disturbance and protect the eyes from excessive blue light, promoting visual comfort and reducing the risk of long-term eye health problems.

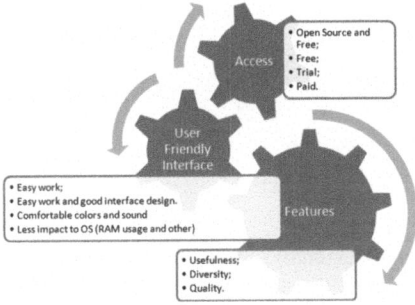

Fig. 3. Requirements for specialized vision software for eye protection.

- Screen adjustments: The brightness, contrast and colour temperature adjustments can help optimise the visual environment, reducing eye strain and discomfort.
- Pause reminders: The reminder option encourage users to take regular breaks from screen time. By encouraging users to rest their eyes and engage in other activities, such as stretching or eye exercises, break reminders help prevent eye fatigue and reduce the risk of CVS. Regular breaks improve circulation to the eyes and reduce the strain caused by continuous screen use.
- Eye exercises and vision therapy: The exercises are designed to improve eye coordination, focus and other visual skills. By practising these exercises regularly, users can strengthen their eye muscles, improve visual acuity, and prevent or alleviate vision problems.
- Ergonomic recommendations: By following recommendations, users can reduce eye strain and maintain better visual ergonomics, thus preventing potential eye health problems associated with poor workstation setup.
- Eye care tips and education: The eye care tips and educational information provide users with guidance on maintaining good visual health habits, such as proper lighting conditions, proper eye hygiene, and healthy viewing habits.
- User feedback and analytics: The feedback allows users to gain insight into their computer usage patterns and make informed decisions to avoid excessive screen time.

The provision of prevention for eye protection through specialized software includes the implementation of specialized applications based on methodologies for conventional visual practices and exercises in real time, which are controlled by the computer operator. Many useful options (implemented as add-ons) for visual exercises with targeted eye strain are the applications included in the specialized Classlesoft Eye Pro v3 (ergo) software. Very useful addons include methods with Saccades Eye Training (Fig. 4 (a) and (b)). It is possible to adjust the parameters of the image (Eye Saccades), as well as the speed of movement. (Reading Saccades). The default time is 2 min.

Method: Eye Saccades: Eye Saccades is an addon included in the Classlesoft Eye Pro v3 (ergo) software, designed to enhance the eye's saccadic movements. This method entails observing a visual representation of an eye as it swiftly moves around the screen. Users are instructed to focus on the eye's movement while ensuring that only their eyes move, without any corresponding head movements. Saccades, a fundamental aspect of oculomotor control, refer to the eye's rapid and accurate shifts between different

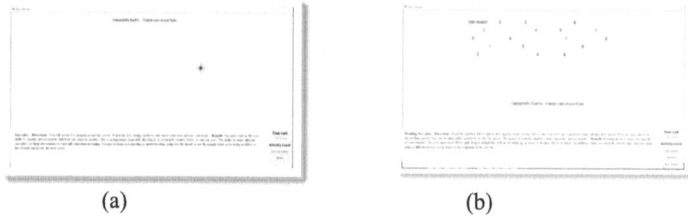

(a)   (b)

Fig. 4. Classlesoft Eye Pro v3 (ergo) software (a) Eye Saccades (b) Reading Saccades.

visual targets. This ability plays a crucial role in visual perception and eye movement coordination. By practicing and improving saccadic movements, users can precisely direct their gaze and control where their eyes aim. It helps users develop and refine their saccadic eye movements, which are especially vital during reading tasks. Efficient saccades prevent overshooting or undershooting, ensuring that the eyes move to the appropriate position when following a line of text and locating the next word. This skill is essential for maintaining a smooth reading flow, preventing disruptions and inaccuracies in the visual tracking process. This method specifically targets the enhancement of saccadic control, contributing to improved visual coordination, accuracy, and efficiency, particularly in reading activities. The focused practice of saccades through this software addon aids users in achieving optimal eye movement control, ultimately enhancing their overall visual performance.

Method: Reading Saccades: Reading Saccades is an addon featured in the Classlesoft Eye Pro v3 (ergo) software, designed to improve the eye movements involved in reading. This method focuses on reading numbers presented on the screen in a specific sequence. Users are instructed to read the numbers from left to right while ensuring that only their eyes move and their head remains still. The method provides different speed settings, starting from slow and progressing to medium and fast speeds, challenging users to read the numbers effortlessly, smoothly, and accurately. Reading Saccades aims to enhance the specific eye movements required during reading tasks. When reading, the eyes must move horizontally from left to right along a straight line of text without deviating upward or downward to the lines above or below. The Reading Saccades method offers several benefits. By practicing and refining reading saccades, users can improve their reading efficiency and accuracy. The method targets the development of precise horizontal eye movements, ensuring that the eyes maintain a steady focus on the current line while smoothly transitioning to the subsequent line without interruptions or errors. By engaging with the Reading Saccades method, users can enhance their ability to read text effortlessly and maintain a consistent reading rhythm. The method challenges users to adapt to different speeds, allowing them to progress from slower speeds to faster ones as they master each level. Incorporating the Reading Saccades method provides users with a targeted exercise to strengthen the specific eye movements necessary for efficient reading. By practicing these saccadic eye movements, users can enhance their reading skills, optimize reading fluency, and improve their overall reading experience.

Other suitable exercise add-ons for vision health prevention are: Bouncing Ball, Circles, Eye Teaming and 3D Stereograms.

3   Results

The results of the analysis of specialised software for visual protection show, firstly, that they are insufficiently popular. Multifunctional software is relatively rare. In terms of technical performance, most of them are limited to regulating the time that a person can work on a computer, allowing the setting of a break time that allows the operator to have a visual rest. Other common features are filter overlays.

In terms of in-depth visual prevention aimed at protecting the eyes and the use of applications based on methods that involve targeted movement of the eye muscles, Classlesoft Eye Pro v3 (ergo) software is the most direct reliable and highly effective. In collaboration with the ergonomic ErgoFellow 3.0 software as an indirect support for the prevention process, the requirements for maintaining a high level and quality of visual health are completed. By integrating with productivity tools and providing resources on eye health, eye-rest software enhances awareness and empowers users to adopt healthier screen habits. With optimized font formats and display settings, users can feel a more comfortable viewing experience, reducing the risk of CVS-related discomfort and promoting long-term eye wellness in the digital age.

4   Conclusions

The research prioritized the provision of accessible digital resources for the prevention of visual health issues. The provided information in the article raising awareness about the significance of visual health and preventive measures, stakeholders were able to adopt proactive approaches in safeguarding their visual well-being. The accessibility of digital resources encompassed the availability of specialized eye software designed to mitigate visual discomfort and address conditions like Computer Vision Syndrome (CVS). The research underscored the importance of promoting optimal ergonomics in the realm of human-computer interaction (HCI) when utilizing digital workstations. After implementation of the specialized ergonomic softwares analyzed in the article, the authors recommend for the purpose of visual health prevention the use of the softwares:

- for anthropometric ergonomics (indirect visual impact): ErgoFellow 3.0
- for visual ergonomics (direct visual impact): Classlesoft Eye Pro v3 (ergo) software

The application of these resources in practice gives users the opportunity for comprehensive informational and digital prevention of visual health when working with computers, which is the most loaded in human-computer interaction. It accentuated the necessity for proactive measures aimed at averting visual discomfort and fostering overall well-being. Through the utilization of accessible digital resources and the implementation of ergonomic practices, stakeholders were able to collaboratively establish work environments that prioritized visual health, user comfort, and productivity within the domain of digital workstations.

Acknowledgments. This paper (result) is supported by the Scientific-Research Project TUV 2023 PD19 "Researching the possibilities of increasing the visual ergonomics of computerized workplaces".

References

1. Pavel, A., et al.: Computer vision syndrome: an ophthalmic pathology of the modern Era. Medicina **59**, 412 (2023). https://doi.org/10.3390/medicina59020412
2. Wangsan, K., et al.: Self-reported computer vision syndrome among thai university students in virtual classrooms during the COVID-19 pandemic: prevalence and associated factors. Int. J. Environ. Res. Public Health **19**, 3996 (2022). https://doi.org/10.3390/ijerph19073996
3. Abuallut, I., et al.: Prevalence of computer vision syndrome among school-age children during the COVID-19 pandemic, saudi arabia: a cross-sectional survey. Children **9**, 1718 (2022). https://doi.org/10.3390/children9111718
4. Balcombe, L., De Leo, D.: Human-computer interaction in digital mental health. Informatics **9**, 14 (2022). https://doi.org/10.3390/informatics9010014
5. Kaewkitipong, L., Chen, C., Han, J., Ractham, P.: Human-Computer Interaction (HCI) and Trust Factors for the Continuance Intention of Mobile Payment Services. Sustainability **14**, 14546 (2022). https://doi.org/10.3390/su142114546
6. Huang, C., Chen, Y., Tong, W., Feng, T., Deng, M.: Research on human-computer interaction technology of large-scale high-resolution display wall system. Appl. Sci. **13**, 591 (2023). https://doi.org/10.3390/app13010591
7. Hipólito, V., Coelho, P.: Blue light and eye damage: a review on the impact of digital device emissions. Photonics **10**, 560 (2023). https://doi.org/10.3390/photonics10050560
8. Nokas, G., Kotsilieris, T.: Preventing keratoconus through eye rubbing activity detection: a machine learning approach. Electronics **12**, 1028 (2023). https://doi.org/10.3390/electronics12041028
9. Artime Ríos, M., Sánchez, F., Suárez, S.A., Iglesias-Rodríguez, J., Seguí, C.: Prediction of computer vision syndrome in health personnel by means of genetic algorithms and binary regression trees. Sensors **19**, 2800 (2019). https://doi.org/10.3390/s19122800
10. Lee, J., Lee, S.: Construction site safety management: a computer vision and deep learning approach. Sensors **23**, 944 (2023). https://doi.org/10.3390/s23020944
11. Panjeti-Madan, V.N., Ranganathan, P.: Impact of screen time on children's development: cognitive, language, physical, and social and emotional domains. Multimodal Technol. Interact. **7**(5), 52 (2023). https://doi.org/10.3390/mti7050052
12. Wolf, C., Wolf, S., Weiss, M., Nino, G.: Children's Environmental Health in the Digital Era: Understanding Early Screen Exposure as a Preventable Risk Factor for Obesity and Sleep Disorders. Children **5**(2), 31 (2018). https://doi.org/10.3390/children5020031
13. Puzio, D., Makowska, I., Rymarczyk, K.: Raising the child—do screen media help or hinder? the quality over quantity hypothesis. Int. J. Environ. Res. Public Health **19**(16), 9880 (2022). https://doi.org/10.3390/ijerph19169880
14. Lua, V.Y.Q., Chua, T.B.K., Chia, M.Y.H.: A narrative review of screen time and wellbeing among adolescents before and during the COVID-19 pandemic: implications for the future. Sports **11**(2), 38 (2023). https://doi.org/10.3390/sports11020038
15. Foerster, M., Henneke, A., Chetty-Mhlanga, S., Röösli, M.: Impact of adolescents' screen time and nocturnal mobile phone-related awakenings on sleep and general health symptoms: a prospective cohort study. Int. J. Environ. Res. Public Health **16**(3), 518 (2019). https://doi.org/10.3390/ijerph16030518
16. Jusienė, R., et al.: Screen use during meals among young children: exploration of associated variables. Medicina **55**(10), 688 (2019). https://doi.org/10.3390/medicina55100688
17. Belton, S., Issartel, J., Behan, S., Goss, H., Peers, C.: The Differential Impact of Screen Time on Children's Wellbeing. Int. J. Environm. Res. Pub. Health **18**(17), 9143 (2021). https://doi.org/10.3390/ijerph18179143

18. Liebherr, M., Kohler, M., Brailovskaia, J., Brand, M., Antons, S.: Screen time and attention subdomains in children aged 6 to 10 years. Children **9**(9), 1393 (2022). https://doi.org/10.3390/children9091393

19. Hao, R., Shao, B., Ma, R.: Impacts of video display on purchase intention for digital and home appliance products—empirical study from China. Future Internet **11**(11), 224 (2019). https://doi.org/10.3390/fi11110224

20. Jain, S., Shrivastava, S., Mathur, A., Pathak, D., Pathak, A.: Prevalence and determinants of excessive screen viewing time in children aged 3–15 years and its effects on physical activity, sleep, eye symptoms and headache. Int. J. Environ. Res. Public Health **20**(4), 3449 (2023). https://doi.org/10.3390/ijerph20043449

21. Liu, J., Li, B., Chen, Q., Dang, J.: Student health implications of school closures during the COVID-19 pandemic: new evidence on the association of e-learning, outdoor exercise, and myopia. Healthcare. **9**(5), 500 (2021). https://doi.org/10.3390/healthcare9050500

22. Chen, J.-Y., Strodl, E., Huang, L.-H., Chen, Y.-J., Yang, G.-Y., Chen, W.-Q.: Early electronic screen exposure and autistic-like behaviors among preschoolers: the mediating role of caregiver-child interaction, sleep duration and outdoor activities. Children **7**(11), 200 (2020). https://doi.org/10.3390/children7110200

23. Dresp-Langley, B.: Children's health in the digital age. Int. J. Environ. Res. Public Health **17**(9), 3240 (2020). https://doi.org/10.3390/ijerph17093240

24. Tian, P., et al.: Effects of paradigm color and screen brightness on visual fatigue in light environment of night based on eye tracker and EEG acquisition equipment. Sensors **22**(11), 4082 (2022). https://doi.org/10.3390/s22114082

25. Zhou, Y., Shi, H., Chen, Q.-W., Ru, T., Zhou, G.: Investigation of the optimum display luminance of an LCD screen under different ambient illuminances in the evening. Appl. Sci. **11**(9), 4108 (2021). https://doi.org/10.3390/app11094108

26. Kim, T., Lee, E.C.: Experimental verification of objective visual fatigue measurement based on accurate pupil detection of infrared eye image and multi-feature analysis. Sensors **20**(17), 4814 (2020). https://doi.org/10.3390/s20174814

27. Erdinest, N., London, N., Lavy, I., Morad, Y., Levinger, N.: Vision through healthy aging eyes. Vision **5**(4), 46 (2021). https://doi.org/10.3390/vision5040046

28. Lem, D.W., Gierhart, D.L., Davey, P.G.: Can nutrition play a role in ameliorating digital eye strain? Nutrients **14**(19), 4005 (2022). https://doi.org/10.3390/nu14194005

29. Victor, V.M., et al.: A web-based cross-sectional survey on eye strain and perceived stress amid the COVID-19 online learning among medical science students. Int. Medi. Edu. **2**(2), 83–95 (2023). https://doi.org/10.3390/ime2020008

30. Zhang, G., He, Y., Liang, H., Chen, X., Deng, D., Zhou, J.: Directional and eye-tracking light field display with efficient rendering and illumination. Micromachines **14**(7), 1465 (2023). https://doi.org/10.3390/mi14071465

31. Mutanu, L., Gohil, J., Gupta, K.: Vision-autocorrect: a self-adapting approach towards relieving eye-strain using facial-expression recognition. Software **2**(2), 197–217 (2023). https://doi.org/10.3390/software2020009

32. Sanchez-Ramos, C., et al.: Retinal protection from LED-backlit screen lights by short wavelength absorption filters. Cells **10**(11), 3248 (2021). https://doi.org/10.3390/cells10113248

33. Qian, Y., et al.: Human eye contrast sensitivity to vehicle displays under strong ambient light. Crystals **13**(9), 1384 (2023). https://doi.org/10.3390/cryst13091384

34. Huyhua-Gutierrez, S.C., et al.: Digital eye strain among peruvian nursing students: prevalence and associated factors. Int. J. Environ. Res. Public Health **20**(6), 5067 (2023). https://doi.org/10.3390/ijerph20065067

35. Johnston, K.: Engagement and immersion in digital play: supporting young children's digital wellbeing. Int. J. Environ. Res. Public Health **18**(19), 10179 (2021). https://doi.org/10.3390/ijerph181910179
36. Li, C., Cheng, G., Sha, T., Cheng, W., Yan, Y.: The relationships between screen use and health indicators among infants, toddlers, and preschoolers: a meta-analysis and systematic review. Int. J. Environ. Res. Public Health **17**(19), 7324 (2020). https://doi.org/10.3390/ijerph17197324
37. Smith, A.C., et al.: Digital overload among college students: implications for mental health app use. Social Sciences **10**(8), 279 (2021). https://doi.org/10.3390/socsci10080279
38. Priftis, N., Panagiotakos, D.: Screen time and its health consequences in children and adolescents. Children **10**(10), 1665 (2023). https://doi.org/10.3390/children10101665
39. Rocka, A., Jasielska, F., Madras, D., Krawiec, P., Pac-Kożuchowska, E.: The impact of digital screen time on dietary habits and physical activity in children and adolescents. Nutrients **14**(14), 2985 (2022). https://doi.org/10.3390/nu14142985
40. Cao, J., Ku, D., Du, J., Ng, V., Wang, Y., Dong, W.: A structurally enhanced, ergonomically and human-computer interaction improved intelligent seat's system. Designs **1**, 11 (2017). https://doi.org/10.3390/designs1020011
41. Estrada, J.E., Vea, L.A., Devaraj, M.: Modelling proper and improper sitting posture of computer users using machine vision for a human–computer intelligent interactive system during COVID-19. Appl. Sci. **13**, 5402 (2023). https://doi.org/10.3390/app13095402
42. da Silva, A.G., Mendes Gomes, M.V., Winkler, I.: Virtual reality and digital human modeling for ergonomic assessment in industrial product development: a patent and literature review. Appl. Sci. **12**, 1084 (2022). https://doi.org/10.3390/app12031084
43. Wróbel, K., Gil, M., Chae, C.-J.: On the influence of human factors on safety of remotely-controlled merchant vessels. Appl. Sci. **11**, 1145 (2021). https://doi.org/10.3390/app11031145
44. Wang, J., Cheng, R., Liu, M., Liao, P.-C.: Research trends of human-computer interaction studies in construction hazard recognition: a bibliometric review. Sensors **21**, 6172 (2021). https://doi.org/10.3390/s21186172

A Diagnosis Model Based on Federated Learning for Lung Cancer Classification

Ann Mary Babu$^{(\boxtimes)}$ and Sivaiah Bellamkonda◉

Computer Science and Engineering Department, Indian Institute of Information Technology, Kottayam, Kerala, India
annmarybabu.eme20@iiitkottayam.ac.in

Abstract. Lung cancer, causing a significant number of fatalities annually, is a prominent contributor to global mortality rates among individuals of both genders, with an estimated five million cases resulting in death each year. The utilization of Computed Tomography (CT) scans contribute valuable data for the detection of lung cancer. The main objectives of this study are to diagnose malignant lung nodules in the provided input lung images and to classify lung nodule based on its level of severity. This study proposes a solution wherein locally computed updates are combined to stimulate the learning of a shared model, while the training data remains dispersed throughout mobile devices. Federated Learning (FL) is an advanced technology that operates in a collaborative and decentralized manner, with the primary objective of preserving privacy. Its purpose is to address the obstacles posed by data silos and the sensitivity of data. Therefore, the FL approach is employed for the classification of medical images in collaborative and real-world circumstances. A new approach is proposed in this paper, where the model is trained on data distributed across multiple institutions, and the training process occurs locally at each institution. The performance of the proposed method in terms of accuracy, specificity and sensitivity is evaluated and compared with that of the existing models such as Googlenet, Alexnet, and SVM. The proposed method performs comparably better in all three performance measures indicating that it works better than other methods.

Keywords: lung cancer · deep learning · Federated Learning · CT Images · X-Ray

1 Introduction

Lung cancer affects 1.8 billion people worldwide and claims the lives of 1.6 million of them, according to a global survey. Lung cancer ranks as the second most prevalent cause of mortality. 17.4% of persons with lung cancer survive for up to 5 years after being diagnosed, according to a survey conducted in the USA. Additionally, according to a report published by the North American Association of Central Cancer Registries, 13 percent of women (112,350) and 14 percent of men (121,680) in the USA were affected by lung cancer in 2020, with 154,040 of those cases resulting in death because of the disease's high risk factors. Lung carcinoma is another name for lung cancer, which

A. Mirzazadeh et al. (Eds.): SEMIT 2023, CCIS 2198, pp. 199–218, 2024.
https://doi.org/10.1007/978-3-031-72284-4_13

develops when cells in the lungs grow abnormally. The chest is typically the main body component impacted by lung cancer. The worst case scenario for the patient's survival occurs when the natural flow of lymph transmits cancer-affected cells to the centre of the chest. Based on the properties of cell development, lung cancer is frequently categorised into two primary classes: small cell and non-small cell. Lung cancer has four stages, numbered from 1 to 4. The stage changes according to the size of the tumour and the lymph node's location. The likelihood of survival is determined based on the cancer cell's stages. Lung cancer can be diagnosed utilizing a range of diagnostic techniques, such as Magnetic Resonance Imaging (MRI), isotope imaging, X-ray, and Computed Tomography (CT). X-ray chest radiography and CT are two commonly employed anatomical imaging methods for the identification of diverse lung pathologies. CT images are utilized by medical professionals, including doctors and radiologists, for the purpose of identifying the presence of diseases. These images allow for direct observation of the morphological dimensions of the diseases, enabling the determination of their patterns and seriousness. Additionally, CT images enable the tracking of disease progression over time and the evaluation of treatment response. Spiral scans, a new feature of the volumetric CT technology, eliminate artifacts brought on by partial volume impacts, heart movement, and uneven breathing rhythms while also speeding up scan times. The utilization of superior quality CT scanning emerged as the preferred imaging method for the detection and characterization of pulmonary diseases, owing to the advancements in CT technology. The process of visually interpreting or evaluating a substantial quantity of CT image slices continues to pose a significant challenge, even with the advancements in anatomic resolution provided by High-Resolution Computed Tomography (HRCT) for lung imaging.

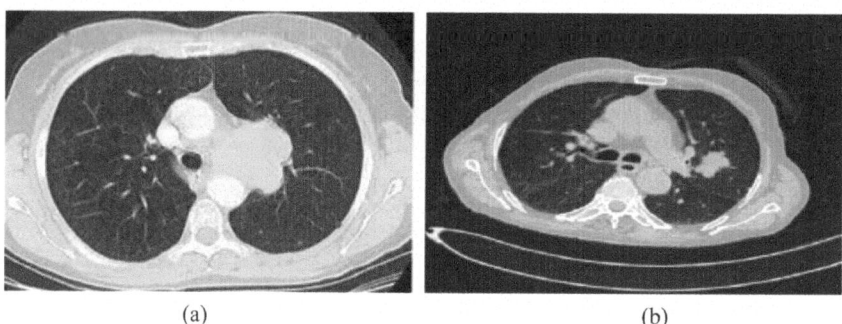

(a)   (b)

Fig. 1. Example of (a) Clear Lung Image and (b) Diseased Lung Image.

As depicted in Fig. 1, lung cancer illness is difficult to detect in CT scans. Low-Dose helical Computed Tomography (LDCT) is currently used as the method for lung cancer screening. To increase the predictive accuracy for lung cancer diagnosis and classification, numerous efforts are being made to build computer assisted diagnosis and detection systems. The development of computer-aided systems was driven by the requirement for trustworthy and impartial analysis. The purpose of the effort is to extract features for diagnosis and classification and intensity determination. The following describes how this report's manuscript is structured: The most recent literature in various relevant fields is discussed in Sect. 2. A thorough explanation of the suggested architecture is presented in Sect. 3. Experimental findings are reported in Sect. 4 along with a discussion of them. Section 5 provides conclusions and recommendations for future work.

1.1 Merits and Demerits of Deep Learning in Lung Cancer Detection

Deep learning possesses a distinct advantage in comparison to traditional machine learning algorithms due to its ability to autonomously perform feature engineering. This study examines the data in order to identify pertinent features and integrates them with the aim of enhancing the learning process. The technique leverages the spatial coherence inherent in the input. The pre-processing of images is conducted prior to the training and testing stages, which occur subsequent to the selection and extraction of features. After the completion of the training and testing phases, Convolutional Neural Network (CNN) algorithm is able to categorize the input lung image as either normal or abnormal, and subsequently displays the obtained results. Consequently, the utilization of a Deep CNN, is employed for the purpose of categorizing lung images in the context of cancer diagnosis.

Merits:

– Improved Accuracy: Deep Learning (DL) algorithms can process vast amounts of data and extract complex patterns, leading to improved accuracy in lung cancer detection. Deep learning models can achieve accuracy rates of up to
– 90%, surpassing the accuracy of traditional lung cancer detection methods.
– Early Detection: DL models can diagnose lung cancer at an early stage,
– enhancing the efficiency of treatment and improving patient outcomes. Early detection is crucial for lung cancer because it is often asymptomatic until it reaches an advanced stage, making it difficult to treat.
– Automation: DL can automate the detection process, reducing the work-
– load of doctors and radiologist and improving the efficiency of lung cancer screening. Deep learning models can analyze medical images and flag potential cancerous lesions, freeing up radiologists' time.
– Scalability: DL models possess the advantageous capability of seamless scalability, enabling efficient processing of extensive datasets. Consequently, these models are highly suitable for the purpose of detecting lung cancer on a population scale. The importance of scalability cannot be overstated, particularly in light of the global prevalence of lung cancer. The efficient processing of extensive datasets holds the potential to significantly enhance the effectiveness of screening programs.

Demerits:

– Data Availability: DL needs large amounts of high-quality data for training, which may not always be available for lung cancer detection. The restricted accessibility of datasets pertaining to lung cancer poses a potential obstacle to the advancement and verification of DL models, thereby constraining their level of accuracy.

- Overfitting: The limited availability of training data can result in overfitting in DL models, thereby compromising the accuracy of predictions. Overfitting is a phenomenon that arises when a model is trained using a limited dataset, resulting in excessive specialisation to that specific dataset and an inability to effectively generalise to novel data.
- Interpretability: The interpretability of DL models poses a significant challenge in effectively communicating the underlying reasoning behind their predictions to medical professionals and patients. The absence of interpretability can pose difficulties in clinical decision-making, as a comprehensive comprehension of the model's rationale is imperative.
- Computational Requirements: Deploying deep learning models in resource-constrained settings can be challenging due to their substantial computational requirements, including the need for high-performance computing systems that may not be readily available.

Although DL offers numerous advantages in the realm of lung cancer detection, it is not without its limitations. Subsequent investigations ought to prioritise the resolution of these constraints in order to enhance the precision and comprehensibility of deep learning models in the realm of lung cancer detection. Furthermore, it is imperative to prioritise the enhancement of accessibility to superior data and computational resources in order to effectively support the advancement and implementation of DL models for the purpose of detecting lung cancer. Despite the inherent limitations, deep learning exhibits the capacity to fundamentally transform the process of lung cancer detection and enhance patient outcomes, thereby establishing itself as a technology of considerable promise in the ongoing battle against lung cancer.

1.2 Why Federated Learning

Federated learning is an algorithmic framework within the field of Machine Learning (ML) that enables multiple entities to collectively train a model while maintaining the decentralisation of their respective datasets, thereby avoiding the need for data sharing with a central server. Federated learning has garnered substantial attention in recent years due to a multitude of factors.

- Privacy: The preservation of data privacy stands as a primary motivation for the adoption of federated learning. In numerous instances, the data utilised for machine learning models encompasses sensitive or personal information, including but not limited to medical records, financial data, or user behaviour. Federated learning allows data to remain locally on each participant's device or server, reducing the desire to share data with a central server, thereby mitigating privacy risks associated with data sharing.
- Data Sovereignty: Federated learning allows organizations to maintain control and ownership over their data. This is particularly important for industries that have strict regulations around data sovereignty, such as healthcare, finance, and government. By keeping data within their own premises, organizations can comply with data protection regulations and maintain sovereignty over their data.

- Scalability: Federated learning can enable large-scale machine learning across a distributed network of devices or servers. Rather than transferring whole data to a central server, which can be resource-intensive and time-consuming, federated learning allows for distributed model training, reducing the amount of data transferred and the associated network overhead.
- Collaboration: Federated learning encourages collaboration among multiple parties, such as organizations, institutions, or researchers, without sharing sensitive data. This enables organizations to pool their resources, expertise, and data to jointly train ML models for mutual benefit, without exposing their data to other parties.
- Data Diversity: Federated learning encourages the training of ML models.
- Cost Efficiency: Federated learning can minimize the cost of data transfer and storage, as it allows data to stay local and reduces the amount of data transferred to a central server. This can be beneficial in scenarios where data transfer costs are high, such as in remote or bandwidth-constrained environments.

1.3 Motivation

The goal of the lung malignant growth identification framework is to recognise and provide trustworthy information to experts and physicians from the clinical picture. Many frameworks have been developed to address this issue using various picture preparation techniques, AI, and deep learning techniques. A reliable tool for clinical screening that is used to locate and analyse lung diseases is registered tomography (CT) imaging. In order to study, comprehend, and analyse the lung malignant growth from lung tissues, doctors and radiologists use CT scan images. However, for some clinicians, acquiring an accurate diagnosis result without using the additional clinical tool known as PC-aided identification. Effective lung disease detection strategies are essential for achieving precise results using your PC-supported analytical framework. To identify and categorise tumours, machine learning algorithms like support vector machines are frequently used. But frequently, they are constrained by the assumptions we make when we describe highlights. This causes a decline in affect ability. While traditional methods may leverage features from basic image data, deep learning emerges as a superior option.

1.4 Objective

Here is a summary of the key goals of this study:

- To utilize Densenet for classifying benign and malignant lung nodules.
- To identify the issue of training on decentralized data from mobile devices
- as a crucial research area and explore the potential of Cross-silo FL for collaborative learning.
- To implement FL client selection, also referred to as participant selection or
- device sampling, in the FL system to mitigate the impact of client heterogeneity.

2 Literature Survey

Lung cancer detection classification has received more research interest recently because of the quick development of pattern recognition and image processing techniques. Although the focus of this section is on works that have made use of the various lung cancer databases, a few other notable works are also mentioned here.

2.1 Image Processing Approach

The image handling method excels in clinical picture studies, enhancing the precision of the order form. The processing of images in knob characterization for lung CT images has been thoroughly researched. For better knob location, various examinations got division, morphological duties, and form channel techniques [6]. Using those approaches, a few analysts were able to precisely propose and implement the lung cancer finding methodology. By using photo handling techniques, Neelima Singh et al. [11] have presented frameworks for identifying lung diseases. The system is used for picture pre-handling, and after picture pre-handling, a clever channel is used for edge detection. The clinical images have been divided using Super Pixel Segmentation, and the images have been denoised using the Gabor channel.Unsupervised feature learning for image registration was one of the main strengths, but there were also several drawbacks, including limited evaluation, no comparison to cutting-edge techniques, and no open-source implementation.

Kiran et al. [10] have also presented a work on lung cancer segmentation technique according to the Sauvola thresholding method and four Gaussian derivatives approach. The approach can be considered a primitive detection procedure. The proposed model mainly consists of six steps. An initial image enhancement procedure is followed by the application of Gaussian derivatives for identifying the outer boundaries of the lung region. Once the data is obtained, the preprocessed image is subjected to Sauvola image thresholding after highlighting the inner areas. Post highlighting, the noise is removed and morphology is carried over to isolate the lung shape. The key benefits included novel hybrid segmentation method, promising results. The limitations were limited evaluation on small dataset, lack of comparison with state-of-the-art methods.

2.2 ML Approach

A Lung-Nodule categorization based on CT Using Taxonomic Diversity Indexes and an SVM is discussed in [1]. The authors make use of taxonomical diversity and taxonomic distinctness-based modules for texture and non-nodule candidate detection. The indices for the same are calculated with the aid of a phylogenetic tree which additionally performs candidate characterization as well. For classification purposes, SVM is employed. The following was listed as a merit for this work were use of taxonomic diversity indexes for nodule classification. One of the flaws was Lack of comparison with other methods, limited sample size.

A similar article by sangamithra [2] discusses a similar work based on EK mean clustering approach. In contrast to existing literature, the article concentrates on the clustering approach employed for isolating non-enhancing lung tumor sessions as well. The first stage of the proposed model involves conducting a preliminary preprocessing procedure utilising median and wiener filters, which is subsequently followed by the application of the EK mean clustering approach. The extraction of features such as entropy, contrast, correlation homogeneity, and others is performed on the tumour region of the image that has been segmented using the fuzzy EK-means algorithm. The process of feature extraction is conducted using a gray level co-occurrence matrix, followed by classification utilising a supervised neural network. A method for lung cancer identification from CT scans has been created by Kulkarni Bagal [15] using image processing and soft computing methods.Anisotropic diffusion filtering and Gaussian filtering are used in this instance for pre-processing. For picture segmentation, the more potent Watershed segmentation algorithm, which has a high success rate, has been used. SVM and K-nearest neighbor (K-NN) classifcation algorithms have been employed for classification, and K-NN technique exhibits approximately 5.5% greater results in classification. The cases are classified into one of three categories at the final step using a support vector machine (SVM): normal, benign, or malignant. We used various SVM kernels and feature extraction methods. The new dataset was subjected to this technique, and the highest accuracy obtained was 89.8876% [17].

2.3 Deep Learning Approach

The article [3] presents a proposed system for classifying lung nodules using a deep neural network. The system architecture utilises a 50-layer ResNet as the initial model, which is subsequently followed by a deep residual network that operates on transfer learning. The proposed model outperforms the existing model and the authors validate the accuracy and performance of the suggested model using the LICC IRDI dataset. Another DNN-based lung cancer detection approach is proposed by Sandhiya and Palani [4]. In contrast to prior models, the approach that was suggested utilizes a unique approach known as the Incremental Feature Selection Algorithm. This approach integrates the principles of Intelligent Conditional Random Field into the feature selection process, as well as the Linear Correlation Coefficient based Feature Selection method algorithm. Additionally, the model incorporates a conventional CNN with temporal features. The model performs well for image-based disease diagnostics and experimental analysis proved the claims. The GoogLeNet DNN is modified using transfer learning to learn medical data. This process entails facilitating the development of the outermost layers of the DNN while constraining the growth of its deeper layers. In this study, the IQ-OTH/NCCD lung cancer dataset was utilised as an initial, raw dataset for the purpose of training and validating the proposed methodology. Based on empirical evidence, the present approach has demonstrated superior performance compared to the standard method actually utilized for this dataset, achieving an accuracy level of 94.38%.

An algorithm developed by CNN outperformed the top outcomes from the PC vision network, was used on ImageNet Classification in 2012 [5]. Additionally, a well-known most recent study using in-depth learning in the field of clinical imaging has produced encouraging results. Another inactive and shared component representation of neuro-imaging data of the brain using the Deep Boltzmann Machine (DBM) was proposed by Suk et al. [6] for the determination of AD/MCI. For deformable enrollment of mind MR images, Xu et al. [7] established the usefulness of applying profound neural systems (DNNs) for highlight extraction in clinical picture examination as a directed methodology. J. Tan et al. [13] developed a framework that employed DNN and CNN techniques to find lung nodules and effectively mitigate the occurrence of false positive results associated with these nodules. The CNN architecture comprises four pooling layers and four convolutional layers. The filter has a 3,5 diameter and a 32 depth. The dataset used in this study was obtained from the LIDC-IDRI and comprised approximately 85 patients. Consequently, the sensitivity yielded a value of 0.82. The authors of the study [16] employed a CNN approach based on the AlexNet architecture. This computer-aided system was developed for the purpose of classifying lung cancer. The dataset used was collected from various hospitals in Iraq. The system was designed to aid in the diagnosis of patients, classifying their condition as normal, benign, or malignant. The proposed model demonstrates a high level of accuracy, achieving a performance of 93.548%.

A CAD framework was put forth by Kumar et al. [8] that uses deep highlights that were taken out of an autoencoder to rank lung knobs on the LIDC dataset as either detrimental or helpful. Suna et al. [9] conducted three distinct deep learning computations, namely CNN, Deep Belief Networks (DBNs), and Stacked Denoising Autoencoder (SDAE). These calculations were scrutinized to the traditional picture-based CAD structure. Eight layers of convolutional and pooling layers are present in the CNN engineering. There were roughly 35 extricated surface and morphological highlights for the conventional method, compared to the calculation approach. For preparation and categorization, these highlights were handled using the bit-based help vector machine (SVM). Calculated precision for the CNN technique was 0.7976, only little better than the traditional SVM's 0.7940. TThey utilized data from approximately 1018 lung cases from the open databases held by the Lung Image Database Consortium and Image Database Resource Initiative (LIDC/IDRI). R. Golan provided a system in [14] for training the CNN weights to recognise lung images in the CT image subsections. The sensitivity of this approach, regarding lung nodules observed by all four radiologists, was found to be 78.9%. The approach resulted in 20 false positives and a specificity of 71.2%.

2.4   Federated Learning Approach

In recent decades, there has been a lot of study and work put into developing DL classification algorithms Lung cancer classification utilising X-rays. However, Google created the FL [33] idea in 2016, which focuses heavily on using different technologies to learn. Google initially used FL to predict future words, emoticons, and search recommendations [33, 36]. After that, FL's scope was expanded to cover cross-silo learning, for instance, for numerous businesses or data centres [34, 35, 45].

With the aid of data on brain tumours gathered from a number of other Hospitals, Sheller et al. [24, 38] developed a segmentation model. Another use for FL is edge computing, such as the job scheduling approach for the Internet of Vehicles [31, 32]. Even though the communication procedure may be created more effectively by giving only model updates instead of raw input, FL systems needed a lot of communication rounds within training to obtain model convergence. This is true even if providing only model changes as opposed to raw data can increase communication efficiency. A wide number of academics are looking into a range of strategies to shorten communication cycles [30]. The majority of the research employed an aggregation technique, such as selective aggregation [27], asynchronous aggregation [28], and aggregation scheduling [29]. Furthermore, compression methods are used to reduce the communication of model's costs when clients and servers send gradients and parameters to the central server [25]. The over-the-air calculation methodology [26] and the multichannel random access communication mechanism [25, 39] are two further communication methods that are suggested to improve communication efficacy. One of the main drivers driving the creation of both of these strategies was the efficiency of communication. Recent reports claim that FL will be crucial for the development of digital health [19, 42]. Without disclosing any raw patient data, FL enables distributed and collaborative DL training [20]. In [37], each client in FL performs local training on their data before sending the model parameters to a server, which collects and combines the client-specific model changes. The accumulated model parameters are again disseminated to clients after a predetermined number of customers have submitted their modifications, and a new round of local training begins. Although outside the purview of this study, FL can potentially be used in combination with additional privacy-preserving techniques to prevent reconstruction of training data by model adversarial in the event that parameters are made available to a contender [21]. Many studies have demonstrated the applicability of FL to tasks involving medical imaging [21, 23, 40]. Kaissis et al. [22] and Ma et al. [12] elaborated that the integration of Federated Learning (FL) with machine learning tasks for classifying medical images can provide security and also preserve privacy. A secure and privacy-preserving method for FL in medical imaging. [] has merits and may make it possible for institutions to work together. Demerits lacked large-scale feasibility testing and actual experimental validation. Overall, the previous studies. [44] explained the potential of FL for improving the accuracy of lung nodule classification, but there is still a need to explore the use of FL on decentralized data from mobile devices.

2.5 Research Gaps

The problem addressed in this proposed study is the classification of benign, normal and malignant pulmonary nodules using Densenet and FL on decentralized data from mobile devices. The study aims to explore the potential of Cross-silo FL for collaborative learning and to reduce the impact of client heterogeneity by implementing FL client selection. The proposed approach is evaluated on the IQ-OTH/NCCD lung cancer dataset, and the usefulness of the approach is compared to other state-of-the-art methods for pulmonary nodule classification.

3 Proposed Methodology

This study proposes a lung cancer detection system that segments the lung region of interest using mathematical morphological operations. From this segmentation, features are retrieved and applied to the categorization of cancer.

3.1 Proposed System Architecture

High-quality data pertaining to advanced technologies such as mobile phones and personal computers can be accessed globally, and are protected by stringent privacy regulations. Federated learning presents an innovative approach to amalgamate datasets for machine learning models, while ensuring compliance with privacy laws, regardless of their hosting location. Typically, in the areas of federated learning, the approach involves training the model using the data, as opposed to training the data using the model. The data-hosting device merely needs to express its willingness to engage in the federation process.

The base of the FL architecture is established by a server responsible for managing the training procedures from a centralized location. Most clients consist of edge devices, potentially reaching a count in the millions. The aforementioned devices establish communication with the server on a minimum of two occasions during each training iteration. The initial step involves requesting the weights of the current global model from the server. Subsequently, the model is trained using individual local datasets to produce updated parameters. Finally, the newly obtained parameters are transmitted back to the server for aggregation. The aforementioned communication cycle persists until a predetermined level of accuracy is achieved or until a specified number of epochs are reached. Within the context of the Federated Averaging Algorithm, the term aggregation denotes a computational process that involves the calculation of an average value. Thus, the training process of a FL model is concluded. The training of all local models will be conducted on a unified system, with clients being solely represented by data shards in this context.

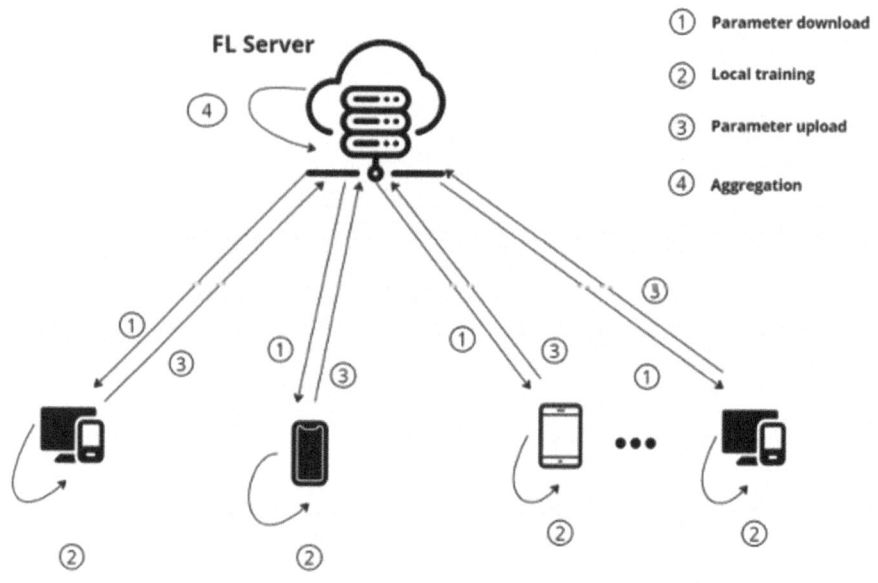

Fig. 2. System Architecture

Figure 2 illustrates a standard federated learning (FL) training process, which encompasses four primary stages. Parameter transmission from the server to the clients (referred to as Parameter Download), local training performed on the clients (known as local training), parameter transmission from the clients back to the server (referred to as Parameter Upload), and model parameter collection conducted on the server (referred to as Aggregation). The training iterations continue until the global model on the server achieves convergence or until a predetermined amount of epochs is attained.

3.2 Federated Members (Clients) as Data Shards

Separate and distinct data from each federated member will be combined in the real-world FL implementation. Always keep in mind that FL collection's goal is to ship models to data. The shard formation process only occurs during experiments. The subsequent step involves the processing of individual client data into a tensorflow dataset and subsequently batching them.

All methods of parameterized learning, including neural networks, are well-suited for FL. FL might not be advantageous for machine learning methods like KNN or similar ones that solely store training data while learning. For our classification task, we employed a 3-layer MLP as the model.

The subsequent step involves the processing of each individual client's data, transforming it into a structured data set, and subsequently grouping them into batches. We propose utilizing a three-layer Multilayer Perceptron (MLP) as the model for the categorization task. The pre-trained DenseNet121 model is added as the first layer, accompanied by a Flatten layer to flatten the output of the DenseNet121 model, and finally a Dense layer with 3 output units and a softmax activation function for multi-class classification.

3.3 Model Aggregation (Federated Averaging)

Now we proceed to Federated Averaging, which is the standard FL method. Since the data is horizontally partitioned, we must take into account parameter averaging that weighs each component's contribution in terms of the percentage of data points it contributed. The federated averaging equation is presented here; it is taken from one of the seminal papers on federated learning [41].

$$f(w) = \sum_{k=1}^{K} \frac{nk}{n} Fk(w), \ where Fk(w) = \frac{1}{nk} \sum_{i \in PK} fi(wk)$$

Here:

- w represents the model parameters (weights).
- K is the total number of clients participating in the federated learning process.
- nk denotes the number of data points held by the kth client.
- n is the total number of data point across all clients i.e. $n = \sum_{k=1}^{K} n_k$.
- Fk(w) is the local objective function of the kth client, computed as the
- average loss over its data points Pk.
- fi(w) is the loss on the ith data point belonging to the kth client.

We are currently conducting weight parameter estimations for each client on the right-hand side. These estimations are based on the loss values that have been recorded for each of the data points they have trained with. We have performed scaling on each of the parameters on the left side and then computed the sum of all the scaled values component-wise.

3.4   Client Selection

Federated Learning (FL) typically operates using a client-server configuration, as shown in Fig. 2. On their own data, each client locally trains the same model architecture. Once a specified number of clients finish a round of local training, the revised model weights are transmitted to the server for aggregation. After collecting the data, the server sends the revised weights to the clients are provided with the revised weight of the server, which initiates the subsequent round of local model training. The convergence of the models at each client occurs following a particular number of Federated Learning rounds. The client can select the best model by observing its performance on a local hold-out validation set. The client can choose the global model returned by the server after averaging. The client can choose any intermediate model that was deemed optimal based on the performance of the model for local training. In our research, we have adopted an approach where the client adopts the global threshold weights when the client chosen weight is below the threshold value. In standard federated learning circumstances, clients exhibit a wide range of data distributions and hardware setups. The various selection parameters such as model's accuracy, convergence rate, and other factors may suffer. Here we have accuracy as the selection parameter. If client's accuracy is below the threshold value, the global models' weights will get updated to the client. Client selection methods, demonstrating promise performance improvement, are used to address the FL client heterogeneity issue.

3.5   Algorithm Client-Server Federated Learning with Federated Averaging

T represents the amount of federated learning rounds and nk represents the number of local training iterations that can be considered to reduce the local loss for a client k. This algorithm [43] trains a global model by averaging the model parameters of multiple clients, each training on their own local data partition. In each round, every client trains their local model for E epochs on a random subset of their data, using the current global model parameters θ as initialization. The local models are then averaged to obtain the new global model parameters for the next round. The process is repeated for T rounds.

Algorithm 1 Federated Algorithm

Step 1 : Initialize weights $\varphi(0)$
for $t \leftarrow 1 \ldots$ **do**
  for client $k \leftarrow 1 \ldots K$ **do**
    Step 2 : Send $\phi(t-1)$ to client k $w_1, w_2, \ldots, w_n$
    Step 3 : Receive from client's $(\Delta\varphi(t)k, n_k)$
    Step 4: Local Training $(\phi(t-1))$
  end for
  Step 4 : $\varphi(t)k \leftarrow \varphi(t-1) + \Delta\varphi(t)$
end for
return φ^t

---

4   Results and Discussion

4.1   Dataset Exploration

The dataset pertaining to lung cancer (See Fig. 3) at the Iraq-Oncology Teaching Hospital/National Centre for Cancer Diseases (IQ-OTH/NCCD) was collected during a three-month duration in the fall of 2019 at the mentioned specialized medical facilities. The dataset comprises computed tomography (CT) scans of both individuals without any medical conditions and individuals diagnosed with lung cancer at various stages of the disease. The slides were marked by oncologists and radiologists in the two previously mentioned centers, IQ-OTHNCCD.

This dataset contains 1048 images of human lung CT images which are classified into 3 classes:

1. Benign-120 images
2. Malignant-561 images
3. Normal-367 images

Approximately 20% of the images are designated for the purpose of model testing, while the remaining majority are allocated for model training. There exists variability in the dimensions of the images within this dataset. The images will undergo pre-processing and the removal of excess margins before being resized to the desired dimensions.

4.2   Experimental Setup

The experimental setup for this study includes both hardware and software components. For hardware, the study utilized Google Colab, a cloud-based platform that provides a free virtual machine environment for running deep learning models. Google Colab provides a GPU-accelerated environment for machine learning, which is ideal for training DL models that require large amounts of computation. The specific hardware configuration used in this study included a Linux operating system with a platform release of 5.10.147 +. The architecture was X86 64, with 13 GB of RAM.

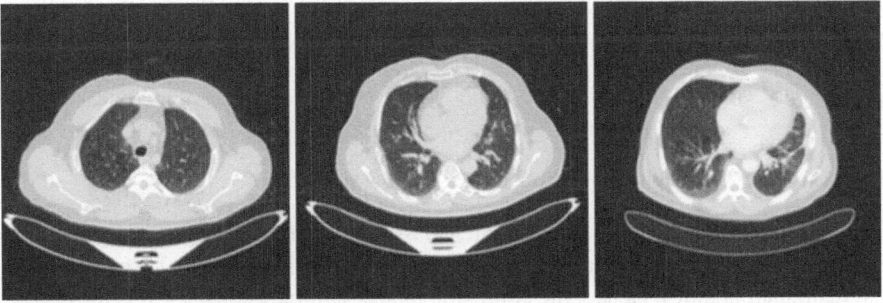

Fig. 3. Example of (a) Normal CT Lung Tissue Image and (b) Benign CT Lung Tissue (c) Malignant CT Lung Tissue image.

The research employed open-source libraries and frameworks such as Tensor Flow, Keras, and Scikit-learn. The TensorFlow machine learning framework, which is open-source, provides support for deep learning models. Keras is an application programming interface (API) for neural networks that is built on top of TensorFlow, a popular neural network learning framework. It provides a high-level abstraction for creating deep learning models, making the process of model creation more straightforward and accessible. Scikit-learn, a widely-used machine learning framework in Python, provides functionalities for data preprocessing, model selection, and assessment.

This work also used the lung cancer dataset from the Iraq-Oncology Teaching Hospital/National Centre for Cancer Diseases. The dataset comprises CT scans of patients with designated cases of lung cancer. The experimental methodology utilized in this study is sufficiently robust to facilitate the development and assessment of deep learning models for the detection of lung cancer. The utilization of Google Colab and open-source modules and frameworks facilitates the expeditious and scalable deployment of deep learning models. Additionally, the IQ-OTH/NCCD dataset offers a comprehensive and varied collection of data for the purpose of evaluation.

4.3 Performance Metrics

The performance criteria that were employed in this study are essential for determining whether or not the strategy proposed for the identification of lung cancer is effective. Accuracy, precision, recall, F1-score, and area under the receiver operating characteristic curve (AUC-ROC) are the measurements that are utilised.

The ratio of samples that were correctly classified to all samples, or accuracy, indicates how accurate the classification findings are overall. The accuracy of 0.9838 shows that the classifier is operating quite effectively. Out of all positive forecasts, precision is the percentage of true positives. It comes to 0.9722. Recall measures the percentage of real positive cases among all positive cases, and its value is 0.9485. The F1-score, which offers a single score to assess the performance of several models, is a harmonic mean of precision and recall. The model has a 99.28% success rate.

ROC measures the ability of the model to identify variations of positive and negative samples, by plotting the true positive rate (TPR) against the false positive rate (FPR) for different thresholds. AUC-ROC values range from 0 to 1, where larger numbers indicate greater efficiency.

The Figs. 4 and 5 are depicting the history of metrics visualization of the global model.

4.4 Analysis of Proposed Method with Confusion Matrix

To assess the effectiveness of the suggested classification method, the confusion matrix is employed as the chosen metric. The three classes are benign nodules, normal nodules, and malignant nodules. Hence, the confusion matrix of dimensions 3×3 is utilised.

The confusion matrix shown in Fig. 6 illustrates the relationship between the actual class and the predicted class. The rows in the matrix correspond to the actual class, while the columns represent the predicted class. Each individual cell within the table denotes

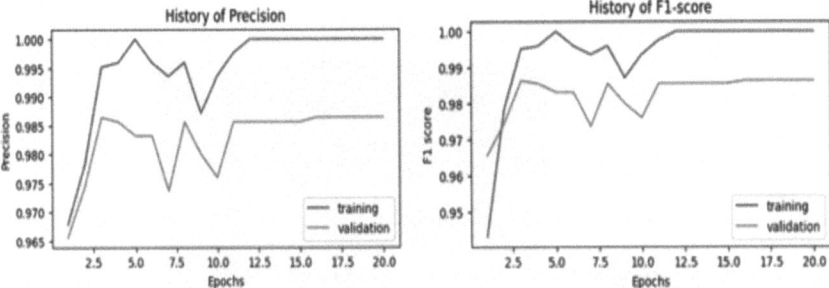

Fig. 4. Curves of (a)Precision and (b) F1 score of the global model.

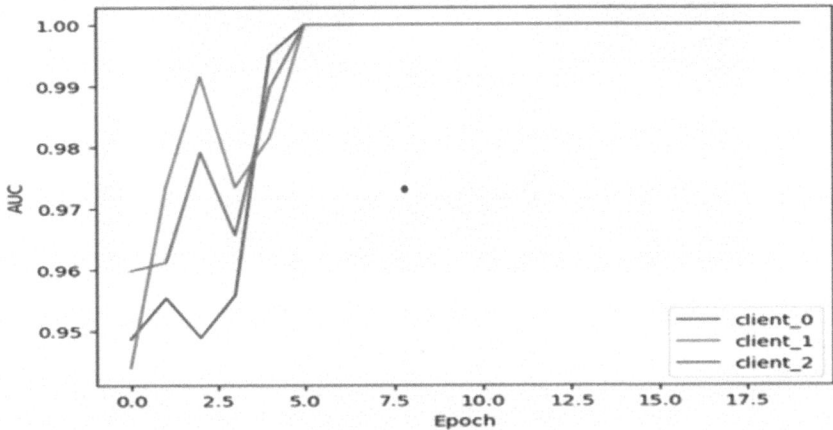

Fig. 5. Model Metrics Visualization.

the count of instances that pertain to a specific actual class and have been identified as belonging to the specific anticipated class. Here Class 1,2,3 are benign, malignant and normal respectively.

4.5 Model Accuracy and Loss Curves

The dataset comprises a total of 1097 CT scans of lung cancer cases, which have been categorized into three distinct groups: benign cases, normal cases, and malignant cases. The dataset was partitioned into two groups for the training process:: 80% for the learning phase and 20% for the testing phase.

The following Fig. 7 displays the model's accuracy: This model provides an overall accuracy of 98.022% following 20 epochs of training.

Upon the completion of training, the model obtained an overall accuracy of 94.15% after 20 epochs. The training and validation loss exhibits a consistent downward trend towards the end of the Loss plot. This suggests that the overall framework has the potential for additional learning and that the training process was terminated prematurely. An overall loss of 0.571908% is achieved.

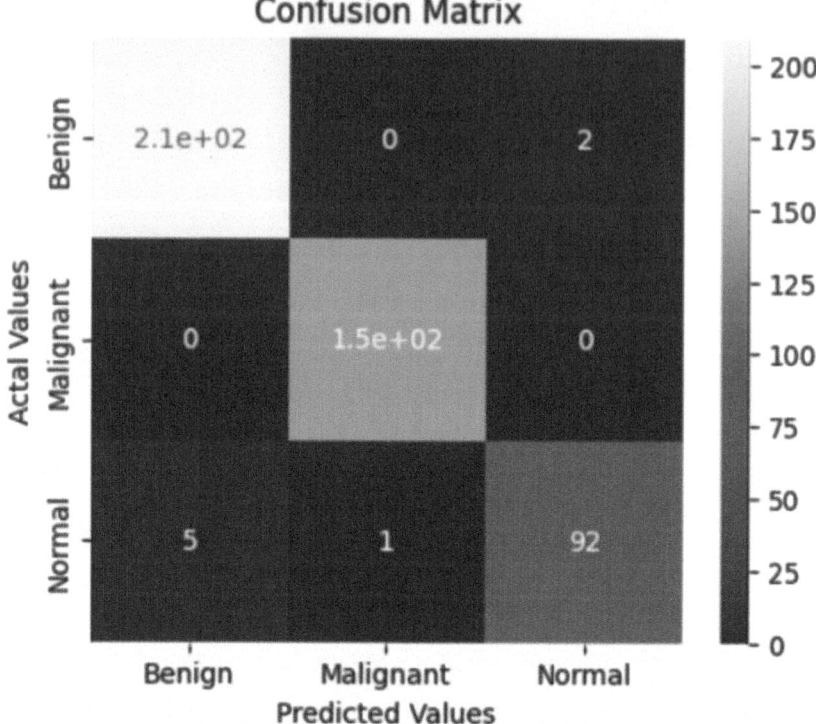

Fig. 6. Confusion Matrix.

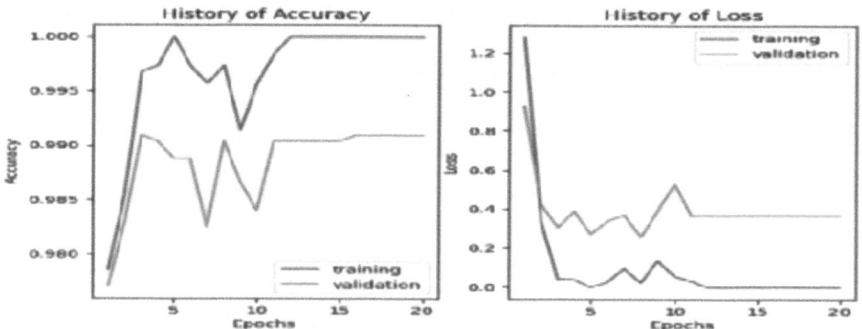

Fig. 7. Model Accuracy and Loss curves.

From Fig. 8 the accuracy of client models exceeded 95% accuracy, with a loss of 0.57% over 20 epochs.

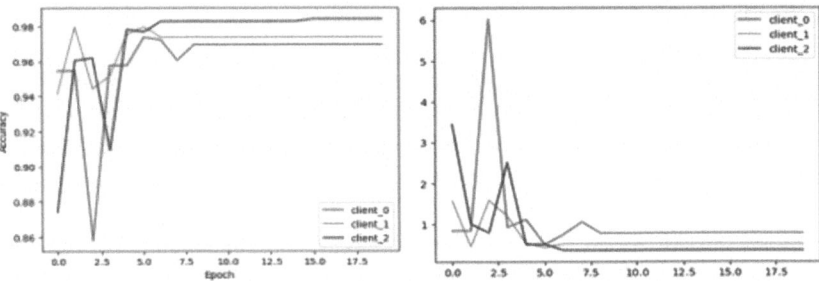

Fig. 8. A(a) Client Accuracy and (b) Loss Curves.

4.6   Comparison Analysis with State-Of-The-Art Models

The performance of the suggested model in terms of accuracy, specificity and sensitivity is evaluated and compared with that of the existing models such as Googlenet, Alexnet, and svm on the same data set. On the IQ-OTH/NCCD dataset, Table 1 compares the accuracy of the suggested model with the current state of the art models. A comparison between the technique employed above and some related works is provided below.

Table 1. Comparison Analysis of Proposed Method with Related Works.

References	Accuracy (%)	Specificity (%)	Sensitivity (%)
GoogLeNet. [18]	94.3%	93.57%	95.08%
SVM. [17]	89.88%	97.14%	97.5%
AlexNet. [16]	93.45%	95%	95.71%
Our Proposed Work	98.39%	97.5%	98.5%

The diagnosis model based on FL is designed to save the privacy of sensitive medical data. In this approach, the model is trained on data distributed across multiple institutions, and the training process occurs locally at each institution. On the other hand, the diagnosis model based on CT scans using CNNs requires access to centralized data repositories, which may pose a privacy risk.

Although the proposed model based on federated learning requires more computational resources and may be challenging to implement in some settings, it offers better privacy protection and interpretability.

It is clear from Table 1 that the suggested method performs comparably better in all three performance measures indicating that it works better than other methods used with datasets other than the current one. However, caution should be used to avoid drawing firm conclusions about how well this algorithm performs in comparison to other algorithms before it has been tested on equal grounds.

5 Conclusion

In conclusion Federated Learning (FL) for medical image classification can improve local accuracy. Using FL, we can develop a generalized model that can yield better results on data from different sources. This enhancement is attributable to the essentially bigger training set that FL made approachable without the requirement for direct data sharing.

Future research could examine how to use histogram equalisation and other approaches [1, 10] to synchronise non-IID data between sites or look into built-in domain adaptation FL framework [15] solutions. In a similar vein, we did not adequately address the challenges of class imbalance and heterogeneity in data size inside our FL framework. For example, due to local labelling requirements imposed by their clinical protocol, client 7 had essentially no category samples. Other mini-batch sampling techniques, loss functions, and client-specific local training iterations could all be used in future work. Also, we did not explore the execution of privacy-preserving methods that could have mitigated the risk of data leaking and inverted models stemming from the trained models. The implementation of differential privacy in our system is straightforward, and it has been shown to yield results that are comparable to those obtained using the default federated learning option.

Despite the challenges encountered, we successfully developed lung cancer detection models within a real-world Federated Learning (FL) environment. These models exhibited superior performance compared to models trained solely on local data. This emphasises the potential of FL in the development of clinically valuable models, eliminating the need for a centralized dataset.

References

1. Carvalho Filho, A., Silva, A., Paiva, A., Nunes, R., Gattass, M.: Lung-nodule classification based on computed tomography using taxonomic diversity indexes and an SVM. J. Sig. Proc. Sys. **87**, 179–196 (2017)
2. Sangamithraa, P., Govindaraju, S.: Lung tumour detection and classification using EK-Mean clustering. In: 2016 International Conference on Wireless Communications, Signal Processing and Networking (WiSPNET), pp. 2201–2206 (2016)
3. Wu, P., Sun, X., Zhao, Z., Wang, H., Pan, S., Schuller, B.: Classification of lung nodules based on deep residual networks and migration learning. Computat. Intell. Neurosci. 2020 (2020)
4. Sandhiya, S., Palani, U.: An effective disease prediction system using incremental feature selection and temporal convolutional neural network. J. Ambient. Intell. Humaniz. Comput. **11**, 5547–5560 (2020)
5. Krizhevsky, A., Hinton, G.E.: B. Imagenet classification with deep convolutional neural networks. Communications of the ACM **60**, 84–90 (2017)
6. Suk, H.: D. Hierarchical feature representation and multi-modal fusion with deep learning for AD/MCI diagnosis. Neuro Image **101**, 569–582 (2014)
7. Xu, Y., Chang, E.: Deep learning of feature representation with multiple instance learning for medical image analysis. In: IEEE International Conference on Acoustics, Speech and Signal Processing. pp. 1626–1630 (2014)
8. Kumar, D., Clausi, D.A.: Lung nodule classification using deep features in ct images. In: 12th Conference on Computer and Robot Vision, pp. 133–138 (2015)

9. Sun, W., Qian, W.: Computer aided lung cancer diagnosis with deep learning algorithms in SPIE Medical Imaging. In: 12th Conference on Computer and Robot Vision, 9785, pp. 97850Z–97850Z (2016)

10. Kiran, M., Ahmed, I., Khan, N., Reddy, A.: Chest X-ray segmentation using Sauvola thresholding and Gaussian derivatives responses. J. Ambient Intell. Human. Comput. **10**, 4179–4195 (2019)

11. Wu, G., Shen, D.: Unsupervised deep feature learning for deformable registration of mr brain images. Medical Image Comput. Comp.-Assis. Intervent. **16**, 649–656 (2013)

12. Ma, Z., et al.: An assisted diagnosis model for cancer patients based on federated learning. Frontiers in Oncology 713 (2022)

13. Tan, J., Huo, Y., Liang, Z., Li, L.: A comparison study on the effect of false positive reduction in deep learning-based detection for juxtapleural lung nodules: CNN VS DNN. Proceedings of The Symposium on Modeling and Simulation in Medicine, pp. 1–8 (2017)

14. Amma, T., Sunny, A., Biji, K., Mohanan, M.: Lung cancer identification and prediction based on VGG architecture. Int. J. Res. Eng. Sci. Manage. **3**, 88–92 (2020)

15. Muthazhagan, B., Ravi, T., Rajinigirinath, D.: An enhanced computer-assisted lung cancer detection method using content-based image retrieval and data mining techniques. J. Ambient Intell. Human. Comput. 1–9 (2020)

16. Al-Yasriy, H., AL-Husieny, M., Mohsen, F., Khalil, E., Hassan, Z.: Diagnosis of lung cancer based on CT scans using CNN. IOP Conference Series: Materials Science and Engineering **928**, 022035 (2020)

17. Kareem, H., Al-Huseiny, M., Mohsen, F., Al-Yasriy, K.: Evaluation of SVM performance in the detection of lung cancer in marked CT scan dataset. Indonesian J. Electr. Eng. Comp. Sci. **21**, 1731 (2021)

18. AL-Huseiny, M., Sajit, A.: Transfer learning with GoogLeNet for detection of lung cancer. Indonesian J. Electr. Eng. Comp. Sci. **22**, 1078–1086 (2021)

19. Rieke, N., et al.: The future of digital health with federated learning. NPJ Digital Medicine. **3**, 119 (2020)

20. McMahan, B., Moore, E., Ramage, D., Hampson, S., Arcas, B.: Communication-efficient learning of deep networks from decentralized data. Artif. Intell. Stati. 1273–1282 (2017)

21. Sheller, M., Reina, G., Edwards, B., Martin, J., Bakas, S.: Multi-institutional deep learning modeling without sharing patient data: A feasibility study on brain tumor segmentation. Brainlesion: Glioma, Multiple Sclerosis, Stroke and Traumatic Brain Injuries: 4th International Workshop, BrainLes 2018, Held in Conjunction With MICCAI 2018, Granada, Spain, September 16, 2018, Revised Selected Papers, Part I 4, pp. 92–104 (2019)

22. Kaissis, G., Makowski, M., Rückert, D., Braren, R.: Secure, privacy-preserving and federated machine learning in medical imaging. Nature Machine Intelligence **2**, 305–311 (2020)

23. Xiong, Y., Du, B., Yan, P.: Reinforced transformer for medical image captioning. Machine Learning in Medical Imaging: 10th International Workshop, MLMI 2019, Held In Conjunction With MICCAI 2019, Shenzhen, China, October 13, 2019, Proceedings 10, pp. 673–680 (2019)

24. Sheller, M., et al.: Federated learning in medicine: facilitating multi-institutional collaborations without sharing patient data. Scientific Reports **10**, 1–12 (2020)

25. Yang, K., Jiang, T., Shi, Y., Ding, Z.: Federated learning via over-the-air computation. IEEE Trans. Wireless Commun. **19**, 2022–2035 (2020)

26. Zhang, C., Xie, Y., Bai, H., Yu, B., Li, W., Gao, Y.: A survey on federated learning. Knowl.-Based Syst. **216**, 106775 (2021)

27. Ye, D., Yu, R., Pan, M., Han, Z.: Federated learning in vehicular edge computing: a selective model aggregation approach. IEEE Access. **8**, 23920–23935 (2020)

28. Xu, C., Qu, Y., Xiang, Y., Gao, L.: Asynchronous federated learning on heterogeneous devices: A survey. ArXiv Preprint ArXiv:2109.04269 (2021)

29. Sun, Y., Zhou, S., Gündüz, D.: Energy-aware analog aggregation for federated learning with redundant data. In: ICC 2020–2020 IEEE International Conference on Communications (ICC), pp. 1–7 (2020)
30. Fu, M., Shi, Y., Zhou, Y.: Federated Learning via Unmanned Aerial Vehicle. ArXiv Preprint ArXiv:2210.10970. (2022)
31. Zhang, W., et al.: Dynamic-fusion-based federated learning for COVID-19 detection. IEEE Internet Things J. **8**, 15884–15891 (2021)
32. Sun, F., Zhang, Z., Zeadally, S., Han, G., Tong, S.: Edge computing-enabled internet of vehicles: towards federated learning empowered scheduling. IEEE Trans. Veh. Technol. **71**, 10088–10103 (2022)
33. Yang, T., et al.: Applied federated learning: Improving google keyboard query suggestions. ArXiv Preprint ArXiv:1812.02903 (2018)
34. Terrail, J., et al.: FLamby: Datasets and Benchmarks for Cross-Silo Federated Learning in Realistic Healthcare Settings. ArXiv Preprint ArXiv:2210.04620 (2022)
35. Terrail, J., et al.: FLamby: Datasets and Benchmarks for Cross-Silo Federated Learning in Realistic Healthcare Settings. Adv. Neur. Info. Proc. Sys. **35**, 5315–5334 (2022)
36. Shaheen, M., Farooq, M., Umer, T., Kim, B.: Applications of federated learning: taxonomy, challenges, and research trends. Electronics **11**, 670 (2022)
37. Nishio, T., Yonetani, R.: Client selection for federated learning with heterogeneous resources in mobile edge. In: ICC 2019–2019 IEEE International Conference on Communications (ICC), pp. 1–7 (2019)
38. Chowdhury, A., Kassem, H., Padoy, N., Umeton, R., Karargyris, A.: A review of medical federated learning: Applications in oncology and cancer research. Brain-lesion: Glioma, Multiple Sclerosis, Stroke and Traumatic Brain Injuries: 7th International Workshop, BrainLes 2021, Held In Conjunction With MICCAI 2021, Virtual Event, September 27, 2021, Revised Selected Papers, Part I, pp. 3–24 (2022)
39. AbdulRahman, S., Tout, H., Ould-Slimane, H., Mourad, A., Talhi, C., Guizani, M.: A survey on federated learning: the journey from centralized to distributed onsite learning and beyond. IEEE Internet Things J. **8**, 5476–5497 (2020)
40. Konečný, J., McMahan, H., Yu, F., Richtarik, P., Suresh, A., Bacon, D.: Federated learning: Strategies for improving communication efficiency. ArXiv Preprint ArXiv:1610.05492 (2016)
41. Pfitzner, B., Steckhan, N., Arnrich, B.: Federated learning in a medical context: a systematic literature review. ACM Trans. Internet Technol. (TOIT). **21**, 1–31 (2021)
42. Xu, J., Glicksberg, B., Su, C., Walker, P., Bian, J., Wang, F.: Federated learning for healthcare informatics. J. Healthc. Info. Res. **5**, 1–19 (2021)
43. Roth, H., et al.: Federated learning for breast density classification: a real-world implementation. Domain Adaptation and Representation Transfer, and Distributed and Collaborative Learning: Second MICCAI Workshop, DART 2020, and First MICCAI Workshop, DCL 2020, Held in Conjunction with MICCAI 2020, Lima, Peru, October 4–8, 2020, Proceedings 2, pp. 181–191 (2020)
44. Malik, H., Anees, T.: Federated learning with deep convolutional neural networks for the detection of multiple chest diseases using chest x-rays. Multimedia Tools and Applications, 1–29 (2024)
45. Caroprese, L., Ruga, T., Vocaturo, E., Zumpano, E.: Lung Cancer Detection via Federated Learning. In: 2023 IEEE International Conference on Bioinformatics and Biomedicine (BIBM), pp. 3862–3867. IEEE (2023)

Arrhythmia Detection from ECG Traces Images Using Transfer Learning Approach

Trupti G. Thite[1,2(✉)] and Sonal K. Jagtap[3]

[1] Department of Electronics and Telecommunication Engineering, G. H. Raisoni College of Engineering and Management, Pune, Maharashtra, India
[2] Department of Electronics and Telecommunication Engineering, Trinity Academy of Engineering, Pune, Maharashtra, India
`truptithite.tae@kjei.edu.in`
[3] Department of Electronics and Telecommunication Engineering, STES's Smt. Kashibai Navale College of Engineering, Vadgaon (Bk.), Pune, Maharashtra, India

Abstract. The increasing prevalence of cardiovascular diseases necessitates efficient and accurate arrhythmia detection methods. Transfer learning offers a powerful technique by leveraging pre-trained neural networks on large image datasets for related tasks. This study proposes an approach for arrhythmia detection from electrocardiogram (ECG) traces utilizing a transfer learning methodology. In this research, pre-trained convolutional neural network architecture is adapted for arrhythmia detection. The Electrocardiogram trace image dataset can be easily obtained using smartphones, making it readily available even in low-resource countries. Hence in this study dataset of labeled traces having five different classes of arrhythmia patterns is used. Data augmentation techniques are applied to enhance the model's ability to generalize to diverse electrocardiogram patterns. The proposed transfer learning model demonstrates good results in terms of accuracy, precision during evaluation on a separate test set with respective convolutional neural network model. The study provides comparative insights into the effectiveness of transfer learning in medical image analysis tasks, particularly in the context of arrhythmia detection.

Keywords: Electrocardiogram · Arrhythmia · Trace Image · Deep learning · Transfer learning

1 Introduction

Cardiac arrhythmias, irregularities in the heart's rhythm, have significant health risks and are a leading cause of cardiovascular-related morbidity and mortality. Electrocardiogram (ECG) traces provide crucial information for diagnosing arrhythmias, but the manual analysis of these traces is time-consuming and can be prone to human error.

Observing properties of ECG signal and classifying types of arrhythmia automatically with computer aided system requires traditional signal processing and also artificial intelligence supported advanced machine learning and deep learning techniques

A. Mirzazadeh et al. (Eds.): SEMIT 2023, CCIS 2198, pp. 219–234, 2024.
https://doi.org/10.1007/978-3-031-72284-4_14

for preventing of cardiac diseases. Improvements in machine learning, deep learning computer-aided design for classifying and diagnosing various diseases have vast applications in medical field such as medical image, signal processing [1–3]. These automated systems has highest accuracy for early detection of tachycardia and reduced workload of cardiologist. Medical experts, particularly cardiologists and electro physiologists, use a variety of parameters/features when manually reviewing electrocardiogram (ECG) images. These features are used to perform analysis of ECG. Traditional machine learning methods are used to extract features of ECG like QRS peak, R peak etc. ECG Features and its normal properties are listed in Table 1. In contrast to this improved deep learning method's learn and extracts features automatically and these methods are less resource and time consuming [4].

In recent years, advancements in deep learning, particularly transfer learning; have shown promise in improving the accuracy and efficiency of medical image analysis tasks [5]. Transfer learning involves leveraging the knowledge acquired by a neural network on a large dataset for one task and applying it to a different but related task. In the context of arrhythmia detection from ECG traces, transfer learning offers the advantage of utilizing pre-trained models on diverse image datasets to extract relevant features without the need for an exhaustive amount of labeled ECG data.

This research aims to explore the application of a transfer learning approach for classification of ECG traces. By adapting a pre-trained convolutional neural network (CNN), which has demonstrated proficiency in image classification tasks, we seek to enhance the model's ability to recognize complex patterns associated with various arrhythmias.

The motivation behind this research lies in the potential to develop a robust and accurate automated system for arrhythmia detection, thereby aiding healthcare professionals in timely diagnosis and intervention. The proposed approach is expected to streamline the diagnostic process, reduce manual workload, and contribute to improved patient outcomes [6–9].

To design any type of ECG arrhythmia detection system; monitoring, detection, recognition, or classification, is different processes steps need to follow. Figure 1 explains flow of ECG analysis. In the first stage we collect the prerecorded clinical dataset from various open source platforms like MIT BIH dataset, PTB database or real time data form wearable ECG sensor. Second stage performs preprocessing of ECG signals to remove noise added during acquisition of ECG signal. To classify signal appropriately for the correct arrhythmia, identifying features like onset, offset, and peak points (fiducial points) of P Wave, QRS wave and T wave is very important which is performed in third stage. These features are used to classify various abnormal heart conditions in fourth stage using signal processing, machine learning methods. In deep learning extraction of features and classification is done by deep learning layers automatically [10].

In this paper, we present the methodology, and results of applying basic Convolutional model and transfer learning to ECG trace image classification. This study also focuses on the preprocessing step on ECG Trace images. The study aims to shed light on the effectiveness of transfer learning approach, effect of its performance metrics with respect to various parameters like number of no of epochs, use of optimizers, Comparison of Evaluation Parameters using CNN 2 Layer Model and Transfer Learning with ResNet50.

Table 1. ECG features

Feature		Normal Duration(ms)	Normal Amplitude(mv)
P Wave	Atrial Depolarization	80	0.1 to 0.2
Q Waves	Premature atrial contractions	25%of R wave	0.1
QRS Complex	Ventricular Contraction simulated By Purkinje fibers	80 to 120	Variable
T Wave	Ventricular repolarization	120 to 160	0.1-0.3
PR Interval	Distance Between P and R Peak	120 to 200	Variable
RR Interval	Distance Between R and R Peak	100 to 120	Variable

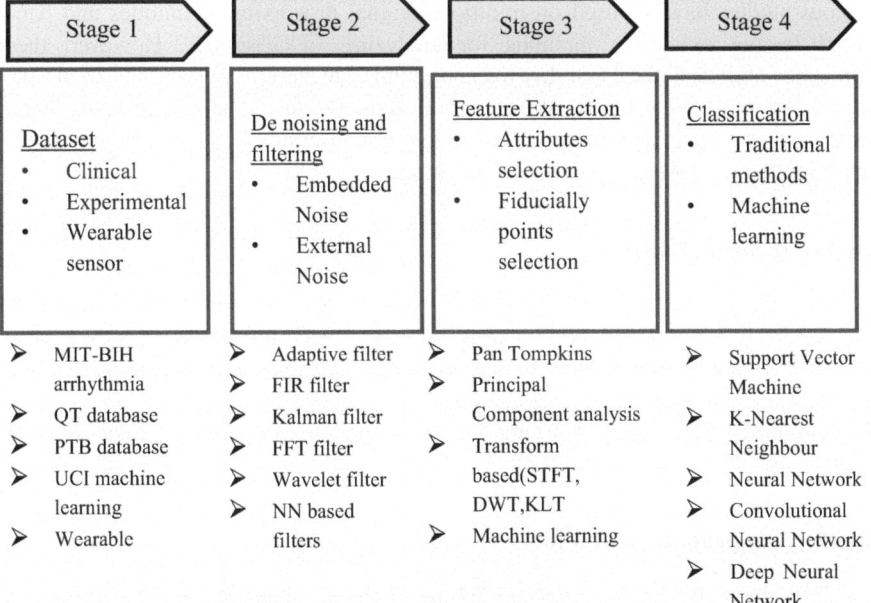

Fig. 1. ECG Analysis Flow

2 Literature Review

Heart arrhythmias are a major worldwide health problem that requires prompt and precise diagnostic techniques in order to manage patients effectively. Conventional methods for diagnosing arrhythmias frequently rely on the laborious and time-consuming manual interpretation of electrocardiogram (ECG) traces. Using machine learning techniques especially transfer learning, to improve the effectiveness and precision of arrhythmia identification from ECG traces has gained popularity in recent years. The research work performed on 2-D Images is summarized in Tables 2 and 3.

2.1 Transfer Learning in Medical Image Classification

Transfer learning has proven to be a powerful tool in medical image analysis due to its ability to transfer knowledge learned from large datasets in one domain to a different but related domain. In the context of arrhythmia detection, this approach has been successfully applied to tasks such as lung cancer detection in radiographic images and diabetic retinopathy diagnosis in ophthalmic images. The effectiveness of transfer learning lies in its capacity to expedite the learning process and improve the generalization of models [1, 3, 11–15].

2.2 Electrocardiogram Signal Processing and Feature Extraction

Previous studies have focused on traditional signal processing techniques and hand-crafted feature extraction methods for analyzing ECG signals. However, these approaches often lack the capability to capture intricate patterns present in arrhythmias. Transfer learning, by contrast, allows neural networks to automatically learn hierarchical representations and discern relevant features from raw ECG images, potentially improving the discriminatory power of the model.

2.3 Pre-trained Models

Several pre-trained convolutional neural network (CNN) architectures, originally designed for generic image classification tasks, have been investigated for their applicability in cardiac imaging. Models such as VGG16, ResNet, and Inception have been employed in various medical image analysis tasks. Their adaptability to ECG traces, when combined with transfer learning, has shown promise in achieving state-of-the-art results in arrhythmia detection [1, 16, 17].

2.4 Data Augmentation Methods

To address the challenges associated with limited annotated datasets, studies have incorporated data augmentation techniques. Augmenting the ECG dataset with variations such as rotations, scaling, and flipping enhances model robustness and aids in generalization. The combination of transfer learning and data augmentation contributes to overcoming the challenges posed by the scarcity of labeled data in medical image analysis [1, 18–22].

2.5   Evaluation Metrics for Arrhythmia Detection

Assessment metrics for arrhythmia detection models typically include accuracy, sensitivity, specificity, precision, and F1 score. Previous research has emphasized the importance of considering both false positives and false negatives, given the critical nature of cardiac diagnoses. A comprehensive evaluation framework is essential to validate the reliability [7].

Table 2. Literature survey on 2D Image classification.

Sr. No.	1	2	3	4	5	6
Reference	(Ullah et al. 2020)	(Kim et al. 2019)	(Ullah et al. 2021)	(Dokur and Ölmez 2020)	(Irmak 2022)	(Rahman et al. n.d.)
Dataset Used	1D ECG(MIT BIH) is transferred to 2D Images				ECG image dataset of cardiac and COVID-19 patients	
Feature Extraction	CNN	CNN	2D CNN Model	2D CNN Model	2D CNN Model	2D CNN Model
Classification	2D CNN	CNN based ensemble network	Hybrid Deep CNN Model	Hybrid Deep CNN Model	CNN model with 20 weighted layers	Six different deep CNN models
Number of Classes	8(NOR, VFW, PVC, VEB, RBB, LBB, PAB, and APC)	2 Classes Sinus Rhythm and Normal	8(8(NOR, VFW, PVC, VEB, RBB, LBB, PAB, and APC)	11 different ECG beat types are classified: N L, R,a, A, V, F, O, E, P, p	3 classes Normal, Abnormal and Myocardial Infarction	Five -Normal, COVID-19, MI) abnormal (AHB), and recovered myocardial infarction
Performance Parameters	Sensitivity: 97.91%, Specificity: 99.61%, Accuracy:99.11%, Precision:98.59%	Accuracy improved by 1%	Accuracy = 97.38%	Training and testing times were quite fast.Average success rates of 99%	Accuracy 98.57%, 93.20% and 96.74% for Normal, Abnormal Heartbeats	Average accuracy for all classes 98.50

3   Proposed Methodology

Following Fig. 2 summarizes the methodology of Multiclass Arrhythmia detection from ECG images of patients with Myocardial Infarction, Covid 19 and normal and abnormal beats. The methodology is described in the following sections.

3.1   Input Images/ECG Data Acquisition

The most commonly available ECG signals are obtained from single-lead and 12-lead ECG recorders. On the other hand, hospital ECG imaging equipment is usually large and supports very accurate and long-term monitoring. However, they limit patient movement and participation. On the other hand, wearable health monitoring systems enable

Table 3. Findings and Limitations on Literature survey.

Sr. No.	Reference	Findings	Limitations/Future Work
1	(Ullah et al. 2020)	Use of spectrograms with the CNN model is a reliable for diagnosis of Cardiac diseases	A one-lead ECG signal is used, multiple lead ECG data can be studied
2	(Kim et al. 2019)	Feature extraction has been done using an ensemble network	Less Number of classes was considered
3	(Ullah et al. 2021)	Wavelet algorithm is used in preprocessing step for enhancing quality of the original ECG signal, to reduce classification error	A single-lead ECG signal is used, multiple lead ECG data can be studied
4	(Dokur and Ölmez 2020)	Training and testing time is reduced using Walsh vector	To identify arrhythmias, the window length will be enlarged to include at least eight heartbeats
5	(Irmak 2022)	Deep learning based fast and accurate diagnosis method is used	Can be used to detect more number of Arrhythmias on real time data
6	(Rahman et al. n.d.)	ECG trace images are used to perform automated diagnosis of COVID-19 and other disorders using Deep CNN based transfer learning strategy	Can be used to detect more number of Arrhythmias on real time data

continuous real-time monitoring of patients using multiple sensors. ECG data can be acquired in different ways for analysis and interpretation by (1) sensor types (eg, wireless or wired), (2) sensor locations, (3) number of sensors, and (4) hardware required for Data collection, storage and transmission the sensors [8]. However, some ECG monitoring systems deal with real-time and continuous acquisition of the ECG sensor. ECG signal acquisition is a complex task because it is sensitive to various quality dimensions, including accuracy, precision, and timeliness. Inaccurate data collection can lead to misdiagnosis and thus influence clinical decisions. However, most researchers involved in ECG monitoring systems prefer to collect data from known databases rather than create their own data collection system, especially when dealing with diagnostic problems and feature extraction techniques that form the last part of the monitoring life cycle [9–11].

Standard ECG databases can be used to estimate algorithms for various test objectives. The MIT-BIH Arrhythmia Database, QT Database, CSE Database, and AHA Database are the most widely utilized databases on published investigations for arrhythmia [12, 13].

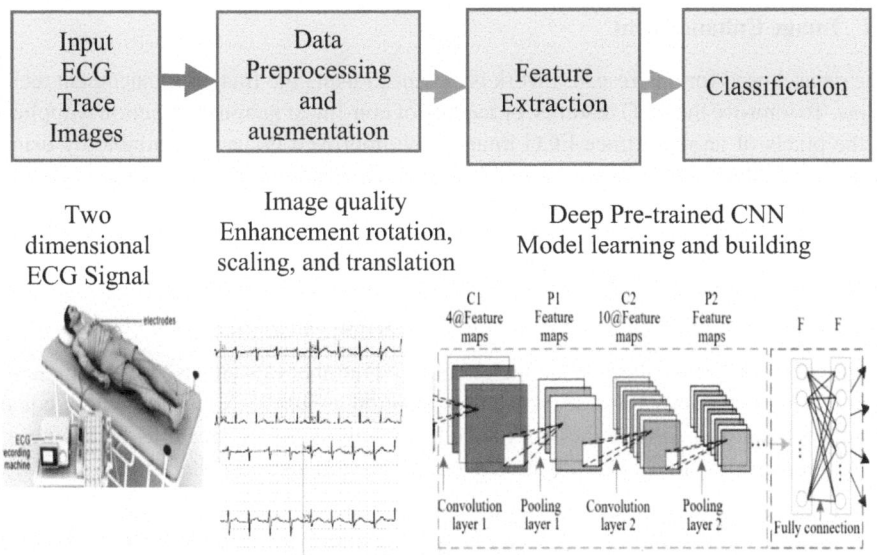

Fig. 2. Proposed Methodology.

Dataset Description. In this study, an cardiac patients ECG image dataset [27] is used which is available in mendeley database (https://data.mendeley.com/datasets/gwb z3fsgp8/2) This dataset has 1937 different patient records with five categories (Normal, COVID-19, myocardial infarction (MI), abnormal heartbeat (AHB), and recovered myocardial infarction (RMI). This dataset is created using the 'EDAN SERIES-3' ECG device. This dataset is formed by manually reviewing twelve lead ECG trace images from medical experts using a telehealth ECG diagnostic system. Table 4 gives details about the data collection process parameters and details about the number of samples available in various classes of this dataset.

Table 4. Dataset Description.

Sr. No.	Category Name	No. of Distinct ECG Images	Sample Rate	Leads
1	COVID-19 Patients	250	500Hz	12 Leads
2	Normal Person ECG Images	859		
3	Myocardial Infarction Patient	240		
4	Patients with Previous History of Myocardial Infarction	203		
5	Patients with Abnormal Heartbeat	548		

3.2 Image Enhancement

The dataset used for this research work is enhanced using the Image enhancement technique. To improve the ECG features; procedure of non-linear gamma correction is applied to the pixels of an input trace ECG image. The improved image is available by using projection relationship between the pixel value and the gamma value as per internal map, Eq. 1 gives Gamma correction function.

$$S(X) = 255(X/255)1/\gamma(X) \tag{1}$$

where s(x) = output pixel correction value (grayscale) and $\gamma(X)$ = Gamma number.

Augmentation. The dataset is having unbalanced number of samples. Hence augmentation technique like rotation, scaling and translation are used to create dataset of equal number of samples. As per the work stated in many recent publications balancing of training dataset improves classification accuracy as well approved stability.

Rotation. Rotation involves rotating the image around its center by a specified angle. This helps the model become invariant to changes in the orientation of ECG traces. It mimics variations that might occur due to changes in electrode placement or differences in the recording setup.

Parameters: The rotation angle can be randomly selected within a predefined range, such as ± 10 °.

Scaling. Scaling involves resizing the image, either stretching or compressing it, along its dimensions. Scaling introduces variations in the size of the ECG traces, simulating different magnifications or resolutions in the recording process. This helps the model generalize to variations in signal amplitude.

Parameters: The scaling factor can be randomly chosen within a range, such as 0.9 to 1.1, where values less than 1 compress the image, and values greater than 1 stretch it.

Translation. Translation involves shifting the image along its x and y axes. Translation mimics variations in the positioning of the ECG trace within the image. It helps the model become robust to slight shifts in the recording position.

Parameters: Randomly choose translation values for both the x and y axes within a specified range, such as ± 5 pixels.

These augmentation techniques are often combined to create a more diverse dataset. For instance, during each training iteration, an ECG image may undergo a random rotation, a random scaling, and a random translation, introducing variability that helps the model generalize well to unseen data.

In Python, using a deep learning library like TensorFlow or PyTorch, you can implement these augmentations using functions provided by the libraries. Additional augmentations like shear, zoom, horizontal flip, and vertical flip, demonstrating the flexibility of data augmentation techniques in enhancing the diversity of the training dataset.

3.3 Feature Extraction and Classification

In the proposed methodology we have decided to use Efficient Neural Network to perform feature extraction and classification. We have used simple CNN and transfer learning for image classification in different classes like abnormal COVID-19, myocardial infarction, abnormal heartbeat, and recovered myocardial infarction. Many researchers focused on use of Transfer learning for classification of Image to tackle the problem of insufficient data samples and time taken for training. Transfer learning uses some of the layers of pertained machine learning models and adds new layer based on problem. These pertained models can be used for feature extraction as well as for prediction.

Basic Steps to use any Transfer Learning models for classification are,

- Use previously trained model Layers
- Freeze the layers, so that weights of that layers will not update, this achieves higher accuracy for small number of image dataset
- Add few new, trainable layers on top of the freezed layers. These new layers will learn to turn old features into predictions on a new dataset.
- Use dataset to train new layers.

There are many deep learning pre trained models available in Keras applications like ResNet50, ResNet152, VGG16, DenseNet121 etc. all these models defer with one another with respect to memory size, Top-5 and Top-1 accuracy, depth of network which includes activation layers, batch normalization layers also time required by GPU and CPU for training. Our Proposed Research used pretrained Keras.tensorflow model ResNet50 to perform feature extraction and classification. ResNet50 uses 1×1 convolutions, known as a "bottleneck", which decreases the matrix multiplications and number of parameters. This results into faster training of each layer.

4 Result and Discussion

To work on proposed methodology each step of proposed algorithm is implemented in Jupiter platform using python language. For experimentation we have used ECG Dataset of images of Cardiac and COVID-19 patients [26]. These Image dataset samples are shown in Fig. 3. The first process implemented on this dataset is Image preprocessing using gamma correction. Gamma values in between 0.5 and 3.0 highlights more pixels of ECG Wave and lightens the Background Noise, the result of gamma correction function applied for various values of gamma number of Myocardial Infraction dataset is illustrated through Fig. 4.

We have applied Basic CNN Binary classifier on above dataset in Python using Colab Platform. Keras python library is used for this implementation. Sequential model from the Keras is used for experimentation. The details about each CNN Layer I have implemented is mentioned in following Table 5.

Training and testing parameters considered for Binary classification to classify Normal and MI class are given in Table 6.

Performance of Classification is measured with the help of parameters like training/testing loss and accuracy with respect to number of epochs which decides number times that the learning algorithm will work through the entire training dataset. As the

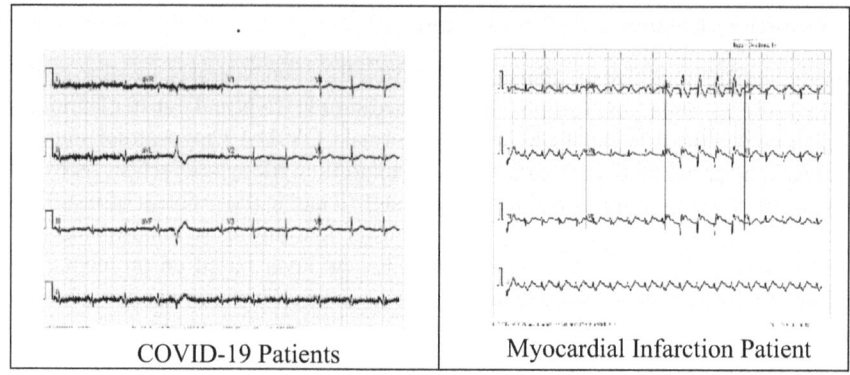

Fig. 3. Image Dataset Samples.

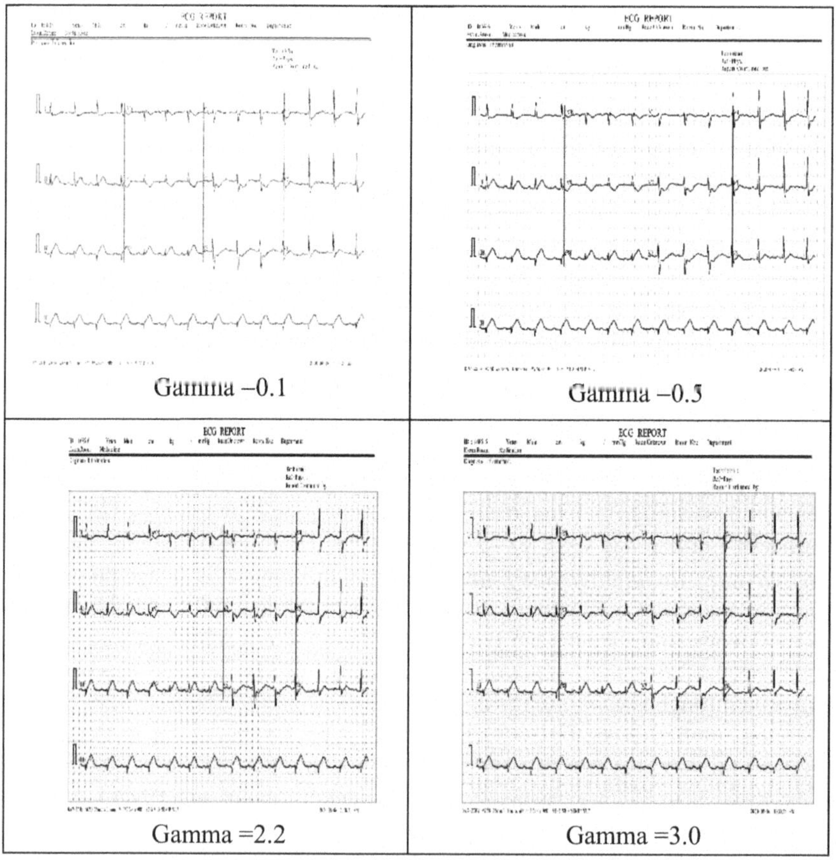

Gamma −0.1

Gamma −0.5

Gamma =2.2

Gamma =3.0

Fig. 4. Gamma Corrected Images.

Table 5. Details about CNN Layers.

Layer	Name	Parameters used
1	Input Layer	Training and Testing data Images of Two classes(Abnormal and MI) image size(500*500)
2	Convolution layer Activation function	Conv2d,Filter with size 32,Activation fuction:Relu
3	Pooling Layer	Pooling layer of size 2*2
4	Output Layer	Activation function: sigmoid
5	Fully Connected Layer	Dense layer

study is based on medical image dataset and medical diagnosis it is very important to predict correct decisions about the abnormal conditions that are considered. Therefore by calculating true positive, true negative, false positive and false negative predictions of classes various parameters like Accuracy, Precision, F1-Score, and Recall are also considered for evaluation [28].

Table 6. Training and testing parameters.

Training sample Count			Testing Sample count	
Normal:687			Normal:172	
MI:192			MI:48	
Total:879			Total:879	
Learning rate	Batch size	Epochs	Optimizer Used	Loss
0.01	10	40	Adam	binary_crossentropy
0.01	10	30	RMSprop	

By using above parameters CNN is applied on Normal and Myocardial infraction dataset using one input layers, 2 hidden layers and output layer for binary classification. Training and testing accuracy with respect to number of epochs is calculated and plotted, same is shown in Fig. 5. For above specification implemented network provides following evaluation parameters given in Table 7.

In second experimentation we have used using transfer learning to learn an accurate image classifier from a relatively small number of training samples available in dataset. Learning new task which relies on the previous task. Using pretrained Keras.tensorflow model ResNet50 Model we performed binary classification for following classes,

1. Abnormal and Myocardial Infraction class
2. Abnormal and PMI class
3. Normal and MI class

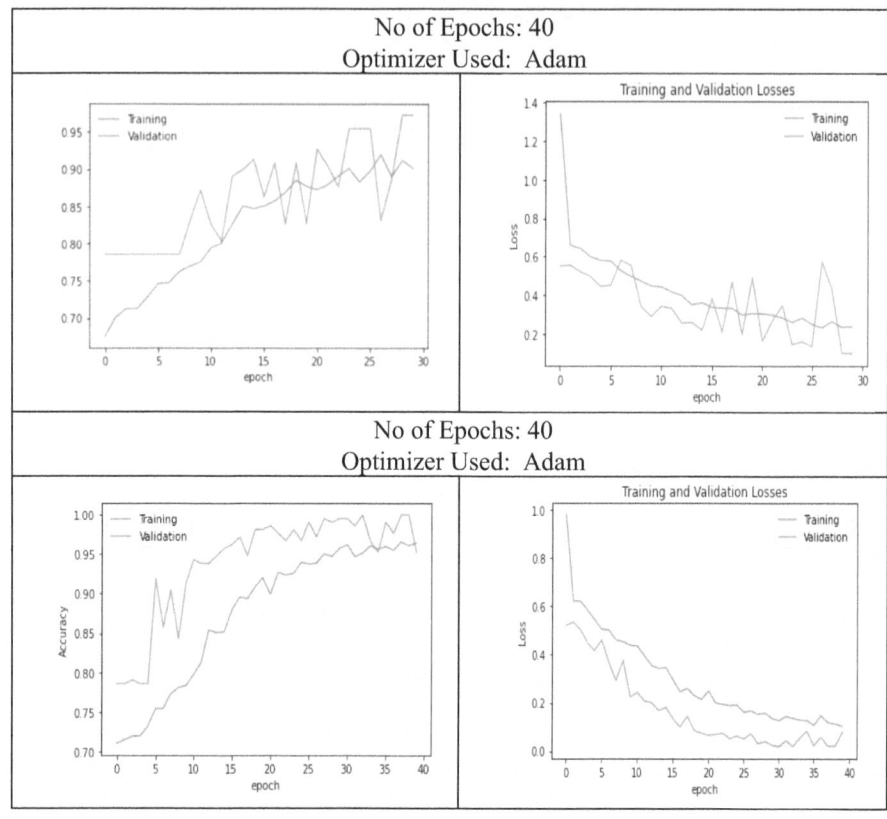

Fig. 5. Training and testing loss and accuracy plots.

Table 7. CNN Evaluation Parameters.

	Accuracy	Precision	F1-Score	Recall
Epoch 30 Optimizer: RMSdrop	0.79	0.79	0.88	1.0
Epoch 40 Optimizer: Adam	0.81	0.80	0.88	1.0

After applying model as per above steps Confusion Matrix obtained for First Binary Class Abnormal and Myocardial Infraction class is as shown in Fig. 6, in which Label 0 is for MI Class and label 1 is for Abnormal heart beat class. There are total 47 images of MI and 46 images of abnormal heart beats used for testing. Evaluation Parameters and training testing dataset for this class are given in Fig. 7.

Combined performance matrix for both experiment performed using CNN and transfer learning model is as shown in Table 8. Which illustrates that classification accuracy by using transfer learning for binary classification is more with respect to CNN Classifier.

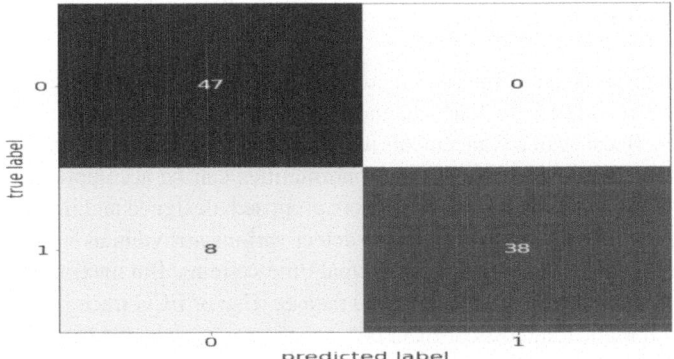

Fig. 6. Confusion Matrix for first class.

```
-----------------------------------------
     Folder_name  Traning Image Numbers
0       MI_Resize                    266
1  Abnormal Train                    187
-----------------------------------------
items in X_train is:    453  items
items in y_train is:    453  items
```

```
-----------------------------------------
     Label_name  Number of samples
0      MI_Resize                 47
1  Abnormal Test                 46
-----------------------------------------
items in x_test is:    93  items
items in y_test is:    93  items
```

```
               precision   recall  f1-score   support

    MI_Resize       0.85     1.00      0.92        47
Abnormal Test       1.00     0.83      0.90        46
```

Fig. 7. Evaluation Parameter for transfer learning Method.

Table 8. Comparison of Evaluation Parameters

Model Used	Class	Epoch	Accuracy	Precision	F1-Score	Recall
CNN	**Normal-MI**	30	0.79	0.79	0.88	1.0
2 Layer Model	**Normal-MI**	40	0.81	0.80	0.88	1.0
Transfer Learning with ReNet50	**AB-MI**	10	0.91	0.92	0.91	91
	AB-PMI	8	0.80	0.81	0.81	0.81
	Normal-MI	8	0.78	0.77	0.80	0.91

5 Conclusion

Electrocardiogram is very important medical signal that can be used to analyze abnormalities of the heart function. Early diagnosis of abnormal heartbeats is challenging as it can save lives. Because of advancements in Computer aided design and machine learning techniques, automated finding of heart abnormalities can be accomplished with ECG analysis and classification. Many researchers proposed, designed and implemented various algorithms for ECG Classification to detect various arrhythmias by means of only software, or hardware or using IoT Based real time systems. But maximum researchers worked on standard one dimensional ECG dataset. Use of ECG trace images is advantageous in automatic diagnosis of ECG because trace image dataset can be easily taken by smartphones and are readily available in cities with low dependent resources. Hence our research concentrates on Multiclass Arrhythmia detection from 2-D ECG Signal. As advanced convolutional neural network can work efficiently on two dimensional datasets without extracting features manually we would identify Deep Convolution Neural Network algorithm using transfer learning for better classification accuracy as compared to one dimensional signal. The proposed transfer learning model with ResNet50 gives accuracy 91%, Precision 92%, F1-Score 91% and 91% recall during evaluation on a separate test set with respective convolutional neural network model.

References

1. Abbas, A., Abdelsamea, M.M., Gaber, M.M.: DeTrac: transfer learning of class decomposed medical images in convolutional neural networks. IEEE Access **8**, 74901–74913 (2020). https://doi.org/10.1109/ACCESS.2020.2989273
2. Fu, F., et al.: Comparison of machine learning algorithms for the quality assessment of wearable ECG Signals Via Lenovo H3 Devices. J. Med. Biol. Eng. **41**(2), 231–240 (2021). https://doi.org/10.1007/s40846-020-00588-7
3. Vallabhajosyula, S., Sistla, V., Kolli, V.K.K.: Transfer learning-based deep ensemble neural network for plant leaf disease detection. J. Plant Dis. Prot. **129**(3), 545–558 (2022). https://doi.org/10.1007/s41348-021-00465-8
4. Somani, S., et al.: Deep learning and the electrocardiogram: review of the current state-of-the-art. Europace **23**(8), 1179–1191 (2021). https://doi.org/10.1093/europace/euaa377
5. Irmak, E.: COVID-19 disease diagnosis from paper-based ECG trace image data using a novel convolutional neural network model. Phys. Eng. Sci. Med. (2022). https://doi.org/10.1007/s13246-022-01102-w
6. Daydulo, Y.D., Thamineni, B.L., Dawud, A.A.: Cardiac arrhythmia detection using deep learning approach and time frequency representation of ECG signals. BMC Med. Inform. Decis. Mak. 1–14 (2023). https://doi.org/10.1186/s12911-023-02326-w
7. Ansari, Y., Mourad, O., Qaraqe, K.: Deep learning for ECG Arrhythmia detection and classification: an overview of progress for period 2017–2023 (2023). https://doi.org/10.3389/fphys.2023.1246746
8. Xiao, Q., et al.: Deep Learning-Based ECG Arrhythmia Classification: A Systematic Review. Appl. Sci. **13**(8) (2023). https://doi.org/10.3390/app13084964
9. Rahman, M.M., Rivolta, M.W., Badilini, F., Sassi, R.: A Systematic survey of data augmentation of ECG signals for AI applications. Sensors **23**(11), 1–22 (2023). https://doi.org/10.3390/s23115237

10. Wasimuddin, M., Elleithy, K., Abuzneid, A.-S., Faezipour, M., Abuzaghleh, O.: Stages-Based ECG signal analysis from traditional signal processing to machine learning approaches: a survey. IEEE Access **8**, 177782–177803 (2020). https://doi.org/10.1109/access.2020.302 6968

11. Wu, Y., Yang, F., Liu, Y., Zha, X., Yuan, S.: A Comparison of 1-D and 2-D Deep Convolutional Neural Networks of ECG, pp. 48–51

12. Kumar, S., Mallik, A., Kumar, A., Del Ser, J., Yang, G.: Fuzz-ClustNet: Coupled fuzzy clustering and deep neural networks for Arrhythmia detection from ECG signals. Comput. Biol. Med. **153**(September 2022), 106511 (2023). https://doi.org/10.1016/j.compbiomed.2022.106511

13. Mhamdi, L., Dammak, O., Cottin, F., Ben Dhaou, I.: Artificial Intelligence for Cardiac Diseases Diagnosis and Prediction Using ECG Images on Embedded Systems. Biomedicines **10**(8), 1–16 (2022). https://doi.org/10.3390/biomedicines10082013

14. Panganiban, E.B., Paglinawan, A.C., Chung, W.Y., Paa, G.L.S.: ECG diagnostic support system (EDSS): A deep learning neural network based classification system for detecting ECG abnormal rhythms from a low-powered wearable biosensors. Sens. Bio-Sensing Res. **31**(January), 100398 (2021). https://doi.org/10.1016/j.sbsr.2021.100398

15. Panganiban, E.B., Paglinawan, A.C., Chung, W.Y., Paa, G.L.S.: ECG diagnostic support system (EDSS): a deep learning neural network based classification system for detecting ECG abnormal rhythms from a low-powered wearable biosensors. Sens. Bio-Sensing Res. **31**(January) (2021). https://doi.org/10.1016/j.sbsr.2021.100398

16. Alom, M.Z., et al.: A state-of-the-art survey on deep learning theory and architectures. Electronics (Switzerland) **8**(3). MDPI AG (2019). https://doi.org/10.3390/electronics8 030292

17. Goh, H.A., Ho, C.K., Abas, F.S.: Front-end deep learning web apps development and deployment: a review. Appl. Intell. **53**(12), 15923–15945 (2023). https://doi.org/10.1007/s10489-022-04278-6

18. Vadillo-Valderrama, A., Goya-Esteban, R., Caulier-Cisterna, R., Garcia-Alberola, A., Rojo-Alvarez, J.L.: Differential Beat Accuracy for ECG Family Classification using Machine Learning. IEEE Access **10**(November) (2022). https://doi.org/10.1109/ACCESS.2022.322 7219

19. Phung, V.H., Rhee, E.J.: A High-accuracy model average ensemble of convolutional neural networks for classification of cloud image patches on small datasets. Appl. Sci. **9**(21) (2019). https://doi.org/10.3390/app9214500

20. Dokur, Z., Ölmez, T.: Heartbeat classification by using a convolutional neural network trained with Walsh functions. Neural Comput. Appl. **32**(16), 12515–12534 (2020). https://doi.org/10.1007/s00521-020-04709-w

21. Kim, M.G., Ko, H., Pan, S.B., Park, K.: A study on user recognition using 2D ECG image based on ensemble networks for intelligent vehicles. Wirel. Commun. Mob. Comput. **2019** (2019). https://doi.org/10.1155/2019/6458719

22. Hao, P., et al.: Multi-branch fusion network for Myocardial infarction screening from 12-lead ECG images. Comput. Methods Programs Biomed. **184** (2020). https://doi.org/10.1016/j.cmpb.2019.105286

23. Ullah, A., Anwar, S.M., Bilal, M., Mehmood, R.M.: Classification of arrhythmia by using deep learning with 2-D ECG spectral image representation. Remote Sens. **12**(10) (2020). https://doi.org/10.3390/rs12101685

24. Ullah, A., et al.: A hybrid deep CNN model for abnormal arrhythmia detection based on cardiac ECG signal. Sensors (Switzerland) **21**(3), 1–13 (2021). https://doi.org/10.3390/s21 030951

25. Rahman, T., et al.: COV-ECGNET: COVID-19 detection using ECG trace images with deep convolutional neural network.

26. Khan, A.H., Hussain, M., Malik, M.K.: Specifications Table. Data Br. **34**, 106762 (2021). https://doi.org/10.17632/gwbz3fsgp8.1
27. Khan, A.H., Hussain, M., Malik, M.K.: ECG Images dataset of Cardiac and COVID-19 Patients. Data Br. **34**, 106762 (2021). https://doi.org/10.1016/j.dib.2021.106762
28. Chen, C., Hua, Z., Zhang, R., Liu, G., Wen, W.: Automated arrhythmia classification based on a combination network of CNN and LSTM. Biomed. Signal Process. Control **57**, 101819 (2020). https://doi.org/10.1016/j.bspc.2019.101819

Smart Production, Transportation and Supply Chain Systems

Enhancing Traffic Flow Prediction in Urban Areas Through Deep Learning and Probe Information: A Comparative Study

Serap Ergün$^{(\boxtimes)}$ ⓘ

Department of Computer Engineering, Isparta University of Applied Sciences, 32260 Isparta, Turkey
serapbakioglu@isparta.edu.tr

Abstract. With the remarkable development of Intelligent Transportation Systems in recent years, the easy collection of traffic information and various vehicle-related data has been made possible. The availability of probe information allows for the acquisition of more extensive traffic data in addition to observation information. In this paper, the traffic flow prediction method on urban roads using probe information is considered. Accurate and real-time traffic information is deemed indispensable for the deployment of high-performance intelligent transportation systems. Traffic flow, being a complicated phenomenon, can be expressed in terms of its characteristics without prior knowledge of site-specific features, thanks to the application of deep learning, which automatically acquires feature quantities. Consequently, a traffic flow prediction model utilizing deep learning is investigated in this research. Additionally, a comparison is made with other traffic flow prediction methods. The research aims to improve prediction accuracy and contribute to the advancement of more efficient intelligent transportation systems.

Keywords: Traffic flow prediction · Intelligent Transportation Systems · Probe information · Deep learning

1 Introduction

Urban areas around the world are grappling with ever-increasing traffic congestion, resulting in a multitude of challenges ranging from increased travel times to environmental concerns. The effective management of urban traffic is critical not only for the convenience and safety of commuters but also for reducing the environmental impact of excessive vehicular congestion. In this context, the fusion of advanced technologies, specifically Deep Learning and Probe Information, presents a promising avenue for enhancing traffic flow prediction and, consequently, the overall efficiency of urban transportation systems (Tao et al., 2020; Sun et al., 2020).

The recent and remarkable advancements in Intelligent Transport Systems (ITS) have greatly facilitated the seamless collection of road traffic data and a wide array of vehicle information (Saleem et al., 2022). This data gathering encompasses various sources,

© The Author(s), under exclusive license to Springer Nature Switzerland AG 2024
A. Mirzazadeh et al. (Eds.): SEMIT 2023, CCIS 2198, pp. 237–252, 2024.
https://doi.org/10.1007/978-3-031-72284-4_15

including observational data procured from sensors embedded in the road infrastructure and probe data gathered from vehicles traversing those roadways.

Probe data, in particular, extends the breadth of road traffic information far beyond what can be obtained from point-specific sensor observations. In this research, it is delved into a traffic flow prediction technique harnessing the potential of probe data.

Urban Traffic Challenges: The complexities of urban traffic are multifaceted. Congestion patterns can vary dramatically depending on factors such as time of day, weather conditions, special events, and road infrastructure. Traditional traffic management systems, which rely on fixed sensors and historical data, often struggle to adapt to these dynamic conditions in real-time. This limitation results in suboptimal traffic management, causing frustration among commuters and contributing to air pollution.

Deep Learning's Potential: Deep Learning, a subfield of machine learning, has gained prominence for its ability to autonomously learn intricate patterns from large datasets. In the realm of urban traffic, Deep Learning models can be trained to recognize and predict traffic flow dynamics based on a wide array of factors, including historical traffic data, weather data, and even real-time probe information (Tran et al., 2020; Perez-Murueta et al., 2019).

Harnessing Probe Information: Probe data, collected from GPS-equipped vehicles traversing urban road networks, is a valuable source of real-time traffic information. These data points offer insights into current traffic conditions, speed variations, and congestion hotspots (Essien et al., 2021; Lv et al., 2014). By integrating probe information into Deep Learning models, it becomes possible to enhance the accuracy of traffic flow predictions and provide real-time updates to commuters.

Benefits and Outcomes: The benefits of enhancing traffic flow prediction in urban areas through Deep Learning and Probe Information are manifold. First and foremost, commuters gain access to more accurate and up-to-date traffic information, enabling them to make informed decisions about their routes and travel times. Additionally, urban planners and transportation authorities can use this predictive capability to implement dynamic traffic management strategies, alleviating congestion and reducing travel times (Koesdwiadyet al., 2016).

Furthermore, reducing traffic congestion contributes to environmental sustainability by lowering fuel consumption and greenhouse gas emissions. As cities worldwide strive to achieve greener and more sustainable transportation systems, improving traffic flow prediction becomes an essential component of this endeavour (Duan et al., 2018).

The fusion of Deep Learning and Probe Information holds immense promise in addressing the intricate challenges posed by urban traffic congestion. By harnessing the power of machine learning and real-time data from probe sources, it can be moved closer to realizing efficient, safe, and environmentally responsible urban transportation systems. In the pages that follow, it is delved into the methodologies, experiments, and results of the research aimed at enhancing traffic flow prediction in urban areas, ultimately contributing to the advancement of smarter and more sustainable cities.

Hence, this study embarks on an exploration of a traffic flow prediction approach founded on deep learning, leveraging probe data. Furthermore, to validate the efficacy of this deep learning-based traffic flow prediction method, a comparative analysis with conventional machine learning techniques is conducted.

The research centers on developing a robust traffic flow prediction model using deep learning techniques. A step further has been taken by conducting comparative analyses with other traffic flow prediction methodologies. The ultimate aim of this research is two-fold: to enhance prediction accuracy and to contribute to the advancement of more efficient intelligent transportation systems.

1.1 Key Research Areas and Contributions

1. Harnessing Probe Data: The research capitalizes on the potential of probe data, a valuable resource for gaining insights into traffic patterns and dynamics. By integrating probe data into the prediction model, it is aimed to improve the accuracy of traffic flow forecasts.
2. Deep Learning Advancements: Deep learning has emerged as a powerful tool in the field of machine learning. In this study, its application in the context of traffic flow prediction is explored. Deep learning's ability to autonomously learn feature representations offers promise in achieving more precise predictions without the need for prior site-specific knowledge.
3. Comparative Analysis: A comparative analysis with conventional machine learning techniques, shedding light on the effectiveness of the deep learning-based approach are conducted. This comparative assessment provides valuable insights into the advantages and limitations of various prediction methods.

The organization of this study is constructed as follows: In Sect. 2, The related research part is presented. Traffic Flow Prediction is given in Sect. 3. The Experiment and the parameters are proposed in Sect. 4 and the results of the experiments are presented in Sect. 5. And finally, the paper ends with the conclusion and outlook part which is given in Sect. 6.

2 Related Research

Significant advancements in the field of traffic flow prediction have been witnessed in recent years, driven by the integration of cutting-edge technologies like Deep Learning and Machine Learning. These innovations have enabled the tackling of intricate challenges posed by urban traffic congestion, resulting in enhanced accuracy and precision in traffic flow prediction. In this comparative overview, a collection of studies that harness the power of these technologies to improve traffic flow prediction is examined. Each study represents a unique approach, exploring diverse applications, methods, and datasets to address the complexities of traffic management in urban areas (Table 1).

A rich tapestry of research endeavors is presented collectively by these studies, shedding light on the potential and limitations of various techniques. From the utilization of Twitter-mined events and weather information to the development of hybrid models integrating attention-based convolutions and Long Short-Term Memory (LSTM) networks, insights are contributed to the realm of traffic flow prediction (Essien et al., 2021). Furthermore, specific aspects, such as urban traffic volume, bus travel time estimation, or congestion avoidance, are focused on by some studies, showcasing the versatility of

Table 1. Comparative Overview of Traffic Flow Prediction Studies Using Deep Learning and Machine Learning Methods.

Study	Application	Methods	Data	Findings
(Koesdwiadyet al., 2016)	Traffic flow prediction with weather information	Deep Learning	Connected car data, weather data	Enhanced traffic flow prediction accuracy with weather information
(Essien et al., 2021)	Urban traffic flow prediction with Twitter-mined events	Deep Learning	Twitter data, traffic events	Improved urban traffic flow prediction by incorporating real-time Twitter events
(Lv et al., 2014)	Traffic flow prediction with big data	Deep Learning	Big traffic datasets	Achieved traffic flow prediction accuracy using deep learning on extensive data sets
(Yang et al., 2019)	Traffic flow prediction using LSTM	Long Short-Term Memory (LSTM)	Traffic data with feature enhancement	Improved traffic flow prediction accuracy by enhancing features with LSTM
(Zheng et al., 2020)	Short-term traffic flow prediction with attention-based conv-LSTM	Hybrid Deep Learning	Traffic data	Enhanced short-term traffic flow prediction with attention-based conv-LSTM networks
(Zheng et al., 2019)	Traffic flow prediction in urban informatics	Deep Learning	Urban traffic data	Enhanced traffic flow prediction using deep and embedded learning techniques

(continued)

Table 1. (*continued*)

Study	Application	Methods	Data	Findings
(Abdullah et al., 2023)	Congestion prediction in smart cities	Soft GRU-Based Recurrent Neural Networks	Smart city traffic data	Optimized traffic flow prediction in smart cities using GRU-based models
(Tao et al., 2020)	Urban traffic volume prediction	Deep Learning	Urban traffic volume data	Improved urban traffic volume prediction using delay-based deep learning
(Tran et al., 2020)	Public bus travel time estimation	Deep Learning	Public bus travel data	Enhanced public bus travel time estimation with deep learning and traffic forecasting
(Perez-Murueta et al., 2019)	Vehicular re-routing and congestion avoidance	Deep Learning	Vehicular data	Improved vehicular re-routing and congestion avoidance using deep learning
(Sun et al., 2020)	City-wide traffic flow forecasting	Deep Learning	City-wide traffic data	City-wide traffic flow forecasting with deep convolutional neural networks
(Saleem et al., 2022)	Traffic congestion control in smart cities	Machine Learning	Vehicular network data	Fusion-based intelligent traffic congestion control system for smart cities
(Duan et al., 2018)	Improved deep hybrid networks for urban traffic flow prediction using trajectory data	Deep Learning	Traffic trajectory data	Improved urban traffic flow prediction using deep hybrid networks
(Yan et al., 2021)	Spatial-temporal Chebyshev graph neural network for traffic flow prediction in IoT-based ITS	Graph Neural Network	IoT-based traffic data	Enhanced traffic flow prediction using spatial-temporal Chebyshev graph neural networks

Deep Learning and Machine Learning in addressing different traffic-related challenges (Yang et al., 2019; Zheng et al., 2020).

As this comparative overview is delved into, the applications, methods, data sources, and key findings of each study will be examined. Through this exploration, a detailed understanding of how these technologies are shaping the future of traffic management in smart cities and urban environments is aimed for, ultimately contributing to more efficient and sustainable transportation systems.

Among the various prediction methods proposed to date, Lv et al. (2014) harnessed deep learning, specifically the Stacked Auto Encoder (SAE), to forecast traffic flow. Their analysis centered on utilizing observational data as the dataset. Their findings demonstrated that this approach yielded greater accuracy compared to models employing traditional machine learning techniques like Support Vector Machine (SVM). However, it had a limitation in that it solely relied on the number of cars as an indicator of traffic flow, failing to capture the nuances accurately.

In the ongoing research, it is adopted a different approach by utilizing "link travel time," which quantifies the time required to travel between intersections. This metric enables us to gain a more precise and elaborate understanding of traffic flow dynamics.

In a separate investigation that incorporated probe information, Zheng and Zuylen (2013) employed a neural network (NN) featuring a single hidden layer to predict link travel time. It's worth noting that Zheng et al.'s study relied on simulated data and information derived from a solitary probe vehicle as their experimental dataset, which, while insightful, may not fully reflect real-world conditions.

In light of this consideration, the current research endeavors to bridge this gap by conducting experiments using link travel time data collected over the course of one year from a more realistic and extensive probe information dataset.

3   Traffic Flow Prediction

The optimization of urban transportation systems and the alleviation of traffic congestion present ongoing challenges in the face of rapid urbanization. Central to addressing these challenges is the field of traffic flow prediction, a crucial component of Intelligent Transportation Systems (ITS). This predictive practice involves leveraging advanced algorithms and models to anticipate future traffic conditions based on historical data, real-time information, and various influencing factors.

At its core, traffic flow prediction serves as a proactive tool for urban planners, transportation authorities, and commuters alike. By foreseeing upcoming traffic patterns, it facilitates the implementation of dynamic strategies to mitigate congestion, improve travel times, and enhance overall traffic management. This predictive capability is of paramount importance as cities continue to grow, emphasizing the need for sustainable and efficient urban mobility solutions.

This study delves into the domain of traffic flow prediction, specifically exploring the application of deep learning techniques and probe data. Prior to delving into the nuances of the approach undertaken, this paper establishes a foundational understanding of the significance of traffic flow prediction in urban environments and its pivotal role in shaping intelligent transportation systems.

As illustrated in Fig. 1, the traffic flow prediction methodology employed in this study leverages a Deep Neural Network (DNN). This DNN serves as the cornerstone of the predictive model. In this framework, the input data consists of link travel times preceding time t derived from probe information sources. During the learning phase, the DNN is trained to produce an output corresponding to the link travel time at time $t + \Delta$ representing the training data.

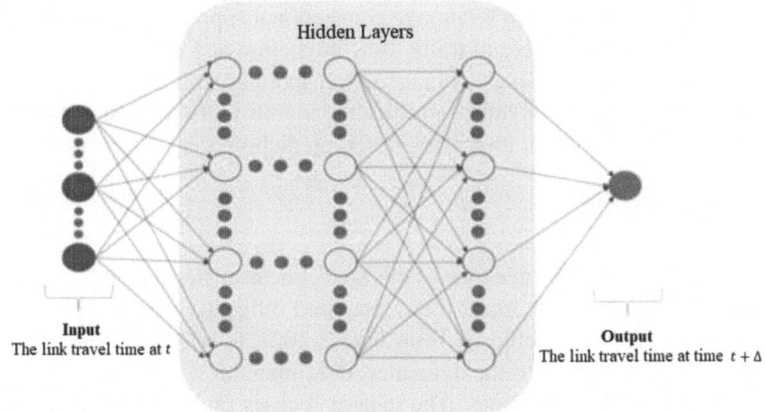

Fig. 1. Configuration of DNNs.

To elucidate further, the input incorporates data from multiple links leading up to time t encompassing the link that is to be predicted. However, the ultimate output of the model pertains exclusively to the link travel time of the target link under consideration. This tailored approach ensures that the predictive system focuses exclusively on the specific link of interest, enhancing the accuracy and relevance of the traffic flow forecasts.

4   Experiment

The forecast of link travel time, as outlined in the preceding section, forms the nucleus of this research's methodology. This anticipatory approach entails employing specialized deep learning techniques designed to meticulously scrutinize and decipher the intricate patterns within the traffic data. By adeptly capturing the inherent dynamics of link travel times, this methodology aims to deliver precise and timely predictions, contributing significantly to the improvement of urban traffic management and the overall commuter experience.

However, the pursuit of scientific rigor and the quest for reliable predictions do not halt at the development of a novel methodology. To validate the credibility and robustness of the predictions generated by the deep learning model, a rigorous comparative analysis is performed. This analysis goes beyond mere validation, delving into a in-depth evaluation of the model's predictive performance.

The comparative analysis goes a step further by juxtaposing the deep learning-based prediction approach with two distinct methodologies: multiple regression analysis and Support Vector Regression (SVR). These established methods have been stalwarts in the field of predictive modeling, and their inclusion in the evaluation serves to benchmark the novel approach against well-established standards.

Through this comparative assessment, the research endeavors to shed light on the effectiveness of the proposed method in capturing and forecasting link travel time dynamics. It goes beyond the confines of mere validation, providing a holistic view of how the deep learning model performs in relation to conventional approaches. This contribution enriches the body of knowledge in traffic flow prediction and offers valuable insights for practitioners and decision-makers in urban transportation management. Ultimately, this comprehensive evaluation aims to affirm the viability of the deep learning-based approach as a valuable tool for improving traffic prediction accuracy in urban areas.

4.1 Dataset Used

The dataset utilized as the cornerstone of this study encapsulates a wealth of invaluable information pertaining to link travel times, acquired diligently over the course of one year. This temporal span, specifically from June 1, 2021, to May 31, 2022, allowed for the elaborate examination of traffic dynamics, encompassing various seasons, weather conditions, and temporal variations. The dataset focuses on a network of 33 distinct links closely situated in the vicinity of the Clermont-Ferrand Prefecture, as visually represented in the illuminating Fig. 2. This strategic selection of links offers a localized yet representative perspective on urban traffic patterns.

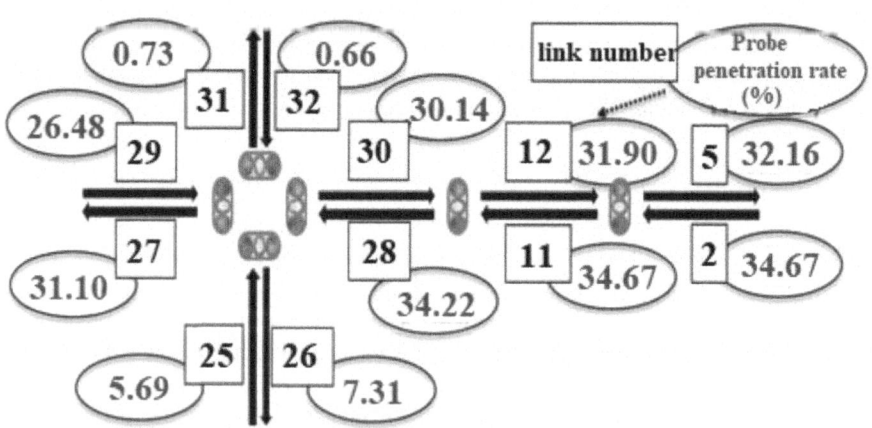

Fig. 2. Example of road link.

To ensure a high degree of temporal granularity and precision, the link travel times within the dataset are thoughtfully aggregated and averaged at 5-min intervals. This meticulous temporal resolution empowers the analysis to capture even the most nuanced variations in traffic flow, acknowledging that urban traffic is a dynamic and ever-evolving system.

In the realm of data preprocessing, meticulous attention has been devoted to addressing missing data points. Through rigorous efforts, gaps in the dataset have been diligently filled, resulting in the creation of a comprehensive and uninterrupted dataset. This proactive approach is pivotal in maintaining the dataset's integrity and ensuring that it aligns with the research's objectives.

The abundance of probe information available for each of the 33 links under scrutiny (Fig. 2). Each link's prevalence is thoughtfully denoted by a numerical value enclosed within an ellipse. Remarkably, the complementation rate of the probe information for these links spans a wide spectrum, ranging from approximately 70% to as high as 99%. This diversity in data completeness ensures that the dataset is both robust and representative, allowing for a thorough and insightful investigation into traffic flow prediction.

In summation, the dataset underpinning this study emerges as a substantial and meticulously curated resource. Its exhaustive nature, high temporal resolution, and diversity in data completeness lay the groundwork for a thorough exploration of traffic flow prediction, enabling the research to provide valuable contributions to the field of urban traffic management.

4.2 Experimental Setup

In the scope of this research, the central objective revolves around the prediction of link travel time with a forward-looking perspective, specifically targeting a 20-min prediction horizon. In this context, the deep neural network (DNN) is meticulously designed to yield predictions corresponding to the anticipated link travel time at time $t + 4$. To facilitate this ambitious undertaking, a itemized dataset spanning an extensive nine-month period is leveraged, commencing from June 2022 and extending to February 2023.

This dataset, which serves as the bedrock of the research, is thoughtfully partitioned into two distinct segments. The initial nine months of data represent the training dataset, providing the fertile ground for the DNN to learn and glean insights into the intricate traffic dynamics of the studied urban area. Following this rigorous training phase, the subsequent three months, spanning from December 2022 to February 2023, are designated for evaluation purposes. This separation of data into training and evaluation sets is instrumental in rigorously assessing the model's predictive performance and ensuring its applicability in real-world scenarios.

The architectural intricacies of the DNN extend beyond the temporal horizon of prediction. The model's input is constructed from multiple link travel time measurements. This input pattern is not limited to the target link earmarked for prediction but also encompasses its neighboring links. This progressive input construction initiates with the target link and its immediate neighbors, gradually extending to encompass links adjacent to the previously considered multiple links. This systematic approach empowers the exploration of a diverse spectrum of parameter combinations, each defined by several crucial factors. These factors encompass the number of links included in the input, which spans from 1 to 33, the consideration of previous time steps (ranging from 1 to 6), the dynamic configurations of hidden layer units (selectable from the set [10, 20,..., 100]), and the potential number of hidden layers (with possibilities ranging from 1 to 3).

Through the meticulous examination of these multifaceted parameter combinations, the research aims to meticulously identify the optimal model configuration that bestows the ability to generate highly accurate link travel time predictions. This effort cultivates a deeper understanding of the complex and dynamic traffic flow patterns inside the urban area, going beyond simple prediction accuracy. By systematically exploring these diverse facets of model configuration, the research contributes to the broader knowledge of urban traffic dynamics, ultimately paving the way for more effective traffic management strategies and enhanced commuter experiences.

4.3 Evaluation Index

The Root-mean-square error (RMSE) serves as a pivotal evaluation index in this research, providing a quantitative measure of the predictive accuracy of the deep neural network (DNN) model. RMSE, denoted by the Eq. (1), is a widely recognized metric for assessing the degree of deviation between predicted values and actual measured values (Yan et al., 2021). Its application in this context is instrumental in objectively quantifying the model's performance.

$$RMSE = \left[\frac{1}{n} \sum_{i=1}^{n} (|f_i - \hat{f_i}|)^2 \right]^{\frac{1}{2}} \tag{1}$$

Here, f_i is the training data (actual measured value), and $\hat{f_i}$ is the output data (predicted value).

f_i represents the actual measured values, which serve as the ground truth data extracted from the training dataset. These values embody the real-world link travel times and act as the reference against which the model's predictions are compared.

$\hat{f_i}$ signifies the predicted values generated by the DNN model. These values represent the model's estimates of link travel times, based on the information it has learned during the training phase.

The RMSE calculation involves the summation of the squared differences between each predicted value and its corresponding actual measured value across the entire dataset. The sum is divided by 'n,' which represents the total number of data points, and then the square root is applied to obtain the final RMSE value. This process effectively quantifies the average magnitude of errors between the predicted and actual values, offering a clear and interpretable measure of the model's accuracy.

By employing RMSE as the evaluation index, this research ensures a rigorous and standardized methodology for assessing the deep learning model's performance in predicting link travel times. This quantitative assessment is essential in objectively gauging the model's reliability and its potential applicability in real-world traffic management scenarios, where accurate predictions are paramount for effective decision-making and congestion alleviation.

5 Experimental Results and Discussion

In the comparative analysis, it is focused on Link31, which exhibits relatively significant variations in link travel time. Through a series of rigorous experiments encompassing the entire range of parameters discussed earlier, the parameter combination that yielded the lowest Root Mean Square Error (RMSE) is identified, as presented in Table 2. The RMSE values obtained were 54.3229 for the training data and 58.4035 for the evaluation data.

Table 2. Optimal parameters.

Parameter	Value
Number of links	33
Number of past times	6
Number of input dimensions	198
Hidden layer unit	[80,50,40]
Number of hidden layers	3

Figure 3 provides a visual comparison between the link travel time predictions generated by the model, trained with the parameter configuration outlined in Table 1, and the actual measured values. Time is plotted on the horizontal axis, while link travel time is represented on the vertical axis. The measured values are depicted by the blue line, while the predicted values are represented by the green line. This comparison spans from March 1, 2022, to March 4, 2022, and from Fig. 3, it's evident that the model effectively captures the overall trends in link travel time variations.

In the pursuit of deeper insights, it is delved into the influence of the number of input links and the historical time steps on RMSE for a DNN specifically designed to predict Link31's travel time. Figure 4 illustrates the RMSE values as a function of the number of input links for various numbers of past time steps included in the input. Remarkably, Fig. 4 demonstrates minimal fluctuations in RMSE as the number of links increases.

Furthermore, Fig. 5 explores the impact of varying the number of past time steps in the input on RMSE. The horizontal axis denotes the changes in the number of past times included in the input, while the vertical axis represents RMSE. Notably, Fig. 5 reveals that the RMSE values tend to decrease as the number of past time steps increases, irrespective of the number of input links. This underscores the significance of the temporal dimension in enhancing prediction accuracy, emphasizing that augmenting the historical context has a more pronounced effect on accuracy than increasing the number of input links.

To validate the deep learning-based prediction method, a comprehensive comparison with multiple regression analysis and an 8-bit model is conducted, including Link30 in the assessment. Table 3 presents the outcomes of this analysis. While the DNN-based prediction exhibited the smallest RMSE for each link, the results did not deviate significantly across the various methods. This suggests that the study successfully demonstrates the validity of the deep learning-based prediction approach; however, no substantial accuracy improvement is observed when contrasted with other methods. This observation

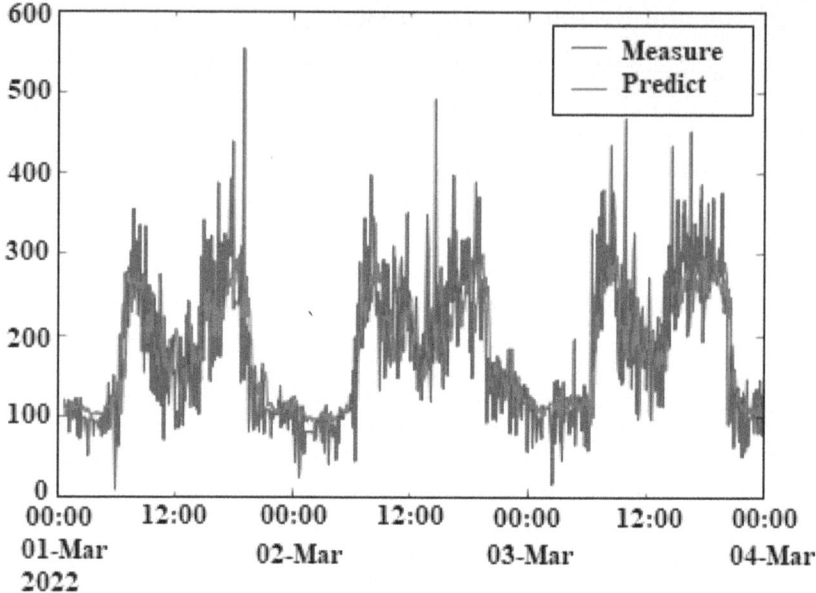

Fig. 3. The comparison of actual measured values and predicted values (Link31) Period: March 1, 2022 to March 4, 2022.

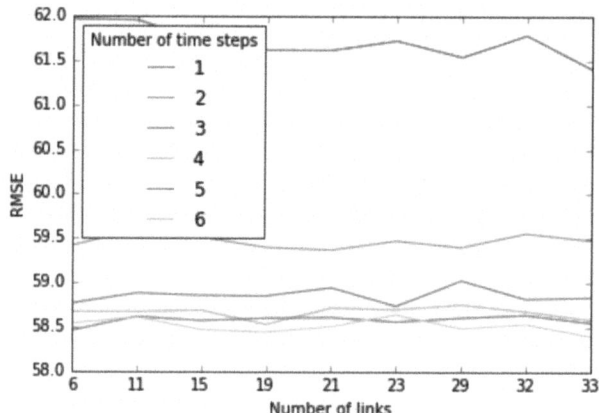

Fig. 4. The changes in RMSE when changing the number of links for each number of past times.

is attributed to the high complementation rate of the dataset, which results in a loss of data diversity. Consequently, the inherent capability of deep learning to approximate nonlinear functions is not fully harnessed in this context.

From the overall analysis presented, several key insights can be derived:

1. **Optimal Parameter Configuration:** The study identified an optimal set of parameters for a Deep Neural Network (DNN) model to predict link travel times effectively.

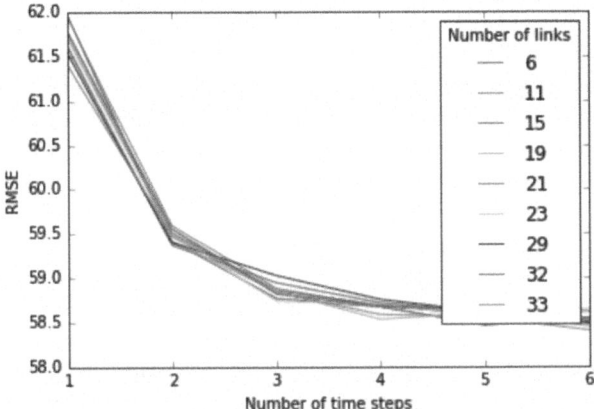

Fig. 5. The changes in RMSE when the number of past times is changed for each number of links.

Table 3. The comparison of prediction results by each method.

Predicted Link		DNN	Multiple Regression Analysis	SVR
RMSE	Link5	37.64	38.10	37.80
	Link30	65.42	65.96	66.12
	Link31	58.40	59.60	58.71

These parameters included the number of links, the number of past time steps, the number of input dimensions, hidden layer units, and the number of hidden layers. This configuration resulted in the lowest Root Mean Square Error (RMSE), indicating improved prediction accuracy.

2. **Model Validation:** The study successfully validated the deep learning-based prediction approach by comparing it with multiple regression analysis and an 8-bit model. While the DNN-based prediction exhibited the smallest RMSE for each link, the differences in RMSE between the methods were not substantial. This suggests that the deep learning-based approach is a valid prediction method, although it did not significantly outperform other methods in this particular dataset.

3. **Temporal Dimension Significance:** The analysis highlighted the importance of the temporal dimension in enhancing prediction accuracy. Increasing the number of past time steps in the input data consistently led to lower RMSE values, indicating that historical context plays a significant role in improving the accuracy of link travel time predictions.

4. **Data Diversity:** It is observed that the high complementation rate of the dataset, which suggests a lack of diversity in the data, may have limited the deep learning model's ability to fully harness its capacity to approximate nonlinear functions. This implies that the dataset used for training and evaluation may benefit from more diverse and varied data sources to further improve prediction accuracy.

In summary, the study's findings emphasize the importance of parameter optimization and the temporal dimension in traffic flow prediction using deep learning models. While the deep learning-based approach is validated as a viable method, its performance may be further enhanced with more diverse data sources. These insights contribute to the ongoing efforts to improve the accuracy of traffic flow predictions, which has practical applications in traffic management and urban planning.

6 Conclusion and Future Prospects

In the context of this study, the task involved applying deep learning techniques to predict link travel times, utilizing probe data as the primary information source. The objective is to scrutinize and validate the efficacy of this approach, particularly in forecasting the link travel time of the target link at time t + 4, using the link travel times of neighboring links leading up to time t as input data.

The meticulous examination of the temporal range for the neighboring links yielded a significant insight: expanding the temporal window encompassing past time intervals had a more substantial impact on improving prediction accuracy than enlarging the scope of peripheral links in the analysis.

To assess the reliability of the deep learning-based predictions, a overall comparative analysis is conducted by contrasting the results with those derived from multiple regression analysis and Support Vector Regression (SVR). Notably, the commendable accuracy achieved with alternative methods highlighted a key observation. The differences in outcomes were not statistically significant, a phenomenon attributed to a high rate of data imputation that led to reduced data diversity, subsequently limiting the discriminative power of the models.

Moreover, the study, primarily focusing on predicting link travel times 20 min into the future, prompts consideration for potential modifications to the prediction period, exploring intervals such as 5, 10, or 15 min. Additionally, in response to the influence of increasing the number of past time steps in the input on prediction accuracy, further experiments are imperative to explore different configurations of past time intervals. These adjustments aim to foster a deeper understanding of link travel time prediction intricacies, potentially enhancing the accuracy of predictive models.

The research not only provides valuable insights into traffic flow prediction through deep learning and probe information but also lays the foundation for future exploration and refinement. Two pivotal avenues for improvement emerge:

Temporal Granularity: Future investigations should delve into the temporal granularity of traffic flow prediction. Shifting from the current 20-min horizon to shorter intervals like 5, 10, or 15 min will offer insights crucial for enhancing the model's real-time adaptability and accuracy, especially for urban traffic management systems.

Optimal Input Configuration: Acknowledging the substantial influence of the number of past time steps on prediction accuracy, further experiments should meticulously explore the optimal configuration of past time steps in the input. This exploration aims to refine the model, allowing it to excel in capturing complex temporal dependencies within traffic data.

Crucially, future research should prioritize addressing the challenge of high imputation rates and limited data diversity. To overcome this, incorporating more diverse datasets is essential, unlocking the full potential of deep learning. This will empower models to handle a broader range of traffic scenarios, providing more accurate predictions.

In conclusion, while this research signifies a significant stride in enhancing traffic flow prediction in urban settings, the journey is far from over. By addressing the specific areas of research and application mentioned above, the field can make distinctive contributions to the development of sustainable, safe, and accessible urban mobility solutions. These endeavors align with the overarching goal of creating smarter and more efficient urban transportation systems, ultimately enhancing the quality of life for city dwellers.

Acknowledgments. The dataset used in this research is provided by https://www.bison-fute.gouv. fr/clermont-ferrand.html and NosDonnees.fr. I would like to express the sincere gratitude.

References

Abdullah, S.M., et al.: Optimizing traffic flow in smart cities: soft GRU-based recurrent neural networks for enhanced congestion prediction using deep learning. Sustainability **15**(7), 5949 (2023)

Duan, Z., Yang, Y., Zhang, K., Ni, Y., Bajgain, S.: Improved deep hybrid networks for urban traffic flow prediction using trajectory data. Ieee Access **6**, 31820–31827 (2018)

Essien, A., Petrounias, I., Sampaio, P., Sampaio, S.: A deep-learning model for urban traffic flow prediction with traffic events mined from twitter. World Wide Web **24**(4), 1345–1368 (2021)

Koesdwiady, A., Soua, R., Karray, F.: Improving traffic flow prediction with weather information in connected cars: A deep learning approach. IEEE Trans. Veh. Technol. **65**(12), 9508–9517 (2016)

Lv, Y., Duan, Y., Kang, W., Li, Z., Wang, F.Y.: Traffic flow prediction with big data: A deep learning approach. IEEE Trans. Intell. Transp. Syst. **16**(2), 865–873 (2014)

Perez-Murueta, P., Gómez-Espinosa, A., Cardenas, C., Gonzalez-Mendoza, M., Jr.: Deep learning system for vehicular re-routing and congestion avoidance. Appl. Sci. **9**(13), 2717 (2019)

Saleem, M., Abbas, S., Ghazal, T.M., Khan, M.A., Sahawneh, N., Ahmad, M.: Smart cities: Fusion-based intelligent traffic congestion control system for vehicular networks using machine learning techniques. Egyptian Info. J. **23**(3), 417–426 (2022)

Sun, S., Wu, H., Xiang, L.: City-wide traffic flow forecasting using a deep convolutional neural network. Sensors **20**(2), 421 (2020)

Tao, Y., Sun, P., Boukerche, A.: A delay-based deep learning approach for urban traffic volume prediction. In: ICC 2020-2020 IEEE International Conference on Communications (ICC), pp. 1–6. IEEE (2020)

Tran, L., Mun, M.Y., Lim, M., Yamato, J., Huh, N., Shahabi, C.: DeepTRANS: a deep learning system for public bus travel time estimation using traffic forecasting. Proceedings of the VLDB Endowment **13**(12), 2957–2960 (2020)

Yan, B., Wang, G., Yu, J., Jin, X., Zhang, H.: Spatial-temporal chebyshev graph neural network for traffic flow prediction in iot-based its. IEEE Internet Things J. **9**(12), 9266–9279 (2021)

Yang, B., Sun, S., Li, J., Lin, X., Tian, Y.: Traffic flow prediction using LSTM with feature enhancement. Neurocomputing **332**, 320–327 (2019)

Zheng, F., Van Zuylen, H.: Urban link travel time estimation based on sparse probe vehicle data. Transport. Res. Part C: Emerg. Technol. **31**, 145–157 (2013)

Zheng, H., Lin, F., Feng, X., Chen, Y.: A hybrid deep learning model with attention-based conv-LSTM networks for short-term traffic flow prediction. IEEE Trans. Intell. Transp. Syst. **22**(11), 6910–6920 (2020)

Zheng, Z., Yang, Y., Liu, J., Dai, H.N., Zhang, Y.: Deep and embedded learning approach for traffic flow prediction in urban informatics. IEEE Trans. Intell. Transp. Syst. **20**(10), 3927–3939 (2019)

An Approach to Multi-agent Deep Q-Network Optimization of Signal Control in Multi-intersection Road Environments to Enhance Urban Traffic Flow

Serap Ergün$^{(\boxtimes)}$ (ID)

Department of Computer Engineering, Isparta University of Applied Sciences, Isparta 32260, Turkey
serapbakioglu@isparta.edu.tr

Abstract. The escalating challenges of urban traffic congestion, resulting in amplified time and economic losses, profoundly impact daily life. Inappropriate signal switching on ordinary roads is identified as a significant contributor to this issue. Traditional approaches relying on human experiences for manipulating parameters in general signal control often yield suboptimal outcomes. To address this critical problem, this research proposes a dynamic traffic signal control system using a multi-agent approach with the Deep Q-Network method. In this urgent scenario, the proposed system aims to achieve precise parameter manipulation within a road environment featuring multiple intersections. A meticulous comparative analysis is conducted against static signal control and non-coordinated multi-agent systems, incorporating detailed numerical results to assess performance metrics. Results from a comprehensive 500,000-step experiment reveal the proposed method's adeptness in balancing performance and computational efficiency, leveraging inter-agent cooperation. "Comparison Method 3," inspired by Joo and Lim's methodology (2021), consistently outperforms others, particularly in congestion reduction.

Keywords: Intelligent transport systems · Traffic congestion and control · Signal switching · Multi-agent system

1 Introduction

In recent years, the severity of time and economic losses attributed to traffic congestion in urban areas has escalated, significantly impacting the lives of residents (Hu et al., 2023) This burgeoning issue has called for innovative solutions to mitigate traffic congestion and improve urban mobility. Two primary approaches can be considered to address traffic congestion within a given traffic volume: one involves traffic dispersion through effective navigation, while the other entails achieving smoother traffic flow through signal control. This study specifically focuses on strategies aimed at optimizing traffic flow through traffic control, with particular attention to intersections, which are notorious bottlenecks for road congestion.

© The Author(s), under exclusive license to Springer Nature Switzerland AG 2024
A. Mirzazadeh et al. (Eds.): SEMIT 2023, CCIS 2198, pp. 253–270, 2024.
https://doi.org/10.1007/978-3-031-72284-4_16

Intersections are crucial points in urban road networks, serving as crossroads where multiple streams of traffic converge. To ensure safety and regulate vehicle flow, traffic lights are commonly employed at these intersections. However, improper signal switching can exacerbate congestion issues. For instance, overly long red-light durations or the absence of adaptive signal timing can lead to extended wait times for drivers and result in traffic gridlock. Conversely, the slow pace of traffic signal changes can lead to traffic jams, especially during right turns, where minor delays can accumulate to create significant bottlenecks. Therefore, the optimization of traffic signal control is of paramount importance in managing urban traffic congestion (Ge et al., 2019; Haddad et al., 2022; Kim and Jeang, 2019).

Presently, signal control parameter adjustments are often based on manual estimations rooted in human experience. Traffic engineers typically rely on historical data, visual observations, and their expertise to fine-tune signal timings. However, this manual approach has limitations, as it cannot adapt swiftly to changing traffic patterns, unexpected events, or variations in demand throughout the day. Moreover, it can be challenging to optimize signal timings for multiple intersections that are interconnected and influence each other's traffic flow.

To address these challenges and alleviate traffic congestion effectively, this study proposes a cutting-edge control system. This system combines the Deep Q-Network (DQN) method introduced by Joo and Lim (2021) with a multi-agent system to facilitate appropriate parameter adjustments in a multi-intersection road environment. The integration of DQN, a powerful reinforcement learning technique, enables the traffic control system to learn and adapt its decisions over time based on real-time traffic data.

DQNs are a type of artificial neural network that have demonstrated remarkable success in solving complex decision-making tasks. In the context of traffic signal control, a DQN-based system can continuously analyze incoming traffic data, such as vehicle counts, speeds, and congestion levels, to make intelligent decisions about signal timings (Zhang et al., 2023). By learning from historical and real-time data, the system can dynamically adjust traffic light parameters, such as green-light durations, cycle lengths, and phase sequences, to optimize traffic flow (Ge et al., 2019).

Furthermore, the integration of a multi-agent system allows for coordination and communication between traffic signal controllers at different intersections. This coordination is essential to avoid conflicts and ensure smooth traffic flow throughout the entire network. For instance, when one intersection detects a surge in traffic demand, it can communicate with neighboring intersections to adapt their signal timings accordingly, preventing congestion from propagating through the road network.

In conclusion, the study's proposed control system represents a significant step toward addressing the escalating issue of urban traffic congestion. By leveraging advanced techniques such as Deep Q-Networks and multi-agent systems, this approach promises to revolutionize traffic signal control, making it more adaptive, efficient, and responsive to the complex dynamics of urban traffic. As cities continue to grow and traffic volumes increase, innovative solutions like this are vital to enhancing urban mobility, reducing travel times, and improving the overall quality of life for urban residents.

The contribution of this paper lies in the introduction of a novel and effective traffic signal control method that integrates a multi-agent system with DQN technology. The key contributions are outlined as follows:

- The proposed method demonstrates a significant reduction in computational demands compared to an ideal method. This is crucial for practical implementation, as it suggests the potential for a traffic management solution that can operate efficiently in complex urban environments without causing congestion.
- A critical feature of the proposed method is its empowerment of individual agents to autonomously manage traffic signals. This decentralization of decision-making allows agents to adapt in real-time to changing traffic conditions, showcasing the potential for a dynamic and responsive traffic signal control system.
- The method facilitates inter-agent information exchange, enabling precise parameter adjustments in road networks with multiple intersections. This collaborative approach enhances overall traffic management effectiveness, providing a robust solution for addressing congestion in urban environments.

The organizational of the paper is structured as follows: The literature review is presented in Sect. 2. Some basic preliminaries of Deep Q-Network algorithm is proposed in Sect. 3. In Sect. 4, a comprehensive experimental setup is proposed to evaluate the effectiveness of the introduced traffic signal control method and this section introduces and meticulously details three comparison methods: static signal control, non-coordinated multi-agent control using DQN, and single-agent control using tapping. Finally, the conclusion and outlook part is presented in Sect. 5.

2 Related Research

Research into signal control has been approached from various perspectives, reflecting the diverse and evolving strategies aimed at managing traffic flow efficiently. These perspectives often incorporate innovative technologies and methodologies to tackle the complex challenge of urban traffic congestion. In Table 1, a comprehensive summary of key studies is provided that have explored the application of multi-agent reinforcement learning in traffic signal control, highlighting their respective applications, methodologies, algorithms, and findings. This table provides a comprehensive overview of recent studies focusing on the application of multi-agent reinforcement learning (MARL) in traffic signal control. Traffic congestion is a persistent issue in urban areas, and MARL offers promising solutions by enabling intelligent and adaptive traffic signal management. The table summarizes various studies, encompassing their specific applications, methodologies, employed algorithms, and key findings. These findings collectively contribute to a deeper understanding of the effectiveness of MARL in optimizing traffic signal control and mitigating urban traffic challenges.

Here, it is delved into some of the notable approaches and developments in traffic signal control research.

Spatharis and Blekas (2022) introduced an intriguing concept where traffic lights at individual intersections are treated as autonomous agents. These "agent" traffic lights collaborate to manage signal control, taking into account real-time traffic conditions and optimizing their actions to alleviate congestion. This approach mimics a decentralized decision-making system, where each traffic light adapts its timing based on local traffic dynamics.

Haimerl et al. (2022) took a unique approach by proposing a multi-element traffic light system featuring 'blue, yellow, red' displays. This creative design aimed to improve the communication between traffic lights and drivers, making signal intentions more intuitive. Genetic algorithms (GAs) are utilized to adaptively adjust and efficiently control these multi-element traffic lights. This approach highlights the importance of human-computer interaction and user-centric design in traffic signal control.

In a separate groundbreaking study, Joo and Lim (2021) harnessed the power of deep learning and reinforcement learning to address traffic congestion. Deep learning, known for its feature extraction capabilities, and reinforcement learning, which facilitates optimal behavior acquisition based on rewards, are combined into a powerful tool. Employing Deep Q Learning, a variant of Q learning, their agent extracted essential features for signal control from high-dimensional data like images. This agent dynamically regulated traffic lights by executing appropriate parameter operations.

However, Joo and Lim (2021)'s research had limitations. It is conducted in a small road environment with a single intersection, limiting the agent's control to all traffic lights within that confined space. This limitation arose because increasing the number of intersections exponentially amplified the variety of traffic light operation patterns, making it challenging to perform comprehensive parameter control. Furthermore, Joo and Lim (2021)'s method involved extensive computational demands, as the agent processed images of the entire road environment. This proved computationally taxing for large road networks with multiple intersections.

To address these limitations and provide a scalable solution for traffic signal control, this study shifts its focus to traffic light operations at intersections. Instead of a single agent controlling all traffic lights, the proposed approach deploys as many agents as there are intersections to manage. Each agent is responsible for overseeing signal control at its designated intersection, reducing the complexity of traffic light operation patterns across agents.

Moreover, through inter-agent cooperation and coordination, computational requirements are mitigated in comparison to Joo and Lim (2021)'s DQN-based approach. This collaborative approach ensures that traffic lights are adjusted in harmony with neighboring intersections, optimizing traffic flow throughout the entire road network.

The primary objective of this study is to minimize the number of traffic lights while executing appropriate parameter adjustments. By doing so, it aims to simplify the traffic control infrastructure and reduce the potential for signal-induced congestion. This approach aligns with the broader goal of enhancing urban mobility, reducing travel times, and improving the overall quality of life for urban residents.

In summary, research in traffic signal control has evolved significantly, drawing inspiration from various methodologies and technologies. From autonomous agent-based control to innovative multi-element traffic lights and deep reinforcement learning, these approaches showcase the ongoing efforts to address the challenges of urban traffic congestion. This study contributes to this ongoing research by introducing a scalable and cooperative approach to traffic light operations, with the ultimate goal of creating more efficient and adaptive urban traffic management systems.

Table 1. Comparative Analysis of Multi-Agent Reinforcement Learning in Traffic Signal Control: A Summary of Key Studies.

Study	Application	Methodology	Algorithm	Findings
Kolat, M. et al. (2023)	Traffic signal control	Multi-agent reinforcement learning	Cooperative approach	Effective traffic signal control, reduced congestion
Zeynivand, A. et al. (2022)	Traffic flow control	Multi-agent reinforcement learning	N/A	Improved traffic flow through multi-agent cooperation
Li, S. (2020)	Traffic signal control	Multi-agent deep deterministic policy gradient	N/A	Enhanced traffic signal control on urban road networks
Zhang, Y. et al. (2023)	Traffic signal control	Nash Deep Q-network Approach	Nash Deep Q-network	Large-scale traffic signal control achieved
Zhang, W. et al. (2022)	Signal control of arterial corridors	Multi-Agent Deep Reinforcement Learning	Distributed signal control	Improved signal control on arterial roads
Wang, T. et al. (2021)	Adaptive signal control	Cooperative Group-based Multi-agent reinforcement learning	Cooperative approach	Adaptive traffic signal control for large-scale scenarios
Zheng, P. et al. (2023)	Traffic signal control system	Multi-agent Deep Reinforcement Learning	N/A	Regional intelligent traffic signal control system
Wang, Z. et al. (2023)	Traffic signal priority control	Shared Experience Multi-Agent Deep Reinforcement Learning	Shared Experience approach	Improved traffic signal priority control
Ge, H. et al. (2019)	Multi-intersection signal control	Cooperative deep Q-learning	Q-value transfer	Cooperative signal control at intersections

(*continued*)

Table 1. (*continued*)

Study	Application	Methodology	Algorithm	Findings
Ge, H. et al. (2021)	Adaptive traffic signal control	Multi-agent transfer reinforcement learning	Multi-view encoder	Adaptive signal control for varying conditions
Wang, Y. et al. (2020)	Cooperative traffic light control	Spatio-temporal multi-agent reinforcement learning	Spatio-temporal approach	Cooperative traffic light control
Jiang, S. et al. (2021)	Adaptive traffic signal control	Distributed multi-agent reinforcement learning	Graph decomposition approach	Adaptive signal control for large-scale scenarios
Xu, J. et al. (2021)	Traffic signal control	Multi-agent reinforcement learning	N/A	Improved traffic signal control method
Huang, X. et al. (2022)	Traffic signal control	Model-Based Multi-Agent Reinforcement Learning	Fairness-aware approach	Fairness-aware signal control
Haddad, T. A. et al. (2022)	Multi-intersection signal control	Deep reinforcement learning-based cooperative approach	Cooperative approach	Cooperative signal control at intersections
Hu, T. et al. (2023)	Traffic signal control	Mean field multi-agent reinforcement learning	Mean field approach	Dynamic signal control in large-scale networks
Song, X. et al. (2023)	Traffic signal control	Counterfactual Multi-Agent Deep Actor Critic Approach	Counterfactual approach	Cooperative traffic signal control
Liu, J. et al. (2023a, Liu et al., 2023b)	Multi-intersection signal control	Cooperative multi-agent reinforcement learning	Cooperative approach	Improved signal control at intersections
Wang, S. et al. (2023)	Traffic signal control	Multi-Agent Deep RL	N/A	Novel approach for traffic signal control

(*continued*)

Table 1. (*continued*)

Study	Application	Methodology	Algorithm	Findings
Kim, D. et al. (2019)	Cooperative signal control	Traffic flow prediction with multi-agent reinforcement learning	N/A	Improved signal control with traffic flow prediction
Liu, J. et al. (2023a, Liu et al., 2023b)	Decentralized signal control	Decentralized Multi-Agent Reinforcement Learning	Decentralized approach	Improved signal control in decentralized settings

3 Proposed Method

3.1 Deep Q-Network Algorithm

Deep Q-Network (DQN) represents a technology that seamlessly integrates deep learning for feature extraction with Q-learning, a foundational approach in the realm of reinforcement learning. This innovative technique involves an agent learning to select an action 'a' that maximizes the expected reward 'r,' also known as the value function. However, in the context of this research, the input data is presented in the form of images, which poses a unique challenge (Wang et al., 2023). To enable reinforcement learning based on image information, the agent must be capable of extracting and leveraging pertinent features from the high-dimensional information contained within previous images.

For this purpose, Convolutional Neural Networks (CNNs), a powerful deep learning method specifically designed for image analysis, are employed to perform feature extraction. CNNs excel at detecting intricate patterns, shapes, and structures within images, making them a natural choice for this task. By utilizing CNNs, the agent gains the ability to convert raw image data into a compact representation of essential features, allowing it to make informed decisions based on the state of the environment captured in the images (Jiang et al., 2021).

However, the complexity of urban traffic management extends beyond the capabilities of a single agent acting in isolation. Traffic networks are dynamic, and the actions of one agent can have ripple effects on neighboring agents. To address this intricacy, this study incorporates inter-agent cooperation as a fundamental aspect of its approach. Agents share critical information regarding "the actions of other agents," allowing them to collaborate effectively and make decisions that benefit the entire traffic network.

Achieving this inter-agent information sharing requires a thoughtful design of the agent's neural network architecture. In this research, values corresponding to the actions taken by other agents are integrated into the fully connected layer of the network. This augmentation results in a total of 513 input values for the agent, a reflection of the comprehensive information exchange between agents within the system.

Consequently, the output action's value, crucial for making decisions, now takes into account not only the agent's own observations but also the actions executed by other agents in the network (Fig. 1). This collective decision-making process ensures that agents respond cohesively to changing traffic conditions and coordinate their actions to optimize traffic flow.

In summary, the integration of DQN with deep learning and reinforcement learning techniques, including the use of CNNs for feature extraction and inter-agent cooperation, represents a powerful paradigm for tackling the challenges of traffic signal control in complex urban environments (Zeynivand et al., 2022). This research not only empowers individual agents to make informed decisions but also enables them to work harmoniously as a collective system. This holistic approach holds the promise of significantly improving traffic management, reducing congestion, and enhancing the overall efficiency of urban transportation systems.

Moreover, the insights gained from this research extend beyond traffic management, offering valuable lessons in the application of artificial intelligence and reinforcement learning to solve complex real-world problems. As technology continues to advance, the fusion of deep learning, reinforcement learning, and inter-agent cooperation has the potential to revolutionize various domains, contributing to more intelligent, adaptive, and efficient systems across industries.

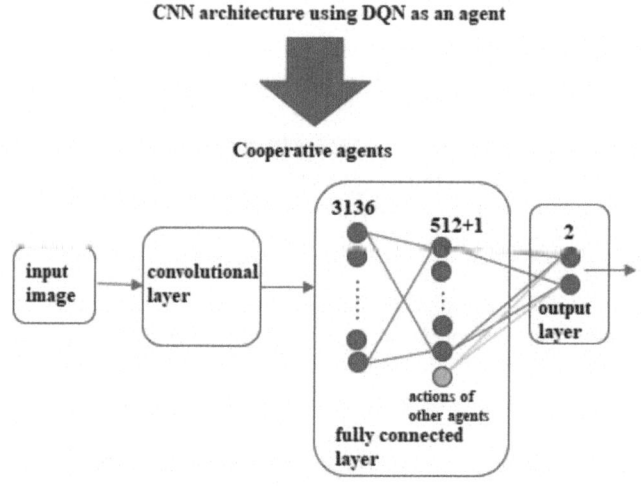

Fig. 1. CNN in non-cooperative/cooperative learning.

4   Experiment and Its Evaluation

To assess the effectiveness and utility of the proposed method for optimizing traffic signal control, a comprehensive comparative experiment is conducted. In this experiment, the number of stationary vehicles within the road environment is chosen as the primary evaluation metric. This metric serves as a tangible indicator of traffic congestion and directly quantifies the count of vehicles that are not in motion, exhibiting a speed of 0. The results of this experiment shed light on the real-world impact of the proposed approach on reducing traffic congestion and improving urban mobility.

The choice of using the number of stationary vehicles as the key evaluation metric is grounded in its direct relevance to the problem of traffic congestion. In urban areas, traffic congestion is a common and frustrating issue that results in delays, increased fuel consumption, and overall negative experiences for commuters. Stationary vehicles are a clear manifestation of congestion, indicating that traffic flow is disrupted, and drivers are forced to come to a halt (Xu et al., 2021). Therefore, by focusing on this metric, the research aims to provide practical insights into the extent to which the proposed method can mitigate congestion and enhance traffic flow.

The comparative experiment involves assessing the performance of the proposed method in contrast to alternative or traditional traffic signal control strategies. It likely considers scenarios with varying traffic volumes, patterns, and complexities to capture a comprehensive view of the method's efficacy. By analyzing and comparing the number of stationary vehicles under different conditions, researchers can discern whether the proposed approach outperforms existing methods and under what circumstances it provides the most significant improvements.

4.1 Environmental Setting

In this study, the experiments are conducted within a simulated micro traffic flow environment, utilizing the widely recognized micro traffic flow simulator known as SUMO (Simulation of Urban MObility). SUMO stands as an open-source platform that has been primarily developed at the German Aerospace Center. It serves as a robust and versatile tool that plays a pivotal role in modeling and simulating complex urban traffic scenarios. This platform has become an essential resource for transportation researchers, urban planners, and traffic engineers, offering a range of capabilities to analyze and optimize urban transportation systems (Krajzewicz et al., 2002).

One of the key strengths of SUMO lies in its extensive configurability. Researchers can finely adjust a multitude of parameters, including vehicle speed, acceleration, driving routes, traffic signal placements, and road layouts (Malik et al., 2019). This level of configurability empowers researchers to create highly customized traffic simulations that closely mimic real-world urban environments, enabling the study of various traffic management strategies under controlled conditions.

The simulation environment employed in this particular experiment encompasses a simulated road network comprising two intersections, as illustrated in Fig. 2. This choice is pivotal in evaluating the proposed method against the comparative approach. Within this simulated environment, researchers can capture valuable data and measurements at defined intervals. Specifically, data on each vehicle's state is recorded at regular intervals, with measurements taken every 3 simulation steps, where one step corresponds to one second of simulated time.

The simulated road network itself spans a total distance of 900 m from left to right, encompassing routes 1 and 2, and 300 m from top to bottom, including routes 3 and 4. This design establishes a vertical-to-horizontal ratio of 1:3 for the traffic flow, mimicking the spatial characteristics of many urban road networks. Notably, the simulation environment is constrained to accommodate only straight-line movement along routes 1, 2, 3, and 4, as depicted in Fig. 2.

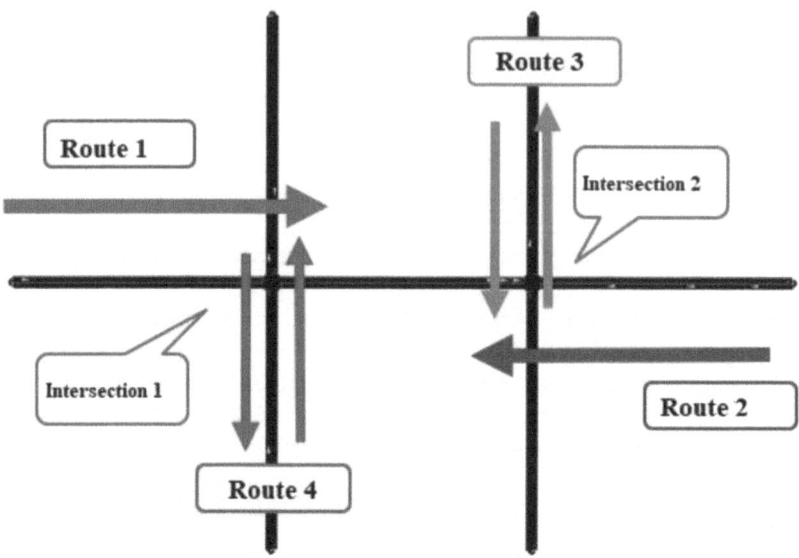

Fig. 2. The illustration of the overall simulation.

4.2 Comparison Method 1: Static Signal Control

To facilitate a comprehensive comparative analysis with the proposed traffic signal control method, a controlled static environment is meticulously configured. In this static environment, traffic lights are programmed to undergo regular interval changes corresponding to predefined traffic flow dynamics. This configuration allowed for a clear contrast with the dynamic and adaptive nature of the proposed method. Here, the details of the static environment setup and the critical parameters taken into account are mentioned:

Static Traffic Light Timing. In the static environment, traffic lights followed a fixed pattern of transitioning at regular intervals. Unlike the proposed method, where traffic signals adapt to real-time traffic conditions, the static environment employed a predetermined schedule for traffic light changes. This configuration provided a benchmark for evaluating the adaptability and effectiveness of the proposed dynamic approach.

Synchronized Traffic Signals. Despite the fixed timing of traffic light transitions, efforts are made to synchronize traffic signals in the static environment with the aim of periodically adjusting them in response to simulated traffic conditions. This synchronization is critical in maintaining some level of responsiveness to changes in traffic flow.

Vertical-to-Horizontal Ratio. Given the vertical-to-horizontal ratio of 1:3 in the simulated traffic flow, the allocation of traffic light phases is thoughtfully established to align with the vehicle flow rates. Specifically, 25% of the traffic light cycle is allocated to the vertical direction, and the remaining 75% to the horizontal direction. This allocation reflected the distribution of traffic volume and aimed to optimize traffic flow across the network.

Traffic Light Phases. Each traffic light cycle consisted of phases representing the transitions from green to yellow to red. The time allocated to each phase is meticulously determined to ensure smooth traffic flow. The distribution of time among these phases played a critical role in regulating vehicle movement and minimizing congestion.

Offset Number for Intersection Timing. To facilitate efficient passage of vehicles between intersections, a novel mechanism is introduced. This mechanism involved staggering the timing for traffic lights to shift to the green phase at each intersection. This temporal shift, referred to as the 'offset number,' is explored across five settings: 0, 10, 15, 20, and 25 s. The objective is to identify the optimal offset number that would promote efficient traffic management and minimize congestion.

Experimental Setup. To empirically evaluate the impact of different offset numbers on traffic performance, a comprehensive comparative experiment is conducted. The number of stationary vehicles is employed as a negative reward criterion to gauge congestion levels. The experiment spanned a total of 12,000 simulation steps, with data averaging performed every 3,000 steps to obtain meaningful insights.

Optimal Offset Number. The findings from the comparative experiment provided crucial insights into the effectiveness of different offset numbers for traffic signal transitions between intersections. The results revealed that the most efficient offset for minimizing the count of stationary vehicles and optimizing traffic flow is 15 s, as illustrated in Fig. 3. Consequently, the proposed method is configured with an offset number of 15 s to achieve the desired traffic management outcomes.

In essence, the meticulous setup of the static environment and the systematic exploration of parameters such as offset numbers allowed for a rigorous assessment of the proposed method's performance.

4.3 Comparison Method 2: Signal Control by Non-coordinated Multi-agent Using Deep Q Network

To facilitate a comprehensive comparison with the proposed traffic signal control method, an intricate multi-agent environment is meticulously constructed. This multi-agent setup represents a significant departure from the proposed method, focusing on the autonomy of individual agents without any inter-agent information sharing or collaboration.

In this multi-agent environment, each agent operated as an independent entity responsible for the management of a specific intersection. The core agents in this setup are DQN, which served as autonomous decision-makers for traffic signal control.

In order to create a basis for comparison with the proposed method, a multi-agent environment is carefully designed. Within this multi-agent setup, DQN assumed the role of agents, each operating autonomously and independently, without any form of information sharing or collaboration. The primary task assigned to each of these agents

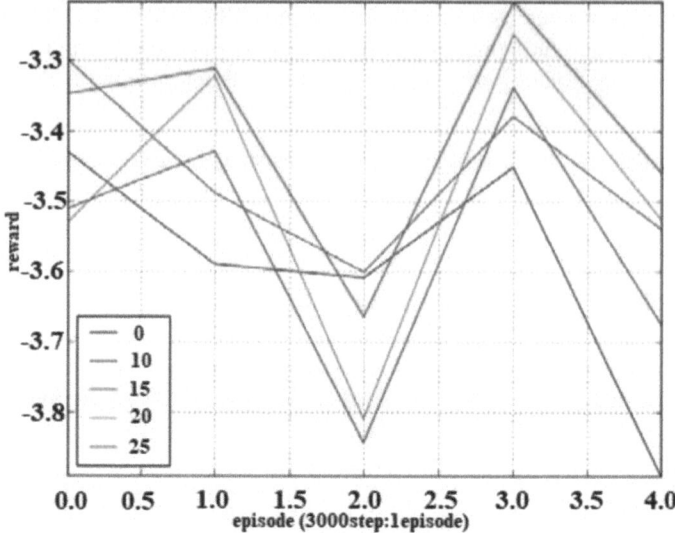

Fig. 3. Comparison of static signal control when shifting the number of offsets

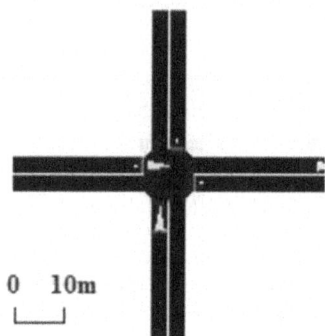

Fig. 4. Input image of intersection 1

is the processing of images captured from various intersections, as exemplified in Fig. 4 and Fig. 5. This image processing served as the foundation for conducting in-depth and comprehensive analyses of the visual data, allowing these autonomous agents to make informed decisions regarding traffic signal control.

4.4 Comparison Method 3: Single Agent Signal Control Using Tapping

To enable a comparison with the proposed method, a single-agent environment is config-ured, adopting the methodology originally outlined by Joo and Lim (2021) In this setup, the singular agent is implemented using DQN technology. The agent's role encompassed the comprehensive analysis of images capturing the entirety of the road environment,

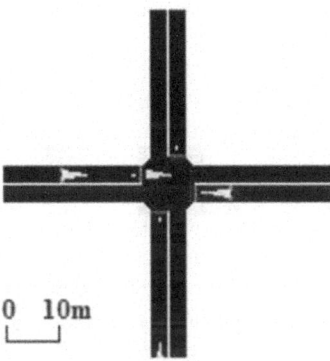

Fig. 5. Input image of intersection 2

adhering to a unified approach. As a result, a solitary agent is responsible for processing images that encompassed the entire road network, leading to the input image configuration illustrated in Fig. 6.

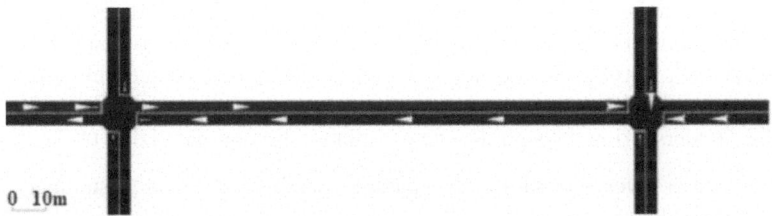

Fig. 6. Input image for single agent.

4.5 Experimental Results and Discussion

Figure 7 encapsulates the results stemming from an exhaustive 500,000-step experimental investigation, conducted to assess both the proposed traffic signal control method and the comparative methods. The central focus of this experiment is to gauge the average count of stationary vehicles at regular 6,000-step intervals. The graphical representation offers insights into how each method performed in this critical aspect of traffic management.

Comparative Methodology. For the purpose of this analysis, between two primary comparative methods are distinguished:

Comparison Method 2 (Designated as "Multi"): This method represents a multifaceted approach, possibly involving multiple agents or strategies.

Comparison Method 3 (Designated as "Single"): This method is based on Joo and Lim (2021)'s approach, known for its effectiveness.

Key Observations

Performance Trends Over Time: While examining Fig. 7 throughout the sections of the experiment, distinct performance trends emerge. Notably, "Comparison Method 3" consistently outperforms all other methods. This demonstrates the robustness of Joo and Lim (2021)'s approach in managing traffic flow and reducing congestion.

Computational Demands: It's important to acknowledge the computational aspects of these methods. Joo and Lim (2021)'s approach, while highly effective, necessitates a simulation duration approximately 1.8 times longer compared to the proposed method. This observation underscores the importance of efficiency in computational resource utilization.

Proposed Method's Performance: The proposed method, despite its computational efficiency, exhibits a noteworthy level of performance. It surpasses the capabilities of "Comparison Method 1" and closely approaches the performance achieved by "Comparison Method 3." This suggests that the proposed method strikes a balance between computational resource demands and effective traffic management.

The Significance of Inter-Agent Cooperation. One of the key takeaways from this comparative analysis is the pivotal role of inter-agent cooperation, as facilitated within the fully connected layer of the Convolutional Neural Network (CNN). This cooperative mechanism empowers agents to work collaboratively, exchange critical information, and enhance their learning capabilities. The proposed method leverages this approach to achieve results that closely align with the more computationally intensive "Comparison Method 3," underscoring the significance of collaboration in optimizing traffic flow.

For a clearer overview of the comparative analysis, here is a summary table summarizing the key findings:

Table 2. Performance and Computational Efficiency Comparison of Traffic Signal Control Methods,

Method	Performance	Computational Efficiency	Learning Mechanism
Proposed Method	High	High (Efficient)	Inter-Agent Cooperation (CNN)
Comparison Method 1	Moderate	-	Independent Agents
Comparison Method 2	Variable	-	Multifaceted Approach
Comparison Method 3	Excellent (Best)	Moderate	Reinforcement Learning (DQN)

Table 2 provides a quick reference to the performance and computational efficiency of each method, highlighting the strengths and trade-offs associated with each approach.

Figure 7 and the accompanying analysis shed light on the varying performance levels and computational demands of different traffic signal control methods. The proposed method stands out for its balance between performance and efficiency, emphasizing the importance of inter-agent cooperation as a catalyst for improved traffic management.

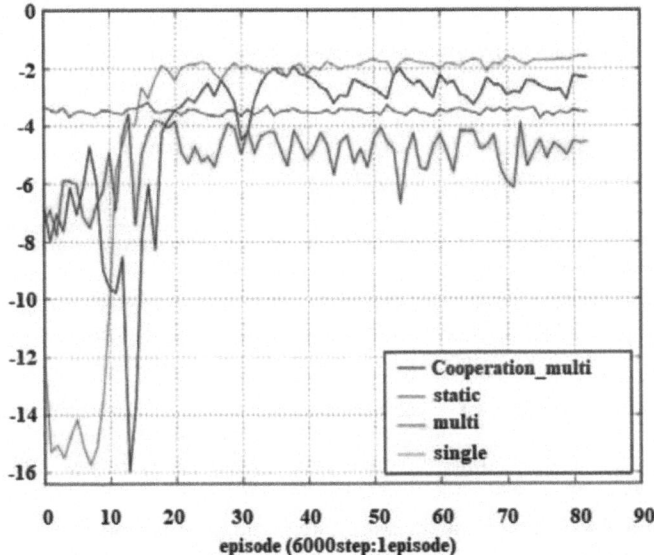

Fig. 7. Comparative experimental results of the proposed method and comparison method.

5   Conclusion and Outlook

In this study, an in-depth assessment of a novel traffic signal control method is conducted, which integrates a multi-agent system with DQN technology. DQN stands out for its fusion of deep learning capabilities, effective feature extraction, and reinforcement learning principles. Our evaluation is focused on understanding how this approach could revolutionize traffic management and mitigate urban congestion while minimizing computational overhead.

The proposed method showcased several key features can be summarized as follow:

Efficient Computational Overhead: Notably, this approach demonstrated a significant reduction in computational demands compared to an ideal method. It managed to maintain traffic flow smoothly without causing congestion, even in complex urban environments.

Autonomous Traffic Signal Management: A critical facet of this method is its empowerment of individual agents to autonomously manage traffic signals. These agents made decisions based on input image data, showcasing the potential for real-time adaptation to changing traffic conditions.

Inter-Agent Information Exchange: Beyond traditional signal control mechanisms, the method facilitated inter-agent information exchange and cooperation. This allowed for precise parameter adjustments in road networks characterized by multiple intersections, enhancing overall traffic management effectiveness.

To further address urban traffic congestion and enhance traffic management, future research endeavors should consider the following directions:

Complex Road Scenarios: Future studies should expand their scope to include complex road scenarios featuring elements such as pedestrian crossings, multi-lane roads with various turning options, and diverse traffic conditions.

Sensor-Enabled Signal Control: Exploring the feasibility of implementing sensor-enabled signal control at major intersections, where measurement sensors are available, can significantly optimize traffic management.

Integration of Emerging Technologies: Leveraging emerging technologies like connected and autonomous vehicles (CAVs) within the signal control system can revolutionize traffic management strategies.

Environmental Considerations: Assessing the environmental impacts of traffic management strategies is crucial, ensuring that they align with sustainability goals.

Scalability and Adaptability: Research efforts should focus on making traffic management systems scalable and adaptable to different urban environments.

Policy Implementation: Collaborating with urban planners and policymakers to translate research findings into effective implementation strategies and policies is essential for improving traffic flow and urban mobility.

In line with these future endeavors, the research will expand to encompass more intricate and lifelike road scenarios. This expansion may include variables such as pedestrians, multiple lanes, and various turning configurations. Additionally, the feasibility of implementing DQN-based traffic signal control at large intersections equipped with measurement sensors only will be investigated. These initiatives will be pursued through additional experiments and comprehensive investigations.

This study presents a novel traffic signal control method integrating a multi-agent system with DQN technology. The method showcases efficient computational overhead, enabling a reduction in demands while maintaining smooth traffic flow in complex urban environments. The autonomy of individual agents in managing traffic signals, real-time adaptation to changing traffic conditions, and inter-agent information exchange contribute to the method's effectiveness.

However, a limitation of this study lies in its focus on controlled simulation setups. While the proposed method excels in these settings, future research should extend its scope to encompass more intricate and lifelike road scenarios, including elements like pedestrian crossings, multi-lane roads, and diverse traffic conditions. The study recommends exploring sensor-enabled signal control at major intersections and integrating emerging technologies like connected and autonomous vehicles (CAVs) for revolutionizing traffic management strategies. Additionally, assessing environmental impacts and ensuring scalability, adaptability, and effective policy implementation are crucial for addressing broader urban mobility challenges.

The controlled simulation setup used in this study offers researchers a systematic way to test and compare the performance of the proposed method and comparative approaches under specific traffic conditions. By recording and analyzing data on vehicle movements, congestion levels, and other relevant parameters, researchers can draw meaningful conclusions about the effectiveness of the proposed method in optimizing traffic signal control.

Beyond the immediate scope of this study, traffic simulation tools like SUMO have broader implications for transportation research and urban planning. They provide a safe and cost-effective means of testing and refining traffic management strategies, assessing the impact of infrastructure changes, and predicting traffic behavior in response to evolving urban environments.

Results obtained from such simulations can inform decision-making processes for urban planners and traffic engineers. This support aids in the development of more efficient and sustainable transportation systems, benefiting urban residents by addressing real-world traffic challenges, reducing congestion, and enhancing overall quality of life.

In conclusion, the use of simulation tools like SUMO represents a vital component of contemporary urban planning and transportation research, promising a brighter future for more efficient and sustainable urban mobility.

References

Ge, H., et al.: Multi-agent transfer reinforcement learning with multi-view encoder for adaptive traffic signal control. IEEE Trans. Intell. Transp. Syst. **23**(8), 12572–12587 (2021)

Ge, H., Song, Y., Wu, C., Ren, J., Tan, G.: Cooperative deep Q-learning with Q-value transfer for multi-intersection signal control. IEEE Access **7**, 40797–40809 (2019)

Haddad, T.A., Hedjazi, D., Aouag, S.: A deep reinforcement learning-based cooperative approach for multi-intersection traffic signal control. Eng. Appl. Artif. Intell. **114**, 105019 (2022)

Haimerl, M., Colley, M., Riener, A.: Evaluation of common external communication concepts of automated vehicles for people with intellectual disabilities. Proc. ACM Hum.-Comput. Interact. **6**(MHCI), 1–19 (2022). https://doi.org/10.1145/3546717

Hu, T., Hu, Z., Lu, Z., & Wen, X. (2023). Dynamic traffic signal control using mean field multi-agent reinforcement learning in large scale road-networks. IET Intelligent Transport Systems

Huang, X., Wu, D., Boulet, B.: Fairness-Aware Model-Based Multi-Agent Reinforcement Learning for Traffic Signal Control (2022)

Jiang, S., Huang, Y., Jafari, M., Jalayer, M.: A distributed multi-agent reinforcement learning with graph decomposition approach for large-scale adaptive traffic signal control. IEEE Trans. Intell. Transp. Syst. **23**(9), 14689–14701 (2021)

Joo, H., Lim, Y.: Intelligent traffic signal control system using deep Q-network. In: 2021 IEEE 3rd Eurasia conference on IOT, Communication and Engineering (ECICE), pp. 285–287. IEEE (2021)

Kim, D., Jeong, O.: Cooperative traffic signal control with traffic flow prediction in multi-intersection. Sensors **20**(1), 137 (2019)

Kolat, M., Kővári, B., Bécsi, T., Aradi, S.: Multi-agent reinforcement learning for traffic signal control: a cooperative approach. Sustainability **15**(4), 3479 (2023)

Krajzewicz, D., Hertkorn, G., Rössel, C., Wagner, P.: SUMO (Simulation of Urban MObility)-an open-source traffic simulation. In: Proceedings of the 4th middle East Symposium on Simulation and Modelling (MESM20002), pp. 183–187 (2002)

Li, S.: Multi-agent deep deterministic policy gradient for traffic signal control on urban road network. In: 2020 IEEE International Conference on Advances in Electrical Engineering and Computer Applications (AEECA), pp. 896–900. IEEE (2020)

Liu, B., Liu, X., Chen, C., Huang, J., Ding, Z.: Decentralized Multi-Agent Reinforcement Learning for Traffic Signal Control. In: 2023 42nd Chinese Control Conference (CCC), pp. 6045–6050. IEEE (2023)

Liu, J., Qin, S., Su, M., Luo, Y., Wang, Y., Yang, S.: Multiple intersections traffic signal control based on cooperative multi-agent reinforcement learning. Inf. Sci. **647**, 119484 (2023)

Malik, F., Khattak, H.A., Shah, M.A.: Evaluation of the impact of traffic congestion based on SUMO. In: 2019 25th International Conference on Automation and Computing (ICAC), pp. 1–5. IEEE (2019)

Song, X., Zhou, B., Ma, D.: Cooperative Traffic Signal Control Through A Counterfactual Multi-Agent Deep Actor Critic Approach. Available at SSRN 4021959 (2023)

Spatharis, C., Blekas, K.: Multiagent reinforcement learning for autonomous driving in traffic zones with unsignalized intersections. J. Intell. Transport. Syst. **28**, 103–119 (2022)

Wang, S., Wang, S.: A Novel Multi-Agent Deep RL Approach for Traffic Signal Control. arXiv preprint arXiv:2306.02684 (2023)

Wang, T., Cao, J., Hussain, A.: Adaptive Traffic Signal Control for large-scale scenario with Cooperative Group-based Multi-agent reinforcement learning. Transport. Res. Part C: Emerg. Technol. **125**, 103046 (2021)

Wang, Y., Xu, T., Niu, X., Tan, C., Chen, E., Xiong, H.: STMARL: A spatio-temporal multi-agent reinforcement learning approach for cooperative traffic light control. IEEE Trans. Mob. Comput. **21**(6), 2228–2242 (2020)

Wang, Z., Yang, K., Li, L., Lu, Y., Tao, Y.: Traffic signal priority control based on shared experience multi-agent deep reinforcement learning. IET Intel. Transport Syst. **17**(7), 1363–1379 (2023)

Xu, J., Zhang, Z., Zhang, S., Miao, J.: An improved traffic signal control method based on multi-agent reinforcement learning. In: 2021 40th Chinese Control Conference (CCC), pp. 6612–6616. IEEE (2021)

Zeynivand, A., et al.: Traffic flow control using multi-agent reinforcement learning. J. Netw. Comput. Appl. **207**, 103497 (2022)

Zhang, W., Yan, C., Li, X., Fang, L., Wu, Y.J., Li, J.: Distributed signal control of arterial corridors using multi-agent deep reinforcement learning. IEEE Trans. Intell. Transp. Syst. **24**(1), 178–190 (2022)

Zhang, Y., Wang, S., Jiang, R.: Large-Scale Traffic Signal Control by a Nash Deep Q-network Approach. arXiv preprint arXiv:2301.00637 (2023)

Zheng, P., Chen, Y., Kumar, B.V.D.: Regional intelligent traffic signal control system based on multi-agent deep reinforcement learning. In: 2023 8th International Conference on Computer and Communication Systems (ICCCS), pp. 362–367. IEEE (2023)

Blockchain-Driven Smart Contracts: An Overview of Application Areas and Gap Identification in Construction Management Literature

Emmanuel Chidiebere Eze[✉], Ernest Effah Ameyaw, and Bahriye Ilhan Jones

Department of Architecture and Built Environment, Northumbria University Newcastle,
Newcastle-Upon-Tyne NE1 8ST, UK
emmanuel2.eze@northumbria.ac.uk

Abstract. The dynamics in Industry 4.0 have continued to transform construction contracts execution. Blockchain and smart contract technologies represent the future of construction contract delivery in the built environment, although they are still in the infancy in the construction sector. While studies on the potentials of Blockchain-based smart contracts in construction have continued to increase, as evident in the extant literature, there is yet to be a consensus on the most crucial application areas in construction. This emerging technology requires more attention; therefore, this study presents the result of a critical review of blockchain-enabled smart contracts studies in construction. Forty documents were obtained from the Scopus and Web of Science databases, and they formed the basis for the review and analysis. The top application areas of smart contract technology were identified and discussed. Furthermore, the application areas that require to be explored are refurbishment contracts, consultancy contracts, long-term PPP projects, circular economy, and waste management. The adoption of blockchain-based smart contracts in these areas will improve sustainable construction targets and enhance the diffusion of blockchain-enabled smart contracts among key built environment experts.

Keywords: Blockchain · construction contract · critical review · Smart contract · Construction projects

1 Introduction

The advancement in Industry 4.0 is driving a major change in the ways construction projects are delivered and stakeholders' relationship management. Inefficiencies and productivity problems in the construction industry are linked to many stakeholders in construction. Centralised systems of management and paper-based, conventional construction systems have been identified as contributors to the drawbacks the industry is experiencing. The lack of trust and transparency among stakeholders, the predominance of claims and disputes, and the lack of satisfaction of clients [1] further worsen the poor productivity and performance inefficiency of the construction sector. Digitalisation is key

© The Author(s), under exclusive license to Springer Nature Switzerland AG 2024
A. Mirzazadeh et al. (Eds.): SEMIT 2023, CCIS 2198, pp. 271–288, 2024.
https://doi.org/10.1007/978-3-031-72284-4_17

to the successes recorded in the operational efficiency and productivity of the aerospace and automotive industries [2]. Blockchain technology (BT) and smart contracts (SC) are industry 4.0 technologies that offer the wide potential to address the numerous problems limiting the construction industry's efficiency and productivity.

Extant studies have shown the potential of smart contracts in the management of construction contracts. SC automate processes and enforce compliance with contractual provisions and conditions when the pre-defined conditions are met [3]. The problems of enforceability, deviance monitoring and tracking, execution and compliance issues, and irregular behaviours that are associated with the traditional paper-based contracts are avoided with the adoption of smart contracts, leading to better productivity, cost and time savings, and reduction in disputes [4, 5]. A smart contract, however, cannot function without being embedded in blockchain technology (BT). BT provides a decentralised, distributed ledger of transactions (blocks) that are immutable, secured and can be tracked across a peer-to-peer network. These attributes of the BT are inherited by the SC when it is embedded in BT. Therefore, Blockchain-enabled smart contracts provide immutability, security and traceability of data exchanged spontaneously amongst stakeholders without an intermediary or centralised authority [6].

Even though the adoption of BT and SC is limited in construction, some review studies exist on various potential areas of application of blockchain technology and smart contacts in the built environment. [7] identified seven areas of application of blockchain in construction, but their study was limited to data obtained from the Scopus database. [8] through a review, found that blockchain can improve construction supply chain performance using only data from the Web of Science (WoS) database. Others used multiple databases but included non-rated, non-index, non-academics/non-peer review sources. For example, [9] reviewed the impact of Blockchain technology characteristics on construction dispute resolution and management, and [10] focused on the challenges and future opportunities of blockchain applications in construction whole life. [11] reported that DLT and smart contact can be applied in eight areas in the construction industry. [12] found that blockchain is not a hype as it has credible potentials in the construction industry. These studies considered grey literature (e.g., web pages, blog posts, conferences, reports, etc.), which may not have gone through rigorous peer review processes like Journal articles, and this could impact the quality of the findings. This present study utilised only peer-reviewed, indexed journal articles from the Scopus and WoS databases, to overcome the domain-specific focus, single database and document choice of previous review studies. Furthermore, there is the likelihood that other potential areas of usage of Blockchain-enabled smart contracts exist that have not been explored in extant literature. This study, through a systematic review, explores smart contracts studies to identify the application areas based on previous studies, identify the gap in the literature, and propose directions for future research. The relevance of BT and SC in other economic sectors were briefly discussed. This is vital as a blockchain-enabled smart contract represents the technology that will drive the future agenda of construction contracts, as it has been found to be in consonance with the industry's contracting system.

2 Research Methodology

This study adopted a systematic review of blockchain-enabled smart contract studies in construction to understand the current status and map out the direction of future research. The systematic review method provides more organised and exploratory outcomes than the conventional review approach [13]. This study was guided by [14] 4-sequence search approaches of articles: (i) identification, (ii)screening, (iii)eligibility evaluation, and (iv)inclusion and analysis. Furthermore, "preferred reporting items for systematic reviews and meta-analyses (PRISMA)" were also leveraged in this study.

Identification of document: 601 articles were initially retrieved from the Scopus and Web of Science (WoS) databases (Scopus = 369; WoS = 232). These databases are the world's leading databases that offer reliable sources of scientific data to researchers undertaking review-based studies [15, 16]. The search took place on August 10 and was updated on October 18, 2022, using the search strings "(*TITLE-ABS-KEY ("smart contract" OR "Smart contracts" OR "Intelligent Contract" OR "Automated Contract" OR "Automated Contract Conditions") AND TITLE-ABS-KEY("Construction Project" OR "Building Projects" OR "Construction")*)".

Screening of documents: The 601 documents were further screened by refining the search to research articles published in the English language, focused on construction management, engineering, and built environment.151 documents were retained after this exercise. Research articles provide detailed scientific knowledge on any subject of interest because of the rigorous review processes they undergo [17]. Smart contract adoption in the Architecture, engineering, and construction (AEC) sector is still in its infancy. Hence, no year limit was set during the search in order to avoid losing vital documents. The 151 datasets were downloaded in CSV file format, since it can open in Microsoft excel. A skim of the titles, abstracts, and keywords led to the elimination of 81 studies on a smart contract that did not focus on the construction industry. Further, the dataset from the two databases were compared for duplicates, and 17 duplicates were removed, leaving 53 documents in total.

Documents inclusion/exclusion criteria: To ensure articles used for the analysis are of high quality, documents from the Scopus database are required to be from rated sources (e.g., Q1 – Quartile 1 ranked journals). Meanwhile, documents from the WOS database are expected to be from SCI- or SCI-E-ranked journals (Source citation index/ Source citation index expanded). These criteria must be met by a document under the two databases. The approach was guided by the studies such as [18]. 40 articles scaled through this stage and were downloaded for critical evaluation, and the results presented in subsequent sections arise from them.

Analysis of retained documents: The retained documents were downloaded and then subjected to a deeper review to extract the themes regarding the application areas of SC studies. The thematic analysis is a deductive and intuitive technique for data analysis, and it is befitting for an 'early researcher' who intends to achieve some level of speed in qualitative analysis [19].

The overall summary of the PRISMA-inspired methodology is presented in Fig. 1 to further give credit to the adopted methodology.

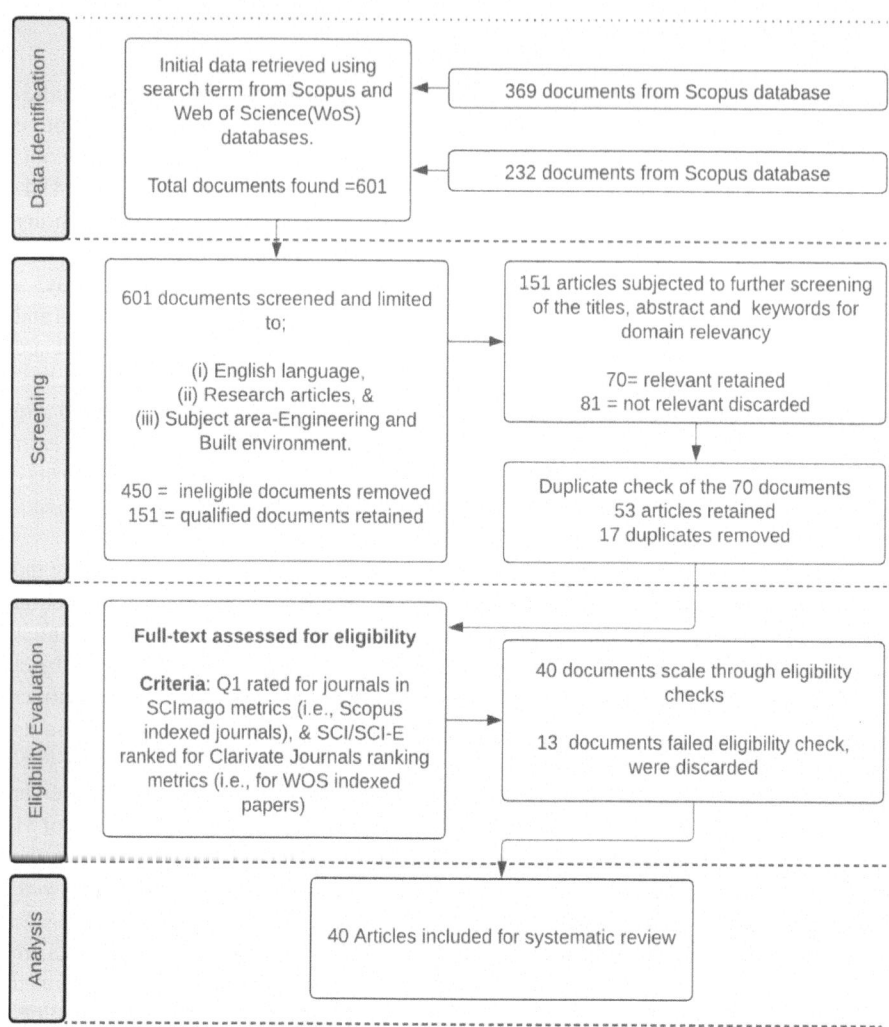

Fig. 1. Summary of Research methodology adopted: PRISMA-inspired flowchart (Source: modified from [20]).

3 Analysis and Findings

3.1 Distribution of Publication

The analysis shows that the retained documents covered publications between 2020 and 2022. It is evident that smart contract studies are growing progressively, as evident in the breakdown, which shows that in 2020, a total of 9 (22.50%) of the articles were published; it grew by another 5% in 2021 to 11 (27.5%), and a sharp jump 20 (50%) was observed in 2022. The trend is expected to continue into the year as interest in a blockchain and smart contract in contract administration and management among practitioners and academics continues to increase.

3.2 Publication by Sources of Articles

The 40 assessed articles came from 12 sources (Fig. 2). "Automation in Construction" has the highest number, 26(65.0%) of the articles, followed by "Buildings" with 3(7.50%) articles and "Journal of Construction Engineering and Management" with 2(5.0%) articles. "Automation in Construction" is the world's leading source of scientific knowledge on technological adoption and innovations in the construction sector. This corroborates the findings of previous construction technologies and innovations review studies [21, 22].

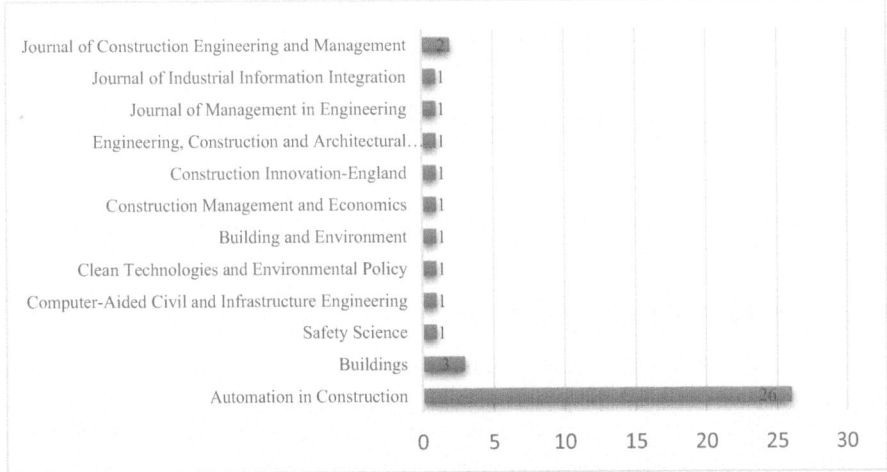

Fig. 2. Sources of the reviewed Articles.

3.3 Distribution of Publications by Country/Continents

In terms of publication by country, China has the highest number with 10 (25.0%) documents; this is closely followed by Australia with 9 (22.50%) documents, then the United States has 5 (12.50%), and Turkey has 4(10.0%) Publications. The United Kingdom and Hong Kong have 3(7.50%) publications each. The continental distribution shows that 18(45%) of studies originated from Asia, followed by Oceania with 10 (25%), then Europe and North America have 5 (22.55) articles each. However, no article emanated from South America, while the African continent has 2(5.0%) (Table 1). This is a clarion call on the academics and researchers in these areas to collaborate and Governments should fund research in smart contract adoption in their built environment. Furthermore, governments and other stakeholders in Africa and South America need to intensify actions to propagate the message of automating construction contract conditions and reducing the over-reliance on the traditional manual construction contract conditions that are prevalent among project stakeholders on the continents.

Table 1. Publications by country/geographical regions.

Countries	Countries	Continents	No of publication	%
Egypt	2	Africa	2	5.00
China	10	Asia	18	45.00
Hong Kong	3			
Turkey	4			
United Arab Emirates	1			
United Kingdom	3	Europe	5	12.50
Netherlands	1			
Italy	1			
United State	5	North America	5	12.50
		South America	0	0.00
Australia	9	Oceania	10	25.00
New Zealand	1			

3.4 Nature and Approach of Studies

An examination of the nature of the studies showed that a larger proportion (32.5%) developed a proof of concept to drive home their ideas. To minimise human errors prone to the traditional communication approach, [23] developed a proof of concept that integrates blockchains and smart construction in a common data environment to improve the communication and information performance of construction stakeholders. A proof of concept was utilised to extend the traceability of and information-sharing potentials of the blockchain and smart contracts to improve the supply chain of prefabricated construction [24]. Studies that utilised conceptual frameworks and surveys approach were the second highest, with 17.5% each and these approaches were used by [25] and [26] respectively. Review studies constitute 12.5% of the evaluated documents, studies that utilised a hybrid approach were about 10.0%, while design science/system designs and experimental studies are each 5.0% of the sampled studies (Fig. 3).

3.5 Smart Contract Application in Construction

The focus of Smart contract studies based on the review is categorised into eight (Fig. 5). Based on the Number of publications per category, the potential of smart contracts in resolving payment issues categorised as "Payment and financial administration" is ranked 1st. Ten studies focused on the potential of smart contracts in resolving payment-related issues in construction contracts. This is the most researched area in construction management literature. This indicates how critical payment is in ensuring the smooth working relationship of parties in contract, going concerns of construction organisations and the successful delivery of construction projects. The blockchain-led smart contract has been advocated as a panacea for payment delays and non-payment problems in the

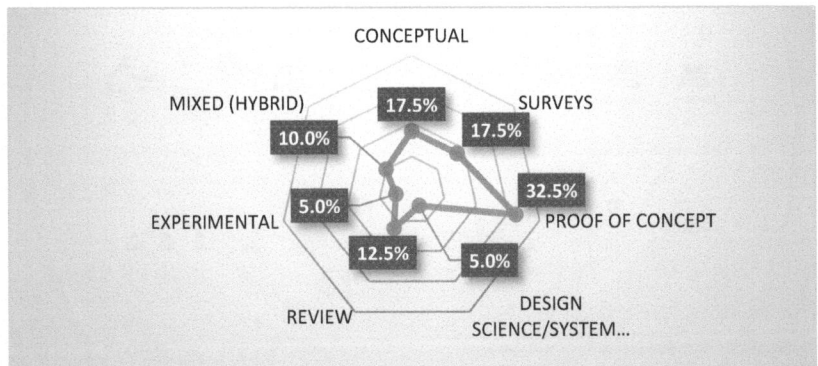

Fig. 3. Methods utilised in Studies.

sector [27]. This is evident in the studies of [25, 26, 28]. In the manufacturing and services sectors, blockchain enhances financial flow among partners in a supply chain, as it facilitates immediate payment as soon as products are sold [29]. BT and SC can improve the logistics performance and payment transactions of the maritime industry due to their ability to produce a transparent and efficient records through the provision of updated secured data that are free from errors and tamper-proof [30].

While it is worthy of note to state that real-world cases or case studies in the use of smart contracts are scarce in construction, there are few cases of implementable models and frameworks that can give a clear idea of how SC works have been developed. For instance, to reduce or eliminate payment issues, [28] proposed a system known as the "smart contract payment security system, SMTSEC" for the construction sector (Fig. 4). Like a normal contract, the employer and main contractor reach agreements on terms of security of payment, the said agreement is coded into a SC using suitable SC language and then deployed on a chosen blockchain platform. SMTSEC ensure that interim progress payments are held and secured for the contractors, subcontractors and suppliers on a monthly basis, and the due amounts are automatically transferred to the beneficiaries' wallets based on planned project cashflows and immediately, the employer gives his approval.

The second is "information and data management," which is covered in six documents. The complex networks of activities, interactions, and many stakeholders have made construction projects information and data laden. A lot of reports are generated throughout the life of a project. The major problems are occurrence of numerous errors, omissions, and lack of clarity [31]. The centralised nature of the traditional contractual system makes tracking of these problems, compliance issues, and controlling activities expensive as a result of the presence of a lot of intermediaries [32]. The smart contract provides information traceability and offers a decentralised, secured, and reliable platform for effective data and information management in construction. The interest in this area of application has grown, as evidenced by studies [33]. In the health sector, the smart contract is one of the five features of blockchain technology that can enhance the exchange of health records of patients in a secure, transparent, and timesaving manner between medical (health) institutions and patients [34, 35]. The data and information

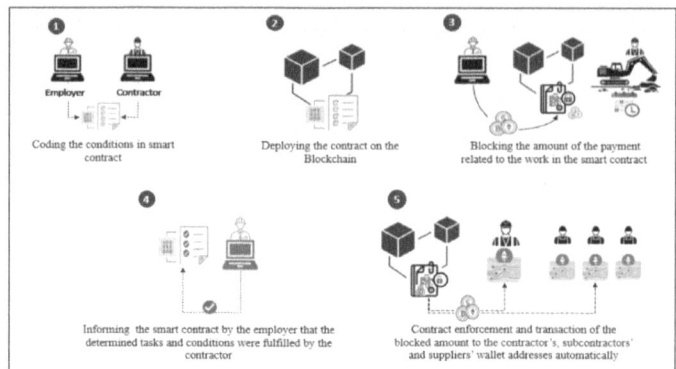

Fig. 4. Smart contract system for security of payment in construction (Source: Ahmadisheykhsarmast and Sonmez (2020)).

management functions of the SC help to prevent valuable information loss and reduce avoidable examinations and treatments of patients in hospitals and in the health industry. Smart systems based on BT have helped to ease paperwork in customs clearance and management, track and locate ships and containers in the maritime sector [36].

Supply Chain Management is the 3rd Category, with Five Publications. Supply chain management (SCM) is founded on the integration of various critical project activities and stakeholders to ensure the success of a project. SCM ensures the smooth execution of project activities, especially in ensuring the balance of the relationship between the suppliers of construction materials, subcontractors, the main contractors, and other stakeholders. Information sharing and data coordination across distances in the paper-based contractual system breeds doubts, trust, and transparency challenges. Tracing of deviances in products and services compliance, quality assurance verification and process control checking present some problems. Blockchain-enabled Smart contracts have the potential to automatically check compliances in a decentralised way through the provision of transparent and trusted data and immutable records across the entire supply chain. The application of Smart contracts (SC) in construction supply chain management has attracted one of the highest interests among construction management researchers and industry practitioners [37]. [37] developed a smart construction objects-enabled blockchain oracles (SCOs-BOs) framework to showcase how blockchain technology can instil and improve traceability and transparency and provide immutable and trusted data throughout the supply chain of construction projects. The framework was validated on high-rise public building projects in Hong Kong. The off-site logistics and on-site assembly of the prefabricated beams meant for the project were studied using the developed framework, and the result shows that more reliable, accurate data were retrieved and showed the real state of health of the project.

In other sectors like manufacturing, production, and services, BT leads as one of the recent innovative financial concepts that have transformed international trades through a speedy settlement of financial transactions and management of supply chains among business partners [29]. In the health sector, BT and SC can help to improve the complicated and sensitive vaccine distribution in pandemic situations (e.g., COVID-19) to help reduce counterfeit vaccines and fraud in vaccine records. This can suitably be achieved through a blockchain-enabled Internet of Things solution for the global distribution of vaccines in a trust, transparent manner where data and records can be traced to effectively monitor the cold chain of the bio-pharmaceutical giants [38].

Dispute Resolution and Management. It is impossible to eliminate disputes in construction, but they can be greatly minimised. This is due to the complex nature and the high number of stakeholders involved in the construction operating environment. A lot of time and finances have been wasted on claims and disputes over the last decades [39]. Disputes can result from external factors, but more often than not, emanates from contractual-related issues such as payments-related, delays and liquidated damages, and variations, among others. Most of these problems can be resolved using blockchain-enabled smart contracts, as evident in extant literature [40]. A blockchain technology-based smart contract (BCT-SmContract) framework developed by [3] revealed that a contract execution rate of 90% can be achieved and 100% precision in the project status information can be guaranteed, which helps to improve stakeholders' relationship and reduced conflicts. A decentralise third party (e.g., Kleros) is blockchain-based and has found use in different sectors, such as insurance, e-commerce, and finance, to arbitrate disputes in a timely and efficient manner [41, 42]. Blockchain and Smart contracts provide a cost-saving, less time-consuming and less tedious and lengthy medium of managing disputes than the lengthy court system [43].

Other applications areas of Smart contracts based on the review include (i) Quality management [44], (ii) Safety management [45], (iii) Energy and Environmental Management [46], and (iv) Procurement management [47].

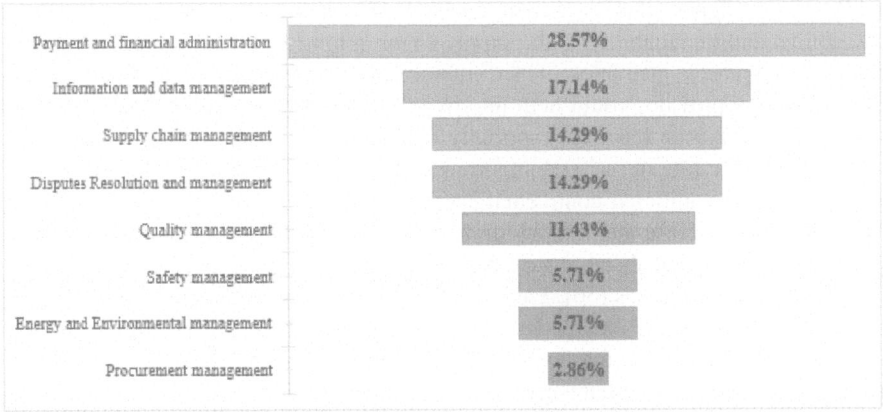

Fig. 5. Focus of Smart contract Studies reviewed.

Problems in Traditional Contracts and the Impact of SC Adoption
Further to the potential application areas of blockchain-driven smart contracts, some of

the critical problems associated with the traditional, paper-based contracting systems that could be mitigated through adopting and implementing blockchain technology and smart contracts were identified and summarised in Table 2 below. It is evident from the roles and impact of SC on construction projects that blockchain-driven smart contracts have the potential to influence a sustainable transformation in the manner construction projects are procured and delivered. Its overall impact lies in enhancing the construction industry's drive towards sustainability objectives.

4   Literature Gaps and Future Research Directions

Smart contracts and public-private partnership (PPP) projects: Successive governments across the world have leveraged PPPs in the delivery of high capital-intensive infrastructures by leveraging the private sector capital and expertise. PPP improves service delivery, reduces government spending, improves economic outlook and enhances risk management and sustainability [48]; these are some of the merits that make PPP more attractive than the traditional system [49]. Despite these benefits, PPP arrangements have failed, and projects have been terminated as a result of performance issues [50], non-achievement of value for money by the public [51], lack of trust and transparency, poor quality, ineffective procurement and environmental performance issues [52]. [53] found that poor contract design and non-adherence to contractual provisions lead to crises and disputes that negatively impact long-term infrastructure projects procured via PPPs. Even though PPP has assumed a global dimension, it is still vulnerable and not a "failureproof business" [54].

Smart contracts promise to overcome these challenges as they help to secure and guarantee payment and enforce contractual compliance that is needed to ensure a sustainable long-term relationship that exists between the private and public sector partners in PPPs [37]. [37] posit that blockchain-enabled smart contracts guarantee transparency, traceability, and immutability in the supply chain in long-term PPP projects. Automation of compliances, guarantee of performance and transparency of transactions that this technology provides could help improve PPP performance and reduce numerous failures that have been reported, especially for long-term infrastructure projects under the PPP route. Despite the critical importance of the Smart contract, most studies have been centred on traditional contractual settings [55], and its potential in PPPs/PFI is yet to be explored in literature. In addition, over 70% of PPP projects failed/terminated and/or were re-municipalised at the operational phase owing to poor services/quality and payment-related issues [56]. Studies on leveraging blockchain-enabled smart contracts to overcome these challenges are lacking in the literature. The application of Smart contracts in long-term infrastructure PPPs/PFI is a critical literature gap that has remained unexplored by researchers and academics in the built environment. Smart contracts would guarantee better PPP project performance as they will drive the future of contracting in long-term Infrastructure projects around the globe.

Blockchain-enabled smart contracts and waste management: Construction waste (CW) constitutes a major drawback to the attainment of environmental, social, and economic sustainability [57]. It impacts construction performance [58] and could be in the form of a waste of time, resources, and materials. There is, however, the absence of

Table 2. Problems in traditional contracts and the impact of SC adoption.

Application areas	Problem(s)	Effect(s) of the problems	Role of SC	Impact of SC
Payment and financial administration	• delay payment • none-payment	• difficulties in acquiring funds from financial institutions • retard the progress of the work • develop adversarial relation-ships between parties	• Automation of the payment system • Decentralize and disintermediate payment execution	• ensure transparent and secure pay-ment/financial data a nd records • reduce payment-related problems to the parties • ensure a healthy cashflow for contractors
Information and data management	• poor quality of information and communications and collaborating information sharing	• lack of propoer tracking of data and information management	• offer a decentralized secured and reliable platform for effective data and information managmenet	• better information sharing • improve collaboration • minimize human errors • improve document quality
Supply chain management	• manual and centralized management of stakeholders in the supply chain • difficulty in tracing deviant product compliance • quality assurance verification and process control evaluation is difficult	• deflection of blame and disputes • poor cost and time performance • slow productivity	• provision of immutable, trusted, transparent data in the supply chain	• enhance the sustainability of the supply chain • improve information sharing • control of the project is in real-time • better dispute tracking

(*continued*)

Table 2. (*continued*)

Application areas	Problem(s)	Effect(s) of the problems	Role of SC	Impact of SC
Dispute resolution and management	• high volume of claims and disputes in contracts • payment delays, quality issues and lack of trust among parties	• cost and time overrun • stoppage of work • damage business relationship	• reduce disputes and lead to speedy dispute resolution	• reduced claims and conflicts • improve trust and information accuracy • healthy business relationships
Quality management	• use of manual, paper-based records that are subject to errors and mistakes • manipulation of the quality inspection report • lack of reliability and integrity of quality information	• use of inferior and substandard materials • failure to follow quality procedure • hoarding of quality information	• produce credible records of quality information • automation of quality compliance checking • tamper-proof record of quality information	• better work quality and continuous improvement • stronger competitive advantages • reduce safety issues • reduced rework and waste
Safety Management	• unsafe working environment • abuse of personal protective equipment (PPE) • behaviours of workers • lack of adequate investment in safety management	• high accidents and fatalities rates • stoppage of work • waste • time and cost overruns	• ensure execution of safety inspection of cranes and other cachinery • monitor PPE compliance among construction workers • tamper-proof safety inspection records • produce transparency and traceability of safety performance records	• skipping of safety inspection is avoided • inspection records and documents are decentralized for accountability purposes • ensure the safe working method is adhered to • decision and mapping out mitigation measure is made easy

(*continued*)

Table 2. (*continued*)

Application areas	Problem(s)	Effect(s) of the problems	Role of SC	Impact of SC
Energy and Environmental management	• Carbon emissions and GHG from construction activities are still high	• Pollutants such as noise, dust, vibrations	• Track environmental and social information across the supply chain	• Automatic monitoring of pollutants • Evaluation of environmental performance • Tracking of energy consumption level of construction products • Energy consumption of construction equipment
Procurement management	• unethical practices such as bid shopping and bid peddling	• claims and disputes • time and cost overruns • quality issues, waste and rework	• eliminate unethical practices by providing a fair playin ground for subcontractors	• transparent procurement of subcontractors

reliable records of the huge quantities of materials that are consumed in the sector, and the waste management approach applied is unreliable. This is a prompt for capitalising on modern, disruptive technologies to achieve a sustainable waste management system [59]. [60] confirm that digital technologies could improve the problems of materials efficiencies. The role of technologies in construction waste management is an underexplored area in literature [61]. Most technology application studies in waste management in construction have been centred on BIM [62, 63]. However, studies on blockchain-based smart contract adoption in construction waste management are lacking. Thus, in meeting the SDG goals and improving project performance, there is a need for studies that would explore the potential of blockchain-enabled smart contracts in construction waste management.

Blockchain-enabled smart contracts and risk management: The busy construction business environment makes achieving effective projects and stakeholder risk management even more difficult. It is even worse as the scale, complexity, and duration of projects increase. Poor risk management is behind the non-attainment of the project's bottom lines [64]. Smart contracts provide real-time records of risk events, track deviant sources, and provide immutable and decentralised records of the outcome of construction processes. Studies on BIM adoption in construction and integration of BIM and VR in risk management have been studied [65, 66]. However, the application of Smart contracts in risk management in the construction sector is lacking and requires investigation.

Other application areas include blockchain-enabled smart contracts in Refurbishment projects.

5   Conclusions

Industry 4.0-driven technologies are at the centre of driving sustainable construction contract administration and delivery. Blockchain-enabled smart contracts are at the core of these technologies. This paper adopted a systematic literature review of smart contract studies in construction to determine the application areas of smart contracts and the gap in the application for future research.

The study revealed that construction management researchers tend to look at financial aspects when studying blockchain technologies and smart contracts. Indeed, there is often a stronger association with, e.g., the fields of automation and computing in construction. Other leading areas of research on the application of blockchain technologies and smart contracts in the construction sector are information and data management, supply chain management, dispute resolution and management and quality management. 'Automation in construction' is the most productive source of blockchain-enabled smart contract studies. Most studies on blockchain and smart contracts emanate from Asia, Europe and the US. A good number of the evaluated studies adopted approaches such as proof of concept, conceptual frameworks and surveys to drive home their ideas. Studies on blockchain-enabled smart contract applications in long-term PPP projects are missing. Also, other unexplored areas in the literature include risk management, waste management and management of refurbishment projects.

Summarily, the two major implications of this study are captured. Firstly, the study highlights some key critical application areas of blockchain-driven smart contracts, and this could guide government and policymakers in their quest to develop digital policies that could transform the way construction projects are delivered in the construction industry with large numbers of stakeholders and complex activities networks. Secondly, it showed that while there has been consistent growth in smart contract studies, a lot more still needs to be done. This study provides a base to guide researchers and academics to build upon in the quest to continue propagating the usefulness of blockchain and smart construction in construction. While this paper presents some critical areas for future research, its reliance on the Scope and WoS databases is a key limitation. Furthermore, a focus on journal articles published in English is another limitation of the study. Therefore, future studies might consider other databases or the addition of more databases and multiple sources (e.g., conferences, book chapters) and expand the language to include others. This study will serve as a basis for further studies on smart contract usage in overcoming the problems associated with the identified unexplored areas. Finally, the scope of future review research could be broadened to include comparative analysis with other industries to see how well these technologies have diffused in various industries of the economies.

Ethical Considerations. This study is part of an ongoing PhD study that has gained ethical approval from the university. Acceptable ethical standards were maintained, and there was no misrepresentation of data or potential biases in the results presented.

References

1. Li, J., Greenwood, D., Kassem, M.: Blockchain in the built environment and construction industry: a systematic review, conceptual models, and practical use cases. Autom. Constr. **102**, 288–307 (2019)
2. Ye, X., Zeng, N., König, M.: Systematic literature review on smart contracts in the construction industry: Potentials, benefits, and challenges. Front. Eng. Manag. **9**(2), 196–213 (2022)
3. Wahab, A., Wang, J., Shojaei, A., Ma, J.: A model-based smart contracts system via blockchain technology to reduce delays and conflicts in construction management processes. Eng. Constr. Archit. Manag. **30**(10), 5052–5072 (2022)
4. McKinsey: Reinventing construction: A route to higher productivity. https://shorturl.at/hrzCM. Accessed 22 september 2022 (2017)
5. Dakhli, Z., Lafhaj, Z., Mossman, A.: The potential of blockchain in building construction. Buildings **9**(4), 1–9 (2019)
6. Bousquin, J.: Tech 101: Blockchain's benefits for construction (2020). https://shorturl.at/eisL6. Accessed 12 Sep 2022
7. Scott, D.J., Broyd, T., Ma, L.: Exploratory literature review of blockchain in the construction industry. Autom. Constr. **132**, 1–18 (2021)
8. Yoon, J.H., Pishdad-Bozorgi, P.: State-of-the-art review of blockchain-enabled construction supply chain. J. Construct. Eng. Manag. **148**(2), 1–19 (2022)
9. Mahmudnia, D., Arashpour, M., Yang, R.B.C.: Blockchain in construction management: applications, advantages and limitations. Autom. Constr. **140**, 1–10 (2022)
10. Wu, H., Zhang, P., Li, H., Zhong, B., Fung, I.W.H., Lee, Y.Y.R.: Blockchain technology in the construction industry: current status, challenges, and future directions. J. Constr. Eng. Manag. **148**(10), 1–16 (2022)
11. Li, J., Kassem, M.: Applications of distributed ledger technology (DLT) and Blockchain-enabled smart contracts in construction. Autom. Constr. **131**, 1–26 (2021)
12. Perera, S., Nanayakkara, S., Rodrigo, M.N.N., Senaratne, S., Weinand, R.: Blockchain technology: Is it hype or real in the construction industry? J. Ind. Inf. Integr. **17**, 1–20 (2020)
13. Green, S., Higgins, J.: Cochrane Handbook for Systematic Reviews of Interventions. Cochrane Collaboration, London (2005)
14. Charles, S.H., Chang-Richards, A., Yiu, K.T.W.: New success factors for construction projects: a systematic review of post-2004 literature. Construct. Innov. **22**(4), 891–914 (2021)
15. Zheng, X., Le, Y., Chan, A.P.C., Hu, Y., Li, Y.: Review of the application of social network analysis (SNA) in construction project management research. Int. J. Project Manage. **34**(7), 1214–1225 (2016)
16. Xu, Y., Chong, H.-Y., Chi, M.: A review of smart contracts applications in various industries: a procurement perspective. Hindawi-Adv. Civ. Eng. **2021**, 1–25 (2021)
17. Jin, R., Gao, S., Cheshmehzangi, A., Aboagye-Nimo, E.: A holistic review of off-site construction literature published between 2008 and 2018. J. Clean. Prod. **20**, 1202–1219 (2018)
18. Elghaish, F., et al.: Blockchain and the 'Internet of Things' for the construction industry: research trends and opportunities. Autom. Constr. **132**, 1–15 (2021)
19. Humble, N., Mozelius, P.: Content analysis or thematic analysis Similarities, differences and applications in qualitative research. In: Proceedings of the 21st European Conference on Research Methodology for Business and Management Studies, vol. 21, issue 1, 76–81 (2022)

20. Moher, D., et al.: Preferred reporting items for systematic review and meta-analysis protocols (PRISMA-P) 2015 statement. Syst. Rev. **4**(1), 1–9 (2015)
21. Aghimien, D.O., Aigbavboa, C.O., Oke, A.E., Thwala, W.D.: Mapping out research focus for robotics and automation research in construction-related studies: a bibliometric approach. J. Eng. Des. Technol. **18**(5), 1063–1079 (2020)
22. Darko, A., Chan, A.P.C., Adabre, M.A., Edwards, D.J., Hosseini, M.R., Ameyaw, E.E.: Artificial intelligence in the AEC industry: scientometric analysis and visualization of research activities. Autom. Constr. **122**, 1–19 (2020)
23. Ciotta, V., Mariniello, G., Asprone, D., Botta, A., Manfredi, G.: Integration of blockchains and smart contracts into construction information flows: proof-of-concept. Autom. Constr. **132**, 1–12 (2021)
24. Wang, Z., Wang, T., Hu, H., Gong, J., Ren, X., Xiao, Q.: Blockchain-based framework for improving supply chain traceability and information sharing in precast construction. Autom. Constr. **111**, 1–13 (2020)
25. Hamledari, H., Fischer, M.: Role of blockchain-enabled smart contracts in automating construction progress payments. J. Leg. Aff. Disput. Resolut. Eng. Constr. **13**(1), 1–11 (2021)
26. Sonmez, R., Ahmadisheykhsarmast, S., Güngör, A.A.: BIM integrated smart contract for construction project progress payment administration. Autom. Constr. **139**, 1–12 (2022)
27. Bolton, S., Wedawatta, G., Wanigarathna, N., Malalgoda, C.: Late Payment to Subcontractors in the Construction Industry. J. Leg. Aff. Disput. Resolut. Eng. Constr. **14**(4), 1–13 (2022)
28. Ahmadisheykhsarmast, S., Sonmez, R.: A smart contract system for security of payment of construction contracts. Autom. Constr. **120**, 1–14 (2020)
29. Goli, A.: Integration of blockchain-enabled closed-loop supply chain and robust product portfolio design. Comput. Ind. Eng. **179**, 1–17 (2023)
30. Alnıpak, S., Toraman, Y.: Analysing the intention to use blockchain technology in payment transactions of Turkish maritime industry. Qual. Quant. **58**(3), 2103–2123 (2023)
31. Liu, Z., Jiang, L., Osmani, M., Demian, P.: Building information management (BIM) and blockchain (BC) for sustainable building design information management framework. Electronics (Switzerland) **8**(7), 1–15 (2019)
32. Adel, K., Elhakeem, A., Marzouk, M.: Chatbot for construction firms using scalable blockchain network. Autom. Construct. **141**, 104390 (2022)
33. Qian, X.A., Papadonikolaki, E.: Shifting trust in construction supply chains through blockchain technology. Eng. Constr. Archit. Manag. **28**(2), 584–602 (2021)
34. Baltruschat, L.M., Jaiman, V., Urovi, V.: User acceptability of blockchain technology for enabling electronic health record exchange. J. Syst. Inf. Technol. **25**(3), 268–295 (2023)
35. Agarwal, A.K., Tiwari, R.G., Kaushal, R.K., Kumar, N.: A systematic analysis of applications of blockchain in healthcare. In: 2021 6th International Conference on Signal Processing, Computing and Control (ISPCC), pp. 413–417 (2021)
36. Li, L., Zhou, H.: A survey of blockchain with applications in maritime and shipping industry. IseB **19**, 789–807 (2021)
37. Lu, W., Li, X., Xue, F., Zhao, R., Wu, L., Yeh, A.G.O.: Exploring smart construction objects as blockchain oracles in construction supply chain management. Autom. Constr. **129**, 1–14 (2021)
38. Yadav, A.K., Shweta, K.D.: Blockchain technology and vaccine supply chain: exploration and analysis of the adoption barriers in the Indian context. Int. J. Prod. Econ. **255**, 1–20 (2023)
39. Lee, J., Ham, Y., Yi, J.-S.: Construction disputes and associated contractual knowledge discovery using unstructured text-heavy data: legal cases in the United Kingdom. Sustainability **13**(16), 1–17 (2021)
40. David. S.: Thoughts for the new decade: smart contracts, blockchain and construction dispute resolution (2022). https://shorturl.at/cjM18. Accessed 18 Sep 2023

41. Gabuthy, Y.: Blockchain based dispute resolution: insights and challenges. Games **14**(3), 1–9 (2023)
42. Aouidef, Y., Ast, F., Deffains, B.: Decentralized justice: a comparative analysis of blockchain online dispute resolution projects. Front. Blockchain **4**, 1–9 (2021)
43. Miller, A.: Blockchain: a new frontier for dispute resolution? (2020). https://shorturl.at/kpsE5. Accessed 18 June 2023
44. Sheng, D., Dinga, L., Zhonga, B., Love, P.E.D., Luoa, H., Chen, J.: Construction quality information management with blockchains. Autom. Constr. **120**, 1–16 (2020)
45. Wu, H., Zhong, B., Li, H., Chi, H.-L., Wang, Y.: On-site safety inspection of tower cranes: a blockchain-enabled conceptual framework. Safety Sci. **153**, 105815 (2022)
46. Shu, Z., Liu, W., Fu, B., Li, Z., He, M.: Blockchain-enhanced trading systems for construction industry to control carbon emissions. Clean Technol. Environ. Policy **24**, 1851–1870 (2022)
47. Pishdad-Bozorgi, P., Yoon, J.H.: Transformational approach to subcontractor selection using blockchain-enabled smart contract as trust-enhancing technology. Autom. Construct. **142**, 104538 (2022). https://doi.org/10.1016/j.autcon.2022.104538
48. Cherkos, F.D., Jha, K.N.: Drivers of road sector public-private partnership adoption in new and inexperienced markets. J. Constr. Eng. Manag. **147**(3), 1–13 (2021)
49. Pellegrino, R., Carbonara, N., Costantino, N.: Public guarantees for mitigating interest rate risk in PPP projects. Built Env. Project Asset Manage. **9**(2), 248–261 (2019)
50. Patil, N., Laishram, B.: Sustainability of Indian PPP procurement process: development of strategies for enhancement. Built Env. Project Asset Manage. **6**(5), 491–507 (2016)
51. Soomro, M.A., Zhang, X.: Roles of private-sector partners in transportation public-private partnership failures. J. Manage. Eng. **31**(4), 04014057 (2015)
52. Nel, D.: Systematic Risk Management and Strategic Control in Public Private Partnerships. Doctoral Dissertation. Johannesburg: University of Johannesburg (2014). https://shorturl.at/axE78
53. Ameyaw, E.E., Chan, A.P.C.: Risk ranking and analysis in PPP water supply infrastructure projects: an international survey of industry experts. Facilities **33**(7/8), 428–453 (2015)
54. Xu, Y., Yeung, J.F., Jiang, S.: Determining appropriate government guarantees for concession contract: lessons learned from 10 PPP projects in China. Int. J. Strateg. Prop. Manag. **18**(4), 356–367 (2014)
55. Das, M., Luo, H., Cheng, J.C.P.: Securing interim payments in construction projects through a blockchainbased framework. Autom. Constr. **118**, 1–21 (2020)
56. Tariq, S., Zhang, X.: Critical failure drivers in international water PPP projects. J. Infrastruct. Syst. **26**(4), 1–17 (2020)
57. Eze, E.C., Awodele, I.A., Egwunatum, S.I.: Labour-specific factors influencing the volume of construction waste generation in the construction industry. J. Project Manage. Pract. **1**(2), 1–16 (2021)
58. Tongo, S.O., Oluwatayo, A.A., Adeboye, B.A.: Factors influencing waste generation in buildings project in South-West, Nigeria. Acad. J. Environ. Sci. **8**(4), 059–063 (2020)
59. Mandičák, T., Mésároš, P., Spišáková, M.: Impact of information and communication technology on sustainable supply chain and cost reducing of waste management in Slovak construction. Sustainability **13**(14), 7966 (2021)
60. Al-Mashhadani, A.F.S., Qureshi, M.I., Hishan, S.S., Saad, M.S.M., Vaicondam, Y., Khan, N.: Towards the development of digital manufacturing ecosystems for sustainable performance: learning from the past two decades of research. Energies **14**(10), 2945 (2021). https://doi.org/10.3390/en14102945
61. Sepasgozar, S.M.E., et al.: Waste management and possible directions of utilising digital technologies in the construction context. J. Clean. Prod. **324**, 1–27 (2021)
62. Liu, Z., Osniani, M., Demian, P., Baldwin, A.: A BIM-aided construction waste minimisation framework. Autom. Constr. **59**, 1–23 (2015)

63. Dantas, H.S., Sousa, J.M.M.S., Melo, H.C.: The importance of city information modeling (CIM) for cities' sustainability. IOP Conf. Series. Earth Environ. Sci. **2019**(225), 1–9 (2019)
64. Iqbal, S., Choudhry, R.M., Holschemacher, K., Ali, A., Tamošaitienė, J.: Risk management in construction projects. Technol. Econ. Dev. Econ. **21**(1), 65–78 (2015)
65. Merzliakov, R., Reshetkina, E.: Reducing risks in construction using innovative technologies. IOP Conf. Series: Mater. Sci. Eng. 753, 1–5 (2020)
66. Alirezaei, S., Taghaddos, H., Ghorab, K., Tak, A.N., Alirezaei, S.: BIM-augmented reality integrated approach to risk management. Autom. Constr. **141**, 1–15 (2022)

Stochastic Optimization Methodology for Production Planning with Uncertain Demand and Lead Time Based on the Digital Twin

Dan Luo[✉], Simon Thevenin, and Alexandre Dolgui

IMT Atlantique, LS2N Nantes, France
dan.luo2@imt-atlantique.fr

Abstract. Due to the manufacturing demand for mass customization and the widespread application of flexible automated production equipment, manufacturers tend to shorten their production cycle. This results in a loss of regularity in the production system, and it becomes difficult for manufacturers to control the product and process quality. To circumvent the issues related with these uncertainties, recent studies showed that using stochastic programming approach in Material Requirement Planning software can yield significant cost saving for the industry. However, there are very few studies that discuss uncertain production demand and lead time simultaneously. To fill these gaps, this paper considers the lot-sizing problems for production planning with uncertainties. We propose a stochastic optimization methodology for production planning with uncertain demand and lead time based on the digital twin. The proposed method is based on the simulation and Bayesian network forecast methods. In addition, we explain how the approach can be integrated with the digital twin systems. More precisely, we integrate the lot-sizing model with the simulation model, domain model, and Bayesian network model to forecast the lead time and improve the lot-sizing model with uncertain demand and lead time.

Keywords: Stochastic optimization · machine learning · simulation · uncertain demand and lead time

1 Introduction

Nowadays, manufacturers are increasingly shortening production cycles and expand-ing product assortments, which results in a volatile production environment characterized by customer demand uncertainties, yields, production capacity, and lead times [1]. To navigate these challenges effectively, manufacturers require production planning tools capable of handling such uncertain parameters [2, 3]. Recent works [4] have shown that the use of stochastic programming in Material Requirement Planning software (MRP) can significantly reduce cost. However, relying on a mathematical or simulation model with a sole unknown parameter is insufficient to offer efficient and accurate decision support in complicated production scenarios [5]. The advanced production environment necessitates a comprehensive approach that considers various uncertainty types. This need

© The Author(s), under exclusive license to Springer Nature Switzerland AG 2024
A. Mirzazadeh et al. (Eds.): SEMIT 2023, CCIS 2198, pp. 289–295, 2024.
https://doi.org/10.1007/978-3-031-72284-4_18

becomes even more pronounced in the context of Industry 4.0, where research efforts increasingly focus on integrating advanced technologies to effectively address complex and uncertain production environment [1]. Therefore, we propose a novel stochastic optimization methodology for production planning with uncertain demand and lead time, which combines simulation and Bayesian network forecast methods. We explain the integration of the lot sizing model with the simulation model, the domain model, and the Bayesian network model to enrich the lot sizing model with probabilistic demand and lead time forecast. The production planning module provides various production plans, and the simulation model determine accurate lead time and planning adherence for each plan. Furthermore, the resulting data can be used to train the Bayesian network model to predict the probability distribution of lead time. In summary, we present an approach that combines stochastic optimization methodology with simulation and Bayesian network methodologies. The resulting tool provide efficient production plans that account for uncertain demand and lead time.

The remaining article is structured with a literature review in Sect. 2, the research problem and mathematical model in Sect. 3, methodology in Sect. 4, and a conclusion in Sect. 5. It is important to note that this paper focuses on describing the conceptual architecture, including the modules and their functionality, rather than providing detailed methodology for each module.

2 Literature Review

The lot-sizing problem is a crucial aspect of production planning [6]. It involves determining the appropriate production lot size and timing, which directly impacts production efficiency, costs, and inventory levels. Solving this problem allows production planners to optimize resource utilization, ensure timely completion of production, and minimize costs. In the context of Industry 4.0, research on lot-sizing is continuously expanding and evolving [1, 7–9]. Initially focused on deterministic lot-sizing problems, scholars are increasingly addressing uncertainty problems. This area of research is primarily concerned with formalizing and modeling uncertainty in manufacturing systems [10, 11]. The literature on production planning provides various approaches and models to deal with different forms of uncertainty. The three main variables that are uncertain in production planning are demand, lead time, and capacity. Our research focuses on demand uncertainty and lead time uncertainty.

Demand uncertainty is a significant challenge for the manufacturing industry, directly impacting the effectiveness and efficiency of production planning [12]. The challenges of demand uncertainty for production planning include the difficulty in predicting actual customer demand, which makes it challenging for production planners to create effective production plans, control inventory, and reduce costs [13]. On the other hand, to maintain competitiveness, the production plan must be flexible enough to respond quickly to changes in market demand. Otherwise, it may result in wasted resources or insufficient supply [14].

In production planning, lead time refers to two types: delivery lead time and production lead time. Delivery lead time is the time it takes from order confirmation to completion of delivery. Long or uncertain delivery lead times can decrease customer service levels, as customers may face longer waiting times [15]. To meet customer demand, firms may need to increase their safety stock, which can affect capital binding and storage space requirements [16]. Uncertain delivery times can also lead to amplified demand fluctuations, which can further impact downstream production planning and inventory management. Production lead time is the duration between the start of production and product delivery. Uncertainty in production lead time can cause planning difficulties and increase the pressure to respond to rush orders and change orders during the production process [17]. It can also result in a mismatch between production and demand, leading to overproduction or oversupply [18]. To minimize the impact of this uncertainty, production plans may need to be adjusted more frequently, additional production capacity may need to be added, or more time buffers may need to be set aside to ensure on-time delivery [19].

For production planning that considers uncertainties, research and applications focus on how to improve the accuracy and resilience of the plan. Stochastic programming and robust optimization have traditionally been the two main approaches in research [20]. Additionally, simulation optimization is widely used to evaluate the performance of different production strategies under the influence of uncertainty [21]. In recent years, scholars have focused on aiding production planning by considering uncertainties with the help of emerging technologies such as machine learning, big data analytics, and especially digital twins. This enables firms to simulate and optimize production processes and predict the impact of uncertain demand and lead time on production by creating virtual copies of physical production systems. This simulation capability can assist firms in adjusting their production strategies promptly when demand and lead time fluctuate, thereby reducing inventory costs and improving market responsiveness [22]. Digital twins can also improve the adaptability and robustness of production planning, enabling production systems to effectively respond to complex and uncertain market environments. Thus, digital twins offer a powerful tool for production planners to dynamically adjust to uncertain demand and lead time.

While the value of digital twins for production planning is widely recognized in both academia and industry, current research has mainly focused on the scheduling domain. Research and application of digital twin-based production planning are still rare [1, 23]. Additionally, qualitative research and applications in real production planning systems, such as MRP, that take into account both demand and lead time uncertainties are difficult and rare to explore [24].

3 Problem Description and Mathematical Model

The typical production planning problem considered in real manufacturing systems or supply chains is a multi-echelon multi-item capacitated lot-sizing problem (MMCLP). The objective of the MMCLP is to determine the suggested production plan, including when to produce, how many items to produce, when to buy materials, how many items to buy, and the amount of extra capacity required. These decisions are made based on the demand, the bill of material (BOM), the production capacity, and the lead time. We choose a generic enough model for MMCLP that would fit in most of the manufacturing industries, detailed described in Luo et al. [25]. In this model, we consider uncertain demand D_{it} for end item $i \in I_e$ in period $t \in T$, and uncertain lead time L_i for both end item and component item, denoted by $i \in I$, where $I = I_c \cup I_e$. Both uncertain demand and lead time can be represented with the probability distribution. The objective of the MMCLP is to determine the suggested production plan. We define three decision variables. Y_{ot}, a binary decision variable, presents if a batch of operation $o \in O$ is performed in period t. Q_{ot} presents the quantity of operation o to perform in period t. w_{rt} presents the amount of extra capacity required for resource $r \in R$ in period t. The objective function is the expected total cost.

$$min \sum_{t \in T} \sum_{i \in I} (h_i I_{it} + b_i B_{it}) + \sum_{t \in T} \sum_{o \in O} (s_o Y_{ot} + v_o Q_{ot}) + \sum_{t \in T} \sum_{r \in R} o_r w_{rt} \qquad (1)$$

$$I_{it-1} - B_{it-1} + \sum_{o \in O} a_{oi} Q_{ot-L_i} - I_{it} + B_{it} = D_{it} \quad \forall i \in I_e, t \in T \qquad (2)$$

$$I_{it-1} + \sum_{o \in O} a_{oi} Q_{ot-L_i} - \sum_{o \in O} b_{oi} Q_{ot} - I_{it} = 0 \quad \forall i \in I_c, t \in T \qquad (3)$$

$$Q_{ot} - M Y_{ot} \leq 0 \qquad \forall o \in O, t \in T \qquad (4)$$

$$\sum_{o \in O} k_{or} \cdot Q_{ot} \leq C_r + w_{rt} \quad \forall r \in R, t \in T \qquad (5)$$

$$Y_{ot} = \{0, 1\}, I_{it} \geq 0, B_{it} \geq 0, Q_{ot} \geq 0 \qquad (6)$$

The objective function (1) is the expected total cost, including inventory cost, backlog cost, setup cost, production cost and extra capacity cost. Constraints (2) and (3) ensure the balance of flow for all items in each period. Constraints (2) ensure that any end item exceeding demand is stored as inventory, while any unsatisfied demand is recorded as backlog. Constraints (3) ensure that component items that are not in production become inventory. Constraints (4) set the production quantities to zero in periods without operations, which means that no setup occurs if there is no production operation in a period. Constraints (5) enforce limits on production capacity.

4   Methodology

The main idea of the digital-twin based methodology is to build the production planning tools, that can automatically generate a production plan on a mid-term or long-term planning horizon. The production planner module, consisting of a series of tools, can be used by a production manager to predict the production demand, and generate long-term and middle-term plans according to the existing demand and demand forecast. The production planning module comprises two sub-modules: the Probabilistic Forecast Tool and the Production Planning Solver. Figure 1 presents the structure of the production planner module, the function and relationship between these modules are introduced as follows:

Probabilistic forecast tool is used to predict the distribution for the uncertain parameters, such as the demand and lead time. For demand, the forecasts in practice are always

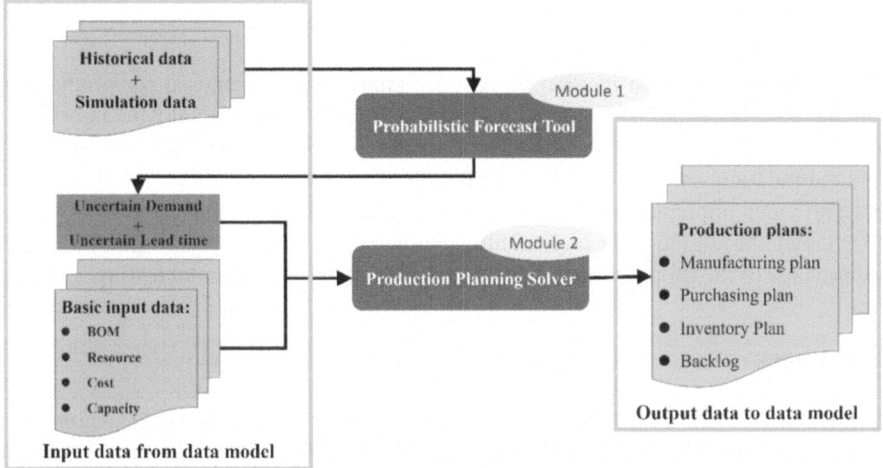

Fig. 1. Digital-twin based production planning tools.

wrong, and the deviation of the actual value of the parameters from the forecast may have a large impact on the quality of the production plan. Therefore, rather than providing a point forecast, the proposed the probability learner estimates the probability distribution of uncertain demand. The tools take as input historical data in the form of a time series, and it outputs the probability distribution of the parameter. The user may choose between several approaches to estimate the probability. For uncertain lead time, we create a Bayesian network using the data from the domain model or simulation model. The Bayesian network is built from the relations in the domain model, and we learn the conditional probability with the pair copula. We compare two methods to optimize the lead time. One is just integrating the simulation model with the production planning model to improve the calculation method of the lead time.

We also integrate the simulation model and Bayesian network with the production planning model to improve the calculation method of the lead time. The production planning module provides different production plans as the input of the simulation model. By running the simulation model with the production plans, we can get the real lead time and planning adherence. Furthermore, we can use the feedback data to train the Bayesian network model for predicting the probability distribution of lead time.

Production planning solver is the main tool that is used to generate mid-term or long-term production plans. First, according to the determined data, we build the general mathematical model for production planning. To consider uncertain demand with distribution, we use Quasi-Monte Carlo methods to generate the scenario tree for uncertain demand. Then, according to the scenario tree, we can get the customized mathematical model, which is the scenario-based mathematical model for the uncertain demand. In the end, we build the basic heuristic algorithm of fix-and-optimize to get the solution of production planning.

5   Conclusion

A stochastic optimization method based on digital twins is proposed for production planning with uncertain demand and lead times. The method uses heuristic algorithms to solve stochastic mathematical models for production planning, and uses Bayesian networks, simulation, and data models to support the optimization of production plans. This paper provides implementation ideas and recommendations for managers to improve MRP under the digital twin architecture. Future work will focus on optimizing the performance of the proposed methods through additional experimental testing.

References

1. Luo, D., Thevenin, S., Dolgui, A.: A state-of-the-art on production planning in Industry 4.0. Int. J. Prod. Res. **61**(19), 6602–6632 (2023). https://doi.org/10.1080/00207543.2022.2122622
2. Khalilpourazari, S., Mirzazadeh, A., Weber, G.-W., Pasandideh, S.H.R.: A robust fuzzy approach for constrained multi-product economic production quantity with imperfect items and rework process. Optimization **69**, 63–90 (2019)
3. Thevenin, S., Adulyasak, Y., Cordeau, J.F.: Stochastic dual dynamic programming for multiechelon lot sizing with component substitution. INFORMS J. Comput. **34**(6), 3151–3169 (2022)
4. Thevenin, S., Adulyasak, Y., Cordeau, J.F.: Material requirements planning under demand uncertainty using stochastic optimization. Prod. Oper. Manag. **30**(2), 475–493 (2021)
5. Zhu, X., Ji, Y.: A digital twin-based multi-objective optimization method for technical schemes in process industry. Int. J. Comput. Integr. Manuf. **36**(3), 443–468 (2023)
6. Haase, K.: Lot Sizing and Scheduling for Production Planning, vol. 408. Springer Science & Business Media (2012)
7. Galbraith, J.: Designing Complex Organizations. Reading, Mass (1973)
8. Suzanne, E., Absi, N., Borodin, V.: Towards circular economy in production planning: challenges and opportunities. Eur. J. Oper. Res. **287**(1), 168–190 (2020)
9. Lohmer, J., Lasch, R.: Production planning and scheduling in multi-factory production networks: a systematic literature review. Int. J. Prod. Res. **59**(7), 2028–2054 (2021)
10. Sethi, S.P., Yan, H., Zhang, H., Zhang, Q.: Optimal and hierarchical controls in dynamic stochastic manufacturing systems: a survey. Manuf. Serv. Oper. Manag. **4**(2), 133–170 (2002)
11. Yano, C.A., Lee, H.L.: Lot sizing with random yields: a review. Operations Res. **43**(2), 311–334 (1995). https://doi.org/10.1287/opre.43.2.311
12. Ivanov, D., Dolgui, A., Sokolov, B.: The impact of digital technology and Industry 4.0 on the ripple effect and supply chain risk analytics. Int. J. Product. Res. **57**(3), 829–846 (2019)
13. Aouam, T., Geryl, K., Kumar, K., Brahimi, N.: Production planning with order acceptance and demand uncertainty. Comput. Oper. Res. **91**, 145–159 (2018)
14. Higle, J.L., Kempf, K.G.: Production planning under supply and demand uncertainty: a stochastic programming approach. Stochastic Programming: The State of the Art In Honor of George B. Dantzig, pp. 297–315 (2011)
15. Slama, I., Ben-Ammar, O., Thevenin, S., Dolgui, A., Masmoudi, F.: Stochastic program for disassembly lot-sizing under uncertain component refurbishing lead times. Eur. J. Oper. Res. **303**(3), 1183–1198 (2022)
16. Shofa, M.J., Moeis, A.O., Restiana, N.: Effective production planning for purchased part under long lead time and uncertain demand: MRP Vs demand-driven MRP. IOP Conf. Ser.: Mater. Sci. Eng. **337**, 012055 (2018). https://doi.org/10.1088/1757-899X/337/1/012055

17. Axsäter, S.: Inventory Control, vol. 225. Springer (2015)
18. Dolgui, A., Ammar, O.B., Hnaien, F., Louly, M.-A.: A state of the art on supply planning and inventory control under lead time uncertainty. Stud. Inform. Control **22**(3), 255–268 (2013)
19. Disney, S.M., Towill, D.R.: The effect of vendor managed inventory (VMI) dynamics on the Bullwhip Effect in supply chains. Int. J. Prod. Econ. **85**(2), 199–215 (2003)
20. Snyder, L.V., Zuo-Jun, M.S.: Fundamentals of Supply Chain Theory. John Wiley & Sons (2019)
21. Metzker, P., Thevenin, S., Adulyasak, Y., Dolgui, A.: Robust optimization for lot-sizing problems under yield uncertainty. Comput. Oper. Res. **149**, 106025 (2023)
22. Aghezzaf, E.-H., Sitompul, C., Najid, N.M.: Models for robust tactical planning in multi-stage production systems with uncertain demands. Comput. Oper. Res. **37**(5), 880–889 (2010)
23. Tao, F., Jiangfeng, C., Qinglin, Q., Meng, Z., He, Z., Fangyuan, S.: Digital twin-driven product design, manufacturing and service with big data. Int. J. Adv. Manuf. Technol. **94**, 3563–3576 (2018)
24. Dolgui, A., Prodhon, C.: Supply planning under uncertainties in MRP environments: a state of the art. Annu. Rev. Control. **31**(2), 269–279 (2007)
25. Luo, D., Thevenin, S., Dolgui, A.: A digital twin-driven methodology for material resource planning under uncertainties. In: Dolgui, A., Bernard, A., Lemoine, D., von Cieminski, G., Romero, D. (eds.) Advances in Production Management Systems. Artificial Intelligence for Sustainable and Resilient Production Systems: IFIP WG 5.7 International Conference, APMS 2021, Nantes, France, September 5–9, 2021, Proceedings, Part I, pp. 321–329. Springer International Publishing, Cham (2021). https://doi.org/10.1007/978-3-030-85874-2_34

Information Technology and Data Science in Industry

Role of Top Management Commitment and Information Technology Investment in Digital Transformation

Pankaj Adatiya Tiwari[✉] [iD]

Department of Management (PG Studies), St. Francis College, Koramangala, Bengaluru, Karnataka 560034, India
adatiya.pankaj@gmail.com

Abstract. In recent times, enterprises have been more focused on information technology (IT) investment to transform digitally. Conversely, the reasons to invest in IT are lacking in literature though it can enhance the overall business. Based on the resource-based view (RBV), this research paper explores the influence of IT infrastructure and investments on the digital transformation of organizations considering the context of the digital transformation strategy. Furthermore, this research paper examines the moderating role of digital transformation strategy on the relationships between top management commitment, IT infrastructure, and digital transformation in business. Through a questionnaire survey of small and medium enterprises, 127 sample data were collected, and the ordinal regression method was used to test the hypothesis and the conceptual framework.

Digital transformation strategy moderates the relationship between top management commitment, IT infrastructure, and organizational digital transformation. Moreover, top management commitment and IT infrastructure significantly positively affect digital transformation. This research paper investigates the moderating role of digital transformation strategy in the relationship between top management commitment, IT infrastructure investment, and digital transformation performance. As a result, the research paper supplements substantially the body of knowledge on business success, IT business value, digital transformation, and strategic management. Also, the findings can help improve managers' perceptions of IT business value and provide theoretical guidance on deriving digital transformation performance with the help of IT infrastructure investments.

Keywords: Information Technology investment · Top management commitment · Digital transformation

1 Introduction

Presently, a new generation of information technology (IT), represented by artificial intelligence, blockchain, cloud computing, big data, and the Internet of Things (IoT), is driving the rise of the digital economy and bringing disruptive changes to organizational structure and business processes, and the business model of companies. Information

A. Mirzazadeh et al. (Eds.): SEMIT 2023, CCIS 2198, pp. 299–322, 2024.
https://doi.org/10.1007/978-3-031-72284-4_19

technology has become a critical factor in driving the digital transformation of businesses. Thus, companies see IT investments as an opportunity to gain a competitive advantage in a difficult and dynamic market competition environment. Companies in almost every industry are taking steps to explore new IT and take advantage of it. According to Gartner's latest forecast, global enterprise IT spending will reach over 4.1 trillion US dollars in the upcoming time. As companies' digital transformation accelerates, their IT costs are expected to continue to rise. However, studies show that only 20% of companies' digital transformation projects are successful, and significant IT spending by companies has not had the desired digital impact. The mismatch between IT input and transformation outputs has once again sparked a new discussion about IT value creation in the context of digital transformation of higher education institutions and industries [1].

Existing studies that have been done on the business value of IT examine how IT affects organizational performance. It has been demonstrated by earlier research that IT may enhance organizational performance. There is general agreement that IT, as a straightforward hardware and software tool, cannot create value on its own, directly, or enhance business performance; rather, it must work in concert with other information systems and organizational elements to create a synergistic effect. [2], for instance, noted that information systems have an impact on company performance by enhancing other enterprise resources or competencies. According to [3], bolstering higher-order business competencies is how IT capabilities affect enterprise performance. Comparably, [4] discovered that IT assets could only influence business performance in concert with IT management, not directly or independently. According to Peng et al. (2016), supply chain management and business process management capabilities can be integrated with IT competence to enhance enterprise performance. Nevertheless, there isn't much agreement in the literature now in publication about how to fully utilize IT's potential benefits and successfully support businesses' digital transformations. Which specific mechanisms IT employs to impact the outcomes of enterprise transformation are still unknown.

According to [1], digital transformation is a strategy response to trends and disruptions in digital technology. It includes significant changes in industry and society brought about using digital technology. It's an intricate path that requires a well-defined digital transformation plan to steer. According to the most recent perspective, strategy—not technology—is what propels digital transformation. Traditional strategic guidelines have completely altered due to digitalization, which has also redefined competitive advantage and its realization plan. In fact, according to [5], digital transformation must consider how technological advancements may alter an organization's business model, structure, and procedures. This includes how new information technologies may affect an enterprise's approach to digital transformation. Thus, how to develop and implement a digital transformation plan is the central problem of enterprise digital transformation. Businesses create a digital transformation strategy to identify new ways to use technology, handle changes brought about by technology, and plan the execution of the complete digital transformation process. Accordingly, some research suggests that organizational change and digital transformation strategy have emerged as a new avenue for IT-driven digital transformation. Nevertheless, despite these insights, it is still unclear how precisely digital transformation strategy fits into the link between IT and digital transformation, and neither its relative strength nor its micro mechanism has been investigated [6].

The focus of the digital transformation strategy is on how new technologies are changing businesses, processes, and products. A digital transformation plan can direct the integration and application of digital technologies to accomplish digital transformation in a dynamic setting. According to research, the strategy for digital transformation has a favorable impact on a company's performance and acts as a mediator between the use of digital technology and performance [7]. Through digital capabilities, a digital strategy can raise an organization's degree of digitalization [8]. Moreover, management attributes predict organizational outcomes. Previous research has demonstrated that digital leadership and support from top management improve the ability to leverage exceptional IT skills, support strategic changes that are successful, and boost business performance [9]. Furthermore, top managers who spearhead and start transformation initiatives are frequently involved in the design and execution of digital transformation strategies. Top managers need to make the right strategic decisions regarding their organization's digital transformation to reduce or eliminate risks associated with improper identification and deployment of IT investment and digital transformation procedures and resources. Businesses might investigate novel approaches to derive value from information technology by implementing digital strategies. IT infrastructure responds to and supports specific business initiatives, which helps to enable digital transformation. Furthermore, IT infrastructure and digital transformation plans work best with top management [10].

In conclusion, this study views top management and digital transformation strategy as the key players in the creation of IT business value within the framework of digital transformation. Theoretically, through adapting to and assisting with digital transformation plans, IT infrastructure affects the results of enterprise transformation. The link between IT infrastructure, Top management commitment, and transformation outcomes can be strengthened by digital transformation strategy. To address the current research needs on the role of digital transformation strategy and the use of new-generation IT in the context of enterprise transformation and upgrading, this study looks at the potential moderating role of digital transformation strategy.

There are theoretical and practical contributions to this topic. First, this paper offers a fresh perspective on how IT infrastructure supports the digital transformation of an organization. The research on IT value creation is expanded and enhanced by including digital transformation strategy as an intermediary condition. Second, this study adds to the body of knowledge on digital transformation by developing and testing an empirical model of IT-driven digital transformation realization. It does this by considering top management commitment, IT infrastructure, and digital transformation strategy as the antecedent configuration of digital transformation. This study suggests that firms cannot execute digital transformation only through IT, despite its practical advantages. Rather, to handle the complicated shift that digital technology has brought about, businesses need to develop a digital transformation plan. Then, they need to integrate an efficient IT strategy to maximize the performance of this transformation. The study's conclusions provide theoretical guidance for companies looking to undergo digital transformation as well as a scientifically supported argument for top management competency training.

After this introduction, the research paper is organized as follows. First, the comprehensive overview of the existing literature, focusing on top management commitment, IT Infrastructure, and digital transformation strategy followed by the theoretical background and support for the present research work. Second, the assumptions are made in the form of hypotheses by describing the conceptual framework and the research methodology used in the study. Then, the results of empirical investigations are presented. From the research findings, a thorough discussion is presented aimed at filling the above-mentioned research gaps. Finally, the conceptual loop is closed by describing the implications, conclusions, limitations of the study, and recommendations for future research.

2   Review of Literature

2.1   Top Management Commitment

In the fields of information systems and business strategic management, the influence of top management has long been a significant area of investigation. Previous studies have demonstrated that leadership, involvement, dedication, and support from upper management are crucial for creating IT value for three primary reasons: According to [11], top managers possessing a wider perspective are more adept at recognizing business opportunities to integrate IT into business processes and offering managerial guidance for organizing, planning, creating, and carrying out tasks. This, in turn, improves the efficiency of the IT management process; Second, to guarantee adequate human, material, and financial input in the IT implementation process [12], senior managers with high levels of management commitment and engagement can undertake significant ownership and are willing to take risks. And finally, by taking part in executive steering committees, forming alliances both inside and between businesses, settling disputes, and maintaining project deadlines, senior management promotes the growth of process capabilities [13]. Theoretically, there is a wealth of literature to support the crucial role that senior management plays in attaining IT performance. A growing body of research has begun to connect the results of innovation or change processes to upper management [14]. Top managers have a direct impact on business innovation because they set the corporate strategy and allocate resources accordingly. One way to think about digital transformation is as a process result built on innovation and change. As a result, current research has begun to concentrate on the role that top management commitment plays in IT investment and digital transformation [15, 16].

2.2   IT Infrastructure

The organizational return on IT investment has been the subject of some useful studies in the field of information systems research. The measurement of IT investment and company performance as well as the mechanism of IT investment on organizational performance are the concerns that these studies need to consider. Because there is little publicly available data on firm-specific IT spending, researchers frequently use a variety of different methods when measuring IT investments. Several key IT investment ideas, including IT spending, IT strategy, and IT capabilities/management, have been identified through a review of prior studies [17, 18]. Financial performance and market performance, such as organizational agility and product innovation performance, are the primary metrics used to quantify the impact of IT investment on a company's performance [19, 20]. There is broad agreement in the literature regarding the relationship between IT investment and organizational performance: IT investments have a positive impact on performance, but how these investments affect performance, and the conditions and contexts must be understood. IT is a component of the corporate value-creating process, working in concert with other complementary resources and organizational competencies to build sustainable competitiveness, even though it cannot do it on its own [2]. Hence, research indicates that there are still areas for improvement in the business value of IT.

2.3 Digital Transformation Strategy

Nearly every area of an organization's internal operations and external environment is being transformed by digital technology, and this digital disruption necessitates the coordination and modification of numerous business strategies [1]. Scholars support the integration of IT business strategy in this regard. [21], for instance, make the case that information systems and organizational plans should be integrated with digital technology and introduce the idea of a digital business strategy. [22] concentrated further on the ways that new technologies are transforming organizations, products, and processes as well as the idea of a digital transformation strategy contending that in a dynamic setting, such a strategy can direct the application and integration of digital technologies to bring about digital transformation [5]. Therefore, formulating and implementing a clear and scientific digital transformation strategy becomes a critical path for the digital transformation practice of enterprises.

Research on digital transformation strategies now mostly focuses on implications, dimensions, dynamics, and effect outcomes. For instance, [22] split the concept of "digital transformation strategy" into four categories: technological use, value creation, structural change, and financial gain. They defined it as supporting the strategic transformation of businesses brought about by the application of digital technology as well as the strategic positioning of the operation and development of businesses during or after transformation. Through case interviews, [5] improved these four dimensions into 11 items and verified and altered them. From the standpoint of digital technology investment, [23] presented two digital transformation strategies: customer engagement and digital solution strategies. From the perspectives of digital technology application and digital operation business model, [24] offered four main strategies for digital transformation: disruptive strategy, business model-led strategy, technology-led strategy, and tailored simulation strategy. Numerous studies investigate the process of creating and executing digital transformation plans, with particular emphasis on the dynamics of digital transformation strategies. [5], for instance, used the successful experiences of three case organizations to identify a set of strategic questions and potential responses that managers should consider when developing a plan for digital transformation. In their construction of an integrated model of the development and implementation of digital transformation strategies, [25] noted that digital transformation strategies involve several critical decision-making activities, are a highly dynamic process of adjustment and change, and integrate information systems and business strategies. Furthermore, some academics are starting to investigate the effects of the digital transformation plan using empirical research methods. These studies offer fresh angles on the topic of digital transformation strategy and implementation. The purpose of this research is to support the claim that strategy and IT collaborate to create a competitive advantage to achieve digital transformation, but there are currently no pertinent empirical studies on the influence of IT on the development and implementation of digital transformation strategy.

3   Theoretical Background

According to the resource-based view (RBV), an organization's long-term competitive advantages come from its distinct resources and competencies. It sees an enterprise as a collection of resources and concentrates on the characteristics and strategic components of those resources to explain the long-term benefits and variations between enterprises [26]. An enterprise's resources are its possessions, including its procedures, technology, expertise, and abilities. Furthermore, RBV highlights that the foundation of competitive advantage can only be composed of valued, uncommon, imperfectly imitable, and non-substitutable resources. RBV is generally acknowledged as the best hypothesis in the information system literature to explain how IT resources create business value [27, 28]. The impact of various IT resources, such as IT infrastructure [27], IT capabilities [10], and management of IT investment [29], on organizational performance, has been the subject of existing studies based on the resource-based view (RBV). These studies consider that IT resources, as a source of competitive advantage, can be used to improve internal communication, increase production efficiency, reduce operating costs, and increase financial performance [12, 30].

In the meantime, other research has cast doubt on the claim that IT resources directly affect company performance [31] and put forth a complementary view based on RBV, which maintains that IT resources only become competitive when they complement other capabilities or resources [19]. Additionally, [32] examined three pathways of the relative influence of firm-specific determinants on performance and offered a composite model. The firm asset effects show how the firm asset affects the strategy, while the RBV-based strategic effect shows how the strategy directly affects performance. This suggests that the firm's resources can improve its capacity to create competitive strategies, which will have an impact on the firm's performance. The perspectives may be extended by the complementary function of digital transformation strategy as an intermediary structure between IT resources and corporate digital transformation. Table 1 summarizes the key literature used in the present research paper.

Table 1. Summary of the Key Literature Review

Author	Summary
[33]	This research work outlines the outcomes of an investigation into the oversight and administration of information technology (IT) within sizable Australian enterprises. The research employed a questionnaire survey distributed to the top-ranking IT officials in each organization. Respondents were classified into three segments depending on the extent of information utilization within the company, namely high-tier, medium-tier, and low-tier industries. A comparison of findings across these groups revealed noteworthy distinctions. Additionally, the results were juxtaposed with those from two other recent studies. Drawing insights from the outcomes, the paper offers tailored recommendations for companies in high, medium, and low-tier industries
[30]	The study develops and tests a theoretical model examining the assimilation of enterprise systems post-implementation. Focusing on top management as a mediator, the model explores how external institutional pressures affect the usage of enterprise resource planning (ERP) systems. Survey data from companies with ERP implementations are used to test hypotheses. Results reveal that mimetic pressures positively impact top management beliefs, leading to increased participation in ERP assimilation. Top management participation, in turn, positively influences ERP usage. Coercive pressures positively impact participation without mediating beliefs, while normative pressures directly influence ERP usage. The study underscores top management's vital role in mediating institutional pressures on IT assimilation, emphasizing the continued importance of institutional pressures in post-implementation assimilation
[21]	Over the past three decades, the prevailing perspective on information technology strategy has positioned it as a functional-level strategy aligned with the broader business strategy. However, as the business landscape transitions into a digital infrastructure with increased interconnections, digital technologies are fundamentally reshaping business strategies, processes, capabilities, and interfirm relationships. This prompts a shift in thinking, advocating for a fusion between IT strategy and business strategy, termed digital business strategy. Four key themes—scope, scale, speed, and sources of business value creation—are identified to guide this perspective. The special issue's papers contribute insights into digital strategies and offer directions for advancing research in this evolving domain

(*continued*)

Table 1. (*continued*)

Author	Summary
[22]	In recent years, organizations across various industries have undertaken numerous initiatives to investigate emerging digital technologies and leverage their advantages. Such endeavors often entail substantial overhauls of critical business operations, influencing both products and processes, as well as organizational structures and management paradigms. Companies find it imperative to institute effective management practices to oversee these intricate transformations. A crucial strategy involves the formulation of a digital transformation strategy, acting as a central concept to streamline the overall coordination, prioritization, and implementation of digital transformations within the organization
[4]	The extensive exploration of the multifaceted role of information technology (IT) in organizations has not fully clarified the interaction between IT assets and IT management and their combined influence on firm performance. This paper adopts a systems perspective to delve into this crucial mechanism. Focusing on IT assets and IT management as integral subsystems within the broader organizational system, the study investigates their joint impact on organizational performance. Drawing on systems theory, particularly the concept of open systems, the research also assesses how the organization and its subsystems are affected by the external environment. The study specifically examines how environmental dynamism moderates the interaction between IT assets and IT management subsystems, utilizing a matched sample of 214 business executives and IT managers for hypothesis testing
[23]	The findings from a study involving 25 companies embarking on digital transformation journeys are outlined in this article. New digital technologies offer both transformative opportunities and potential existential threats to companies established in the pre-digital economy. The study identifies two key digital strategies—customer engagement and digitized solutions—as guiding principles for digital transformation. Execution of these strategies relies on two essential technology-enabled assets: an operational backbone and a digital services platform. The article elucidates how a sizable, established company can integrate these elements to navigate its digital transformation effectively

(continued)

Table 1. (*continued*)

Author	Summary
[17]	Industry 4.0, heralded as a new industrial phase, integrates vertical and horizontal manufacturing processes, aiming to enhance industrial performance through connectivity. In emerging countries like Brazil, understanding how industries perceive the potential contributions of Industry 4.0 technologies remains limited. Utilizing secondary data from a survey across 27 industrial sectors representing 2225 Brazilian companies, this study explores the adoption of Industry 4.0 technologies and their association with anticipated benefits in product, operations, and side-effects aspects. Regression analysis reveals that certain Industry 4.0 technologies are seen as promising for industrial performance, challenging conventional wisdom. The study provides insights into contextual conditions in Brazil, suggesting a nuanced implementation of Industry 4.0 concepts developed in advanced economies. The findings are synthesized in a framework, contributing to discussions on real industry expectations and fostering future research on the tangible benefits of Industry 4.0
[34]	The emergence of novel and potent digital technologies, along with digital platforms and infrastructures, has brought about transformative effects on innovation and entrepreneurship. Going beyond the creation of new opportunities for innovators and entrepreneurs, these digital technologies hold broader implications for both value creation and capture. Research focused on comprehending the digital transformation of the economy must encompass multiple levels of analysis, drawing upon ideas and concepts from diverse fields and disciplines, while explicitly acknowledging the role of digital technologies in reshaping organizations and social relationships. To advance this research agenda, three key themes—openness, affordances, and generativity—associated with digitization are identified, and comprehensive research issues related to each are outlined. These intrinsic themes of digital technologies are proposed as a unifying conceptual foundation, facilitating connections between issues at different levels and the integration of ideas from various disciplines and areas

(*continued*)

Table 1. (*continued*)

Author	Summary
[1]	The existing body of literature has contributed to a deeper comprehension of specific facets within digital transformation. However, there is a notable absence of a comprehensive depiction of its nature and ramifications. Through a review encompassing 282 scholarly works, the researchers construct an inductive framework delineating digital transformation across eight foundational elements. The framework accentuates digital transformation as a dynamic process wherein digital technologies induce disruptions, prompting strategic responses from organizations. These responses aim to reshape their paths of value creation while concurrently managing the associated structural changes and organizational obstacles that influence the positive and negative outcomes of the transformation process. Expanding on this framework, the authors present a research agenda that advocates for (1) investigating the role of dynamic capabilities and (2) addressing ethical considerations as pivotal avenues for future strategic Information Systems (IS) research on digital transformation
[35]	This study investigates the impact of Digital Transformation Strategy (DTS) on organizational performance in the context of Chinese enterprises, drawing on perspectives such as "Skewed conflict," "minority dissent theory," and "too-much-of-a-good-thing." Using a large sample of Chinese enterprises, empirical analysis through multiple linear regression with SPSS reveals a positive relationship between DTS and both short- and long-term financial performance. The study introduces the moderating role of cognitive conflict, indicating that moderate cognitive conflict enhances the relationship between DTS and short-term financial performance, while higher cognitive conflict significantly influences long term financial performance. The research contributes a theoretical perspective for future studies in the IT/IS, DTS, and digital strategy domains
[7]	Extensive research in both academic and industrial contexts has delved into the utilization of digital technology. A more profound analysis of corporate performance reveals that the effective use of digital technology contributes to the facilitation of both digital transformation strategy and organizational innovation. This investigation goes a step further by exploring the mediating impact of digital transformation strategy and organizational innovation on the correlation between digital technology usage and firm performance. Through an empirical study conducted via a survey targeting supervisors in the financial sector in Taiwan, responses were gathered from 227 companies. The results suggest that the positive influences of digital technology usage extend to digital transformation strategy and organizational innovation, subsequently impacting firm performance. Moreover, digital transformation strategy and organizational innovation act as complete mediators in the relationship between digital technology usage and firm performance

(*continued*)

Table 1. (*continued*)

Author	Summary
[36]	In the digital economy, IT investment is crucial for enterprise digital transformation, yet understanding why and how it enhances this transformation is lacking in the literature. This study, grounded in the resource-based view (RBV), investigates the impact mechanism of IT infrastructure on enterprise digital transformation through the lens of digital transformation strategy. Surveying 180 Chinese enterprises, the study utilizes partial least squares-structural equation modeling (PLS-SEM) to test hypotheses. Findings reveal that digital transformation strategy fully mediates the relationship between IT infrastructure and enterprise digital transformation. Additionally, top management positively moderates the links between IT infrastructure and digital transformation strategy, and between digital transformation strategy and enterprise digital transformation. The study contributes to knowledge on IT business value, digital transformation, and strategic management, offering valuable insights for managers and theoretical guidance for deriving performance from IT infrastructure investments
Present Study	This research, grounded in the resource-based view (RBV), explores the impact of IT infrastructure and investments on organizational digital transformation, emphasizing the role of digital transformation strategy. Examining 127 small and medium enterprises through a questionnaire survey, the study utilizes ordinal regression to test hypotheses. Findings indicate that digital transformation strategy moderates the relationship between top management commitment, IT infrastructure, and organizational digital transformation. Top management commitment and IT infrastructure significantly positively influence digital transformation. The study contributes to understanding business success, IT business value, digital transformation, and strategic management, offering insights for managers and theoretical guidance on deriving digital transformation performance through IT infrastructure investments

4 Conceptual Framework and Hypotheses Development

To clarify the value creation mechanism of IT investment in the context of enterprise digital transformation, this study—which is based on the IT business value paradigm and RBV theory—proposes an IT-driven digital transformation model with a digital transformation strategy acting as the moderator and top management acting as the boundary condition. Figure 1 illustrates the conceptual research framework.

4.1 Top Management Commitment, IT, and Digital Transformation Strategy

The critical significance that top management practices have in the effectiveness of information systems has been extensively researched. Effective information system (IS) planning appears to have resulted from senior management's involvement [33]. The dedication of upper management to IT initiatives enhances IT performance by offering

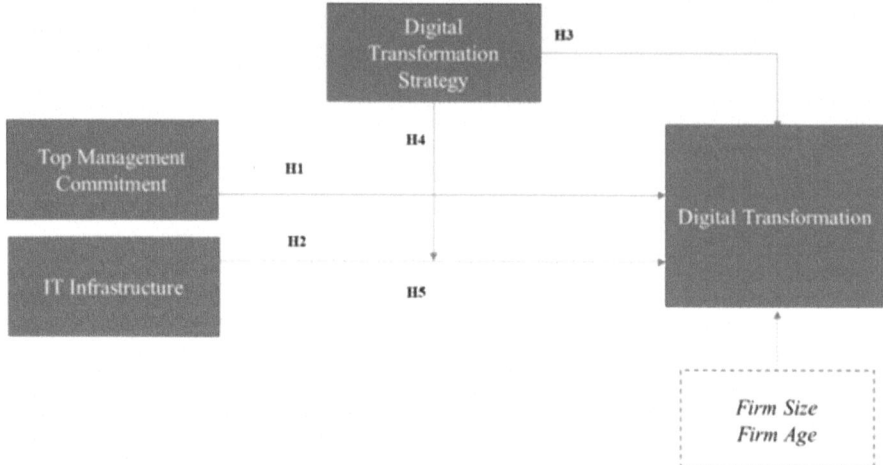

Fig. 1. Conceptual Framework (Author's interpretation).

resources, support, and direction on IS tasks. Additionally, by ensuring the continuity of IT expenditures, this commitment aids in the integration of IT with corporate plans and procedures [2]. According to [37], effectively managed IT investment can foster an environment where IT resources and enterprise strategy are aligned. Top managers support their performance as strategic executors by coordinating the efforts of various business units, synchronizing IT and business units, streamlining operational procedures, cutting production costs, regularly reviewing IT priorities, and allocating IT resources on time. The resource complementary theory, as put forth by [2], contends that integrating various complementary resources can result in synergies that improve outcomes. Better digital transformation performance can be achieved by using top management as a supplementary resource to direct the development of IT value and the execution of digital transformation strategies.

The process of digital transformation is a complicated social undertaking that requires the backing of upper management. However, the strategic orientation of digital transformation can be influenced by top management practices, which can also provide the resources and capability required to support the strategy's effective implementation, increasing the likelihood that digital transformation will be realized. According to research, there may be opposition to the adoption of a digital transformation plan from various departments within the organization. For this reason, senior management must be able to encourage the active involvement of many stakeholders. Additionally, putting into practice a digital transformation strategy is a highly dynamic process that calls for ongoing iterations between learning and practice. Top management must be involved in leading and initiating transformation efforts [38], and the results could vary in terms of performance.

Hence, proposed:

H1. Top management commitment has a substantial impact on digital transformation.

Resources are the fundamental unit of analysis in Resource-Based Viewing (RBV), whereas capabilities are how resources can carry out an action or task jointly. A company with significant IT resources could be able to increase its capabilities by utilizing these resources [11]. According to [22], an enterprise digital transformation plan may be thought of as a capacity that shows the ability to use digital technology in business. Thus, it is suggested that the strategy for digital transformation should take IT infrastructure into consideration. An organization's strategy reaction to the disruptive changes brought about by digital technologies is known as digital transformation [1]. Organizations must orchestrate their innovation and change processes as technology continues to permeate them. This requires a strategy that enables IT investments to produce value along a performance dimension that is in line with transformation goals. To accomplish the intended goals of digital transformation, a digital transformation strategy directs the integration and acceptance of digital technologies and focuses on the changes that new technologies bring about in organizations, products, and processes [22]. Consequently, a digital transformation strategy offers guidance on how to best utilize emerging technology to support an organization's digital transformation. Furthermore, the use of new technologies modifies organizational structures and practices, promotes the development of innovative products and business models, and serves as a primary catalyst for strategic change and innovation within the company [34]. It also offers technical assistance to ensure successful implementation [1]. According to research, digital technology drives strategic transformation by altering the shape, nature, value, and structure of an organization's initial resource base in four ways: standardization, process, data, and resource interconnectivity. According to [32], a company's ability to establish strategies that create value increases with its technology resources, and developing a digital transformation strategy is made easier when a company has more technological resources [7]. This study contends that a company's digital transformation plan starts with its IT infrastructure. Businesses with more advanced IT infrastructure are more adept at creating and executing digital transformation plans.

Hence, proposed:

H2. IT infrastructure has a substantial impact on digital transformation.

4.2 Digital Transformation Strategy and Digital Transformation

According to [32], digital transformation is the process of upending conventional methods of creating value while looking for innovation and change. To accomplish the intended goals of digital transformation, this intricate systemic engineering requires a digital transformation strategy that will organize, direct, and coordinate the implementation of all relevant operations [7]. Additionally, the RBV highlights how crucial organizational capabilities are to the process of giving the company a competitive edge [20]. The ability to use the IT infrastructure to increase the company's competitive advantage is reflected in the digital transformation strategy, which can aid with the digital transformation. Many studies emphasize that enterprise leaders should do top-level design, create new value propositions by combining digital technology capabilities with existing resources and stuff, and realize digital transformation. They view digital transformation strategy as a crucial antecedent condition for digital transformation. By emphasizing the innovation and change brought about by technology and coordinating all organizational resources and competencies, a digital transformation plan can assist an enterprise's digital transformation. A company that has implemented effective digital transformation processes demonstrates a well-defined and transparent digital transformation plan. On the other hand, businesses without a digital transformation plan exhibit poor and inefficient resources and decision-making. Using a sizable sample of data, [22] also confirmed the beneficial effect of the digital transformation plan on the performance of the company. Competitive advantage and long-term performance are possible outcomes of successful digital transformation projects [1, 17].

Hence, proposed:

H3: Digital transformation strategy has a substantial influence on digital transformation.

4.3 Digital Transformation Strategy as Moderator

According to RBV, a company's precious, uncommon, distinctive, and irreplaceable resources are what provide it a competitive advantage [26, 27]. Although IT infrastructure is a replicable resource, it does not directly produce sustained firm performance. Instead, organizational competencies or resource complementarities have an indirect effect [7]. Stated differently, when examining the influence of IT on enterprise-level results, such as company performance, it is necessary to consider the supplementary benefits of additional organizational resources or capacities acting as middlemen [32, 35].

IT-savvy businesses are more driven and equipped to carry out their digitally focused innovation projects. Research from the past has demonstrated that strategy and company assets, particularly IT resources, combine to produce firm performance. A company's capacity to create a utility-creating strategy that offers enough circumstances for performance sustainability increases with the number of resources it possesses [14, 19]. The essential components of enterprise digital transformation are digital technology and digital transformation strategy. The utilization of novel technologies has the potential to enhance an organization's capacity for digital transformation, hence impacting its innovation endeavors and overall performance [12].

The critical significance that top management practices have in the effectiveness of information systems has been extensively researched. Effective information system (IS) planning appears to have resulted from senior management's involvement [21]. The dedication of upper management to IT initiatives enhances IT performance by offering resources, support, and direction on IS tasks. Additionally, by ensuring the continuity of IT expenditures, this commitment aids in the integration of IT with corporate plans and procedures [17]. According to [5], effectively managed IT investment can foster an environment where IT resources and enterprise strategy are aligned.

Top managers support the organization's performance in their capacity as strategic executors by coordinating the efforts of various business units, synchronizing IT and business units, streamlining operational procedures, cutting costs associated with production, regularly reviewing IT priorities, and promptly allocating IT resources [21]. The resource complementary of RBV theory, as put forth by [7], contends that integrating various complementary resources can produce synergies that improve outcomes. Better digital transformation performance can be achieved by using top management as a supplementary resource to direct the production of IT value and the execution of digital transformation strategies. Therefore, this study argues that Top management commitment and IT infrastructure resources and capabilities are influencing digital transformation through digital transformation strategies.

Hence, proposed:

H4. Digital transformation strategy moderates the relationship between top management commitment and digital transformation.

H5. Digital transformation strategy moderates the relationship between IT infrastructure and digital transformation.

5 Research Methodology

5.1 Sampling

For hypotheses analysis, a sample size of 127 data is collected. The data were collected from managers of small and medium-sized enterprises having designations such as manager, senior manager, director and above, etc., and only one response was collected from each organization since the unit of analysis was individual companies. These companies are identified based on their market existence (i.e. *firm age*) and number of employees (i.e. *firm size*) [39]. A convenience sampling technique was used when collecting data. In total, approximately three hundred respondents were emailed to answer a questionnaire based on Google Forms. The data cleansing and analysis process involved thoroughly validating each response and considering the participants from the targeted organizations [40]. The rate of response to the survey was 26.8%. There were no significant differences (alpha 5%) among the earlier and subsequent responses [41]. Participants at various positions/roles were contacted to reduce the bias risk as per the common-method variance to assess the study variables.

5.2 Sample and Respondents' Profiles

Figure 2 indicates the sample attributes. Most of the respondents were from a firm size between 300 and 1000 employees and belonged to Directors and above considering firm age of 6 to 10 years.

5.3 Study Variables/Measures

The measures were constructed on multiple-item scales as reviewed from information system literature and the latest studies performed. Some of the items were re-phrased and altered to fit into the scope of the present research. Three domain experts relating to the sample organization were inquired to evaluate measures [40], and a pilot test was carried out to validate the appropriate meaning to the respondent [42]. By using PCFA, the validity of all item scales was confirmed, followed by CFA. The PCFA was

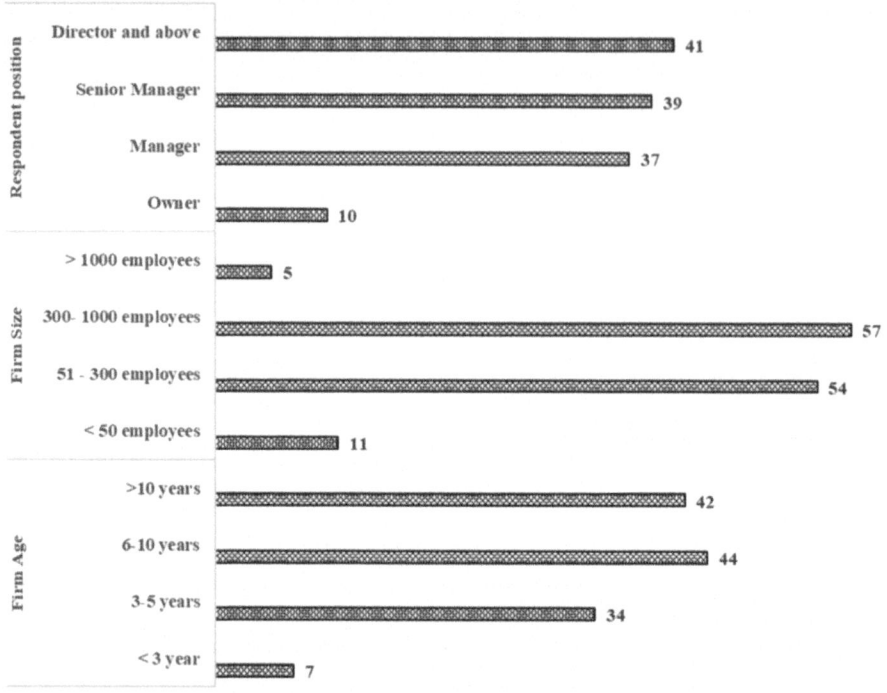

Fig. 2. Sample Profile.

accomplished to examine all items loaded in one factor. Cronbach's alpha (α) appropriate values were found to be greater than 0.7 for the scale reliability. A confirmatory factor analysis (CFA) was performed to validate the measurement model and is considered satisfactory at CMIN/DF = 2.807, CFI = 0.916, RMSEA = 0.071, and SRMR = 0.029 [43].

The instrument was developed by adapting items from similar previous studies. The independent variables Top Management Commitment is assessed with three items (α = 0.789) [36] and IT Infrastructure is assessed with four items (α = 0.882) [36]. The dependent variable Digital Transformation is determined by applying a three-item scale (α = 0.875) [36]. The moderating variable of the digital transformation strategy is calculated using five items (α = 0.885) [36]. The control variable used in the study is Firm size and firm age are important metrics of business value and are evaluated with a scale reformed by [45] and denoted by the natural logarithm of the average of the number of employees and number of years of existence.

6   Research Outcomes

This study adds value to information systems literature and different practices by examining the moderation effect of digital transformation strategy on top management commitment, IT infrastructure, and digital transformation in small and medium-sized organizations using descriptive statistics. Table 2 indicates the descriptive statistics with the mean and standard deviation values along with the correlation between different study variables.

Table 2. Descriptive Statistics.

Variables	0	1	2	3
Mean	3.574	3.152	3.043	3.267
Std. Dev	1.153	1.318	1.233	1.786
Reliability	0.875	0.798	0.882	0.885
Kendall's tau_b				
0 (Digital Transformation)	1			
1 (Top Management Commitment)	0.563***	1		
2 (IT Infrastructure)	0.489***	0.431***	1	
3 (Digital Transformation Strategy)	0.435***	0.374***	0.389***	1
Spearman's rho				
0 (Digital Transformation)	1			
1 (Top Management Commitment)	0.634***	1		
2 (IT Infrastructure)	0.598***	0.513***	1	
3 (Digital Transformation Strategy)	0.545***	0.469***	0.465***	1
*** Correlation is significant at the 0.01 level (2-tailed)				

6.1 Ordinal Regression Method for Moderation Analysis

The association between ordinal outcome variables is examined in the current study i.e., top management commitment, IT infrastructure, digital transformation, and digital transformation strategy. An ordinal, categorical, and five-point Likert scale was used for assessing the study variables. The ordinal categorical results could not be assumed to be normal or to have homogeneous variance. The ordinal regression method was used given that it requires the assumption of parallel lines across each stage of the categorical outcome rather than constant variance and normality [46]. Before running the regression analysis, diagnostic tests were run to check for any preconceived notion violations. There were none of the variables that had values that were missing. Additionally, the SPSS tool was used to analyze the findings using the ordinal regression method. Table 3 represents the outcomes of the ordinal regression method used for data analysis. The variation inflation factor (VIF) was found with a value of 2.16. Figure 3 represents the moderation interactions.

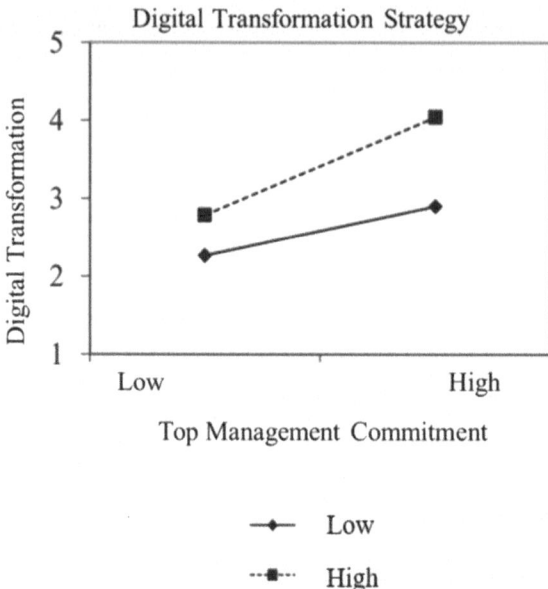

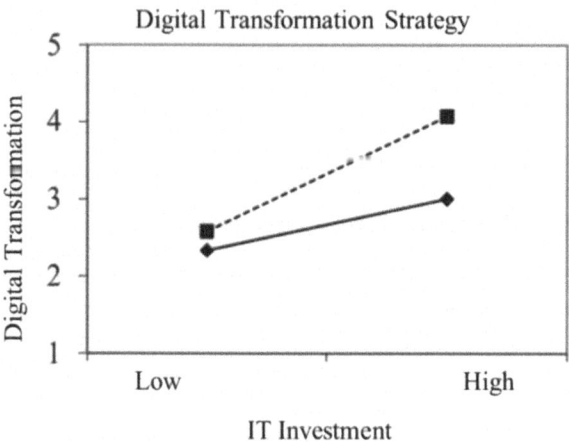

Fig. 3. Moderation Interactions.

7 Discussion

This study aims to explore a new path for IT resources and top management commitment to empowering the digital transformation of enterprises by empirically testing the moderating role of the digital transformation strategy. The findings enrich the insights on IT value creation in the context of digital transformation and the path to achieve digital transformation in enterprises. In this study, the impact of top management commitment, and IT infrastructure on an enterprise's digital transformation is direct and the digital

Table 3. Ordinal Regression (Moderation Analysis).

Variables	Digital Transformation		
Control Variable	Model 1	Model 2	Model 3
Firm Size	0.125***(0.011)	.112***(0.021)	0.026***(0.012)
Firm Age	0.143*** (0.035)	0.167**(0.024)	0.096**(0.008)
Independent Variable			
Top Management Commitment	0.338***(0.016)	0.268***(0.017)	0.145***(0.089)
IT Investment	0.465*** (0.987)	0.321**(0.014)	0.195** (0.091)
Moderating Variable			
Digital Transformation Strategy		0.279***(0.034)	0.178***(0.076)
Interaction			
Top Management Commitment * Digital Transformation Strategy			0.213***(0.086)
IT Investment * Digital Transformation Strategy			0.209***(0.065)
-2 log-likelihood	447.768	472.771	473.754
Likelihood ratio (Chi-Square)	87.256***	113.636***	125.283***
Pesudo R^2 Cox and Snell	0.534	0.597	0.689

Notes: N = 127 1. Unstandardized regression coefficients and standard errors are shown in parentheses.
2. *** Significance at 0.001 level (2-tailed). 3. **Significance at 0.05 level (2-tailed).

transformation strategy plays a moderating role in this process. This result reaffirms that IT investment alone does not guarantee improvement of the firm performance and that business value can only be created when IT resources are integrated with other capabilities, but top management commitment is important. It would be more beneficial and significant to concentrate on strategic capabilities related to digital transformation. This study shows that businesses can achieve a higher degree of digital strategic capabilities by better integrating digital resources to respond to and support the selection and execution of firm strategies. Businesses that have an advantage in their IT infrastructure can do this [1]. Better expectations for digital transformation are met and organizational change and transformation are supported. This outcome fully aligns with certain business value studies on IT. For instance, several academics have demonstrated that various organizational resources and competencies that serve as intermediaries must be used in conjunction with IT to maximize its impact on firm-level outcomes [36] and that strategic competencies have a greater influence on IT-driven business performance as a crucial component of the company's innovative development.

Second, the research demonstrates that digital transformation strategy and IT infrastructure are workable avenues for businesses to pursue digital transformation. Enterprises on this road must have the IT infrastructure skills and resources to support digital transformation objectives. Digital technology is extensively integrated into organizational processes, enabling innovation and change inside the organization and serving as the basis for developing and executing strategies for digital transformation. Enterprise IT can be guided by the digital transformation strategy to produce value that is in line with the transformation objectives. According to [21], they work in tandem to propel enterprise digital transformation. Thus, to adapt and innovate the value generation route that businesses traditionally relied on to preserve competitiveness, this study encourages businesses to invest more in new technologies and use digital technologies [1]. In answer to the present queries for research on digital transformation strategy, this study was conducted. According to some perspectives, businesses must create a digital transformation strategy to handle the complexity of digital technologies and make use of their advantages. This research offers both theoretical and empirical support for these opinions. Third, the process of building IT infrastructure can be facilitated by top management, which is a necessary border condition that allows for digital transformation. Previous research has demonstrated that having strong managerial skills can help implement strategic changes like digital transformation that are successful and boost company performance. The study's findings corroborate this theory and demonstrate how stronger top management participation, support, and leadership may maximize the strategic value of IT investments and convert them into successful digital transformation initiatives. Redesigning company processes, investing in organizational capacities, and putting strategic solutions into practice are just a few of the management concerns that must be addressed to meet digital transformation. According to [47], a top management team possessing the requisite expertise, knowledge, and abilities is therefore more likely to recognize and capitalize on opportunities and steer the effective execution of digital transformation.

7.1 Implications for Research

This study advances the fields of digital transformation and information systems research. First, by examining the value generation path of IT infrastructure in digital transformation, this study expands on research on IT business value. For scholars and practitioners in the IT/IS industry, how businesses develop competitive advantages based on their IT investments has always been a crucial topic. Few studies have examined the role of IT in the context of digital transformation, despite the numerous studies demonstrating the beneficial effects of IT resources on firm performance [23]. Using a digital transformation approach, this study offers concrete proof of the influence of top management commitment and IT infrastructure on digital transformation, generating fresh concepts for IT value generation. Additionally, earlier investigations of moderating factors between IT and firm-level outcomes aid in the development of a research stream on imperative strategic perspective by illustrating the moderating role of digital transformation strategy between top management commitment, IT infrastructure, and transformation performance. Second, by illustrating the influence of the complementary effects of IT resources and digital transformation strategy on digital transformation, this study adds to the body of knowledge already available on the subject. Earlier research has looked at factors including technology utilization and digital transformation strategy that are associated with effective enterprise digital transformation [33]. According to [21], this research has not produced a definitive result regarding the micro-level mechanisms connecting IT, digital transformation strategy, and transformation performance. The impact of IT and digital transformation strategy on digital transformation is examined in this study. Based on a strategic viewpoint, it creates a new avenue for IT-driven digital transformation, which has important theoretical implications for expanding on current research on the mechanics of digital transformation. Third, by examining the role of top management in the process of digital transformation, this study adds to the body of knowledge on organizational management and differentiated value generation. It has been observed that the influence of IT infrastructure on digital strategy and the extent to which it results in digital transformation performance are contingent upon the competencies of upper management. Digital transformation strategy and IT resources can work better together when top management is involved. It can improve how well IT supports the digital transformation strategy and how the strategy encourages the implementation of the digital transformation. With explicit theoretical frameworks for IT investment and digital transformation, these findings improve the boundaries for the development of value from IT resources and their application [18].

7.2 Implications for Practice

This research offers significant perspectives for businesses making IT investments and executing digital transformation. First, businesses going through a digital transformation need to invest in IT infrastructure. Instead of just focusing on the outward appearance of IT investment returns, managers need to concentrate on digital transformation initiatives to realize IT business value. By bolstering businesses' ability to implement digital transformation strategies, IT infrastructure indirectly promotes digital transformation. Therefore, digital strategy should direct managers' decisions about future IT investments. The degree to which IT facilitates and advances the digital transformation plan ought to be a crucial factor. This aids managers in directing the activities of their IT department, assessing the impact of IT investments on their transformation success, streamlining IT resources, and taking advantage of this infrastructure to maximize its relative strength. Secondly, this research can assist managers in tackling the increasing difficulties brought about by new digital resources and skills. According to the report, having a strong IT infrastructure may be a prerequisite for digital transformation, but it may not be sufficient. When employing IT resources for transformation, a digital strategy must provide competitive advantages to steer digital transformation. Managers should therefore seek out chances to invest in digital resources and develop the strategic digital capabilities of their companies. To plan and carry out digital transformation, businesses might create digital transformation strategies through external collaboration and consultation or internal innovation and change. These results can help practitioners manage the enterprise's digital transformation process. Thirdly, it facilitates senior managers' methodical practice and efforts in IT management as well as the creation and execution of strategies. To enable the execution of the digital transformation, top management is crucial for overseeing transformation operations and extracting value from IT. Managers must support, engage, and possess the necessary skills to direct IT in this environment so that it delivers value in a way that is consistent with the strategic objectives of digital transformation. To adapt to the constantly changing external environment, businesses should therefore introduce new leadership roles and update the digital skills and capabilities of their top management teams, either internally (through training) or externally (through recruitment, collaboration, and consulting).

8 Limitations and Future Research Directions

Future research endeavors and the interpretation of our findings must consider several constraints. First off, the validation of this study is limited to a sample of 127 SMEs. Further research must expand the sample data sources and compare the obtained and available results, since such geographical and sample size restrictions may jeopardize the generalizability of the research findings to some degree. Secondly, the nature of digital transformation strategy is the exclusive focus of this study; strategic classification is not considered. Based on the research findings, managers could be unable to pinpoint precise strategic activities. This restriction enables researchers studying digital transformation strategies in the future to examine the mechanisms underlying strategy type differentiation. Third, without delving further into more intricate situational elements in diverse industries, the study's findings are a synopsis and distillation of pertinent theoretical research and the real-world experience of digital transformation in a variety of businesses. Since digital transformation is an industry phenomenon, it is critical to examine conceptual models' micro-foundations in many scenarios. As a result, it is recommended for new academics to build upon and improve the present study findings by establishing additional situations.

Conflict of Interest.   None.

References

1. Vial, G.: Understanding digital transformation: a review and a research agenda. J. Strateg. Inf. Syst. **28**(2), 118–144 (2019)
2. Wade, M., Hulland, J.: The resource-based view and information systems research: review, extension, and suggestions for future research. MIS Q. **28**(1), 107–142 (2004)
3. Mithas, S., Rust, R.T.: How information technology strategy and investments influence firm performance: conjecture and empirical evidence. MIS Q. **40**(1), 223–245 (2016)
4. Wang, Y., Shi, S., Nevo, S., Li, S., Chen, Y.: The interaction effect of IT assets and IT management on firm performance: a systems perspective. Int. J. Inform. Manage. **35**(5), 580–593 (2015)
5. Hess, T., Matt, C., Benlian, A., Wiesb Ck, F.: Options for formulating a digital transformation strategy. MIS Q. Executive **15**(2), 123–139 (2016)
6. Svahn, F., Mathiassen, L., Lindgren, R.: Embracing digital innovation in incumbent firms: how Volvo Cars managed competing concerns. MIS Q. **41**(1), 239–253 (2017)
7. Tsou, H.-T., Chen, J.-S.: How does digital technology usage benefit firm performance? Digital transformation strategy and organizational innovation as mediators. Technol. Anal. Strateg. Manag. **20**(1), 1–14 (2021)
8. Proksch, D., Rosin, A.F., Stubner, S., Pinkwart, A.: The influence of a digital strategy on the digitalization of new ventures: the mediating effect of digital capabilities and digital culture. J. Small Bus. Manag. **11**(2), 1–29 (2021)

9. Li, L., Su, F., Zhang, W., Mao, J.Y.: Digital transformation by SME entrepreneurs: a capability perspective. Inform. Syst. J. **28**(6), 1129–1157 (2018)
10. Chae, H.-C., Koh, C.E., Park, K.O.: Information technology capability and firm performance: role of industry. Inform. Manag, **55**(5), 525–546 (2018)
11. Liang, H., Saraf, N., Hu, Q., Xue, Y.: Assimilation of enterprise systems: the effect of institutional pressures and the mediating role of top management. MIS Q. **31**(1), 59–87 (2007)
12. Hu, Q., Dinev, T., Hart, P., Cooke, D.: Managing employee compliance with information security policies: the critical role of top management and organizational culture. Decis. Sci. **43**(4), 615–660 (2012)
13. Cragg, P., Mills, A., Suraweera, T.: The Influence of IT management sophistication and IT support on IT success in small and medium-sized enterprises. J. Small Bus. Manag. **51**(4), 617–636 (2013)
14. Oreg, S., Bartunek, J.M., Lee, G., Do, B.: An affect-based model of recipients' responses to organizational change events. Acad. Manag. Rev. **43**(1), 65–86 (2018)
15. Talke, K., Salomo, S., Kock, A.: Top management team diversity and strategic innovation orientation: the relationship and consequences for innovativeness and performance. J. Product. Innov. Manag. **28**(6), 819–832 (2011)
16. Osmundsen, K., Iden, J., Bygstad, B.: Digital transformation: drivers, success factors, and implications. In: MCIS 2018 Proceedings, AIS eLibrary, Corfu, p. 37 (2018)
17. Dalenogare, L.S., Benitez, G.B., Ayala, N.F., Frank, A.G.: The expected contribution of Industry 4.0 technologies for industrial performance. Int. J. Product. Econ. **204**, 383–394 (2018). https://doi.org/10.1016/j.ijpe.2018.08.019
18. Karhade, P., Dong, J.Q.: Information technology investment and commercialized innovation performance: dynamic adjustment costs and curvilinear impacts. MIS Q. **45**(3), 1007–1024 (2020)
19. Ravichandran, T.: Exploring the relationships between IT competence, innovation capacity and organizational agility. The J. Strateg. Inform. Syst. **27**(1), 22–42 (2018)
20. Sabherwal, R., Sabherwal, S., Havakhor, T., Steelman, Z.: How does strategic alignment affect firm performance? The roles of information technology investment and environmental uncertainty. MIS Q. **43**(2), 453–474 (2018)
21. Bharadwaj, A., Sawy, O.A.E., Pavlou, P.A., Venkatraman, N.: Digital business strategy: toward a next generation of insights. MIS Q. **37**(2), 471–482 (2013)
22. Matt, C., Hess, T., Benlian, A.: Digital transformation strategies. Bus. Inform. Syst. Eng. **57**(5), 339–343 (2015)
23. Sebastian, I.M., Ross, J.W., Beath, C., Mocker, M., Moloney, K.G., Fonstad, N.O.: How big old companies navigate digital transformation. MIS Q. Executive **16**(3), 197–213 (2017)
24. Tekic, Z., Koroteev, D.: From disruptively digital to proudly analog: a holistic typology of digital transformation strategies. Bus. Horiz. **62**(6), 683–693 (2019)
25. Chanias, S., Myers, M.D., Hess, T.: Digital transformation strategy making in pre-digital organizations: the case of a financial services provider. J. Strateg. Inform. Syst. **28**(1), 17–33 (2019)
26. Barney, J.: Firm resources and sustained competitive advantage. J. Manag. **17**(1), 99–120 (1991)
27. Barney, J.B., Ketchen, D.J., Jr., Wright, M.: The future of resource-based theory: revitalization or decline. J. Manag. **37**(5), 1299–1315 (2011)
28. Shibin, K., Dubey, R., Gunasekaran, A., Hazen, B., Roubaud, D., Gupta, S., Foropon, C.: Examining sustainable supply chain management of SMEs using resource-based view and institutional theory. Ann. Operat. Res. **290**(1), 301–326 (2020)
29. Ilmudeen, A., Bao, Y.: IT strategy and business strategy mediate the effect of managing IT on firm performance: empirical analysis. J. Enterp. Inform. Manag. **33**(6), 1357–1378 (2020)

30. Devaraj, S., Kohli, R.: Performance impacts of information technology: is actual usage the missing link. Manag. Sci. **49**(3), 273–289 (2003)
31. Peng, J., Quan, J., Zhang, G., Dubinsky, A.J.: Mediation effect of business process and supply chain management capabilities on the impact of IT on firm performance: evidence from Chinese firms. Int. J. Inform. Manag. **36**(1), 89–96 (2016)
32. Spanos, Y.E., Lioukas, S.: An examination into the causal logic of rent generation: contrasting Porter's competitive strategy framework and the resource-based perspective. Strat. Manag. J. **22**(10), 907–934 (2001)
33. Sohal, A.S., Fitzpatrick, P.: IT governance and management in large Australian organisations. Int. J. Product. Econ. **75**(1–2), 97–112 (2002)
34. Nambisan, S., Lyytinen, K., Majchrzak, A., Song, M.: Digital innovation management: reinventing innovation management research in a digital world. MIS Q. **41**(1), 223–238 (2017)
35. Wang, H., Feng, J., Zhang, H., Li, X.: The effect of digital transformation strategy on performance: the moderating role of cognitive conflict. Int. J. Conflict Manag. **31**(3), 441–462 (2020)
36. Zhang, X., Xu, Y.Y., Ma, L.: Information technology investment and digital transformation: the roles of digital transformation strategy and top management. Bus. Process Manag. J. **29**(2), 528–549 (2023)
37. Mao, H., Liu, S., Zhang, J., Deng, Z.: Information technology resource, knowledge management capability, and competitive advantage: the moderating role of resource commitment. Int. J. Inform. Manag. **36**(6), 1062–1074 (2016)
38. Haffke, I., Kalgovas, B. and Benlian, A. The role of the CIO and the CDO in an organization's digital transformation. In: Thirty Seventh International Conference on Information Systems, Dublin, pp. 1–20 (2016).
39. NASSCOM (2023). Indian technology industry overview – FY2024E. https://nasscom.in/knowledge-center/publications/technology-sector-india-strategic-review-2024
40. Hair, J.F., Ringle, C.M., Sarstedt, M.: The use of partial least squares (PLS) to address marketing management topics. J. Market. Theory Pract. **19**(2), 135–138 (2011)
41. Podsakoff, P.M., MacKenzie, S.B., Lee, J.Y., Podsakoff, N.P.: Common method biases in behavioral research: a critical review of the literature and recommended remedies. J. Appl. Psychol. **88**(5), 879 (2003)
42. Nunnally, J.C.: An overview of psychological measurement. In: Wolman, B.B. (ed.) Clinical Diagnosis of Mental Disorders, pp. 97–146. Springer US, Boston, MA (1979). https://doi.org/10.1007/978-1-4684-2490-4_4
43. Guide Jr, V.D.R., Ketokivi, M.: Notes from the Editors: Redefining some methodological criteria for the journal★. J. Operat. Manag. **37**(1), v–viii (2015).
44. Arora, K.K., Kapila, R., Kapila, S., Patra, A., Chaudhary, P., Singal, A.: Management of lateral epicondylitis: a prospective comparative study comparing the local infiltrations of leucocyte enriched platelet-rich plasma (L-aPRP), glucocorticoid and normal saline. Malays. Orthop. J. **16**(1), 58 (2022)
45. Mikalef, P., Gupta, M.: Artificial intelligence capability: conceptualization, measurement calibration, and empirical study on its impact on organizational creativity and firm performance. Informat. Manag. **58**(3), 103434 (2021)
46. Tiwari, P., Suresha, B.: Moderation effect of flexibility in projects on senior management commitment in achieving success in financial services IT projects. Int. J. Proj. Organ. Manag. **15**(1), 77–98 (2023)
47. Ukko, J., Nasiri, M., Saunila, M., Rantala, T.: Sustainability strategy as a moderator in the relationship between digital business strategy and financial performance. J. Cleaner Prod. **236**(1), 117626 (2019)

Hashtag and Marketing Campaign on Twitter: From the Spectrum of Smartphone Industry Perspective

Prashant Chaudhary[1]([✉]), Prabha Kiran[2], and Sarika Sharma[3]

[1] WPU School of Business, Dr. Vishwanath Karad MIT World Peace University, Pune, India
prashant.vchaudhary@gmail.com
[2] Westminster International University, Tashkent, Uzbekistan
[3] Symbiosis Institute of Computer Studies and Research, Symbiosis International (Deemed University), Pune, India

Abstract. Social media has completely revolutionized how companies promote their products and engage with their target audience. Traditionally, platforms like X (formerly Twitter) were used for advertisement and promotion of products and brands. Today these platforms are used to run marketing campaigns, known as 'Hashtag Campaign'. The focus is essentially on the propagation of the brand message and promises and engaging the target audience with the brand story and narrative. In this context, the present research focused on sentiment analysis of Indian Smartphone brands' engagement on Twitter with the help of a hashtag marketing campaign. The five major smartphone brands were selected based on the level of customer engagement on Twitter. The data was collected by developing a Twitter account and mining tweets with R language. After the collection of tweets, sentiment analysis was done with the Microsoft Azure Machine Learning tool. The findings were derived from an analysis of nearly 18000 tweets and 87 hashtags. Based on the results it was suggested that the brands need to engage directly with the consumers to build strong brand salience and equity. The brands fetching negative sentiments must focus more on streamlining the delivery of high-quality and feature-loaded products and related services. Here creativity and innovations play crucial roles with the right brand narrative.

Keywords: Hashtag · social media marketing · marketing campaign · Sentiment Analysis · Smartphone industry · Customer engagement

1 Introduction

The world of business is changing swiftly and so are the marketing and branding done by businesses. As we move into the 21st century, it becomes of utmost importance for all businesses to make their statements, promotion campaigns, appeals and offers effective and engaging along with creativity and distinctiveness. Today social media platforms like Twitter, Facebook (Rebranded as Meta in 2021), WhatsApp and so on have emerged as effective marketing channels where there is a vast presence of an audience

A. Mirzazadeh et al. (Eds.): SEMIT 2023, CCIS 2198, pp. 323–342, 2024.
https://doi.org/10.1007/978-3-031-72284-4_20

belonging to different segments [1]. In India, Twitter was launched in 2006 as a micro-blogging platform [2] that allowed users to share short, 140-character posts (also known as "tweets"). In the coming years, the popularity of Twitter increased phenomenally and the number of users subsequently reached around 24 million in 2022. When looking at its audience worldwide, data shows that Twitter has 353 million users so far in 2023. Although it may fall behind platforms like Facebook and Instagram, which have users in the billions, Twitter still has a loyal audience of those who log in regularly [3]. Demographically, India is a young country and according to the United Nations (the UN), almost one-fifth of the world's 15- to 64-year-olds are expected to be Indian by 2030 [4].

The sentiment of tweets in real-time helps to gain insights into what people think and feel about your brand, product, or services. The Twitter sentiment analysis helps to determine whether a tweet is positive, negative, or neutral. Hence, it is valuable for understanding people's feelings and perceptions about your marketing mix elements [5]. However, the major challenge today faced by the companies is 'How' to make a powerful impact on the minds of the customers. This is essential for catching the eyeballs. It is increasingly becoming very difficult for brands to catch and hold the customer's attention and then engage them with the brand. The use of hashtags all started back on August 23, 2007, with a tweet by San Francisco techie and former Google developer Chris Messina. He wrote on Twitter, "How do you feel about using # (pound) for groups. As in #barcamp [msg]?" and the rest is history [6].

1.1 Rationale and Objectives

The major objective of this paper was to delve deep into consumer engagement behaviour, in the context of drastically reducing attention span. This study primarily deals with the way Indian consumers interact with brands and brand campaigns on different social media websites. Here the focus is on Twitter as a medium to run marketing campaigns through hashtags. In the past, it has been observed, especially in the US, the response to online campaigns with hashtags and a message to appeal to the target consumers with prominent brands such as Coca-Cola, Burger King, Redbull, etc. to name a few of those who effectively run such campaigns. Conclusively, the result of the study would make the marketers understand the response of the consumers towards online marketing campaigns on Twitter and the major factors that influence them.

In this study focus was on leading Mobile Phone brands in India that have a significant presence and consumer engagement on Twitter. The secondary data was derived from Statista, to choose the top 5 mobile phone brands for the year 2020, i.e. Samsung, OnePlus, Realme, Vivo and Mi. It was interesting to observe how the way brands communicate with consumers has changed after the upsurge of social media channels.

While earlier marketing and branding campaigns were run through traditional channels like Television, Radio, print media and so on, now been significantly shifted to social media platforms such as Twitter [7]. With the new campaign launched on Twitter, every mobile phone brand wants to increase its engagement with the audience, especially in a country like India. With its huge demographic dividend and increasing number of internet users, the opportunities are endless for all the brands. Twitter was gaining popularity more quickly than Instagram within the Gen Z demographic in India [8].

Even though Twitter has been around for quite some time, it continues to see growth in its user base. Not only that but there are tons of tweets being posted daily, ensuring there's always something interesting being shared. In this study. The major focus was to analyse such hashtag campaigns and analyse the sentiment of the people as in whether they are positive about the campaign, indifferent to the campaign or neutral and finally, whether they have more negative sentiment towards the campaign launched.

1.2 Background and Practical Utility

The study concentrated on 5 major mobile phone brands in India on Twitter and the hashtag campaigns being run by these brands regularly. These brands include Samsung, OnePlus, Vivo, Mi, and Realme. As the mobile Industry is changing constantly as new brands, and improved models are being launched with technical and design upgrades. This scenario has made the consumers spoilt-for-the-choices, since there are numerous options at their disposal. Hence, it becomes imperative for smartphone brands to make their mark in the market which grew even by 9 per cent during the third quarter of 2020 despite Covid-19 [9]. Marketing managers need to concentrate on building an omnichannel approach as it is the best way to appeal to a wide audience, engage with them effectively and convert prospects into customers down the funnel [10, 11]. As Twitter allows the users of different devices to come together, here the marketers can leverage their strengths and competitor's weaknesses.

1.3 Hashtag Commerce

At the most basic level, hashtag commerce relates to the use of hashtags to facilitate and generate commerce across a range of economic situations. As a result, one definition of hashtag commerce is the delivery of commerce capabilities using hashtags, typically in the context of social media. Hashtag commerce involves users including hashtags in their communications to facilitate a range of economic activities, ranging from simply making others aware of an economic opportunity (e.g. a product/service or campaign) to initiating and completing transactions. Since transactions are executed in social media, typically, there will be some structure developed independent of the social media. For example, user credit card information likely is set up on a secured site and linked to the social media site.

Hashtags potentially play a critical role in social commerce. [12] suggested that hashtags were breathing life back into social commerce. Hashtags are versatile; they can be used in different social communication settings, ranging from social media to email to reports or even verbal exchanges. As an example, Chirpify had developed hashtag commerce so that users could gather information from a television ad to order a product: "Brands include a hashtag with their advertising campaign, and when consumers use that hashtag in a Facebook, Twitter or Instagram post, they get to be sent a link to a page with a purchasing form or other related information." [13].

1.4 Relevance and Importance of Hashtags

With the emergence of digital technologies like social media, AI (Artificial Intelligence), ML (Machine Learning), NLP (Natural Language Processing), metaverse and so on;

brands and marketers are not constrained by geography when it comes to diffusion of brand messages, mission and ethos [14]. With digital commerce and social media, practitioners and researchers have become increasingly trying to understand the newer ways and approaches to leverage all these technologies to understand consumer behaviour, psychology and perception. Sentiment analysis is one of the emerging techniques that have the potential to bring precise actionable insights regarding what happening in the minds of the consumers [15].

According to the research by Ad Espresso having at least one hashtag can increase engagement by up to 12.6% [16]. Therefore, this research is expected to be beneficial for marketers who are mulling to increase online engagement on X (Twitter). By concentrating on the reasons why consumers tend to post negative comments or feedback, one can get deep insights into how to improve customer engagement. The overarching objective of this research study was to identify rational and emotional reasons [17] behind negative feedback and find ways that help brands turn negative feedback into positive sentiments. Here the objective is to improve online engagement and generate positive and insightful user-generated content.

2 Review of Literature

2.1 Key Concepts Theories and Studies

Social media has become one of the most valuable sources of data and insights for businesses regarding consumer perception in many industries and sectors such as finance, retail, E-commerce, hospitality and so on. It has also emerged as a valuable source of information for the users. They can obtain information about the product and brands from the reviews and comments posted by other users. This phenomenon has led businesses to adopt the omnichannel approach and thereby strengthen their presence on different social media portals depending on the category in which they are operating. For instance, various research studies have been conducted on Twitter sentiment analytics focused on different brands across industries [18]. Researchers studied interesting patterns and various insights to help digital marketers and brand managers understand the trend of viral tweets. For this purpose, millions of tweets are being analysed in the categories of content, sentiment, motive and richness including social learning and activism [19]. One other significant aspect of campaigns can be seen in political propaganda promoted by different political parties as was seen in the US investigation into Russian interference in the US election where the results were significant as it was estimated about 4.9 per cent of liberal tweets were done by bots followed by 6.2 per cent of conservative tweets [20]. The researchers are now upscaling the research to appeal to the people from where the tweet originated.

The twitter was being used for the analysis of brand image at different times and locations through a Support Vector Machine (SVM). The objective was to enhance accuracy and it went up to 80 per cent in feature selection labelling tweets as positive, negative and neutral [21]. The research study focusing on SVM usage in the analysis part reportedly increased the accuracy by 80 per cent. In this research study authors focused more on sentiment analysis of hashtag campaigns. One of the proposed models was framed for Online Social Networks (OSN) where the data was collected from Twitter,

Facebook, MySpace, and Blogs where the informal conversation was recorded instead of formal surveys. The study carried out was on Samsung Galaxy and the model framed was for high-end managers where they can easily understand the public pulse and market share [22].

According to researchers, big data of user-generated content (UGC) on social media are equipped with potential value-driven drivers for brand managers. The researchers did text mining with Latent Dirichlet Allocation (LDA) and Sentiment Analysis on 1.7 million unique tweets for 20 brands in categories of fast food, Department Store, Footwear, electronics, and Telecommunications. It was found that product launches, service specifications and promotional offers were the topics of interest to consumers, followed by new brand launches in different industries. Hence, more accurate results can be obtained by doing a company-specific analysis of positive and negative tweets [23]. The major focus here is on user-generated content for brands across industries and sectors not of a similar nature which formed the major research gap in the study. In many research studies based on the correlation between a brand's social media presence and performance and the resulting Marketing Outcomes; it was found that the buying decision is positively influenced by positive comments and reviews [24]. However, the majority of these research studies conducted were about Facebook and Instagram. Hence, the Research Gap was very evident. Since many research studies focused more on Facebook, the same study if applied to Twitter, might result in different results. Hence this research primarily focuses on the sentiments developed by the users of different mobile phone brands on the hashtag campaign run by these brands.

2.2 Identified Research Gap and Knowledge Construction

Prior research studies have majorly focused on financial analysis, banking and other trends of viral tweets, covering more generalised trends instead of a focused area study. In this study authors focused on the leading mobile phone brands and the data was collected from a mix of tweets, and retweets related to a particular mobile phone brand. There were research studies that categorically involved opinion mining. In this study, authors categorically focused on hashtag campaigns of the companies. The major challenge in the collection of data through Twitter is the limitation and comparison of data available for different brands such as mobile phones because the different features are promoted by different brands.

The research study by [25] focused largely on different features promoted by brands. However, this study faced certain limitations as information related to features of all these smartphone brands was not well organised on Twitter. Such a scenario makes the comparison difficult. In this research, the author's major focus was on the analysis of hashtag campaigns by these mobile phone brands and their impact on users' perceptions. Here the perception of the users that are active on Twitter can only be assessed. For instance, various research studies were conducted to analyse the impact of hashtag campaigns on Twitter on US politics after the 2016 presidential elections and the type of tweets that were able to influence the voter's perceptions and ideological inclinations. In the context of marketing management, according to Customer Experience Report 2023 published by NTT DATA [26], enabling easy collection of feedback across integrated touchpoints is the key to creating a hyper-personalised experience.

A review of these research studies formed the research scope for this study as that has a business angle, specific to the smartphone industry on Twitter in India. Few research studies were conducted on the online engagement of Twitter users with major gambling brands. The intensity of engagement was measured with a sole focus on tweets posted by the companies and retweets by the users. The major focus of this research work was on sentiment analysis on hashtag campaigns on Twitter of major smartphone brands in India that have a strong fan following on their Twitter handles. [27].

2.3 Key Debates and Controversies

The application of Big Data plays an important role in analysis. A Twitter analysis was done on HSBC, and 45 per cent of tweets expressed positivity, 28 per cent of negative opinions followed by 26 per cent of neutral tweets. This data could further be used in analysing why there were more positive tweets on a specific date and why the negative tweets increased during certain days consecutively. It also included the identification of that factors were there in competition or exogenous variables [28]. The researchers are working on a technique to provide automatic feedback based on data collected from Twitter through opinion mining. The data was analysed for mobile phones with 80 per cent accuracy in sentimental analysis with fast and valuable feedback to the respective brands and business entities [29]. The major advantage of online engagement through platforms like Twitter is continuous user engagement as was evident in a study done on gambling brands on Twitter where 7 well-known gambling brands in the UK such as Bet 365, Betfair, Betfred, Coral, Ladbrokes, Paddy Power, and William Hill posted between 89 and 202 tweets a day for continuous consumer engagement. [30].

As the popularity of Twitter is increasing, it is proving to be massively popular for both informal communication and decisive strategy in politics and business. In the 2008 U.S. presidential election, it was estimated that the use of Twitter was done to target key constituencies to enable continuous engagement with potential voters by maintaining mass communication [31]. One such speech was given by Barrack Obama where he mentioned 'Twitter Town Hall' to engage citizens of the United States. He even went on to launch the hashtag campaign #AskObama to ask him questions and many citizens utilized this unique way to communicate from anywhere across the United States. [32].

It has been observed by many researchers that social media platforms will be at the core of the economy in the future. A study was carried out on Dutch Tweets for 24 different brands, including goods and services. The findings indicated that services received more negative sentiment tweets than products. Thus, the managers for the services-oriented brand can understand as to what are the reasons why the customers are receiving negative feedback and work on improving the services for the same [33]. The major focus of the research paper was on products and services and the comparison of negative feedback, but the topic of our research is more of a comparison among mobile phone brands. The research is done on the role of social media in consumer decision-making and the advertisements which lead to buying actions. The research gap here is that the concentration is on advertisement and different social media platforms and we are majorly focused on Twitter hashtag campaigns with a focus on mobile brands across India.

2.4   Industry Profile

The smartphone market in India was growing at a faster pace and has overtaken the US to become the 2nd largest smartphone market in the world. This market witnesses around 7 per cent year-on-year (Y-o-Y) growth. This growth in the adoption of smartphones was supported by increased internet penetration, access and cheaper rates. According to Ericsson's Mobility Report 2023, India had roughly 10 million 5G subscriptions by the end of 2022. It was expected to reach 700 million, or 57 per cent of all mobile subscribers, by the end of 2028. This would make India the fastest-growing 5G region globally [34]. This owing to the key investment initiatives by different Mobile phone brands in India. Under the 'Make in India' scheme, Xiaomi started its manufacturing in India and also started exporting from India. In 2018, Samsung initiated manufacturing in Noida, by opening the world's largest mobile phone factory then with the capacity to produce around 12 million mobile phones every year. The phones manufactured here comprised both low-end end as well as flagship smartphones like the Samsung Galaxy S9 series. In 2020, Samsung announced the manufacturing plant in India for manufacturing smartphone displays to leverage different benefits announced by the Ministry of Electronics and Information Technology, which consequently increased its in-house production of smartphones. Joining this growth spree, OnePlus also invested around INR 1000 crore in a research and development facility in Hyderabad. Further, it expanded its exports from the Noida plant to the US and European Union markets from India [35]. Meanwhile, Oppo and Nokia resolved the global patent dispute and forged the cross-license agreement [36].

Apple has been selling iPhones in India since 2008, held a mere 2 per cent market share in the Indian smartphone market in 2019 subsequently increased its market share to 4 per cent by 2022 [37]. Looking at the appetitive for premium smartphones among young Indian consumers and as part of its China + 1 strategy, Apple was Apple also concentrating its supply chain in and around the Indian market. By the beginning of 2023, Apple captured almost 58 per cent of the market share in India in the ultra-premium smartphone segment. India emerged as one of the very few countries where smartphones of almost all smartphone brands are being manufactured, which could happen because of the development of the entire value chain and ecosystem [38].

This is evident smartphone companies are deriving benefits from programs and initiatives run by the Government of India coupled with the Production-Linked Incentive (PLI) scheme. With rising geopolitical tensions and burgeoning trade wars, reconfiguration of the supply chains is happening across the world [39]. The major challenge thereby lies in promoting and branding in the highly competitive smartphone market. Here one of the keys to success is to leverage social media platforms to create the required buzz and consumer engagement. This leads to positive sentiments about the marketing campaigns and thereby enhances brand equity.

3   Research Methodology and Data Analysis

Following were the steps followed to create a Twitter developer account:

STEP 1: Authors logged into https://developer.twitter.com/ with their Twitter handle credentials this was followed by clicking on Apply for a developer account.

STEP 2: Now primary reason for using the Twitter developer tools needs to be selected. For this research study, the primary motive was Academic.

STEP 3: After selecting the purpose, verifying the Twitter Username, was done to a developer account.

STEP 4: Step 4 involves filling in all the data for the organization for this study data was the Christ University and the motive filled was for the Master Thesis.

STEP 5: Describing Intended Use of Twitter API. The current study used the hashtags generated by the five mobile companies and scrapping the tweets to analyse the positive, negative and neutral sentiments of the people.

STEP 6: Describe the planned use of the features of the developer account. Here since the publishing of the master thesis was also taken into account, the information might be published in Government entities such as public universities. Therefore 2nd option was selected as shown below.

STEP 7: Accepting the Developer Agreement and verifying the email account.

STEP 8: The application is under review and within a few days confirmation as to your account has been verified and the developer account is approved.

3.1   Analysis and Interpretation Tools

Data Collection.   This is the first step when data is collected from different social media platforms. The data is a row that needs to be refined and converted into meaningful insights. Therefore, here text analytics and natural language processing are used to extract and classify the data.

Text Preparation.   This step involves cleaning data so that irrelevant content such as signs doesn't act as a hindrance for extracting tools in processing correct outcomes.

Sentiment Detection and Classification.   This step involves the extraction of sentences with reviews, comments, and opinions. Sentences with subjective expressions (opinions, beliefs, and views) are retained and sentences containing objective communication (facts and factual information) are removed. These sentences are classified in sentiments of positive, negative and neutral characteristics. For the current study, Microsoft Azure Learning was used to perform sentiment analysis on the collected data.

Following are the Steps Followed in Sentiment Analysis

Step 1: Copying the text column which we need for sentiment analysis to a separate sheet. Here we take the example of #AskMadhav.

Step 2: Removing Duplicate Values in the text so that the analysis is as accurate as possible.

Step 3: Select Microsoft Azure Machine Learning Tool from Add-ins.

Step 4: After selecting the tool, the following steps need to be followed. Once Azure Machine Learning Tool opens up, select Text Sentiment Analysis.

Step 5: Once the command is run, information will be displayed as follows, giving the score and sentiment.

3.2 Data Analysis

SAMSUNG. For the Samsung Brand, a total of 24 Hashtags were collected and the following are the results:

The highest count of tweets extracted was for the hashtag #GalaxyS20FE with 2937 tweets and scores as shown in Fig. 1.

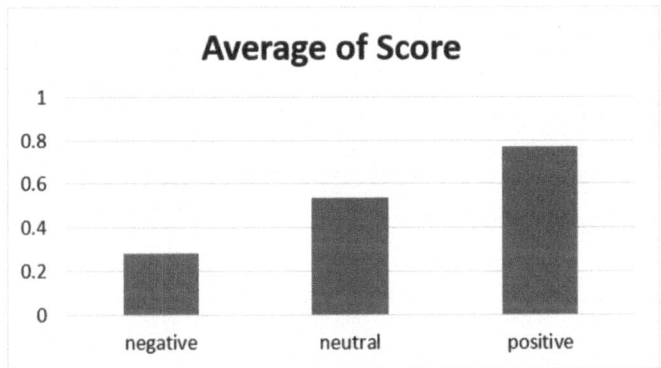

Fig. 1. Average Score for #GalaxyS20FE

The major reason this hashtag received so much reaction was due to the following factors:

Buzz Creator. Samsung GalaxyS20FE is also known as Fan Edition and this was the prime reason there was so much buzz unlike the S20 Ultra which was initially doing well but then the sales volume of S20 and S20 plus rose along the volume and Samsung decided to launch the S20 fan edition.

Price Differentiator. Samsung Galaxy S20 FE, price range was around INR 50,000, in India and it is interesting to note that Samsung has phones in almost all the price range but this phone was kept at neither too costly nor too cheap. It is also interesting to note that in December 2020, renowned tech Youtuber MKBHD also gave the best phone award to Samsung S20 FE, thus indicating that the positive sentiment was justi-fied.

Below are the top 10 hashtags with positive sentiment and the greatest number of count of tweets from the 24 hashtags for Samsung (Refer to Fig. 2). It was impera-tive to see overall positive sentiment in the tweets with maximum sentiment touching close to 78 per cent. Though #GalaxyNote20Ultra has the highest positive score than #GalaxyS20FE, its count of tweets was less. The most negative sentiments were received for #GalaxyBudsPro and #SamsungUnpacked. If it is analysed further major reason for negative sentiment in these hashtags is that many consumers were not able to receive the buds ordered on time and Samsung's unpacked event was to create the buzz for the surprise products which may have let down the consumers as they might have been demanding more.

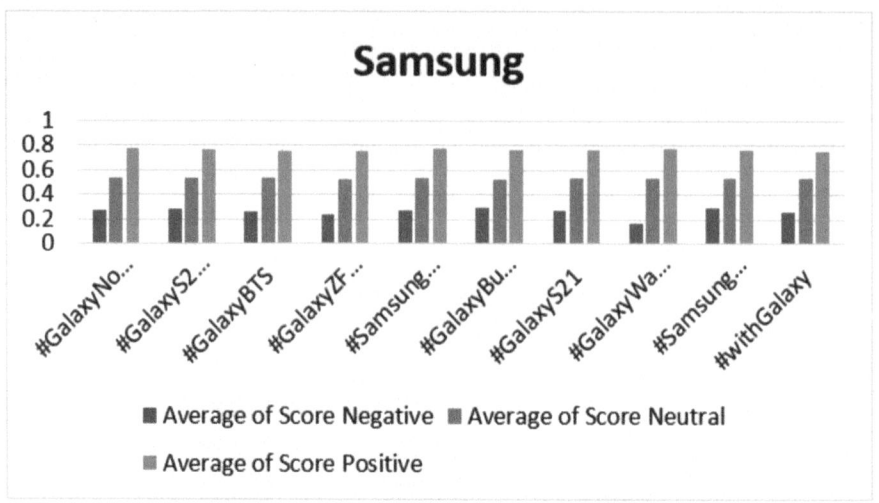

Fig. 2. Top 10 hashtags based on counts of Tweets for Samsung

REALME. For the Realme brand, 28 hashtags were collected for analysis and the following were the results: The highest count of tweets extracted was for the hashtag #realme with 2001 tweets Refer to Fig. 3.

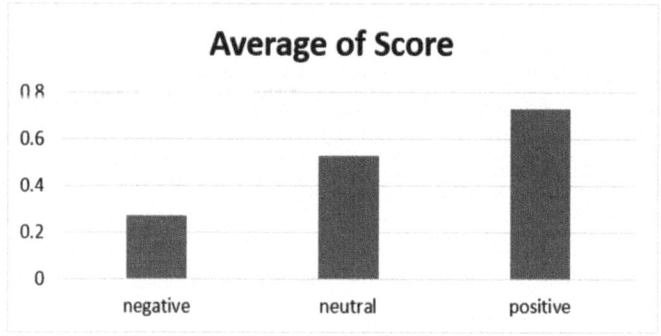

Fig. 3. Average Score for #realme

The #realme hashtag was the general hashtag used by its users for different products and services as well as engagement. By using #realme, users engaged with the brand with topics such as Realme smart TV and Smart Watch, asking the CEO of the company about the latest rollout of 5G smartphones and the after-sale services of the products.

The average score of the top 10 hashtags for Realme is shown in Fig. 4. It can be seen from the figure that #AskMadhav had the highest positive sentiment from all the hashtags. The reason for such engagement was the direct interaction of the CEO of the company with the consumers. When he listened to the queries and responded to them, it enhanced the consumer trust. When the information or insight directly comes from the CEO, it becomes easy to apprehend it and make a positive impact. While analysing the negative sentiment, it was found that #realmeUI and #realme7 series had the highest score. Such insights and feedback need to be studied by brands and improvements need to be made.

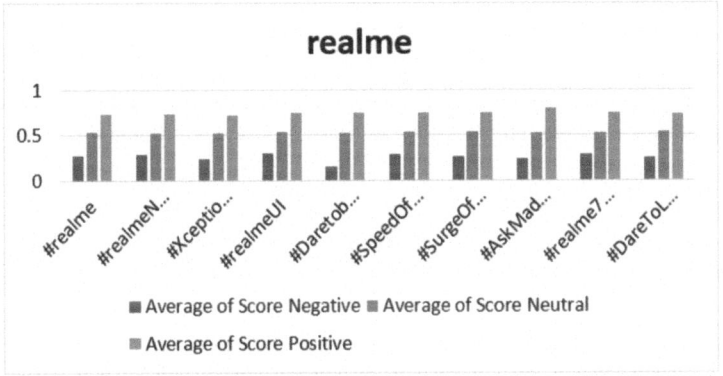

Fig. 4. Top 10 hashtags on the basis of counts of Tweets for Realme

XIAOMI. For the MI brand, 15 hashtags were collected for analysis and the following were the results. The highest count of tweets extracted was for the hashtag #Mi10i tweets. Refer to Fig. 5.

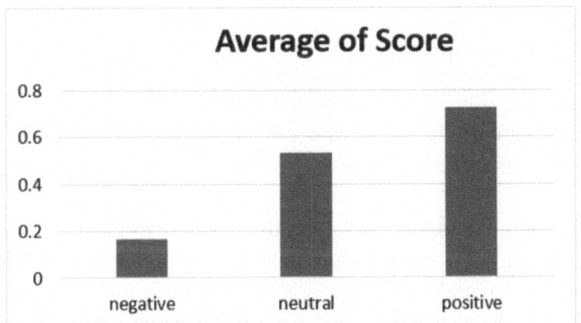

Fig. 5. Average Score for #Mi10i10

As shown in Fig. 5, it can be observed that there were more negative sentiments with a total count of 283 and from them 186 as negative and only 44 responses were positive. MI10I was launched in the Indian market in 2021. The phone was one of the flagship products launched by Mi. According to the MI, "I" in the phone stands for India and according to the experts, it is said to be curated especially for Indian Markets. This model was reportedly competing with OnePlus Nord, and according to the tech experts, the phone was indeed giving competition to OnePlus Nord significantly. One of the prime reasons was the pricing range of this product, which plays a crucial role in value-conscious markets like India.

However, it was difficult to figure out the exact reasons for such negative sentiment. Figure No. 6, depicts the average score of the top 10 hashtags for Xiaomi. The highest positive sentiment aggregator for the MI was #PatchWall and #PowerYourCreativity. #PatchWall was the campaign used for Smart TV promotion by Xiaomi. #PowerYour-Creativity was the hashtag campaign used for promoting the Mi10 Tone the flagship phone launched by Xiaomi. The brand message was to power creativity using Mi10T. The highest negative sentiment score can be seen for the #NoMiWithoutYou which was used as a gratitude campaign to the users as Xiaomi turned 6 to thank the users (Fig. 6).

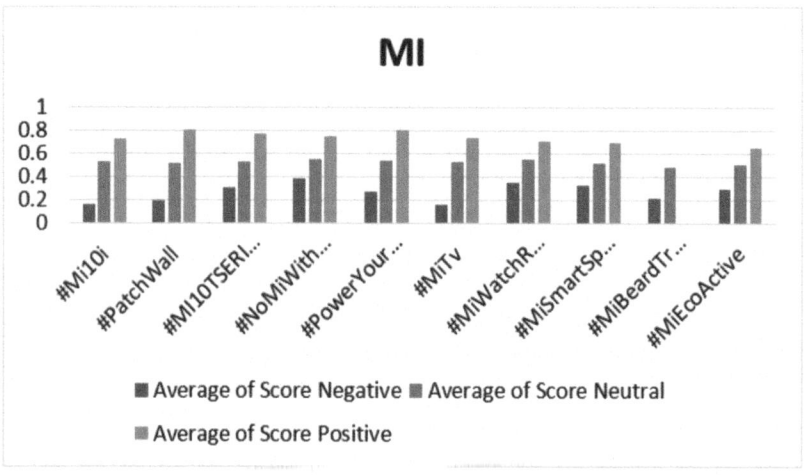

Fig. 6. The top 10 hashtags based on counts of Tweets for Xiaomi

For the OnePlus brand, 11 hashtags were collected for analysis and the following were the results. The highest count of tweets was extracted for the hashtag #TheChosenOne as shown in Fig. 7.

The #TheChosenOne campaign was run by OnePlus to promote Ear Buds and the main aim was to promote at least 100 sets by retweeting. It was observed that there were 501 positive tweets and the average score was also high for the brand with 73 per cent. According to the report by Counterpoint Research, Oppo, along with OnePlus and Realme, captured an overall market share of around 16 per cent [40]. With this, Oppo emerged as the second-biggest smartphone brand in the world, overtaking Apple in terms of market share by mid-2021 [41]. The focus target group of these Buds was the OnePlus customer base. According to a major tech blog, 'Android Authority', OnePlus was successful in the campaign because OnePlus had done a great job tailoring the earphones to the pre-existing customer base. Figure No. 8 shows the top 10 hashtags for the OnePlus and the Count of tweets for the same.

#BreakTheLoop was the campaign launched by OnePlus for the launch of the One-Plus 8 smartphone. The major reason for such a launch was to create a Buzz in the market with the launch of the OnePlus 8. The #BreakTheLoop implies that the launch

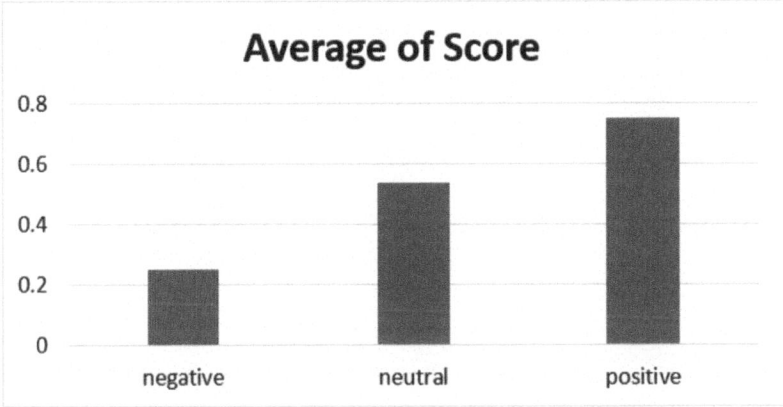

Fig. 7. The Average Score for #TheChosenOne for Xiaomi

will include something unique or out of the box. The highest negative sentiment was also seen for the same hashtag, indicating higher consumer engagement with a mix of views by the consumer (Fig. 8).

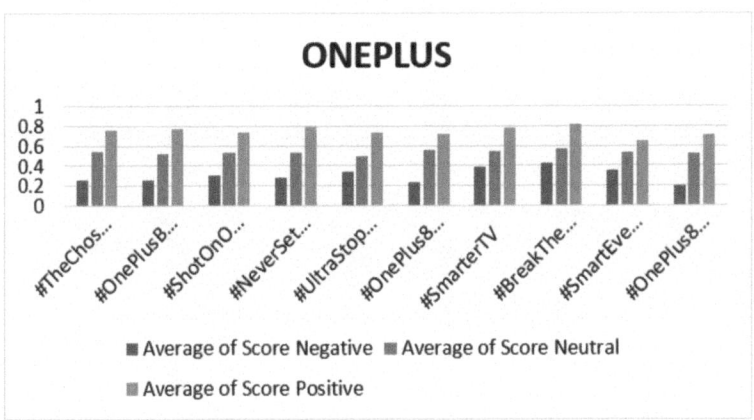

Fig. 8. The top 10 hashtags based Top 10 hashtags based on counts of Tweets for OnePlus

VIVO. For the VIVO mobile phone brand, a total of 9 hashtags were analysed and the results are as follows. The highest count of tweets was extracted for #PhotographyRedefined with 484 tweets as shown in Fig. 9.

The #PhotographyRedefined campaign was run by Vivo to promote the flagship feature of its smartphones, the camera. As given in Fig. 10 there were 8 hashtags used for vivo. It also shows a count of Tweets for the same. As is indicated in Fig. 10, #PotraitOnvivoX50Series got the maximum average score indicative of the photography campaign launched by the company. When it comes to negative sentiment, it was highest

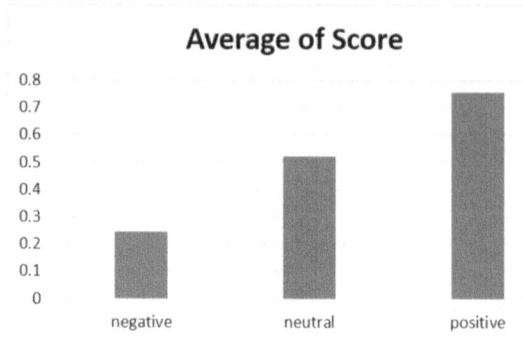

Fig. 9. Average score for #PhotographyRedefined based on the count of Tweets for Vivo

for #Slimmest5G phones which was indicative that people did not accept the slim design launched by Vivo to the level expected by the brand.

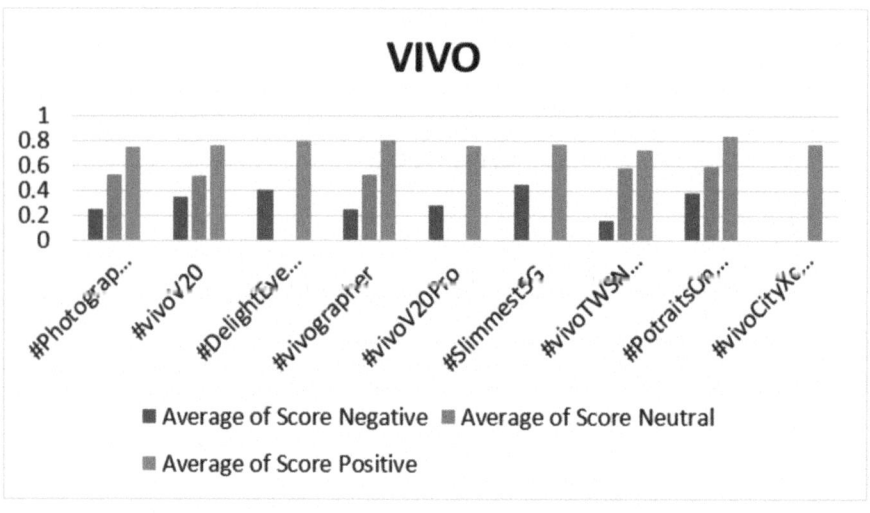

Fig. 10. The Top 10 hashtags based on count of Tweets for vivo

4   Findings

In this research, undertaken on hashtag and marketing campaigns, various factors were found to be influencing the customer engagement level and quality [42]. Firstly, creativity plays a very decisive role for the brands to create the desired level of online engagement with the consumer. For instance, in the case of OnePlus, "#TheChosenOne" and Vivo "#PhotographyRedefined". However, a standard tweet using the product name or the brand name may also be sufficient to enable a connection between the brand and audience as was seen in the case of Samsung (#GalaxyS0FE), Realme (#realme) and Xiaomi (#Mi10i).

When it comes to negative sentiment expressed by the consumers such as for Galaxy Unpacked, it could initially act as the event where the company is trying to raise buzz in their favour. Still, if the products are not according to expectations, it might generate negative sentiments. It was also evident from the #GalaxyBudsPro that consumers expressed negative sentiment because delivery for many consumers was late. This was the direct message for the company executives as to what level of efficiency the consumers want such brands to deliver. Looking at the case of Realme phones, it was seen that #realme had the highest positive sentiment, indicating that the brand was successful in creating its positive image among consumers.

In the case of #AskMadhav, where CEO of Realme, Madhav Sheth took questions directly from the consumers and addressed them one-on-one, creating a positive perception of the brand in the minds of the consumers. This essentially leads to winning the mind share and subsequently the wallet share. This type of engagement enhances the positive sentiments through a direct dialogue between the CEO happened with the target audience, which consequently leads to the establishment of trust between the brand and consumers.

During the COVID-19 pandemic and standoffs at the border, consumer sentiments for Chinese brands were not very favourable in India because of the rising geopolitical tension between the two neighbouring countries [43]. Hence, in such a scenario, the CEO interacting with the customers through a crucial touchpoint such as Twitter engagement can be seen as a positive step to create a positive image of the brand and maintain customer loyalty. Hence the success of any hashtag campaign depends on creativity, quality, and relevance of the content. The product features and quality should go hand in hand with the brand promise. The brands need to understand customer sentiments, tastes, priorities, preferences and so on to make them sustainably resonate with their brands [44].

5   Conclusion and Theoretical Implications

It is evident that every generation wants self-expression, but for Gen Z customers, self-expression is significantly different from previous generations. They are increasingly aligning their preferences with considerations like brand image, brand ethos, social responsibility initiatives, sustainability aspects, ethical marketing, corporate governance practices, and many more [45, 46]. They are getting huge exposure to information at the click of a button and at the same time every aspect of their life is documented through various social media channels. On top of that their self-expression is not singular but multi-faceted and complex [47]. In this context, marketers and sales professionals need to have a razor-sharp focus not only on the data but on consumer sentiments as well. Marketers should analyse and leverage it on a real-time basis to obtain actionable insights and make data-led decisions [48, 49]. For long-term success, businesses need to constantly leverage emerging digital technologies and tools to innovate on how they can provide personalised, one-on-one conversations with their customers [50]. In this context, techniques like sentiment analysis play a crucial role in winning over consumer trust. Traditionally, there used to be a marketing department which used to overlook and control the digital marketing function as a sub-section. But today every marketer is essentially a digital marketer and needs to gather, organise, and transform data into insights, continuously. Hence, it should be hailed as an organic process with an agile approach.

6   Practical Implications

In today's business world, market dynamics are increasingly being shaped by consumer conversations. The strategic integration of Direct-to-consumer (D2C), social media and E-commerce has brought unparalleled opportunities for marketers. Social Media Platforms like Facebook, YouTube, WhatsApp, X (Twitter) and Instagram are not only facilitating communication between brands and consumers but also virtual marketplaces [51]. In this context, this research study helps brands to recognise the distinct preferences of consumers across platforms like Twitter. It is not just a nuance but a strategic imperative to leverage human co-marketing and positive E-Word-of-mouth (E-WoM), which is key to success in today's connected world. Techniques of sentiment analysis are taking a paradigm shift as without programming, one can perform sentiment analysis on the data with tools from Excel. Marketers can work on improving the sentiment analysis and more new techniques can be explored for data scrapping and sentiment analysis which provide more accurate results in the data [52].

In this study, it was observed that to make the hashtag campaign to be successful, the hashtags need to be creative, concise and clear. Besides that, the campaign needs to be supported by direct engagement of the key people of the company, which translates into enhancement in trust and value of engagement. Brands like Realme and OnePlus are using the strategy to engage with consumers by bringing in their top leaders to directly interact with the audience. Madhav Sheth of Realme, and Pete Lau using the #TheChosenOne, also indicate the confidence the leaders have in their product and brand. In the context of the current geopolitical scenario, ongoing trade wars, complexities in trade negotiations, and the multi-polarisation of the world; brands must engage with consumers of different nationalities with a polycentric approach. This would help them to resonate with the customers and build trust. For instance, the launching of the all-new flagship #Mi10i where the 'I' stands for India creates sustainable goodwill for the brand [53].

7   Limitations and Scope for Future Research

The major challenge in the collection of data through Twitter is the limitation and comparison of data available for different brands such as mobile phones, because of the different features being promoted by different brands. The limitation of the study was the limited data extracted from the Twitter API as it only lets you extract the past 1 per cent of the data of the last 7 days. If this limitation could be reduced, researchers may observe significant changes in results and more accurate analysis of the hashtags can collected. The study was limited by the data collection as Twitter only lets users mine 1 per cent of the past seven days' data. The sentiment analysis of hashtags collected can be studied further and trends can be studied continuously for a year for more accurate and comprehensive analysis. The research can also be focused on different geographical regions of the country and sentiments can be studied in depth to understand the highest number of tweets from which part of the country. Besides that, sentiment analysis by using tools like Microsoft Azure Machine Learning may not recognize and analyse the sarcasm, context, facial expression, voice tone and modulation and metacommunication aspects of the post.

This research highlights the scope of similar kinds of studies that can be conducted for other industries and sectors. This can be very useful for business organisations in industries like telecom, retail, hospitality and so on to get on the pulse of the consumers. More comprehensive, holistic and accurate results can be achieved if the mining is done consistently for an extended period.

Some of the future research studies can be taken on these emerging areas such as smartphone consumer behaviour and hashtag adoption, innovation in hashtag strategies for smartphone launch, social media influencers and brand alliances, real-time analytics and hashtag performance metrics, and global trends and cultural sensitivity. It would be interesting to explore whether short-term strategies may impact long-term brand loyalty in another research study [54].

References

1. Wang, Y., Guo, J., Yuan, C., Li, B.: Sentiment analysis of twitter data. Appl. Sci. **12**, 11775 (2022). https://doi.org/10.3390/app122211775
2. Chaudhary, P., Kiran, P., Kate, N., Pandey, S.: Experiential tourism – role and application of micro-targeting in enhancing customer experience, engagement and loyalty. J. Inf. Optim. Sci. **43**, 1463–1473 (2022). https://doi.org/10.1080/02522667.2022.2139929
3. Rosário, A.T., Dias, J.C.: Marketing strategies on social media platforms. Int. J. E-Bus. Res. **19**, 1–25 (2023). https://doi.org/10.4018/IJEBR.316969
4. Mandavia, M.: Why India Isn't the New China. https://www.livemint.com/economy/why-india-isn-t-the-new-china-11705651235391.html#:~:text=Summary,investors'%20and%20manufacturers'%20radar (2024)
5. Chaudhary, P., Kiran, P., Shimpi, S.: Understanding the impact of marketing outcomes from the hashtags of the wellness industry: twitter perspective. J. Content Community Commun. **16**(8), 92–105 (2022). https://doi.org/10.31620/JCCC.12.22/08
6. Jenders, M., Kasneci, G., Naumann, F.: Analyzing and predicting viral tweets. In: Proceedings of the 22nd International Conference on World Wide Web. pp. 657–664. ACM, Rio de Janeiro Brazil (2013). https://doi.org/10.1145/2487788.2488017
7. Blackburn, K., Boris, K.: Social media data analytics – using big data for big consumer reach. SSRN J. (2020). https://doi.org/10.2139/ssrn.3707859
8. Sharma, A., Ghose, U.: Sentimental analysis of twitter data with respect to general elections in India. Procedia Comput. Sci. **173**, 325–334 (2020). https://doi.org/10.1016/j.procs.2020.06.038
9. Kaur, H., Ahsaan, S.U., Alankar, B., Chang, V.: A proposed sentiment analysis deep learning algorithm for analyzing COVID-19 tweets. Inf. Syst. Front. **23**, 1417–1429 (2021). https://doi.org/10.1007/s10796-021-10135-7
10. Chaudhary, P.V.: Retail marketing in the modern age. SAGE, Los Angeles (2016)

11. Chaudhary, P., Singh, A., Sharma, S.: Understanding the antecedents of omni-channel shopping by customers with reference to fashion category: the Indian millennials' perspective. YC. **22**, 104–124 (2021). https://doi.org/10.1108/YC-05-2021-1327

12. O'Brien, C.: How to Use Hashtags Effectively on Social Media, https://digitalmarketinginstitute.com/blog/how-to-use-hashtags-in-social-media. Last accessed 28 Dec 2023

13. Soper, T.: Chirpify lets you purchase products seen on TV by using a hashtag. https://www.geekwire.com/2014/chirpify-actiontags/ (2014)

14. Chakraborti, J., Chaudhary, P., Dutta, A.: Antecedents to the Creation of Effective and Disruptive Business Models for Start-Ups by Leveraging Metaverse – An Interpretive Structural Modelling Approach. JCCC. 17, (2023). https://doi.org/10.31620/JCCC.09.23/16

15. Taherdoost, H., Madanchian, M.: Artificial Intelligence and Sentiment Analysis: a review in competitive research. Computers **12**, 37 (2023). https://doi.org/10.3390/computers12020037

16. Gotter, A.: The 29 Instagram Statistics You Need to Know in 2021. AdEspresso by Hootsuite (2021)

17. Stieglitz, S., Dang-Xuan, L.: Emotions and information diffusion in social media—sentiment of microblogs and sharing behavior. J. Manag. Inf. Syst. **29**, 217–248 (2013). https://doi.org/10.2753/MIS0742-1222290408

18. Souza, T., Kolchyna, O., Treleaven, P., Aste, T.: Twitter Sentiment Analysis Applied to Finance: A Case Study in the Retail Industry (2015)

19. Samuel, J., Garvey, M., Kashyap, R.: That Message Went Viral?! Exploratory Analytics and Sentiment Analysis into the Propagation of Tweets. http://arxiv.org/abs/2004.09718 (2020)

20. Badawy, A., Ferrara, E., Lerman, K.: Analyzing the digital traces of political manipulation: the 2016 Russian Interference Twitter Campaign. In: 2018 IEEE/ACM International Conference on Advances in Social Networks Analysis and Mining (ASONAM), pp. 258–265. IEEE, Barcelona (2018). https://doi.org/10.1109/ASONAM.2018.8508646

21. Cho, S.W., Cha, M.S., Kim, S.Y., Song, J.C., Sohn, K.-A.: Investigating temporal and spatial trends of brand images using twitter opinion mining. In: 2014 International Conference on Information Science & Applications (ICISA), pp. 1–4. IEEE, Seoul, South Korea (2014). https://doi.org/10.1109/ICISA.2014.6847417

22. Das, T.K., Acharjya, D.P., Patra, M.R.: Opinion mining about a product by analyzing public tweets in Twitter. In: 2014 International Conference on Computer Communication and Informatics, pp. 1–4. IEEE, Coimbatore, India (2014). https://doi.org/10.1109/ICCCI.2014.6921727

23. Liu, X., Burns, A.C., Hou, Y.: An investigation of brand-related user-generated content on Twitter. J. Advert. **46**, 236–247 (2017). https://doi.org/10.1080/00913367.2017.1297273

24. John, L.K., Emrich, O., Gupta, S., Norton, M.I.: Does "liking" lead to loving? the impact of joining a brand's social network on marketing outcomes. J. Mark. Res. **54**, 144–155 (2017). https://doi.org/10.1509/jmr.14.0237

25. Arora, D., Li, K.F., Neville, S.W.: Consumers' sentiment analysis of popular phone brands and operating system preference using twitter data: a feasibility study. In: 2015 IEEE 29th International Conference on Advanced Information Networking and Applications, pp. 680–686. IEEE, Gwangiu, South Korea (2015). https://doi.org/10.1109/AINA.2015.253

26. NTT DATA: 2023 Global Customer Experience Report The rise of AI, cloud and employee experience in shaping the CX of the future. NTT DATA, Inc. (2023)

27. O'Leary, D.E.: Hashtag commerce: "Order by Tweet." J. Inform. Technol. Teach. Cases **9**, 26–37 (2019). https://doi.org/10.1177/2043886918819310

28. Bhoi, A., et al.: Mining social media text for disaster resource management using a feature selection based on forest optimization. Comput. Ind. Eng. **169**, 108280 (2022). https://doi.org/10.1016/j.cie.2022.108280

29. Anto, M.P., Antony, M., Muhsina, K.M., Johny, N., James, V., Wilson, A.: Product rating using sentiment analysis. In: 2016 International Conference on Electrical, Electronics, and Optimization Techniques (ICEEOT), pp. 3458–3462. IEEE, Chennai, India (2016). https://doi.org/10.1109/ICEEOT.2016.7755346
30. Bradley, A., James, R.J.E.: How are major gambling brands using Twitter? Int. Gambl. Stud. **19**, 451–470 (2019). https://doi.org/10.1080/14459795.2019.1606927
31. Antypas, D., Preece, A., Camacho-Collados, J.: Politics, sentiment and virality: a large-scale multilingual twitter analysis in Greece, Spain and United Kingdom. SSRN J. (2022). https://doi.org/10.2139/ssrn.4166108
32. Antypas, D., Preece, A., Camacho-Collados, J.: Negativity spreads faster: a large-scale multilingual twitter analysis on the role of sentiment in political communication. Online Soc. Netw. Media. **33**, 100242 (2023). https://doi.org/10.1016/j.osnem.2023.100242
33. Hornikx, J., Hendriks, B.: Consumer tweets about brands: a content analysis of sentiment tweets about goods and services. J. Creative Commun. **10**, 176–185 (2015). https://doi.org/10.1177/0973258615597406
34. IBEF: India's 5G user base is expected to reach around 700 million by 2028 end: Ericsson. IBEF and Ericsson (2023)
35. Kumar, N.R.: OnePlus plans to invest ₹1,000 crore in R&D facility in Hyderabad The global R&D facility, the company's first in India, will have a headcount of 1,500. https://www.thehindu.com/business/oneplus-plans-to-invest-1000-crore-in-rd-facility/article29260745.ece (2019)
36. Mallick, S.: Oppo, Nokia resolve global patent dispute with cross-license agreement, https://brandequity.economictimes.indiatimes.com/news/business-of-brands/oppo-nokia-resolve-global-patent-dispute-with-cross-license-agreement/107130873?utm_source=Mailer&utm_medium=newsletter&utm_campaign=etbrandequity_news_2024-01-27&dt=2024-01-27&em=cHJhc2hhbnQudmNoYXVkaGFyeUBnbWFpbC5jb20= (2024)
37. Singal, N.: Apple's winning formula in India: iPhone's market share on track to touch 7% by year end. https://www.businesstoday.in/technology/news/story/apples-winning-formula-in-india-iphones-market-share-on-track-to-touch-7-by-year-end-392823-2023-08-04 (2023)
38. Kawoosa, F.: All smartphone brands, including Chinese cos, have helped develop a thriving ecosystem in India, https://telecom.economictimes.indiatimes.com/blog/all-smartphone-brands-including-chinese-cos-have-helped-develop-a-thriving-ecosystem-in-india/105921663. Last accessed 12 Dec 2023
39. Trivedi, R.: What Makes India Suitable Market for Apple? https://sputniknews.in/20231213/what-makes-india-a-suitable-market-for-apple-5813737.html. Last accessed 13 Dec 2023
40. Counterpoint Quarterly: Oppo emerged as the second-biggest smartphone brand in the world, overtaking Apple in terms of market share by mid-2021. Counterpoint Quarterly (2023)
41. Counterpoint Research: Oppo, OnePlus, and Realme together overtake Apple to rank second in global smartphone market. India Today (2021)
42. Chaudhary, P.: Online influencer marketing – an effective marketing technique for strategic branding, resonating communication and customer engagement. Manag. Dyn. **22**(1), 36–42 (2022). https://doi.org/10.57198/2583-4932.1296
43. Chaudhary, P.V.: Selling and Negotiation Skills: A Pragmatic Approach. SAGE Publications India Pvt Ltd, Thousand Oaks (2019)
44. Puri, R.: Digital tools transforming approach to omnichannel: Cloud, AI ensure seamless customer experience, data security. https://www.financialexpress.com/life/technology-digital-tools-transforming-approach-to-omnichannel-cloud-ai-ensure-seamless-customer-experience-data-security-3376769/ (2024)
45. Chaudhary, P., Kate, N.: The coalescence effect: Understanding the impact of customer value proposition, perceived benefits and climate change sensitivities on electric vehicle adoption in India. Bus. Strat. Dev. **6**(4), 843–858 (2023). https://doi.org/10.1002/bsd2.282

46. Kate, N., Chaudhary, P., More, M.: Antecedents to organic tea buying behavior and consumption among millennials in India: through the lens of theory of planned behavior. Indian J. Market. **54**(1), 44 (2024). https://doi.org/10.17010/ijom/2024/v54/i1/173382

47. Tellis, S.: Brands need to co-create with consumers: Coach CMO. https://brandequity. economictimes.indiatimes.com/news/marketing/brands-need-to-co-create-with-consumers-coach-cmo/107092757?utm_source=Mailer&utm_medium=newsletter&utm_campaign= etbrandequity_news_2024-01-28&dt=2024-01-28&em=cHJhc2hhbnQuY2hhdWRoYXJJ5 QG1pdHdwdS5lZHUuaW4= (2024)

48. Raut, N., Chaudhary, P., Patil, H., Kiran, P.: Understanding the contribution of artificial intelligence. In: Garg, V., Goel, R., Tiwari, P., Döngül, E.S. (eds.) Handbook of Artificial Intelligence Applications for Industrial Sustainability: Concepts and Practical Examples, pp. 64–73. CRC Press, Boca Raton (2024). https://doi.org/10.1201/9781003348351-5

49. Chaudhary, P., Raut, N., Patil, H., Kate, N.: Up-skilling in fashion retail. In: Malik, R., Sharma, A., Chaudhary, P. (eds.) Transforming Education with Virtual Reality, pp. 323–336. Wiley (2024). https://doi.org/10.1002/9781394200498.ch19

50. Parveen, N., Chakrabarti, P., Hung, B.T., Shaik, A.: Twitter sentiment analysis using hybrid gated attention recurrent network. J Big Data. **10**, 50 (2023). https://doi.org/10.1186/s40537-023-00726-3

51. Nagar, A.: Customers to take centre stage. https://www.financialexpress.com/business/bra ndwagon-customers-to-take-centre-stage-3352224/ (2024)

52. Elmas, T., Stephane, S., Houssiaux, C.: Measuring and detecting virality on social media: the case of twitter's viral tweets topic. In: Companion Proceedings of the ACM Web Conference 2023. pp. 314–317. ACM, Austin TX USA (2023). https://doi.org/10.1145/3543873.3587373

53. AminiMotlagh, M., Shahhoseini, H., Fatehi, N.: A reliable sentiment analysis for classification of tweets in social networks. Soc. Netw. Anal. Min. **13**, 7 (2022). https://doi.org/10.1007/s13 278-022-00998-2

54. Qi, Y., Shabrina, Z.: Sentiment analysis using Twitter data: a comparative application of lexicon- and machine-learning-based approach. Soc. Netw. Anal. Min. **13**, 31 (2023). https:// doi.org/10.1007/s13278-023-01030-x

Antecedents of Mobile Banking Apps Adoption Among Consumers in Ghana

Masud Ibrahim[1]([✉]) [iD] and Dora Yeboah[2]

[1] Akenten Appiah-Menka University of Skills Training and Entrepreneurial Development, Box 1277, Kumasi, Ghana
Imasud10@gmail.com
[2] GIMPA School of Business, Accra, Ghana

Abstract. In this study, Ghanaian bank customers' usage of mobile banking apps was investigated. A modified Technological Acceptance Model (TAM) paradigm served as the foundation for a conceptual framework. Nine different hypotheses were created and put to the test using structural equation modeling. Design/Methodology: A convenient sampling technique was employed to select 700 bank customers using the mobile banking app from Kumasi, the Ashanti Region of Ghana. After the initial screening, 450 responses were deemed to be usable out of a total of 554 completed questionnaires received. Results: This study's findings showed that design and perceived security have a favourable influence on the perceived usefulness and ease of use of mobile banking apps. Additionally, perceived ease of use, social influence, and perceived security risk were discovered to have a significant impact on the intention to embrace mobile banking apps. Originality/Novelty: This study explores mobile banking app adoption in a developing country context, where the study seems sparse.

Keywords: Mobile banking app · Perceived ease of use · Perceived usefulness · Perceived security risk · Technology acceptance model

1 Introduction

In recent times, entities such as businesses, organizations, institutions, and even states have taken to social media networks such as Facebook, twitter, LinkedIn, etc. as a means of communicating with their various audiences. The rise of the social media has led to the adoption of various technologies to help in various business processes to have seamless as well as coherent productions and services (Dwivedi et al., 2022). Banking institutions are noted to be among the firms that have always been associated with the adoption of technology to augment their service provisions (Damanpour and Gopalakrishnan, 2001). For instance, the first set of technology outlined by banks included ATMs, internet banking, smart cards, voicemail interfaces etc. ((Karjaluoto, 2002), and these were mostly used by consumers from developed worlds (Donner, 2008). Accordingly, these were the days when customers had to queue for longer hours to be served, especially those from developing nations (Abor, 2005; Donner, 2008). However, today, banks have started using applications also known as banking apps to provide banking services to teeming customers, both far and near. This explains extant literature which suggests that mobile banking apps are not only provide innovative business approaches but also could become one of m-commerce's value-added apps in service encounters (Muñoz-Leiva et al., 2017; Lee et al., 2003).

Ghana has undergone significant transition in recent years, with most banks attempting to serve Ghanaians in a timely manner rather than wasting valuable hours in most banking halls in order to obtain any type of financial service (Dzogbenuku, 2013; Coffie et al., 2020). To this end, crucial variables such as technological advancements and fierce competition have compelled banks to adapt to the issues that the banking public faces. Thus, resulting in the rapid adoption of technology innovation and tactics to please consumers while lowering operational costs becomes imperative (Sohail and Shanmugham, 2003; Gai et al., 2018; Coffie et al., 2021). In Ghana, for example, mobile phone adoption and use surged from 17.44 million customers in 2010 to almost 404.62 million subscribers in 2020 (ITU, 2021). Also, the internet penetration rate moved from 11 million in 2007 to 37.88 million in 2017 (ITU, 2020). Chatterjee (2020) suggests that this can provide a platform for not only financial inclusion but also economic growth. Consequently, given the nature of rapid technological change within industries, it is not surprising that firms are responding adequately by remodelling their business models to take advantage of the opportunities to remain competitive (Coffie et al., 2021). In other words, a firm that does not know how to respond adequately to this new technological change losses out among the crowd. This implies that, while technology provides opportunity for new service offerings, at the same time technological transformation poses challenges to current business models (Favoretto et al., 2022). For instance, challenges such as consumer scepticism (Chan et al., 2022), leading companies frequently try to influence the progress of technical applications for their own benefit (Lai, 2007; Lovelock, 2001) and learning challenges to older CEOs (Coffie et al., 2021) have been identified.

This study conceptualises a business model as how a firm design and delivers value with an aim to capture value in return (Tecee, 2010). It means that to be able to achieve this goal, firms that aim at employing technology as innovative strategy for success must also understand the associated challenges. There have been a number of studies focusing on consumers' adoption of new technologies (Dapp et al., 2012; Lai, 2016; Lai and Zainal, 2014). Yet, considering the overwhelming usage of apps by businesses including the banking sector, it would be important to empirically test the willingness of consumers to adopt this new banking process (Son et al., 2020; Haritha, 2022; Shaikh et al., 2023) This will provide practitioners and academics with contemporary evidence on why consumers would patronize new technologies such as the mobile banking apps.

To address this issue, earlier studies investigated into the TAM model suggested by Davis, Bogozzi, and Warshaw (1989). However, only a handful of these studies have concentrated on the variables that affect the adoption of these mobile apps, with particular attention paid to social influences or subjective norms as well as trust, risk, and social image (Muoz-Leiva et al., 2017; Liébana-Cabanillas, 2012); and social influences or factors. In addition, these studies have been restricted to specific subjects and contexts, which rendered the application of the findings to separate environments challenging.

The current research offers a novel conceptual model that integrates the major factors influencing user behaviour in relation to the adoption of an innovative technology in an online banking app to fill this gap. Therefore, the purpose of this study is to investigate what influences consumers in Ghana to utilize mobile banking apps.

The rest of the paper is structured as follows; the next section presents the review of the theory supporting this study as well as relevant conceptual model of the study. The next section discusses the key method employed in undertaking this study. Next is the presentation of the results as well as the discussion of the main findings. The conclusion as well as managerial implications of the study's findings are discussed last.

2 Theoretical Review

The most well-known theories for examining behavioural intention and technology use are the Technology Acceptance Model (TAM) and Theory of Planned Behaviour (TPB). Davis (1989) introduced the TAM as a method for predicting user acceptance and use of any information technology. Due to its sound influence on the acceptability of behaviour (Lymperopoulos and Chaniotakis, 2005), "the TAM has been explicitly introduced to model the acceptance of Information Technologies and Information Systems" (Davis, 1989, p.4). In terms of empirical evidence, it has also been asserted that the theory performs better than others, such as the Theory of Planned Behaviour (Mathieson, 1991).

The TAM has been used extensively in studies including the adoption of mobile services (Jiang et al., 2015; Narteh et al., 2017; Wei, Xinyan and Yue, 2011; Wei et al., 2009), online shopping (Gefen, Karahanna and Straub, 2003) and e-commerce (Ibrahim, Mensah and Asare, 2021). Perceived ease of use (PEOU) and perceived usefulness (PU), according to Davis (1989), are two beliefs that have an impact on technology adoption intention and behaviour (TAI B). In the subsequent sections, we will discuss how these two viewpoints affect new technology, like mobile banking apps.

2.1 Perceived Usefulness (PU)

The belief of customers that using technology will improve the outcome of their purchasing and information seeking is referred to as PU (Chen, Gillenson, and Sherrell, 2002; Verma, Bhattacharyya and Kumar, 2018; Akdim et al., 2022). The first belief, PU, is the user's "subjective probability that using a specific application system will increase his or her job performance within an organizational context" (Davis et al., 1989, p. 985). PU was first described in the context of job performance, but it has since been applied to any common task in non-organizational settings, such as online purchasing. PU is incorporated into the image components of product selection, customer service, and delivery or fulfilment in the role of functional ascribed in a similar model created by Dennis et al. (2009). That is, consumers' willingness to adopt technology is contingent on their perceptions of the technology's utility. As such, we hypothesize that;

H1: Perceived usefulness of the mobile banking apps will influence customer's intention to adopt it.

2.2   Perceived Ease of Use (PEOU)

PEOU, the second belief, is "the degree to which the user expects the target system to be free of efforts" (Davis et al., 1989, p.985). PEOU has also been defined as a person's conviction that a system will be easy to use and that it shouldn't be complicated in order to promote adoption (Carter and Belanger, 2005; Chen et al., 2002; Rogers, 2003; Akdim, Casalo and Flavian, 2022). This indicates that the user should have to exert minimal effort in order to use a certain type of technology (Liu et al., 2010). This endeavour might be both physical and mental in nature (Davis, 1993; Taylor and Todd, 1995). PEOU has been found to have a positive effect on user intention in previous studies (Carter and Belanger, 2005; Davis, 1989; Guriting and Ndubisi, 2006; Narteh et al., 2017; Ramayah, Jantan and Aafaqi, 2003; Kim et al., 2019). With regards to the adoption of mobile banking apps, PEOU considers how simple the interface is, how quickly the service loads, how easy it is for customers to engage in banking transactions, the minimum steps required to make a transfer, and how usable the service is with basic features and software on mobile devices (Qing and Haiying, 2021). This study therefore hypothesized that:

H2: Perceived ease of use of the mobile banking apps will influence customer intention to use it.

2.3   Conceptual Review

Design. In this study, design refers to the system's features, capabilities and performance. User interface (UI) and user experience (UX) are two aspects of app design (UX). The UI refers to the app's entire appearance (including the colors, fonts, and general look and feel). The UX, on the other hand, focuses on the app's real operation and usability. After using an app for the first time, a huge majority of users abandon it. Consequently, because consumers are discriminating about which apps they use and are quick to abandon those that they do not like, it is critical that enough time and effort be put into establishing an excellent user experience. This suggests that the layout and functionality of an app would not only entice customers to adopt but also good aesthetics or design in mobile apps can capture the attention and possible user engagement of mobile apps (Qing and Haiying, 2021; Tiongson, 2015). Based on this, the following are stated;

H3: Design features will have a positive impact on users' perceived ease of use of mobile banking app.

H4: Design features will have a positive impact on users' perceived usefulness of mobile banking app.

Perceived Security risk (PS). The belief in the uncertainty of possible negative repercussions (dangers) in using a physical object or service is known as perceived security (PS) (Featherman and Pavlou, 2003). When a users' private information is known to others, the users' risk exposure is perceived to be high (Aldás-Manzano et al., 2009; Cox and Rich, 1964; Featherman and Pavlou, 2003). Consumers' perception of security will increase if they perceive potential losses resulting from the uncertainties associated with adopting a new technology, such as a mobile banking app, for banking purposes. Any negative implications for consumers, such as identity theft, hacking, and financial risk, are possible security concerns (Chan et al., 2022).

Hacking is the possibility of another person or hackers gaining an authorized access to the clients account by posing as the customer to steal their money (Alsayed and Bilgrami, 2017). Identity theft is the possibility of another user posing as the customer by using the customer's credentials online without the authorization of the customer (Lynch, 2005). Financial risk refers to the danger of a client losing money as a result of unlawful access to their mobile banking account (Merritt, 2011).

Previous studies have found perceived security to influence users' intention to adopt technology. Research findings conclude that perceived security, influences users' intention to adopt mobile-payment services (Johnson et al., 2018; Oliveira et al., 2016). In addition Liebana-Cabanillas et al. (2014) show that fears linked to financial losses could negatively impact mobile-payment system usage. This is consistent with the findings of Vess, Richard, Wenjun, and Joseph (2020) that perceived privacy and security positively influences consumers' behavioural intention. Based on this, the following hypotheses are stated:

H5: Perceived security risk will have an impact on users' perceived ease of use of mobile banking app.

H6: Perceived security risk will influence users' perceived usefulness of mobile banking app.

H7: Perceived security risk will influence consumers' intention to use mobile banking apps for banking transactions services in Ghana.

Perceived Social Influence (PSI). The conviction that an individual holds about the expectations of others, as well as the individual's incentive to meet these expectations, is referred to as social influence (SI) (Dunn et al., 2011). An individual's perception of what others (family and friends) think about his or her use of a mobile banking app and the degree to which the person feels inclined to comply with this feeling. It also refers to how important it is for a persons' close relations to adopt the new system (Venkatesh et al., 2003). The societal influences on individuals to perform or not execute a given action are represented by SI (Narteh et al., 2017).

According to a study on SI by Thomas, Robert, and Wiggins (2015), people in a certain social group are more likely to conceal their consumption behaviour when there is extreme non-conformity of certain consumption to that group. In a similar vein, Mohd Suki (2013) found that increasing smartphone demand is influenced by SI and the product's brand identity. This suggests that users may be afraid to use the mobile banking app because of their social group's severe non-conformity, or they may embrace the use of mobile money services because of their social group's great conformity (Mohd Suki, 2013; Zimand Sheiner, Kol and Levy, 2021). Hence, this study hypothesized that:

H8: Social influence has a positive effect on intention to adopt and use the mobile banking app for banking transactions.

Figure 1 shows the conceptual model for the study was adapted from Lai (2016) to explore the adoption intention and usage of mobile banking app by consumers. The design is the interface of the App which supposed to be user friendly. Perceived security and design are the stimuli that depict the capabilities of the system and feature. Perceived ease of use and perceived usefulness represent the motivation to use the system that leads to consumers' responses to use technology, whereas actual ease of use and actual usefulness represent the motivation to use the system.

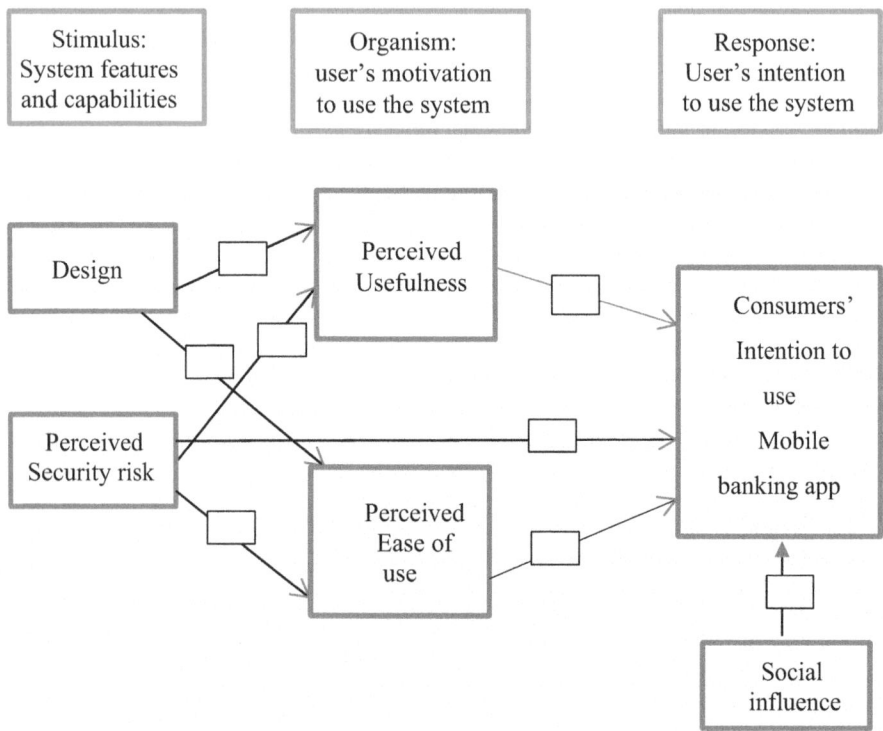

Fig. 1. Conceptual model for the study.

3   Methodology

This section describes the research methods utilized to carry out the study. The study used a cross-sectional design, which allowed the researchers to take one or more samples from the population at one time and investigate the relationship between variables in more depth (Sekaran, 2000). The study population consisted of bank customers using mobile banking apps in Kumasi in the Ashanti Region of Ghana. Since it was difficult obtaining the total population of the bank customers using the mobile banking apps, the convenient sampling technique was used to select the sample for the study. About 700 questionnaires were printed and issued to bank customers at various locations including bank premises, offices and homes. In all 554 completed questionnaire was received from the respondents. After the initial screening, 450 responses were deemed to be usable out of a total of the 554 completed questionnaire received (Malhotra and Birks, 2007).

A Likert scale ranging from 1 to 5 where 1 = strongly disagree and 5 = strongly agree was used to gather the data. The scale used to design the questionnaire were adopted from similar studies conducted in the past. The PU and PEOU questionnaire scale were adapted from Davis (1989); Davis et al. (1989) and Moore and Benbasat (1991); the behavioural intention (BI) scale was adapted from (Davis, 1989) and (Davis et al., 1989); and the perceived security (PS) and design (Ds) scales were also adopted from Lai (2016). Nine components were measured using a total of 18 items. PEOU, BI, Ds, and PS were all measured using three items each, while PU was assessed using five items.

There were three (3) parts to the questionnaire. The first segment (section A) examined the respondents' demographic characteristics; the second (section B) and third (section C) examined both adoption factors and the BIs of mobile banking app adoption intention. The data was collected over the course of four weeks. SPSS version 22 and SmartPLS v3 were used to analyse the data acquired in this study. The data was coded and inspected for outliers and other data set variations. For demographic variables, descriptive analysis was employed, and hypotheses were evaluated using structural equation model (SEM).

A pre-test of the study instrument was conducted for quality control to ensure its face validity and reliability. The Cronbach's (alpha) test was used to ensure that the questionnaire was accurate and complete. Cronbach alphas of 0.7 or above was considered significant in this study. In addition, content validity was employed to confirm the instrument's validity and reliability. The instruments were provided to experts on the topic to assess the suitability of the questions to measure what they intended to measure or not as it had been done in prior studies to avoid being imprecise and ambiguous. Cronbach's alpha reliability coefficients greater than 0.7 were utilized to ensure internal consistency (Collis and Hussey, 2009).

To evaluate the model, the partial least squares (PLS) technique was used, which led to the use of the Smart PLS software (Ferreira, Sayago and Blat, 2016). When predicting a dependent variable from a (very) large set of independent variables (i.e., predictors), the PLS approach is very useful (Abdi et al., 2013; Liébana-Cabanillas, 2012).

4   Results of the Study

4.1   Demographics of Respondents

Gender, age, education level, and job position were some demographic factors that were gathered for this study. From Table 1, 38.5% of the respondents were female and 61.5% of the respondents were male; also, 51.9% of respondents identified as being between the ages of 18 and 24; 31.8% between the ages of 25 and 29; 7.5% between the ages of 30 and 34; 5.9% between the ages of 35 and 39; and 2.9% who identified as being beyond the age of 40. About 85.8% of them had undergraduate degrees; 5.4% had master's degrees; 3.8% had doctoral degrees; and 48% had other credentials. Regarding the respondents' employment situation, 1.7% are involved in trading; 9.2% are teachers; 74% are students; and 14.6% are involved in other activities.

With regards to the mobile banking app awareness 82.8% of the respondents are aware of the mobile banking app; and the remaining 17.24% are unaware of the mobile banking app. Also, in terms of the app usage, 25.9% indicated they use it; whiles the remaining 74.1% indicated they do not use it.

4.2 Confirmatory Factor Analysis (CFA)

To assess for common method variance, the researchers utilized Harmann's Single-Factor test. This test was carried out with the help of exploratory factor analysis (EFA) and the loading of 19 items into a single factor. Initially, 21 items were entered, however three of them were eventually removed, leaving 19 items. Together, these factors account for almost 74% of the variance in the sample.

4.3 Reliability and Validity of Scales

The data were initially examined for convergent and discriminant validity to guarantee instrument quality. The exploratory factor analysis (EFA) was performed using SPSS to determine the underlying dimension linked with 19 items. The validity of the constructs was assessed using Bartlett's test of sphericity and the Kaiser–Mayer–Olkin (KMO) measure of individual variable sampling adequacy. To perform factor analysis, the KMO should be at least 0.6 according to Özdamar (2002). According to the results of Bartlett's Sphericity and KMO tests, the constructs are suitable for factor analysis (see Table 1).

Again, results from Table 1 shows that cumulative to be 93%, which exceeds the minimum threshold of 60% (Özdamar, 2002). Also, Bartlett's test of sphericity indicates that the variables are sufficiently correlated (Chi square = 4505.510; $p > 0.000$). All items on each scale have a factor loading greater than 0.5. Which exceeds the minimum threshold of 0.4 (Hair, Hult, & Ringle, 2016; Hair Jr, Sarstedt, Ringle, & Gudergan, 2017). As a result, these figures show convergent validity (see Table 1).

Table 1. KMO and Bartlett's Test

Kaiser-Meyer-Olkin Measure of Sampling Adequacy		.930
Bartlett's Test of Sphericity	Approx. Chi-Square	4505.510
	Df	66
	Sig	.000

4.4 Measurement Model Reliability and Validity

Item factor loadings with an acceptable value of 0.70 and Cronbach's alpha with a level of 0.7 are used to determine construct reliability, which evaluates the degree of internal consistency of the employed measures (Hair et al., 2016; Ringle, Wende and Becker, 2015). The reliability of the items used to assess the constructs is demonstrated by the fact that all of the variables in Table 2 have Cronbach's alphas larger than 0.70. Construct validity on the other hand refers to how accurately a measurement captures the observable reality and logically connects it to the construct through the underlying theory (Fornell and Larcker, 1981). The validity of the constructs is assessed using convergent and discriminant validity (Ringle et al., 2015). Convergent validity was accomplished in this investigation because the average variance extracted (AVEs) and composite reliability (CR) both satisfied the minimum requirements of 0.50 and 0.70, respectively (Fornell and Larcker, 1981; Ringle et al., 2015).

Table 2. Item loading and construct reliability

	FL	CA	CR	AVE
Dsgn1	0.866	0.801	0.883	0.716
Dsgn2	0.837			
Dsgn3	0.761			
PSec1	0.845	0.740	0.853	0.659
PSec2	0.805			
PSec3	0.837			
Peou1	0.847	0.775	0.869	0..690
Peou2	0.786			
Peou3	0.706			
Si1	0.524	0.889	0.931	0.818
Si2	0.862			
Si3	0.862			
bi1	0.733	0.810	0.882	0..714
bi2	0.829			
bi3	0.838			
pu1	0.709	0.719	0.928	0.811
pu2	0.753			
pu3	0.719			

Notes: FL – Item Loadings; PEOU – Perceived ease of use, PU – Perceived usefulness, DGN – Design, PSEC – Perceived security, BI – Behavioural intention, Si – Social Influence; AVE-Average variance extracted, CR- Composite reliability, CA – Cronbach's alpha

4.5   Result of the Structural Model

The results of the structural model's evaluation of the variable relationships in the study are shown in Fig. 2. The evaluation takes into account the path coefficients, which calculate the relationship between the variables. From Fig. 2, design and perceived security (PS) related positively with PEOU and PU. Design related positively with both PEOU and PU (0.409) and (0.231) which means that, design influences PEOU and PU by about 40.9% and 23.1% respectively. Also, PSEC related positively with both PU and PEOU (0.121) and (0.496) respectively; which means that, PSEC influences PU and PEOU by about 12.1% and 49.6% respectively. Also, PEOU, PU, PSEC and SI related positively with BI (0.618), (0.128), (0.136) and (0.012) which means that, PU, PEOU, PSEC and SI influence by BI by about 61.8%, 12.8%, 13.6% and 1.2% respectively.

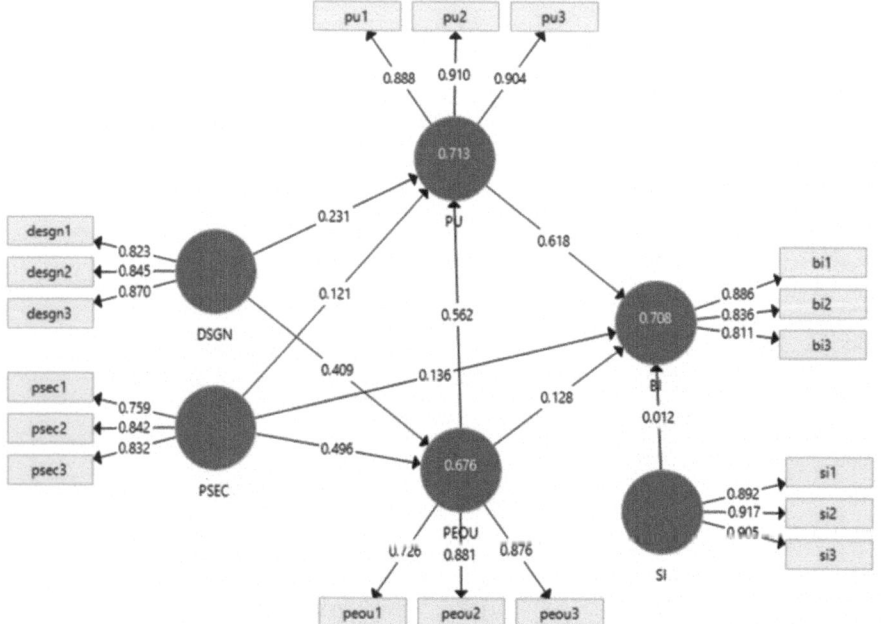

Fig. 2. Structural model showing relationship among the variables

It therefore means that, perceived usefulness of the mobile banking app has the largest influence on consumer intention to adopt the app followed by perceived security and perceived ease of use. Banks should therefore focus more on the perceived usefulness of the mobile banking app as it influences intention of consumers to use their mobile banking app more than other factors (see Fig. 2).

4.6 Hypothesis Test

To evaluate the factors influencing customers' adoption of mobile banking apps in Ghana, a hypothesis test utilizing the bootstrapping approach with 5000 samples was carried out. Table 3 demonstrates the support for each of the stated hypotheses. The test results indicate a substantial and favourable correlation between the variables (H1-H8; $p < 0.001$). According to Table 3, the findings support both hypothesis H1 and H2, respectively, by demonstrating that design positively correlates with PU ($\beta = 0.231$; $p < 0.001$)

and PEOU ($\beta = 0.409$; $p < 0.001$). Additionally, PU and PEOU showed positive and substantial relationships with perceived security ($\beta = 0.121$; $p < 0.001$) and ($\beta = 0.496$; $p < 0.001$), leading to the acceptance of hypotheses H3 and H4, respectively. PEOU, PU, and PSEC once more showed favourable correlations with BI ($p < 0.05$). PU had a positive and significant relationship with BI ($\beta = 0.618$; $p < 0.001$) and this led to the acceptance of H5. Again, PEOU and PSEC both revealed positive and significant relationship with BI ($\beta = 0.128$; $p < 0.05$) and ($\beta = 0.136$; $p < 0.10$) and this led to the acceptance of Hypotheses H6 and H7 respectively. Hypothesis H8 was accepted since PU likewise showed a favourable and significant relationship with PEOU ($\beta = 0.562$; $p < 0.001$).

Table 3. Test of Hypothesis

Paths	Beta	Mean	STDEV	t-value	p-value
DSGN -> PEOU	0.409	0.410	0.049	8.290	0.000
DSGN -> PU	0.231	0.231	0.052	4.469	0.000
PEOU -> BI	0.128	0.127	0.088	1.454	0.146
PEOU -> PU	0.562	0.561	0.063	8.946	0.000
PSEC -> BI	0.136	0.135	0.072	1.886	0.059
PSEC -> PEOU	0.496	0.495	0.048	10.369	0.000
PSEC -> PU	0.121	0.122	0.052	2.324	0.020
PU -> BI	0.618	0.614	0.075	8.187	0.000
SI -> BI	0.012	0.018	0.066	0.182	0.856
	R Square	R Square Adjusted			
BI	0.708	0.704			
PEOU	0.676	0.674			
PU	0.713	0.711			

The R squared figure shows that, together, the independent variables (perceived security, perceived usefulness and social influence) explain about 70.8% of the variance in the dependent variable BI. Also, the R-squared figure of 0.673 and 0.713 indicate that, the independent variables, Design and Perceived security together explain about 67.6% of the variance in PEOU as well as 71.3% variance in PU respectively.

4.7 Model Fit Summary

The overall model fitness of this investigation was determined from Table 4 to be suitable. Although the model appears to be sound, it is still appropriate to examine the value of the Chi-square statistic, which is $\chi 2$ divided by the Degrees of Freedom (DF), as the $\chi 2$ statistic is typically sensitive to the sample size. But it is suggested that $\chi 2$ divided by DF makes for a better fit. A satisfactory model fit was determined from Table 4 by the value of $\chi2$ / DF, which was 3.082 (less than the 5.0 criterion). Additionally, the model showed a high significance level (.001). All the indices were approved within the suggested range, which is indicative of good performance, according to Hair Jr et al. (2017)'s recommendation that the cut-offs for the individual indices be set at NFI (0.90), SRMR (0.08), and RMS Theta (<1).

Table 4. Model fit Measurement

	Saturated Model	Estimated Model
SRMR	0.074	0.086
d_ULS	0.0928	1.259
d_G	0.0530	0.600
Chi-Square	993.274	1,077.400
NFI	0.781	0.736
RMS Theta		0.209

5 Discussion

This study evaluated the factors that influence customer adoption of mobile banking apps in Ghana. The findings from the research showed that design and perceived security have a favourable and significant impact on users' perceptions of the usefulness and usability of mobile banking apps in Ghana. The results of this study showed a favourable and significant correlation between the mobile banking app's design and its PEOU and PU. This finding supports similar research finding by Wang and Li (2017) who found icon appearance to influence the download behaviour of users. The design of the app in particular is very important in the determinants of perceived ease of use and usefulness of the mobile banking app among the consumers. Design features including the colours, fonts, and general look and feel of the app. The design therefore entices the customer to try the app. Again, the study found that perceived security has a positive and significant effect on PEOU and PU of mobile banking app. ed ease of use and perceived security are the main determinants of mobile banking app adoption among consumers in Ghana.

A positive and significant association between the variables was also found in this study's findings regarding the influence of perceived usefulness, perceived ease of use, perceived security, and perceived social influence on consumers' propensity to embrace mobile banking apps. First, research into the impact of perceived ease of use on customers' inclinations to embrace mobile banking apps in Ghana found a positive but insignificant correlation between PEOU and BI. The results of these research by Muoz-Leiva et al. (2017) and Narteh et al. (2017) are in contrast to this finding. Perceived ease of use is recognized as one of the key factors influencing the adoption of new technologies. However, this finding suggest that consumer do not base their adoption of mobile banking app on perception of how easy it is to use the app. May be, Ghanaian consumers are influenced by factors other than the perceived ease of use of the mobile banking app.

In contrast to the finding on the effect of PEOU on mobile banking app adoption intention by consumers, findings from this study revealed that perceived usefulness has a positive and significant effect on consumers adoption of mobile banking apps in Ghana. This finding unlike the previous finding indicates that, consumer intention towards adoption of mobile banking apps is influenced largely by perceived usefulness of the app. This finding supports earlier findings with regards to the influence of perceived usefulness in technology adoption studies (Davis et al., 1989; Dennis et al., 2009; Merrilees et al., 2011; Muñoz-Leiva et al., 2017). This finding suggests that, perceived usefulness of the mobile banking app is an important determining factor in consumers mobile banking app adoption decision or intention.

Additionally, the findings revealed a positive and significant relationship between social influence and mobile banking app adoption intention. Most consumers' decision to use a new service or purchase new products/service is influenced by their peers and family members due to societal view or thinking about the decision. However, relatives and friends who already use a mobile banking app can persuade others to do the same. This result supports the claim made by Narteh et al. (2017) that people's views, feelings, and behaviour are influenced not just by their unique personalities but also by what pertinent other people believe, feel, or do. This finding suggests therefore that, consumers intention to adopt mobile banking app in Ghana would be influenced by what other people say or do. It is therefore imperative to communicate to the right people at the right time for the right response on adoption of the mobile banking apps.

Furthermore, findings with regards to the effect of perceived security and adoption intention of mobile banking app by consumers revealed a positive and significant relationship. Perceived security is an important aspect of any technology adoption consideration due to the risk involved. This finding supports earlier findings (Johnson et al., 2018; Liebana-Cabanillas et al., 2014; Oliveira et al., 2016; Vess et al., 2020). The mobile banking app for instance as a financial service technology is prone to higher risk as its tied to consumers money. If care is not taking and the account is exposed, the consumer is left at the mercy of fraudsters who would not hesitate to siphon the funds into their own accounts. It is imperative therefore to have a robust system that makes it difficult for fraudsters to get access to people's accounts in trying to use the app.

Finally, findings with regards to the effect of perceived ease of use on perceived usefulness indicate that, PEOU influences PU significantly. This finding supports earlier studies that found that PEOU has a positive and significant influence on PU (Ibrahim et al., 2021; Lai, 2014, 2016; Liebana-Cabanillas et al., 2014; Muñoz-Leiva et al., 2017; Narteh et al., 2017). PEOU is regarded as one of the important determinants of new technology adoption. Bank customers would therefore adopt mobile banking app when they perceive the app usage to be easy and convenient than going to the banking halls. Therefore, the app should be created in a way that makes it simple and enjoyable for users to use. Customers will readily adopt the new banking app's use once they discover how simple it is to use compared to standing in line in the banking halls or driving longer distances to visit their bank branches.

6 Conclusion

This study explored the determinants of mobile banking app adoption among consumers in Ghana. Findings with regards to the determinants of mobile banking app adoption indicate that perceived usefulness and perceived ease of use are both influenced by design as well as perceived security of the mobile banking app. Again, the findings suggest that the major determinants of mobile banking app adoption are perceived usefulness, social influence and perceived security. Perceived ease of use even though is important in technology acceptance, is not an important factor in adoption mobile banking app as this study found. The adoption of mobile banking app is therefore dependent to a large extent by its perceived usefulness, social influence and to some extent how secured the system is.

6.1 Managerial Implications

This research provides management with key determinant factors for mobile banking app adoption among consumers in Ghana. The following findings and managerial implications can be drawn:

First, mobile banking app adoption in influenced by several factors including, design, perceived security, perceived ease of use, perceived usefulness and social influence. There should be strategies put in place to ensure the app provides customers all these.

Second, out of the factors that influence intention to adopt mobile banking app by consumers, perceived usefulness is the most important determining factor followed by social influence and perceived security. That means the banks and other organizations seeking to develop mobile apps should focus more on creating good content that offer the usefulness experience of the app that would resonate more with customers.

Also, the study found that social influence is one of the factors that influence the adoption of mobile banking apps. Banks should be able to design a suitable communication or promotion campaign to target the influencers in the society as customers mostly are influenced in their decision by these people.

Finally, both usefulness and perceived ease of use were found to be influenced by design. The app's design should be simple and comfortable for users to use. Users would have no trouble transitioning from the traditional banking system to digital banking option once they discover the new technology to be simple to use and also realize the benefits as indicated above.

6.2 Limitations and Suggestions for Future Studies

This study has limitations regarding the following. Firstly, this study employed quantitative methods and a cross-sectional design on a population consisted of bank customers from four banks that are currently operating the mobile banking app in Ghana. Regarding the gender of respondents, 61.5% were male and 38.5% female. This suggests that males' views not only dominate but also might strongly reflect in the results to render generalisation of the findings challenging. Secondly, about 500 questionnaires were distributed among bank customers in Kumasi in the Ashanti Region of Ghana, out of which 450 usable questionnaire was obtained after data cleaning. This means that the study's findings are based on data from only 450 participants to represent the population of study.

Also, conclusions of the study can be compromised since a relatively smaller sample population of 450 participants cannot be said to be adequate representation of the study population. It is possible that future studies using relatively bigger sample sizes within different subject areas and contexts could generate different results. Thirdly, purposive sampling technique was employed to select the various banks operating the mobile banking. It means that not following from probability sampling design provided the researchers some level of control over the sampling process regarding who to include and who not to include in the study. This can lead to biases. Future studies can consider sample selection techniques (e.g., systematic random sampling) that tend to provide all respondents with equal chance of being selected while at the same time limiting researchers' control over the selection process.

References

Abdi, H., Chin, W.W., Esposito Vinzi, V., Russolillo, G., Trinchera, L.: New Perspectives in Partial Least Squares and Related Methods In, vol. 56. Springer Science+Business Media, New York, NY (2013)

Abor, J.: Technological innovations and banking in Ghana: An evaluation of customers' perceptions. Am. Acad. Financ. Manage. **13**, 170–187 (2005)

Akdim, K., Casaló, L.V., Flavián, C.: The role of utilitarian and hedonic aspects in the continuance intention to use social mobile apps. J. Retail. Consum. Serv. **66**, 102–888 (2022)

Aldás-Manzano, J., Lassala-Navarré, C., Ruiz-Mafé, C., Sanz-Blas, S.: The role of consumer innovativeness and perceived risk in online banking usage. Int. J. Bank Market. **27**(1), 53–75 (2009)

Alsayed, A., Bilgrami, A.: E-banking security: Internet hacking, phishing attacks, analysis and prevention of fraudulent activities. Int. J. Emerg. Technol. Adv. Eng. **7**(1), 109–115 (2017)

Bashir, I., Madhavaiah, C.: Trust, social influence, self-efficacy, perceived risk and internet banking acceptance: an extension of technology acceptance model in Indian context. Metamorphosis A J. Manage. Res. **14**(1), 25–38 (2015)

Carter, L., Belanger, F.: The utilization of e-government services: citizen trust, innovation and acceptance factors. Inf. Syst. J. **15**(1), 5–25 (2005)

Chan, R., Troshani, I., Rao Hill, S., Hoffmann, A.: Towards an understanding of consumers' FinTech adoption: the case of open banking. Int. J. Bank Market. **40**(4), 886–917 (2022)

Chatterjee, A.: Financial inclusion, information and communication technology diffusion, and economic growth: a panel data analysis. Inform. Technol. Dev. **26**(3), 607–635 (2020)

Chen, L., Gillenson, M.L., Sherrell, D.L.: Enticing online consumers: a technology acceptance perspective. Inform. Manag. **39**(8), 705–719 (2002)

Coffie, C.P.K., Zhao, H., Adjei Mensah, I.: Panel econometric analysis on mobile payment transactions and traditional banks effort toward financial accessibility in sub-Sahara Africa. Sustainability **12**(3), 895 (2020). https://doi.org/10.3390/su12030895

Coffie, C.P.K., Hongjiang, Z., Mensah, I.A., Kiconco, R., Simon, A.E.O.: Determinants of FinTech payment services diffusion by SMEs in Sub-Saharan Africa: evidence from Ghana. Inf. Technol. Dev. **27**(3), 539–560 (2021)

Collis, J., Hussey, R.: Business research: a practical guide for undergraduate & postgraduate students. Palgrave Macmillan, Basingstoke, Hampshire (UK) (2009)

Cox, D.F., Rich, S.U.: Perceived risk and consumer decision-making: the case of telephone shopping. J. Market. Res. **1**, 32–39 (1964)

Damanpour, F., Gopalakrishnan, S.: The dynamics of the adoption of product and process innovations in organizations. J. Manage. Stud. **38**(1), 45–65 (2001)

Dapp, T., Stobbe, A., Wruuck, P.: The future of (mobile) payments – New (online) players competing with banks. Retrieved from (2012)

Davis, F.D.: Perceived usefulness, perceived ease of use, and user acceptance of information technology. MIS Q. **13**(3), 319–340 (1989)

Davis, F.D.: User acceptance of information technology: system characteristics, user perceptions and behavioral impacts. Int. J. Man Mach. Stud. **38**, 475–487 (1993)

Davis, F.D., Bogozzi, R., Warshaw, P.R.: User acceptance of computer technology: a comparison of two theoretical models. Manage. Sci. **35**, 982–1003 (1989)

Dennis, C., Merrilees, B., Jayawardhena, C., Wright, T.L.: E-consumer behaviour. Eur. J. Mark. **43**(9/10), 1121–1139 (2009)

Donner, J.: Research approaches to mobile use in the developing world: a review of the literature. Inf. Soc. **24**, 140–159 (2008)

Dwivedi, Y.K., et al.: Metaverse beyond the hype: multidisciplinary perspectives on emerging challenges, opportunities, and agenda for research, practice and policy. Int. J. Inf. Manage. **66**, 102–542 (2022)

Dunn, K.I., Mohr, P., Wilson, C.J., Wittert, G.A.: Determinants of fast-food consumption. An application of the Theory of Planned Behaviour. Appetite **57**(2), 349–357 (2011)

Dzogbenuku, R.K.: Banking Innovation in Ghana: insight of students' adoption and diffusion. J. Internet Bank. Commer. **18**(3), 2–20 (2013)

Favoretto, C., Mendes, G.H.D.S., Filho, M.G., Gouvea de Oliveira, M., Ganga, G.M.D.: Digital transformation of business model in manufacturing companies: challenges and research agenda. J. Bus. Ind. Market. **37**(4), 748–767 (2022)

Featherman, M., Pavlou, P.: Predicting e-services adoption: a perceived risk facets perspective. Int. J. Hum Comput Stud. **59**(4), 451–474 (2003)

Ferreira, S.M., Sayago, S., Blat, J.: Going beyond telecenters to foster the digital inclusion of older people in Brazil: lessons learned from a rapid ethnographical study. Int. Technol. Dev. **22**(1), 26–46 (2016)

Fornell, C., Larcker, D.F.: Evaluating structural equation models with unobservable variables and measurement error. J. Mark. Res. **18**(1), 39–50 (1981)

Gefen, D., Karahanna, E., Straub, D.W.: Trust and TAM in online shopping: an integrated model. MIS Q. **27**, 51–90 (2003)

Guriting, P., Ndubisi, A.: Borneo online banking: evaluating customer perceptions and behavioral intention. Manag. Res. News **29**(1/2), 6–15 (2006)

Haritha, P.H.: Mobile payment service adoption: understanding customers for an application of emerging financial technology. Inform. Comput. Secur. (ahead-of-print) (2022)

Hair, J.F., Hult, G.T.M., Ringle, C.M.: A primer on Partial Least Squares Structural Equation Modeling (PLSM), 2nd edn. Sage Publications, Kennessaw, US (2016)

Hair Jr., J.F., Sarstedt, M., Ringle, C.M., Gudergan, S.P.: Advanced issues in partial least squares structural equation modeling. Sage Publications (2017)

Ibrahim, M., Mensah, A.F., Asare, F.: Exploring online marketing adoption factors among used car sellers in Ghana. In: Association, I.M. (ed.) Research Anthology on E-Commerce Adoption, Models, and Applications for Modern Business, pp. 1377–1390. IGI Global (2021)

ITU: Percent Individuals using Internet. Retrieved from itu.int (2020)

ITU: Mobile Cellular Subscriptions 2000–2020. Retrieved from (2021)

Jiang, G., Peng, L., Liu, R.: Mobile game adoption in China: the role of TAM and perceived entertainment, cost, similarity and brand trust. Int. J. Hybrid Inform. Technol. **8**(4), 213-232 (2015)

Joa, C.Y., Magsamen-Conrad, K.: Social influence and UTAUT in predicting digital immigrants' technology use. Behaviour & Information Technology **41**(8), 1620–1638 (2022)

Johnson, V., Kiser, A., Washington, R., Torres, R.: Limitations to the rapid adoption of m-payment services: understanding the impact of privacy risk on m-payment services. Comput. Hum. Behav. **79**, 111–122 (2018)

Karjaluoto, H.: Selection criteria for a mode of bill payment: empirical investigation among Finnish bank customers. Int. J. Retail Distribut. Manag. **30**, 331339 (2002)

Kim, B.G., Kim, K.W., Seo, H.I.: Effects of mobile app service characteristics on user satisfaction and continuance usage intention. J. Inform. Technol. Appl. Manag. **26**(3), 99–120 (2019)

Lai, P.C.: The chip technology management implication in the era of globalization: Malaysian consumers' perspective. Asia Pac. Bus. Rev. **31**(1), 91–96 (2007)

Lai, P.C.: Factors influencing consumers' intention to use a single platform E-payment System. UNITEN (2014)

Lai, P.C.: Design and Security impact on consumers' intention to use single platform E payment. Interdiscip. Inf. Sci. **22**(1), 111–122 (2016)

Lai, P.C., Zainal, A.A.: Perceived Enjoyment of Malaysian consumers' intention to use a single platform E-payment. Paper presented at the International Conference on Liberal Arts & Social Sciences, Hanoi, Vietnam (2014)

Lee, M.S., McGoldrick, P.J., Keeling, K.A., Doherty, J.: Using ZMET to explore barriers to the adoption of 3G mobile banking services. Int. J. Retail Distrib. Manae. **31**(6), 340–348 (2003)

Liébana-Cabanillas, F.: El papel de los medios de pago en los nuevos entornos electrónicos. (Doctoral dissertation). Universidad de Granada, Granada, Espanha (2012)

Liebana-Cabanillas, F., Sanchez-Fernandez, J., Munoz-Leivan, F.: Antecedents of the adoption of the new mobile payment systems: the moderating effect of age. Comput. Hum. Behav. **35**, 464–487 (2014)

Liu, I.-F., Chen, M.C., Sun, Y.L., Wible, D., Kuo, C.-H.: Extending the TAM model to explore the factors that affect intention to use an online learning community. Comuput. Educ. **54**(2), 600–610 (2010)

Lovelock, C.: Services Marketing, People, Technology, Strategy. Prentice Hall, New Jersey (2001)

Lymperopoulos, C., Chaniotakis, I.E.: Factors affecting acceptance of the internet as a marketing-intelligence tool among employees of Greek bank branches. Int. J. Bank Market. **23**(6), 484–505 (2005)

Lynch, J.: Identity theft in cyberspace: crime control methods and their effectiveness in combating phishing attacks. Berkeley Tech. LJ **20**, 259 (2005)

Malhotra, N., Birks, D.: Marketing Research: An Applied Approach. Prentice Hall (2007)

Mathieson, K.: Predicting user intentions: comparing the technology acceptance model with the theory of planned behavior. Inf. Syst. Res. **2**(3), 173–191 (1991)

Merrilees, B., Rundle-Thiele, S., Lye, A.: Marketing capabilities: antecedents and implications for B2B SME performance. Ind. Mark. Manage. **40**(3), 368–375 (2011)

Merritt, C.: Mobile money transfer services: the next phase in the evolution of person-to-person payments. J. Payments Strategy Syst. **5**(2), 143–160 (2011)

Mohd Suki, N.: Students' dependence on smart phones: the influence of social needs, social influences and convenience. Campus-Wide Inform. Syst. **30**(2), 124–134 (2013). https://doi.org/10.1108/10650741311306309

Moore, G.C., Benbasat, I.: Development of an instrument to measure the perceptions of adopting an information technology innovation. Inf. Syst. Res. **2**, 173–191 (1991). https://doi.org/10.1287/isre.2.3.192

Muñoz-Leiva, F., Climent-Climent, S., Liébana-Cabanillas, F.: Determinants of intention to use the mobile banking apps: an extension of the classic TAM model. Spanish J. Market. **21**(1), 25–38 (2017)

Narteh, B., Mahmoud, M.A., Amoh, S.: Customer behavioural intentions towards mobile money services adoption in Ghana. Serv. Ind. J. **37**(7–8), 426–447 (2017). https://doi.org/10.1080/02642069.2017.1331435

Oliveira, T., Baptista, G., Thomas, M.A.M.M.A., Baptista, G., Campos, F.: Mobile-payment: understanding the determinants of customer adoption and intention to recommend the technology. Comput. Hum. Behav. **61**, 404–414 (2016)

Özdamar, K.: Paket Programlar ile İstatistik Veri Analizi. Kaan Kitapevi, Eskişehir (2002)

Qing, T., Haiying, D.: How to achieve consumer continuance intention toward branded apps—from the consumer–brand engagement perspective. J. Retail. Consum. Serv. **60**, 102486 (2021)

Ramayah, T., Jantan, M., Aafaqi, B.: Internet Usage among Students of Institutions of Higher Learning: The Role of Motivational Variables. Paper presented at the the Proceedings of the 1st International Conference on Asian Academy of Applied Business Conference, Sabah, Malaysia (2003)

Ringle, C.M., Wende, S., Becker, J.M.: SmartPLS 3. SmartPLS, Hamburg (2015)

Rogers, E.M.: Diffusion of Innovation. The Free Press, New York (2003)

Sekaran, U.: Research Methods for Business: A Skill Business Approach. New York (2000)

Slade, E.L., Dwivedi, Y.K., Piercy, N.C., Williams, M.D.: Modeling consumers' adoption intentions of remote mobile payments in the United Kingdom: extending UTAUT with innovativeness, risk, and trust. Psychol. Mark. **32**(8), 860–873 (2015)

Shaikh, A.A., Alamoudi, H., Alharthi, M., Glavee-Geo, R.: Advances in mobile financial services: a review of the literature and future research directions. Int. J. Bank Market. **41**(1), 1–33 (2023)

Sohail, M., Shanmugham, B.: E-banking and customer preferences in Malaysia: an empirical investigation. Inf. Sci. **150**(3/4), 207–217 (2003)

Son, Y., Kwon, H.E., Tayi, G.K., Oh, W.: Impact of customers' digital banking adoption on hidden defection: a combined analytical–empirical approach. J. Oper. Manag. **66**(4), 418–440 (2020)

Taylor, S., Todd, P.A.: Understanding information technology usage: a test of competing models. Inf. Syst. Res. **6**, 144–176 (1995)

Teece, D.J.: Business models, business strategy and innovation. Long Range Plan. **43**(2–3), 172–194 (2010)

Thomas, V., Robert, J., Wiggins, J.: Hidden consumption behaviour: an alternative response to social group infuence. Eur. J. Mark. **49**, 512–531 (2015)

Tiongson, J.: Mobile app marketing insights: How consumers really find and use your apps. Think with Google (2015)

Venkatesh, V., Morris, M.G., Davis, G.B., Davis, F.D.: User acceptance of information technology: toward a unified view. MIS Q. **27**(3), 425–478 (2003)

Verma, S., Bhattacharyya, S.S., Kumar, S.: An extension of the technology acceptance model in the big data analytics system implementation environment. Inf. Process. Manage. **54**(5), 791–806 (2018)

Vess, L.J., Richard, W.W., Wenjun, W., Joseph, R.B.: The impact of perceived privacy, accuracy and security on the adoption of mobile self-checkout systems. J. Innov. Econ. Manag. **1**(31), 221–247 (2020)

Wang, M., Li, X.: Effects of the aesthetic design of icons on app downloads: evidence from an android market. Electron. Commer. Res. **17**(1), 83–102 (2017)

Wei, G., Xinyan, Z., Yue, M.: Literature Review on Consumer Adoption Behavior of Mobile Commerce Services. Paper presented at the International Conference on E-Business and E-Government (ICEE), Shanghai (2011)

Wei, T., Marthandan, G., Chong, A., Ooi, K., Arumugam, S.: What drives Malaysian m-commerce adoption? An empirical analysis. Ind. Manag. Data Syst. **109**(3), 370–380 (2009)

Zimand Sheiner, D., Kol, O., Levy, S.: It makes a difference! Impact of social and personal message appeals on engagement with sponsored posts. J. Res. Interact. Mark. **15**(4), 641–660 (2021)

Designing a Data Pipeline Architecture for Intelligent Analysis of Streaming Data

Iryna Mysiuk[1] , Roman Mysiuk[1,1(✉)] , Roman Shuvar[1] ,
Volodymyr Yuzevych[2] , Anatolii Pavlenchyk[3] , and Volodymyr Dalyk[4]

[1] Ivan Franko National University of Lviv, 1 Universytetska Str., Lviv 79000, Ukraine
mysyukr@ukr.net
[2] Karpenko Physico-Mechanical Institute of the NAS of Ukraine, 5 Naukova Str., Lviv 79060, Ukraine
[3] Ivan Boberskyi Lviv State University of Physical Culture, 11 Kostiushka Str., Lviv 79000, Ukraine
[4] Lviv Polytechnic National University, 12 Stepana Bandery Str., Lviv 79013, Ukraine

Abstract. The paper describes the process of creating a data pipeline architecture. Based on multiple data sources and processing through intermediate data warehouses and end-to-end business intelligence. This study is a continuation of the previously considered approaches in the context of the generalization of the entire chain of data interaction. The analysis used pre-collected data from social media news sites, which can be considered as one of the most popular streaming data. The information collection consists of automated work with a large amount of information from several web pages using the Selenium tool, and the data warehouse is implemented on the Elasticsearch, Kibana, and Logstash (EKL) technology stack. The analysis and classification of the results are based on working with a machine learning model and data visualization methods. The developed data pipeline architecture can be useful for developing data processing processes, highlighting vulnerabilities and advantages of methodologies of data selection, processing, and analysis.

Keywords: data pipeline · intelligent analysis · data streaming · business analysis

1 Introduction

Designing a data pipeline architecture for streaming data is a challenge especially considering the moments of real-time data storage and analysis. Streaming data can be both media data and real-time data. Media data can be considered films that are streamed and processed with filters and effects. In addition, streaming data can be collected from the environment and transmitted using Internet of Things to a central server to indicate actions or perform analysis. This filtered information can signal changes in parameters in the home or environment and warn of danger.

The amount of information, especially in the social network, is increasing due to new users, bots, business pages of new brands. Often, collected data is stored in files

A. Mirzazadeh et al. (Eds.): SEMIT 2023, CCIS 2198, pp. 361–372, 2024.
https://doi.org/10.1007/978-3-031-72284-4_22

of various formats, but searching for data and their further processing requires actions and time for opening, reading, and processing. Therefore, in order to analyze such a large amount of data, it is necessary to divide them by topic and save them in the data warehouse for further analysis. Designing a universal architecture for various tasks and topics is possible if there are similar data structures and a unified approach to gathering from sources. However, in such systems, reducing the data to one format is unnecessary as a complicating step.

In this work, a conceptual solution for the interaction of streaming data is proposed for the design of streaming system solutions. The gap in the research is to create a sequence of actions for the design of complex systems of data selection, processing and analysis. This topic is interesting in terms of real-time data analytics applications. Analysis of the application of data storage on the design of relevant systems is considered in [1]. The test data for use in this pipeline is used from the collected elements of a Facebook post about news information that characterizes the behavior of users in social networks [2, 3].

Building a complete data pipeline involves understanding all the steps involved. Such types of architecture are usually developed by solution architects and accompany the development until the pipeline reaches the required level. Commonly known tools are often used, but such a set of tools can be optimized taking into account the pricing policy and integration between the existing set of tools. The full pipeline cycle is not always the same and standardized. Usually, some stages may be omitted in it. This behavior can be applied in the case of simpler architectural construction or in projects of lesser complexity.

2 Literature Review and Problem Statement

The result of the work is to design a system based on the data pipeline from the stage of collection to visualization and conducting data analytics. Data from social networks (comments, likes, and connections), which are collected in a data warehouse for further business analysis, were selected as the main design topic. Many studies [4, 5] work with data using a file and directly process the data but storing it will allow more reliable and faster processing of the results. Especially works [6, 7] with natural language processing (NLP), intermediate results are calculated several times each time.

Tools for processing streaming data change quite dynamically and the specifics of their use are different [8]. The main differences between streaming tools can be the way they work with data. For example, Apache Kafka writes data to dedicated topics with several partitions, Spark allows you to make batch tables as a result, and Apache Storm - through several spouts and bolts.

As a result, the architecture is developed according to certain requirements and convenience of data description. Recently, Elastisearch, Kibana and Logstash (EKL) stack has gained popularity among the search engines of various websites [9, 10]. In this case, requests through the developed Application Program Interface (API) are sent to the Elasticsearch database and a list of products or records is generated in response.

The main implementations are based on the use of Apache Kafka and Spark technologies with their respective advantages and disadvantages [11, 12]. The difference in the proposed architecture, among others, is the EKL technology stack, which have advantages in data retrieval and stored data visualization.

In work [13], a review of various tools was carried out, from graphical representations of relations in databases (such as neo4j) to various visualization tools (in particular Tableau). This means that there are different techniques for data analysis and a large number of tools that help to do it in different ways. However, from the point of view of the interaction between data flows, it is worth using the developed software interfaces for the processes of ingest (pushing data), preprocessing and searching.

The data pipeline described in [14] is more difficult to configure and the considered components (in particular, semantics). Given certain rationales for effectiveness, however, this solution is more related to the medical field. Some aspects described in this source can be used to improve the proposed data exchange scheme. Some aspects of attracting customers, impact on business and features of working with big data and the Extraction–Transformation–Loading (ETL) process are discussed in [15]. This shows the high relevance and interest of solutions in this field of research.

3 The Purpose and Objectives of the Research

The purpose of this work is to design a data pipeline architecture based on the EKL stack of technologies for processing data from social networks. Among the main tasks is to describe the process of collecting data, saving it in the data warehouse and visualizing the results of the analysis. An option for data analysis is data classification based on user comments or likes on Facebook and Instagram social media posts.

The main stages of data pipeline are data ingestion (selection and loading of data), data storage (saving the received information in the database and related tools) and visualization (presentation of processed texts).

As an example, collect information from Instagram and Facebook regarding search by tags using defined locators to web page elements. In addition to design, one of the goals is to test such an architecture with data shared between indexes in the database. The plan is to test the system by running the data flow from the data collection to the analysis step.

It is also worth describing the work process of the entire system in the form of algorithm steps and schemes. In this way, it will be easier to understand the dependencies and the sequence of actions.

4 Methodology of Data Analysis Based on EKL Stack

The main components of such an architecture can be divided into the following layers: data collection, data processing, data storage, and analysis with visualization. At each stage, certain instruments were used to ensure the next step (see Fig. 1) in the general data flow scheme.

The work uses methods of data selection, processing, and analysis. Several means have been used to solve the problem of integration. At the same time, Selenium, Kibana processing and visualization were used among the selection tools. The main sample of data was selected data read from news pages in social networks [2, 3]. The work uses the Python programming language, which contains many possibilities with connected libraries, from data transformation to the application of machine learning algorithms. At the stage of collecting data from the comments and likes of users in the post, the Selenium tool is used. This library allows specifying the locators of web elements in the Document Object Model (DOM) of a web page.

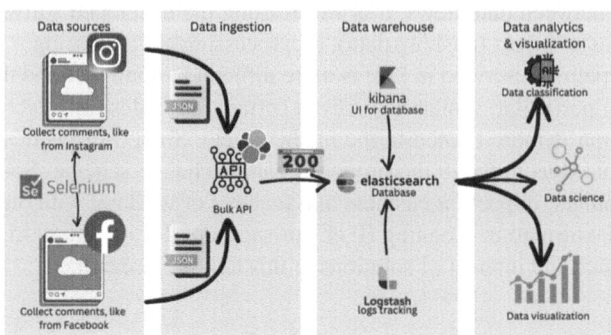

Fig. 1. Visualization of the data pipeline for social network analysis

Among the possible ways of describing the path to the web elements of a web page are by identifier, tag, class, or CSS or XPath. Access to the browser is implemented through the connected web driver of a specific browser. In the test case of this system, Google Chrome. In addition to standard locators, JavaScriptExecutor is used for various interactive scrolling of the comment page to work with them. This method of data collection is based on the direct collection of data from the web page, as if simulating the actions of a real user. Reading data from the required element on the page is incredibly fast. Often the speed of the Internet is lower than the speed of the browser. Various types of waiters are used for this. In our case, the most common waiter is an implicit wait. This type of waiter allows you to implicitly wait for an element until it appears. There are still many opportunities to stop the page to have time to collect data. But all of them are used only when necessary. At the collection stage, other data may be used, either collected from devices or generated for testing.

Since it is possible to execute the curl command from the command line to perform http requests to create an index and load data, the process is automated using bash scripts. This method is simple and fast to run any set of commands and the order of execution in it. The first step is to read the data and generate datasets for download. Pre-created request body templates with all necessary settings. After that, a check is made for the success of downloading this batch file. As data is transferred in batches, the data is converted to JavaScript Object Notation (JSON) format in preparation for submission to the database through the ingest process. Elasticsearch is implemented based on the REST architectural style (RESTful web service), so all communication with it is implemented using client-server interaction based on the HTTP protocol. REST is characterized by the specialization of using this protocol to communicate with the server, which gives it flexibility in requests and responses to him. The response to each request from the server can be understood using the corresponding status codes. In case of incorrect settings or server errors, 400 and 500 errors will be displayed, and successful downloads or data updates will be displayed with 200 status codes. In the non-relational database Elasticsearch, there is a Bulk API for sending a file with changes. This method allows more records to be sent using fewer repeated requests and reduces the load on the database.

The main part for data storage is a data, warehouse based on Elasticsearch. Data indexes can be dynamically created according to the specified configuration values of names and parameters of shards and replicas from a JSON file.

This database is often used as a search engine because it can search by Domain Specific Language queries. Elasticsearch works as an API, and Kibana is a tool that visualizes actions to the database. There is also the possibility of tracking metrics of parameter changes, setting filters for data visualization. However, separate parts of the code have been developed for more complex and specific data processing and analysis.

5 Results of the Component Analysis of the Designed Data Pipeline

5.1 Data Ingestion

The process of data ingestion consists in preparing and filling databases with information (see Fig. 2).

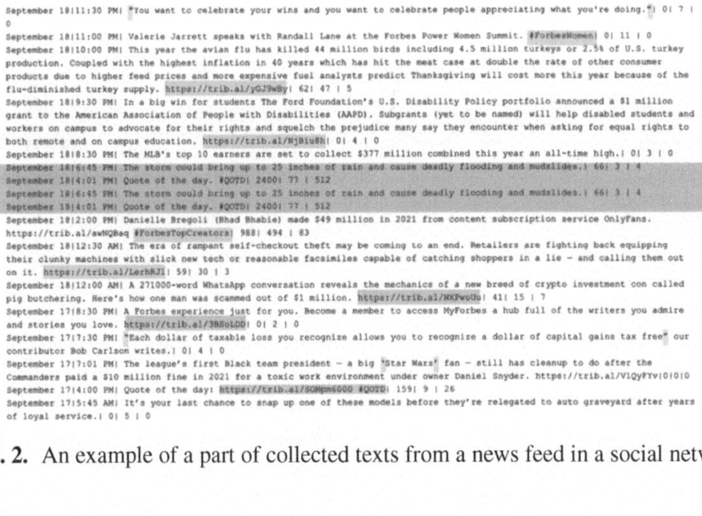

September 18|11:30 PM| "You want to celebrate your wins and you want to celebrate people appreciating what you're doing."| 0| 7 | 0
September 18|11:00 PM| Valerie Jarrett speaks with Randall Lane at the Forbes Power Women Summit. #ForbesWomen| 0| 11 | 0
September 18|10:00 PM| This year the avian flu has killed 44 million birds including 4.5 million turkeys or 2.5% of U.S. turkey production. Coupled with the highest inflation in 40 years which has hit the meat case at double the rate of other consumer products due to higher feed prices and more expensive fuel analysts predict Thanksgiving will cost more this year because of the flu-diminished turkey supply. https://trib.al/yGJ9wBy| 62| 47 | 5
September 18|9:30 PM| In a big win for students The Ford Foundation's U.S. Disability Policy portfolio announced a $1 million grant to the American Association of People with Disabilities (AAPD). Subgrants (yet to be named) will help disabled students and workers on campus to advocate for their rights and squelch the prejudice many say they encounter when asking for equal rights to both remote and on campus education. https://trib.al/NjBiu8h| 0| 4 | 0
September 18|8:30 PM| The MLB's top 10 earners are set to collect $377 million combined this year an all-time high.| 0| 3 | 0
September 18|6:45 PM| The storm could bring up to 25 inches of rain and cause deadly flooding and mudslides.| 66| 3 | 4
September 18|4:01 PM| Quote of the day. #QOTD| 2400| 77 | 512
September 18|6:45 PM| The storm could bring up to 25 inches of rain and cause deadly flooding and mudslides.| 66| 3 | 4
September 18|4:01 PM| Quote of the day. #QOTD| 2400| 77 | 512
September 18|2:00 PM| Danielle Bregoli (Bhad Bhabie) made $49 million in 2021 from content subscription service OnlyFans. https://trib.al/awNQBaq #ForbesTopCreators| 988| 494 | 83
September 18|12:30 AM| The era of rampant self-checkout theft may be coming to an end. Retailers are fighting back equipping their clunky machines with slick new tech or reasonable facsimiles capable of catching shoppers in a lie - and calling them out on it. https://trib.al/LerhRJl| 59| 30 | 3
September 18|12:00 AM| A 271000-word WhatsApp conversation reveals the mechanics of a new breed of crypto investment con called pig butchering. Here's how one man was scammed out of $1 million. https://trib.al/NXPwoUu| 41| 15 | 7
September 17|8:30 PM| A Forbes experience just for you. Become a member to access MyForbes a hub full of the writers you admire and stories you love. https://trib.al/3BSoLDD| 0| 2 | 0
September 17|7:30 PM| "Each dollar of taxable loss you recognize allows you to recognize a dollar of capital gains tax free" our contributor Bob Carlson writes.| 0| 4 | 0
September 17|7:01 PM| The league's first Black team president - a big "Star Wars" fan - still has cleanup to do after the Commanders paid a $10 million fine in 2021 for a toxic work environment under owner Daniel Snyder. https://trib.al/V1QyFYv|0|0|0
September 17|4:00 PM| Quote of the day: https://trib.al/SOMpm6000 #QOTD| 159| 9 | 26
September 17|5:45 AM| It's your last chance to snap up one of these models before they're relegated to auto graveyard after years of loyal service.| 0| 5 | 0

Fig. 2. An example of a part of collected texts from a news feed in a social network.

There are often problems with the processing of read data that needs to be handled. For example, a photo may be added there without a description of the picture, which leads to writing an empty line in the database. It can also be a time and date conversion to one type of data representation. Data trimming is used to overcome the problem of extra spaces. After collecting part of the content, such as textual information from comments, there is a need for data preprocessing. This is due to the existence of emoticons, punctuation marks and link tags. These characters make it difficult to process when training a machine learning model to classify comments and text from a post. Since scrolling is used for the collection, at some point in time there may be repetitions of texts. In this case, such information should be filtered and checked for uniqueness.

Before sending, the file must be prepared and converted to the desired JSON format (see Fig. 3). Therefore, the collected data array in the preparation process is filtered for the presence of repetitions and unnecessary characters. Date, time, post text, number of comments, number of posts and number of distribution fields are wrapped with additional brackets and quotation marks for JSON format. Accordingly, the keys of such values with names are added: "date", "hour", "text", "number_of_likes", "number_of_comments", "number_of_shares" [2].

Since at the first stage the data is saved from the console logs to files, the data is raw and contains a lot of unnecessary information. Partially unnecessary data is filtered out, however, to save loading time, work with texts takes place in the following stages. Data Ingestion process has its limitations. For example, the volume of data that can be loaded at one time must have its own size (in the Elasticsearch example, it can be 100 MB of http payload.). Accordingly, the number of records added to the database has its limits. In general, you need to find the optimal time and resource values for working with a large amount of data. This way of uploading data in batches is much faster than adding data one by one. A special feature of working with Elasticsearch is configuring configuration maps. This means that the pre-structured data schema is loaded into the created indexes.

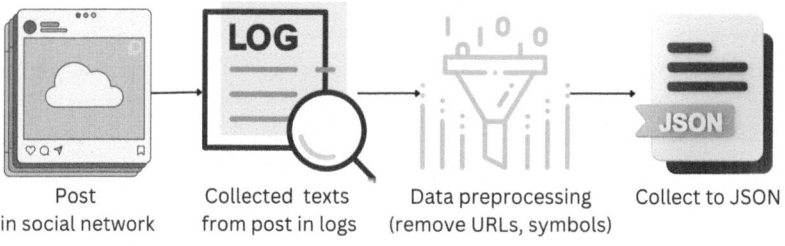

| Post in social network | Collected texts from post in logs | Data preprocessing (remove URLs, symbols) | Collect to JSON |

Fig. 3. Stages of data transformation and preparation for data ingestion

When using a request to the Bulk API, events are logged, and the response shows the success or failure of downloading certain data with added HTTP status codes. Indexes in databases can be populated with specific configurations of shards and replicas. This operation is performed once before filling the database and is automated using a Bash script.

5.2 Data Warehouse

All data collected from social networks should be stored in a separate place to avoid their loss. It is desirable that this place is protected and that it is possible to add, delete and move this data. Since this is user data, the information may have different vulnerabilities. A necessary condition is the use of a Data warehouse. This approach ensures not only the preservation of data, but also the possibility of its interpretation in graphic form. Such data is easier to work with by avoiding the process of reading from large files each time.

In addition, the data warehouse has a very good way of filtering, sorting, and displaying the results of these functions. Given the division of data into separate tables or indexes, data analytics is simplified with distributed data. Storing data in a data warehouse allows you to reuse the stored data in analysis. The created indexes contain names according to the selected social networks and are divided according to the topic of the collected information (for example, several news sources) [3]. A similar infrastructure can be deployed in cloud environments. Thanks to the provision of support for Elasticsearch in cloud environments such as Opensearch, such an integration is possible.

The approach of storing data in a data warehouse is chosen due to the fact that storing data in a simple file is quite dangerous. After all, the collected data may contain confidential, sometimes sensitive information collected from social network pages. Due to the described principle, the data is protected and cannot be used for illegal purposes against users, influence or harm them.

The system of the actual applied data warehouse can be modified or expanded according to the use of the new approach. In addition, this approach is modern and widely used in the world, which means that it is supported according to new developments.

The process of setting up the data warehouse environment and recording data was performed based on a news feed collected from social networks [1].

5.3 Data Analytics and Visualization

The stored data is used for the analysis of the results. Among the possible visualizations is the possibility of working with texts, highlighting the most used words in the texts. In addition, it can be visualizing the most popular hours of user activity [2] and analyze the dependence of the number of likes on comments [3]. As a test data set for a trained machine learning model, it can be used to classify text on a certain topic. The most popular words can also be displayed during analytics (see Fig. 4). Stop words were previously removed from the sentences and the most frequently used ones were displayed with the largest font using the WordCloud library. In this way, additional data analysis can be performed. As a result of the Word Cloud analysis, we can see that the words with the highest frequency are year, Forbes, power, summit, million and billion, and the words Ukraine, Americans, speaks and business are also often found. Considering the period of data collection of newspaper news, it can be asserted that during this period a summit was held at which issues of capacity, business, relations between countries and the situation in the world were discussed. Based on such an analysis, it is possible to understand the main accents of the world during this time period. Of course, such emphases may change over the time of data collection, depending on the collection period and the amount of data collected.

Regarding test data for machine learning models, data from a database can be used. From the sklearn library, you can train and use this data for validation. Information from the used news feed needs to be tokenized, cleaned, stop words added, and lemmatized.

The process of pre-processing texts in natural language processing involves removing punctuation and URLs, using lowercase text, tokenization, removing stop words, and lemming. This process is necessary to clean the data from redundant information. This method makes it possible to speed up the work of text analysis and visualization algorithms and avoid additional symbols during data processing. This is since in social networks texts are usually saturated with various additional symbols to attract the attention of users. In this way, the image and the intriguing text or description below it will be attractive to ordinary users. To remove punctuation from a sentence, you need to define a list of unwanted characters and remove them using the string methods of the Python library. To bring all words to the same form, lower case is used for them. And the tokenization process consists in dividing the text into words. Among those tokenized words, there may be words that do not carry any information but are used for stylistics and grammar of the language. Such a list of stop words is also removed from the list of words. As a result, we get a set of words ready for further text analysis. However, in the text there are stemmed words or diminished words to the main form. it is also worth performing lemmatization of the dictionary, i.e. converting words to their original form.

After performing these processes, you can create new indexes in the database and work directly with the processed data. As a result of such an analysis, it is possible to classify the collection by topics: sports, politics, disasters [16].

Fig. 4. An example of presenting the most popular words from one of news feed [2] from social networks.

The support system for making innovative business decisions regarding the implementation of investment projects [1, 17, 18] in this direction is also important here. This is especially relevant in conditions of uncertainty, risk and instability [19–21]. At the same time, when solving these tasks, it is necessary to take into account the specifics of the use of information systems and technologies, compliance with management and data processing standards [22–26], as well as the assessment of project parameters taking into account the values of sustainable development [27, 28]. An important element is also the modeling of conditions and aspects [29–33] that affect the success of innovative investment initiatives.

In addition to visualizing words in the form of Word Cloud, the text can be analyzed using graphical dependencies. For example, it can be the dependence of the text of the book on the number of unique characters. Dependencies can be represented as N-Gram Word Cloud Frequency, Bubble Line, Barcode, Tree Diagram, Network Diagram and Circular Line Diagram. Such visualizations make it possible to highlight the main statistical differences of the texts for further data analysis. Often, the Tableau library is integrated with the Python programming language for such visualizations. In addition, machine learning classifiers are often used to divide into certain groups. In this way, similar texts can be highlighted and the approach of working with new ones is automated. VADER (Valence Aware Dictionary and Entiment Reasoner) or Afinn library is also often used for semantic analysis, which helps to classify texts according to certain dictionaries. Clustering of the main keywords can be done using the k-means algorithm. This is a well-known algorithm for data processing, in which the steps of working with text consist of preprocessing, verticalization of text, reduction of text volume using Principal Component Analysis (PCA).

6 Discussion

The developed architecture can be used for data analytics. The proposed system was tested based on the news feed collected from social networks. The advantage of the proposed solution is the possibility of more complex searches and data visualization. The disadvantages of this approach include the process of data preparation with transformations and data processing.

The proposed set of tools allows you to process streaming data from the stage of collection to visualization. All tools are free and freely accessible and allow you to collect, process and visualize the results obtained from social networks. The design of such a solution can be applied to much larger projects. The described features of working with data at each stage make it possible to fully use the set of data pipeline tools without additional restrictions.

Some of the approaches considered can have a greater impact on the visualization of the results [13], which helps to better conduct the analysis. More complex approaches for data pipelines [14, 15] allow more thorough intermediate data processing. However, in the context of a complex solution, it is worth paying attention to modern technologies and their integration with each other to obtain a full cycle of working with data.

Compared to similar systems, this data pipeline architecture allows extensibility and analysis of stored data. Testing based on data from social networks made it possible to evaluate the specified architecture.

7 Conclusions

The modern development of science and technology allows designing systems for data analysis, in particular for streaming data from news resources of the Facebook social network. Based on the literature review, we can conclude that a lot of attention is paid to collection and analysis, but there are no conceptual flows of data exchange. Considering the significant influence of information from social networks, it is worth paying attention to the analysis of the content of posts, the data reading of which is proposed to be performed using Selenium. Although this tool allows you to flexibly configure the path to web page elements and its content, there are some restrictions related to the policy of social networks regarding unauthorized users.

In this work, a data pipeline for working with streaming data is designed. The main stages of development are shown and tested based on data from social networks. The methods of visualization and data analysis are analyzed. Also, the process of working with data sources, pre-processing of data, and working with a database is considered. It is revised features of using the Elasticsearch, Kibana, Logstash technology stack when working with the data pipeline. Data partitioning in the Elasticsearch database is configurable, allowing you to add and delete queries almost independently. Comparing the described possibilities of data presentation for visualization with the implemented method, it can be considered that this Word Cloud method and others are no less informative, clearly showing trends and emphasis during a certain time of data collection.

In addition, the possibilities of data analysis according to various parameters and criteria are described. The proposed architecture can be used on similar topics and systems. In addition, possible areas of future research include the application of this methodology and framework for data mining.

References

Mysiuk, I.: Designing a data warehouse for collected data about user activity in social networks using Elasticsearch. Path Sci. 9(7), 4001–4005 (2023). https://doi.org/10.22178/pos.94-13

Mysiuk, I., Mysiuk, R., Shuvar, R.: Collecting and analyzing news from newspaper posts in facebook using machine learning. Artif. Intell. 28(1), 147–154 (2023). https://doi.org/10.15407/jai 2023.01.1472

Mysiuk, I., Mysiuk, R., Shuvar, R., Yuzevych, V.: Methods of analytics of big data of popular electronic newspapers on facebook. Electron. Inf. Technol. 19, 66–74 (2022). https://doi.org/ 10.30970/eli.19.6

Abdukhamidov, E., Juraev, F., Abuhamad, M., El-Sappagh, S., AbuHmed, T.: Sentiment Analysis of Users' Reactions on Social Media during the Pandemic. Electronics 11(10), 1648 (2020). https://doi.org/10.3390/electronics11101648

Conway, M., Hu, M., Chapman, W.W.: Recent advances in using natural language processing to address public health research questions using social media and consumer generated data. Yearb. Med. Inform. 28(1), 208–217 (2019). https://doi.org/10.1055/s-0039-1677918

Jiao, Q.: A brief survey of text classification methods. In: 2023 IEEE 3rd International Conference on Information Technology, Big Data and Artificial Intelligence (ICIBA), Chongqing, China, pp. 1384–1389 (2023). https://doi.org/10.1109/ICIBA56860.2023.10165621

Hodorog, A., Petri, I., Rezgui, Y.: Machine learning and Natural Language Processing of social media data for event detection in smart cities. Sustain. Cities Soc. 85, 104026 (2022). ISSN 2210-6707. https://doi.org/10.1016/j.scs.2022.104026

Samosir, J., Indrawan-Santiago, M., Delir Haghighi, P.: An evaluation of data stream processing systems for data driven applications. Proc. Comput. Sci. 80, 439–449 (2016). ISSN 1877-0509. https://doi.org/10.1016/j.procs.2016.05.322

Mu, C., Zhao, J., Yang, G., Zhang, J., Yan, Z.: Towards Practical Visual Search Engine within Elasticsearch (2019). arXiv, https://doi.org/10.48550/arXiv.1806.08896

Devi, F., Thomson, P., Umniy, S.: Implementation of ElasticSearch search engine on order management system data. Int. J. Comput. Appl. 181, 25–35 (2018). https://doi.org/10.5120/ijca20 18917617

Iqbal, D.A., Faqih, H.: The implementation of stream architecture for handling big data velocity in social media. J. Phys. Conf. Ser. 1641 (2020). https://doi.org/10.1088/1742-6596/1641/1/ 012021

Podhoranyi, M., Vojacek, L.: Social media data processing infrastructure by using apache spark big data platform: twitter data analysis. In: Proceedings of the 2019 4th International Conference on Cloud Computing and Internet of Things (CCIOT '19). Association for Computing Machinery, New York, NY, USA, 1–6 (2019). 1https://doi.org/10.1145/3361821.3361825

Sebei, H., Hadj Taieb, M.A., Ben Aouicha, M.: Review of social media analytics process and Big Data pipeline. Soc. Netw. Anal. Min. **8**, 30 (2018). https://doi.org/10.1007/s13278-018-0507-0

Bono, C.A., Cappiello, C., Pernici, B., Ramalli, E., Vitali, M.: Pipeline design for data preparation for social media analysis. J. Data Inf. Qual. **15**, 4, Article 42, 25 pages (December 2023). https://doi.org/10.1145/3597305

Rustum, R., Kavitha, J., Rao, P.V.R.D.P., Bhargav, J., Babu, G.C.: Customer engagement through social media and big data pipeline. In: Chen, J.IZ., Tavares, J.M.R.S., Shi, F. (eds.) Third International Conference on Image Processing and Capsule Networks. ICIPCN (2022). Lecture Notes in Networks and Systems, vol. 514. Springer, Cham. https://doi.org/10.1007/978-3-031-12413-6_47

NLP Tutorial for Text Classification in Python. URL: https://medium.com/analytics-vidhya/nlp-tutorial-for-text-classification-in-python-8f19cd17b49e. Accessed 19 Aug 2023

Skrynkovskyi, R.M.: Methodical approaches to economic estimation of investment attractiveness of machine building enterprises for portfolio investors. Actual Probl. Econ. **118**(4), 177–186 (2011)

Skrynkovskyi, R.: Investment attractiveness evaluation technique for machine-building enterprises. Actual Probl. Econ. **7**(85), 228–240 (2008)

Pavlenchyk, N., et al.: The influence of management creativity on the optimality of management decisions over time: an innovative aspect. J. E. Eur. Cent. Asian Res. (JEECAR) **10**(3), 498–514 (2023). https://doi.org/10.15549/jeecar.v10i3.1318

Popova, N., Kataiev, A., Nevertii, A., Kryvoruchko, O., Skrynkovskyi, R.: Marketing aspects of innovative development of business organizations in the sphere of production, trade, transport, and logistics in VUCA conditions. Stud. Appl. Econ. **38**(4) (2021). https://doi.org/10.25115/eea.v38i4.3962

Popova, N., et al.: Development of trust marketing in the digital society. Econ. Ann.-XXI **176**(3–4), 13–25 (2019). https://doi.org/10.21003/ea.v176-02

Mysiuk, R., Mysiuk, I.m Pawlowski, G., Yuzevych, V., Yasinskyi, M., Tyrkalo, Y.: Video-based concrete road damage assessment using JetRacer kit. In: 17th International Conference on the Experience of Designing and Application of CAD Systems (CADSM) (2023). https://doi.org/10.1109/cadsm58174.2023.10076528

Babych, M., et al.: Substantiation of economic efficiency of using a solar dryer under conditions of personal peasant farms. E. Eur. J. Enterp. Technol. **6**(8) (84), 41–47 (2016). https://doi.org/10.15587/1729-4061.2016.83756

Mysiuk, R.V., et al.: Determination of conditions for loss of bearing capacity of underground ammonia pipelines based on the monitoring data and flexible search algorithms. Arch. Mater. Sci. Eng. **115**(1), 13–20 (2022). https://doi.org/10.5604/01.3001.0016.0671

Yuzevych, V., Klyuvak, O., Skrynkovskyy, R.: Diagnostics of the system of interaction between the government and business in terms of public e-procurement. Econ. Ann.-XXI **160**(7–8), 39–44 (2016). https://doi.org/10.21003/ea.v160-08

Yuzevych, L., Skrynkovskyy, R., Koman, B.: Development of information support of quality management of underground pipelines. EUREKA: Phys. Eng. **4**, 49–60 (2017). https://doi.org/10.21303/2461-4262.2017.00392

Dzhala, R., et al.: Simulation of corrosion fracture of nano-concrete at the interface with reinforcement taking into account temperature change. In: 4th International Workshop on Modern Machine Learning Technologies and Data Science, MoMLeT&DS 2022, CEUR Workshop Proceedings 3312, Leiden–Lviv, The Netherlands–Ukraine, pp. 123–133, Nov., 25–26 (2022). https://ceur-ws.org/Vol3312/paper10.pdf

Sumets, A., et al.: Methodological toolkit for assessing the level of stability of agricultural enterprises. Agri. Resour. Econ.: Int. Sci. E-J. **8**(1), 235–255 (2022). https://doi.org/10.51599/are.2022.08.01.12

Mysiuk, R., Yuzevych, V., Koman, B., Yasinskyi, M.: High availability system for monitoring material degradation processes at the concrete-polymer interface. In: 2022 12th International Conference on Advanced Computer Information Technologies (ACIT) (2022). https://doi.org/10.1109/acit54803.2022.9913086

Skrynkovskyy, R., Pavlenchyk, N., Tsyuh, S., Zanevskyy, I., Pavlenchyk, A.: Economic-mathematical model of enterprise profit maximization in the system of sustainable development values. Agri. Resour. Econ.: Int. Sci. E-J. **8**(4), 188–214 (2022). https://doi.org/10.51599/are.2022.08.04.09

Ji, Z., Wu, P., Ling, C., Zhu, P.: Exploring the impact of investor's sentiment tendency in varying input window length for stock price prediction. Multimedia Tools Appl. **82**(18), 27415–27449 (2023). https://doi.org/10.1007/s11042-023-14587-830

Bouadjenek, M.R., Sanner, S., Wu, G.: A user-centric analysis of social media for stock market prediction. ACM Trans. Web. **17**(2), 1–22 (2023). https://doi.org/10.1145/353285631

Hsieh, T.-Y., Lin, T.-Y., Li, F., Huang, Y.-T.: Analyst's target price revision and dealer's trading behavior analysis: evidence from Taiwanese stock market. Sustainability **15**(4), 3593 (2023). https://doi.org/10.3390/su15043593

Employee-Engagement Level as a Predictor of Organizational Performance: A Study of Information Technology Companies in Telangana-India

Asma Bano[1](✉), Ayesha Khatun[2], and Dinesh Kumar[1]

[1] Mittal School of Business, Lovely Professional University, Punjab, India
asmabanu_522@yahoo.in

[2] Symbiosis Law School, Symbiosis International University, Nagpur, India

Abstract. Employee performance, dedication, competitive advantage, etc. all stem in large part from the level of engagement present inside a business. The current study consists of Employee Engagement (EE) and Organizational Performance (OP) with their own dimensions. EE consists of organizational engagement and job engagement and OP consists of emotional, financial, and non-financial components. The current work aimed at determining the levels, factors and relationship of the study variables in Information Technology Companies in Telangana. A total of 440 responses gathered within the time frame. The sample is grouped into two levels primary and secondary levels. In light of the study's primary emphasis on the viewpoint of the employee engagement, only minor adjustments to the engagement and performance questionnaires were made in consultation with IT Company workforce like managers, assistant managers, administrators, team leaders and employee. Factor analysis by Varimax orthogonal rotation followed by Kaiser Normalization Factor analysis was conducted by using latest version of SPSS 21. Employee engagement is favourably related to emotional, financial, and nonfinancial components of organizational performance. Employees' levels of involvement and dedication did not vary greatly across the different departments, between employees of different types of working hours and schedules, between employees with different designations, and between employees with different degrees of experience, as revealed by this study.

Keywords: Employee Engagement · Telangana · Information Technology Employees · Organizational Performance

1 Introduction

There are total more than 1500 IT Companies in Hyderabad. The IT/ITES Companies in Hyderabad consists of 6,00,000 employees. All the IT companies are well versed with vast area, multiple disciplines, well equipped with tools & techniques and machines & labs, good infrastructures, properly designed strategies, policies, programs and objectives and highly talented and skilled employees (engineers and manager). Several regulating bodies have been established by the government of Telangana to control the activities to be performed by the IT Sector. This results in providing opportunities for 5.3 million jobs for IT people in Telangana. The government of Telangana has come up with valid incentives and grants for the information technology sector to pull the new, multi talents and skills to meet the challenges of IT industry. Information Technology companies and other affiliated entities have made efforts to address the importance and growth of IT sector by raising awareness, enhancing the quality of training, growing and developing strategies and bettering the standard of living at rural, remote areas and so on. A career in the field of IT sector is unlike any other. According to the establishment and maintenance of standards in IT sector 2020 about sixty-five and sixty-nine per cent of IT employees operate in a multicultural setting and different personal makeups. They come up with different creed and caste and had to conclude on a common knowledge sharing platform where the concept of engagement has given due importance. Managing personnel is made more difficult by the diversity problem and the severe staffing deficit. When discussing the management of people, employee involvement is crucial. Active workers care about their jobs and their company, and they are dedicated to doing a good job. Employees that are invested in the success of their business are more likely to go above and beyond their normal duties in order to achieve corporate goals, and can serve as a driving force in the (Khan, 1992).

India is always been a key contributor to quality work. By the end of 2023 total 905715 employees are working in IT sector in Hyderabad. The new starts up in 2014 were 400 which have increased to 2000 in the year 2022 with the advancement in technology. The relevance of gauging the dedication of IT employees is emphasized by predictions of hard work scarcity in the future and rising IT/ITES sector. The most important objective of this research paper is to find out the impact of engagement level of employees on to the organizational performance as well as to pinpoint the relationship among them.

1.1 Employee Engagement (EE)

Initiated by Khan, the internal communication movement is based on a multi-dimensional framework for engagement. One definition of employee engagement is that condition of an individual where he puts his 100% towards his job and job role. (Khan, 1992). Positive assertiveness occurs when an employee moves upward and beyond the need or availability to demonstrate greater personal investment in the success of the company and to advocate on behalf of the company's bottom line. An individual's engagement with their employer can take the shape of either outside work or performance in addition to their regular duties, both of which foster positive transformation for the company's future success. Employee and customer satisfaction, as well as the organization's bottom line, are directly tied to how invested workers are in their jobs and in the success of the company as a whole (Cohen, 1991). Engaged and committed workers are more likely to be productive, profitable, retained, and safe, as demonstrated by a plethora of research (Hay Group, 2001).

If a company has dedicated workers who are invested in its success, it may create a workplace where those workers want to spend their time, which in turn boosts productivity. Workplace engagement is the desire to do one's best work with full understanding of the organization's needs, while workplace commitment is the desire to continue as a fellow caretaker. There has been a lot of focus on employee engagement in the last two decades from both the academic and business worlds. This is because it is seen as the metric that best predicts how invested and productive an employee will be at their workplace (Sundaray, 2011). Numerous studies had confirmed about the significant correlation between employee and the engagement in different economies; however, the effects of engagement on employees' likelihood of staying with the company and their willingness to adhere to its norms have received much less attention. Despite the abundance of research on employee connection and its effects on businesses, there is a significant vacuum in this area of study, prompting the need for more field research from a variety of perspectives and contexts. Participation, satisfaction, commitment, dedication, communication, work culture, involvement and needs and wants of employees are few factors that crucial and significant in bringing out the engagement in the employees and enhanced improved engagement. Most of the organizations consider these elements simple and mostly overlooked which could disengage the employees.

1.2   Employee Engagement in the Information Technology Industry

Despite of growth in education and its development to the global economy, very less is understood how to apply the concepts of engagement in the global scenario and its effects on industry. In addition, the study is motivated by factors specific to the IT sector, such as the distinctive challenges it presents (isolation, difficulties in socializing, communication problems, cultural disagreements, etc.). There is no way around it: companies must increase productivity while decreasing employee input, even while the workforce is shrinking and has its own unique challenges. In order to achieve this goal, IT companies must not only keep their personnel actively working, but also engage their minds and the entire essence of their selves. There is a desperate need for an inquiry like this to be undertaken, henceforth the current research aim to fill the gaps raised from the literature of employee engagement and organizational performances in IT sector. To do this, it investigated concepts of EE and its outcomes on the organizations. As such, we took into account the Saks' model of talent management and made some minor adjustments so that it would fulfil the requirements of current work (Saks, 2006). Engagement in IT sector is also equally important as to other sectors. The quality of production has changed due rising of advance technology, multinational exposures, purposive knowledge, scoring and ranking in a highly competitive and complex world, designing and development, training and placement, reward and recognition and financial growth and stability, which are the essential challenges for the employees to stay engaged and involved which in turn enhances organizational performance.

Information Technology Companies are placed with several challenges like strict budgetary control, result driven, task orientation, fixed working schedule and overtime working depending on security and networking reasons, hence it become essential for the employees to become communicated, dedicated and engaged otherwise there are deprived outcomes. Engagement is an essentiality and leads to the below mentioned outcomes.

Outcomes of Employee Engagement in Information Technology Sector are advance technology, multinational exposures, purposive knowledge, scoring and ranking, designing and development, training and placement, reward and recognition, financial growth and stability, organizational performance.

2 Literature Review

By considering title of study widespread collected works remained on construct of research such as employee engagement and organizational performance acting as independent and dependent variable of the study. The author detects effects and execution dynamics of connected ideas. Analysis from diverse periodical including google scholar, research gate, emerald publication, Francis and Taylor and springer set of databank. The review studied the theories of the study constructs at juncture of their connection through each other and their influence on the personnel and establishments. A comprehensive examination of every constant laterally using its elements, procedure connection and consequences is revised by a methodical evaluation technique.

2.1 Employee Engagement

Several researches in the past several years have shown involvement as a crucial success factor. It has also been shown that employee involvement significantly contributes to organizational performance, creativity, and competitive advantage. Leaders and managers care a great deal about achieving maximum employee engagement for the reasons stated above. Prior to the 1990s, the engagement was viewed solely as practical consultancy work; however, since academics recognized its research significance in the early 20th century, it has attracted a rising quantity of academics in arenas such as con sciousness, corporate, and administration, as well as organizational conduct (Xu and Copper Thomas 2011). Numerous studies under the direction of academics and professionals have been conducted, yet dearth of students' acute writings on the theme (Kular et al. 2008). The breadth of employee participation was examined in a distinct study. It resulted in advancement of several descriptions on drivers of engagement. Strong ties exist among EE and other well-studied conceptions, such as satisfaction, obligation, citizenship behaviour, involvement and participation; as a result, our understanding of engagement must draw on the findings of many other studies.

Role theory became popular in the late 1960s, and one definition of employee engagement is "impulsive role participation," as described by Goffman, while another definition, by Wildermuth and Pauken, is "noticeable venture of concentration and powerful determination" (Pauken, 2008). Csikszentmihalyi defined employee engagement as the emotional state of having one's "whole being" devoted to one's work. Academic trailblazer W.A. Kahn used the term "personal engagement" to describe the trend of encouraging workers to feel invested in their jobs. Work that allows the employees to invest physically, mentally, and emotionally towards their job roles proved to have the highest engagement levels (Khan, 1992). Employee involvement is a key factor that has been highlighted by the research of Schaufeli et al. and Robinson et al. For them, EE is a condition of conscious that involves taking pride in and actively contributing to one's job and one's company. "Engagement" is defined by Hewitt Associates as "the situation where people are enthusiastic knowledgeable and get engaged to work, checked by 3 behavior displays of individuals namely tell, connect, and struggle" (Hewitt Associates LLC, 2004).

Employee engagement, as conceptualized by Saks as the level that an employee is determined and assessed on work. He distinguishes work engagement from organizational engagement as a distinct category. How invested a person is in carrying out the duties of their position is referred to as "job engagement." However, organizational engagement refers to an employee's level of emotional investment as a sense of belongingness to the company (Saks, 2006). "The capability to arrest the intelligence, emotions, and personalities of employees to develop a primary purpose of quality and result," write Fleming and Asplundh of Gallup. In addition, they show that employees who are truly invested in the success of their company have a strong emotional, social, and even spiritual connection to the organization's goal, vision, and purpose. Newman and Harrison's definition of employee engagement took the employee's actions as a whole into account, with special emphasis on the employee's performance, their level of participation, and their citizenship (Newman and Harrison, 2008). According to Cook (2012), employee engagement occurs when workers have a favourable impression of their company and take initiative to help their employer, co-workers, and other stakeholders reach their goals.

According to E. Kaviya and S.Purushothaman (2020) the elements of employee engagement like employed situation, greater provision, structural guidance and colleague's care, recompenses and acknowledgment and profession development. Ascertaining the happiness of personnel pointers to worker retaining, comprising in what way to encourage and preserve personnel etc., assist the IT companies toward marking their workforces completely engaged and dedicated to organization. According to P. Lakshmi Narayanamma et al., (2022) employee engagement accomplish vigorous role in any establishments as it is associated by means of production, work gratification, commitment originates when individuals understand their responsibility and meeting the demands of one's profession. According to Priyashantha et al., (2023), outcomes of employee engagement are care, interaction, and emotional wealth, prospects aimed at knowledge and expansion, communal conversation and managerial enactment, CSR accomplishments and worker retaining, work role optimistic arrogances, profession capitals and transformational management elegance, feel right and appropriate and faith, and chances meant for resourcefulness. According to Ting Yao & Preecha Methavasaraphak (2023), recompense, profession progression, work fulfilment, and structural obligation considerably inclined to employee engagement, suggests that staffing corporations must order improving work fulfilment. Executing systematic worker fulfilment reviews and response assemblies identify extents demanding development, such as work-life balance, job circulation, and response of undertaking. Contribution of strong profession development prospects and career growth also allow personnel, showcasing the business's promise to their development. Hence the study touches the core aspects of current work. According to Alam, J. et al., (2023), prognostic elements of employee engagement were remuneration supervision, shadowed by enactment administration, universal supervision and corporate governance and regulating element of engagement was age, where elder workers described superior commitment. Hence displays different elements of employee engagement of the study. According to Jindain, C. and Gilitwala, B. (2023), perceived organizational support, faith and esteem in the business delivered a substantial constructive influence on employee engagement in turn showing a significant effect on employee performance in a hybrid working model. Hence the above study provides the relation of engagement on employee performance, an important consideration for the above work. According to Bhat, S.A., Bashir, M. and Jan, H. (2024), work engagement is related to three facets of perceived job performance (PJP). Employee engagement to develop the general work presentation for improving their commitment and outcome generation, focus on the connection of employee engagement in making employees committed and improving job performance.

2.2 Organizational Performance (OP)

An employee's dedication to their job may be broken down into three categories: emotional, ethical, and long-term. According to Meyer and Allen, each level of an organization's staff demonstrates all three types of dedication separately and independently. Organizational performance is the capability of an association to stretch its objectives and heighten outcomes. In today's labour force, organizational performance can be distinct as a business's ability to attain aims in a state of constant change. A person's level of performance to an organization is measured by how strongly he connects, participates, trust and embrace organization along with its aims and ideals. Dedicated workers have a strong desire to remain organizational members and are more likely to put in extra effort on its behalf (Steers, 1982). Employee engagement is favorably related to emotional, financial, and non-financial components of organizational performance; it contradicts previous research by finding that engagement is not substantially related to the non-financial component of organizational performance.

According to Mukherjee S et al., (2024), the implementation of industrialized Internet of things (IIoT) in SMEs to attain and accomplish improved organizational performance. By the newest tools, small and medium-sized enterprises (SMEs) generate an economical power in marketplace besides improved functional patrons. Hence innovation and technology lead to increased organizational performance by supporting the significance of above research. According to Mukaro, C.T., Deka, A. & Rukani, S. (2023), the connotation of intellectual capital (IC) and company performance display the prominence of debit and total money in rising organizational performance along with long-standing obligation and rational wealth decrease company productivity. Hence this review is helpful in determining financial aspects of the organizational performance of current work. According to Pandey, N., Bhattacharyya, S.S. and Kharat, M.G. (2023), several precursor factors like structural obligation, managerial positioning, worker authorization and top most administration provision lead and affect organizational performance. Hence outlines the factors of organizational performance of existing research. According to Alshahrani, I., et al., (2024), healthcare, novelty, knowledge explores innovative work behaviour's (IWB's) that stimulates transformational leadership. Healthcare specialists observe the rudiments of independence, capability, understanding, inspiration and awareness distribution are important structures that impact great competence in managerial productivity. IWB too consumed a substantial and straight affirmative impact on organizational performance. Hence the above work provides an insight into the theoretical concepts of the study.

2.3 Employee Engagement and Organizational Performance

Due to their positive associations with employee actions that boost both organizational performance and financial success, corporate commitment and employee engaged have emerged as a thriving concept in the field of business studies (Chalofsky and Krishna, 2009). According to the research, across the different categories performance, affective performance has the most direct effect on worker productivity. EE originated to have significant relation with emotional organizational performance across a number of studies, but its effect on the other two dimensions financial, and non-financial components of organizational performance—has received much less attention in recent years (Schaufeli, 2001). Schaufeli and Salanova's research on the subject of EE's effect on OP found a positive correlation between the two; moreover, they found that higher levels of engagement led to gains in productivity, contentment, regularity, creativity, and motivation.

The increased degree of employee involvement affects not just their ability to learn, but also their drive to do so (Gilliland et al., 2007). According to research by Brown and Leigh, employees are more invested in their jobs and more willing to put in extra time and effort if they feel like they can be themselves at work. They have also shown that there is a favourable correlation between one's emotional and mental states of dedication, contentment, and desire. Exhaustion was shown to have a significant mediation function in the link with job stress and ill health, while engagement was found to play a significant mediating role of job resources and corporate performance in two separate studies (Schaufeli, 2006). As part of an effort to assess the Work Demands-Resources (JDR) model and see how facilities and pressures affect impetus and physical disability in due time, shown that work demands forecast occupational stress in very less time, resulting in prediction of impending pain. The performance of an employee to an organization is influenced by the resources available to them in their jobs (Ahola, 2008). Since cost-awareness associated with leaving an organization is what Meyer and Allen mean by "continuance performance," it seems to reason that these two authors would use this term. They state that research shows a negative correlation between employees' degree of engagement and their performance to staying with their current employer. On the other hand, an employee who is in a more optimistic frame of mind is more likely to show emotional and organizational performance to their work. So, it can be concluded EE is linked favorably with emotional organizational performance but unfavorably with financial and nonfinancial performance.

To develop an atmosphere where personnel remain inspired to attach through their exertion and honestly concern regarding executing fit inside the business, employee engagement should be enhanced on large scale. The link amid employee engagement and organizational performance is proved to be positively correlating and is substantial (Mansor et al., 2023). According to Satata &Dian Bagus Mitreka. (2021), employee engagement is a somatic and mental situation connected to job intellectual, passion, and performance to get successful both the employee and the company. It is an element for refining effort presentation inside the institute and powers specific job role; hence managerial objectives can be attained. According to Oyebanji et al., (2023), employee engagement and job satisfaction bear a strong and optimistic relation with organizational performance. Supervisors of companies must generate the functioning background that nurtures worker commitment and job satisfaction, when wanted to accomplish improved organizational performance. According to Emmanuel Akanpaadgi & Felicia Binpimbu (2021), employee engagement has an optimistic and constructive influence on organizational performance. Organizations are prejudiced through the operative commitment of workforce. Work engagement remained to inspire worker inspiration therefore impacting the overall organizational performance. According to Khusanova R, Kang S-W and Choi SB (2021), an optimistic relationship among occupation consequence and commitment and also points out the association amid employee engagement and organizational performance which gives a broad connection to the above research. Engagement clarified the effect of consequence on presentation and to detect the important and leading factors of job commitment as well as inspect the significance of relevance in the public sector. According to Otoo, F.N.K. and Rather, N.A. (2024), extremely dedicated, encouraged and promised personnel guarantee organizational accomplishment and effectiveness. Personnel management strategies lead to improved employee engagement which in turn leads to organizational performance. Plan and application of active personnel management strategies result toward extremely involved and dedicated employees for enhanced and increased organizational performance. Therefore the above study generates coherence between the variables of the study which could be a valid consideration.

3   Conceptual Framework of the Study

The study consists of two variables Employee Engagement and Organizational Performance.

Employee Engagement includes dimensions like Organizational Engagement and Job Engagement is taken as independent variable. Organizational Performance includes dimensions like Emotional Performance, Financial Performance and Non-Financial Performance is taken as dependent variable. The study will first find out the level of each variable. Secondly find out the relationship between the variable individually from which two relationships are developed. One is correlation relationship between EE and OP. Second is the impact of EE on OP. The study involves the analysis of organizational performance with the help of employee engagement.

Elaboration: To find out the impact of employee engagement and on organizational performance. The research is done in following ways- i) identify levels of EE, ii) identify levels of OP, iii) correlation analysis between EE and OP and iv) impact of EE on OP by regression analysis (Fig. 1).

Fig. 1. Relationship between Employee Engagement and Organizational Performance (Source: Developed by the Authors)

4   Research Design

Research design highpoints statistics description, showing how, when and where information is composed, the techniques of investigation besides in what way you understands the results. Henceforth a study protocol is an explanation of the exploration, study method and methodologies tangled. The approaches implemented aimed at discovering the investigating extent over outlining study theory. It is a scientific application for inspection significances to accomplish clarifications to study interrogations.

4.1   Sample

There were a total of 440 responses gathered within the time frame. The sample consists of two groups of IT employees namely assistant managers, and managers who are grouped under two levels namely primary and secondary levels. The secondary level involves assistant managers who are concerned with information and technology, theories and practices, the most important role is the implementation of knowledge and knowledge sharing by means of tools and technologies. The primary level includes Managers who are concerned with all five managerial functions like planning, organizing, staffing, directing and controlling. Who are concerned with planning and decision making, research and development? It also includes the objectives of these particular levels are planning structures, objectives, implementation of strategies, policies and procedures. Research and development is at the prime in this. Enough care was made to avoid reusing volunteers and to ensure that their responses were not influenced. Only 413 viable replies were received after excluding 27 due to missing information. Factor analysis in the engagement and dedication model was used, and the sample size was deemed appropriate since models using this method require between five and ten respondents per variable. In order to further explore the diversity issue in future research, this study employed on five IT companies in Telangana.

All the employees of five IT companies of Telangana, who are currently serving the positions of assistant managers and managers, made up the sample population. 200 assistant managers (48.4%) and 213 managers (51.6%), made up the sample of 413. Of them, 113 were fresher (secondary level), 300 were senior and experienced (primary level). Among all the employees, 26.9% were assigned to planning and decision making, 24.9% assigned departmental planning and activities, 19.4% assigned to course structure and objectives planning, 16.6% assigned to feedback development, result analysis and research improvement, and 12.8% to training and placement. The age of the sample consists 30 and 30+ years. When asked to respondents to who they report directly inside their organization, 66.3% of respondents said they report to assistant managers, while 33.7% said they report to the next upper level employees in the company.

4.2 Questionnaire/Procedure

An all-inclusive, three-part questionnaire was developed to collect data on motivation, dedication, and demographics linked to both the workplace and the individual. The Saks, instrument (Saks, 2006) served as the foundation of employee engagement scale, while the Allen and Meyer instrument served as the basis for the development of survey questionnaires relating to organizational performance, with a few modifications made to suit the needs of the IT industry. The final survey, which included their feedback, had twenty factors for measuring performance, two more than the standard model. These 10 questions were used to gather demographic information, in addition to measuring organizational engagement (with six items) and job/work engagement (with five items). Cronbach's alpha for items measuring organizational engagement was 0.878, while for measures measuring job engagement, it was 0.896. Cronbach's alpha results are over the threshold of significance, showing adequate internal consistency reliability. During the course of three months, both in and out of class, respondents were given a three-part questionnaire to fill out, which asked for demographic information as well as their level of participation with and dedication to the organization.

4.3 Scoring Methodology

Eleven and twenty items, recorded on a 5 point Likert scale, were used to create an engagement and performance scale, respectively. Assigned points from five (strongly agree) to one (strongly disagree) for each answer choice in every survey question. A respondent with a perfect score of 55 on both work and organizational involvement would have rated each item a 5. Similarly, if each item is scored "1," the sum of the points would be 11. Based on their results, respondents are classified as either "High," "Medium," or "Low." A high category score would fall between 44 and 55. Participants with scores of 44 and 33 are classified as medium, and those with scores of 33 or below are classified as low. To categorize levels of commitment, we also applied the same scoring system.

4.4 Statistical Analysis

All statistical analysis in this study was performed in SPSS 21. It was found that the best method for extracting factors from a factor analysis was to use Varimax orthogonal rotation followed by Kaiser Normalization. The standard threshold for eigenvalue was 1, however research by Jolliffe found that this was too stringent and instead recommended keeping all components with an eigenvalue of 0.7 or above (Jolliffe, 1972). By seeing outcomes that account for sixty per cent of the variation in social sciences is recommended, while Hair et al. work's says that an Eigenvalue criteria of less than 0.7 is not credible if the number of variables utilized in the study is fewer than 20 and just a few components may be recovered. In this analysis, an Eigenvalue of 0.9 was used to maintain sufficient components for predicting 60% of the variation while still ensuring sufficient reliability. Low loading (less than 0.5) were disregarded to guarantee a limited number of variables were responsible for a sizable portion of the variation. The researchers used a regression analysis to measure the impact of employee interest in their business and their dedication to their work.

5 Data Analysis

It is the process of systematic and significant analysis that involves statistical and logical tools to describe, illustrate, relate and evaluate the data used in the study. The current study uses a sample of 413 employees working in five different IT companies of Hyderabad. The employees were grouped in two categories i.e., Managers and Assistant managers on whom engagement and performance levels are studied.

The respondents were from companies namely Wipro, Infosys, HCL, TCS and Techmahindra of Telangana. Of them, 51.6% are between the ages of 31 and 40, 27.3% are older than 40, and 21.1% are in the 21- to 30-year-old range. A total of 39.9% of respondents had experience ranging from 6–9 years, while 37.8% had experience spanning >10 years, and 22.3% had experience spanning 2–5 years. Of the sample,.26.9% were assigned to administration activities, 24% assigned departmental planning and activities, 19% assigned to strategy planning, 16% assigned to performance analysis and 12% to training and placement. The majority (52.3%) of respondents worked in the planning and development of course structures and objectives (primary level), while the remaining (42.7%) worked on implementation of knowledge and showing guidance& support (secondary level) employees. When asked about their income, 30.8% said they made more than $5,000 per year, 30.1% said they made between $4,001 and $5,000, 22.3% said they made between $2,000 and $3,000, and 17.2% said they made between $3,000 and $4,00 (Table 1).

5.1 Scores of Employee Engagement and Organizational Performance

Average score of employee involvement, calculated by adding together their answers to all 55 questions, ranged from 14 on the low end to 52 on the high end. The standard deviation was 11.56 points, while the mean was 30.86. Using a histogram, able to determine that the sample's distribution followed a normal distribution (Fig. 2).

Table 1. Demographic Analysis (Source: Developed by the Authors).

Demographics	Percentage (%)	Frequency/Activities
Age	21.1	21 and 30
	51.6	31 and 40
	27.3	40 above
Experience	22.3	2–5 years
	39.9	6–9 years
	37.8	>10 years
Activities performed	26.9	Administration activities
	24	Departmental planning
	19	Strategy planning
	16	Performance analysis
	12	Training and placement
Managers	52.3	Planning and development
Assistant Managers	42.7	Implementation and guidance
Income	22.3	between $2,000 and $3,000
	17.2	between $3,000 and $4,000
	30.1	between $4,001 and $5,000
	30.8	more than $5,000 per year

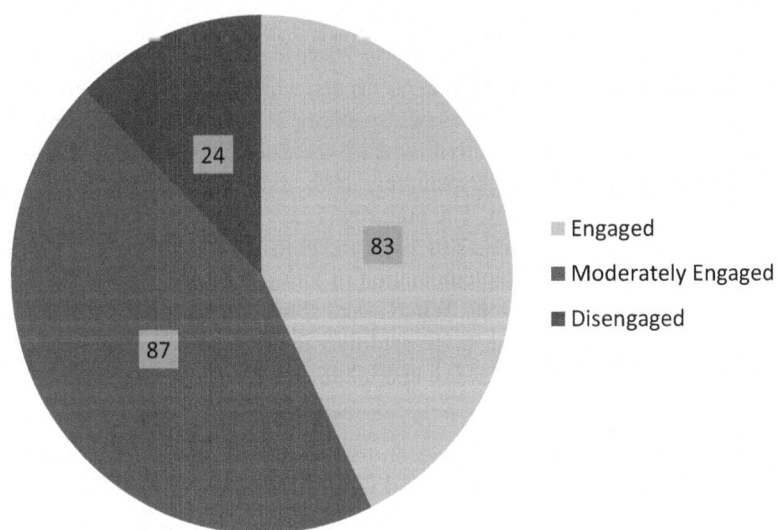

Fig. 2. Levels of Engagement (N = 413) (Source: Developed by the Author)

The analysis of 413 replies showed 20.1% (N = 83) of employees were regarded to be engaged, 21.6% (n = 87) were thought to be engaged moderately and the remaining 58.8% (n = 24) were deemed to be disengaged. When compared to the findings of Bhattacharya's study, which revealed that there were more partially engaged employees, this finding was unexpected (Fig. 3).

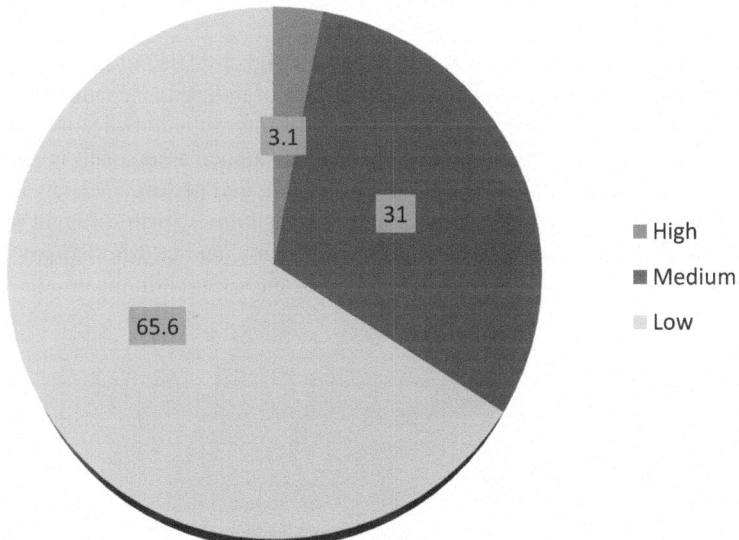

Fig. 3. Levels of Organizational Performance (N = 413) (Source: Developed by the Author)

Similarly, the range of scores for organizational performance was wide, from 25 to 92 out of 100, by a mean of 50.8 and standard deviation of 15.753. Only 3% of respondents (n = 14) were discovered to show an extremely high level of performance, whereas 31% of respondents (n = 128) showed a medium level of performance, and 65.6% (n = 271) showed a low level of performance (Table 2).

Table 2. Engagement Levels and Organization Performance Details (Source: Developed by the Author)

Employee Engagement(N = 413)			Organizational Performance (N = 413)		
N	Percentage (%)	Engagement level	N	Percentage (%)	Performance level
83	20.1	Engaged	14	3.1	High
87	21.6	Moderately engaged	128	31.0	Medium
24	58.8	Disengaged	271	65.6	Low

5.2   Descriptive Statistics for Employee Engagement and Organizational Performance

This used to find out the averages of mean, standard deviation variances and distribution of the taken dataset. The basic criterion is to provide an overall view of the data and help identify patterns and relationships. The current research uses the descriptive of Managers and Assistant Managers of the variables under the study i.e., Employee engagement and Organizational Performance.

The present works finds out managers showed a higher degree of interest and dedication, as indicated by values above the mean. T-test of independent samples was used to test the significant statistical difference in level of interest and dedication shown by Managers and Assistant mangers level employees. Variance assessment is performed to determine if any important variances in engagement and performance levels among officers serving on distinct types of roles and responsibilities, with different levels of experience, in different designations, across age groups, and at different pay grades. Analysis using F-values found no statistical significant variation in mean scores of the sample (Fig. 4).

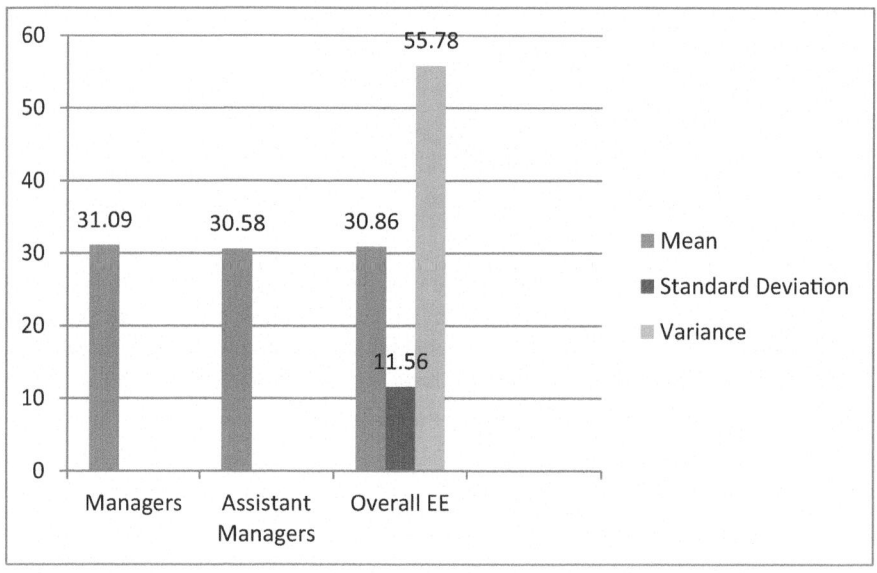

Fig. 4. Descriptive Statistics of EE (Source: Developed by the Author).

Assistant managers (n = 197) had an overall average engagement score of 30.588, while Managers (n = 216) had a mean engagement score of 31.0972. The t-values for engagement is t = .446. Overall mean of the EE is 30.86 (n = 413) with standard deviation 11.56 and variance 55.78. The mean engagement and performance ratings of assistant managers and managers are not statistically different (Fig. 5).

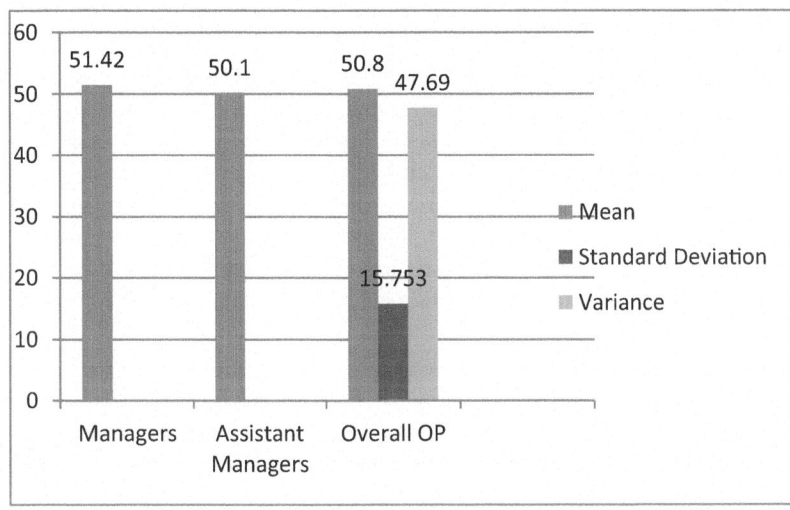

Fig. 5. Descriptive Statistics of OP (Source: Developed by the Author).

Meanwhile, assistant managers had a mean performance score of 50.1015, while managers had a mean performance score of 51.4213. As shown by the t-values of performance, t = 0.850. Overall mean of the OP is 50.8 (n = 413) with standard deviation 15.753 and variance 47.69. The mean engagement and performance ratings of assistant managers and managers are not statistically different (Table 3).

Table 3. Descriptive statistical details of Employee engagement and Organizational performance (Source: Developed by the Author).

		N	Mean	Standard Deviation	Variance	Skewness (Std Error)	Kurtosis (Std Error)	t value
Employee Engagement	Managers	216	31.09					
	Assistant Managers	197	30.58					
	Overall EE	413	30.86	11.56	55.78	-1.165 (.152)	1.498(.319)	.446
Organisational Performance	Managers	216	51.42					
	Assistant Managers	197	50.10					
	Overall OP	413	50.8	15.753	47.69	-1.310 (.152)	1.399(.319)	0.850

5.3   Factors of Employee Engagement and Organizational Performance

Eleven factors were used to determine employees' level of engagement, while twenty were used to evaluate their level of organizational performance to the company. KMO and Bartlett's test, used to assess whether or not a sample is large enough, found a level of involvement and performance at the 93% and 92% significance levels, respectively. All of the considered variables had communities greater than 0.5, with a mean engagement of 0.73 and a mean performance of 0.69. Dimension reduction analysis revealed two latent variables/factors explaining the variation in levels of engagement by 73%, and three latent variables explaining the variation in levels of organizational performance by 70%.

5.4   Reliability and Correlation Analysis

Cronbach's alpha value for the engagement and performance factors was 0.878 and 0.896 respectively, indicating high levels of internal consistency. An emotional, non-financial, and financial performance score of 0.891, 0.903, and 0.863, respectively, is very dependable and should be taken into account for further study (Table 4).

Table 4.   Reliability Analysis (Source: Developed by the Author).

Reliability	Cronbach's alpha	No of items	Sample size
Employee Engagement	0.878	11	413
Organizational Performance	0.896	20	413

Emotional and financial performance characteristics were shown to have a favourable correlation with engagement. The results of the current work contradict with previous studies, which revealed negative correlation between Non-financial performance and participation level of employees (Table 5).

Table 5.   Correlation analysis between EE and OP (Source: Developed by the Author).

	Employee Engagement (413)	Organisational Performance (413)
Employee Engagement (413)	1	.234*
Sig. (2-tailed)		0.00
Organisational Performance (413)	.320	1
Sig. (2-tailed)	0.01	

5.5   Regressions Analysis

A very good correlation (r = 0.848, N = 413, p = 0.00) was found between employee engagement and loyalty to the company. According to the results of a regression study, employee involvement accounts for 72.0% of the variable in institutional dedication (R2 = .720). On the basis of rank order regression analysis, no control variables considered—years of experience, salary, type of roles and responsibility, or division—have any significant associations with the variables we were looking at, which are all related to employees' dedication to the organization. Effective and normative devotion of IT companies in Telangana was shown to be favorably associated to employee effectiveness and work/job engagement elements. There was no correlation between employee engagement and loyalty to the company (Table 6).

Table 6. Regression analysis (Source: Developed by the Author).

		R	R^2	Adjusted R^2	Std. Error of Estimate	B Coefficient	Std, Error	β	t-value	P value
PV	EE	0.848	.720	.072	10.59	.580	0.15	0.848	.446	0.00
CV	OP	.259	.067	.063	6.76	.240	0.06	.259	4.01	.001

PV - Predictor Variable, CV - Criterion Variable,
EE – Employee Engagement, OP – Organization Performance.

6   Results and Discussion

Two variables explaining 73% of the variance in employee engagement levels were found using a factor analysis. The study indicated that OE was the most reliable predictor. OE is especially important for both primary and secondary employees because the company is their home and place of employment. Support from management, fair procedures, equitable distribution of resources, a common goal, a positive atmosphere, and the chance to advance professionally are all components of an enabling organizational environment (OE).

The workplace has deteriorated and employees' attachment to their employer and the industry as a whole has been weakened due to the prevalence of repetitive work routines, stressed environment, complexity of working schedules, procedures and protocols, time management, course completion and result orientation. The inability to take up multiple tasks, role performance and fixed schedules is often cited as a major deterrent to organizational engagement. Once an employee executes a contract and start her\he curriculum, he or she seldom hears from the higher authorities again. Until he finishes his contract, he won't be able to reconnect with almost anybody. The employee sense of belonging to the firm is weakened as a result of this disconnect. An employee in an education sector might feel more like a valued member of the team if his or her complaints are heard and handled promptly. Considering the quality nature of learning and development of the education system, many teachers experience feelings of uneasiness. Staff morale is boosted when they know their jobs are secure.

7 Practical Implications and Conclusions

On the basis of the results of above researches it can be said that less interest and dedication leads to low engagement levels. The difficult working conditions of complex mind and methods of the environment are due to lack of cohesion. This obstacle is often seen as the lower or decreased involvement for the movement. It sheds focus on relevance of enhancing work environment and organizational involvement as a means to boost engagement, which is a precursor to most work and organizational outcomes. Primary level employee turnover is common in the IT companies since most companies in the sector perform essentially the same types of labour. If employees aren't fully invested in their work, they'll be more likely to jump the work role at the first sign of dissatisfaction.

Future retention rates will be high because of the growing interest in research and publication careers and the increased public understanding of them. Personnel in the IT industry have a lot of room to grow in a variety of areas, all of which have the potential to boost teachers' enthusiasm for their work and their dedication to the organization. Impartial pay scheme provide equality among employees, the construction of new recreational facilities, the extension of maternity leaves, the provision of extra assistance for far-flung teaching and learning, etc., are all possibilities to consider in order making every teacher feel appreciated in the workplace. There are a number of things that IT companies can do to encourage employee attachment to their work and the organization, including maintaining regular motivation, award and reward, appraisal and compensations, recognizing their contributions to the organizations immediately, meeting with top management or owners' lawmakers before and after each contract period to discuss organizational needs and the employees' perspectives, providing courteous service, and facilitating regular contact with loved ones back home.

The study has a few limitations. The first limitation is that only Telangana IT sector is included in this study. Only the significant impact of engagement on performance is analysed, despite the truth that other factors, such as organizational effectiveness, organizational efficiency, competitive advantage, organizational atmosphere, etc., might also affect the performance. The impact of moderators and mediators, such as emotional quotient, job satisfaction, employee participation, etc., was not analyzed because it would be outside the scope of this study. Nonetheless, more research on the degree of participation and dedication among employees of various other sectors in the state and other states may be considered in future studies.

8 Suggestions for Future Research

The current work emphases the effect of employee engagement and organizational performance and its relationship in the IT sector, yet could not discover the backgrounds of engagement. Hence it is suggested that upcoming investigation comprises antecedents of employee engagement for having a stronger considerate of the correlation in the middle of employee engagement and organizational performance. Forthcoming exploration including additional fundamentals for engagement must be occurred in different role and performance situations to make a vivid literature of employee engagement. The existing research helps the readers to develop inferences about how employee engagement relates to the outcomes and for improved organizational performance. Upcoming scholars might attempt to inspect the connection among these modules in diverse enormous government affiliating societies besides where the facility is straightly delivered through staffs. Future studies might be directed on drivers and factors of employee engagement and organizational performance and a cross sectional group of participants whose findings and extrapolations are continued to advance prototypes and implements that could be important for the field of Personnel Management and Behavior. There is vast absence of research of employee engagement and organizational performance in small and medium sized enterprises; hence it is worthwhile to explore this concept in that particular field. It is also advisable to do research of employee engagement and its impact with leadership styles along with its negative impacts on overall success of the organization. Upcoming research can provide explorations on why the impact of supreme manager negatively influences employee engagement and organizational performance.

References

1. Alam, J., Mendelson, M., Ibn Boamah, M., Gauthier, M.: Exploring the antecedents of employee engagement. Int. J. Organ. Anal. **31**(1), 1–6 (2023)
2. Allen, N., Meyer, J.: The measurement and antecedents of affective, continuance, and normative commitment to the organisation. J. Occup. Psychol. **63**, 1–18 (1990)
3. Allen, N.J., Meyer, J.P.: Affective, continuance, and normative to the organization: an examination of construct validity. J. Vocat. Behav. **49**(3), 252–276 (1996)
4. Alshahrani, I., Al-Jayyousi, O., Aldhmour, F., Alderaan, T.: Towards understanding the influence of innovative work behavior on healthcare organizations' performance: the mediating role of transformational leaders. Arab Gulf J. Sci. Res. **42**(1), 198–216 (2024)
5. Bhat, S.A., Bashir, M., Jan, H.: Work engagement and perceived job performance: does information communication technology orientation matter? Glob. Knowl. Mem. Commun. (2024)
6. Bhattacharya, Y.: Employee engagement as a predictor of seafarer retention: a study among Indian officers. Asian J. Ship. Logist. **31**(2), 295–318 (2015)
7. Brown, S.P., Leigh, T.W.: A new look at psychological climate and its relationship to job involvement, effort and performance. J. Appl. Psychol. **81**, 358–368 (1996)
8. Buchingham, M., Coffman, C.: First, Break All the Rules: What the World's Greatest Managers Do Differently. Simon & Shuster, New York: NY (1999)
9. Buckingham, M.: Canadian Government Executive. Available at: http://www.tbs-sct.gc.ca/rp/pstc-eng.asp (accessed 2009\07\01)
10. Chalofsky, N., Krishna, V.: Meaningfulness, commitment, and engagement: the intersection of a deeper level of intrinsic motivation. Adv. Dev. Hum. Resour. **II**(2), 189–203 (2009)
11. Cohen, A.: Career stage as a moderator of the relationship between organizational commitment and its outcomes: a meta-analysis. J. Occup. Psychol. **64**, 253–268 (1991)
12. Cook, S.: The Essential Guide to Employee Engagement. Kogan Page (2012)
13. Corrigan, P., Kerr, A., Knudsen, L.: The stigma of mental illness: explanatory models and methods for change. Appl. Prev. Psychol. **11**, 179–190 (2005)

14. Csikszentmihalyi, M.: Beyond Boredom and Anxiety. Jossey Bass (1982)
15. Demerouti, E., Bakker, A.B., Nachreiner, F., Schaufeli, W.B.: The job demands-resources model of burnout. J. Appl. Psychol. **86**(3), 499–512 (2001)
16. Lakshmi Narayanamma, P., Neelima, S., Mounika, K.: Employee engagement and organizational performance: a literature review. J. Positive School Psychol. **6**(3), 3558–3563 (2022)
17. Akanpaadgi, E., Binpimbu, F.: Employee engagement and organizational performance. Bus. Manag. Econ. Res. **7**(3), 93–100 (2021)
18. Flemming, J.H., Asplund, J.: Where employee engagement happens. Gallup Manag. J. (2007)
19. Gbadamosi, G.: HRM and the commitment rhetoric: challenges for Africa. Manag. Decis. **41**(3), 274–280 (2003)
20. Gilliland, S.W., Steiner, D.D., Skarlicki, D.P.: Research in Social Issues in Management: Managing Social and Ethical Issues in Organizations, vol. 5. Information Age Publishers, Greenwich, CT (2007)
21. Hakanen, J., Bakker, A.B., Schaufeli, W.B.: Burnout and work engagement among teachers. J. Sch. Psychol. **43**, 495–513 (2006)
22. Hakanen, J., Schaufeli, W.B., Ahola, K.: The job demands-resources model: a three year cross-lagged study of burnout, depression, commitment, and work engagement. Work Stress. **22**, 224–241 (2008)
23. Hewitt Associates LLC. Employee engagement higher at double digit growth companies, Research brief at www.hewitt.com (2004)
24. Jindain, C., Gilitwala, B. The factors impacting the intermediating variable of employee engagement toward employee performance in a hybrid working model. Rajagiri Manag. J. (2023)
25. Jolliffe,I. T.: Discarding variables in a principal component analysis .I: Artificial data. J. R. Stat. Soc. Ser. C (Applied Statistics) **21**(2), 160–173 (1972)
26. Karrasch, A.I.: Antecedents and consequences of organizational commitment. Mil. Psychol. **15**(3), 225–236 (2003)
27. Khan, A W.: To be fully there: psychological presence at work. Hum. Relat. **45**, 321–349 (1992)
28. Khusanova, R., Kang, S.-W., Choi, S.B.: Work engagement among public employees: antecedents and consequences. Front. Psychol. (2021)
29. Kular, S., Gatenby, M., Rees, C., Soane, E., Truss, K.: Employee Engagement: A Literature Review. Kingston University (2008)
30. Macey, W.H., Schneider, B.: The meaning of employee engagement. Ind. Organ. Psychol. **1**(1), 3–30 (2008)
31. Mansor, F., Huzaimi, Y., Hashim, M., Muhammad, N., Omar, S.: Employee engagement and organizational performance (2023)
32. Maslach, C., Schaufeli, W.B., Leiter, M.P.: Annu. Rev. Psychol. **52**, 397–422 (2001)
33. Mowday, R.T., Porter, L.W., Steers, R.M.: Employee–Organization Linkages: The Psychology of Commitment, Absenteeism and Turnover. Academic Press, San Diego, CA (1982)
34. Mukaro, C.T., Deka, A., Rukani, S.: The influence of intellectual capital on organizational performance. Fut. Bus. J. **9**, 31 (2023)
35. Mukherjee, S., Baral, M.M., Chittipaka, V., Nagariya, R., Patel, B.S.: Achieving organizational performance by integrating industrial Internet of things in the SMEs: a developing country perspective. TQM J. **36**(1), 265–287 (2024)
36. Munro, B.H., Williams & Wilkins.: Statistical methods for health care research. Lippincott, Philadelphia (2005)
37. Murlis, H., Schubert, P.: Engage employees and boost performance, S.L.: Hay Group – Working paper (2001)

38. Newman, D.A., Harrison, D.A.: Been there, bottled that: Are state and behavioural work engagement new and useful construct; wines'? Ind. Organ. Psychol. **1**, 31–35 (2008)
39. Otoo, F.N.K., Rather, N.A.: Human resource development practices and employee engagement: the mediating role of organizational commitment. Rajagiri Manag. J. (2024)
40. Oyebanji, O., et al.: Organizational Performance: The Imperatives Of Employee Engagement And Job Satisfaction, vol. 24 (2023)
41. Pandey, N., Bhattacharyya, S.S., Kharat, M.G.: Explicating the factors influencing firm performance: study of social enterprises in India. Int. J. Organ. Anal. **31**(6), 2811–2829 (2023)
42. Porter, L.W., Steers, R.M., Mowday, R.T., Boulian, P.V.: Organizational commitment, job satisfaction, and turnover among psychiatric technicians. J. Appl. Psychol. **59**(5), 603–609 (1974)
43. Priyashantha, K.G., De Alwis, A., Welmilla, I.: Common methods and outcomes of employee engagement: a systematic literature review towards identifying gaps in research. **46**, 39–64 (2023)
44. Robinson, D., Perryman, S., Hayday, S.: The Drivers of Employee Engagement. Institute for Employment Studies. IES Report 408, UK (2004)
45. Saks, M.A.: Antecedents and consequences of employee engagement. J. Manag. Psychol. **21**(7), 600–619 (2006)
46. Salanova, W.B., Shaufeli, M., Gonzalez, R.V., Bakker, A.B.: The measurement of engagement and burnout: a two sample confirmatory factor analytic approach. J. Happiness Stud. **3**, 71–92 (2002)
47. Satata, D.B.M.: Employee engagement as an effort to improve work performance: literature review. Int. J. Soc. Sci. **2**, 41–49 (2021)
48. Schaufeli, W.B., Salanova, M.: Work engagement: an emerging psychological concept and its implications for organizations (2007)
49. Purushothaman, S., Kaviya, E.: A study on employee engagement in a IT company. J. Manag. (JOM) **7**(3) 1–7 (2020)
50. Sundaray, B.: Employee engagement: a driver of organizational effectiveness. Eur. J. Bus. Manag. **3**(8), 53–60 (2011)
51. Urner, B.A., Chelladurai, P.: Organizational and occupational commitment, intention to leave, and perceived performance of intercollegiate coaches. J. Sport Manag. **19**(2), 193–211 (2005)
52. Wildermuth, C., Pauken, P.: D.A perfect math: decoding employee engagement – part I: engaging cultures and leaders. Ind. Commer. Training **40**(3), 122–128 (2008)
53. Xu, J., Cooper Thomas, H.: How can leaders achieve high employee engagement? Leadersh. Organ. Dev. J. **32**(4), 399–416 (2011)

Comparative Study of Data Compression Algorithms: Zstandard, zlib & LZ4

Alysha Puti Maulidina, Rachel Anastasia Wijaya, Kimberly Mazel, and Maria Seraphina Astriani[✉]

Computer Science Department, School of Computing and Creative Arts, Bina Nusantara University, Jakarta 11480, Indonesia
seraphina@binus.ac.id

Abstract. Data compression continues to grow more important in the era of rapid communication and transfer of data. Compression algorithms allow this to happen, but many different options are available. This comparative study investigates three lossless compression algorithms: Zstandard, zlib, and LZ4. This study has a unique aim to provide insight into the performance of each algorithm to identify their strengths and weaknesses in different applications. Previous studies have been done; however, this study evaluates the latest modern options for lossless compression algorithms with a larger variety of data types and measured benchmarks. The algorithms are tested with a corpus consisting of different files; text-based, image, PDF, CSV, and JSON. The tests are done a set number of times, and the average is taken to increase reliability. The benchmarks used to evaluate the algorithms are the compression ratio, size savings, compression speed, decompression speed, and respective space complexities. Through these values, it was found that zlib had the highest compression ratios, despite its generally slower compression speed. Zstandard's compression ratios and size savings are slightly below zlib, however, it has higher speeds. LZ4 has the worst compression ratios out of the three but has the highest speeds due to its low overhead, making it suitable for small microprocessors. Each algorithm has its strengths and weaknesses, but zlib had the best overall performance in this study. Further research can be done to improve the generalizability and reliability of the findings.

Keywords: Data Compression · Algorithm Analysis · Compression Algorithm · Zstandard · zlib · LZ4

List of Abbreviations

AE	Autoencoder
CSV	Comma-Separated Values
HTTP	Hypertext Transfer Protocol
IoT	Internet of Things
JPEG	Joint Photographic Experts Group
JSON	JavaScript Object Notation
LEC	Lossless compression algorithms
LZMA	Lempel-Ziv-Markov chain Algorithm

A. Mirzazadeh et al. (Eds.): SEMIT 2023, CCIS 2198, pp. 394–406, 2024.
https://doi.org/10.1007/978-3-031-72284-4_24

PDF   Portable Document Format
PPMd   Prediction by Partial Matching
PPMonstr   Prediction by Partial Matching Monster
PNG   Portable Network Graphics

1   Introduction

Data compression refers to the conversion of data into a more compact form of representation that has fewer storage requirements [1]. Fundamentally, the process involves eliminating and interpreting excessive or redundancy in data. The goal of data compression is to represent the data in as few bits as possible while maintaining the minimum requirements of the original. For example, in a successful text compression, unnecessary characters are removed and replaced with a single character as a reference for a string of repeated characters. With the right function, compression algorithms can effectively reduce the size of a text file by 50 percent or more, significantly lower than its original size [2].

In the digital multimedia revolution era and rapid communication, where massive amounts of data are generated each day, data compression algorithms have been critical in enabling the ease of data transmission. Many data compression software is available to compress files of different formats, with each vendor providing different methods to optimize compression and offering different trade-offs. This research aims to focus on comparing the performance of three different compression algorithms, examining each strength, best-case uses, and efficiency.

The main problem that this paper aims to address is the lack of a comprehensive comparison of different data compression algorithms. While each algorithm has its own unique characteristics, it is difficult to determine which algorithm is the most effective overall.

To address this problem, this study will thoroughly compare and analyze different data compression algorithms. This study will compare the most popular algorithms, namely Zstandard, zlib, and LZ4, and evaluate them in terms of compression ratio, compression and decompression speed, and memory usage. This study will use a variety of data sets, including text, images, and other file types to ensure that the results are representative of a wide range of data types.

Zstandard, also known as zstd, is a fast lossless compression algorithm that targets real-time compression scenarios at the zlib-level and better compression ratios. According to the developers of Facebook, Zstandard provides high compression ratios as well as great compress and decompression speeds and allegedly offers the best-in-kind performance in many conventional situations [3]. However, there are two alternatives to Zstandard, namely zlib, and LZ4.

Similarly to Zstandard, zlib, and LZ4 claim to offer the same benefits of high compression ratios and speeds. Although these algorithms have the same purpose, no two algorithms are identical. Each algorithm will have its strengths and weaknesses, and this project aims to measure and compare them to find out what they are.

Previous studies have already compared different compression algorithms; however, different algorithms and methods were used in this paper. N. A. Khairi and A. B. Jambek

[4] compared algorithms consisting of autoencoder lossy Compression, Huffman coding, and simple lossless compression. Moreover, the study did not describe the benchmarks used to compare the algorithms, as only the advantages and disadvantages were shown. The scope of the paper was in the context of IoT applications so the findings may not be applicable to general usage. M. J. Haque and M. N. Huda [5] established the effectiveness of Repeated Huffman coding, Huffman Run-length, and Run-length Huffman using only text and image files. The study used compression ratio as a measure of comparison. A. Gupta, A. Bansal, and V. Khanduja [6] also compared different compression algorithms, namely: Deflate, Bzip2, LZMA, PPMd, and PPMonstr. It used more measures such as compression ratios, compression speed, and decompression speed. Although the baselines are similar to this paper, previous studies have not evaluated the modern options for lossless algorithms, which are Zstandard, zlib, and LZ4. Additionally, more benchmarks and data types were used in this paper to evaluate the performance of each algorithm. This is summarized in Table 1.

Table 1. Comparing previous research.

References	Algorithms	Measures
N. A. Khairi and A. B. Jambek [4]	Autoencoder (AE) lossy compression, GAS-LEC, FAS-LEC, Huffman coding, MAS (Minimal, Adaptative, and Streaming Compression Algorithm), Simple lossless compression algorithm	Advantages and Disadvantages, no benchmarks
M. J. Haque and M. N. Huda [5]	Repeated Huffman coding, Huffman Run-length, and Run-length Huffman	Compression Ratio
A. Gupta, A. Bansal, and V. Khanduja [6]	Deflate, Bzip2, LZMA, PPMd, and PPMonstr	Compression Ratio, Compression Speed, and Decompression Speed

2 Literature Study

In theory, data compression algorithms work by reducing the redundancy of data, thereby allowing it to be stored or transmitted more efficiently. Compression algorithms are used to reduce the size of a file without removing information [7]. Zstandard, zlib, and LZ4 use different theories and techniques to compress data.

A common approach used by compression algorithms is to identify and remove redundant patterns or sequences of data [8]. For instance, the Zstandard algorithm uses a combination of techniques, including dictionary compression and entropy encoding, to achieve elevated levels of compression. These metrics were chosen because they work by creating a dictionary of commonly occurring patterns in the data and replacing these patterns with shorter references to the dictionary, resulting in a smaller representation of the data [9]. This method is particularly effective for types of data that contain repetitive patterns, such as natural language text or source code. Dictionary compression algorithms are typically faster than other compression techniques; however, the research by Lasch et. al. Revealed that such dictionaries consume a significant amount of memory due to the need to store the dictionary [10]. Dictionary-based algorithms, such as LZ4, are often used in combination with other compression techniques, such as Entropy coding, to further improve the compression ratio. Zstandard is designed to be highly versatile and can be used in a variety of applications, such as file compression, network communication, and data storage.

Entropy coding is a technique that uses statistical properties of data to encode it more efficiently. It adopts the theory that symbols that occur more frequently on the data should be assigned shorter code words than symbols that occur less frequently. This is based on the principles of entropy, which states that the amount of information in a message is inversely proportional to the probability of each symbol [11]. Huffman coding and arithmetic coding are typical algorithms of this kind.

zlib is a data compression library that uses the DEFLATE algorithm - a combination of the LZ4 algorithm and Huffman encoding [12]. It works by using a sliding window technique that replaces the repeated sequences of data with a reference to the original data. A sliding window is comprised of a search buffer and a look-ahead buffer, where the search buffer contains the dictionary (recently encoded data), and the look-ahead buffer contains the next portion of the input data sequence to be encoded [12]. Zlib is widely used in many applications, such as the PNG image format and HTTP compression.

LZ4 uses a dictionary-matching scheme like the LZ4 byte-oriented compression algorithm [13]. LZ4 has been found to be extremely fast both in compression and decompression and is often used in applications such as data backup, data archiving, and in-memory data storage.

3   Measurement

There are three standard metrics for comparing data compression algorithms, which are as follows: compression ratio, compression speed, and decompression speed. In compression ratio, the original size of the data compared with the compressed size. Measured in unitless data as a size ratio of 1.0 or greater.

$$CompressionRatio = OriginalFileSize/CompressedFileSize \qquad (1)$$

The rate at which data can be made smaller is called compression speed. The compression speed measured in MB/s of input data consumed.

$$CompressionSpeed = OriginalFileSize/CompressionTime \qquad (2)$$

The decompression speed is the rate at which the original data from the compressed data can be reconstructed. This metric measured in MB/s for how quickly data is produced from compressed data.

$$DecompressionSpeed = CompressedFileSize/DecompressionTime \qquad (3)$$

However, two metrics have been added for additional analytical purposes: space complexity and space savings. Space complexity is the amount of space/memory taken up by an algorithm to run input to completion and measured in Bytes. It is the amount of space required to execute an algorithm [14]. Space savings mean the amount of space/memory saved from compressing the data (measured in percentages).

The reason these metrics were chosen is that using the three-standard metrics of compression ratio, compression speed, and decompression speed is standard practice when comparing data compression algorithms. Alongside the addition of space complexity and space savings, the collected information can be used to decide when to use specific algorithms. For example, one algorithm might be able to compress data very quickly, but at the cost of taking up a large amount of space.

4   Methodology

To rigorously evaluate the different algorithms, certain variables must be controlled to ensure that the measured variables are only affected by the algorithms alone, not external factors. For example, the test data and device should be the same for each algorithm. Since all three algorithms are open-sourced, the code can be easily found online.

A corpus, or dummy data, is used to test these algorithms. This research has been based on the Silesia corpus, which is a set of files from the Silesia Compression Test Suite, a well-established benchmark for data compression research, of distinctive characteristics to test how the algorithms perform on common data types used every day. The Silesia corpus is a collection of open-source data files gathered from various sources such as software distributions, text documents, and image files. The Silesia corpus is widely used in the field of data compression as it provides a standardized and representative dataset for evaluating the performance of compression techniques [15]. This corpus was chosen as a basis for the one used in this study because of its diverse file types and sizes, making it an ideal dataset for testing the efficiency of different compression algorithms.

In this research, 6 different file types were used, including PNG images, JPG images, PDF documents, CSV files, JSON files, and plain text files. The files were sourced from various sites such as Project Gutenberg, Kaggle, Tumblr, NASA Hubblesite, OneSky, and World Health Organization (WHO) - South-East Asia Indonesia. The description and file sizes for each file can be seen in Table 2.

These file types were chosen to represent a diverse set of data types commonly encountered in real-world applications. The files were downloaded directly from the Silesia website without any pre-processing, to ensure that the results would be an accurate representation of the actual performance of the compression techniques on these specific file types. By using a diverse set of file types, this research evaluated the effectiveness of the compression algorithms across a wide range of data types and sizes, including image, document, and structured data. The data sets vary in size as this will allow the algorithms to be tested on both small and large data sets.

Samples from the corpus can be seen in Fig. 1. The corpus is then used to test each of the algorithms. To improve accuracy, the testing for each algorithm will be done three times, and the average of each algorithm will be used instead of the pure value for one trial. The results will be documented in tables and represented in various graphs to be able to compare the difference more clearly.

Table 2. Data types used.

Data type	File size (MB)	Description	Source
Text	0.063	.txt file containing the poem The Raven by Edgar Allan Poe	Project Gutenberg [16]
PDF	2.373	.pdf file containing a report by the World Health Organization (WHO) Indonesia documenting the 60th COVID-19 situation report	World Health Organization (WHO) - South-East Asia Indonesia [17]
CSV	2.073	.csv file containing a spliced data set of 1000 movies from IMDb	Kaggle [18]
JSON	0.000903	.json file containing example code	OneSky [19]
JPG	0.308	.jpg file picturing a Kirby doll seated in a car	Tumblr [20]
PNG	130.916	.png file picturing Spiral Galaxy UGC 2885 captured by the Hubble Space Telescope	NASA Hubblesite [21]

After the comparison, a conclusion can then be properly made about each algorithm's strengths and weaknesses, alongside the presentation of the results. A general overview of the methodology employed in this research has been visualized using a flowchart, as shown in Fig. 2.

5 Findings and Analysis

After testing each data compression algorithm and obtaining the raw data from each run, the average was then calculated for each measurement. Table 3 shows the average figures of the different corpus tests on the three compression algorithms.

According to the findings, the file types that were compressed best were text-based and JSON files. As shown in Table 3f, the highest compression ratios were from JSON files, with text-based files falling second in Table 3a. This is further supported by the high value of size savings for both JSON and text-based files. However, the compression and decompression speeds of both file types are the lowest. This may be the result of the low size threshold of JSON and text-based files. The speeds are measured in MB/s (megabytes per second), so the recorded speed values are low as there are few megabytes to compress in the first place. To support this hypothesis, a Pearson's Correlation test was done to see if there was any correlation between the original file size and compression speed. With basing the classification for the strength of correlation on [22], the results show that there exists a positive correlation for all algorithms tested, with a moderate correlation for zlib, a strong correlation for Zstandard, and a strong correlation for LZ4. These results can be seen in Table 4.

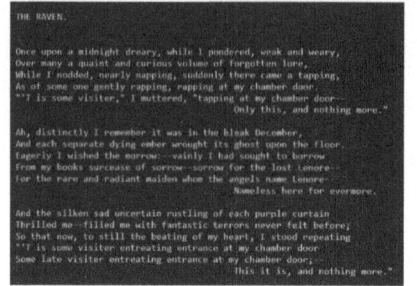

a. Text   b. PDF

c. CSV

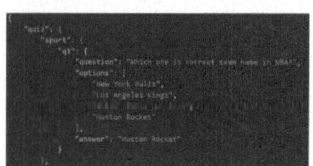 

d. JSON   e. JPG   f. PNG

Fig. 1. Data type samples.

On the other hand, the worst compressed file types were PDFs and images, specifically JPEGs. It has the lowest compression ratios and size savings, as shown in Table 3d, Table 3b, and Table 3c. They have higher compression and decompression speeds, but this may be attributed to their larger file sizes. Interestingly, the smaller-sized images have negative values of size savings. JPEGs are already compressed file type. As a result, attempting to compress the size again did not lower the original size of the file. Instead, the size became larger due to the compression algorithms' overhead adding onto the original file size. This is why JPEGs were compressed poorly throughout the trials. The file sizes are already compressed to the point that no compression can decrease the file size further unless it is lossy.

Overall, zlib had the best performance for most data types. It had the best compression ratios and size savings except for CSV files, where they fell short of Zstandard. The LZ4 algorithm had the worst compression ratios and size savings out of the three,

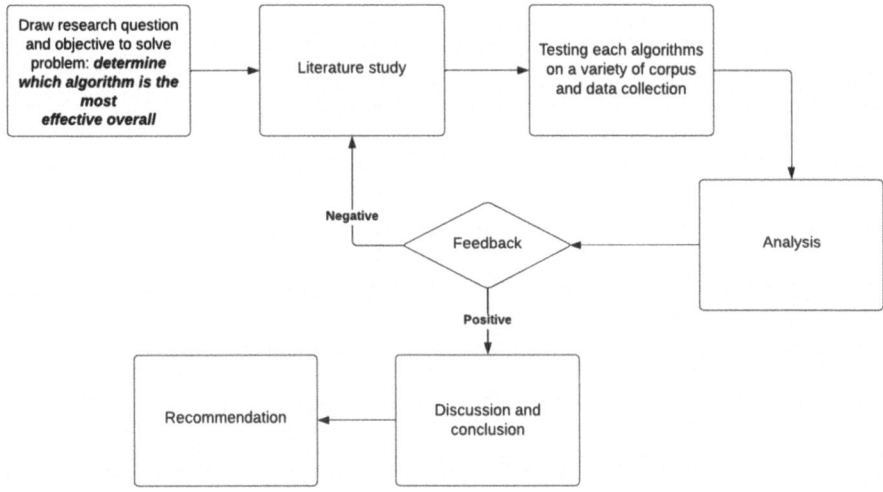

Fig. 2. Flow of research.

however, it had the best compression speeds. This is because LZ4 has a small overhead and relatively simple decoding. It provides high compression speeds at the cost of low compression ratios. To view whether there was a significant difference between the algorithms' compression speed, a paired one-tailed t-test was done between the algorithms. The null hypothesis was there no difference between the paired algorithms, while the alternative hypothesis was that the LZ4 compression speed would be higher than the Zstandard and zlib. The results of both tests can be seen in Table 5 and Table 6.

The absolute values for the t-test statistics from both tests were found to be larger than the one-tailed t-test critical value of 2.015, by which the null hypothesis can be rejected. In addition, with a confidence (alpha) value of 0.05, the p-value for both tests were also found to be significant, which also supports the rejection of the null hypothesis and gives sufficient evidence to conclude that the LZ4 algorithm has the fastest compression speed.

As for decompression speeds, zlib had the best performance except for larger images and PDFs, where Zstandard took the lead. For space complexities, LZ4 and Zstandard have identical values across all data types. Interestingly, both algorithms share the same creator. Zlib only had the advantage of the space complexity of compressing images and decompressing JSON files.

6 Conclusions and Future Work

This report presents a comparison between three lossless data compression algorithms, Zstandard, zlib, and LZ4; carrying out analyses of five different data types: text, images, PDF, CSV, and JSON. This research provided deeper insight into the field of compression algorithms due to the variety of data types and benchmarks and reveals distinct strengths and optimal use cases for each algorithm when considering different data types.

It is crucial to acknowledge notable differences with studies such as those by N.A. Khairi and A.B. Jambek [4], M.J Haque and M.N. Huda [5], and A. Gupta, A. Bansal,

Table 3. Results of tests across data types.

Measurement	Zstandard	zlib	LZ4
a. Text			
Compression Ratio	2.60	2.62	1.67
Size Savings (%)	61.60	61.78	40.20
Compression Speed	12.47	6.89	38.20
Decompression Speed	12.97	13.35	10.05
Space Complexity (c)	768.00	770.00	768.00
Space Complexity (d)	736.00	740.00	736.00
b. small image			
Compression Ratio	1.00	1.00	1.00
Size Savings (%)	-0.01	1.00	-0.01
Compression Speed	153.78	34.18	205.81
Decompression Speed	41.31	43.16	35.69
Space Complexity (c)	1,020.00	686.00	1,020.00
Space Complexity (d)	866.00	734.00	730.00
c. Large image			
Compression Ratio	1.00	1.00	1.00
Size Savings (%)	0.00	0.01	0.00
Compression Speed	398.42	39.19	527.90
Decompression Speed	692.38	247.69	585.48
Space Complexity (c)	1,052.00	718.00	1,052.00
Space Complexity (d)	746.00	750.00	746.00
d. PDF			
Compression Ratio	1.09	1.10	1.08
Size Savings (%)	8.26	9.48	7.11
Compression Speed	244.950	33.758	512.77
Decompression Speed	239.886	159.869	229.91
Space Complexity (c)	772.00	774.00	772.00
Space Complexity (d)	738.00	742.00	738.00
e. CSV			
Compression Ratio	2.52	2.43	1.54
Size Savings (%)	60.29	58.87	35.02
Compression Speed	50.84780732	7.87	176.57

(*continued*)

Table 3. (*continued*)

Measurement	Zstandard	zlib	LZ4
Decompression Speed	222.6286971	141.78	271.71
Space Complexity (c)	780.00	782.00	780.00
Space Complexity (d)	742.00	746.00	742.00
f. JSON			
Compression Ratio	3.38	3.71	2.54
Size Savings (%)	70.43	73.07	60.61
Compression Speed	0.20	0.24	0.36
Decompression Speed	0.41	0.75	0.60
Space Complexity (c)	774.00	776.00	774.00
Space Complexity (d)	740.00	744.00	740.00

Table 4. Pearson Correlation Coefficient results.

Compression algorithm	Pearson's Correlation Coefficient (r)
Zstandard	0.8075886369
zlib	0.5446006575
LZ4	0.622371913

Table 5. Zstandard and LZ4 One-tailed t-test results.

Data type	Compression speed - Zstandard	Compression speed – LZ4	Differences
Text	12.47	38.20	−25.7307
Image - Small	153.78	205.81	−52.0364
Image - Big	398.42	527.90	−129.4832
PDF	244.95	512.77	−267.8170
CSV	50.85	176.57	−125.7222
JSON	0.20	0.36	−0.1595
Mean of Differences			−100.1582
Standard Deviation of Differences			97.44523657
t-test statistic			−2.517685235
One-tailed t-test critical value			2.015048342
p-value			0.02666

Table 6. Zlib and LZ4 One-tailed t-test results.

Data type	Compression speed - zlib	Compression speed – LZ4	Differences
Text	6.89	38.20	−31.3028
Image - Small	34.18	205.81	−171.6348
Image - Big	39.19	527.90	−488.7127
PDF	33.76	512.77	−479.0096
CSV	7.87	176.57	−168.7043
JSON	0.24	0.36	−0.1166
Mean of Differences			−223.2468
Standard Deviation of Differences			213.6141485
t-test statistic			−2.55994631
One-tailed t-test critical value			2.015048342
p-value			0.02532

and V. Khanduja [6]. In the work of N.A. Khairi and A.B. Jambek [4], autoencoder (AE) lossy compression, GAS-LEC, FAS-LEC, Huffman coding, MAS (Minimal Adaptive, and Streaming Compression Algorithm), and simple lossless compression algorithm were explored. However, their study did not provide benchmarks, and the advantages and disadvantages of the algorithms were outlined without specific performance measures. Similarly, M.J. Haque and M.N. Huda [5] focused on repeated Huffman coding, Huffman Run-length, and Run-length Huffman. They primarily evaluated compression ratios without comprehensive benchmarks. Lastly, A. Gupta, A. Bansal, and V. Khanduja [6] investigated into Deflate, Bzip2, LZMA, PPMd, and PPMonstr, considering compression ratio, compression speed, and decompression speed. While their study provided a multifaceted analysis, the specific algorithms and metrics differ from our investigations.

In comparison, our study employed a distinctive methodology with different algorithms and benchmarks, which revealed nuanced strengths and optimal use cases for each algorithm. These distinctions highlight the novelty of our study and offer a fresh perspective on the performance of compression algorithms in diverse scenarios. Based on the findings, it can be concluded that while among the three compression algorithms, Zstandard has a higher encoding speed with consistent compression ratios, it being a recently released algorithm (stable release in 2022) with a lack of open sources can make it less reliable in general use cases compared to zlib, which uses the universally adopted DEFLATE algorithm and has been developed and improved upon since 1995. Zstandard offers a balanced performance of compression ratio and speed, which makes it a versatile choice for a variety of data types, especially for medium to large-sized files. Zlib has demonstrated superior performance with text-based and JSON files, where maximizing space savings is critical. On the other hand, it can also be concluded that LZ4 had the worst compression ratio in comparison to zlib and Zstandard but had the fastest decoding speeds by a significant margin due to its low overhead and simple decoder. This makes it particularly useful in scenarios where speed is crucial, such as real-time data processing or systems with limited computational resources.

In future research, a larger variety of data types and sizes can be used to improve generalizability. More benchmarks can also be used to further determine the usability for different cases and observe whether the current findings are still valid. There are still many different options of compression algorithms and techniques that are not covered within this study, so it would be beneficial to conduct further research to compare their performances with the current algorithms.

Acknowledgement. This work is supported by Research and Technology Transfer Office, Bina Nusantara University as a part of Bina Nusantara University's International Research Grant entitled Teaching and Learning Augmented Reality Installation with Hologram Special Effect with contract number: 029/VRRTT/III/2023 and contract date: 1 March 2023.

References

1. Colett, Y., Turner, C.: Smaller and faster data compression with Zstandard, https://engineering.fb.com/2016/08/31/core-infra/smaller-and-faster-data-compression-with-zstandard/ (2016)
2. Anup, A., Ashok, R., Raundale, P.: Comparative study of data compression techniques. Int. J. Comput. Appl. **178**, 15–19 (2019)
3. Compression techniques, https://isaaccomputerscience.org/concepts/data_compr_loss?examBoard=all&stage=all, last accessed 2023/10/15
4. Khairi, N.A., Bahari Jambek, A.: Study on data compression algorithm and its implementation in portable electronic device for internet of things applications. In: EPJ Web of Conferences, vol. 162 (2017)
5. Haque, M.J., Huda, M.N.: Study on data compression technique. Int. J. Comput. Appl. **159**, 6–13 (2017)
6. Gupta, A., Bansal, A., Khanduja, V.: Modern lossless compression techniques: review, comparison and analysis. In: 2017 Second International Conference on Electrical, Computer and Communication Technologies (ICECCT), 1–8 (2017)
7. Wayner, P.: Disappearing Cryptography: Information Hiding: Stenography & Watermarking. Morgan Kaufmann, Amsterdam (2009)
8. Jayasankar, U., Thirumal, V., Ponnurangam, D.: A survey on data compression techniques: From the perspective of data quality, coding schemes, data type and applications. J. King Saud Univ. Comput. Inf. Sci. **33**, 119–140 (2021)
9. Data compression, https://www.barracuda.com/support/glossary/data-compression, last accessed 2023/10/15
10. Lasch, R., Oukid, I., Dementiev, R., May, N., Demirsoy, S.S., Sattler, K.-U.: Faster & strong: string dictionary compression using sampling and fast vectorized decompression. VLDB J. **29**, 1263–1285 (2020)
11. LZ4: LZ4: Extremely fast compression algorithm, https://github.com/lz4/lz4, last accessed 2023/10/15
12. Chen, E.: Compression Algorithm, https://www.euccas.me/zlib/, last accessed 2023/10/15
13. Lu, Z.-M., Guo, S.-Z.: Lossless Information Hiding in Images. Elsevier, Cambridge, MA (2017)
14. Goswami, T., Sinha, G.R.: Statistical Modeling in Machine Learning: Concepts and Applications. Academic Press, Oxford (2023)

15. Deorowicz, S.: Silesia compression corpus, https://sun.aei.polsl.pl/~sdeor/index.php?page=silesia, last accessed 2023/10/15

16. Poe, E.A.: The Raven, https://www.gutenberg.org/ebooks/17192, last accessed 2023/10/15

17. World Health Organization: Coronavirus disease 2019 (COVID-19) situation reports, https://www.who.int/indonesia/news/novel-coronavirus/situation-reports, last accessed 2023/10/15

18. Banik, R.: The movies dataset, https://www.kaggle.com/datasets/rounakbanik/the-movies-dataset, last accessed 2023/10/15

19. C, B.: https://support.oneskyapp.com/hc/en-us/articles/208047697-JSON-sample-files, last accessed 2023/10/15

20. Soitsu: https://soitsu.tumblr.com/post/126146797740/proper-driving-safety-even-if-youre-soft-enough, last accessed 2023/10/15

21. NASA, ESA, Holwerda, B.: Spiral Galaxy UGC 2885. NASA (2020)

22. Evans, J.D.: Straightforward Statistics for the Behavioral Sciences. Brooks/Cole Publishing Company, Pacific Grove (1996)

Category Sort with TODIM Method an Application for Retail Sector E-Commerce Site

Ayşe Hümeyra Akar[1]([⊠]) and Babek Erdebilli[2]

[1] Department of Industrial Engineering, TOBB ETU University, 06200 Ankara, Turkey
aysehumeyraakar@etu.edu.tr
[2] Department of Industrial Engineering, Ankara Yıldırım Beyazıt University, 06010 Ankara, Turkey

Abstract. In recent years, various classical multi-criteria decision-making methods have been developed and frequently used to solve real-life problems. One such method is Topsis-Based Multi-Criteria Decision-Making (TODIM), which is used to solve ranking problems. In today's world, e-commerce has become essential for businesses due to the increasing volume of online sales, changing world balances, and the pandemic. Consequently, taking part in the digital world has become indispensable for companies. The easiest way to establish a digital presence is through successful e-commerce sites. The success of an e-commerce site depends on the proper ranking of product categories to enable users to navigate easily and improve their shopping experience. Therefore, strategically aligning product categories is critical for improving user experience and increasing sales performance. In this study, conducted using real data of the company in the retail sector in Turkey, we use the TODIM method to rank product categories on e-commerce sites to increase customer satisfaction and sales. Thanks to the applied method, categories are made more visible and contribute to the organization of the site's home page.

Keywords: Topsis · Based Multi-Criteria Decision-Making · e-commerce · sorting problem · MCDM

1 Introduction

E-commerce is a rapidly growing and developing sector with the increase in digitalization these days. With consumers' increasing online shopping habits, e-commerce sites are adopting various strategies to improve customer experience and gain a competitive advantage. One of these strategies is to organize the product categories offered on the home page of e-commerce sites.

E-commerce sites have a wide range of options to offer a variety of user experiences to attract users' attention and enable them to find their products easily. These experiences include many options such as sorting products by gender, color options, and displaying customer-based ads. Also, there are studies conducted for product ranking [4, 41]. These studies were conducted to rank the products directly, but while the products were listed,

© The Author(s), under exclusive license to Springer Nature Switzerland AG 2024
A. Mirzazadeh et al. (Eds.): SEMIT 2023, CCIS 2198, pp. 407–420, 2024.
https://doi.org/10.1007/978-3-031-72284-4_25

the categories and the products related to these categories were not directly evaluated. Additionally, live sales data obtained from the website of a supermarket in the retail sector was used in this study. Sorting product categories correctly, allows users to find the products they are looking for more easily and improves site navigation. Therefore, e-commerce sites need to have a user-friendly interface.

As a result, this study will enable the ranking of product categories on the e-commerce site with the TODIM method and it will be possible to determine which category should be highlighted for the layout of the home page. The TODIM method has been preferred due to its assumption of homogeneous user preferences and criteria, treating all users' preferences and criteria equally.

In the study, which consists of seven sections in total, a literature summary is presented as the second section after the introduction. In the third part of the study, the TODIM method is explained. The TODIM method was applied to the data obtained in the fourth section. In the fifth section, another method, the AHP method, was applied. Then, sensitivity analyses were conducted in the sixth section. Finally, there is the last section where the results obtained are evaluated, and suggestions for future studies are presented.

2   Literature Review

Multi-criteria decision-making (MCDM) problems arise in different areas of science and engineering [31]. Various researches have been conducted to develop new methods or improve existing methods. Typical challenges of MCDM methods are uncertainty, risk, etc.

This study will be based on the TODIM method, which is one of the multi-criteria decision-making methods. In this context, there are many studies conducted in the past. The TODIM method is a method based on the "Expectation Theory" first put forward by Kahneman and Tverski in the 1970s. Unlike other multi-criteria decision-making methods, in the TODIM method, the measurement value calculated by applying the "Expectation Theory" paradigm is used instead of the highest value [1]. Figure 1 shows the loss and gain function of expectation theory. Cumulative expectancy theory is also an effective approach to reflect people's psychological behavior [2]. The TODIM method can be used effectively in decision-making problems based on objective and imprecise data. This method can assist decision makers in their decisions by combining fuzzy logic and an analytical hierarchy process.

Although there is no direct study on the category ranking of e-commerce sites, there are many studies on product ranking. While the volume of online product reviews has increased in recent years [3], some studies in this field have investigated product ranking according to customer feedback [5] by obtaining information about emotional tendencies [4]. There are also studies in the literature to rank monthly sales by categories [6].

In a study conducted by Jia-Wei Gong, Hu-Chen Liu et al. [7], the TODIM method was used to determine the best e-learning website using network teaching. In the study, the TODIM method was used to evaluate and rank the sites in order to make a choice among the sites providing online education. The results obtained show that the TODIM method is an effective tool in this regard.

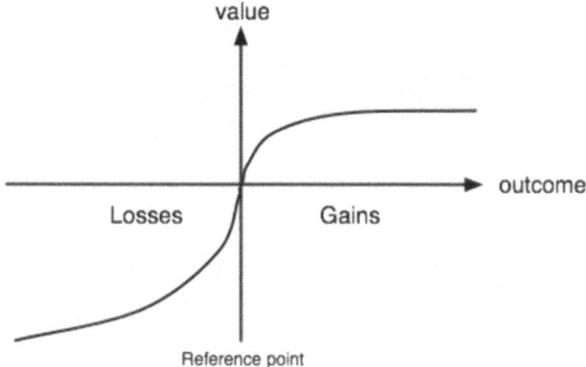

Fig. 1. Expectation Theory.

In another study conducted by Karakış (2022) [8], BMW and the fuzzy TODIM method were used together in the supplier selection process. In the research, suppliers were evaluated by using these two methods together to select the most suitable one among the suppliers in different retail food sectors.

In another study; fuzzy TODIM was used as a hybrid with fuzzy AHP to measure the performance of retail companies traded in Borsa Istanbul [9]. In the study, the criteria are measured from the Balance Scorecard perspective. Blur was also used in this study. The main goal of this study is to reach the most successful company. The table below provides information about some studies conducted in the past.

Another study, Bellman and Zadeh [30], introduced fuzzy sets theory in MCDM problems as an effective approach to treating uncertainty, lack of information, and ambiguity inherent in human decision-making, known as fuzzy multi-criteria decision-making (FMCDM).

Examples for further studies applying traditional TODIM include application of setting priorities in health care [33], rental evaluation of residential properties [1], selecting the natural gas destination in Brazil [34], evaluation of real estate properties [35], evaluation of broadband internet plans [36], behavioral multi-criteria decision and analysis [37], a case study on the forecasting of property values for rent in a Brazilian city [38], supply chain selection and oil spill in the sea [39], ERP software Selection [40], these can be given as examples (Table 1).

3   TODIM Method

TODIM is a Portuguese abbreviation that stands for Interactive and Multi-criteria Decision Making. At the same time, this method uses global value measurements with the application of Expectation Theory (Gomes et al., 2009) [1]. By using this method, a decision can be made in risky situations. The value function of this method is similar to the loss-gain function in prospect theory. [27, 28].

Traditional TODIM uses the square root function to reproduce the S-shaped value function of gains and losses of prospect theory. The dominance values of all criteria

Table 1. Past Studies

Paper Name	Author	Place of Publication	Application area	Method Used
Probabilistic linguistic TODIM method for selecting products through online product reviews	Liu Peide, Teng Fei	Information Sciences Volume 485, June 2019, Pages 441–455	Making purchasing decisions easier based on online product reviews	Linguistic TODIM (PL-TODIM)
Product selection based on sentiment analysis of online reviews: an intuitionistic fuzzy TODIM method	Zhenyu Zhang, Jian Guo, Huirong Zhang, Lixin Zhou & Mengjiao Wang	Complex & Intelligent Systems	Product ranking based on online reviews	intuitive fuzzy TODIM (IF-TODIM)
A decision framework for cultural and creative products based on IF-TODIM method and group consensus reaching model	Ning Ding, Sui-Huai Yu, Jian-Jie Chu, Chen Chen, Xin-Yi Shu	Advanced Engineering Informatics Volume 55, January 2023, 101891	Cultural and creative products with localized styles	IF-TODIM
Multicriteria Classification with TODIM-FSE	Renato Monte Araújo	Procedia Computer Science Volume 55, 2015, Pages 559–565	Choosing a suitable location for store opening	TODIM-FSE (TODIM and the Fuzzy Synthetic Evaluation)
TODIMSort: A TODIM based method for sorting problems	Liang Wang, Zi-Xin Zhang, Alessio Ishizaka, Ying-Ming Wang, Luis Martínez	Omega Volume 115, February 2023, 102771	Proposing a TODIMSort method built on the TODIM method	TODIM
Fuzzy TODIM method based on alpha-level sets	Liang Wang a b, Ying-Ming Wang a, Luis Martínez	Expert Systems with Applications Volume 140, February 2020, 112899	Improving the disadvantages of dealing with fuzzy information in existing fuzzy TODIM methods	Fuzzy TODIM
Hybrid TODIM Method for Law Enforcement Possibility Evaluation of Judgment Debtor	Zhenyu Zhang, Jie Lin, Huirong Zhang, Shuangsheng Wu, Dapei Jiang	Mathematics 2020, 8, 1806	Evaluation of enforcement possibilities of enforcement debtors	Hybrid TODIM
An analysis of the generalized TODIM method	Bonifacio Llamazares	European Journal of Operational Research Volume 269, Issue 3, 16 September 2018, Pages 1041–1049	Simplifying the model by avoiding calculating the relative weights of criteria to a reference criterion	TODIM
TODIM and TOPSIS with Z-numbers	Renato A. Krohling, André G. C. Pacheco & Guilherme A. dos Santos	Frontiers of Information Technology & Electronic Engineering volume 20, pages283–291 (2019)	Considering Z-numbers in the context of multi-criteria decision-making problems	Z-TODIM

(continued)

Table 1. (*continued*)

Paper Name	Author	Place of Publication	Application area	Method Used
TODIM Method for Picture Fuzzy Multiple Attribute Decision Making	Guiwu Wei	Informatica, Volume 29, Issue 3 (2018), pp. 555–566	Picture Fuzzy MADM Problems	TODIM and pictorial fuzzy numbers (PFNs)
Development of TODIM with different types of fuzzy sets: A state-of-the-art survey	Xiaoli Tian, Wanqing Li, Li Liu, Gang Kou	Applied Soft Computing Volume 111, November 2021, 107661	Combination of TODIM with different fuzzy sets	fuzzy TODIM
Study on the Selection of Pharmaceutical E-Commerce Platform Considering Bounded Rationality under Probabilistic Hesitant Fuzzy Environment	Zixue Guo and Sijia Liu	*Mathematics* 2023, *11*(8), 1859	Selection of E-Commerce Platform	Probabilistic unstable fuzzy multi-attribute group decision-making based on TODIM
Fuzzy TODIM for ELICIT Information	Álvaro Labella, Diego García-Zamora, Rosa M. Rodríguez & Luis Martínez	INFUS 2022. Lecture Notes in Networks and Systems, vol 504	Building a multi-criteria group decision-making model based on fuzzy TODIM dealing with Extended Comparative Linguistic Expressions with Symbolic Translation (ELICIT) values	Fuzzy TODIM
IF-TODIM: An intuitionistic fuzzy TODIM to multi-criteria decision making	Renato A. Krohling, André G.C. Pacheco, André L.T. Siviero	Knowledge-Based Systems Volume 53, November 2013, Pages 142–146	Supply chain selection and offshore oil spill	IF-TODIM
Portfolio allocation with the TODIM method	Fatih Alali, A. Cagri Tolga	Expert Systems with Applications Volume 124, 15 June 2019, Pages 341–348	Portfolio allocation process	TODIM
Comparing Rankings from Using TODIM and a Fuzzy Expert System	Valério Antonio Pamplona Salomon, Luís Alberto Duncan Rangel	Procedia Computer Science Volume 55, 2015, Pages 126–138	Proving that the TODIM method can produce good results from fuzzy sets with a mixed qualitative-quantitative research strategy	TODIM
Interval-valued Intuitionistic Fuzzy TODIM	Renato A. Krohling, André G.C. Pacheco	Procedia Computer Science Volume 31, 2014, Pages 236–244	Extending TODIM to interval-valued intuitionistic fuzzy (IVIF) environments	Interval-valued Intuitionistic Fuzzy MCDM
A hybrid model for remanufacturing facility location problem in a closed-loop supply chain	Ali Alimoradi, Rosnah Mohd. Yussuf, Norzima Zulkifli	INTERNATIONAL JOURNAL OF SUSTAINABLE ENGINEERING	Supply Chain	Fuzzy TOPSIS

between any two alternatives are compared pairwise and summed as global dominance values to rank the alternatives. [32].

The main purpose of the TODIM method is to determine the degree of dominance of each alternative over the others by using the potential theory-based utility function [29]. Pairwise comparisons are made to calculate the relative dominance of one alternative over another [1].

The mathematical formulations can be systematically summarized as follows:

Step 1: The first step of the research is to create the decision matrix. This stage forms the basis of the decision-making process and is an important step for the further stages of the research.

Step 2: Normalization of the values in the matrix is done by calculating the value of an alternative for useful criteria by dividing it by the sum of all alternatives for each criterion in formula (1). Likewise, formula (2) is used for criteria that are unbeneficial. Formula (1) and (2) are shown below.

$$\text{Beneficial Criterion Pij} = \frac{Xic}{\sum_{i=1}^{n} Xic} \tag{1}$$

$$\text{Unbeneficial Criterion Pij} = \frac{1/Xic}{\sum_{i=1}^{n} 1/Xic} \tag{2}$$

Step 3: In the TODIM method, in a problem where n alternatives are ranked according to m criteria, it is assumed that one of these criteria is the reference criterion. For this reason, a reference criterion should be selected among the criteria, taking into account the previously determined weight values. The selected reference criterion "r" should be the criterion with the highest degree of importance.

The relative weights of the criteria are calculated using formula (3) below.

$$Wcr = \frac{Wc}{Wr}(c = 1,2,3,..n) \tag{3}$$

$w_r = \max\{w_c \,|c = 1,2,...,n\}$ indicates the reference criterion weight, w_{cr} indicates the relative criterion weight, wc indicates the criterion weight.

Step 4: The following formulas (4) and (5) are used to calculate the degree of superiority of the A_i alternative over the A_j alternative, taking into account the C_c criterion.

$$\delta(Ai, Aj) = \sum \Phi cmc = 1(Ai, Aj) \tag{4}$$

$$\Phi c(\,Ai,\,\,Aj) = \begin{cases} \sqrt{\frac{Wcr(Pic-Pjc)}{\sum_{c=1}^{m} Wcr}} & \text{if } (\,P_{ic} - P_{jc}) > 0 \\ 0 & \text{if } (\,P_{ic} - P_{jc}) = 0 \\ \frac{-1}{\theta}\sqrt{\frac{\sum_{c=1}^{m}(Wcr)(Pic-Pjc)}{Wcr}} & \text{if } (\,P_{ic} - P_{jc}) < 0 \end{cases} \tag{5}$$

here θ is the loss reduction factor.

Step 5: The following normalization formula is used to calculate the global value of ith alternative.

$$\varepsilon = \frac{\sum_{j=1}^{n} \delta(Ai - Aj) - mini(\sum_{j=1}^{n} \delta(Ai - Aj))}{maxi(\sum_{j=1}^{n} \delta(Ai - Aj) - mini\sum_{j=1}^{n} \delta(Ai - Aj)}$$

(6)

Step 6: In the last stage, the results are listed and evaluated.

4 Case Study

The flowchart for the TODIM method study conducted for a retail company's e-commerce website is visually represented as follows. This research involves a process in which the data used to evaluate the performance of the e-commerce site is obtained through SQL queries and then these data are processed and analyzed. The data processing step enabled the obtained information to be made more meaningful and, conclusions to be drawn (Fig. 2).

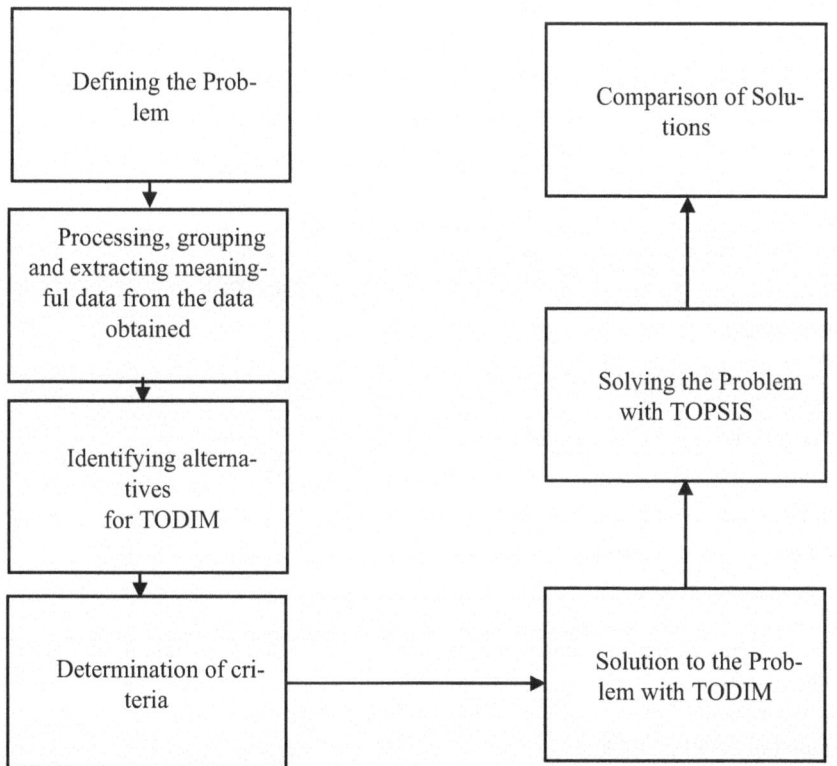

Fig. 2. Flowchart of the Project.

Steps for category sorting with the TODIM method are shown below. Data for the 12 top categories and 6 criteria existing on the site are shown in Table 2.

The criteria used in this study are the number of customers shopping from the category, the average shopping amount (TL) of the category, the amount purchased from the category, the amount of stock of the products, the age range and product type of the customers purchasing products by category.

Individuals within the age range of 18–24 are represented by the number 1, while those between 25–34 years of age are denoted as 2. People aged 35–44 are indicated as 3, and individuals in the 45–64 age group are defined as 4. Those aged 65 and older are represented by the number 5.

Table 2. Decision Matrix

	Beneficial			Non Beneficial		
Category Name	Number of Customers	Average Amount (TL)	Quantity	The amount of stock	Age range	No. of Product Types
Baby	3562	756702,34	7034,00	578487	3	4498
Meat-Chicken-Fish and Seafood	17270	3427899,45	51823,97	15173466,36	4	34015
Food	36993	8052296,25	323430,6	168337155,9	3	205862
Non-Food Products	33606	530364,83	218354	36487704	1	47572
Beverages	33003	4115302,59	233169,3	92831677,84	2	100182
Paper- Cosmetics	24865	3433588,18	92050	17125405	2	63330
Greengrocer	27218	3339204,27	336314,6	255660284	5	214803
Healthy Living Products	351	18740,08	602	123746	3	424
Salad Dressings	2047	47457,12	3148	72746	2	2285
Milk, Breakfast	34380	6817943,35	166307,4	142174481,7	4	114340
Cleaning	24080	3473696,39	89499,36	13460561	2	70066
Bakery products	15144	506058,8	58660,23	49123770	1	34834
Weights	0,268865	0,20682	0,17235	0,156681	0,104454	0,09083

The weights were determined by an expert by the SWARA method in this study.

The data for beneficial and non-beneficial criteria were subjected to normalization using the formula below, and the matrix obtained after this normalization process is presented in detail in Table 3.

Then, the weights of the criteria were calculated with the formula W_{cr} (1).

The calculated values are as follows.

W_{cr}	1	0,76923363	0,641028	0,582749707	0,3885	0,337827534

Table 3. Normalized Matrix

0,014105869	0,021921167	0,00445079	7,25E-02	5,85E-02	7,04E-02
0,068390893	0,099303985	0,032791815	2,77E-03	4,39E-02	9,32E-03
0,146495907	0,233269709	0,204651914	2,49E-04	5,85E-02	1,54E-03
0,133083055	0,015364319	0,138164326	1,15E-03	1,75E-01	6,66E-03
0,130695116	0,1192176	0,14753877	4,52E-04	8,77E-02	3,16E-03
0,098467838	0,099468784	0,058244988	2,45E-03	8,77E-02	5,00E-03
0,107785949	0,096734544	0,212804358	1,64E-04	3,51E-02	1,48E-03
0,001389994	0,000542888	0,000380918	3,39E-01	5,85E-02	7,47E-01
0,008106321	0,001374801	0,001991909	5,77E-01	8,77E-02	1,39E-01
0,136148171	0,19751132	0,105231667	2,95E-04	4,39E-02	2,77E-03
0,095359161	0,100630692	0,056631061	3,12E-03	8,77E-02	4,52E-03
0,059971725	0,01466019	0,037117484	8,54E-04	1,75E-01	9,10E-03

As a 3rd step, using the formula (2), the degree of superiority of alternative A_i over alternative A_j is calculated, taking into account the criterion C_c. After calculating one by one for 12 categories, the following values were obtained (Table 4).

Table 4. Degrees of Distinction.

Baby	−25,81
Meat-Chicken-Fish and Seafood	−23,4
Food	−10,86
Non-Food Products	−13,32
Beverages	−11,69
Paper- Cosmetics	−16,45
Greengrocer	−18,69
Healthy Living Products	−19,8
Salad Dressings	−18,58
Milk, Breakfast	−16,02
Cleaning	−16,71
Bakery products	−21,2

As the last step, the global values of the alternatives were calculated using formula (3).

As a result of this calculation, it was understood that the Food category is the category that should be displayed most on the home page. The food category is followed by the beverage category. The suggested category order is given in Table 5.

Table 5. Recommended Category Ranking.

Food
Beverages
Non-Food Products
Milk, Breakfast
Paper- Cosmetics
Cleaning
Salad Dressings
Greengrocer
Healthy Living Products
Bakery products
Meat-Chicken-Fish and Seafood
Baby

5   Evaluation of Data with TOPSIS Method

Additionally, based on the same data, the TOPSIS method was applied together with the TODIM method. In this method, the similarity of each alternative to the ideal solution is calculated for each criterion. These similarity values are determined by two different distance measures of the alternatives called "S+" (similarity to ideal solution) and "S-" (similarity to anti-ideal solution).

In this applied method, s+, s- values, and p values are shown in detail in Table 6. According to these values, the results obtained from the TOPSIS method and the results obtained from the TODIM method are similar In particular, the Food category has the highest value of 0.68017 and is therefore recommended as the category that should be displayed most on the home page.

According to the TOPSIS method, the categories that should be highly visible on the home page are shown in Table 7.

6   Sensitivity Analysis

In this section, sensitivity analysis will be discussed in order to evaluate sensitivity to variability, sensitivity, and uncertainty of the measures and weights used in decision-making processes. Through sensitivity analysis, it is aimed to determine the reliability of the methods used in their application to reality, and it will be discussed whether they will help decision makers to make more solid and reliable decisions.

Table 6. Values According to the TOPSIS Method.

Categories	s+	S–	p score
Baby	0,182202	0,127121	0,410964
Meat-Chicken-Fish and Seafood	0,129027	0,139025	0,518648
Food	0,093251	0,198314	0,68017
Non-Food Products	0,123995	0,166533	0,573207
Beverages	0,084871	0,161238	0,65515
Paper- Cosmetics	0,108902	0,151551	0,581874
Greengrocer	0,154	0,137544	0,471778
Healthy Living Products	0,19629	0,126808	0,392475
Salad Dressings	0,191704	0,12883	0,401923
Milk, Breakfast	0,092084	0,168032	0,645988
Cleaning	0,110017	0,151094	0,578657
Unlu Mamüller	yön0,159119	0,120838	0,431631

Table 7. Category Sorting According to the TOPSIS Method.

1	Food
2	Beverages
3	Milk, Breakfast
4	Paper- Cosmetics
5	Cleaning
6	Non-Food Products
7	Meat-Chicken-Fish and Seafood
8	Greengrocer
9	Unlu Mamüller
10	Baby
11	Salad Dressings
12	Healthy Living Products

6.1 Taking the Criterion Weights Equally

If the weights are taken equal, all of the W_{cr} values, that is, the criterion weights, change to 0.17. In this case, no criterion will have any superiority over the other criterion. An increase was observed in all global values of the alternatives, but there was no change in the ranking. The table below shows the normal value of the first milk and the calculated values of the second milk with equal weights (Table 8).

Table 8. Equal Criterion Weights.

Baby	−25,81	−25,73
Meat-Chicken-Fish and Seafood	−23,4	−21,99
Food	−10,86	−8,58
Non-Food Products	−13,32	−12,50
Beverages	−11,69	−10,17
Paper- Cosmetics	−16,45	−15,34
Greengrocer	−18,69	−16,24
Healthy Living Products	−19,8	−20,25
Salad Dressings	−18,58	−19,30
Milk, Breakfast	−16,02	−13,64
Cleaning	−16,71	−15,61
Bakery products	−21,2	−21,18

6.2 Taking Criterion Weights as 60% - 40%

Some differences in the ranking occurred as a result of distributing the weights to the beneficial ones by 60% and to the non-beneficial ones by 40%. The greengrocer and Salad Dressings, which were in sixth and seventh place, changed places.

7 Conclusion and Future Research

With the acceleration of e-commerce due to the pandemic and the increasing sales volume, studies in this field have gained importance. In this study, the TODIM method was applied to cope with the problem of ranking the categories of websites and to suggest a more effective ranking. Sales data from the e-commerce site was used to sort between categories. The data was obtained via SQL, and a business intelligence platform was used to process and categorize the data. In this way, it was possible to determine how many orders were received from which category.

When comparing the results obtained from the TODIM method and the TOPSIS method, they are similar in both and the most visible category should be the food category. At the same time, we can say that the results obtained are consistent. In this context, we can say that the study achieved its purpose. Ensuring the home page layout according to the given order can help increase sales. In this study, external factors such as market trends, seasonality or competitive analysis were not taken into account in TODIM's ranking process; however, these can be examined in future studies.

For future studies, in addition to home page editing in the field of e-commerce, many areas such as gender-based home page editing, color editing, and advertising campaigns can be studied. Having customers browse websites designed for them can increase customer loyalty and also bring in new customers. Also, as an extension of this study, user behavior and satisfaction can be examined. Multi-criteria decision-making methods are a good method that can be used when decisions need to be made in this field.

References

1. Gomes, L., Rangel, L.: An Application of the TODIM method to the multicriteria rental evaluation of residential properties. Eur. J. Oper. Res. **193**(1), 204–211 (2009)
2. Kahneman, D., Tversky, A.: Prospect theory: an analysis of decision under risk. Exp. Env. Econ. 143–172 (2018)
3. Zha, Z.J., Yu, J., Tang, J., Wang, M., Chua, T.S.: Product aspect ranking and its applications. IEEE Trans. Knowl. Data Eng. **26**(5), 1211–1224 (2014)
4. Wu, C., Zhang, D.: Ranking Products with IF-Based Sentiment Word Framework and TODIM Method. School of Management, Harbin Institute of Technology, Harbin, China. ISSN: 0368–492X (2028)
5. Santhana Preethi, J., Abirami, A.M., Askarunisa, A., Sathya Priya, G., Sankaragomathy, E.: Applying MCDM techniques for ranking products based on online customer feedback. Int. J. Knowl. Based Comput. Syst. **3**(2) (December 2015)
6. Response Magazine March 2002 Page 21
7. Gong, J.-W., Liu, H.-C., You, X.-Y., Yin, L.: An integrated multi-criteria decision making approach with linguistic hesitant fuzzy sets for E-learning website evaluation and selection. Appl. Soft Comput. J. **102**, 107118 (2021)
8. Engin KARAKIŞ, BWM VE BULANIK TODIM YÖNTEMLERİ İLE PERAKENDE SEK-TÖRÜNDE TEDARİKÇİ SEÇİMİNİN GERÇEKLEŞTİRİLMESİ. Int. J. Econ. Admin. Stud. ISSN 1307-9832 (2022)
9. Erdoğan, N.K., Onay, A., Karamaşa, C.: Measuring the performance of retailer firms listed in BIST under the balanced scorecard perspective by using interval valued pythagorean fuzzy AHP based pythagorean fuzzy TODIM methodology. J. Oper. Res. Stat. Econ. Manag. Inf. Syst. **7**(2) (2019)
10. Probabilistic linguistic TODIM method for selecting products through online product reviews. Inf. Sci. **485**, 441–455 (2019)
11. Zhang, Z., Guo, J., Zhang, H., Zhou, L., Wang, M.: Product selection based on sentiment analysis of online reviews: an intuitionistic fuzzy TODIM method. Complex Intell. Syst. 3349–3362 (2022)
12. Ding, N., Sui-Huai, Y., Chu, J.-J., Chen, C., Shu, X.-Y.: A decision framework for cultural and creative products based on IF-TODIM method and group consensus reaching model. Adv. Eng. Inform. **55**, 101891 (2023)
13. Araújo, R.M.: Multicriteria classification with TODIM-FSE. Procedia Comput. Sci. **55**, 559–565 (2015)
14. Wang, L., Zhang, Z.-X., Ishizaka, A., Wang, Y.-M., Martínez, L.: TODIMSort: A TODIM based method for sorting problems. Omega **115**, 102771 (2023)
15. Wang, L., Wang, Y.-M., Martínez, L.: Fuzzy TODIM method based on alpha-level sets. Expert Syst. Appl. **140**, 112899 (2020)
16. Zhang, Z., Lin, J., Zhang, H., Shuangsheng, W., Jiang, D.: Hybrid TODIM method for law enforcement possibility evaluation of judgment debtor. Mathematics **2020**, 8 (1806)
17. Llamazares, B.: An analysis of the generalized TODIM method. Eur. J. Oper. Res. **269**(3), 1041–1049 (2018)
18. Krohling, R.A., Pacheco, A.G.C., dos Santos, G.A.: TODIM and TOPSIS with Z-numbers. Front. Inf. Technol. Electron. Eng. **20**, 283–291 (2019)

19. Wei, G.: TODIM method for picture fuzzy multiple attribute decision making. Informatica **29**(3), 555–566 (2018)
20. Tian, X., Li, W., Liu, L., Kou, G.: Development of TODIM with different types of fuzzy sets: a state-of the-art survey. Appl. Soft Comput. **111**, 107661 (2021)
21. Guo, Z., Liu, S.: Study on the selection of pharmaceutical E-Commerce platform considering bounded rationality under probabilistic hesitant fuzzy environment. Mathematics **11**(8), 1859 (2023)
22. Labella, A., García-Zamora, D., Rodríguez, R.M., Martínez, L.: Fuzzy TODIM for ELICIT Information, INFUS 2022. Lecture Notes in Networks and Systems, vol. 504
23. Krohling, R.A., Pacheco, A.G.C., Siviero, A.L.T.: IF-TODIM: an intuitionistic fuzzy TODIM to multi-criteria decision making. In: Knowledge-Based Systems, vol. 53, pp. 142–146 (2013)
24. Alali, F., Cagri Tolga, A.: Portfolio allocation with the TODIM method. Exp. Syst. Appl. **124**, 341–348 (2019)
25. Salomon, V.A.P., Rangel, L.A.D.: Comparing rankings from using TODIM and a fuzzy expert system. Procedia Comput. Sci. **55**, 126–138 (2015)
26. Krohling, R.A., Pacheco, A.G.C.: Interval-valued intuitionistic fuzzy TODIM. Procedia Comput. Sci. 31, 236–244 (2014)
27. Gomes, L.F.A.M. ve Lima, M.M.P.P., TODIM: Basics and application to multicriteria ranking of projects with environmental impacts. Found. Comput. Decis. Sci. **16**, 113–127 (1992a)
28. Gomes, L.F.A.M. ve Lima, M.M.P.P.: From modeling individual preferences to multicriteria ranking of discrete alternatives: a look at prospect theory and the additive difference model. Found. Comput. Decis. Sci. **17**, 171–184 (1992b)
29. Qin, J., Liu, X. ve Pedrycz, W.: An extended TODIM multi-criteria group decision making method for green supplier selection in interval type-2 fuzzy environment. Eur. J. Oper. Res. **258**(2), 626–638 (2017)
30. Bellman, R.E., Zadeh, L.A.: Decision-making in a fuzzy environment. Manage. Sci. **17**, 141–164 (1970)
31. Hwang, C.L., Yoon, K.: Multiple Attribute Decision Making. Springer-Verlag, Berlin (1981)
32. Lee, Y.-S., Shih, H.-S.: Incremental analysis for generalized TODIM. Cent. Eur. J. Oper. Res. **24**, 901–922 (2016)
33. Nobre, F.F., Trotta, L.T.F., Gomes, L.F.A.M.: Multi-criteria decision making—an approach to setting priorities in health care. Stat. Med. **18**(23), 3345–3354 (1999)
34. Gomes, L.F.A.M., Rangel, L.A.D., Maranhao, F.J.C.: Multicriteria analysis of natural gas destination in Brazil: an application of the TODIM method. Math. Comput. Model. **50**, 92–100 (2009)
35. Moshkovich, H., Gomes, L.F.A.M., Mechitov, A.I.: An integrated multicriteria decision-making approach to real estate evaluation: case of the TODIM method. Pesqui. Oper. **31**(1), 3–20 (2011)
36. Rangel, L.A.D., Gomes, L.F.A.M., Cardoso, F.P.: An application of the TODIM method to the evaluation of broadband internet plans. Pesqui. Oper. **31**(2), 235–249 (2011)
37. Gomes, L.F.A.M., González, X.I.: Behavioral multi-criteria decision and analysis: further elaborations on the TODIM method. Fund. Comput. Decis. Sci. **37**(1), 3–8 (2012)
38. Gomes, L.F.A.M., Machado, M.A.S., Costa, F.F.D., Rangel, L.A.D.: Criteria interactions in multiple criteria decision aiding: a Choquet formulation for the TODIM method. Procedia Comput. Sci. **17**, 324–331 (2013)
39. Krohling, R.A., Pacheco, A.G.C., Siviero, A.L.T.: IF-TODIM: an intuitionistic fuzzy TODIM to multi-criteria decision making. Knowl.-Based Syst. **53**, 142–146 (2013)
40. Kazancoglu, Y., Burmaoglu, S.: ERP software selection with MCDM: application of TODIM method. Int. J. Bus. Inf. Syst. **13**(4), 435–452 (2013)
41. Zhang, D., Li, Y., Chong, W.: An extended TODIM method to rank products with online reviews under intuitionistic fuzzy environment. J. Oper. Res. Soc. **71**(2), 322–334 (2020)

Social Networks and Privacy Concerns: An Insight into IT Industry User Experience

Maria Anjum[1($\boxtimes$)], Maria Anum[1], Humaira Kosar[1], and Mariam Rehman[2]

[1] Department of Computer Science, Lahore College for Women University, Lahore, Pakistan
maria.anjum@gmail.com, humaira.kosar@lcwu.edu.pk
[2] Department of Information Technology, Government College University, Faisalabad, Pakistan

Abstract. Information systems in the form of social networks provide a virtual place where people share ideas, information, personal feelings and experiences with family, friends and colleagues. This virtual environment provides an opportunity to develop social relationships with people around the world and make sustainable virtual communities. The sustainability of these virtual communities is critical especially in the time of globalization and increased adoption of virtual work environments to access and utilize best resources around the globe. This has encouraged academics and practitioners to study user behavior in relation to social networks and has now become an important research area. Various studies have been conducted to understand social networks and user behavior in the context of personality traits, cultural differences, adoption of technology, gender differences, usage patterns, employee's performances, etc. However, these studies largely focus on user intentions in adoption of technology and there is little evidence that information systems are analysed from a perspective of actual use (which considers user's experience over time) to form a trustworthy and sustainable social network and virtual community. Therefore, in this research efforts are made to analyse 'actual use' of virtual environments and the factors that affect towards the sustainability of such platforms. The research has proposed a conceptual framework and evaluation is carried out through statistical analysis. The findings show that actual experience is positively related to ease of use, self-disclosure, performance expectancy, and hedonic expectancy. However, perceived risk was not found significant towards actual use of social networks.

Keywords: User Behavior · Sustainability · Information systems · Social Networks · Social Networking Sites · SNS · UTAUT · Structured Equation Modeling (SEM)

1 Introduction

Sustainability is an important concept to measure the effectiveness of information systems. This becomes particularly important in the context of globalization and formation of virtual communities to integrate ideas, skills and experiences. The virtual communities exist in various forms (social groups, educational, service led, professional etc.) and make

A. Mirzazadeh et al. (Eds.): SEMIT 2023, CCIS 2198, pp. 421–436, 2024.
https://doi.org/10.1007/978-3-031-72284-4_26

use of social networking sites (SNSs) as a platform to construct social relations by communicating with other individuals or groups through forums, posts and other provided features [1, 2]. The social networks formed through these virtual communities facilitate individuals and groups to break social barriers and engage in activities of mutual or community interest. This has made SNS an important common public forum to disseminate information related to areas such as education, politics, religion, sports, world events, healthcare, epidemic outbreak etc. [3]. Therefore, the use of information systems in the form of SNS has equally gained popularity among various institutions including government organizations, private firms, law enforcement agencies, healthcare, academia, disaster management etc.

The usage of SNS varies from user to user and platform to platform. Users share their personal information, experiences and interests through profiles to make themselves visible on social media and to socialize with others (who could be their friends, relatives, workplace colleagues or strangers). The level of information shared on SNS however varies depending on the purpose of using that particular SNS platform. The large companies such as Microsoft Corporation, IBM, Oracle, Accenture, SAP, etc. make use of SNS to provide their employees more comfortable environment to share information and opportunity to know each other in an informal way [4].

The popular SNS platforms among users include Facebook, Twitter, Google, LinkedIn, and Foursquare [5]. These SNS provide various features some of which are similar and others are different depending on the purpose for which they are being developed. For example, Facebook is used for various purposes such as to establish personal connections, increase company's internal communication with employees, bring social awareness regarding certain issues etc., whereas, LinkedIn is largely used for professional purposes and users provide their work experiences, establish connections with companies, seek or offer job opportunities etc. [6].

SNS also provides an opportunity to teachers, students and learners to share informative articles, experiences, lectures and videos with each other. It facilitates the students and learners to contact teachers, mentors, and experts that belong to different geographical areas around the globe. In this way, SNS provides e-learning opportunity to these learners [1, 7]. Further, SNS has made users to learn new ways of forming virtual communities of their own interest. This is a bottom up activity where one user finds another user with the same area of interest and make their collaboration easy, effective and efficient [8].

SNS has both positive and negative impact on society. The benefits associated with SNS include access to information, educational opportunities in the form of course forums, quick and easy communication with family, friends and colleagues; professional networks and opportunity to extend friend circle [9]. However, there are negative effects associated with the use of SNS. Students are largely benefited by SNS however, there are studies that highlight that the students spending too much time on SNS, have negative effects on their studies. Similarly, relationships, and trust could easily be effected by the comments or the posts made by friends and colleagues. Sometimes users provide false information in their profiles which is misleading and arise trust issues in individuals and community [10]. There is no doubt that SNS is a medium where people break their relations but it is also the largest platform where users build relations [11]. Therefore,

SNS platforms have now made world a connected area where we can interact with anyone, at any time [12].

The continued growing trend of using SNS has made research community to investigate the behaviour of users in relation to use of SNS platforms. While using SNS, users exhibit certain behaviors that represent their personality traits. The study of these traits can help to understand the behaviour of certain community for various purposes such as education, crime and drug control, healthcare awareness, elderly care, and altitude towards certain technology and its adoption. In this regard, the research carried out on SNS and user behavior can be classified into three categories, observed during our previous study [17] and stated here:

a. Comparative analysis of real-life experiences and virtual environment such as: comparing real life communication and socialization pattern with that of exhibited on SNS.
b. Identifying relationship between personality traits and user behavior on SNS.
c. Identifying behavioral patterns and effectiveness of SNS in different communities of professionals, students, cultures; and special user groups such as elders, patients etc.

In this research, the focus is on the third category where behavior of a particular community is investigated in relation to 'actual use' of SNS in forming sustainable virtual community.

In, information systems, individual acceptance and use of technology is a prominent research area [13]. The same trend also exists in studies of SNS where technology acceptance and use models are employed to understand influential factors of user behavior on the use of SNS. The technology acceptance models include Theory of Planned Behavior (TPB), Technology Acceptance Model (TAM) and Unified Theory of Acceptance and Use of Technology (UTAUT). Among these models, UTAUT is a more concrete model that combines various constructs of others models and provides a comprehensive framework [14].

The UTAUT model has four key constructs that include performance expectancy, effort expectancy, social influence, and facilitating conditions. These constructs could be used along with the constructs of other technology adoption models to understand the usage of a particular technology. In this way, the model facilitates technology providers to understand intentions or actual use of users towards any particular technology and make improvements in their product or services.

The studies on user behavior and the use of SNS are being conducted to identify influential factors that shape behavior of the user in virtual social environment. These studies have not only identified behavioral elements largely related to personality traits but have also identified technical aspects that lead to form certain usage and behavioral patterns. For example, information disclosure is a factor that not only depends on user's personal choice of sharing information but also is constrained by the ability of user to customize SNS settings. Similarly, privacy, a well-known research area in SNS studies carries both perspective. Studies have been conducted to identify when and where privacy is considered important by SNS users. In these studies, participants are largely taken from non-technical background. The lack of knowledge or skill to use social networking environment raise concerns such as trust, privacy, ease of use, self-disclosure etc.. However, what behavior is exhibited by the users who have skill in using technology is yet to explore. Current literature on SNS and user behavior lacks studies where behavior of professionals are being studied in relation to SNS use. With rapid development in technology and its early adoption by younger communities requires involvement of participants having skill in technology to better understand relationship of 'actual use' of technology and user behavior.

Therefore, in this research, relationship of 'actual use' of SNS and user behavior is investigated by considering the community of professionals having background in information technology. The purpose of this study is different from that of previous studies in two ways. First, instead of evaluating 'user intentions' towards technological use and more specifically towards SNS, this research investigates the 'actual use' of SNS by considering user experience. Second, the participants engaged in this research are professionals from software industry which implies that participants are skilled in technology use. This is different from previous studies where, participants involved largely lack technological skills (e.g. privacy setting, profile editing, control over interface etc.) which effected their behaviour towards SNS use. In the absence of this limitation, what would be the behaviour of users towards SNS use and what will be the concerns raised by such community; are the dimensions in which this research is focused.

In next section, research process is explained in detail. Section 3, provides proposed framework and associated hypothesis. In Sect. 4, results and findings are discussed and Sect. 5, provides conclusion. Subsequent paragraphs, however, are indented.

2 Research Process

To conduct this research a systematic process is adopted by analyzing the existing literature and constructing a conceptual framework by integrating user behaviour features with technology adoption and use model i-e UTAUT. To evaluate the proposed framework, hypothesis are constructed. A protocol was designed by following guidelines provided by Evidence Based Software Engineering (EBSE) to conduct survey and collect data to evaluate proposed framework and associated hypothesis. The complete research process is provided in Fig. 1.

The details of survey instrument, sampling techniques, and data collection are discussed be-low.

Instrument Development: The survey instrument is developed in the form of questionnaire and was validated by two educational experts to eliminate the chances of inconsistency. A five point likert scale was used where 1 was for strongly disagree, and 5 for strongly agree. The five point likert scale best suits for long questionnaires [15].

Sampling Technique: Purposive sampling technique [16] is employed to identify target population. This technique is well suited with our research since we were targeting community consisting of IT professionals working in software industry. The sample size was determined by employing two minimum sample size formulas to best fit model.

$50 + 8K$ (I)

$50 + 8K$, k is the number of independent variables in the model

$50 + 8(5) = 90$

$104 + K$ (II)

$104 + K$, k is the number of independent variables in the model

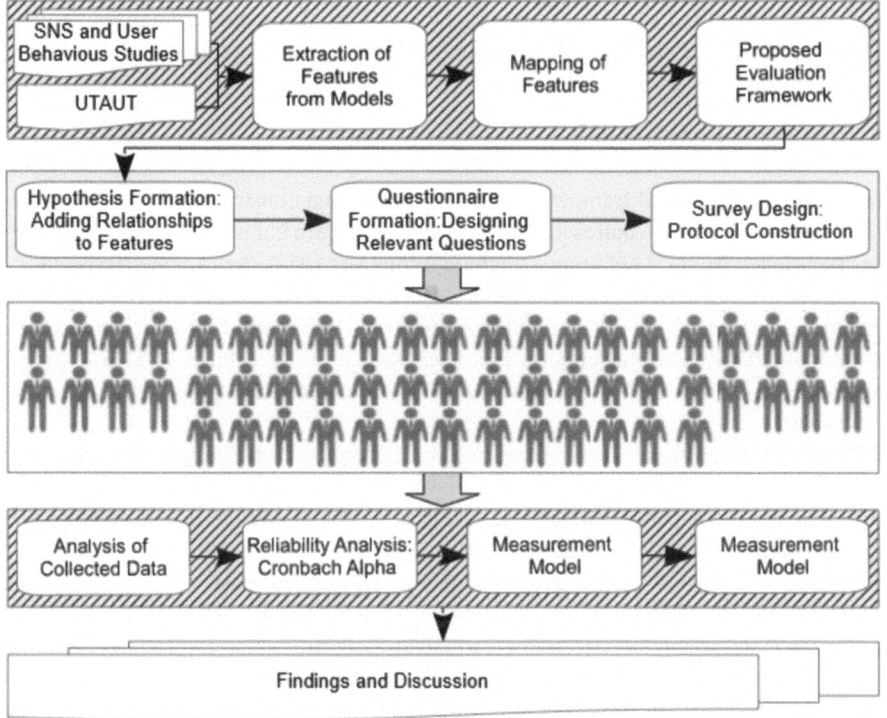

Fig. 1. Research Process.

$104 + 5 = 109$

It is recommended that sample size should not be less than 110 for appropriate results and to converge model.

Data Collection: Data is collected by developing online questionnaire which was made available through Google forms. The survey link is available at https://docs.goo gle.com/   forms/d/14MGx\ nDzLdE6dNNnPJRgysFPTFnPLhnIl6kNnHK7k4/formResponse. Data collection process was completed approximately in four months to collect maximum responses. During this time, reminder emails were sent to IT professionals and company CEOs. In some cases, respondents requested for further details as they thought some questions are personal. To address this, supporting documents were provided to facilitate them in understanding the nature of research. This was also important to build the trust, and bring clarity into their responses. The concerns related to data privacy were also addressed and ethical statements were shared as part of survey. A total of 288 responses were collected. The responses were saved in spread sheet through google form. To avoid missing data, all the fields in the questionnaire were made mandatory. The collected data was analyzed for inconsistency and accuracy of data in terms of provided responses. There were 17 responses that were completed with irrelevant information, therefore, discarded. The final dataset consisted of 271 responses which was used for further analysis. In next section, proposed framework and associated hypothesis are discussed.

3 Proposed Framework

The proposed conceptual framework is based on original constructs of UTAUT model [13] and user behaviour features identified from literature in our previous study [17]. The constructs taken from UTAUT model include Actual Use (AU), Performance Expectancy (PE), and Ease of use (EOU) whereas constructs associated with user behaviour include Hedonic Expectancy (HE), Perceived Privacy Risk (PPR), and Self Disclosure (SD). The framework evaluates the effects of these constructs on 'actual use' of SNS. Figure 2 provides relationship of these constructs with 'actual use' in proposed conceptual framework.

In the proposed framework, actual use is a dependent variable whereas other five constructs are considered independent variables. Actual use is considered dependent as it relates to the experience of the user with a particular SNS over certain period of time. Therefore, this study of user experience is different from the ones where user intentions are evaluated. Such studies lack depth and user responses are constrained by lack of experience. The experience of user is affected by various factors which are taken as independent variables in the framework such as Performance Expectancy, Ease of use, Hedonic Expectancy, Perceived Privacy Risk, and Self-disclosure. Self-disclosure represents user trust and satisfaction towards SNS use. The user's comfort to disclose personal information on SNS will make the relationship of this construct significant towards actual use. In contrast, non-significant relationship indicates lack of trust and dis-satisfaction towards SNS. Such users will be very conscious and hesitant in sharing information.

Hedonic Expectancy is described as enjoyment and pleasure that user experience while using SNS. The positive relationship of Hedonic expectancy towards actual use shows that user is having pleasant experience with SNS while negative relationship represents discomfort and displeasure towards SNS experience. Performance expectancy describes to what extent user considers the use of SNS can improve job performance. Since SNS are used in many companies to facilitate employees in overcoming communication barriers, resolve issues and engage in discussions, therefore, this construct is included in the proposed framework. Further, the population under consideration includes professionals therefore, this construct has its own significance. Another construct, ease of use is included in the framework. This construct is about user's level of comfort towards SNS use. This could include use of SNS features such as control over information sharing, finding particular information, updating profiles, using various features of SNS, etc. If user finds SNS easy to use then this construct will have a positive relationship towards actual use. Perceived privacy risk is related to what user thinks about his/her personal space on SNS and feels secure while communicating and sharing information. This is an important construct as previous studies have highlighted it as a main concern raised by users towards SNS. How far user consider an SNS secure, effects his/her activities on SNS and level of information sharing. Therefore, it is important to evaluate this construct in relation to actual use of SNS.

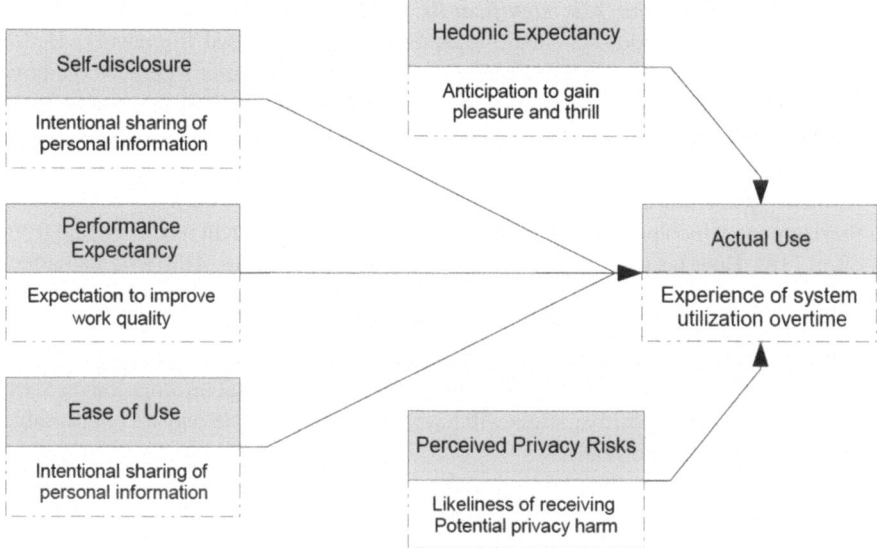

Fig. 2. Proposed Conceptual Framework.

To evaluate the relationship among constructs described in the proposed framework, five hypotheses have been formulated. The hypothesis and their relationship paths are provided in Table 1.

Table 1. Proposed Hypothesis

Proposed Hypothesis	Relationship Path
H1 Performance expectancy has a positive impact on actual use of SNS	PE → AU
H2 Hedonic Expectancy is significantly related to actual use in SNS	HE → AU
H3 Ease of use has significant effect on actual use of SNS	EOU → AU
H4 Self-Disclosure has a positive impact on actual use of SNS	SD → AU
H5 Perceived Privacy Risk has a positive impact on actual use of SNS	PPR → AU

- ***H1 Performance expectancy has a positive impact on actual use of SNS.*** Performance expectancy is the degree to which a person believes that using SNS would enhance his job performance [18, 19]. Performance expectancy is the core construct of UTAUT model for determining the actual use of SNS with respect to user. SNS could be used for formal and informal communication, therefore, its usage could improve working relationships and understanding the job related activities.

- *H2 Hedonic Expectancy is significantly related to actual use in SNS.* Hedonic expectancy provides schematic representation of proposed framework. Hedonic expectancy has been broadly seen as a way to measure user's perceived enjoyment, fun, and perceived entertainment [20]. This hypothesis indicates that hedonic expectancy has positive influence towards actual use of SNS which means users enjoy their time on SNS.
- *H3 Ease of use has significant effect on actual use of SNS.* This hypothesis shows the degree to which person believes that using a particular system would be free from effort [18]. How far user is comfortable in using SNS features. This will also affect the time user spend on SNS. The actual use is closely related to the comfort of user towards the usage of SNS.
- *H4 Self-Disclosure has a positive impact on actual use of SNS.* This implies that users have concerns while disclosing and sharing their personal information on SNS. If the relationship is positive, users will have strong trust on SNS and are comfortable in disclosing their information.
- *H5 Perceived Privacy Risk has a positive impact on actual use of SNS.* Perceived Risk, in general, can alter an individual's feelings [21], and could cause negative feelings such as anxiety, discomfort and uncertainty [22, 23]. Also, the privacy risk can effect users activities on SNS for example, sharing of personal information, locations, opinions etc.

In the next section, analysis of data collected through questionnaire from IT professionals is provided. The results of applying statistical model and findings are discussed in detail.

4 Results and Discussion

The data was analyzed by employing structured equation modeling using IBM SPSS 20. The descriptive statistics, reliability analysis, measurement model and testing of hypothesis are discussed below.

a) **Descriptive Statistics**

For descriptive statistics, data related to age, qualification, gender, and frequency of use of SNS was collected from participants and summarized in Table 2. The 44% of respondents belonged to age group of 20–25, 30% fall under 26–30 year age group and 17% came under the age group of 31–35 years. Remaining 9% were above the age of 36 years. The participants who volunteered in this study were largely male 83% whereas female respondents were 17%. In this research, the focus was to evaluate user behaviour therefore we did not categorize the population based on gender. The results carry two interpretations. Either female participants were not comfortable to share information or the employment of female in software industry is low when compared to males. The qualification of the majority of the participants was undergraduate and graduate. Only 2% were PhD and 3% were having experience of post-doctorate. This shows an interesting trend that professionals with doctorate degree prefer to join academia and very few join industry. However, graduates and undergraduates who join industry from the very beginning of their career prefer to stay in industry and improve their skill through professional certifications and experience. Very few software professionals decide to go for higher education such as doctorate. The participants qualification in this survey represents the same trend.

In case of SNS selection, Facebook was the most popular SNS among participants. Twitter was also used by almost half of the participants. The respondents were using more than one SNS however, among all mentioned SNS these two were preferred. Regrading SNS usage, majority of the participants shared use of SNS for 1–2 h every day. The usage of SNS once a month was significantly low.

The participants responses related to conceptual framework were evaluated for internal consistency and to construct measurement model discussed below.

Table 2. Descriptive Statistics.

Factors	Ranges	Responses	Frequency
Age			
	20–25 years	122	44%
	26–30 years	82	30%
	31–35 years	46	17%
	36–40 years	16	5%
	40–45 years	3	2%
	45–50 years	1	1%
	above 50	1	1%
Gender			
	Male	225	83%
	Female	46	17%
Education			
	Under Graduate / Graduate	260	95%
	Doctorate	3	2%
	Post Doctorate	8	3%
SNS Category			
	Facebook	250	95%
	Twitter	129	49%
	Orkut	17	7%
	Hi5	2	0.8%
	My Space	2	0.8%
	Other	72	27%
SNS experience			

(continued)

Table 2. (*continued*)

Factors	Ranges	Responses	Frequency
	04+ years	227	83%
	03 years	10	4%
	02 years	24	9%
	01 year	10	4%
SNS Usage Frequency per Day			
	1–2 h	206	76%
	2–3 h	32	12%
	3–4 h	21	8%
	More than 4 h	12	4%
SNS Usage Frequency			
	Once a month	8	3%
	<month	3	1%
	Once every two week	12	4%
	2–4 times each week	61	23%
	Everyday	187	69%

b) **Reliability of Instrument**

To evaluate instrument reliability, Cronbach alpha reliability test was employed. This test measures correlation of psychometric items in a survey by using IBM SPSS 20. The alpha coefficient ranges from 0 to 1 to check reliability factors where;

- greater than 0.9 is consider excellent (a > 0:9)
- greater than 0.7 but smaller than 0.9 is consider good (0:7 < a < 0:9)
- greater than 0.6 but smaller than 0.7 is consider acceptable (0:6 < a < 0:7)
- greater than 0.5 but smaller than 0.6 is consider poor (0:5 < a < 0:6)
- smaller than 0.5 is consider unacceptable (a < 0:5)

Table 3 provides details about constructs, value of Cronbach Alpha and reliability level achieved for each construct. Liu 2010, mentioned that value of Cronbach Alpha greater than 0.7 is considered as reliable value of coefficients [24]. The alpha values provided in Table 3 are above 0.7 threshold which represent good consistency level and good level of reliability of instrument.

Table 3. Cronbach Alpha for internal consistency of constructs.

Construct	Cronbach Alpha Value	Reliability Level
Actual Use	0.719	Good
Self-Disclosure	0.826	Excellent
Hedonic Expectancy	0.746	Good
Performance Expectancy	0.753	Good
Ease of Use	0.712	Good
Perceived Privacy Risk	0.814	Excellent

c) Measurement Model

Confirmatory factor analysis (CFA) is used to assess measurement model. CFA is employed to test latent variables which cannot be measured directly and estimation of these variables is carried out through observed variables. In this research, maximum likelihood estimation (MLE) is used for structured equation modeling (SEM). The CFA is carried out through MLE by using Amos tool. In Table 4, model fit indices are presented. The results of the CFI, provides a good measurement model fit for the data.

Table 4. Measurement Model Fitness Indices.

Fit Indices	Recommended Value [25]	Measurement Model
Goodness-of-Fit Index (GFI)	>0.90	0.956
Adjusted Goodness-of-Fit Index (AGFI)	>0.80	0.934
Comparative Fit Index (CFI)	>0.90	0.997
Root Mean Square Error of Approximation (RMSEA)	<0.08	0.012
Normed Fit Index (NFI)	>0.90	0.912
Parsimony Normed Fit Index (PNFI)	>0.60	1.00

d) Hypothesis Testing

Hypothesis testing describes whether constructed hypothesis is significant or not by using P values in which the significant value of p is $p < .001$, $p < .01$, $p < .05$ and *** representing a significant hypothesis. In Table 5, hypothesis test results are provided. Out of five, four hypothesis (H1, H2, H3 and H4) were found significant. One hypothesis H5 related to perceived risk was not found significant towards actual use which is an interesting finding.

Table 5. Hypothesis Testing.

Hypothesis	Path	Estimates	C.R	P	Analysis
H1	PE → AU	0.360	4.053	***	Highly Significant
H2	HE → AU	.367	3.324	***	Highly Significant
H3	EOU → AU	.179	1.735	.083	Significant
H4	SD → AU	.198	3.353	***	Highly Significant
H5	PPR → AU	-.062	-1.515	.130	Non-significant

***Significant at p <.05.
Significant at p < .01.
* Significant at p < .001.

A fuzzy cognitive map shown in Fig. 3 is designed to show significance of Self-Disclosure, Hedonic Expectancy, Performance Expectancy, Ease of Use and Perceived Privacy Risk with Actual Use of SNS. Highly significant relationship is represented with (+++), significant relationship is shown with (+) and non-significant is represented with (–).

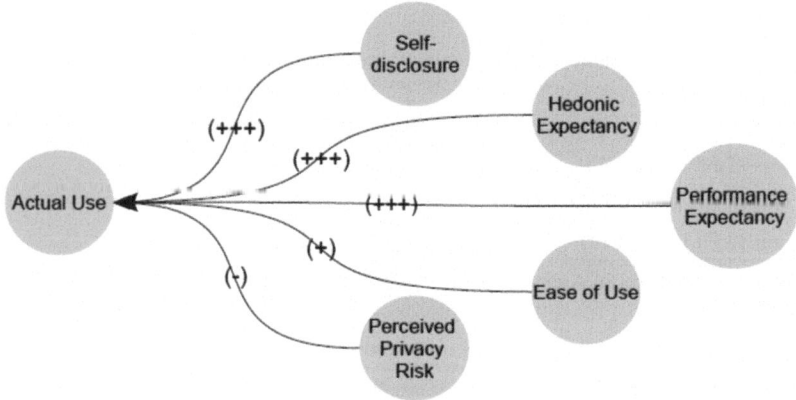

Fig. 3. Fuzzy Cognitive Map.

The findings show that H1, H2, H3 and H4 are found significant towards actual use however, H1 was not found significant. H1 associated with performance expectancy has significant effect towards actual use. Performance expectancy is the direct predictor of actual use. This shows that respondents who could associate SNS with their work-related activities are more inclined to continue using SNS.

H2 is associated with hedonic expectancy is found highly significant towards actual use, which means IT professionals use SNS as leisure activity and enjoy their time using this platform. The results of this study are found consistent with previous study on UTAUT and social networking sites [26].

H3 related to ease of use, was found significant towards actual use. This means SNS interfaces and settings are not constraining users to use different features of SNS. Therefore, user is comfortable in spending time on SNS. However, this finding is not consistent with previous study [27]. One reason for this could be the background of participants. In this study, the participants are IT professionals and are familiar with complicated interfaces. Therefore, identifying settings, dealing with new interfaces and changes made over the time are not an issue when compared to users who are not skilled in technology.

H4 is associated with self-disclosure of users on SNS. Self-disclosure is described as when user feels secure and comfortable to disclose their personal information on SNS. The findings show highly significant relationship with actual use. This means that participants feel comfortable in disclosing their information on SNS which also represent their level of trust towards SNS. This finding is inconsistent with previous studies where users' have expressed their concerns over information disclosure and were hesitant in sharing information [26, 28]. This behaviour could be associated with a number of factors that may include trust towards SNS, cultural context or the competency of the user to control digital environment. In our case, the relationship was found significant due to the later reason.

H5 is related to perceived privacy risk which was not found significant. In this case the competency of using digital environment could be the reason. This finding was found consistent with [29] where participants were college students. This is interesting as young users are more open and less cautious towards sharing information. However, the findings in this study are not age related rather focus is on users' ability to use technology. Therefore, the findings of this study reflect that users having more knowledge of technology are less concerned about privacy issues and are comfortable in using SNS platform. This could be associated with their skill to use SNS platforms, understanding of the privacy risks associated with SNS and control over information disclosure.

5 Conclusion

Information systems are playing an important role in forming Social Networks to create virtual communities of various forms. The information systems particularly in the form of SNS have become important platforms for information sharing (both formal and informal) among individuals, groups, and organizations. Various companies including government and private sector have adopted SNS platforms particularly to increase employees productivity through informal virtual community. Therefore, the study of user behaviour in relation to SNS use has become an active research area in past decade. Research community has focused on various areas of SNS use such as education and counseling for teenage groups, drug control, elderly health monitoring and help forums, cultural effects in social groups, crime control, marketing strategies, relationship formation, personality traits in SNS users and finding user intentions towards continuous use of SNS etc.. The studies conducted on adoption of SNS are largely focused towards the 'intention' of users to use SNS for any particular purpose mentioned earlier. To capture user behaviour by assessing user 'intention' limits the understanding of user behavior toward a particular technology. Further, user behaviours are transformed over the time and without the 'actual use' of a technology it is challenging to analyse user behvaiour in depth.

In this research, 'actual use' of SNS is evaluated in relation to user behavior. The study includes participants with background in technology to understand user behavior in the absence of technological threats which also makes this study different from previous ones where technological constraints constrained user exposure towards SNS use and hence effected their behavior towards SNS.

A conceptual framework is proposed by combining features of user behaviour and UTAUT technology model to identify relationship towards actual use of SNS. The proposed conceptual framework is evaluated by constructing hypothesis that associated 'actual use' with Self-Disclosure, Hedonic Expectancy, Performance Expectancy, Ease of Use and Perceived Privacy Risk. The findings show that four out of five hypothesis were found significant. From the results, we conclude that the users having technological understanding and skill exhibit different behavior towards SNS use. They are more confident and comfortable to use this virtual platform and are able to relate it with their professional activities. Therefore, performance expectancy is found significant towards actual use. Since users are technologically skilled, therefore, they get pleasure in using SNS and enjoy its features. This also encourage them to disclose more information without getting concerned about privacy risk. In this study, perceived privacy risk was not found significant towards actual use which is largely due to the background of the users. With more technological understanding, users consider they have more control over what they share hence they feel less concerned towards privacy risks.

The findings of this research are important for practitioners and SNS service providers. With the advancements in technology, and its rapid adoption by the young users are changing the behavior of users towards technology. Therefore, the concerns raised in last decade regarding SNS use in terms of its interfaces, controls, settings etc. might not be a concern in coming years. However, security of information disclosed by users on SNS is and will remain a challenge. Therefore, on one hand technological awareness and skill is opening more opportunities for SNS providers to offer their services and being adopted by users. On the other hand, it is also bringing more challenges for practitioners to design secure SNS platforms to maintain Trust!

The privacy and trust are important factors that made this research challenging. In future, case based longitudinal studies may be conducted to analyse the behavior of technologically skill users on social network sites and its impact on their personal life, society and workplace.

Acknowledgements. We would like to thank all IT and Software companies involved in this research especially thanks to CEOs of the companies who encouraged their employees to take part in the research. We also thank and appreciate the time and suggestions provided by the IT and Software professionals during this research and sharing their experiences and suggestions on social media.

References

1. Valenzuela, S., Park, N., Kee, K.F.: Is there social capital in a social network site?: Facebook use and college students' life satisfaction, trust, and participation1. J. Comput.-Mediat. Commun. **14**(4), 875–901 (2009)
2. Cheon, J., Lee, S., Crooks, S.M., Song, J.: An investigation of mobile learning readiness in higher education based on the theory of planned behavior. Comput. Educ. **59**(3), 1054–1064 (2012)
3. Hashemi, M., Azizinezhad, M., Najafi, V., Nesari, A.J.: What is mobile learning? Challenges and capabilities. Procedia Soc. Behav. Sci. **30**, 2477–2481 (2011)
4. Greenhow, C., Robelia, B.: Informal learning and identity formation in online social networks. Learn. Media Technol. **34**(2), 119–140 (2009)
5. Danah, M.B., Eliison, N.B.: Social network sites: definition, history, and scholarship. J. Comput. Mediat. Commun. **13**(1), 210–230 (2007)
6. 梁媛, 虞孝成, et al.: Social dating site for example Friendster.com, PhD thesis (2007)
7. Rennie, F., Morrison, T.: E-Learning and Social Networking Handbook: Resources for Higher Education. Routledge (2013)
8. Nicol' o, P., Carmine, G., Michael, U., Tony, G., Pekka, A.: Software development in startup companies: a systematic mapping study. Inf. Softw. Technol. **56**(10), 1200–1218 (2014)
9. Lin, K.-Y., Lu, H.-P.: Why people use social networking sites: an empirical study integrating network externalities and motivation theory. Comput. Hum. Behav. **27**(3), 1152–1161 (2011)
10. Al-Mushasha, N.F., Hassan, S.: A model for mobile learning service quality in university environment. Int. J. Mobile Comput. Multimedia Commun. (IJMCMC) **1**, 70–91 (2009)
11. Richardson, K., Hessey, S.: Archiving the self? facebook as biography of social and relational memory. J. Inf. Commun. Ethics Soc. **7**(1), 25–38 (2009)
12. Xu, C., Ryan, S., Prybutok, V., Wen, C.: It is not for fun: an examination of social network site usage. Inf. Manag. **49**(5), 210–217 (2012)
13. Venkatesh, V.Y., Thong, J., Xu, X.: Consumer acceptance and use of information technology: extending the unified theory of acceptance and use of technology. MIS Q. 157–178 (2012)
14. Teo, T.: Factors influencing teachers' intention to use technology: model development and test. Comput. Educ. **57**(4), 2432–2440 (2011)
15. Armstrong, R.L.: The midpoint on a five-point likert-type scale. Percept. Mot. Skills **64**(2), 359–362 (1987)
16. Atkinson, R., Flint, J.: Accessing hidden and hard-to-reach populations: snowball research strategies. Soc. Res. Update **33**(1), 1–4 (2001)
17. Waheed, H., Anjum, M., Rehman, M., Khawaja, A.: Investigation of user behavior on social networking sites. PLOS ONE **12**(2), 1–19 (2017)
18. Davis, F.D., Bagozzi, R.P., Warshaw, P.R.: User acceptance of computer technology: a comparison of two theoretical models. Manage. Sci. **35**(8), 982–1003 (1989)
19. Venkatesh, V., Morris, M.G., Davis, G.B., Davis, F.D.: User acceptance of information technology: toward a unified view. MIS Q. 425–478 (2003)
20. Weijters, B., Rangarajan, D., Falk, T., Schillewaert, N.: Determinants and outcomes of customers' use of self-service technology in a retail setting. J. Serv. Res. **10**(1), 3–21 (2007)
21. Y¨ uksel, F., Bramwell, B., Y¨ uksel A.: Centralized and decentralized tourism governance in turkey. Ann. Tourism Res. **32**(4), 859–886 (2005)
22. Dowling, G.R., Staelin, R.: A model of perceived risk and intended risk handling activity. J. Consum. Res. **21**(1), 119–134 (1994)
23. Featherman, M.: Extending the technology acceptance model by inclusion of perceived risk. In: AMCIS 2001 Proceedings, vol. 148 (2001)

24. Tan, G.W.-H., Ooi, K.-B., Sim, J.-J., Phusavat, K.: Determinants of mobile learning adoption: an empirical analysis. J. Comput. Inf. Syst. **52**(3), 82–91 (2012)
25. Hair, J.F., Ringle, C.M., Sarstedt, M.: Pls-sem: indeed a silver bullet. J. Mark. Theory Pract. **19**(2), 139–152 (2011)
26. Ntlatywa, P., Botha, R.A., Haskins, B.: Claimed vs observed information disclosure on social networking sites. In: Information Security for South Africa (ISSA), 2012, IEEE, pp. 1–6 (2012)
27. Jin, C.: The perspective of a revised tram on social capital building: the case of facebook usage. Inf. Manag. **50**(4), 162–168 (2013)
28. Wang, J.-L., Jackson, L.A., Gaskin, J., Wang, H.-Z.: The effects of social networking site (sns) use on college students' friendship and well-being. Comput. Hum. Behav. **37**, 229–236 (2014)
29. Zhang, S., Chen, H., Zheng, D.: Empirical study on users' participation behavior in sns based on theory of perceived risks and involvement degree. In: Service Systems and Service Management (ICSSSM),10th International Conference on, IEEE, pp. 424–429 (2013)

Association Between Demographic Factors and Internet Banking Usage

R. Muthukumar[1]([✉]), Lalitha Ramakrishnan[1], A. Poongodai[2],
and C. S. G. Krishnamacharyulu[3]

[1] Department of Management Studies (Karaikal Campus), Pondicherry University, Puducherry,
India
muthu.r.kumar@gmail.com

[2] Department of CSE (AI), Madanapalle Institute of Technology and Science, Madanapalle, AP,
India

[3] Sri Venkateswara University, Tirupati, India

Abstract. Internet banking, an innovative way of banking delivery, plays an important and major role in the banking industry worldwide. Almost all the banks in India provide such innovative internet banking services. But, despite the banks' efforts towards increasing internet banking customers, it is yet to reach its desired levels and attract all customers. This study made an attempt to identify the association between demographic factors and the internet banking usage among the internet banking users. Using convenience sampling 429 responses were collected from the internet banking users in India. Descriptive analysis was used to understand the profile of sample respondents. In addition, Chi-square analysis was used to find out the relationship between demographic factors and the internet banking usage. From the analysis results, it was found that there is a significant association between demographic characteristics and internet banking usage.

Keywords: Demographic factors · Internet banking · Chi-square analysis · Descriptive analysis · Banking services

1 Introduction

One of the technological developments in the information technology revolution is online banking or internet banking. The birth and evolution of IT and the internet paved the path for internet banking, which unites a bank and its customers over the internet to access essential financial services. It is an advanced technological application which is used to share the financial information resources available in electronic form. This development of IT empowers the banks to quickly as well as efficiently serve their customer without the need for their physical presence at the service branches. Internet banking is considered to be an effective accounting and payment system that enables the banks to provide quick, speedy, safe and secure delivery of banking services [1].

The human involvement required for financial transactions is a key distinction between traditional and Internet banking [2]. Users must be physically available at their bank location to access bank services in traditional banking for the transactions that include information inquiry, bank account opening, transaction status inquiry, etc. However, with online banking, customers may conduct transactions and access banking services from wherever they are, at any time of day, using their own computer, laptop, tablet, or smartphone.

Today's banks are producing a vast number of new services and products through internet banking. For instance, it has transformed the way of paying bills, filing income tax returns, etc. Users may now conduct financial transactions without the need for human interaction because to technological advancements. The information is now available on the mere mouse or a button click. This provision promoted competitiveness in the banking industry throughout the world. Furthermore, there is fierce competition between banking and non-banking enterprises. Many non-banking companies have recently established themselves as strongholds and have begun to compete with core banking companies.

As a result, one of the issues that banking organisations face is, sustaining or retaining clients. As the products or services provided by a banking firm are more or less very standard ones, banks are feeling an increasing need to differentiate themselves from the rivalry firms. Banks may now provide practically all of their products and services online thanks to the adoption of internet banking. In recent years, the number of research papers on the acceptance and use of Internet banking in India has increased. However, many concerns remain unresolved, resulting in a disconnect between what banks have been giving in the form of Internet banking services and what actual bank customers demand.

In India, banks are facing competition and finding it tough to attract and retain customers. They are facing tough challenge in terms of new product introductions, technology developments and raising customer expectations. In post demonetization scenario, the competition shifted from off-line to on-line banking services, as government has been encouraging on line transactions and businesses. In this context, strategies are essential for internet banking, through which banks can retain the existing customers and to attract new users. For that, they need to understand the demographics of the internet banking users. Hence, this study is proposed to get the understanding of internet banking users' demographics.

2 Review from Past Studies

Internet banking is doing banking transactions through or via internet. It is also called web banking or online banking or e-banking or electronic banking. It is becoming one of the major general types of delivery channel of banking. Users can use internet banking to check their account balances, transfer funds, and pay bills at their convenience. Internet banking also enables the customers to apply for and manage loans, do the investments including stocks or mutual funds, etc., conveniently without any difficulties. However, it can be noted that the nature of services through Internet banking varies from bank to bank.

As defined by Daniel (1999), electronic banking delivers banks' information and services to banks customers. The electronic banking uses various platforms including personal computer, mobile phone, telephone and digital television. The term e-banking or electronic banking can be used as an umbrella term for the transactions done through various delivery channels without visiting any bank branch [3].

As a major delivery channel of banking, internet banking has been providing numerous benefits to the banks and their customers [4]. The following are few benefits of internet banking to the banks: Cost savings, increased client population, increased efficiency, improved bank reputation, and improved customer satisfaction and customer service [5].

Internet banking enables the customers to manage their banking affairs at their convenience, and the privacy is ensured during their interaction with their bank. As reported by many researchers and experts, internet banking customers or users receives various benefits at lower costs [6]. As propounded by Turban et al. (2000), customers benefit greatly from internet banking because of the cost, time, and space benefits it provides [7].

Internet banking provides a value to the customers through various benefits. As its boundary is beyond time and geography, customers across the world can able to get easy access to their bank accounts at their convenient place and time. Some of the services that are not offered at bank branches are also provided through internet banking. Internet banking also makes customers to avoid bank branch visit. Thus, it ensures convenience and accessibility along with saving time and money [4].

Internet banking offers many advantages that traditional banking cannot provide, as given below:

Convenience: Traditional banking requires customers to be physically present at their bank location to access services such as cash withdrawals and deposits, information inquiries, bank account opening, and so on. However, with online banking, customers may conduct transactions and acquire banking services from any location at any time of the day (24x7 access) using their own computer, laptop, tablet, or smart phone. Internet banking is therefore more user-friendly, efficient, and simple to use.

Ubiquity: It is the state of presence everywhere. Internet banking is available or accessible everywhere wherever internet connection is present.

Wide range of services: With internet banking, a vast variety of innovative services and products are being developed by banks. Smart cards, electronic funds transfer, ATM, phone banking, and internet banking are virtual electronic banking services. Banks provide wholesale products to corporate customers and retail & fiduciary products to its retail customers. Moreover, products and services available through internet banking may be similar to those available through conventional bank delivery methods.

No human interaction: Users may now do financial transactions without needing to engage with a human. The information is these days available through machine interaction with a mere click of a button.

High speed and low cost: Internet banking reduced the transaction cost and improved the speed of services than in conventional banking. Internet banking enables users to enjoy the customized banking services conveniently. Moreover, internet banking assists banks to offer their service to many customers in a cost-effective way [8].

Efficiency: In general, with an aim to attract new customers and retain them, the banks provide various promotions and deals via online. In addition, most of the banks that offer internet banking are transparent in their offerings and pricing. This helps in quick searching and comparing prices of offerings of different banks in a short time.

Effectiveness: From internet banking portal, customers can download the available data for reviewing at a later point of time when needed. With the given sophisticated tools and features one can manage his/her accounts and transactions in a more effective way.

The retail and wholesale services provided by banks through internet banking are given in Table 1.

Table 1. Internet Banking Services.

Retail Services	Wholesale Services
Account Aggregation and Management	Account Management
Account Opening	Loan-related Services
Fund Transfer	Cash Management
Bill Payment	Tax Payment
Investment/Brokerage services	Commercial wire transfers
Loan application and Loan approval	Employee benefits/pension Administration
E-shopping, Ticket booking, Paying taxes	Business-to-business payments and Bill presentments
Other value-added services	Automated Clearing House (ACH) Transactions

Srivastava (2007) in his study made an attempt to investigate the perception of customers towards internet banking. He listed few of the influencing factors that impact customer acceptance towards Internet banking. The following are the factors that influence the use of Internet banking: Gender, income and education. He also recommended measures to improve the usage of internet banking services [9]. Agarwal, Rastogi and Mehrotra (2009) found that customers are influenced by the kind of account they hold, their age and profession [10].

Dixit and Dutta (2010) in their study determined that few demographic factors affect the acceptance of internet banking service by adult customers, and customers with ≥35 years of age [11]. Jayaraman Munswamy (2012) also examined the existence of impact by demographics factors on Internet banking adoption. This study conducted a survey on the retail customers of banks in the Klang valley. It was concluded that the analysis results did not support hypotheses stated on gender, race, educational level and occupation [12].

Elavarsi and Surulivel (2014) made an attempt to investigate customer awareness among State Bank of India customers in Kumbakonam, a city of Tamil Nadu, India. The authors found that the internet banking preference is identified more in the younger age group of customers as against older age group customers [13]. Online banking is an inexpensive delivery channel of banking to offer various banking products to bank customers. Customers are increasingly using the internet to conduct their financial transactions, because of rapid technological advancements [14].

Arora and Sandhu (2018) conducted a study to find the factors that influence customers' usage of e-banking services. The research was conducted among Punjab bank customers in India. Amritsar, Jalamdhar, and Ludhiana were chosen as the locations for a sample of 10 private and 10 public most profitable scheduled commercial banks. A sample size of 600 customers, with 10 customers from each bank and five customers from each branch considered for data collection. The study relied on primary data obtained directly from the selected respondents via a questionnaire that had been pre-tested for construct and content validity. E-banking services were chosen by 524 of the 600 bank customers surveyed. Age, gender, income and education are all found to have a major impact on customers' use of e-banking services. According to the findings, younger female, middle-income and more educated clients are the most likely to use e-banking. Only six (experience, information, self-interest, service quality, performance and satisfaction) of the 11 perceptual characteristics were found to be positively associated with E-banking usage [15].

The research paper by Rupesh Roshan Singh and Navneet Kaur (2019) is based on the financial performance of the top ten public sector banks. To properly examine the data, basic focus is done on ROA and ROE (2018 and 2019). To make the comparison, data is obtained from the 10 largest public sector banks, as reported in Money Control, as well as from different websites and RBI statistics, including online data for NEFT and RTGS [16].

Kaur and Arora (2020) investigated the effect of perceived risk on behavioural intention in online banking, using trust as a moderator. With this purpose in mind, a conceptual model was developed to look at the impact of perceived risk on behavioural intention both directly and indirectly through a unified theory of technology acceptance and use. Data was collected from 800 bank customers in the three cities of Amritsar, Jalandhar, and Ludhiana using a convenience sample technique. A structural equation modelling technique was utilised to evaluate the data. According to the findings, perceived risk, as a multi-dimensional construct, had a direct and indirect impact on behavioral intention [17].

Muthukumar and Lalitha Ramakrishnan (2019) quoted the report by Facebook and The Boston Consulting Group, saying that with the ongoing digital drive in India, the number of online banking users would be 150 million by 2020, as against 45 million active online banking users of urban India in 2017. Due to the existence of hidden charges and lack of trust, around 50% of users are not satisfied with their online banking [18]. Yesildag (2019) studied the factors influencing bank customers' internet banking preferences and the correlations between demographic features of bank customers and internet banking usage in Usak, Turkey [19].

Naaz Gorowara (2020) made an attempt to identify that the demographic factors are correlated with the acceptance of internet banking services. Based on the survey conducted in the state of Haryana and the analysis, the author determined that age, occupation, income and location were the factors that significantly affect or impact the acceptance of respondents towards internet banking products and services [20].

Chaudhary, Mandaviya, Salah, Maroor and Bharti (2021) made an attempt to ascertain the role of demographic variables on the preferences of the users opting for online services offered by the banks. The respondents were provided with a structured questionnaire. The data so collected was analysed using statistical tools like frequency tables, cross tabulation, and the chi-square test. The results of the said study indicated that majority of the users opting for internet banking services were male with education being minimum of high school diploma [21].

Kirti, R., Suman, K. and Ashok, P. (2022) made an attempt to determine demographic factors that influence the adoption of internet banking services through an empirical study. The research was done among 372 respondents in Ganjam district of Odisha, India. It was found that there are relationships between demographic factors such as age, gender, income, educational level, and job status have a substantial impact on customers' technological banking services and various technological banking services provided by the banks to the customers [22].

According to Shetty, A., and Suresh, G. (2023), demographic factors such as age, education, and income level were found to have a positive impact on customers' awareness, while gender had no significant impact. Furthermore, the study found that the level of awareness of banking services varied among different demographic groups, with younger, more educated, and higher-income customers having higher levels of awareness [23].

Several past studies suggest that consumer adoption and usage of internet banking technologies are linked to the particular consumer's attributes as well as the technology itself. The following are the few related factors that impact internet banking adoption and usage: socio-economic, demographic characteristics and perception of Internet technologies. Age, income, educational background, and years of involvement with the Internet are the few demographic characteristics. Hence this study proposed to find the association between internet banking usage and the demographic characteristics.

Though there are many studies on the association between demographics and the internet banking adoption, there are very minimal studies on the real usage of internet banking usage. So, this was the gap identified from the literature review. Also there are no studies specifically on the association of demographics with frequency of internet banking and the experience of internet banking.

3   Objectives and Hypotheses

The aim of this research paper is to examine the relationship between demographic factors of internet banking users and their usage details and to present the descriptive analysis of internet banking users. Based on the above-mentioned studies on the influence of demographic factors on the e-banking usage, the following hypotheses are proposed.

Hypothesis 1: There is significant association between demographic factors (Age, Gender, Education, Occupation and Income of the customers) and frequency of internet banking.
Hypothesis 2: There is significant association between demographic factors (Age, Gender, Education, Occupation and Income of the customers) and their experience of internet banking.
Hypothesis 3: There is significant association between demographic factors (Age, Gender, Education, Occupation and Income of the customers) and the account types.

4   Methodology

In this paper, primary data is collected from internet banking customers to investigate the available literature focusing on the internet banking in India and worldwide. The survey method of data collection is employed to collect demographics of internet users and other variables. Data is collected from secondary sources to describe internet banking and review literature. Primary data is the key to the study. It is collected from internet users who have been using internet banking over a period of one year or more.

In 2020, the total number of internet banking users in India was around 150 million. The total internet banking users in India is the population for the study. The target population is defined as internet users who have been using internet banking over a period of one year or more.

The required sample size for an unknown population or a very large population size is calculated using the following formula:

$$SampleSize = \frac{(Zscore)^2 \times StdDev \times (1 - StdDev)}{marin\ of\ error^2} \tag{1}$$

For the present study, as used in many past studies, the confidence level is 95%, the acceptable standard deviation is –5, and the margin of error (confidence interval) is ±5%.

Sample Size = $3.8416 \times 0.25/0.0025 = 0.9604/0.0025 = 384.16$.

Hence it was targeted to have the final sample size of 400 to 500. Table 2 displays the total number of questionnaires gathered from the respondents.

Table 2. Summary of Responses Collected.

Standard Sample Size (As calculated from formula)	Distributed Nos	Responses received	Responses accepted
384	500	466	429

With the anticipation that some of the responses would be rejected, the researcher distributed 500 questionnaires in total. After carefully examining the responses, the researcher eliminated roughly 37 of them altogether, leaving a final sample of 429. The calculated rejection rate is 8%, which is substantially below the expected rejection rate of 10%.

The convenience sampling and snowball sampling methods are used during the process of data collection. A structured questionnaire with close-ended questions is used for the primary data collection. The questionnaire was sent to 566 customers through email. Out of which responses from 429 respondents were received and they were complete and in order. The questionnaire contained the questions on demographics: (1). Gender, (2). Age, (3). Education, (4). Profession and (5). Income and internet banking usage: (1). Account type, (2) Duration, (3). Frequency of use and (4). Place of access. Before the actual study, a pilot study was conducted. It is a smaller-scale version of a larger study that lasts for a shorter amount of time and involves a smaller group of people. It is used in the present study to check the questionnaire.

5   Results and Discussion

5.1   Profile of Respondents

The purpose of this section is to understand the personal profile of the customers and get an insight into their few banking habits. The demographic or personal profile of the respondents includes gender, age, education, profession and income. Table 3 gives a description of the personal profiles of the customers.

Table 3. Personal Profiles of Customers.

Demographic Profile	Item	Frequency	Percentage
Gender	Male	238	55.5
	Female	191	44.5
Age	Below 31 years	71	16.6
	31–40 years	111	25.9
	41–50 years	86	20.0
	51–60 years	31	7.2
	Above 60 years	16	3.7
Education	Schooling	38	8.9
	Diploma	5	1.2
	UG	131	30.5
	Professional	1	.2
	PG	218	50.8
	Scholar	3	.7
	Doctorate	33	7.7
Profession	Retired	14	3.3
	Professionals	45	10.5
	Student	80	18.6
	Employee	243	56.6
	Businessmen	32	7.5
	Self-employed	2	.5
	Scholar	5	1.2

(*continued*)

Table 3. (*continued*)

Demographic Profile	Item	Frequency	Percentage
	Homemaker	8	1.9
Income	Below Rs.25,000	137	31.9
	Rs.26,000 - Rs.50,000	109	25.4
	Rs.51,000 - Rs.75,000	68	15.9
	Rs.76,000 - Rs.1,00,000	55	12.8
	Above Rs.1,01,000	60	14.0

Table 3 shows the description of the personal profiles of the customers. The following are the observations: Gender wise analysis shows that 55.5 per cent of respondents are males. The educational qualifications were post graduate (50.8%), followed by graduate (30.55%). The less educated are about 10.1% having school and diploma education. A majority of customers (56.6 per cent) are employees. The next larger segment of respondents (18.6 percent) belongs to students. The rest of them belong to professionals (10.5 per cent) and businessmen (7.5 per cent).

From the Fig. 1, it can be observed that a large no. of respondents is in the group of 31–40 years of age. This illustrates that a majority of middle-aged people have participated in the survey. The sample is dominated by male customers. The majority of the respondents are well qualified post graduates. The larger segment of respondent is employees. Very few respondent customers are in the retired, housewife, and other categories. The distributions of the respondents are across different income categories.

5.2 Internet Banking Usage Profile

Table 4 includes details about the type of account that the customer have with the bank, and the number of years they are dealing with the banks. Duration is important to the study as most respondents have used internet banking for long enough time to elicit representative judgment on the quality of the provided internet banking services. Most of the respondents have accessed internet banking from home and that majority of them use internet banking frequently.

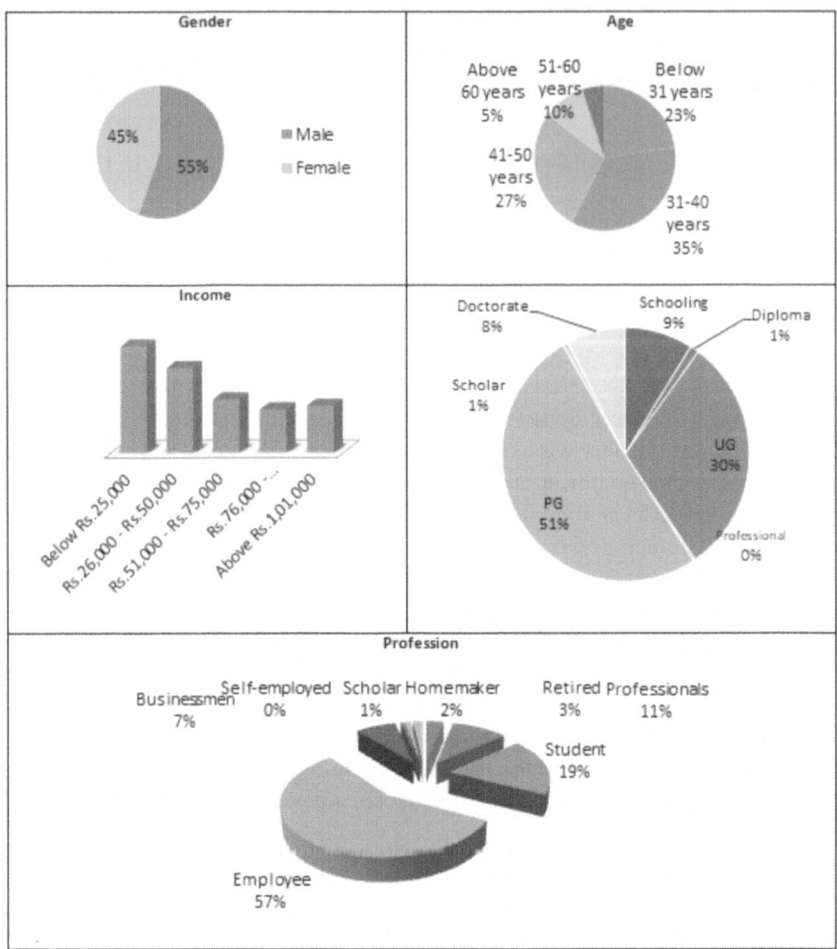

Fig. 1. Personal Profile of Customer.

From the Table 4, it can be seen that only 23% respondents have been using Internet banking for 1 – 2 years and the rest (77%) have been using internet banking for more than 2 years. A significant part of them (34.6%) have been using it for more than 5 years. This specific aspect is important to the study as most respondents have used internet banking for a sufficient amount of time to make an accurate assessment of the quality of the service provided in turn leading to satisfaction and loyalty on these services. Majority of the respondents have used internet banking from home (89%). The next location is the workplace/institution, about 47% access from here. The users of internet banking from cybercafe are very less (7%).

Table 4. Details of Internet Banking Usage Profile.

Internet Banking Usage Profile	Item	Frequency	Percent
Account Type	Savings	381	88.8
	Current	32	7.5
	Deposit	16	3.7
Duration	1–2 years	98	22.8
	2–3 years	73	17.0
	3–4 years	50	11.7
	4–5 years	52	12.1
	Above 5 years	156	36.4
Frequency of use	Very Frequently	121	28.2
	Frequently	161	37.5
	Occasionally	73	17.0
	Rarely	74	17.2
	Total	429	100.0
Place of Access	Home	382	89.0
	Workplace/ Institution	203	47.3
	Cybercafe	31	7.2

Also from the Fig. 2, it can be noted that 28.2 percent of respondents use internet banking services very frequently, whereas 37.5% respondents use internet banking services frequently. About 17% use it either occasionally or rarely.

The analysis of influence of demographic factors of respondents on their account type is presented in Table 5 and it shows that chi-square value of all the demographic factors except gender and income are significant ($p \leq 0.05$). From this, it can be concluded that there is no difference between gender of (male and female) respondents with account type and account type does not vary among the different income group of respondents.

The chi-square values of all the demographic factors except gender are significant ($p \leq 0.05$). This indicates that there is no difference between gender of (male and female) respondents in the number of years of using internet banking. (see Table 6).

From Table 7, the chi-square value for age indicates that the value is significant leading to the inference that frequent use of internet banking varies among the different age groups of respondents. As the chi-Square value for gender is not significant at 0.05 level, there is no difference between gender of (male and female) respondents in the use of internet banking. The chi-square value of education, occupation and income are significant ($p \leq 0.05$) as shown in Table 7. Hence it can be said that those factors have association with the frequency of use of internet banking.

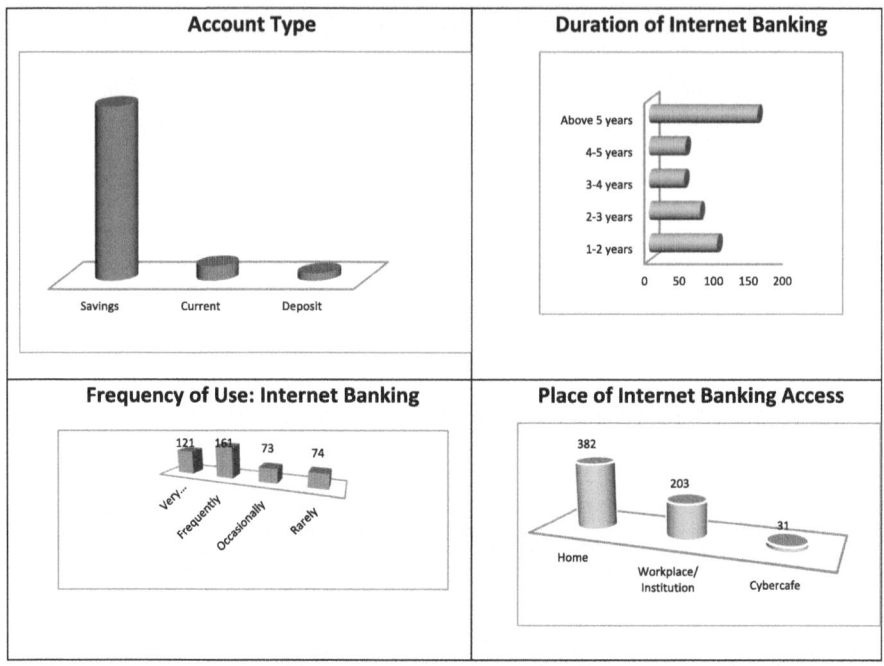

Fig. 2. Internet Banking Profile.

Table 5. Account Type – Across Demographic Factors.

Demographic factors	Chi Square		
	Value	Df	Significance
Age	18.903	10	.042
Gender	3.090	2	.213
Education	22.665	12	.031
Occupation	27.801	14	.015
Income	7.161	8	.519

The findings are as follows: The frequency of internet banking use is significantly influenced by age, education, occupation, and income. There is no significant difference in internet use between males and females. The frequent users are 21–50 years old, college educated holding UG or PG degrees, both employees and students, and predominantly having a monthly income of Rs 50,000 or less.

Table 6. No. of Years using net banking – Across Demographic Factors.

Demographic factors	Chi Square		
	Value	Df	Significance
Age	1.347E2	20	.000
Gender	9.188	4	.057
Education	1.090E2	24	.000
Occupation	92.691	28	.000
Income	1.608E2	16	.000

Table 7. Frequency of Internet Banking Use – Across Demographic Factors.

Demographic factors	Chi Square		
	Value	Df	Significance
Age	55.613	12	.000
Gender	1.676	3	.642
Education	66.461	18	.000
Occupation	65.672	21	.000
Income	84.695	12	.000

6 Conclusion

The Indian banking industry is undergoing a digital transformation. Almost all banks now provide internet banking services, which benefit both banks and customers. ATMs, credit cards, ECS, NEFT, debit cards, mobile banking, internet banking, and other innovative services have fundamentally transformed the Indian financial landscape. At this point, banks must focus on building and sustaining a loyal client base. From this study it can be concluded that there is association between demographic factors age, income and occupation and the internet banking usage of the customers in India (Naaz Gorowara, 2020; Kirti, R., Suman, K. and Ashok, P., 2022; Arora and Sandhu, 2018). The study findings can be generalized to the entire country as the data was collected from the people from all over the country. However, there are certain drawbacks like demographic factors restricted to only three aspects were tested for their association with internet banking usage. The study reveals a path to explore in the same area with respect to aspects other than demographics that might influence the internet banking usage. It is strongly recommended that the banks should consider to concentrate on the significant demographic factors so that the loyalty of customer towards using internet banking may be improved in future. As there is a possibility of dynamic change in the internet banking usage behaviour, it is proposed to do a longitudinal study which is a repeat collection of data from the same sample over an extended period of time. With the longitudinal study, the association between the internet banking usage and the demographic variables can be examined and understood in a better way. It will help the banks in making appropriate decisions in retaining their respective customers and increase the loyalty among their customers through different ways.

References

1. Subramanian, S.: E-Banking - a study on awareness and satisfaction of customers with reference to commercial bank of Ethiopia. RJSSM **6**(2) (2016)
2. Sree Krishna, T., Murty, T.N., Challa, S.K.: Impact of demographic variables of users on internet banking. Int. J. Bus. Admin. Res. Rev. **1**(9), 14 (2015)
3. Daniel, E.: Provision of electronic banking in the UK and the Republic of Ireland. Int. J. Bank Mark. **17**(2), 72–82 (1999)
4. Karjaluoto, H., Mattila, M., Pento, T.: Factors underlying attitude formation towards online banking in Finland. Int. J. Bank Mark. **20**(6), 61–72 (2002)
5. Jayawardhena, C., Foley, P.: Changes in the banking sector: The case of internet banking in the UK. Internet Res.: Electron. Netw. Appl. Policy **10**(1), 19–30 (2000)
6. Niels, M.: The Behavioural Consequences of PC banking. Int. J. Bank Mark. **16**(5), 195–201 (1998)
7. Turban, E., Lee, J., King, D., Chung, H.M.: Electronic Commerce: A Managerial Perspective. Prentice-Hall, Upper Saddle River, NJ (1999)
8. Amin, M.: Internet banking service quality and its implication on e-customer satisfaction and e-customer loyalty. Int. J. Bank Mark. **34**(3), 280–306 (2016)
9. Srivastava, R.K.: Customer's perception on usage of internet banking. Innov. Mark. **3**(4), 67–73 (2007)
10. Agarwal, R., Rastogi, S., Mehrotra, A.: Customers' perspectives regarding e-banking in an emerging economy. J. Retail. Consum. Serv. **16**, 340–351 (2009)
11. Dixit, N., Datta, K.S.: Acceptance of E-banking among adult customers: an empirical investigation in India. J. Internet Bank. Commer. **5**(2), 1–17 (2010)
12. Munusamy, J., De Run E., Chelliah, S., Annamalah, S.: Adoption of retail internet banking: a study of demographic factors. J. Internet Banking Commer. **17**(3) (2012)
13. Elavarasi, R., Surulivel, S.T.: Customer awareness and preference towards e-banking services of banks (A study of SBI). Int. Res. J. Bus. Manag. **4**, 59–67 (2014)
14. Firdous, S., Farooqi, R.: Impact of internet banking service quality on customer satisfaction, http://www.icommercecentral.com, last accessed 2023/09/19
15. Arora, S., Sandhu, S.: Usage based upon reasons: the case of electronic banking services in India. Int. J. Bank Mark. **36**, 680–700 (2018)
16. Singh, R.R., Kaur, N.: Interaction between online banking and its impact on financial performance of banking sector:- evidence from Indian public sector banks. Int. J. Recent Technol. Eng. (IJRTE) **8**(2S11) (2023)
17. Kaur, S., Arora, S.: Role of perceived risk in online banking and its impact on behavioural intention: trust as a moderator. J. Asia Bus. Stud. **15**(1), 1–30 (2020)
18. Muthukumar, R., Lalitha, R.: A study of E-service quality and its influence on internet banking usage and customer satisfaction in India: a literature review. IJRAR **6**(2) (2019)
19. Yeşildag, E: Factors affecting internet banking preferences and their relation to demographic characteristics. In: Contemporary Issues in Behavioral Finance (Contemporary Studies in Economic and Financial Analysis, vol. 101, pp. 187–203). Emerald Publishing Limited, Bingley (2019)
20. NaazGorowara: Impact of demographic correlates on internet banking acceptance. Int. J. Future Gen. Commun. Netw. **13**(3), 932–958 (2020)

21. Chaudhary, V., Mandaviya, M., Salah, H., Maroor, J., Bharti, A.: A study on effect of various demographic factors on preference of consumers towards online banking usage. Mater. Today: Proc. **51**(1) (2021)
22. Kirti, R., Suman, K., Ashok, P.: Impact of demographic variables on consumers' adoption of e-banking services in Ganjam District of Odisha: an empirical investigation. J. Manag. Res. Anal. **9**(4), 210–217 (2022)
23. Shetty, A., Suresh, G.: A study of the impact of demographic factors on customers' awareness of banking services. J. Entrep. Educ. **26**(S5), 1–12 (2023)

Correction to: Science, Engineering Management and Information Technology

A. Mirzazadeh⑩, Zohreh Molamohamadi⑩, Babek Erdebilli⑩, Erfan Babaee Tirkolaee⑩, and Gerhard-Wilhelm Weber⑩

Correction to:
A. Mirzazadeh et al. (Eds.): *Science, Engineering Management and Information Technology*, **CCIS 2198,**
https://doi.org/10.1007/978-3-031-72284-4

The book was published with a typo in the 4th editor's name in this book. The name of the editor as "Efran Babaee Tirkolaee", whereas it should read "Erfan Babaee Tirkolaee" correctly. This has been corrected in the book accordingly.

The updated version of this book can be found at
https://doi.org/10.1007/978-3-031-72284-4

Author Index

The manufacturer's authorised representative in the EU is Springer
Nature Customer Service Centre GmbH, Europaplatz 3, 69115 Heidelberg,
Germany. If you have any concerns regarding our products, please
contact ProductSafety@springernature.com

Printed and bound by CPI Group (UK) Ltd, Croydon, CR0 4YY
29/04/2026
02099532-0014